New
Caribbean
Thought

New Caribbean Thought

A Reader

Edited by

Brian Meeks

and

Folke Lindahl

THE UNIVERSITY OF THE WEST INDIES PRESS

Jamaica • Barbados • Trinidad and Tobago

University of the West Indies Press
1A Aqueduct Flats   Mona
Kingston 7   Jamaica

05 04 03 02   5 4 3 2

CATALOGUING IN PUBLICATION DATA
New Caribbean thought : a reader / edited by Brian Meeks
and Folke Lindahl
p. cm.
Includes bibliographical references.

ISBN: 976-640-103-9

1. Caribbean, English-speaking – Politics and government.
2. Ideology – Caribbean, English-speaking. 3. Democracy – Caribbean,
English-speaking. I. Meeks, Brian. II. Lindahl, Folke.

F1623.N48 2001   972.905

Set in Adobe Garamond 11/ 14 x 24
Cover and book design by Robert Harris

Contents

PART II CONJUNCTURES

PART III CRITIQUE

Chapter 13

Chapter 14

Chapter 15

Chapter 16

PART IV   CONSTRUCTION

Chapter 17

Chapter 18

Chapter 19

Chapter 20

Introduction

On the Bump of a Revival

BRIAN MEEKS

In the brilliant afternoon sun of 19 October 1983, on the highest parade ground of the old fort recently renamed after his father, Maurice Bishop, prime minister of revolutionary Grenada, was shot to death alongside some of his closest comrades. At the other end of the Soviet-built AK47 automatic rifles were soldiers of the People's Revolutionary Army, of which Bishop, only days before, had been the respected commander in chief.

In a bizarre sequence of events – the exact order of which remains an issue of bitter dispute sixteen years later[1] – Bishop's prestige had, in the eyes of many of his supporters in the ruling New Jewel Movement, plummeted: from the unassailable position of *jefe maximo*, he had in the weeks before been placed under house arrest and was now being described as a potential counterrevolutionary. To the average man in the street, this volte-face, without either reason or explanation and without any prior warning, was completely unacceptable. Firm supporters of the revolution rallied to its leader and leading symbol of the social and economic gains of the previous, hectic, four years; firm opponents – many of whom had always been wary of the cocky, freewheeling élan of the 'Jewel Boys' – saw the detention as proof of their worst fears and joined the groundswell against the party and its remaining leaders.

Then, in a massive outpouring of popular support, they marched to free Bishop from his residence, located on one of the many hills overlooking the beautiful St George's Harbour. Meeting no resistance from the soldiers of the People's Revolutionary Army, they released him and headed back to Market Square in the centre of the town, where an even larger throng awaited its liberated hero. But on the way to the market, there is a fork in the road: one prong leads down Market Hill to the square; the other to Fort Rupert – the main military base, still under the full control of the party and People's Revolutionary Army. With the fateful decision to change course and attempt to capture the fort from the army, the stage had been set for the bloody confrontation that led to Bishop's death and, in that act, buried the tender revolution. Five days later, during the night of 24 October, United States Navy SEALS – the advanced detachment of an invasion force – landed stealthily near the capital. After three days of bitter fighting,[2] the first Marxist regime in the anglophone Caribbean to take power by insurrection had passed into the history books.

Long before the symbolic collapse of the Berlin Wall, the invasion of Panama to purportedly capture its President Noriega, and the Iraqi conflict, the collapse of the Grenada Revolution and the US invasion signalled not only the end of a particular variety of Caribbean Marxism but the demise of an entire notion of sovereignty and nonalignment. Along with these, though far less evident, the Grenada debacle eclipsed a new, but palpably present, sense of self-confidence that had been growing among the small island and contiguous mainland territories of the wider Caribbean. For my generation, radicalized in the popular awakening that accompanied the Black Power movement in the late 1960s, our hopes for a different, more equal and more just Caribbean, were at first raised and then dashed by the course of events in the following decade and a half. Grenada was the last nail in the coffin, but before that deadening seal there had been the revelation of the corrupt Burnham regime in Guyana and the death by assassination of that country's first son Walter Rodney and the running to ground of the Manley government in Jamaica by a brutal, relentless process of financial, psychological and military destabilization.[3]

Many previously idealistic and committed young men and women withdrew from politics. Some, without resources, education or family to support them, sunk deep into poverty; others went insane. Some, starting with a firmer social foundation, reincarnated themselves as businessmen and entrepreneurs and, with the tools of organization forged in a decade of political activity, performed extremely well. Others sought to disavow Marxism and parallel streams of revolutionary thought, seeking solace and refuge in that old, unfailing place of solace and refuge – religion. Others – quintessential political animals – shifted remarkably smoothly from radical to traditional politics, their gaze firmly affixed on the ultimate prize of the political kingdom.

At the heart of this ragged retreat of the serried ranks was the collapse of a paradigm that had, at one time with significant authority, insisted that it was possible for small states with radical, egalitarian policies to survive and flourish. The critical thing that made this possible, at least in one particular interpretation of the paradigm, was the existence of a powerful, committed and altruistic socialist bloc, which would never allow revolutionary regimes to be overcome by the manoeuvres of 'reaction' and 'imperialism'. The socialist bloc, however, turned out to be a house built on shifting sands. By the early 1990s, with the notable exception of China and relatively small, isolated Cuba, Vietnam and North Korea, 'really existing socialism' had passed into the history books.

Then, in the 1980s, with the rise and triumph of neoliberalism in Britain and the United States and the success stories emanating from the newly industrialized countries in Southeast Asia, not only was the notion of revolution no longer on the agenda but the entire history of the engagement with radical transformation took on the appearance of a flight of ideological vanity, so disconnected from the real world as to verge on lunacy. At the apogee of neoliberalism, then, somewhere before 1995, to many former opponents of global capitalism, resistance seemed futile. This was the phase when even the mildest notions of statist intervention, as from the Japanese who argued, in effect, for regionally specific models of capitalism, were dismissed out of court by the ideological guardians as being irrelevant and beneath sensible discussion. The neoliberal model has, however, also turned out to be built on shifting sands.

The collapse of many Southeast Asian economies after the summer of 1997; the discrediting, both from within and without, of neoliberal International Monetary Fund prescriptions;[4] the growing alarm at the untrammelled power of the World Trade Organization and its potential effect to destroy the economies of vulnerable, small and medium-sized states; the fear of the Multilateral Agreement on Investment – the shady, investment-centred twin to the World Trade Organization arrangements – and the recent outpouring of international opposition to it;[5] and the growing global inequality, both in a secular sense as well as within many of those states that have otherwise prospered in this phase of globalization,[6] all point towards the ideological and political exhaustion of a paradigm.

The Caribbean region, perhaps due to its smallness and vulnerability, has been at the receiving end of the momentous events that characterize this particular moment. Since the collapse of the Grenadian revolution, political and economic development in the region have been variegated and contradictory. The very smallest territories, in many instances following a model of tourism and offshore banking and utilizing the seal of approval of a continuing colonial presence, have done remarkably well. The British Virgin Islands and the Cayman Islands, for instance, have today average levels of income and social development that are the envy of their larger, independent neighbours.[7] The question, however, as to whether the models appropriate to microstates can be replicated in far larger territories with more complex economies remains moot, though the weight of opinion is probably leaning to the view that there can be no simple equation of the two. Yet one might argue that Barbados, which, while tiny on any count, is still generally considered as being on a different scale from the smallest islands, has managed to do exceptionally well. In the mid 1990s Barbados went through a period of economic contraction in the wake of the North American Free Trade Agreement arrangements, but it has since managed to pull out of this contraction and is once again on a growth path. Barbados, more than anywhere else in the region, suggests the complex nature of the global system, which, while generally hostile to small developing economies, has niches and crevices that allow for growth under very specific circumstances, however tentative this may turn out to be.[8]

Beyond these examples, however, the situation quickly becomes more pessimistic. Trinidad and Tobago continues to respond to the rhythms of the global petroleum economy though the lateral expansion into gas has given that twin-island republic greater elbowroom and flexibility. Trinidad, however, like its far more encumbered neighbour to the south, Guyana, is increasingly mired in a politics of ethnicity that has embedded within it the possibility of open racial conflict.[9] Such a situation, unless it is resolved through new and unprecedented social and political initiatives, does not bode well for the future of either of these countries. Jamaica, despite its respected history of electoral transition, is undergoing a sea change in its social and political life. The economy is caught in a vicious cycle of deflationary high interest rates and underinvestment. Three decades of structural adjustment have yielded few benefits for the poor, and there is now a new disenchantment with conventional politics along with a demand for thoroughgoing social and political change.[10] The failure of the Lavalas movement and its leader, Jean Bertrand Aristide – who in the 1990s offered a new, post–cold war approach to social transformation – to make any serious dent in the social order of Haiti suggests the limitations of popularly supported, radical movements operating in a single country in the present global order.[11]

Perhaps most illustrative, yet surprisingly with an element of optimism, is the case of revolutionary Cuba. It is remarkable how wrong were the prophets of doom who argued at the beginning of the decade that the Cuban Revolution was about to fall. Cuba has survived, though it has had to make social and economic accommodations that may yet undermine the egalitarian premise of the revolution. With the inevitable passing of Fidel Castro and a new, unfavourable internal social situation, Cuba could well follow the model of Eastern European countries, in which the population rises up in opposition to a small privileged political elite. But Cuba has always been more complex than this. The themes of nationalism and race, exemplified in the hostility to the Miami-based Cuban political machine, the pride in having survived the special period, the hostility to the United States for its forty-year attempt to exclude Cuba from the world, are all deep, unifying themes in Cuban political life. With the bottoming out of the Cuban economy and a return to growth, it would be difficult to conclude that the revolution, however modified, will not survive Castro's death.[12]

If one were to try to identify critical events that characterize the state of the region in this period, two would come to mind. The first would undoubtedly be the various 'Shiprider' agreements, through which a number of governments have given the United States the right to interdict ships in the search for drugs within the territorial waters. The ease and limited resistance with which independent states ceded the right to police their own jurisdictions suggests, more than anything else, the extent to which the old idea of sovereignty has been undermined in the new order.[13] Second, the highly publicized battle between the European community and the United States/Chiquita over the protected market for Lomé bananas in Europe, ending with the inevitable defeat, suggests the increased marginalization of the small and poor and the continuing fragility of the economies of small island states. The Caribbean Windward Islands now face uncertain futures as the protected banana industry, the cornerstone of their relative success stories in the 1980s and 1990s, has been effectively knocked out from under them, with no clear alternatives.[14]

At the start of the twenty-first century, then, in a world increasingly divided into large economic blocs, from which most of the tiny nations are excluded, it is a far more bleak than optimistic future that the Caribbean faces. And yet, within this, there are interesting new developments. The new regional initiatives associated with the deepening of the Caribbean Community and Common Market (CARICOM) and the widening of regionalism in the Association of Caribbean States suggests that there is an increasing recognition that the countries of the Caribbean will either hang together or hang separately.[15] These initiatives suffer from the old, well-established ailment of the West Indies Federation, that is, too many decisions from the state and too few discussions with the people. Yet even here, there is a greater recognition that without popular support there will be no regional integration. At the level of individual states, there is a generational change taking place that is worth close observance. Particularly in the Eastern Caribbean – in St Lucia, Dominica, Barbados, Grenada and elsewhere – a new, younger cohort of leaders has been elected, with renewed interest in regional cooperation, in developing new strategies for intervening in international affairs and in forging new relationships with the Caribbean diaspora. At the popular level, there is a new restless mood that, while anarchic in its outward manifestation, has within the possible engine of a new social and political renewal (see Meeks 2000 and Munroe 1999). This is perhaps best manifest in Jamaica, the place with which I am most familiar. The April 1999 popular demonstrations over the price of gas suggest a growing and healthy critique of the limitations of representative democracy and a concern on the part of the people to be involved in the inner affairs of their own government.

This nascent development is in no small measure enhanced by the fact that Caribbean populations are increasingly mobile and transnational. The physical and virtual movement between Kingston and Miami, Santo Domingo and New York, Bridgetown and Toronto are rapidly changing the rules of engagement of Caribbean political economy.[16] Nation, if it was ever the case, can no longer be confined to territorial space. This simple fact will have the most profound implications for the next century, though whether the outcome will be positive or negative is still not yet clear. It is already evident, however, that the new waves of migration have changed the patterns of foreign exchange earnings in many Caribbean countries. Returning citizens bring less hierarchical attitudes to social mobility and to politics. They have new, enhanced material expectations and demand that bureaucracies function in more efficient, less particularistic, ways. Residents overseas have the potential – in those places where they are concentrated in sufficient numbers – and the ability to influence local and, as with the example of the Miami Cubans, foreign policy of their host nation.

Alongside these new currents there has been an early, though as yet mild, renaissance of Caribbean social, economic and political thought. In the months and years after the defeat of the Manley regime and the collapse of the Grenadian revolution, intellectuals and intellectualism went into retreat. There was the obvious political dimension in which radical intellectuals, closely linked to the policies and politicians of democratic socialism and Caribbean Marxism-Leninism, suffered from the demoralization that follows defeat. But there was also a profoundly economic dimension. Under the impact of structural adjustment, the stable Afro-Creole salariat of the 1950s and 1960s rapidly disintegrated. This was especially felt in established areas such as the civil service, teaching and nursing. Teachers and civil servants – never rich, but previously able to buy modest cars and houses – were, in the face of raging inflation, slashed budgets and ubiquitous 'downsizing', suddenly pauperized. Pensioners were hit particularly hard. An entire generation of retired, stable, 'decent' middle class pensioners was bereft.

The University of the West Indies – the premier higher education institution in the anglophone Caribbean – was not excluded from these tectonic movements.[17] Highly respected professors with international reputations suddenly found themselves in massive debt, their buying power reduced to a mere fraction of its former size. Along with the devaluation of the currency went the devaluation of the intellectual endeavour. For some with the necessary credentials, the answer was to migrate to a place where the university professors and their projects were still valued; for others the answer was to leave the profession at whatever cost. Local private sectors were the beneficiaries of many of the brightest as they fled the poverty-stricken halls of academe.

Those who remained discovered that the framework for intellectual production had been drastically narrowed. The coincidence of the rise of neoliberalism placed a virtual damper on what was considered the acceptable field for research. For if the terms of engagement with the world economy were already set, why waste time exploring failed paradigms when the task at hand was really to make the local economy more efficient and to get the already predetermined essentials 'right'? From the perspective of creative, exploratory research, the result was a lost decade, in which technical consultancies replaced heated denominational quarrels and out of which few single studies with lasting content emerged. If the 1960s, then, can be considered as the decade in which a new, resident Caribbean intellectualism flourished, then the 1970s was the time when the debate was transferred to the plane of politics with, in the end, disastrous effect. The 1980s, however, witnessed the debilitating retreat of the intellectual both from politics and the project of serious inquiry.

The 1990s, as earlier mooted, was the beginning of a new phase. Foremost among the contributory factors has been the rapid parabolic trajectory of neoliberalism. Even at its moment of utter triumph, the model had already begun to fray at its edges. In Jamaica, located at the epicentre of the long regional engagement with structural adjustment, it was evident from at least the early 1990s that the classic devaluation and privatization prescription from the International Monetary Fund was not working. An alternative was adopted, in the deflationary model of high interest rates, but it has proven to be even more catastrophic (see Levitt 1998 and LeFranc 1994). The result has been a popular upsurge of unprecedented proportions, threatening, as nothing has done since the 1970s, the already seriously tattered social structure of that island. Another specifically Jamaican factor was the return of the Manley government to power in 1989. While the People's National Party came back with an entirely new agenda, closely wedded to the International Monetary Fund, it remained, and continues to be, far more open to the academy and free expression than the Seaga-led Jamaica Labour Party regime that preceded it. Salaries at the University of the West Indies at Mona, as well as those of teachers, policemen and other segments of the old middle classes, improved significantly, against the current of the deteriorating economy. At the University of the West Indies, Mona, somnolence once again began to give way to thoughtful, if at first tentative, critique. A third factor is to be found in the massive movement of the middle classes to the United States and Canada in the previous two decades. An entire new generation of Caribbean academics is emerging in North America. The older members are products of the University of the West Indies; the younger members have gone to school and college in North America. Many of those located in the humanities are influenced by the prevailing currents in the North American academy. They are sensitive to the debates within Afrocentricity and 'critical race theory' discourses. They have been exposed to the somewhat transient fashions of post Marxism, postmodernism and postcolonial thought which pervade many humanities departments. They have been insulated from the worst corrosive effects of the economic adjustment programmes that undermined the academy in the Caribbean in the 1980s, with both the positive and negative effects of distance. Most importantly, they bring to their academic work the exile's enhanced concern for the lost homeland.

The articles in this volume, it is hoped, capture some of the flavour of this early revival.[18] The immediate origin is a series of encounters that took place between 1993 and 1997 at annual Caribbean Studies Association conferences.

A diverse group of persons, including Folke Lindahl, Charles Mills, Rupert Lewis, Obika Gray and myself, critical of the limited presence of political theory at the annual Caribbean Studies Association conference, sought to fill this lacuna with a regular panel sensitive to issues concerned with theory and philosophy. An early product of this collaboration was the special issue of the journal *Social and Economic Studies* entitled "New Currents in Caribbean Thought" (Meeks 1994). "New Currents", in addition to publishing articles by the above-mentioned persons, included critical comments on gender from Pat Mohammed alongside controversial essays from Horace Campbell, Barry Chevannes and Trevor Munroe. After the positive reception that followed the publication of the special issue, Folke Lindahl and myself agreed to jointly host a larger, interdisciplinary group at Michigan State University in April 1997. That conference had the similar title "New Currents in Caribbean Thought: Looking Towards the Twenty-first Century". It turned out to be a rich and long overdue event. The core of the papers in this volume was presented at that encounter, though some are taken from the earlier panels and a few are later acquisitions.

The volume itself is divided into four sections. Part 1, Context, seeks both to re-examine definitions of the Caribbean and to introduce some of the broad questions confronting the region at both levels of theory and policy. The second part, Conjunctures, shifts emphasis from macro issues to focus on specific territories and important theoretical issues surrounding class, race, gender and culture. In part 3, Critique, an attempt is made to sample some of the historic as well as contemporary quarrels within the sphere of Caribbean theory. The final part, Construction, includes recent attempts to resurrect a relevant critical theory in the context of globalization and begins a conversation on an alternative policy agenda for the future.

While it would be wrong to suggest that these papers represent a typical sampling of new thought from the Caribbean, they do, nonetheless, mirror some of the newly emerging or reconsolidating trends. There is a sharp critique of Caribbean Marxism, coming from a liberal/postmodernist perspective, which is reflected mainly in the work of Folke Lindahl. There is a new race-centred discourse – perhaps most evident in the work of Charles Mills, which seeks to rethink the role of race, as opposed to class, as a central phenomenon in the project of modernity. There is a widespread concern for the place of gender in understanding and transforming Caribbean society, reflected in the chapters by Rhoda Reddock, Pat Mohammed, Cecilia Green, Clive Thomas, Maribel Aponte-Garcia and others. Issues are raised in relation to the deteriorating state of Caribbean politics and society, as in Selwyn Ryan's chapter. There is an attempt to rethink class itself and infuse it with the specific realities of Caribbean society, in chapters by Rupert Lewis, Percy Hintzen, Obika Gray and Linden Lewis. There is a concerted attempt to rescue and reorganize the critical elements in that fruitful school of thought captured under the rubric of the New World/Plantation School. This is again evident in the work of Thomas, Green and Aponte-Garcia. In keeping with the relocation of many thinkers in the North, there is an attempt to engage with broader African diaspora debates. Winston James' critique of the social character of early Caribbean migrants to the United States is an example of this. There is, perhaps as the dominant element of this volume, an attempt to come to terms with the radical political ideas that dominated the recent past. Thus, Lindahl's chapter, the sharp (and yet to be contested) critique of Meeks by Hilbourne Watson, and Paget Henry's reading of contemporary Caribbean Marxism all ask the questions as to whether Marxism, and what kind of Marxism, might still be theoretically useful. There is an attempt to, as it were, 'shift the goalposts' and rethink foundational concepts, as in David Scott's rereading of the Caribbean interpretation of freedom. There is throughout, though most evidently in the articles by Norman Girvan, Gordon Rohlehr and Stuart Hall, an attempt to redefine the Caribbean and secure its conceptual space in the New World at the end of the century. Despite the overt and unapologetic attempt to come to terms with theoretical issues, there is also a necessary concern with more practical issues of policy and direction for the immediate future of the beleaguered region. Clive Thomas, Maribel Aponte-Garcia and Alex Dupuy, among others, all raise matters that, while arising from rich theoretical discussion, contain solid implications for policy.

If one were to seek to find a commonality in this broad and diverse presentation, then it would have to be the eclectic interdisciplinary search for appropriate modes of research and attendant solutions, which is a direct product of the political crises of the tragic past as much as it is the necessary response to the increased marginalization of the hectic present. Throughout, there is a persistent attempt to grasp the political economy of a complex, if shrinking, world. Thankfully, this approach is tempered by a sensitivity to the unique social, cultural and political realities of the Caribbean matrix. If such an open, plural and unfettered conversation can be sustained and extended beyond the academy to the wider Caribbean, then, while nothing is ever certain, there must, inevitably, be greater room for optimism in the future.

Notes

1. Now that there is more distance, it is perhaps time for a new, critical review of what exactly happened in Grenada in those momentous days in October. The last serious round of analyses is already a decade old. See, for some differing perspectives, Lewis 1987; Marable 1987; and Meeks 1993.

2. Sterling proof of the fact that it is the victors who write history is evident in the persistent myth that the invading US troops met resistance primarily from Cuban regulars and irregulars. The truth is that there were no regular Cuban troops in Grenada. The armed irregulars – construction workers trained as militiamen in the typical Cuban manner – had been given strict instructions not to engage the US troops and only begun a rearguard defence after being attacked and virtually overwhelmed by the Americans. That fighting that did take place – unexpectedly fierce and prolonged beyond any prior assessment – involved members of the People's Revolutionary Army and the Grenadian militia. This fact of history is in urgent need of documentation, obviously beyond the purposes of this introduction.

3. See, for an initial attempt to survey the Anglo-Caribbean Left, Mars 1998.

4. Two recent studies from former disciples of the neoliberal paradigm most poignantly suggest the extent to which it is growing out of favour. See Gray 1998 and Krugman 1999.

5. For a discussion of the ongoing course of the anti-Multilateral Agreement on Investment skirmishes, see Chomsky 1999.

6. Nowhere else is the danger of growing global inequality more passionately discussed than in the annual *Human Development Report* of the United Nations Development Programme. See, for example, UNDP 1996: 12–37.

7. However, this spectacular growth is now threatened by new initiatives from within the European Community to remove the offshore banking privileges that have been at the heart of their success.

8. Ian Boxill, in a short paper has argued that the success of the Barbadian model lies in the fact that opposed social interests have found ways to compromise with each other rather than engage in debilitating conflict. This approach, he advances, is in contrast to other examples, such as Jamaica, where social conflict has retarded development. Assuming his initial argument to be substantial, the relevant question is whether, given the peculiar history of sharp social and political confrontation in Jamaica, such a model can at all be transferred (see Boxill 1999).

9. For a general discussion of Caribbean Politics which includes a focus on both Trinidad and Guyana, see Selwyn Ryan, "Democratic Governance in the Anglophone Caribbean: Threats to Sustainability", chapter 4 in this volume. For a somewhat pessimistic perspective on the state of ethnically based conflict in Guyana, see Thomas 1998.

10. For various assessments of the Jamaican crisis, see Levitt 1998; Munroe 1999; Girvan 1999b; and Meeks 2000.

11. See, for example, Dupuy 1997.

12. For two insightful comments supportive of this position, see Allahar 1999 and Girvan 1999a.
13. See, in particular, Elliott Abrams' argument for a new, evidently neocolonial relationship between Washington and the small Caribbean islands (Abrams 1996). For an initial response, see Lewis 1996.
14. See, for example, Lewis 1997.
15. For a rich assessment of the need for Caribbean integration, see West Indian Commission 1992; for an update on the state of wider Caribbean integration, see Serbin 1999.
16. See, for example, Basch, Schiller and Blanc 1994.
17. For a discussion of some of the changes at the University of the West Indies, Mona, see Goulbourne 1992: 21–49. For a more recent update, see Meeks, forthcoming.
18. It is reasonable to suggest that between the time of the first draft of this introduction and its publication that the revival is maturing. Thus, Paget Henry's novel and important study, *Caliban's Reason: Introducing Afro-Caribbean Philosophy* (New York: Routledge, 2000); David Scott's *Refashioning Futures* (Princeton: Princeton University Press, 2000); and Charles Mills' well-received *The Racial Contract* (Ithaca: Cornell University Press, 1997) all suggest a flowering of the discourse around 'Caribbean thought'. It is to the credit of this volume that many of the ideas present in those larger works are to be found in condensed form here.

References

Abrams, Elliott. 1996. "The Shiprider Solution: Policing the Caribbean". *National Interest*, Spring.

Allahar, Anton. 1999. "Cuba and the collapse of world socialism in the 1990s". Paper presented at the Caribbean Studies Association Annual Conference, Panama City.

Basch, Linda, Nina Glick Schiller, and Cristina Szanton Blanc. 1994. *Nations Unbound: Transnational Projects, Postcolonial Predicaments and Deterritorialized Nation States*. Pennsylvania: Gordon and Breach.

Boxill, Ian. 1999. "Crisis of an intellectual tradition". *Vistas* 6, no. 2 (June–August).

Chomsky, Noam. 1999. *Profit Over People: Neoliberalism and Global Order*. New York: Seven Stories Press.

Dupuy, Alex. 1997. *Haiti in the New World Order: The Limits of the Democratic Revolution*. Boulder: Westview Press.

Girvan, Norman. 1999a. " 'Ours is an autonomous revolution': Impressions from a visit to Cuba, March–April 1999". Typescript.

Girvan, Norman. 1999b. "Thoughts on the gas price riots". Typescript.

Goulbourne, Harry. 1992. "The institutional contribution of the University of the West Indies to the intellectual life of the anglophone Caribbean". In *Intellectuals in the Twentieth Century Caribbean*. Volume 1, *Spectre of the New Class: The Commonwealth*

Caribbean, edited by Alistair Hennessy. Warwick University Caribbean Studies Series. London: Macmillan.

Gray, John. 1998. *False Dawn: The Delusions of Global Capitalism.* New York: The New Press.

Krugman, Paul. 1999. *The Return of Depression Economics.* New York: W.W. Norton.

LeFranc, Elsie, ed. 1994. *Consequences of Structural Adjustment: A Review of the Jamaican Experience.* Kingston, Jamaica: Canoe Press.

Levitt, Kari. 1998. "Lessons of the seventies for the nineties in international context". Paper presented at symposium, Jamaica in the Seventies. University of the West Indies, Mona.

Lewis, Gordon. 1987. *Grenada: The Jewel Despoiled.* Baltimore: Johns Hopkins University Press.

Lewis, Patsy. 1996. "The Caribbean and the restructuring of the United Nations' alternatives to Abrams' Shiprider solution". *Journal of Commonwealth and Comparative Politics* 34, no. 3.

Lewis, Patsy. 1997. "Surviving beyond bananas: Revisiting size and viability in the Windward Islands". Working Paper no. 38, Center for Afro-American and African Studies, University of Michigan Colloquium Series.

Marable, Manning. 1987. *African and Caribbean Politics: From Kwame Nkrumah to Maurice Bishop.* London: Verso.

Mars, Perry. 1998. *Ideology and Change: The Transformation of the Caribbean Left.* Kingston, Jamaica: The Press, University of the West Indies.

Meeks, Brian. 1993. *Caribbean Revolutions and Revolutionary Theory: An Assessment of Cuba, Nicaragua and Grenada.* Warwick University Caribbean Studies Series. London: Macmillan.

Meeks, Brian, ed. 1994. "New Currents in Caribbean Thought". Special issue. *Social and Economic Studies* 43, no. 3 (September).

Meeks, Brian. 1999. "Saving the soul of the University". In *Celebrating the Past, Charting the Future: Proceedings of the Fiftieth Anniversary Symposium, 22 July 1998.* Kingston, Jamaica: Caribbean Quarterly.

Meeks, Brian. 2000. *Narratives of Resistance: Jamaica, Trinidad, the Caribbean.* Kingston, Jamaica: University of the West Indies Press.

Munroe, Trevor. 1999. *Renewing Democracy into the Millennium: The Jamaican Experience in Perspective.* Kingston, Jamaica: The Press, University of the West Indies.

Serbin, Andres. 1999. *Sunset Over the Islands: The Caribbean in an age of Global and Regional Challenges.* London: Macmillan.

Thomas, Clive. 1998. "Exception and rule: Racial constructs and dynamics of the Africian diaspora experience". Paper presented at Conference on African Diaspora Studies on the Eve of the Twenty-first Century. University of California, Berkeley.

UNDP (United Nations Development Programme). 1996. *Human Development Report, 1996.* New York: Oxford University Press.

West Indian Commission. 1992. *Time for Action: Report of the West Indian Commission.* Bridgetown, Barbados: West Indian Commission.

Abbreviations

ACP	Association of Concerned Policyholders
ACS	Association of Caribbean States
BMLAS	Barbados Mutual Life Assurance Society
CARICOM	Caribbean Community and Common Market
IMF	International Monetary Fund
NAFTA	North Americian Free Trade Agreement
PNP	People's National Party
PPM	People's Progressive Movement
PRG	People's Revolutionary Government
PRO	Public Record Office
UNDP	United Nations Development Programme
UNIA	Universal Negro Improvement Association
WPJ	Workers' Party of Jamaica

PART 1

Context

1

Reinterpreting the Caribbean

NORMAN GIRVAN

Definition

What constitutes the Caribbean? The answer is often a matter of perspective and of context. Anglophones in the region usually speak and think of the Caribbean as meaning the English-speaking islands, or the member states of the Caribbean Community and Common Market (CARICOM). Sometimes the phrase 'the wider Caribbean' is employed to refer to what is, in effect, 'the others'. In the Hispanic literature, *El Caribe* refers either to the Spanish-speaking islands only or to *Las Antillas* – the entire island chain. More recently, a distinction is being made between *El Caribe insular* – the islands – and *El Gran Caribe* – the Greater Caribbean, or entire basin. Among scholars, 'the Caribbean' is a sociohistorical category, commonly referring to a cultural zone characterized by the legacy of slavery and the plantation system. It embraces the islands and parts of the adjoining mainland – and may be extended to include the Caribbean diaspora overseas. As one scholar observes, there are many Caribbeans (Gaztambide-Geigel 1996: 84).

This distinction between 'Caribbeans' is reflected at the level of regional organizations. CARICOM is primarily an anglophone grouping, recently expanded to include Suriname and, in principle, Haiti. CARIFORUM, which

groups the Caribbean signatories to the Lomé Convention, includes CARI-
COM, Haiti and the Dominican Republic. The Association of Caribbean
States (ACS) embraces the entire basin. The majority of the dependent
territories in the Caribbean do not belong to CARICOM, CARIFORUM or
the ACS; but most are members of the Caribbean Development and Cooperation Committee of the Economic Commission for Latin America and the
Caribbean. The Caribbean Development and Cooperation Committee ex-
cludes the majority of the basin states; its membership corresponds roughly to
that of the insular Caribbean.

In short, the definition of the Caribbean might be based on language and
identity, geography, history and culture, geopolitics, geoeconomics, or organization. The term itself has an interesting history. It originated with the desire
of the Spanish invaders to demonize those groups of the earlier inhabitants
that chose to resist them. *Los Caribes* were allegedly the maneaters (after the
Spanish *carne,* for meat) and therefore deserving of no mercy. Gaztambide-
Geigel (1996: 76, 83) has shown that the derivative name only began to be
applied to the entire region towards the end of the nineteenth century, in the
context of the United States expanding its 'southern frontier'. Later expressions
of this were the Anglo-American Caribbean Commission (later simply the
Caribbean Commission) of 1942 and Ronald Reagan's Caribbean Basin
Initiative of the 1980s. Both the name itself and its later application to a
geographical zone were inventions of imperial powers.

What is significant is the subsequent *reinvention* of the concept of Caribbean
by native scholars as expressions of intellectual and political resistance. This
was especially notable in the case of the New World Group, which emerged
in the anglophone Caribbean in the 1960s. Drawing on the insights of the
American anthropologist Charles Wagley and building on the earlier work of
the radical nationalists C.L.R. James (1938)[1] and Eric Williams (1944, 1970),[2]
the group articulated a vision of the Caribbean as an integral part of 'Plantation
America'. Similarities of history and culture were held to outweigh differences
in language or colonial power. In the words of Lloyd Best (1971),[3]

Certainly [the Caribbean] includes the Antilles – Greater and Lesser – and the Guianas . . . But
many times the Caribbean also includes the littoral that surrounds our sea . . . what we are
trying to encompass within our scheme is the cultural, social, political and economic
foundation of the 'sugar plantation' variant of the colonial mind. (7)

For Best, this definition was the foundational step in establishing the link
between intellectual thought and Caribbean freedom. Striking parallels exist

Table 1.1 Many Caribbeans

Name	Scope	Characterization	Institutions
Caribbean Basin (United States)	Mainland and islands	Geopolitical/ hegemonic	CBI
Greater Caribbean 1 (*El Gran Caribe*)	Mainland and islands	Geoeconomic/ cooperative	ACS
Greater Caribbean 2 (*El Gran Caribe*)	Mainland and islands	Geosocial/ counterhegemonic	CRIES, Civil Forum
Plantation Caribbean or "African Central America"	Islands, the three Guianas, and "Caribbean"/black communities on the mainland	Ethnohistoric/ counterhegemonic	CSA
Insular or Island Caribbean	Islands, the three Guianas and Belize	Ethnohistoric	CDCC, ACE, CPDC
Caribbean of CARICOM	Anglophone states, Suriname, Monsterrat	Economic cooperative, strong cultural and linguistic ties	CARICOM
Caribbean of ACP	CARICOM, Dominican Republic, Haiti	Neocolonial/ negotiation, in transition	CARIFORUM

Notes:

ACE	Association of Caribbean Economists
ACP	African, Caribbean and Pacific Group of Countries. Members are signatories to the Lomé Convention with the European Union.
CARICOM	Caribbean Community and Common Market. Members are thirteen anglophone states, Suriname and Montserrat, a British dependent territory. Haiti has been admitted in principle but the formalities have not yet been completed.
CARIFORUM	Caribbean members of the ACP Group. Members are CARICOM, the Dominican Republic and Haiti
ACS	Association of Caribbean States. Members are all states of the Greater Caribbean plus three French dependencies (nonratified associate members).
CBI	Caribbean Basin Initiative
CDCC	Caribbean Development and Cooperation Committee of the Economic Commission for Latin America and the Caribbean. Members are all states of the insular Caribbean only, plus the Dutch- and US-dependent territories and three British-dependent territories.
Civil Forum	Forum of Civil Society of the Greater Caribbean
CPDC	Caribbean Policy Development Centre, an umbrella grouping of nongovernmental organizations of the insular Caribbean.
CRIES	Regional Coordination of Economic and Social Research, a network of research centres linked with nongovernmental organizations.
CSA	Caribbean Studies Association

in the positions taken by the Haitian anthropologist Jean Casimir (1991: 75–77) and the Puerto Rican historian Gaztambide-Geigel (1996: 90–92). The latter regards the Caribbean as constituting *Afro-America Central* ('Central Afro-America'); and calls this the *ethnohistoric conception* of the region.

Yet the counterhegemonic concept of Caribbean is not limited to the ethnohistoric perspective. The 'basin' perspective of the hegemonic power has been inverted by some as a sphere of resistance. This vision, which Gaztambide-Geigel characterizes as *Tercermundista* ('Thirdworldist') dates back at least to the 1940s and has been articulated by the elite in Mexico, Colombia and Venezuela, the so-called G3 (Group of Three) countries. In contemporary times it finds expression in the ACS and in the Civil Society Forum of the Greater Caribbean, a nongovernmental organization grouping. However, these organizations emphasize cooperation in furtherance of common interests as their objective; any counterhegemonic aspirations, if they are present, are muted rather than explicit.

Hence the notion of Caribbean has been, and is being, continuously redefined and reinterpreted in response to external influences and to internal currents. A plausible position is that there is no one 'correct' definition: content depends on context, but it should be clearly specified whenever used for descriptive or analytical purposes (see, for instance, Table 1.1). Conceptually, we find it useful to distinguish just the two variants of the *insular Caribbean* (a sociohistorical rather than geographic category that includes the islands, the three Guianas and Belize); and the *Greater Caribbean* (the entire basin). Organizationally, it is necessary to distinguish the Caribbean of CARICOM, of CARIFORUM, and of the ACS. Culturally, the growing importance of the diaspora of the insular Caribbean in North America and Europe has to be recognized. The Caribbean is not only multilingual, it has also become transnational.

Identity

A parallel ambiguity arises regarding the existence of a common Caribbean 'identity'. Certainly, the inhabitants of the region have been ambivalent about accepting a definition that was originally imposed from without and is still today very much an intellectual or political creation. Central Americans have always preferred to identify themselves as belonging to 'the isthmus' and to call their eastern coast 'the Atlantic'. In the Hispanic islands, the nationalist current identified itself with Latin America on cultural, linguistic and historical grounds. Self-definition as 'Caribbean' was problematic in so far as it connoted a denial of their Hispanic identity historically associated with US expansionism. It also meant being grouped with islands that were non-Hispanic, still under colonial rule and overwhelmingly black. As recently as 1987, Edgardo Rodríguez Julio, a leading Puerto Rican writer, was asserting:

For us Puerto Ricans the term *antillean* has clear significance, but not the terms *Caribbean* or *Caribbeanness*. The former makes us part of the historical and cultural experience of the Greater Antilles, the latter . . . imposes on us a suprahistorical category, an invented object of a sociological, anthropological and ethnological character that is anglophone in origin, and that functions against the colonized person, as Fanon pointed out. (Rodríguez Julio 1988 quoted in Gaztambide-Geigel 1996: 85)

Fidel Castro must have been acutely aware of the divisiveness and implicitly ethnic orientation of this current when he declared in 1976 that Cuba is a "Latin African" rather than Latin American nation, and more recently when he asserted that "the Caribbean people of African origin are a part of Our America" (Castro 1999).

An analogous ambivalence is evident among the non-Hispanics. Up to the middle of the twentieth century most of these islands remained simply 'the West Indies' or 'the Antilles' – British, French and Dutch – and their inhabitants were known as West Indians or Antilleans. Haiti, which had been isolated since its independence a century earlier, was African, francophone and uniquely Haitian. It was not until the 1940s that 'the Caribbean' began to acquire some currency in the European West Indian colonies. This was originally as a result of the activities of the (Anglo-American) Caribbean Commission and subsequently that of the work of regional historians and social scientists.

For anglophones, the terminological transition was signalled when the ill-fated *West Indies* Federation of the 1950s was replaced by the *Caribbean* Free Trade Association in the 1960s and CARICOM and the Caribbean Development Bank in the 1970s. The first two were, however, founded as exclusively anglophone clubs. Anglophones still display a certain discomfort with the expansive definition of the region: they guard their 'West Indian' identity jealously and appear to fear domination by the more populous Hispanic counties. This was reflected in the name, and the report, of the Independent West Indian Commission, set up by the CARICOM Heads of Government in 1992. The commission recommended that the integration efforts of CARICOM should be deepened rather than widened; the objective of widening regional cooperation would be pursued through the formation of the ACS, a looser form of association (West Indian Commission 1992).

It might be said that Hispanics tend to see themselves as Caribbean and Latin American, anglophones as Caribbean and West Indian. 'West Indian' might also incorporate elements of pan-Africanism or pan-Hinduism that are either weak or nonexistent in the Hispanic societies. Identity may overlap in name but may be in contradiction in content. The process of forming a common Caribbean psychocultural identity that transcends barriers of language and ethnicity is at best slow and uneven.

For their part, the Dutch islands still call themselves 'Antilles' although they have joined several Caribbean regional organizations. The French territories have the status of Overseas Departments of the French Republic and their inhabitants are French citizens. Here, self-definition as 'Caribbean' is still relatively rare and, when used, might connote an assertion of distinct cultural identity and perhaps a demand for greater autonomy.

In what follows we examine the principal socioeconomic characteristics of the Greater Caribbean and the insular Caribbean.

Socioeconomic Characteristics

Within the countries of the Greater Caribbean there are wide disparities in size, population and per capita income (see Appendix 1.1 for detailed data). The grouping is dominated by the G3 countries, which together account for between two-thirds and three-quarters of the total population, gross domestic product (GDP) and land area (Table 1.2). Mexico alone, with ninety million

Table 1.2   Greater Caribbean: Major Country Groups

	Per Capita GDP US$	Share in Population	GDP	Land Area
G3	2,713	68	73	77
Isthmus	1,447	15	8	9
Insular Caribbean	2,759	17	18	14

Note: Insular Caribbean includes Belize, Guyana, Suriname and French Guiana. GDP per capita are averages weighted by population.
Source: Based on Appendix 1.1.

people, has a greater population than all the other countries combined and 46 percent of the aggregate GDP. The population of Colombia is about equal to that of entire insular Caribbean with a GDP that exceeds that of the sixteen independent states. Venezuela has over three times the population and four times the GDP of the whole of CARICOM. Per capita income in the G3 is also higher than that of Central America and the non-CARICOM insular states and slightly below that of CARICOM. Given the wide disparities in size between the G3 and the rest, it is understandable that they should be regarded as "Latin American powers in the Caribbean" with the potential to be significant economic and political players in the region.

The balance of the regional population is divided fairly evenly between the isthmus states and the insular Caribbean. As a group, the isthmus states are the poorest in the region, with an average per capita income that is only about half that of the G3 and of CARICOM. There are wide income disparities among countries, Costa Rica and Panama having income levels that are four to five times the level in Nicaragua and Honduras. The last two are among the poorest countries in the hemisphere.

The insular Caribbean has a higher per capita income than that of the Greater Caribbean as a whole. Within this group, there are wide income disparities between the non-CARICOM and the CARICOM states, among CARICOM states, and between the independent states and the dependent territories. These income differentials are associated with size, location and political status. The next section discusses these and other socioeconomic characteristics of the insular Caribbean in greater detail.

The Insular Caribbean

The insular Caribbean is an extremely fragmented and heterogeneous subregion. With just thirty-seven million people it contains twenty-eight distinct political entities and these vary widely with respect to size, political status, income and language. Twenty-two countries have populations of under one million, and these include eleven independent states. Fourteen of the sixteen independent states attained sovereignty only in the past forty years,[4] some as recently as the 1980s. Their political systems vary from multiparty parliamentary democracies in most of the anglophone countries to executive presidential systems in several and the one-party popular democracy of Cuba.

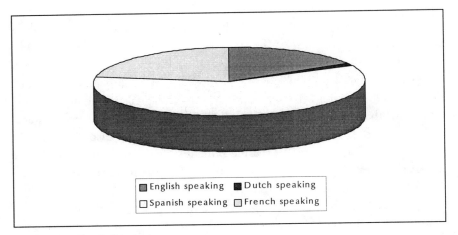

Figure 1.1   The Caribbean: Language

The dependent territories belong to four metropolitan powers. Constitutional arrangements range from virtually full internal autonomy, as in Puerto Rico and the Netherlands Antilles, to the sharing of responsibility between locally elected administrations and the metropolitan authorities, as in the British and French dependencies. There are at least six official languages and several local Creoles are also spoken.[5] Here there is a paradox: although the majority of Caribbean entities are English speaking, the majority of the population is Spanish speaking, with French being second in importance. The distribution of population by language is shown in Figure 1.1 above.

In analysing socioeconomic characteristics, we have found it useful to distinguish four subgroups that combine the attributes of political status, size and location, while ignoring distinctions of language, political system and regional association. The subgroups are:

1. Larger island states: four states in the Greater Antilles containing three-quarters of the population, with an average population of nearly seven million. These are Cuba, the Dominican Republic, Haiti and Jamaica.
2. Smaller island states: nine states, mostly in the eastern and southern Caribbean with populations under one and a half million each and an average population size of 260,000. These are Trinidad and Tobago, Barbados, the Bahamas, and the six members of the Organization of Eastern Caribbean States.
3. Mainland states: Suriname, Guyana and Belize.
4. Dependent territories, which number twelve in all.

Table 1.3   Insular Caribbean: GDP, Population and Land Area

	Per Capita GDP 1995[a]	GDP	Percent total Population	Land Area
Larger Island States	1,101	30.3	75.9	27.6
Smaller Island States	5,215	12.0	6.4	3.0
Mainland	1,174	1.6	3.8	55.0
Dependent Territories	11,099	56.1	13.9	14.4
Total	2,759	100.0	100.0	100
Memo note: CARICOM	2,923	18.0	17.0	59.6
Non-CARICOM states	1,036	25.0	69.1	26.0

[a] Weighted averages

Summary information on the subgroups is provided in Table 1.3, with additional details on human development and poverty in Table 1.4.

Larger Island States

The group of four island states with 75 percent of the population of the subregion has relatively low per capita incomes and modest levels of human development. It includes Haiti, one of the poorest countries in the world with very low human development.[6] Cuba, the Dominican Republic and Jamaica are all in the $1,000 to $2,000 range of per capita income. Cuba has done best in terms of level of human development compared to level of per capita income,[7] followed by Jamaica. The incidence of poverty is very high in Haiti, where two-thirds of the population live below the poverty line, and significant in Jamaica and the Dominican Republic where one-third and one-fifth of the population, respectively, are estimated to be in absolute poverty. In Cuba one-sixth of the urban population is estimated to be at risk of being unable access their basic needs requirements.

All four countries have experienced low or negative real per capita growth over much or most of the last two decades. This is due to falling commodity prices and debt and adjustment crises (the Dominican Republic and Jamaica) exacerbated by the effects of political turmoil (Haiti) and the collapse of the Soviet Union (Cuba). As a result, they have lost substantial ground in their human development ranking in the world during the 1990s.

Table 1.4   Insular Caribbean: Human Development, Growth and Poverty

	GDP Per capita 1995 US$		Human Development Category	Human Development Index Change 1991–1998[g]	Growth[b]		Poverty[c]
	Current	Real PPP$[a]			1965–80	1980–95	
Larger Island States							
Cuba	1,113	3,100	Medium	-23	0.6	–	15[e]
Dominican Republic	1,663	3,923	Medium	-8	3.8	1.1	21
Haiti	285	917	Low	-34	0.9	-4.0	65[d]
Jamaica	1,762	3,801	Medium	-25	-0.1	1.4	32
Smaller Island States							
Antigua and Barbuda	6,640	9,131	High	17	-1.4	5.2[f]	12
Bahamas	12,258	15,738	High	-4	1.0	-0.1	5[d]
Barbados	7,120	11,306	High	-2	3.5	1.2	8[d]
Dominica	2,574	6,424	High	12	-0.8	4.3	33
Grenada	2,344	5,425	High	13	0.1	3.0	20
St Kitts and Nevis	3,083	10,150	High	15	4.0	4.9	15
St Lucia	4,642	6,503	High	10	2.7	4.4[f]	25
St Vincent	2,032	5,969	High	22	0.2	4.5	17
Trinidad and Tobago	4,101	9,437	High	-1	3.1	-1.5	21
Mainland							
Belize	2,696	5,623	High	4	3.4	1.7	35
Guyana	809	3,205	Medium	-11	0.7	-1.7	43
Suriname	1,066	4,862	Medium	-10	5.5	3.4	47[d]

[a] Adjusts GDP for differences in purchasing power between countries (from UNDP 1998).

[b] Average annual real per capita GDP growth for period (from UNDP 1998).

[c] Proportion of population below income poverty, national poverty line estimate, 1989–94, except where otherwise indicated (from UNDP 1998).

[d] Head Count Poverty Index, mid 1990s, as reported by World Bank 1996: 164.

[e] Urban population at risk of not accessing supply of essential goods and services (from Ferriol 1998: 19).

[f] 1980–93 (from UNDP 1998).

[g] Change in global Human Development Index rank, 1991–98.

Smaller Island States

This group of nine mini-states,[8] with less than 7 percent of the population of the subregion, enjoys levels of per capita income and of human development considerably higher than in the larger island and mainland states. Their average per capita income is 4.7 times that of the larger island states, and they are all classified as having high human development in the United Nations Development Programme tables. Economic growth in the last two decades or in the 1990s has been propelled by the expansion of tourism, offshore banking services, manufacturing, banana exports and energy-based industries. Investment has also been strong due to political and social stability and successful macroeconomic management in the majority of cases. In some of the smallest islands the fruits of economic growth have been fairly widely distributed due to the small populations, the dispersal of tourism and banana cultivation, and strong public spending on social services.

Yet problems of poverty and vulnerability cast a shadow over the future of these countries. In six of the nine countries the incidence of poverty is 15 percent or over, and the rate reaches over 20 percent in Trinidad and Tobago and two of the Windward Islands and over 30 percent in Dominica. The Windward Islands' banana-producing economies are also threatened with severe dislocation due to a World Trade Organization ruling against the preferential treatment they receive under the European Union banana import regime (Lewis 1999). Vulnerability to natural disasters is evident in the damage sustained in the Windward and Leeward Islands during the annual hurricane season and in episodes such as the volcanic eruptions in Montserrat, which have dislocated an entire island community. The strategic location of the islands on the principal drug trafficking routes from South America to North America and Europe has also exposed them to the activities of large international criminal organizations whose resources vastly exceed those of the local state systems.

Mainland States

The three mainland states contain 55 percent of the land area but only 4 percent of the population of the subregion. In spite of their low population densities they are relatively poor. Per capita incomes are similar to those of the larger islands, though Belize is considerably richer on average than the other two. Both Guyana and Suriname have an export structure that is dominated by primary commodities – bauxite in the case of Suriname and bauxite and sugar in the case of Guyana – and both have been negatively affected by the weakening of commodity markets since the 1980s. Internal political conflict has also contributed to economic decline. Suriname experienced an abrupt withdrawal of Dutch aid in the 1980s following a military coup; while the economy of Guyana suffered from brain drain and capital flight during the Burnham dictatorship of the 1970s and the 1980s.

Dependent Territories

The twelve dependent territories contain 14 percent of the population of the subregion and have relatively high per capita incomes. Puerto Rico predominates in this subgroup in terms of population and GDP. This territory has 10 percent of the population and 42 percent of the GDP of the insular Caribbean as a whole.

The factors behind the high incomes of the dependent territories are similar to those applying to the smaller island states, with the additional advantages of dependent status. Resource transfers to support social services are substantial in the US and French dependencies. The British and Dutch dependencies have become major offshore banking centres, taking advantage of their political attractiveness associated with colonial protection. Most of the dependent territories have large tourist industries and small populations – a combination that inevitably results in high per capita incomes.

The Caribbean Diaspora

One consequence of these trends has been the continued growth of intraregional migration as well as of external migration flows. This is not a new phenomenon, as intraregional migration dates back to the end of the nineteenth century. Contemporary flows are oriented to the expanding tourism and service economies of the smaller island and dependent territories from the labour surplus, crisis-affected economies such as Haiti, Jamaica, the Dominican Republic, Guyana, Dominica and, more recently, Cuba. External migration has also continued on a substantial scale. Although this phenomenon is not as well researched as it ought to be, especially intra-Caribbean migration, the following indicators are illustrative of its importance.

The net loss of population from the region in the period from 1950 to 1989 has been estimated at five and one half million (Guengant 1993, cited in Samuel 1996: 8), which is about 15 percent of the present population within the region. Haiti, Cuba, Jamaica and Puerto Rico each had close to one million of their native-born population living abroad at the close of the 1980s. In relation to the resident population, the overseas population at the end of the 1980s stood at 40 percent for both Jamaica and Guyana, 36 percent for Suriname, 23 percent for Puerto Rico, 21 percent for Trinidad and Tobago, 15 percent for Haiti, and 10 percent for Cuba. By the early 1990s the overseas population was sending home in remittances an amount equal to 71 percent of the value of exports in the case of the Dominican Republic, 32 percent in the case of Haiti, 29 percent in Jamaica and 17 percent for Barbados (Samuel 1996: Table 6). In Jamaica remittances have been the fastest growing source of foreign exchange inflows in the 1990s. Hence the Caribbean diaspora is undoubtedly an important source of household income in many of these societies as well as a major aspect of people-based integration within the social life of the region itself.

To summarize, the insular Caribbean has a small number of densely populated states whose living conditions are not too dissimilar from those in the rest of the Greater Caribbean, and a large number of mini-states and dependent territories, some of which have been able to secure relatively high incomes by specializing in tourism and financial services. It is likely that income differentials within the subregion have widened in the past two decades, intraregionally if not intranationally. Pressures arising out of shifts in the world economy and other developments, generally referred to as globalization, are evident in the difficulties experienced in the most populous countries during the 1990s and the uncertainties now faced by some of the smaller states. Poverty is a major problem in the larger countries and in several of the smaller societies, notwithstanding their higher per capita incomes. Even the relatively prosperous societies – including the dependent territories – are highly vulnerable to events not of their own making and to forces outside of their control. Caribbean people continue to move in search of survival and a better life, as they always have. But for the subregion, vulnerability, differentiation and fragmentation continue to be major issues.

Regionalism in the Insular and the Greater Caribbean

Regional integration, or at least cooperation, is frequently advanced as a strategy of confronting the challenges of globalization and the risks of marginalization facing the insular and the Greater Caribbean. In the 1990s there has been renewed interest in regionalism, as shown by the report of the Independent West Indian Commission, the expansion of CARICOM, the formation of CARIFORUM and the creation of the ACS. In the wider hemisphere there have been efforts to consolidate Mercosur, the Andean Community, and the Central American Integration System in response to the formation of the North American Free Trade Agreement (NAFTA) and the drive towards the European Union single market.

Regional integration cannot substitute for what is lacking at the national level. Essential foundations of effective regionalism are internal political and social cohesiveness and policy coherence. Several societies in the insular Caribbean are facing severe problems of governance and political legitimacy, including Haiti, Guyana, Suriname, Jamaica, and possibly Trinidad and Tobago. These are rooted in ethnic and class conflict and, in some instances, in the fragility and erosion of national institutions. These problems will make it difficult to embark on regional projects that require negotiated compromises, concessions on national sovereignty and consistent implementation. In the Greater Caribbean the movement towards effective regionalism will also be conditioned by success in resolving problems of internal legitimacy in several of the G3 and Central American states.

CARICOM is often referred to as one of the more successful integration groups in the developing world. But the community has disappointed many who saw in it the possibility of organizing a cohesive economic grouping with coordinated economic policies. Initiatives that failed to be completed include the harmonization of fiscal incentives, the regional industrial policy, joint strategies of agricultural development and the organization of joint industrial enterprises. By the early 1990s CARICOM had opted for the newly fashionable strategy of 'open regionalism'. The common external tariff was reduced steeply and the process of forging the CARICOM Single Market and Economy was launched. Progress towards the CARICOM Single Market and Economy has been steady, but agonizingly slow; and the target date for completion has been put back several times. CARICOM cooperation has been more successful in the field of external negotiations focusing on relations with the European

Union under Lomé and with the United States under the Free Trade Area of the Americas. The CARICOM governments continue to be driven by the immediate requirements of preserving and enhancing existing external trade privileges; the organization is not seen primarily as a cooperation mechanism to assist the transformation of internal social and economic relations.

A significant development in 1997 was the bid by the new Fernandez administration in the Dominican Republic to become a bridge between the Caribbean and Central America in the forging of a "strategic alliance" between the two subregions (Girvan 1998). The proposal is for a free trade agreement between the two subregions and between both and the Dominican Republic, with cooperation in business enterprise development, in tourism and investment promotion, and in external trade negotiations. Initial response has been lukewarm, as both subregions see little scope for the expansion of intraregional trade and are preoccupied with the more immediate issues of NAFTA parity and the European Union post-Lomé negotiations. Yet as the small countries of the insular Caribbean and the isthmus discover the limits of their leverage in the post–cold war era, interest in a strategic alliance of this kind is likely to grow.

The emergence of the ACS as an intergovernmental organization of the Greater Caribbean, may also be significant (Byron 1998). The ACS aims to foster cooperation in trade, transport and tourism. The principal ACS members already belong to integration groups: Mexico with NAFTA, Colombia and Venezuela with the Andean Group, and Central America and the anglophone states to Sistema Económico Latinoamericano (Latin American Economic System) and CARICOM, respectively. An ACS free trade area is therefore unlikely, as is joint external negotiations on trade agreements. But the very existence of the ACS, whose headquarters are in Port of Spain, is stimulating interest in educational exchange, language training, trade facilitation, and sustainable tourism.

Another notable development is the growing role of nongovernmental organizations in effecting regionalism at the level of civil society. In the insular Caribbean there is the Caribbean Policy Development Centre and in Central America there are several, including the Civil Initiative for Central American Integration (Serbin 1998). In recent years there have been two meetings of the Permanent Forum of Greater Caribbean Civil Society, which is promoted by the Regional Coordination of Economic and Social Research. The emergence of these new actors is part of a wider hemispheric and global phenomenon in the 1980s and 1990s. It corresponds to the growth of the women's and environmental movements and of community organizations as well as to the erosion of the state and the decline of conventional Left parties due to shrinking labour union membership and the fall of the USSR. By being less bureaucratic and more flexible, visionary and voluntaristic than the existing official structures, these movements may be better placed to promote integration processes at the popular level.

Towards the Future

At the close of the nineteenth century the Caribbean had not yet been invented. The nation state was very much a privilege of the imperial powers. The British, French and Dutch West Indies were sleepy backwaters of European empires. Haiti and the Dominican Republic were relatively isolated. José Martí had died fighting for a free Cuba and *Nuestra America*, but Cuba and Puerto Rico were in the process of exchanging one imperial overlord for another. Few could have guessed at the momentous changes the twentieth century would bring.

Yet these changes were already in the making. The European powers were enmeshed in a deadly imperialist rivalry that would lead to two world wars that were to change the political map of the world and set the stage of decolonization. In Jamaica, Garvey had already started to question the racially stratified order of the colonial society, the first step towards his vision of a united Africa as home for black people liberated from mental slavery and racial discrimination. All over the British West Indies the second generation of free blacks had secured education and were now manning the teaching profession, which gave birth to the Trinidadian C.L.R. James and others who were to launch the labour and independence movements of the 1930s. In Cuba, Martí's dream refused to die; sixty years later it would inspire Fidel Castro and the Cuban Revolution. The social foundations for a Sandino, a Manley I and II, a Williams, a Jagan and a Bishop had already been established.

The foundations of the changes of the early twenty-first century have already been laid, even if the changes themselves cannot be predicted. Capitalist globalization and the ideology of progress are being questioned, as was imperialism one hundred years ago. But so are the legacies of ideas and institutions of the political movements of the twentieth century, such as national sovereignty and its expressions of nation state, national development, and regional (interstate) cooperation. Sovereignty and identity are being detached from a defined physical space, while culture and common interest are emerging as important frames of reference. To be sovereign in the age of global community

Appendix 1.1   Basic Statistics on the Greater Caribbean

	Population Thousand	Area km^2	Density Pers/km^2	GDP 1995 per capita	GDP 1995 US$M	Indepen- dence	Language
Mexico	90,100	1,967,183	46	2,775	250,038	1810	Spanish
Venezuela	21,852	916,445	24	3,433	75,016	1811	Spanish
Colombia	35,900	1,141,748	31	2,120	76,112	1810	Spanish
G-3	147,852	4,025,376	37	2,713	401,166	–	
Costa Rica	3,424	51,000	67	2,697	9,233	1821	Spanish
El Salvador	5,662	21,040	269	1,673	9,471	1821	Spanish
Guatemala	10,621	108,889	98	1,364	14,489	1821	Spanish
Honduras	5,654	112,080	50	696	3,937	1821	Spanish
Nicaragua	4,124	130,700	32	464	1,913	1821	Spanish
Panama	2,622	75,517	35	2,827	7,413	1903	Spanish
Isthmus	32,107	499,226	64	1,447	46,456	–	
Cuba	10,964	114,525	96	1,113	12,200	1959	Spanish
Dominican Republic	7,250	48,308	150	1,663	12,055	1844	Spanish
Haiti	7,180	27,750	259	285	2,043	1804	French
Insular non-CARICOM	25,394	190,583	133	1,036	26,298	–	
Antigua & Barbuda	64	440	146	6,640	427	1981	English
Bahamas	279	13,864	20	12,258	3,420	1973	English
Barbados	264	431	613	7,120	1,883	1966	English
Belize	217	22,966	9	2,696	584	1981	English
Dominica	74	751	98	2,574	190	1978	English
Grenada	98	344	285	2,344	230	1974	English
Guyana	780	216,000	4	809	631	1966	English
Jamaica	2,500	11,424	219	1,762	4,406	1962	English
St Lucia	145	616	236	3,083	448	1979	English
St Kitts & Nevis	42	269	156	4,642	195	1983	English
St Vincent & Grenadines	110	389	283	2,032	224	1979	English
Suriname	409	163,820	2	1,066	436	1975	Dutch

Table continues

Appendix 1.1 (contd') Basic Statistics on the Greater Caribbean

	Population Thousand	Area km^2	Density Pers/km^2	GDP 1995 per capita	GDP 1995 US$M	Indepen- dence	Language
Trinidad & Tobago	1,262	5,066	249	4,101	5,175	1962	English
CARICOM	6,244	436,380	14	2,923	18,249		
Aruba	82	188	434	16,810	1,370		Dutch
Netherland Antilles	207	783	265	7,871	1,632		Dutch
Dutch Territories	289	971	298	10,388	3,002		
Anguilla	10	91	113	5,932	61		English
Montserrat	10	102	98	5,155	52		English
British Virgin Islands	18	150	122	18,487	339		English
Cayman Islands	32	260	123	28,125	900		English
Turks and Caicos Islands	15	417	35	7,021	103		English
British Territories	85	1,020	83	17,106	1,454		
French Guiana[1]	141	91,000	2	9,908	1,397		French
Guadeloupe[1]	447	1,705	262	7,585	3,390		French
Martinique[1]	360	1,060	340	10,895	3,922		French
French Departments	948	93,765	10	9,187	8,709		
Puerto Rico	3,700	9,065	408	11,450	42,364		Spanish
US Virgin Islands	102	342	298	13,163	1,340		English
USA Territories	3,802	9,407	404	11,495	43,704		
Insular Caribbean[2]	36,762	732,126	50	2,759	101,416		
Greater Caribbean	216,721	5,256,728	41	2,533	549,038		

[1] 1992 GDP data
[2] CARICOM members, Cuba, the Dominican Republic, Haiti and the dependent territories.
Source: Based on data in Ceara 1997, Annex Table 1.

will be less a matter of formal state authority and more a matter of developing the capacity for autonomous and proactive strategies at all levels, beginning with the community. To be regional will imply discovering a shared identity and interests and acting in function of those.

If the Caribbean was an invention of the twentieth century, it seems certain to be reinterpreted and perhaps transcended in the twenty-first. The Caribbean of tomorrow will not be an exclusively anglophone or Hispanic conception, and it will not be tied exclusively to geographic space or definition. If it survives at all, it will be a community of shared economic, social and political interests and strategies that encompasses different languages and cultures and the Caribbean diaspora. It might well include interstate cooperation, but if so, this will be only one of a number of spheres of interaction.

It is by no means clear to this writer that all or most of these societies will survive as viable entities – units that provide for the basic social, economic and community needs of a collection of defined citizens and with some capacity for autonomous action. Some may become just places to reside in for a while, to visit, to holiday in and to retire to. In any case, only those legacies of the twentieth century that are found to be in the interests of the people of the region will be retained and reshaped. The rest will be discarded and forgotten, and our people will move on.

Notes

1. James' book on the Haitian Revolution, *The Black Jacobins,* was reissued in 1962 with a new appendix called "From Toussaint L'Ouverture to Fidel Castro". It has gone through many editions, has been published in French and Italian, and strongly influenced the consciousness of several generations of anglophone Caribbean intellectuals.

2. Williams, a Trinidadian historian who later led the nationalist movement and became the first prime minister of Trinidad and Tobago, analysed the connection between slavery, the slave trade and the rise of British industrial capitalism. He worked for the Caribbean Commission in Puerto Rico before entering Trinidadian politics. In 1970, the same year that Williams' *From Columbus to Castro* came out, the Dominican Republic nationalist leader Juan Bosch published a book in Spanish with a virtually identical name (Bosch 1983).

3. Originally published in 1967. The same passage makes clear that Best's conception of the Caribbean stretched as far as Recife in Brazil and the Carolinas in the United States. See also Beckford's classic *Persistent Poverty* (1972).
4. This includes Cuba, whose official date of independence is 1 January 1959.
5. Spanish, French, English, Dutch, Haitian Creole and the Creole of the Netherlands Antilles.
6. Haiti was ranked 159th in the world Human Development Index tables in 1998. It has slipped thirty-four places in ranking since 1991.
7. This is measured by the difference between the country's GDP per capita rank and its Human Development Index rank. For Cuba this was 18 in 1998, for Jamaica 9, for the Dominican Republic 1.
8. The official United Nations classification of a mini-state is one with a population of less than one and a half million.

References

Beckford, George. 1972. *Persistent Poverty: Underdevelopment in the Plantation Economies of the Third World*. New York: Oxford University Press.

Best, Lloyd. 1971. "Independent thought and Caribbean freedom". In *Readings in the Political Economy of the Caribbean*, edited by Norman Girvan and Owen Jefferson. Kingston, Jamaica: New World Group. (Originally published 1967 in *New World Quarterly* 3, no. 4.)

Bosch, Juan. 1983. *De Cristóbal Colón a Fidel Castro: El Caríbe, Frontera Imperial*. 1970. Reprint, Havana: Editorial de Ciencias Sociales.

Byron, Jessica. 1998. "The Association of Caribbean States: Growing pains of a new regionalism?" *Pensamiento Propio*, year 3, no. 7 (May–August).

Casimir, Jean. 1991. *La Caraïbe: une et divisible*. Comision Económica Para America Latina y El Caribe Nations Unies–Éditions Henri Deschamps.

Castro Ruz, Fidel. 1999. Intervention on the Caribbean. "Encuentro internacional sobre globalización y problemas del desarrollo". Palabras Sobre El Caribe al Encuentro Internacional sobre Globalización y Problemas del Desarrollo. Havana, 20 January. (Informal English translation by N. Girvan.)

Ceara Hatton, Miguel. 1997. "The insular Caribbean and hemispheric integration". *Pensamiento Propio*, year 2 (September–December).

Clarke, Lawrence, ed. 1997. *Essays in Honour of William Demas*. St Augustine, Trinidad: Caribbean Centre for Monetary Studies.

CRIES (Regional Coordination of Economic and Social Research). 1997. *1er Foro de la Sociedad Civil del Gran Caríbe*. Managua: CRIES–Instituto Venezolano de Estudios Sociales y Politicos.

Ferriol, Angela. 1998. "La reforma económica en Cuba en los 90" ("Economic reform in Cuba in the 1990s"). *Pensamiento Propio*, year 3, no. 7 (May–August).

FES/ACE (Friedrich Ebert Siftung/Association of Caribbean Economists). 1998. *CARI-COM, Central America and the Free Trade Agreement of the Americas: Two Contributions.* Kingston, Jamaica: FES and ACE.

Gaztambide-Geigel, Antonio. 1996. "La invención del Caríbe en el siglo XX: las definiciones del Caríbe como problema histórico e metodológico". *Revista Mexicana del Caríbe,* year 1, no. 1.

Girvan, Norman. 1998. "Towards a Caribbean-Central American strategic alliance". *Pensamiento Propio,* year 3, no. 7 (May–August).

Guengant, J. 1993. "Whither the Caribbean exodus? Prospects for the 1990s". *International Journal* 48 (Spring).

James, C.L.R. 1938. *The Black Jacobins: Toussaint L'Ouverture and the San Domingo Revolution.* London: Secker and Warburg.

Lewis, Patsy. 1999. "Beyond bananas: Globalization, size and viability in the Windwards Islands". Paper presented at Department of Government seminar, Globalization and Small States, University of the West Indies, Mona, 13 January.

Rodríguez Julio, Edgardo. 1988. "Puerto Rico y el Caríbe: história de una marginalidad". *El Nuevo Día,* 20 November. (Quoted in Gaztambide-Geigel 1996: 85; informal English translation by N. Girvan.)

Samuel, Wendell. 1996. "The contribution of remittances to social and economic development in the Caribbean". Typescript, Eastern Caribbean Central Bank, St Kitts, January.

Serbin, Andres. 1998. "The integration processes in the Greater Caribbean". *Pensamiento Propio,* year 3, no. 6 (January–April).

UNDP (United Nations Development Programme). 1998. *Human Development Report, 1998.* New York: Oxford University Press.

Wagley, Charles. 1960. "Plantation America: A culture sphere". In *Caribbean Studies: A Symposium,* edited by Vera Rubin. Seattle: University of Washington Press.

West Indian Commission. 1992. *Time for Action: Report of the West Indian Commission.* Bridgetown, Barbados: West Indian Commission.

Williams, Eric. 1944. *Capitalism and Slavery.* Chapel Hill: University of North Carolina Press.

Williams, Eric. 1970. *From Columbus to Castro: The History of the Caribbean, 1492–1969.* London: Harper and Row.

World Bank. 1996. *Poverty Reduction and Human Resource Development in the Caribbean.* Washington, DC: World Bank.

2

Negotiating Caribbean Identities

STUART HALL

In this article I will address questions of Caribbean culture and identity. I want to suggest that such questions are not in any sense separate or removed from the problems of political mobilization, of cultural development, of economic development and so on. The more we know and see of the struggles of the societies of the periphery to make something of the slender resources available to them, the more important we understand the questions and problems of cultural identity to be in that process. I want to examine some of the themes of a topic that has been richly explored by Caribbean writers and artists – cultural identity presenting itself always as a problem to Caribbean people.

Why cultural identity should be a problem is not a mystery, but I want to probe this question of identity and why Caribbean writers, politicians, civic leaders, artists and others have been unable to leave worrying away at it. In doing so, I want to problematize to some extent the way we think about identity. I want to explore the term 'myth' itself – the English are not good at myth, always opposing it, on the one hand, to reality and, on the other hand, to truth, as though one has to choose between them. I specifically do not want to choose between myth and reality but to talk about the very real contemporary and historical effects of myths of identity. And I want to do so with one other purpose, which I hope will come through more clearly at the end. The issue of cultural identity as a political quest now constitutes one of the most serious global problems at the start of the twenty-first century. The re-emergence of questions of ethnicity, of nationalism – the obduracy, the dangers and the pleasures of the rediscovery of identity in the modern world, inside and outside of Europe – places the question of cultural identity at the very centre of the contemporary political agenda. What I want to suggest is that despite the dilemmas and vicissitudes of identity through which Caribbean people have passed and continue to pass, we have a tiny but important message for the world about how to negotiate identity.

The Search for Essence

There is a very clear and powerful discourse about cultural identity, especially in the West. Indeed, most of us have lived through, and are still living through, an exercise in the definition and defence of a particular kind of British cultural identity. I was puzzled when Norman Tebbit asked which cricket team you would support, in order to discover whether you were "one of us", "one of them" or maybe neither.[1] My own response to that was, if you can tell me how many of the four hundred members of the British athletics team are properly British, I would be ready to answer the question about the cricket team; otherwise not. But the discourse of identity suggests that the culture of a people is at root – and the question of roots is very much at issue – a question of its essence, a question of the fundamentals of a culture. Histories come and go, peoples come and go, situations change, but somewhere down there throbs the culture to which we all belong. It provides a kind of ground for our identities: something to which we can return, something solid, something fixed, around which we can organize our identities and our sense of belongingness. And there is a sense that modern nations and peoples cannot survive for long and succeed without the capacity to touch ground, as it were, in the name of their cultural identities.

Now, the question of what constitutes a Caribbean cultural identity has been of extraordinary importance, especially in the twentieth century. Partly because of the dislocations of conquest, of colonization and slavery, partly because of the colonial relationship itself and the distortions of living in a world culturally dependent on and dominated by some centre outside the place where the majority of the people lived. But the question has also been important for counter-identities, providing sources on which the important movements of decolonization, of independence, of nationalist consciousness in the region have been founded. In a sense, until it is possible to state who the subjects of independence movements are likely to be, and in whose name cultural decolonization is being conducted, it is not possible to complete the process. And that process involves the question of defining the people. In *Black Skin, White Masks*, Frantz Fanon speaks of what he calls a passionate research directed to the secret hope of discovering beyond the misery of today, beyond self-contempt, resignation and abjuration, some beautiful and splendid area whose existence rehabilitates us both in regard to ourselves and others (Fanon 1970). And as I have said, that passionate research by Caribbean writers, artists and political leaders, that quest for identity, has been the very form in which much of our artistic endeavour in all the Caribbean languages has been conducted in this century.

Cross-Currents of Diaspora

Why, then, is the identity of the Caribbean so problematic? It is a very large question, but let me suggest some of the reasons. First of all, if the search for identity always involves a search for origins, it is impossible to locate in the Caribbean an origin for its peoples. The indigenous peoples of the area very largely no longer exist, and they ceased to exist very soon after the European encounter. This is indeed the first trauma of identity in the Caribbean. Take the coat of arms of Jamaica, for example: it has two Arawak Indian figures supporting a shield in the middle, which is crossed by pineapples surmounted by an alligator. In 1983 the then prime minister of Jamaica, Edward Seaga, wanted to change the coat of arms on the ground that he could not find represented in it a single recognizable feature of Jamaican identity. "Can the crushed and extinct Arawaks," he asked, "represent the dauntless inhabitants of Jamaica? Does the low-slung near-extinct crocodile, a cold-blooded reptile, symbolize the warm soaring spirits of Jamaicans? Where does the pineapple, which was exported to Hawaii, appear prominently either in our history or in our folklore?" I mention this simply as a reminder that questions of identity are always questions about representation. They are always questions about the invention, not simply the discovery, of tradition. They are always exercises in selective memory, and they almost always involve the silencing of something in order to allow something else to speak.

Morris Cargill, a famous commentator on Jamaican affairs in the *Gleaner,* responded to Prime Minister Seaga, "What about a design containing entwined marijuana plants? Against a background of US dollar bills with Toyotas rampant and ladies couchant?" (Cargill 1987: 285). Silencing as well as remembering identity is always a question of producing in the future an account of the past; that is to say, it is always about narrative, the stories cultures tell themselves about who they are and where they came from. The one way in which it is impossible to resolve the problem of identity in the Caribbean is to try looking at it, as if a good look will tell you who the people are. During the period in which I was preparing my series on the Caribbean for the British Broadcasting Corporation, I had the occasion, in a relatively short space of time, to visit a large number of Caribbean islands, several of them for the first time.[2] I was staggered by the ethnic and cultural diversity I encountered. Not a single Caribbean island looks like any other in terms of its ethnic composition, including the different genetic and physical features and characteristics of the people. And that is before you touch the question of different languages and different cultural traditions that reflect the different colonizing cultures.

It may surprise some people to know that there are several Caribbean islands, large ones, in which blacks are nowhere near a majority of the population. There are now two important formerly British Caribbean societies where Indians are in the majority. In Cuba what you are struck by first of all is the continued persistence of white Hispanic settlement, then of the mestizo population, and only later of the black population. Haiti, which is in some ways the symbolic island of black culture, where one feels closer to the African inheritance than anywhere else, has a history in which the mulattos have played an absolutely vital historical role. Martinique is a bewildering place; it is, in my experience, more French than Paris – just slightly darker. The Dominican Republic is a place where it is possible to feel closer to Spain and to the Spanish tradition of Latin America than anywhere else I have been in the Caribbean. The melting-pot of the British islands produced a different combination of genetic features and factors everywhere, and in each island elements of other ethnic cultures – Chinese, Syrian, Lebanese, Portuguese, Jewish – are present. I know because I have a small proportion of practically all of them in my own inheritance. My background is African, also I am told Scottish – of pretty low descent, probably convict – East Indian and Portuguese Jew.

What is more, in another sense, everybody in the Caribbean comes from somewhere else, and it is not clear what has drawn them to the region and certainly not whether their motives were ever of the highest level of aspiration.

That is to say, their true cultures, the places they really come from, the traditions that really formed them, are somewhere else. The Caribbean is the first, the original and the purest diaspora. These days, blacks who have completed the triangular journey back to Britain sometimes speak of the emerging black British diaspora, but I have to tell them that they and I are twice diasporized. This is more than just a diaspora and living in a place where the centre is always somewhere else: we are the break with those originating cultural sources as passed through the traumas of violent rupture. I do not want to address the nature of this rupture, with the majority of the populations wrenched from their own cultures and inserted into the cultures of the colonizing plantation relations of slavery. I do not want to address the trauma of transportation, of the breaking up of linguistic and tribal and familial groups, or the brutal aftermath of Indian indenture. I simply want to make the point that in the histories of the migration, forced or free, of peoples who now compose the populations of these societies, whose cultural traces are everywhere intermingled with one another, there is always the stamp of historical violence and rupture.

Of course, the peoples thus inserted into these old colonizing plantation societies instantly polarized. And if anyone is still under the illusion that questions of culture can ever be discussed free from and outside of questions of power, one has only to look at the Caribbean to understand how for centuries every cultural characteristic and trait had its class, colour and racial inscription. One could read off from the populations to the cultures, and from the cultures to the populations, and each was ranked in an order of cultural power. It is impossible to approach Caribbean culture without understanding the way it was continually inscribed by questions of power. Of course, that inscription of culture in power relations did not remain polarized in Caribbean society, but I now understand that one of the things I was myself running away from when I came to England to study in 1951 was a society that was profoundly culturally graded, which is what the old postcolonial society I grew up in was like. Of course, those cultural relations did not remain fixed, and the relative cultures were quickly open to integration, assimilation and cross-influence. They were almost never self-contained. They became subject at once to complex processes of assimilation, translation, adaptation, resistance, reselection and so on. In a deep sense they became diasporic societies. For wherever one finds diasporas, one always finds precisely those complicated processes of negotiation and transculturation that characterize Caribbean culture. I do not want to try and sketch the cultural relations of that period, simply to identify three key processes that are at work creating the enormously refined and delicate tracery, the complexities of cultural identification, in Caribbean society in that time.

Survival and Assimilation

The first process, and especially with respect to the populations that had been enslaved, has been the retention of old customs, the retention of cultural traits from Africa; customs and traditions that were retained in and through slavery, in plantation, in religion, partly in language, in folk customs, in music, in dance, in all those forms of expressive culture that allowed men and women to survive the trauma of slavery. The customs have not remained wholly intact, never pure, never untouched by the culture of Victorian and pre-Victorian English society, never outside of Christianity or entirely outside the reach of the church, never without at least some small instruction in the Bible. Rather, they have been always surrounded by the colonizing culture, but importantly – and to some extent today, imperatively – retaining something of the connection. They have been often unrecognized, often evident only in practice, or often unreflected. Nevertheless, in everyday life, in so far as it was possible, the traditions were maintaining some kind of subterranean link with what was often called 'the other Caribbean': the Caribbean that was not recognized, that could not speak, that had no official records, no official account of its own transportation, no official historians, but it had an oral life that retained an umbilical connection with the African homeland and culture.

But let us not forget that retention characterized the colonizing cultures as well as the colonized. For if you look at the Little Englands, the Little Spains and the Little Frances that were created by the colonizers, if you consider this kind of fossilized replica, with the usual colonial cultural lag – people are always more Victorian when taking tea in the Himalayas than when taking tea in Leamington – they were keeping alive the memory of their own homes and homelands and traditions and customs. This very important double aspect of retention has marked Caribbean culture form the earliest colonial encounters.

The second profound process is that of assimilation, of dragging the whole society into some imitative relationship with this other culture that one could never quite reach. When one talks about assimilation in the Caribbean, one always feels Caribbean people constantly leaning forward, almost about to tip over, striving to reach somewhere else. My mother used to tell me that if she could only get hold of the right records, she would be able to stitch together a kind of genealogy for her household – not one that led to the West Coast of Africa, believe me, but a genealogy that would connect her, she was not quite sure, to the ruling house of the Austro-Hungarian Empire or the lairds of Scotland, one way or the other. She probably thought that in the quadrangle of Merton College, Oxford, I might stumble across one of these secret stones that would somehow convert me into what clearly I was formed, brought up, reared, taught, educated, nursed and nurtured to be: a kind of black Englishman. When I first went home in the mid 1960s, my parents said to me, "I hope they don't take you to be one of those immigrants over there." And the funny thing is, I had never called myself or thought of myself as an immigrant before. But having once been hailed or interpellated, I owned up at once: that is what I am. In that moment I migrated. Again, the word 'black' had never been uttered in my household or anywhere in Jamaica in my hearing, in my entire youth and adolescence – though there were all kinds of other ways of naming, and large numbers of people were very black indeed. So it was not until the mid 1960s, on another visit home, that my parents said to me, "There's all this black consciousness, black movement in the United States. I hope it's not having an influence over there", that I realized I had just changed identity again. I owned up once more and said, "Actually, you know, I am exactly what in Britain we are starting to call black." Which is a sort of footnote to say identity is not only a story, a narrative we tell ourselves about ourselves; it is a set of stories that change with historical circumstances, and identity shifts with the way in which we think, hear and experience them. Far from only coming from the still small point of truth inside us, identities actually come from outside; they are the way in which we are recognized and then come to step into the place of the recognitions others give us. Without the others there is no self, there is no self-recognition.

Given the skewed structures of growing up in such a society, of attempting, whatever social rank or position in the racial colour structure you occupy, to negotiate the complexities of who out of these complicated sets of stories you could possibly be, where you find in the mirror of history a point of identification or recognition for yourself, it is not surprising that Caribbean people of all kinds, of all classes and positions, experience the question of positioning themselves in a cultural identity as an enigma, as a problem, as an open question. There are many writings about this question, but for me, the overwhelmingly powerful statement is to be found in Fanon's *Black Skin, White Masks*, for only in Fanon does one understand the internal traumas of identity that are the consequence of colonization and enslavement: not just the external processes of pressures of exploitation but the way that, internally, one comes to collude with an objectification of oneself that is a profound misrecognition of one's own identity. Consequently, against this background in the New World and in the Caribbean – the attempts in the twentieth century to reach for independence, to decolonize, the movements in the nineteenth century in the Hispanic Caribbean societies for independence from Spain, the attempts to regenerate and ground the political and social life of the society not in an absent picture or image that could never be fulfilled or in the nostalgia for something outside the society but in the complicated realities and negotiations of that society itself – is a question that had to entail the redefinition of identity. Without it there could have been no independence of any kind. And one of the complexities of perplexities of the independence movement – certainly in the British Caribbean islands – is that, in the early phases of those movements, so-called political independence from the colonial power occurred but the cultural revolution of identity did not.

Africa and Modernity

For the third process, which will form the rest of my chapter, I want to start by looking at some of the other attempts to name the unnameable, to consider the possibilities of cultural identification, of the different traditions of the peoples for whom, on the whole, there were no cultural models, the peoples at the bottom of the society. That process involved a renegotiation, a rediscovery of Africa. The political movements in the New World in the twentieth century have had to pass through the re-encounter with Africa. The African diasporas of the New World have been in one way or another incapable of finding a place in modern history without the symbolic return to Africa. It has taken many forms; it has been embodied in many movements both intellectual and popular. Perhaps best known, in an intellectual sense, is the movement around the notion of Negritude, around the discovery of blackness, the affirmation of an African personality, very much associated with the name of Aimé Césaire, and of the group around Césaire in Paris and afterwards, coming out of Martinique (that tiny society described above, in a rather pejorative way, as the most French place I have encountered in the Caribbean, certainly, but also the birthplace of both Fanon and of Césaire). Césaire's work lay in plucking out of that Caribbean culture with which he was familiar, the strands

that related most profoundly back to the valorization of the African connection, the rediscovery of the African connection, of African consciousness, of
African personality and of African cultural traditions.

I was fortunate enough in the programme on Martinique to be able to
include an interview with Aimé Césaire, who must be nearly twice my age and
looks about half of it, wonderfully fit and resilient. In that interview one can
see the enormous pleasure with which he describes the story of having gone to
Africa and discovered for the first time the source of the masks of the
Martinique carnival which he had played in and helped to make when he was
a boy. Suddenly there was the flash of recognition, the continuity of the broken
and ruptured tradition. The enormously important work that flowed from his
involvement in the Negritude movement – not only the poems and the poetry
and the writing which has come out of that inspiration, of the recognition of
a Caribbean consciousness with the African past, but also the work he has
inspired in Martinique, amongst the poets and painters and sculptors – is a
profound revelation of how creative this symbolic reconnection has been.

And yet, of course, the paradox is that when Aimé Césaire opens his mouth
he speaks the most exquisitely formed, beautifully articulated lycée French. "I
am," he says, "French, my mind is French." Looking for the right parallel, he
says, "Like if you went to Oxford you would be English. I went to a French
school, I was taught the French language, I wasn't allowed to use *kreyole* at
home, I learned only French classical literature. There's a strong tradition of
assimilation; I went, of course, to Paris where all bright young Mariniquans
went." And because of the tradition of political assimilation, he has in fact done
what no black British Caribbean person has ever done, which is to sit in the
parliament of his own metropolitan society. Nevertheless, when Aimé Césaire
started to write poetry, he wanted, because of his interest, alerted and alive to
the subterranean sources of identity and cultural creativity in his own being,
to break with the models of French classical poetry. His notebook, *Return to
My Native Land,* shows how much that is a language that, in its open roaring
brilliance, has broken free from those classical models. He becomes a surrealist
poet.

Aimé Césaire has never, as you perhaps know, argued for the independence
of Martinique. Martinique has a very particular position: it is an internal
department of France. Those of you who want to be crude and materialist
about it had better see the kinds of facilities that status gives Martiniquan
people and compare these with the facilities available to most of the other
peoples of the Caribbean islands before you decide that their department status

is terrible. Nevertheless, my own feeling, though I have no enormous evidence for this, is that the reluctance of Césaire to break the French connection is not only a material one but also a spiritual one. He went to the Schoelcher lycée. Schoelcher was an important early Martiniquan figure, and in celebrating an anniversary of Schoelcher, Césaire said, "He associated in our minds the word France and the word liberty, and that bounds us to France by every fibre of our hearts and every power of our minds." He said, "I know only one France: the France of the Revolution, the France of Toussaint L'Ouverture. So much for the Gothic cathedrals."

So much indeed for Gothic cathedrals. The France with which Césaire identifies, and it has played, of course, a most profound role in Caribbean history, is one France and not another. It is the France of the revolution, the France of *liberté, egalité, fraternité,* the France that Toussaint L'Ouverture heard, of course, the France that mobilized and touched the imagination of slaves and others in Haiti before the revolution. And yet in the actual accounts of the revolution that we have, one of the most difficult historical passages to negotiate is precisely how much, in the spark of the various things that went into the making of the Haitian Revolution, can be attributed to the ruptures sweeping out in the wake of the French Revolution, on the one hand, and to the long experience of a severe and brutal regime on the plantations themselves, what one might call the revolutionary school of life itself, on the other. There were also, of course, the traditions of Africa and of African resistance, and of marronage in the plantation villages themselves. We do not know. It is an impossible enigma to sort out, in one of the most momentous historical events of Caribbean history, to what the different elements that come together in that revolutionary conjuncture can be attributed.

Césaire was influenced in part by his contact at an early age with an important movement in the United States that now goes under the title of the Harlem Renaissance. It was an important movement among writers, such as Langston Hughes, Countee Cullen and Van Vechten, intellectuals and artists in New York in the early years of the twentieth century, and it had an important influence on a variety of Caribbean writers, poets and artists. One of the important things that the movement of the Harlem Renaissance did was to speak about the importance and the cultural and aesthetic distinctiveness of the black American contribution to American culture. The other important thing that movement did was to stake a claim for the American blacks in the centre and at the heart of modernism itself. The writers of the Harlem Renaissance did not wish to be located and ghettoized as ethnic artists only able to speak on behalf of a marginal experience, confined and immured in the past, locked out of the claim to modern life. They said that the experience of blacks in the New World, their historical trajectory into and through the complex histories of colonization, conquest and enslavement is distinct and unique and it empowers people to speak in a distinctive voice. But it is not a voice outside of and excluded from the production of modernity in the twentieth century. It is another kind of modernity. It is a vernacular modernity; it is the modernity of hybrid black music in its enormous variety throughout the New World – the sound of marginal peoples staking a claim to the New World. I say that as a kind of metaphor, just in case you misunderstood the point I was trying to make about Aimé Césaire. I do not see him as an assimilationist Frenchman, deeply in bad faith because he is invoking Africa. I am trying to do something else. I am talking about the only way in which Africa can be relived and rediscovered by New World blacks who are diasporized irrevocably, who cannot go back through the eye of the needle.

A Cultural Revolution

Finally, a point about going back through the eye of the needle. There was a famous moment during the explosion of Rastafarianism in Jamaica in the 1960s when a somewhat beleaguered prime minister said, "Well, perhaps you ought to go back to Africa. You've talked about it so much, you say you came from there, you say you're still in slavery here, you're not in a free land, the promised land is back there where somebody took you from, perhaps you ought to go back and see." Of course, some people did go back and see. Of course, they did not go back to where they came from; that was not the Africa they were talking about. Between the Africa that they came from and the Africa that they wanted to go back to, two absolutely critical things had intervened. One is that Africa had moved on. One has to say it now and again to somewhat nostalgic and sentimental nationalists in the Caribbean, Africa is not waiting there in the fifteenth or seventeenth century, waiting for you to roll back across the Atlantic and rediscover it in its tribal purity, waiting there in its prelogical mentality, waiting to be awoken from inside by its returning sons and daughters. It is grappling with the problems of acquired immune deficiency syndrome, underdevelopment and mounting debt. It is trying to feed its people; it is trying to understand what democracy means against the background of a colonial regime that ruptured and broke and recut and reorganized peoples and tribes and societies in a horrendous shake-up of their entire cognitive and social world. That is what twentieth-century Africa is trying to do. There is no fifteenth-century Mother Africa waiting there to succour her children. In that literal sense, they wanted to go somewhere else, they wanted to go to the other place that had intervened, that other Africa constructed in the language and the rituals of Rastafarianism.

The language and rituals of Rastafarianism speak indeed of Africa, of Ethiopia, of Babylon, of the promised land and of those who are still in suffering. But like every chiliastic language that has been snatched by the black people of the New World diasporas out of the jaws of Christianity and then turned on its head, or read against the grain, or crossed by something else – and the New World is absolutely replete with them – it is impossible, in my experience, to understand black culture and black civilization in the New World without understanding the cultural role of religion, through the distorted languages of the one Book that anybody would teach them to read. What they felt was, "I have no voice, I have no history, I have come from a place to which I cannot go back and which I have never seen. I used to speak a language which I can no longer speak. I had ancestors whom I cannot find, they worshipped gods whose names I do not know." Against this sense of profound rupture, the metaphors of a new kind of imposed religion can be reworked and become a language in which a certain kind of history is retold, in which aspirations of liberation and freedom can be expressed for the first time, in which what I would call the 'imagined community' of Africa can be symbolically reconstructed.

When I left Jamaica in the 1950s it was a society that did not and could not have acknowledged itself to be largely black. When I went back to Jamaica at the end of the 1960s and in the early 1970s, it was a society even poorer in material terms than when I had left it, but it had passed through the most profound cultural revolution. It had grounded itself where it existed. It was not any longer trying to be something else, trying to match up to some other image, trying to become something it could not. It had all the problems in the world sticking together, finding the wherewithal to get to the next week, but in terms of trying to understand ordinary people – the important thing was the new realization that they could speak the language that they ordinarily spoke to one another anywhere. The biggest shock for me was listening to Jamaican radio. I could not believe my ears that anybody would be quite so bold as to speak patois, to read the news in that accent. My entire education,

my mother's whole career, had been specifically designed to prevent anybody
at all, and me in particular, from reading anything of importance in that
language. Of course, you could say all kinds of other things, in the small
interchange of everyday life, but important things had to be said, goodness
knows, in another tongue. To encounter people who can speak with one
another in exactly that transformation of Standard English which is patois,
which is creole – the hundreds of different creole and semi-creole languages
that cover the face of the Caribbean in one place or another – that these have
become, as it were, the languages in which important things can be said, in
which important aspirations and hopes can be formulated, in which an
important grasp of the histories that have made these places can be written
down, in which artists are willing, for the first time, the first generation, to
practise, that is what I call a cultural revolution.

And it was, in my view, one made by the cultural revolution of Rastafarianism. Certainly, not everybody became Rasta, although there was a moment
in the 1960s when it was pretty hard not to be Rasta. I once interviewed a very
old Rastafarian figure about the large numbers of Kingston intellectuals and
students who were growing their locks down to their ankles. And I asked him,
as part of a long interview about the nature of Rastafarianism, how he had got
into it, and so on: "What do you think of these weekend Rastas, these middle
class Rastas? Do you think they're up to anything? Do you think they can
reason?" And he said, "You know, I don't say anything against them, I don't
think anything against them, because in my church everybody reasons for
themselves. So if they want to reason in that way, that's their business." Well,
I thought, that was a nice gentle remark; but I wanted to nail him, so I said,
"Listen to me now, isn't Haile Selassie dead? He's dead, how can the Son of
God be dead?" And he said to me, "When last you hear the truth about the
Son of God from the mass media?"

You see, it was not the literal Africa to which people wanted to return, it
was the language – the symbolic language for describing what suffering was
like; it was a metaphor for where they were, as the metaphors of Moses and
the metaphors of the train to the North, and the metaphors of freedom, and
the metaphors of passing across to the promised land, have always been
metaphors, a language with a double register, a literal and a symbolic register.
The point was not that some people, a few, could only live with themselves
and discover their identities by literally going back to Africa – though some
did, not often with great success – but that a whole people symbolically

re-engaged with an experience that enabled them to find a language in which they could retell and appropriate their own histories.

I have mentioned the intellectual movement of Negritude. I have referred to another important movement, not in the Caribbean, the Harlem Renaissance of the 1920s, and I have talked about the cultural revolution in the wake of Rastafarianism. One of the most important things that people outside the Caribbean know about Rastafarianism is that it produced the greatest reggae artist in the world, Bob Marley. And I think many Europeans believe that reggae is a secret African music that we have had tucked in our slave knapsacks for three or four centuries, that we have hid out in the bush, practised at night when nobody was looking; and gradually as things changed we brought it out and began to play it a little, feed it slowly across the airwaves. But as anybody from the Caribbean would know, reggae was born in the 1960s. Actually, it was the answer to ska. When I returned to Jamaica I heard these two musical traditions. In *The Invention of Tradition*, the collection edited by Eric Hobsbawm and Terence Ranger, it is explained that many British traditions people believe have been around since Edward I were actually developed by Elgar or Disraeli, the day before yesterday. Well, reggae is a product of the invention of the tradition. It is a music of the 1960s, its impact on the rest of the world comes not just through preservation – though it is rooted in the long-retained traditions of African drumming – but by being the fusion, the crossing, of that retained tradition with a number of other musics. The most powerful instruments of its world propagation were those deeply tribal instruments: the transistor set, the recording studio, the gigantic sound system. That is how this deeply profound spiritual music of Africa that we have been treasuring got here.

Reggae music and Rastafarianism not only provided a kind of black consciousness and identification for people in Jamaica but it saved the second generation of young black people in British society. Is this an old identity or a new one? Is it an ancient culture preserved, treasured, to which it is possible to go back? Is it something produced out of nowhere? It is of course none of those things. No cultural identity is produced out of thin air. It is produced out of those historical experiences, those cultural traditions, those lost and marginal languages, those marginalized experiences, those peoples and histories that remain unwritten. Those are the specific roots of identity. On the other hand, identity itself is not the rediscovery of them but what they as cultural resources allow a people to produce. Identity is not in the past to be found but in the future to be constructed. And I say that not because I think therefore that Caribbean people can ever give up the symbolic activity of trying to know more about the past from which they come, for only in that way can they discover and rediscover the resources through which identity can be constructed. But I remain profoundly convinced that their identities for the twenty-first century do not lie in taking old identities literally but in using the enormously rich and complex cultural heritages, to which history has made them heir, as the different musics out of which a Caribbean sound might one day be produced.

I want to end by quoting a passage from C.L.R. James, about a talk he had just heard by the Guyanese novelist Wilson Harris:

I went the other day to the West Indian students' hostel to hear Wilson Harris speak on the West Indian novel. Well, in the end, we decided we should print it. I was told I could write an introduction [a wonderfully C.L.R. James phrase, that!]; Learie Constantine had paid for it, and I have the proofs here. Harris is speaking about the West Indian novel, and I want to read one extract, because we can't have a talk about Wilson Harris without your hearing something that Harris says for himself. Harris says, "The special point I want to make in regard to the West Indies is that the pursuit of a strange and subtle goal, melting pot, call it what you like, is the mainstream, though the unacknowledged tradition, of the Americas. And the significance of this is akin to the European preoccupation with alchemy, with the growth of experimental science, the poetry of science, as well as the explosive nature which is informed by a solution of images, agnostic humility, and essential beauty rather than vested in a fixed assumption and classification of things." (James 1980: 167–68)

Notes

1. Norman Tebbit was then a member of Margaret Thatcher's Conservative cabinet.
2. Stuart Hall, *Redemption Song* (BBC/Ambrose Video, 1991).

References

Cargill, Morris. 1987. *Morris Cargill: A Selection of His Writings in the* Gleaner, *1952–85.* Kingston, Jamaica: Tropical Publishers.

Césaire, Aimé. 1968. *Return to My Native Land.* Paris: Presence Africaine.

Fanon, Frantz. 1970. *Black Skins, White Masks.* London: Palladin.

Hobsbawm, Eric, and Terence Ranger. 1983. *The Invention of Tradition.* Cambridge: Cambridge University Press.

James, C.L.R. 1980. *Spheres of Existence: Selected Writings,* vol. 2. London: Allison and Busby.

3

Caribbean Dependency Theory of the 1970s

A Historical-Materialist-Feminist Revision

CECILIA GREEN

Introduction: Colonialism, Modes of Production and the Caribbean

At the risk of oversimplification, it may be noted that the problem of Caribbean economy has been *either* tackled through frames derivative of historical problems at least once removed *or* directly posed within the context of the colonial experience and 'New World' social formation. The result has been a characteristic split in the literature between more universalizing idealist paradigms and more specifying empiricist paradigms. In the first tendency, history is subordinated to universal theory; in the second, theory is custom-built to fit specific history. The results are mixed in both cases.

'Universalizing' paradigms have tended to emanate from the dominant centre and to operate in hegemonic ways with regard to peripheral or 'Third World' formations as objects of study. This is notwithstanding the fact that theories encompassed within this general classification may have radically opposed epistemological and political starting points. Classical Marxism and neoclassical theory, ranged as they are against each other, both contain a tradition of seeking universals that posit the core societies of Euro-capitalism as the ideal type and end of 'development' (even when, therefore, that end is seen as neither desirable nor ultimate). The vision of development projected by the classical versions of both paradigms remains uninterrupted by the messy historical realities of colonialism, dependency and continuously reproduced heterogeneity or hybridity. In both cases, the problem of colonialism and its peculiar impact on political economy at both the centre and the periphery is, in effect, elided.

Specifying paradigms have tended to emanate from the dominated periphery. Whatever their methodological or political oversights, these paradigms have been marked by a centring in the historical experience of colonialism and the geosocial space of the periphery. The most prominent among them are dependency theory, the more narrowly focused 'plantation economy' thesis and various Third World Marxist adaptations such as theories of 'colonial modes of production'. The important qualification linking these sometimes significantly different frameworks is that they all centre the periphery and privilege the colonial experience as a historical baseline. There is no possibility of racism and dependency ever becoming 'extraneous' variables here.

This broad division between paradigms may seem artificial, but it has been remarkably consistent with reality. The result has been schools of thought that should be informing each other instead talking past each other. This was keenly illustrated during the 'modes of production controversy' of the 1970s, when Euro/American Marxist scholars criticized Latin American and Caribbean dependency scholars, sometimes correctly, for bad theory or lack of theoretical rigour, without ever truly engaging or foregrounding the historical problem with which the latter were grappling (see Foster-Carter 1978). The criticism often prompted the simple and appropriate response, "Here I am struggling with these urgent and complex historical problems and here you come talking about abstract modes of production." George Beckford, for example, classic theoretician of the plantation economy school, openly chose enriched ideal types abstracted from a specific historical experience over the historicizing of universal models. In the preface to his seminal text on plantation economy, he states unequivocally that

the question of whether one is absolutely right or wrong is really a phony issue. I do not mind being charged with over-generalization and under-documentation. This is an 'ideas' book. What we need most are studies pregnant with ideas, not studies full of sterile detail. Ideas are what help people to understand problems and to pursue further inquiry. (Beckford 1972: vii)

He is unapologetic in his choice, because, in his view,

[t]oo often we view our problems through the eyes of metropolitan man; and our analyses of these problems depend too inordinately on analytical constructs developed for, and appropriate to, North Atlantic society but which may be inappropriate for the Third World . . . No apology is necessary for directing the book to a Third World readership. (vi)

The resonances of that earlier nonexchange, particularly between Euro-Marxism and Third World dependency theory, are still with us today. Indeed, that nonexchange would appear to represent a permanently lost opportunity because of the amnesia surrounding the rich heritage of that period's intellectual struggle against neocolonialism, or, at least that of the struggle's authorship. One would not be exaggerating too much to say that a large proportion of the revolutionary, social-scientific and literary intellectual production of the Third World in the postwar decades has been appropriated, displaced, subverted and anonymously reconfigured within the polar (but closely related) trends of globalization and postmodernist theory. It was only when Third World humanity began to intrude on the physical habitat of First World humanity that 'difference' began to be embraced and celebrated (from a final unbreachable distance). Similarly (and conversely), the export of First World jobs to the Third World in the era of 'deindustrialization' has prompted unprecedented gestures of international solidarity and organizing. However cynical these assertions may sound, they are meant to signify *actual* historical conjunctures and not necessarily to judge them.

While the division between universalizing and specifying paradigms is a critical one, it is not the only one that is relevant here. Indeed, the theories belonging to both paradigmatic types suffer in common from badly foreshortened definitions of the economy and the 'political economic'. There are two parts to this absence. In the first place, there has been a narrowing of the socio-spatial and institutional field of the economy to include only the public sphere of commodity production-circulation and bureaucratic and juridical governance, or, the 'marketplace', the 'law' and the 'government'. It is important to acknowledge, however, that this limitation has been significantly mitigated by a longstanding and sustained focus on the informal economy, whose field of operation tends to span and integrate the domestic and public realms. But, even here, because theoreticians do not begin with a concept of the economy as comprising, first and foremost, a community of re/producers and consumers and the activities by which they reproduce themselves as such, the informal economy has tended to be seen as an aberrant or anomalous addendum to the mainstream or formal economy, not as an integral part of the matrix of social reproduction. In the second place, political-economic relations are, or *were*, seen to be about the business of class, race and colonial or nation-state relations; gender was never seriously factored in as part of the equation.

Two types of literature can be – and, to some extent, have been – enlisted to help fill the gaps. The first is a vast anthropological literature that focuses on less differentiated preindustrial societies in which material production is critically embedded in kinship structures and the domestic-community domain. This literature reveals to us in particularly clear ways the intimate connection between the production and circulation of goods and the reproduction and circulation of persons. It also immediately posits, even when it misrecognizes, the cultural nature of the 'embedded' economic. The second type of literature comprises reams of feminist scholarship, which seeks to activate and foreground gender as a major social relation across the entire social field and to locate women as both actors and acted upon.

It can be concluded, therefore, that the pieces of the theoretical puzzle might be provided by the following: periphery/Caribbean-specific historical typologies (foregrounding the impact of colonialism), dialectical materialist epistemology or 'ways of knowing', and an expansion of the field of economic determination to include reproduction (encompassed within household/family/kinship relations) and gender.

I have already devoted a considerable amount of effort in other work to exploring and analysing the last-mentioned of the three components (Green 1986, 1992–93, 1994, 1995b, 1996); in this chapter I wish to go back, as it were, to the first two areas of concern. These will be accessed by means of a revisiting, reassessment, and historical-materialist reworking of Caribbean dependency theory.

Dependency Theory and Plantation Economy

In this chapter I will broadly survey the ideas of three or four major theorists of dependency and underdevelopment, as these phenomena relate to Caribbean society and, in particular, those aspects most relevant to my own concerns. George Beckford (1972), perhaps the premier exponent of plantation economy, focused on the institution, mode of production and social

Table 3.1   Patterns of Colonial Conquest and Social Formation

Type of Colony	Ecology/Region	Mode of Colonization	Colonial Economy
Colonies of Settlement (Euro-America)	Temperate lowland America – North America (excluding the US South), Brazilian centre-south, Argentina, Uruguay and Chile	Genocide or marginalization of small-scale, gatherer-hunter or horticultural communities; largely European settlement on 'free' soil	Family farm; artisanal, small-scale and maritime industries; 'provisioning trade' to the plantation colonies; free or indentured European labour; slave minority
Colonies of Conquest (Indo/Mestizo-America)	Highland America – area of high plateau stretching generally from Mexico to Chile (former land of the Aztecs, Inca, Maya and others)	Subjugation of densely populated, state-centred, class-stratified indigenous societies; European settler landowning and bureaucratic oligarchy replaces indigenous elite	Semi-feudal agricultural estates (haciendas) producing staples for limited local or regional markets; subjugated local communities of dependent labourers/clients/tenants
Colonies of Exploitation (Afro-America)	Tropical Lowland America – area stretching from the Brazilian northeast through the Caribbean basin to the US South	Genocide or marginalization of small-scale gatherer-hunter or horticultural communities; large-scale importation of enslaved African workers; European settler owners and supervisors	'Mono-crop' plantation production of tropical staples for export to Europe; enslaved African labour; minority European owning and supervisory class (plus European smallholding class in the US South)

Source: Adapted from Girvan 1991, among others.

relations of the plantation as *the* dominant nexus of colonial production. Lloyd Best (1968), together with Kari Levitt (1975), focused on the reproduction of dependency and disarticulation – through different historical stages – in the plantation-dominated colonial economy and social formation as a whole, generated by institutional colonial and neocolonial trade linkages. Norman Girvan (1991 [1975]) focused on the reproduction of race and class structures peculiar to the colonized society and the generation of a racially mediated anticolonial nationalist consciousness, leading to a (flawed) version of independence. A fifth member of this pantheon of radical Caribbean (or Caribbeanist)[1] political economists is Clive Thomas, whose work will not be discussed here, but whose greatest contribution lies in the realm of prescriptive theory, that is, prescription for transformation (see especially Thomas 1974).

Beckford (1972) followed a number of his predecessors in classifying the different forms that colonial takeover and occupation took in the colonized countries:

The colonization activities of the metropolitan countries took three general forms, the establishment either of colonies of 'settlement', of 'conquest', or of 'exploitation'. In the first case, people migrated (individually, as families, and as groups) from the metropole and settled in the colony. In the second case, metropolitan interest was simply in establishing sufficient administrative and military organization to facilitate the transfer of wealth (chiefly precious metals) from the colony to the metropole. In the third case, metropolitan interest was in production for trade. North America, Australia, and New Zealand were representative of colonies of settlement; mainland Spanish America of colonies of conquest; and the Caribbean islands and those of Southeast Asia of colonies of exploitation. The plantation was the institution best suited to metropolitan needs in colonies of exploitation. (8)

In keeping with the above schema, scholars of American patterns of colonization and settlement have differentiated the resulting colonies or dependencies into three historical and geocultural regional types: 'colonies of settlement' corresponding to temperate lowland America and Euro-American ethnic predominance, 'colonies of conquest' in highland America, with its Indo/Mestizo-American ethnic predominance, and the 'colonies of exploitation' of tropical lowland America, prominently featuring Afro-American ethnicity. The seminal definition of the latter culture sphere as 'Plantation America' was the work of Charles Wagley (1957). This general classification, which has undergone considerable variation in its real-life version in more recent times but is still appropriate as a 'foundational' model, is rendered schematically in Table 3.1.

George Beckford's Plantation Economy

"The plantation was an instrument of colonization," wrote George Beckford (1972: 30). Plantations remade the entire social and natural landscape of the countries in which they were installed, mobilizing and transplanting vast amounts of capital and technology, as well as diverse botanical specimens and ethnonational populations uprooted from various far-flung 'foreign' habitats, into new socioeconomic and institutional configurations under European hegemony. The major areas of plantation economy are Tropical Asia (comprising the countries of Southeast Asia) and Tropical America. However, the birth of plantation economy in the latter area ushered in more truly neoteric or New World societies, since the 'total institution' of the colonial plantation completely – and violently – replaced earlier ecological, social and ethnohuman life systems, leaving hardly a trace of them behind. The plantation has a longer history in the Caribbean than elsewhere. Sidney Mintz (1989) has pointed out that even the peasantry that is so prominent a feature of some Caribbean countries today cannot be fitted into traditional precapitalist definitions since it originated, for the most part, as a peculiar modern adaptation to and struggle against the capitalistic monopoly represented by the plantation. According to Beckford (1972), the postslavery peasantry that emerged in many areas of the Caribbean is itself dependent in one way or another on the plantations. He insists that "[t]he peasant sectors of these economies are really sub-sectors within the general framework of the plantations", and that "the development of the peasantry is interwoven with that of the plantation". He amplifies upon this point:

In most of the countries in which plantations are important they co-exist with peasant producers who normally are engaged in farming cash crops (sometimes the same crop as the plantation) in addition to providing for their own subsistence. These peasant farmers are affected by the plantations in at least two important ways: competition for land and other resources and the provision of wage work on the plantations to supplement their incomes from the main pre-occupations of farming on their own account. (13)

"Plantation economy" describes those countries "where the internal and external dimensions of the plantation system dominate the country's economic, social, and political structure and its relations with the rest of the world" (Beckford 1972: 12). However, the emergence of a peasantry "in the crevices" of these societies does modify the social structure and, indeed, defines the relative limits or failure of the plantation system. The extent to which the growth of a peasantry interrupted, compromised or even aborted the hegemony of the plantation system became the major criterion differentiating the postslavery economies of the anglophone Caribbean, so that while some territories remained essentially 'pure plantation economies', others became essentially 'dual economies' under varying degrees of plantation hegemony. As such, the dual economies differed among themselves with regard to both the pre-existing and continuing levels of development of plantation hegemony. Barbados, Antigua and St Kitts emerged as examples of pure plantation economy (eventually modified), while Jamaica and the Windwards became unambiguously dual economies. While Jamaica's strong plantation heritage was sustained, modified and renewed, Dominica maintained a plantation framework without the plantations, or, at least, without *viable* plantations. Dominica provides perhaps the best example of a weak plantation economy. In both islands, the peasants quickly comprised a numerical majority of the rural population but remained a 'jural minority'. Postemancipation Barbados, on the other hand, has always been overwhelmingly dominated by wage labour, even in its early feudal-like forms.

Before Beckford, Wagley (1957) had summed up the common features of plantation America as follows: "monocrop cultivation under the plantation system, rigid class lines, multi-racial societies, weak community cohesion, small peasant proprietors involved in subsistence and cash-crop production, and a matrifocal type family form" (5). Beckford goes beyond Wagley's rich but static typological paradigm to investigate the *persistence* of poverty and the dynamics of the *reproduction* of underdevelopment in plantation economy. Like Wagley, he develops a checklist of the fundamental features which characterize plantation economy (paraphrased and summarized as follows):

- Specialized 'monocrop' production undertaken solely for (foreign) sale
- Plantation monopoly over major factors of production and privileged access to auxiliary infrastructural and institutional resources
- Export orientation, capital specificity and rigidity, foreign 'metropolitan' ownership and/or control, and economic, political and psychological dependence on the mother country
- Import dependence (on both consumer and producer goods and inputs); persistently unfavourable terms of trade between specialized tropical agro-exports with low-income elasticities of demand and food and industrial imports with high-income elasticities of demand (however, this is irrelevant to the metropolitan plantation enterprise; it is, literally, not its problem)
- Masses of unskilled labour

- A caste system based on race and colour (and white bias)
- Plural societies (but Beckford [1972: 28] points out that the "plantation societies of the New World have the rather unique characteristic of exhibiting both cultural pluralism and [economically and hegemonically mediated] social integration")
- Peasant-plantation conflict
- Concentration of power in a tiny elite; authoritarian, highly centralized government

Beckford demonstrates how the needs of the domestic economy are subordinated to the needs of the metropolitan plantation enterprise that dominates it. Their respective circuits of reproduction fundamentally diverge from each other, beyond the colonial locus in a parasitical and exploitative relationship which drains resources away from the domestic economy into the metropolitan plantation enterprise. These resources are therefore unavailable to the domestic economy for its social reproduction. Profits and multiplier effects from plantation production accrue primarily outside of the national economy, while resource use in the national economy is skewed ('misallocated') towards the plantations. The origins of this pattern lie in the colonial relationship. Beckford (1972) follows Best (1968) in reminding us that the slave plantation economy

is structurally a part of an 'overseas economy' consisting of a metropole which is the locus of initiative and decision, of product elaboration and disposal, and of the provisioning of capital, technology and managerial skill, and other services. This means that the plantation colony is simply a locus of production of the export staple. (45–46)

There is therefore no reinvestment in a social infrastructure that results in the extended and internally linked reproduction of capital, labour and consumer markets, or what others have called an autocentric form of capitalism.[2] As Beckford points out, backward and forward linkages "have been canalized within the complex of metropolitan plantation enterprise and thus have largely served to generate incomes in metropolitan, not plantation, economy" (1972: 198). The colony is left with (regressive) taxation, subsistence wages, import trade, metropolitan state welfare, and (quantitatively and qualitatively) marginal land for food cultivation. It is locked into world capitalism and dependent upon it for generative and realization capacities but is incapable of reproducing an independent capitalist mode of production (or *any* independent mode of production for that matter). Domestic modes of re/production and the enclave-capitalist sector(s) do not merely coexist; they are directly at odds with each other. The ensuing tug-of-war encompasses much more than class struggle; it combines national-racial-class struggle.

The plantation economy thesis and its various modifications, constituting a major example of dependency theory, reveal a not-so-hidden kernel of colonial relations of production which is every bit as significant as the labour theory of value. It provides a major modification to Marxist political economy which assumes that social formation and social reproduction are coterminous and autocentred, barring 'foreign trade', which is further assumed to consist of free – if not always equal – exchange of domestic products on the international market (see Green 1980). The whole Marxist debate about exchange versus production fails to make a distinction between what might be termed 'institutional trade' and 'market' or 'free trade' (Laclau 1971; Brenner 1977). The former involves institutionally fixed transactions within a single, inter-linked centre/periphery *production* complex, while the latter entails free market *exchange* between independent and roughly coequal production centres.[3] The Marxist model assumes too that mode of production can always be isolated as an internally generated phenomenon within social formations, and that modes of production encompass simple class relations between antagonists who share, however unequally, a single socioeconomic (and sociocultural) habitat and common circuit of extended reproduction. Except for Marx's insightful empirical-political treatment of the national-class relationship between England and Ireland, there is no accounting of combined national-class (that is, colonial) systems of exploitation within his capital-logic framework. Even coexisting modes of production within the Marxist model are assumed to relate to each other only as relatively simple linear-historical points of transition or *evolution* from one stage of development to the other (implicit in the notion of uneven development). The problem is, of course, conflation between historico-logical 'model' and general methodology, for which Marx is perhaps less to blame than his followers. Despite his own careful delineation of the absolutely contingent relationship between historical reality and dialectical materialist abstraction, among many of his followers, modes of production have been reduced to their universal, classificatory 'surface' forms and abstracted away from their historical conditions of (extended) reproduction.

While Beckford's plantation economy thesis allows for some adaptations of its own and has been further modified from the outside, several valid criticisms have been made of it. The modifications that Beckford himself accounts for include peasant-plantation dualism and struggle, the metropolitan corporatization of the old family-based plantations, and the emergence of a small middle class based on the acquisition of education. Norman Girvan, who is to the mineral-export sector in the Caribbean and other parts of the Third World what Beckford is to plantation economy, has further added to and updated the staple-export model by elaborating on modern mining enclaves (particularly bauxite in Jamaica) that have been juxtaposed to the plantation sector and replicate its transnational-corporate dynamic in even more advanced form. Those countries in which transnationals exploiting mineral resources such as bauxite and oil developed alongside transnationals in sugar production have been characterized as "mixed plantation-mineral export economies" rather than just "plantation economies" (Girvan 1971).

Although Beckford does acknowledge, in some detail, the social-infrastructural development benefits of plantations, he weighs them against the generative indices of underdevelopment in a zero-sum equation and comes up with a negative balance. Following from this zero-sum approach, many problems with the model can be identified. Four, in particular, stand out:

1. The thesis is underconsumptionist and stagnationist to a fault, and needs to factor in more realistically both the gains achieved through struggle and the dynamic of dependent development. Dependency, not underconsumption, may be the overriding feature of the model. Beckford trivializes real gains made in income and standard of living as a result of both 'modernization' and anticolonial agitation, followed by independence. While underconsumption and stagnation are important and enduring features of the peripheral-capitalist reality, it is also important to historically and theoretically account for the elevation of many postplantation economies to middle-income country status.

2. The notion of 'total institution' and lack of interplantation linkages is clearly exaggerated. Verene Shepherd (1988) has challenged this thesis of total enclavization in her re-examination of links between sugar and nonsugar properties, particularly pens (livestock farms), in pre-emancipation Jamaica. Also, Mintz (1989) has long popularized the notion of a proto-peasantry and a relatively autonomous sub- or alternative economy during slavery. Both the original notions of total economic enclavization and total institutional incorporation need to be modified and at least problematized.

3. Beckford does not make enough allowance for diversity and divergence of historical experience in the application of his model. It seems to be predominantly based on the experience of Jamaica. To illustrate this

criticism, Barbados and Dominica serve as cases in point. Barbados, with its successful retention of a resident plantocracy, demonstrates the greater level of 'spread effects' from the plantation sector that occurs wherever the planter class is locally domiciled (even if the social reproduction of plantation capital is not entirely internal). Thus, the social-infrastructural development effects are greater, although here plantation economy is actually more monolithic (and the world market dependency quotient greater). In Dominica the plantation framework of land and institutional monopoly was retained without a viable plantation economy and the staple-export economy was eventually predominantly sustained by a peasantry. Both these situations introduce considerable variation into the plantation economy thesis.

4. Beckford is too cavalier in his dismissal of the possibilities for social mobility, class advancement and middle class development, mentality and agency. First, he understates the impact and agency of the nationalist middle class which led the plantation colonies into independence. Recently, Thomas, critical of such understatement, has reminded us of a number of changes introduced by independent governments, including "development of state productive sectors; labour force training; macroeconomic management and regulation: . . . social welfare programmes; population policies; land settlement programmes; investments in Research and Development, as well as the pursuit of 'independent' national roles in the world economy" (1997: 7). Second, Beckford understates the extent of social mobility into the middle class from the labouring classes; he particularly understates the potential for class advancement and internal stratification among smallholders and cash-crop cultivators. In his 1980s survey research on Jamaica, Gordon (1987: 24) found that roughly 30 percent of middle class men and women came from small farming households and another 30 percent came from working class origins. Beckford pays little attention to the class origins and consciousness of these sections of the middle class, assuming a universal reproduction of the assimilationist, intermediary role among all class members.

Having noted the limitations of Beckford's plantation economy thesis, it is important to point out that his model takes us beyond a bare explication of plantation economy to plantation *society*. Using a multidisciplinary mode of analysis, he examines the social structures and local institutional framework that attend upon plantation economy and ensure its reproduction. Some of the features he highlights have been listed above. On a whole, Beckford sacrifices flexibility and dialectical dynamism in his paradigm for holism or what might be referred to today as metanarrative. His metanarrative, however, adheres assiduously to the rule of historical specificity, and is ultimately far superior to 'dialectical' models constructed upon universal typologies.

The Best-Levitt Model

Best (1968) and Levitt and Best (1975) are also concerned with institutional factors that originate in the colonial relationship and continue to reproduce dependency in modified form. Best is one of the original formulators of the plantation economy thesis. His seminal and classic piece, "Outlines of a Model of Pure Plantation Economy" (1968), has been followed by numerous efforts on his part, and in conjunction with Kari Levitt, to update and diversify the foundation model. Whereas Beckford focuses on the intersection of the transnational enterprise and the domestic economy, Best and Levitt are more strictly concerned about the distortion of and potential for the development of a national economy. Best's plantation economy model is therefore founded on a more strictly nationalist framework than that of Beckford, and, in that sense, it is more amenable to the possibilities of dependent development, even though he too unequivocally rejects the latter trajectory. Moreover, his investigation of dependent development in the Caribbean ultimately assesses it to be an advanced and extended reproduction of the old dependency. His prognosis seems even less hopeful than Beckford's since it does not allow for transformatory class struggle.

The Best-Levitt model is less class-conscious and dichotomous than that of Beckford, but it is in some ways more dialectical within a narrower nationalist and institutionalist framework. There is no doubt that both formulations share a common plantation economy framework. For Levitt and Best (1975), this is fundamentally defined by the domination of the "hinterland economy" by branch plant subsidiaries of multinational corporations and the enduring tendency of this kind of economy to remain "passively responsive to metropolitan demand and metropolitan investment" (36–37). The coauthors' "primary interest lies in isolating the institutional structures and constraints" of the plantation legacy, and specifying the historical stages or "the successive layers of inherited structures and mechanisms which condition the possibilities of transformation of the present economy" (37–39). Their framework allows for diversification of the plantation economy model and various alternative routes of development. They talk, for example, of "mainland versus island plantation hinterlands" which differ in the level of autonomy of the "residentiary sector".[4] In the island variety, the residentiary sector is "principally an adjunct of the plantation sector" (40). They also speak of closed versus open island hinterlands. The closed island hinterland is one in which all available land is engrossed by plantations and is fully under cultivation. Barbados, St Kitts and Antigua are typical examples. The open island hinterland is characterized by an abundance of "unsettled virgin land suitable for plantation cultivation" and the importation of significant additional labour supplies to ensure plantation hegemony (40). This situation is typified by Trinidad and the Guyanas,[5] as well as by Cuba, Puerto Rico and the Dominican Republic. The intermediate or mixed cases are best exemplified by Jamaica. But there are also "territories which never came under the influence of the full plantation system, and where the local producers began early to be predominant" (40). This situation is characteristic of some of the Windward Islands, particularly Grenada, St Vincent and Dominica.

All plantation or semi-plantation hinterlands came into being within an "overall mercantilist framework" defined by "institutional rules of exclusivist trading arrangements" between hinterland and metropole. Levitt and Best classify the rules of the game establishing and perpetuating these arrangements under four broad headings: Muscovado Bias, Navigation Provision, Metropolitan Exchange Standard, and Imperial Preference. Broadly speaking, these rules of the game do the following, respectively: confine the hinterland to 'terminal activity' ("primary production at the one end of the spectrum, and distribution or assembly of consumer goods at the other end" [Levitt and Best 1975: 41]) and proscribe advanced local processing of staple export-products or local development of manufacturing industry, the latter being designated a prerogative of the metropole; establish the metropolitan market as the exclusive destination of colonial products and metropolitan carriers as the exclusive means of their transportation; provide for metropolitan financial backing of hinterland currency at a fixed exchange standard; and establish a mutual system of preferences in metropole-hinterland 'trade'.

The 'national economy' that emerges at the end of the first staple cycle (the end of the exclusive dominance of sugar and the old colonial system) is an adjunct to the plantation sector and is severely circumscribed by the plantation legacy and new or refurbished mercantilist arrangements. The refurbished arrangements are executed, for the most part, within the setting of the multinational corporation and relations between the parent company and the hinterland subsidiary. Levitt and Best present four alternative paths of development, depending on the fates of the metropolitan-hinterland relationship and the traditional export sector and staple. The four alternative paths and countries that exemplify them are briefly listed below:

1. Old metropolitan ties are cut, but the traditional export sector is maintained intact (Cuba).
2. Old metropolitan ties are cut and the traditional export sector disintegrates (Haiti).
3. Metropolitan ties are maintained or restored and a 'quasi-staple' is developed. The quasi-staple economy specializes in finishing touch assembly manufacturing, tourism and the provision of labour to the metropole by emigration. The more extreme case of a quasi-staple economy is Puerto Rico. Barbados and Antigua can also be characterized as quasi-staple economies.
4. Metropolitan ties are maintained and reinforced by the entry of a new staple (the new mineral export sectors of Trinidad [oil] and Jamaica, Guyana and Suriname [bauxite]). (Levit and Best 1975: 48–49)

Levitt and Best choose to explore the development trajectory typical of the fourth case, characterized by a plantation-mineral export economy or the entry of an additional new staple into the old plantation framework, and the pursuit of an import-substitution industrial strategy. This scenario is relevant as the applied form of a development strategy that has been pursued by all the postwar Caribbean economies, but with lower success or implementation rates in 'less developed' islands such as Dominica.

Although, "[i]n theory, the hinterlands are free to adopt more independent monetary systems, to establish their own facilities for production elaboration and import-displacement, to engage in multinational trading beyond the frontiers of the metropolitan system, to pursue commercial policies which discriminate against metropolitan suppliers and to arrange their carriage in the cheapest bottoms", in practice the old mercantilist rules of the game prevail. Indeed, they have become more sophisticated:

The control of the modern corporation over primary production is tighter than that of the old time merchants over the planter-producers. Their time horizon is longer and their allocation of investments between hinterlands forms part of an overall competitive strategy.

. . . The *incalculability* of the old merchant-planter transactions has asserted itself in an international economy in which corporate strategy requires the elimination or suppression of price determining markets in the service of creating and securing quasi-monopoly rents and transferring them to the metropole. (Levitt and Best 1975: 50; emphasis in orginal)

The new staple-exporting hinterland subsidiaries are direct offshoots of advanced, modern multinational corporations. As such, they are capital- and technology-intensive, occupy a disproportionate space in the local economy, and have a low propensity to generate employment, while enjoying the right to repatriate profits. Lack of control over the national economy inhibits the government from using the increased tax and royalty yields, in conjunction with regulatory mechanisms, for long-term development purposes. Organized labour is primarily concerned with preserving the high wages enjoyed by workers in the newer export operations, while subsidiaries of metropolitan banks are more interested in making the increased domestic savings available to higher-income consumers or the distribution sector for import purchases than in financing local entrepreneurial initiatives (except when they are joint ventures with foreign companies).

Because of the overwhelming nature of the institutional constraints and the absence of political will to challenge the plantation legacy, the government is forced into a strategy of 'industrialization by invitation' which relies on external borrowing and investment concessions. The residentiary sector then becomes involved in 'finishing touch', licensee-manufacturing of consumer goods, or branch plant management.

The outcome is the emergence of a residentiary sector which engages in import-replacement rather than import displacement. The importation of parts and components takes the place of the importation of finished articles. What is more, 'finishing touch' consumer goods industries catering for the domestic market create a new rigidity in the import bill in the form of political pressure from wage-earners employed in these assembly-type industries and from consumers who come to regard these products as necessities of life. (Levitt and Best 1975: 56)

Import-substitution manufacturing firms "typically employ few workers, import a large part of their supplies, . . . contribute little or nothing to government revenues" and enjoy substantial, unearned, concessions and sub-sidies (Levitt and Best 1975: 57). The local economy therefore continues to engage in terminal activity, entrepreneurial initiative is discouraged, and few linkages are generated between sectors. With the inevitable slowdown of the economy (and with more funds going out than coming in), the government is forced to turn to external borrowing. Perennial indebtedness to metropolitan bankers becomes a new form of dependency:[6] "When the export sector slows its growth, as inevitably it must, the entire burden of adjustment falls on the public sector. Having failed to effect transformation when conditions were more favourable, the government is forced to turn to increased external borrowing to meet its rapidly rising development expenditures" (Levitt and Best 1975: 58). Levitt and Best conclude that "structural transformation is not possible without breaking the traditional plantation patterns whereby Caribbean economy is incorporated into metropolitan economy" (58).

First, it is important to acknowledge the theoretical progress represented by the Best-Levitt model. It accounts for diversification of the plantation economy paradigm and its historicization or 'modernization'. The coauthors recognize different kinds of plantation hinterlands and different trajectories beyond the common first staple cycle (characterized, for the most part, by slavery and indentured labour, a monocrop export economy, and the old colonial system). While they do not, strictly speaking, talk about class relations – since they are more interested in the dialectic of national versus foreign or metropolitan actors and interests – they identify four categories of actors or interest groups: the (postcolonial) government or public sector, the residentiary sector (which appears to refer to local *or* domestic-market business operations), organized labour, and the export sector. These actors all benefit from and participate in the dominant export and import-substitution activities, but do so unequally and, in the case of the national actors, in contradictory and equivocal ways. For workers in the export[7] and import-substitution sectors and for middle class citizens, income and consumption grow. Generally speaking, therefore, the Best-Levitt model can be defined as one of dependent development, even though it does not (and should not) preclude the feature of the 'development of underdevelopment' in relation to certain parts of the economy.

Although the model nominally accounts for diversity in the plantation economy paradigm, the coauthors choose not to explore the divergent cases represented by Barbados and Dominica. This becomes a real weakness since the differences are theoretically significant yet completely accommodatable within the main paradigm. In the case of Barbados, the residentiary sector and the export sector would be collapsed into each other, and in the case of Dominica the export sector would consist of a mediated relationship between a metropolitan trading conglomerate and small owner-producers.

The more significant inadequacy of the Best-Levitt model lies in its total and exclusive focus on the dominant mode of production and formal national economy. While the model correctly shows that the dominant mode of production cannot be grasped at the level of the domestic economy[8] or local social formation, it fails to demonstrate, and indeed denies, that the domestic economy, the domestic economic community or social formation, has meaning beyond the dominant mode of production. The model does not even register the continuously reproduced dualism of the economy or the plantation-peasant dichotomy and conflict. More generally, as noted above, it does not begin with a concept of the economy as comprising a community of re/producers and consumers and the activities by which they reproduce themselves as such. Levitt and Best (1975) are explicit in the notion that only the dominant, mainstream, formal hegemonic-national economy needs to be operationalized in their paradigm: "The national economy must be distinguished from the domestic economy as it refers to economic activity organised by foreigners. The latter is a technical concept relating to productive activity with[in] a defined geographic area. The former is the relevant unit for discussions of economic welfare" (39).

The domestic economy is therefore a mere technical concept, not a phenomenon that embraces a bounded community of re/producers and the activities by which they reproduce themselves, whether or not these activities fall within the ambit of the codified national economy. This is particularly problematic in highly fragmented dependent capitalist economies where staple export operations may be dominant in national economic profiles but are enclavized and not pervasive throughout the domestic economy. In fact, after the first staple cycle, the majority of livelihoods are typically produced outside the export sector, and a large percentage of them may be produced outside the formal economy altogether. The nature of dependency is fundamentally defined not just by the relationship between the hinterland subsidiary and the metropolitan firm but also by that between the subsidiary operations and the rest of the domestic economy, *beyond* the 'national' actors Levitt and Best allow into their model. The latter relationship is precisely characterized by exploitation of a reserve army of labour without extensive subsumption of labour, extended reproduction of capital, or autocentric generation of sectoral and market linkages. The domestic economy is reproduced *because of, in spite of,* and *against* the subsidiary operations. This complex, dis/articulated national-class-modes-of-re/production dynamic needs to be an integral part of an explanatory model of Caribbean economy. Some of the features that need to be included in such a model will be more fully explored below. As dependency theorists, therefore, Levitt and Best have challenged 'metropolitan' economic models in fundamental and decisive ways, yet the scope of their work has remained very much within formal, mainstream parameters. The problem is not that they highlight the dominant economic operations and mode of production (they should) but that they omit from their terms of reference and boundaries of analysis the modes of re/production of the majority of living, breathing members of the 'domestic community', sustained in varying degrees of tension with the dominant sector. As such, class, reproduction (in human terms) and informal economy are all excluded from their line of vision.

Girvan's Political Economy of Race and Class

Certain dimensions of class and the need to fit in or define the specific historical status of the marginal populations of the periphery are fortunately among the focal concerns of Norman Girvan (1991),[9] predominantly known for his scholarly expertise on dependent mineral-export economies. His wider sociological exploration has led him to compose one of the most important analytical notes on the peculiarities of class forms and relations in colonial settings, and in particular those of the Americas. Girvan gleans considerable comparative insight from an examination of the commonalities and differences between colonies of settlement and colonies of exploitation and conquest. Colonies of settlement have reproduced, in the main, the economic and class systems of core or autocentric capitalism, with the twist that subcolonial developments enabled the physical integration of plantation hinterlands into the new centres or core nations, producing a situation of internal rather than overseas colonialism. The key factor is that class systems occupying the *centre* of (ex-)colonies of settlement reproduce the historical situation that provided the model for Marx's theories of capitalism. However, the marginal populations of the 'internal colonies' or contiguous plantation hinterlands are engaged by that centre in different and oblique ways. One of Girvan's contentions regarding that difference is that white labour tended to be proletarianized while non-whites were 'lumpenproletarianized'. This process, facilitated by an ideology of racism, was also "characterized by a powerful alliance of attitudes and actions within the white community as a whole in relation to non-whites" (Girvan 1991: 17).

While there are critical and rather obvious differences between overseas and internal colonies, the commonalities form an important basis for understanding the 'Third World' experience, particularly in the Americas. Ethnonational and racial divisions profoundly modify all pre-existing conceptualizations of class systems. Class is 'overdetermined', to use an Althusserian term, by racial-economic segmentation (its context embracing both transnational and internal dimensions). As such, European labour is profoundly differentiated from African and 'Indian' (Native American) labour with regard to socioeconomic status:

In the first place it was free labour – more properly wage-labour – rather than slave labour; and in the second place it had a high degree of ethnic and cultural similarity with the employer class. This had important implications for the nature of the ideology which was to be established. Ethnic-cultural similarity meant that it was not feasible to use a racist ideology as a means of social control; a regime of wage-labour meant that this was in any case not necessary. Indeed, so far as the white community was concerned, the required ideology was precisely the opposite of one which taught that membership of the labouring group automatically condemned one to permanent underdog status: i.e. – it was necessary to establish the ideology that *any* white worker, no matter how poor, illiterate and unskilled he might be, could by his own efforts achieve middle-class and big-capitalist status. For by promoting the belief in the possibilities for vertical mobility for the whites – of which the United States represents the fullest development – the class struggle could be dampened and the European migrants could be persuaded to accept the consolidation of national bourgeoisies in these countries. (Girvan 1991: 9–10; emphasis in orginal)

Structural racism maintained non-white labour as a virtually unlimited source of "unskilled, cheap and quiescent manpower", while European workers were assigned the role of a skilled and relatively high-income workforce, "providing both the skills required by the dynamic sectors of the expanding economy and the market to consume its products and thereby permit more accumulation" (Girvan 1991: 14). Also, European migrants supplied the individuals who would become big and small capitalists. Because "whites never had the experience of being a subjugated race . . . the struggles of white people against white capital would have a class content only" (23–24). Moreover, the class relations among whites have been considerably mitigated by cross-class racial solidarity – or white nationalism – against non-whites. White nationalism, based on "the ideology of white supremacy or superiority which is the implicit and explicit correlate of the ideology of non-white inferiority . . . generated, as a dialectical response, non-white nationalism" (24). In the first half of the twentieth century, the most important, certainly the most widespread (pan-American), form assumed by Afro-American nationalism was

Garveyism, based on the ideas and organizational activities of the Jamaican, Marcus Garvey.

In those countries where non-whites were a numerical majority, they nonetheless remained a politico-jural minority, and continued white domination did not depend on a large or ethnically 'pure' physical presence. Girvan (1991) assures us that "in both Indo-America and Afro-America economic and political power remained squarely in the hands of so-called *creole* elites, who were ethnically either of pure or mixed European stock and culturally of decidedly Euro-North American orientation, and who preyed upon the Indian and Black masses" (17–18; emphasis in orginal).

The reproductive propensities of the socio-economic structure along racial lines are further confirmed by the pattern of immigration into these societies in the 19th and early 20th centuries. Those European migrants [who] did end up in those societies tended to be rapidly absorbed into the warm embrace of the ruling classes, typically through the route of commercial and matrimonial activity. They thus came to occupy within a generation or so places of privilege and power in relation to non-whites who had been native to the habitat for centuries, sometimes millennia. On the other hand, non-white immigration to these societies, principally from Asia, came in at the bottom. It took the form of indentured labour to do low paid, unskilled work as on the plantations, which native Indians or Black labour could not be induced to do. (18)

Post-1930 developments in global capital and industry, the emergence of capital-intensive mineral-export sectors, and anticolonial struggles have led to the selective social advancement of non-white strata "in certain countries where European populations are not present in large numbers".

The struggles of non-whites and the requirements of international capital have therefore overlapped *in certain specific areas* . . . to incorporate pockets of non-whites into the more highly-paid and socially prestigious occupations in the socio-economic order, such as skilled labour, the professions, and the governmental bureaucracies. Hence we have the appearance of a so-called Black bourgeoisie or Indian middle class in certain countries, which has on the face of it loosened the tight correlation between race and the occupational status which previously existed. (25–26; emphasis in orginal)

According to Girvan (1991), the incidence of vertical mobility among some non-whites needs to be subjected to careful political consideration, since "such developments . . . form the basis of claims that a decisive break has been made with the system of a racial division of labour and its definite, if slow, erosion will take place spontaneously as a result of economic expansion" (27). Does this mean that "the racial content in political ideologies would cease to be relevant and should be replaced by a class content"? First, as Girvan points out, "the situation is complicated by the existence of a large racially-mixed intermediate group – mestizos and mulattoes – which was strategically placed to be the first to profit from the assault by the non-white masses on the white politico-economic hegemony" (26). Second, "the condition of the large majority of the non-whites has been changed not a jot by the creation of a non-white bourgeoisie: they still remain relegated and restricted to the role of suppliers of cheap, unskilled labour" (27). Moreover, accession to the ranks of the bourgeoisie requires the shedding of Afro-Creole folk identity and the adoption of white Western cultural attributes (or whiteness as 'social race'). Rejection of blackness and punishment of black racial solidarity are still critical components of the social structure: "the creation of a non-white bourgeoisie in this context, instead of constituting a fundamental break with the socio-economic order, represents a modification in form which permits substantial reinforcement in its content, both on the structural and ideological level" (29).

However, a diagnosis of the cause of poverty and exploitation can no longer be cast in purely racial terms. It must operationalize in analysis the following:

(1) the *class* question in these societies in so far as it is no longer identical to the question of phenotypical race; (2) the *structural* question relating to the political economy, i.e., the existence of a structure which requires the mass of the population to be oppressed, whatever their race, (3) the question of *imperialism*, i.e., the insertion of the political economy into the international capitalist system which continually reproduces a structure of dependent and oppressive underdevelopment. (Girvan 1991: 29–30; emphasis in orginal)

It would nonetheless be wrong to conclude that "revolutionary politics and ideology can be 'de-racialized' in content to any significant degree". To the extent that there persists "a high correlation between income, occupational status, ownership of property and socio-economic power on the one hand, and 'physical' and 'social' race on the other . . . it is inevitable that class conflict should be expressed at least partly in racial terms". In any event, the continued wielding of an ideology of physical and cultural racism to legitimate the socioeconomic order calls for the mobilization of black nationalist ideologies in counterhegemonic and transformatory movement (30).[10]

Although not noted by Girvan, the case of Barbados is interesting since it incorporates features of a settler colony while remaining a predominantly exploitation colony. In Barbados the tiny 'European settler' group was divided into a tenacious and exclusive residentiary bourgeoisie and an economically marginal (even lumpenized) group which acquired increasingly privileged proletarian status and enhanced opportunities for social mobility in the postslavery period as a result of the closing of racial ranks against the black and no-longer-captive majority. An intermediate, mixed group did not acquire the same historic (sub)hegemonic significance that it did elsewhere in the Caribbean.

The thrust of Girvan's thesis, like that of Beckford, is expressed in the radical political terms of the 1960s and 1970s, which might be considered somewhat undernuanced today. However, it remains a classic statement of the way in which imperial capitalism articulates class systems – transnationally and internally – that are 'necessarily' mediated through racial-national divisions and identities. More specifically, it provides a basic understanding of how the peripheral-capitalist formations of the Caribbean develop class systems that are mediated through the colonial relationship (racial imperialism) and modern dependent development/underdevelopment (dependent insertion into the global economy). It is a necessary contextual starting point that combines sociological and economic dimensions[11] and focuses, at some basic (if undifferentiated) level, on the oppressed majority of the peripheral social formation.

Below, I want to offer some preliminary and general comments demonstrating how a 'dependency' perspective might be more fruitfully integrated with a historical materialist methodology, and how gender *must* be a critical component of that synthesis.

A Third World Marxist Synthesis

One result of efforts to adapt a Marxist framework to the historical reality of colonized formations has been the formulation of theories of 'colonial' modes of production or modes of production of dependent or peripheral capitalism.[12] The common thread running through these efforts is a concern to 'centre' in theory the historical experience of social formations whose core contradictions are not 'autocentrically' generated and whose principal conditions of reproduction are dependent on an external centre, which engages them, moreover, in a functionally peripheral and one-sided way. The idea is to understand modes of production whose matrix of reproduction is mediated, *in a dependent and subordinate way,* through peripheral capitalism locally and corporate capitalism transnationally. The purely 'dependency' perspective tells us:

The point here is that it is an insufficient diagnosis simply to note that in the Caribbean the units of production have, for the most part, been externally owned. What has also to be taken into account is that these units have usually been minor and dependent partners in wider international systems of resource mobilization and allocation. The lines of interdependence run, not laterally, between local firms, but vertically to the metropole. As a consequence, the territorial economy is really comprised of a number of unintegrated segments held together by the political system. Production and pricing and other decisions are made more with reference to international than national considerations. (Levitt and Best 1975: 54)

   This characterization defines the dominant dimensions of Caribbean political economy, although, again, its explanatory power is somewhat diminished in the cases of Barbados and Dominica. The main problem, however, with this kind of exclusive focus on the branch plant or multinational corporation-subsidiary[13] economy is that it elides the interstitial functioning of domestic modes of re/production and the vast numbers of human subjects who occupy or 'people' those modes. This invisibility is particularly harsh to women, who are not the workers in the mineral-export or major import-substitution operations; who are not the principal entrepreneurs in the residentiary sector; who are not the leading party, government and union officials; and who tend to specialize in the nurturing or lowest-paid, lowest-prestige 'mass' professions. On the other hand, they play critical roles in the household-domestic and informal economies, as well as in nonexport sectors such as small-scale food production and marketing (among other sectors, of course). In general, Caribbean political economy must be understood (as well) at the level of the social formation or from the perspective of the social reproduction of the domestic economy (the domestic articulation of modes of re/production). The social formation is coterminous with a bounded (and sociologically meaningful) community of re/producers and their matrix of social practices, although it is not the generator of the dominant mode of production.

   To repeat a point made earlier, it is particularly important to understand the dependent economy at the level of the (abstracted) social formation *because the dominant mode of production is not always pervasive throughout the society*: it may act as a dominant fragment that blocks rather than transforms the rest of the economy. Beyond this, however, it is an indispensable, universal, methodological rule that dominant economic relations and practices are never coextensive with the whole of economic life (which inevitably incorporates residual and secondary hegemonies, as well as modes of re/production that are relatively independent of and in tension with the hegemonic relation). The extraordinary observations made by Raymond Williams (1977) below, which are meant to apply to 'normal', noncolonial situations, provide a hint as to the complexity of the analytical framework required by our type of society:

What has really to be said . . . is that *no mode of production and therefore no dominant social order and therefore no dominant culture ever in reality includes or exhausts all human practice, human energy and human intention.* This is not merely a negative proposition, allowing us to account for significant things which happen outside or against the dominant mode. On the contrary it is a fact about the modes of domination, that they select from and consequently exclude the full range of human practice. What they exclude may often be seen as the personal or the private, or as the natural or even the metaphysical. Indeed it is usually in one or other of these terms that the excluded area is expressed, since what the dominant has effectively seized is indeed the ruling definition of the social. (125; emphasis in original)

Williams' observation contains an implied criticism of Marxist orthodoxy, whose explanatory scope has often corresponded too closely to the self-selected and 'given' highlights of the hegemonic order. This tendency towards reductionism and economism is common to Marxist and dependency theory. Even as their respective foci on capitalism-class and colonial-racial-imperialism correct and counterbalance each other, they share a conscious or subconscious tendency to relegate other aspects of socioeconomic life to the realm of "the personal or the private, or . . . the natural or even the metaphysical", thus placing them beyond the boundaries of scientific inquiry.

At one level, this kind of reductionism is native to what has been called malestream theory, or, more accurately, theories cast in the malestream mould. However, I want to approach this line of argument with circumspection and caution. Feminist theory, which undoubtedly corrects, completes and enriches both orthodox Marxist and dependency theory, battles its own demons of reductionism and essentialism, sometimes in an exact mirror image of the most maligned Marxist orthodoxy. Furthermore, there are two kinds of reduction that we need to distinguish. One involves a process of determinate abstraction which strips socioeconomic structure down to its core, but maintains *historical specificity* and reveals historical and social meaning in all its most fundamental dimensions. This kind of methodological reduction is necessary to all social analysis, but can be overdone or mis-done – such as in an economistic reading of politics that fails to respect the 'relative autonomy' and 'own integrity' of the latter realm. Here, different levels of social structure or social analysis are collapsed into each other; or all levels are read off from an 'ultimate' core. The other kind of reduction, though not unrelated, is much more problematic and involves unguarded omission from a determinate and critically interconnected social field of human/social subjects, practices, relations, institutions, and their social venues or spaces of operation. This involves the exclusion of certain fundamental social relations and practices (and their protagonists) from the core matrix of social reproduction and social determination. I refer here, of course, to genuine blind spots, which consciously or unconsciously confer harmful invisibility upon whole human groups and human practices (as essential components of the social dialectic), *not* to the deliberate and properly acknowledged selection from a range of social concerns and topics in intellectual production. Euro-Marxists (Euro-feminists) have sometimes made rebuttals on the basis of claims to superior methods of dialectical-materialist (dialectical-feminist) reduction, when the criticisms to which they were responding were aimed rather at the empirico-historical and ideological blind spots generated by Eurocentric vision.

My concept of 'mode of re/production' (in keeping with a number of earlier equivalents)[14] represents a feminist-materialist improvement upon the old mode-of-production formulation with its exclusive attention to class (between male antagonists) and goods-production. Instead, the reformulated concept immediately presumes a historically specific articulation between the two productions (human reproduction and goods production) and, correlatedly, between the sexual division of labour and the class division of labour, involving interlocking and differentiated social, institutional and spatial dimensions (for example, household/market, private/public, family/job, kinship/class). This web of complexity is further compounded in peripheral-capitalist situations. In the Caribbean, a veritable structural maze is produced by the so-called dualism of the economy, historically correlated with a racial economic division of labour and racial-ethnic division of re/productive enclaves, a transnational/local split that occurs between as well as within sectors, and a gender-based dualism that occurs across as well as within sectors.

Thus all the previously ignored or analytically suspended relations must come into play – race/ethnicity, gender, human reproduction, informal economy and subsidiary modes of production. The dualism of the economy has less to do with the misconceptualized traditional/modern dichotomy than with the dis/articulation (connoting connection and fragmentation at the same time) of enclave-capitalist (or colonial-capitalist) and domestic modes of re/production, or the heterogeneous peculiarities of dependent capitalism. Acosta and Casimir (1985) put it very simply for St Lucia:

St Lucian society appeared as a dual structure: a colonial one, imposed by the political authorities through public administration, import-export trade and plantation activities, and a local one emerging around inward-oriented agriculture, family and community life. At no time had the bearers of the local structure been able to develop fully the model which can be designed on the basis of their practices, nor had they been able to isolate themselves from the dominant plantation system, to create a distinct peasant economy. (38)

They add later:

Other sets of rearrangements are taking place in the urban areas with the development of tourism and enclave manufactures. The convergence of these trends will be responsible for the ability of the country to respond to a third system of processes, namely international trade and politics. (59)

The dual or multiple structure identified by Acosta and Casimir and others has historically corresponded to a racial-ethnic division of economy and society in the Caribbean represented by the locally situated but transnationally connected Euro-colonial ruling classes, 'intermediary' race/class groups, and peasant-proletarian labouring classes constituting the majority of descendants of African slaves and Asian indentured labourers. In one of its most basic forms as postemancipation modification of slave society, the dual structure represented two societies of distinct racial-ethnic character, organized in part within relatively distinct spaces and circuits of re/production but confronting each other from opposite sides within the single spatial circuit(s) of the dominant colonial-capitalist relation. Within the latter spatial circuit, the two societies met as opposed and mutually dependent classes. The re/productive orbits of both race/class communities were, in a sense, spatially and socially split: that of the colonial ruling classes was split transnationally between core and periphery, and that of the labouring classes was split locally between the dominant capitalist export enclaves and the domestic hinterland economy.[15] Barbados and Jamaica represented somewhat different variants of the dual-society structure (that is, within the majority-African model). In Jamaica (and the Windward Islands) social dualism encompassed a pronounced plantation/peasant divide and therefore had a clear correspondence with different modes of production, whereas in Barbados (and the Leeward Islands) social dualism correlated with divisions of race, culture and class, but, in the context of the pervasiveness of the capital-labour relation and the plantation-type economy, did not extend to a segmented dualism of the economy: black labour has been effectively integrated into the orbit of white capital, locally and transnationally.

To sum up, the legacy of colonial capitalism in the Caribbean is a dual social structure. This duality has been externalized in an articulation/split between dominant and subordinate modes of production in Jamaica and Dominica and has been almost wholly incorporated in class and ethnocultural relations within the dominant and pervasive labour/property form in Barbados. Everywhere in the Caribbean, colonial capitalism developed one-sidedly within transnationally linked, mutually disarticulated enclaves which fulfilled the specialized, primary-export production requirements of dominant metropolitan or 'core' capitalists and the import-consumption and commercial requirements of settler colonialists (see Green 1980). Thus the driving force of (local) colonial capitalism was (global) imperialism; the former 'serviced' core capitalists and settler colonialists in a system that largely ignored the full range of reproductive needs of the oppressed race/class majority that provided the unfree or semi-free labour inputs. The persistent underdevelopment of commodified labour and consumer markets among the oppressed majority was ensured by the casualized, informal and episodic ways in which they were incorporated into dominant production processes once they were no longer a captive labour force.

Locally, export- and commercial-capitalist enclaves comprise the dominant forms and the driving force of dependent or peripheral capitalism. The social descendants of settler colonialists, a tiny group of merchant-industrial capitalists, constitute its dominant class. During slavery and increasingly in postemancipation society, small-scale domestic modes of production and circulation sprouted up and developed within the interstices of the dominant enclaves, directed by small-propertied or self-employed cultivators (or 'proto-peasants'), artisans and traders from the oppressed race/class group, and oriented towards its own needs. The resulting complex of domestic modes forms a subeconomy or re/productive enclave that is often vast in human terms but remains, to varying degrees, subsidiary to and dependent on the dominant modes of peripheral capitalism. At the same time, this subeconomy has become essential to the 'stable' functioning of peripheral capitalism itself.

The one-sided, static and externally oriented character of export- and merchant-capitalist enclaves severely limits their capacity to subsume the mass of the dispossessed under a self-expanding capitalist mode of production based on the dynamic generation of internal linkages and interdependent mass labour and consumer markets. Significant numbers of the dispossessed are precariously located – as producers or consumers or both – on the outer margins of the capitalist enclaves. Self-employment and self-provisioning remain indispensable means of survival for huge sections of the population. These subsidiary modes of providing goods and services must be understood on their own terms, but also as fulfilling 'primary' economic functions in 'secondary' forms and as having the effect of subsidizing the cost of labour to the capitalist enclaves. Petty commodity and subsistence production and exchange form coexisting *and* subsidiary, dominated *and* semi-autonomous modes of production in relation to dependent capitalism. The coexisting dominant/subordinate forms lend the character of duality and heterogeneity to the class structure and are correlated in critical and complex ways with a division of labour by gender.

Conclusion

In conclusion, it must be pointed out that the need for an inclusive and complex framework is no mere intellectual self-indulgence. Such a framework must do no less than inform a new politics of decolonization and empowerment, no matter how difficult and off-the-agenda this may seem in the current conjuncture.

All the radical anti-imperialist movements and civil insurgencies of the twentieth century anglophone Caribbean have sought both decolonization and popular empowerment, but have done so in uneven and fluctuating ratios. This was true of the mass riots and rebellions of the 1930s, which led to independence and formal democracy, and of the Black Power protests, militant economic nationalism and various socialist initiatives of the 1960s and 1970s, which led to nationalizations, Third Worldist anticapitalist rhetoric, and a short-lived period of grass-roots organizing, either against or in uneasy alliance with the state. The subsequent derailing of the would-be Caribbean revolution and the painful lessons accompanying it have demonstrated that popular empowerment can no longer continue to be the stepchild of political decolonization. One is an integral and inextricable condition of the other. And a key tool in the pursuit of empowerment is understanding how ordinary people – women and men – have invented themselves, their lives and their livelihoods, and how they both suffer and evade victimization on an everyday level. We need to understand not only the commanding heights of the economy and its hegemonic force but also the nooks, crannies and living networks of the popular and domestic economy and its creative potential. I am not suggesting that with such understanding something magical will occur; politics (and different kinds of politics, in different arenas) has to be built, devised, strategized, organized according to its own logic, not just inferred. However, it is only on the basis of this understanding and the infrastructure it reveals that a politics of empowerment can be sturdily built. I suggest that a theoretical framework based on a historical-materialist and popular-feminist reworking of Caribbean dependency theory can be one powerful route to that understanding.

Notes

1. Levitt is the only non-Caribbean national of the group.
2. See Amin's early work (1974; 1976) for an explication of autocentric versus disarticulated or peripheral capitalism.
3. Best (1968) has referred to this as the "incalculability" of transactions between hinterland and metropole according to market criteria. This *incalculability* has deepened in the transactions between the parent companies of transnational corporations and their hinterland subsidiaries: "They have largely internalized transactions relating to the 'purchase' and 'sale' of products between scores of subsidiaries and the parent companies. Similarly, 'borrowing', 'lending', 'repayment', 'remittance of profit', and 'transfer of capital' between subsidiaries and parent companies are transactions with no clearly determined counterpart on a market" (Levitt and Best 1975: 50).
4. Although there are mainland-*located* plantation hinterlands that mimic the model of island hinterlands (the Guyanas, Suriname, Belize).
5. See note 4 above.
6. The Best-Levitt model is predictive with regard to the post-1970s, post–import-substitution phase generated by the trap of external indebtedness. I refer to the current phase of International Monetary Fund–induced "structural adjustment" and export-orientation, which have produced new and continuing forms of dependency. I have treated these phenomena and associated case studies in Green 1990, 1995a, 1996, 1998.
7. In the first staple cycle, only the minority of skilled workers in the sugar factories and supervisory field personnel enjoyed relatively high incomes, not the vast majority of field workers, who were always desperately poor.
8. Here I refer of course to the *hinterland*-domestic economy as a whole as opposed to the metropolitan economy, not to the *household*-domestic economy. Later, I depart from the specialized Best-Levitt terminology in referring to the domestic 'hinterland economy', that is, the (internal) hinterland of the local social formation.

9. Girvan's important monograph *Aspects of the Political Economy of Race in the Caribbean and the Americas* was first published in 1975 by the Institute of Social and Economic Research, University of the West Indies, Mona, as a working paper. It languished for almost two decades before being republished in Lewis and Bryan 1991. My references to Girvan's work are based on the 1991 reprint of the 1975 working paper.
10. The need to assert racial and cultural pride becomes more complicated where the oppressed majority comprises multiple ethnic groups, particularly Asians and blacks, but this will not concern us here.
11. Which is what a true 'political economy' should do.
12. For early initiatives in this regard, see Banaji 1972, 1977; Alavi 1975; Green 1980.
13. Multinational corporation (MNC) is interchangeable with transnational corporation (TNC).
14. One of the best and most inspiring feminist-materialist reformulations of mode of production can be found in the work of Wally Seccombe (1983, 1986, 1992, 1993).
15. Best (1968) and Levitt and Best (1975) always use 'hinterland economy' to describe the entire peripheral economy, but here I refer to an internal hinterland, relative to the modern capitalist enclaves.

References

Acosta, Yvonne, and Jean Casimir. 1985. "Social origins of the counter-plantation system in St Lucia". In *Rural Development in the Caribbean,* edited by P.I. Gomes. New York: St Martin's Press.

Alavi, Hamza. 1975. "India and the colonial mode of production". *Socialist Register.*

Amin, Samir. 1974. *Accumulation on a World Scale.* New York: Monthly Review Press.

Amin, Samir. 1976. *Unequal Development.* New York: Monthly Review Press.

Banaji, Jairus. 1972. "For a theory of colonial modes of production". *Economic and Political Weekly* 8, no. 52 (23 December).

Banaji, Jairus. 1977. "Modes of production in a materialist conception of history". *Capital and Class,* no. 3 (Autumn).

Beckford, George. 1972. *Persistent Poverty: Underdevelopment in the Plantation Economies of the Third World.* New York: Oxford University Press.

Best, Lloyd. 1968. "The mechanism of plantation-type economies: Outlines of a model of pure plantation economy". *Social and Economic Studies* 17, no. 3 (September).

Brenner, Robert. 1977. "The origins of capitalist development: A critique of neo-Smithian Marxism". *New Left Review,* no. 104 (July–August).

Foster-Carter, Aidan. 1978. "The modes of production controversy". *New Left Review,* no. 107 (January–February).

Girvan, Norman. 1971. *Foreign Capital and Economic Underdevelopment in Jamaica.* Kingston, Jamaica: Institute of Social and Economic Research.

Girvan, Norman. 1991. "The political economy of race in the Americas: The historical context of Garveyism". In *Garvey: His Work and Impact,* edited by R. Lewis and P. Bryan. Trenton, NJ: Africa World Press. First published as *Aspects of the Political Economy of Race in the Caribbean and the Americas* (Kingston, Jamaica: Institute of Social and Economic Research, 1975).

Gordon, Derek. 1987. *Class, Status and Social Mobility in Jamaica.* Kingston, Jamaica: Institute of Social and Economic Research.

Green, Cecilia. 1980. "Toward a theory of 'colonial' modes of production: A Marxist approach". Master's thesis, University of Toronto.

Green, Cecilia. 1985. "Marxist-feminism and Third World liberation". *Fireweed,* no. 20 (Spring). Also published in *Fireworks: The Best of Fireweed,* edited by Makeda Silvera (Toronto: The Women's Press, 1986).

Green, Cecilia. 1990. *The World Market Factory: A Study of Enclave Industrialization in the Eastern Caribbean and its Impact on Women Workers.* Kingstown, St Vincent and the Grenadines: Caribbean People's Development Agency.

Green, Cecilia. 1992–93. "Gender and re/production in British West Indian slave societies". Parts 1–3. *Against the Current* 7 no. 4 (September–October); no. 5 (November–December); no. 6 (January–February).

Green, Cecilia. 1994. "Historical and contemporary restructuring and women in production in the Caribbean". In *The Caribbean in the Global Political Economy,* edited by Hilbourne A. Watson. Boulder: Lynne Rienner.

Green, Cecilia. 1995a. "Export-processing industry and the new peripheralization of the Commonwealth Caribbean". *Twenty-first Century Policy Review* 2, no. 4 (Spring–Summer).

Green, Cecilia. 1995b. "Gender, race and class in the social economy of the English-speaking Caribbean". *Social and Economic Studies* 44, nos. 2 and 3 (June–September).

Green, Cecilia. 1996. "At the junction of the global and the local: Transnational industry and women workers in the Caribbean". In *Human Rights, Labor Rights, and International Trade,* edited by Lance Compa and Stephen Diamond. Philadelphia: University of Pennsylvania Press.

Green, Cecilia. 1998a. "The Asian connection: The US–Caribbean apparel circuit and the evolution of a new model of industrial relations". *Latin American Research Review* 33, no. 3 (Fall).

Green Cecilia. 1998b. "Labouring women: A historical, sociological and comparative analysis of the Afro-Caribbean women's economic roles in three islands". PhD diss., University of Toronto.

Green Cecilia. 1999. "A recalcitrant plantation colony: Dominica, 1880–1946". *New West Indian Guide/Nieuwe West-Indishe Gids* 73, nos. 3 and 4.

Laclau, Ernesto. 1971. "Feudalism and capitalism in Latin America". *New Left Review,* no. 67 (May–June).

Levitt, Kari, and Lloyd Best. 1975. "Character of Caribbean economy". In *Caribbean Economy,* edited by G. Beckford. Kingston, Jamaica: Institute of Social and Economic Research.

Mintz, Sidney W. 1989. *Caribbean Transformations.* 1974. Reprint, New York: Columbia University Press.

Seccombe, Wally. 1983. "Marxism and demography". *New Left Review,* no. 147 (January–February).

Seccombe, Wally. 1986. "Patriarchy stabilized: The construction of the male breadwinner wage norm in nineteenth-century Britain". *Social History* 11, no. 1 (January).

Seccombe, Wally. 1992. *A Millennium of Family Change.* London: Verso.

Seccombe, Wally. 1993. *Weathering the Storm.* London: Verso.

Shepherd, Verene. 1988. "Pens and pen-keepers in a plantation society: Aspects of Jamaica's social and economic history 1740–1845". PhD diss., University of Cambridge.

Thomas, Clive Y. 1974. *Dependence and Transformation: The Economics of the Transition to Socialism.* New York: Monthly Review Press.

Thomas, Clive Y. 1997. "On reconstructing a political economy of the Caribbean". Paper presented at symposium New Currents in Caribbean Thought: Looking Towards the Twenty-first Century. Kellogg Center, Michigan State University, 4–5 April. (Appears as chapter 19, this volume.)

Wagley, Charles. 1957. "Plantation America: A culture sphere". In *Caribbean Studies: A Symposium,* edited by V. Rubin. Seattle: University of Washington Press.

Williams, Raymond. 1977. *Marxism and Literature.* Oxford: Oxford University Press.

4

Democratic Governance in the Anglophone Caribbean

Threats to Sustainability*

SELWYN RYAN

The anglophone Caribbean is frequently seen by observers as an area in which Westminster-style democracy had succeeded, perhaps beyond expectations. Jorge Dominguez, for example, in an essay entitled "The Caribbean Question: Why Has Liberal Democracy (Surprisingly) Flourished?", observes that

No other region in what has been called the Third World has had, for so long, so many liberal polities . . . The Caribbean's capacity to sustain liberal democratic polities is impressive. Since independence (beginning with Jamaica and Trinidad and Tobago in 1962) ten of the twelve (Guyana and Grenada excepted) Anglophone Caribbean Countries have consistently held fair elections and have been free from unconstitutional transfers of power. Also since independence a majority of the ten consistently constitutionalist Anglophone Caribbean countries have witnessed at least one election as a result of which the

* This chapter is a substantially modified version of an earlier paper prepared for the United Nations Development Programme in 1996 and presented to that agency in Mexico City in March 1996. That paper was published in December 1996 by the Caribbean Division of the Regional Bureau for Latin America and the Caribbean of the United Nations Development Programme.

governing party peacefully turned power over the hitherto opposition party; in Barbados and Belize this democratic achievement has occurred twice, and in Jamaica, thrice . . . This Caribbean achievement is far superior to that of Latin America and also to that of the countries of Africa and Asia that acquired their formal independence from European powers after the Second World War. Some have noted that former British colonies have had a better record than the former colonies of other major powers at sustaining liberal democracy. (1993: 3)

The question now being anxiously asked by many has to do with the extent to which the achievements of the Caribbean can be sustained, given the powerful forces that are now serving to undermine and subvert them. Is the 'historically favourable political culture', which was inherited together with a sophisticated complex of liberal democratic institutions, sufficiently well entrenched to withstand the hurricane-like social storms that are roaring throughout the region? Is there sufficient democratic renewal taking place to compensate for the diminution in the stock of social capital that is rapidly taking place, or is the decline of democracy secular and irreversible? The argument of this chapter is that liberal democracy is in grave danger in the anglophone Caribbean and that unless drastic steps are taken to bolster and renew the democratic character and institutional capability of the political and social systems of the island states in the region, they will be lumped with other states that are negatively classified along the governance continuum.

Size and Good Governance

'Good governance' has become one of the most widely used concepts in the contemporary political lexicon, replacing traditional concepts such as law and order, political order, stability, peace and good government, civic culture, and other such terms previously favoured by philosophers and political commentators. What in fact does the term mean? Clearly, the way the term is being used suggests that it means something more than democracy, or rule by the people, however those terms might be defined. It is popular democracy in its broadest sense, plus good political, financial and administrative management. It also assumes a high level of transparency and morality in public affairs as well as a politically vibrant civil society that interacts continuously with state officials.

The United Nations Development Programme, in its "Strategy Paper on Governance" (1995), has defined the concept of good governance in the following terms:

Governance is the exercise of political, economic and administrative authority to manage a nation's affairs. It is a broad concept that encompasses the organizational structures and activities of central, regional and local government, the parliament and the judiciary. Importantly, the concept of governance also incorporates the institutions, organizations and individuals that comprise civil society, insofar as they actively participate and influence the shaping of public policy that affects people's lives. (1)

The United Nations Development Programme document also seeks to define the concept of civil society. Civil society is described as the "social mode of life, the customs and organization of an ordered community". The term is also used to identify that part of "the public realm occupying the space between the state and the individual or the family" (3).

One of the questions that needs to be addressed is whether the concept of good governance means the same thing in all societies or whether it must vary from society to society and depend for its meaning on the specifics of each society. There is also the issue of whether the concept could mean the same thing in small societies, such as those in the Caribbean, as it does in the larger democracies of Western Europe and North America. In sum, is there one model of good governance against which all performance could be judged? A related question is whether or not there is anything peculiar to small states that makes them hospitable or inhospitable environments for 'good governance'. Is small in fact always beautiful?

Before we attempt to answer these questions, it is important to note that the concept of small as it relates to states is subject to various definitions. Some definitions advert to geographical space; others use demographic data such as size and spatial distribution of the population; while yet others use determinants such as the size, scope, diversity, complexity and viability of the economy, the structure of the elite clusterings, or the spatial distribution of political power grids in the social system.

Economists often use the concept of viability, resource sufficiency and size of national income to classify societies; that is, whether the society has an economy of sufficient scope and scale to allow it to sustain a 'decent' standard of living for its inhabitants. Some have used per capita income to measure viability. Others have argued that the use of this criterion presents more difficulties than it solves since raw per capita figures tell us little about human priority ratios, that is, the percentage of social spending devoted to basic human needs such as shelter, nutrition, education, primary health care or safe drinking water. In sum, the figures tell us little about distribution of that income, the economic and social well-being of the citizenry, the sustainability of such welfare system as exists, and the adaptability of the economy in the context of a rapidly changing world economic system (UNDP 1993: 70).

Sociologists and anthropologists use notions such as the nature and quality of role relationships in their discussion of the concept of size. They observe that small societies are characterized by the predominance of primary relationships over those that are secondary. In such societies, critical decision-making roles are invariably preformed by a limited number of individuals. To use the jargon, there is a tendency towards role diffuseness rather than role specificity. Interpersonal and intergroup relationships are also intense and relationships of anonymity and impartiality are the exception rather than the norm.

While smallness may facilitate social cohesion and harmonious mediation of conflicting interests, it often serves to intensify individual and group rivalry which serves to fragment and paralyse a community and its basic institutions. Group, family or clan rivalry or feud affect perception of issues, and positions are taken not in terms of merits of the matter but how they impact on group positions. There is also a tendency to privatize and personalize issues. Matters of policy are not viewed in terms of their generalized impact but in terms of how they affect key personalities and primary relationships in the system. Policy options are therefore not assessed in terms of whether they are 'rational', administratively implementable, or adequate to the problems that they are designed to address but in terms of how they affect notables in the system.

Legislative and bureaucratic institutions also function differently in small states. Opposition parliamentarians and out elites in the Commonwealth Caribbean are of the view that one of the most effective ways of securing good governance in general, and financial accountability and transparency in particular, is to have the legislature exercise greater control of the executive through the creation of an elaborate system of standing parliamentary committees such as those that obtain in the United States and some mature democracies. Those who hold such views note with concern that the balance of power in political systems the world over was progressively shifting to the executive to the point where parliamentary democracy was now seriously threatened. This was particularly so in small states such as those in the Caribbean.

The Spoils System and Governance

One of the most troubling developments in the postindependence politics of many, if not all, Caribbean states is the tendency of newly elected governments to assume that winners are entitled to all the spoils of office. As such, they let it be known that they expect the chairmen, members and even chief executive officers of all statutory boards, commissions and state enterprises to resign or at least offer their resignations to allow them to fill these posts with persons presumed to be loyal or sympathetic to them. The heads of these organizations are in turn expected to ensure that the organizations under their control extend the process by providing jobs and resources to persons known or assumed to be loyal to the party and the prime minister who sees himself, anthropomorphically, as personifying the state (Ryan 1996: 359–64). In a number of jurisdictions (Grenada, St Kitts and Nevis, and St Lucia), heads of state have been replaced with persons deemed more sympathetic to the new political directorate. The spoils system has probably become most highly developed in Jamaica. As Figueroa (1996: 27) notes:

Within the garrisons, the value system promoted is one that accepts the right of the party supporters to undertake all manner of illegal acts, so long as they are seen to be contributing towards the ultimate goal of party victory. The winner takes all; if the party wins, the spoils of victory are expected to redound to its supporters. But win or lose, living in a garrison often brings with it certain privileges not enjoyed by other citizens. These come in the form of such things as the right to live in rent/mortgage free accommodation with free water and light. The unfair distribution of jobs, houses and contracts to the party faithful are all accepted as normal. This sharing in the spoils provides a basis for community support for the justification of the hatred, murder and mayhem against the opposition. Thus a psychological and social basis is created for the terrorism that is part and parcel of Jamaican politics. But the garrison is more than a psychological fortress; it is a veritable military base, a haven for those who engage in illegal activities on behalf of the political parties. From these bases it is possible to do the 'outreach work' involving the intimidating of the opposition and manipulating the electoral process. It is from the garrisons that the paramilitary attacks are launched in the positional warfare associated with turf politics. In general, these are carried out with impunity as the nexus between the corrupt police, the politicians and the gunmen protects the perpetrators from prosecution.

Postelection competition for state office is of course not unique to small or poor Third World states, and its best illustration is to be found in the United

States of America. Its effects are, however, more damaging in the former. The intensity that characterizes the scramble for spoils has to do with the fact that resources in these poor societies are scarce and politics is viewed as a means of earning a livelihood. Many people live 'off' politics rather than 'for' politics. The fact that the private sector is weak and that the state has to serve as a major source of employment, both salaried and otherwise, intensifies the preoccupation. Where the state and the commanding heights of the private sector are dominated by the same community, the problem becomes even more complex. Individuals and groups thus develop a vested interest in having their parties retain office in perpetuity while the parties themselves develop a corresponding interest in the monopolistic retention of office.

While this arrangement may benefit those individuals and parties that control the state, it becomes socially and economically dysfunctional for the society at large. For one thing, it means that the society is divided into warring political factions (and in the case of Guyana and Trinidad into ethnic camps) that seek to delegitimize whatever one group has to offer or attempt to do. For another, it means that the pool of high-calibre personnel, which is small at the national level and smaller still at local government levels, cannot be fully utilized for the benefit of the society as a whole. The result is a tremendous wastage of scarce human and social capital, to say nothing of the damage inflicted on the social and institutional fabric of the state during and between elections as accusations of corruption are hurled at incumbents by out elites, each side seeking to discredit the other. The damage done to the reputations of families and individuals as a result of these conflicts is also substantial.

If standards of good governance are to be raised or even maintained, serious consideration must be given to the issue of which public offices are to be depoliticized and made 'permanent' and occupiable by professionals without reference to political affiliation on some form of performance-oriented tenure and which, if any, are to be determined on the basis of electoral outcomes. It does not of course mean that such permanently appointed officials must be 'neutral' in the sense in which that term has conventionally been understood – that is, they are delinked from and disinterested in the political objectives of their political bosses (Nunes 1990). Professionals must take those on board. However, they should also seek to retain their independence and professionalism. In sum, the social choices of the elected politician should count for as much as the technical expertise of the professional; the latter should bring both factors to bear on the advice he proffers.[1]

A way clearly needs to be found to abort the process of elite circulation that automatically follows a change of government. The assumption that it is the done thing the world over is also mistaken. The problem, of course, is how to overcome the suspicion, driven by embedded mistrust, that leads the politician to suspect that the advice being given by the professional is designed to subvert or sabotage rather than to further his political goals.

The professional might also assume that what the politician is doing is not in the interest of the community or the party to which he is sympathetic. The problem is a difficult one, but we cannot assume that it cannot be resolved or attenuated. Mechanisms should thus be put in place to change the etiquette and the protocols that inform the relationship between elected officials and professionals, both of whom should be made to appreciate that the society is better served if each respects his sphere of influence while working together for the common good. If a platform of good governance is going to be regained or maintained in the region, Caribbean societies must begin the process of fashioning postelectoral arrangements that are more inclusive than exclusive.

Structural Adjustment and Good Governance

The economic and social consequences of structural adjustment for Caribbean societies have been well documented and need not be detailed here. Less has been said of the impact of adjustment on the manner in which the political system functions, particularly as it relates to the balance between the state and civil society generally, and in particular to the relationship between the executive and the legislature and the elites who speak for groups negatively influenced by the imperatives of adjustment (Munroe 1996).

While executive ascendancy has invariably been the norm in Westminster-patterned states, new developments have served to increase such ascendancy even more in developing states. For one thing, many of these states are under the tutelage of multilateral lending agencies which have members of their staff inserted in the bureaucracy, often on a continuing basis. These parallel agencies not only dictate macroeconomic policy as a condition of debt restructuring. They also write detailed policy and budget proposals and monitor in microscopic detail the implementation of such proposals to ensure that governments fulfil the terms of the conditionalities attached to the loan.[2] Because many of these proposals are likely to upset popular and vested interests, governments are driven to withhold critical information from Parliament and public, and at times even from members of their own party for fear of public disclosure.

The growing need to attract investment capital also requires the state to seek to dominate elements in civil society that, in their quest to improve the economic well-being of their constituents, take action that, in the view of governing elites, threatens to destabilize the society and scare off would-be investors. In doing so, they often unwittingly provoke confrontations which serve to fast-forward the very crises they seek to prevent. The crises in 1990, 1994 and 1995 in Trinidad and Tobago, Barbados and St Lucia illustrate this point well.[3] As this occurs, democratic governance progressively deteriorates, and with it the attractiveness of the destination to potential investors. 'Good governance', one of the prerequisites often demanded by international agencies and investors as a collateral conditionality for aid and investment capital (the so-called donor democracy), may thus be incompatible with the imperatives of structural adjustment (Chossudovsky 1994: 17–18).[4]

Regionalization and globalization are also serving to reduce the ability of parliaments and local groups to control important areas of policy. What Sally Washington says of the problem in Organization for Economic Cooperation and Development countries is equally true, perhaps more so, of small states which do not have the capacity to influence international decision making significantly and thus perhaps enlarge their sovereignty:

Governments may take policy issues into the international arena as a strategy to escape domestic opposition. Claiming 'tied hands' from being party to international agreements may allow them to present policies at home that are unpalatable to some groups, and therefore politically difficult to implement. There may also be a power shift from elected to non-elected bodies. The tendency to resort to international decision-making (including treaties and international agreements) seems to increase the power of executive government at the expense of legislatures, putting such fora beyond democratic control . . . The erosion of parliamentary supervision is likely to be a central issue in the debate on the future of democracy. Parliaments are already demanding more say in the international undertakings of their governments. But can parliamentary oversight be built into international decision-making without adding costs and delays? (OECD 1996: 25–26)[5]

Parliamentary Accountability and Control

One of the problems faced by small states in securing parliamentary accountability is that the size of parliaments and the trained elite does not allow certain conventional mechanisms of control to be utilized. In larger political systems, it is possible to put in place elaborate committee systems to monitor and scrutinize government budgets and other activities. It is even the norm in some countries to have such committees chaired by back-benchers or members of rival parties. Such arrangements do not work in small states, either because parliaments meet too infrequently or because the opposition was too small and too weak to provide the manpower and expertise needed to staff such committees. Party loyalty and party discipline also mean that back-benchers would invariably support the executive on such committees since they would wish to avoid scoring their own goals, which embarrass their party.

Trevor Munroe has also drawn attention to the parliamentary distortions that derive from the operation of the first-past-the-post electoral system and the tendency this system – which, he notes, is often enforced by force, fraud and violence – has to overrepresent one party and to underrepresent others. The result is that governments are rarely ever put in danger by motions of no confidence. Munroe also shares the concern about the manner in which the legislature in the Caribbean is dominated by the executive and the prime minister:

[T]he power of the executive and of the prime minister in particular over the candidacy, the electoral fortunes and the legislative tenure of the parliamentary members of the governing party, reinforces the subordinate nature of the legislature in relation to the executive. The combination rather than the separation of powers between the executive and the legislature is carried to an extreme in the Commonwealth Caribbean even as far as parliamentary systems are concerned. (1996: 18)

Similar observations about the limited utility of parliamentary control on executives in small states were made by Dr Ralph Gonzales, the leader of an opposition party in St Vincent. In an article written in 1977, Gonzales (1993: 17) itemized the weakness as follows:

the small size of parliament with few or not critical back-benchers; the high percentage of parliamentarians as ministers and parliamentary secretaries; the dominant position of the executive in managing the economy and polity; the political imperatives of a competitive party system; the tendency of the electorate to hold party leaders in reverence; and the spoils system of politics which encourages executive patronage and corruption.

The small size of Parliament also limits the ability of prime ministers to reshuffle cabinet ministers or call for the resignation of ministers who embarrass the government. In large parliaments the prime minister can bring in competent back-benchers to replace ministerial incumbents. In small parliaments this option is not normally available unless an appointment is made via the senate, where such an institution exists and constitutional arrangements allow.

Gonzales sagely observed that improving the machinery for scrutiny by introducing more specialized committees would not do much to ensure accountability unless one were to go further and change the formal powers of committees and party behaviour. Gonzales in fact argued that the only way to ensure greater accountability would be to abandon the Westminster model and replace it with 'genuine' representative institutions that could exercise meaningful control of the bureaucratic apparatuses of the state. Gonzales's proposals included provision for more democracy at the local level and, more importantly, the institution of a one-party system. The latter would, in his view, serve to eliminate the fruitless and damaging party divisions that render the mechanisms of scrutiny unworkable. Others have endorsed the call for the modification of the Westminster model and have urged the acceptance of a consociational alternative.

While it is conceivable that some of the difficulties identified above might be overcome by a commitment to bipartisanship and consensus, the reality is that political and group competition in small states is invariably fierce and personalized. Those who wish to remain within the narrow elite circle or to benefit from state patronage, either for themselves or for firms that they own or represent, are generally disinclined to challenge a potentially punitive officialdom. The problem is exacerbated in plural societies where the government has its centre of gravity in one community and opposition parties in others. The problem of loyalty in such cases becomes not merely one of the loyalty to party or leader but also to community. Critics remain silent out of concern that they might be viewed as betrayers of their kin or ethnic group. Such inhibitions affect individuals in the private sector as well as those in the public sector.

Societies that are small are also generally characterized by the narrowness of their resource base. There are few free-floating material assets. In order to secure a share of the small resource pie, interest groups, real or potential, feel compelled to forge links with and become clients to those who are in a position to allocate valued resources. Clientelism has in fact served to transform the workings of the Westminster parliamentary system in the anglophone Caribbean. Those who are under the clientelistic umbrella are either suborned to stay mute, at least in public, or do so in the hope of being incorporated or shaded by the political banyan tree.

Public administration specialists have also observed that while smallness has advantages, in that bureaucratic coordination, penetration of the society and conflict resolution may be rendered easier, small scale also constitutes a serious constraint on bureaucratic capability and effectiveness.[6] There are certain functions that all states in the international system, whether large, medium sized or small, are expected to undertake on behalf of citizens whose expectations are inflated by their exposure to the international media and modern consumption patterns. The range of such functions often requires a level of structural differentiation and complexity that is invariably beyond their ability to generate, given their limited material and human resource capabilities.[7] They are in fact unable to take advantage either of economies of scale or scope. The result is that their administrative systems become overloaded and overwhelmed by the demands placed on them and consistently underperform.[8]

Caribbean Youth and Good Governance

Growing unemployment among youth, and the inflation of credential requirements have served to marginalize youth in the conventional labour market and have disposed many to turn to petty crime and drug distribution as alternative mechanisms for earning the income to sustain the lifestyles to which they aspire or indeed to meet basic needs. For some, crime has become a functional equivalent to work and is no longer perceived as deviant behaviour by many parents or dispossessed elements within the community in which the under-class live.

Studies done at the Institute of Social and Economic Research have also linked the behaviour of youth to wider processes in the society – the decline of community and the family. The decline of community is seen to be a by-product of internal and external migration, greater social mobility, the disappearance of institutions that served as poles around which community action took place (the village shop, the community standpipe, harvests, Sunday schools, village sporting events), the increase in the incidence of female-headed one-parent families, the growing prevalence of agnosticism, the corresponding decline in attendance at church-related activities by youth (and male youth in particular), and the appearance of the 'block' or the 'street corner lime' as an alternative mechanism for transmitting norms as to which values and forms of dress are 'cool' and which are not. What Richard Carter (1997) observes in relation to Barbados is true across the region:

There has clearly been a shift in the patterns of authority relating to youth in a range of institutional contexts over the last three decades. In the family, the school and at the community level the open acceptance of the authority of the institution, particularly as expressed through the adults in those institutions, has been replaced by a greater predisposition to question the legitimacy of such authority. (41)

Community-based adults generally, and political elites in particular, are not now seen as the source of knowledge and moral tutelage as was the case in the past. In their place have emerged the gang and its leader and the drug dons as competing founts of authority.

Modernizing Caribbean States

In recent years there has been much talk about downsizing the state and the need to have it withdraw from active management of the development process. Good governance, however, requires the existence of a state system that is capable of implementing such policies as have been agreed upon. State capacity is in fact now being recognized as the central precondition of development (Grindle 1997). Development is also facilitated by the existence of a complex legal system that is independent of the executive and not beholden to power elites in civil society. Attention has been drawn to the problems being faced by the judiciary in the Caribbean, both in terms of the excessive delays involved in getting matters heard and adjudicated and the attempts that are being made by drug traffickers to suborn and intimidate judges, magistrates, police officers and state witnesses as well as to tamper with documents, some of which are made to 'disappear' (Ryan 1996). A US State Department report published in February 1997 observed in respect of the judiciary in Trinidad and Tobago, that "despite serious efforts to improve the judiciary, severe inefficiency remains in many areas. Several criminal cases were dismissed due to judicial or police inefficience." What was said by the report of the US State Department is equally true of almost all jurisdictions in the Caribbean.

The World Bank (*The State in a Changing World '97*) and other lending and reform agencies have recently begun to pay closer attention to the need for strengthening judicial capacity, which is seen as a prerequisite for the enforcement of contracts and property rights that are in turn regarded as crucial if investment is to be encouraged. It is widely agreed that a slow and inefficient legal system erodes confidence in an economy, and that this in turn facilitates corruption and discourages business transactions that may require impartial adjudication in the event that there are contractual disputes. An arbitrary legal environment can also have the effect of driving would-be entrepreneurs into the informal sector or into short-term investments.

The 1993 Nobel Prize winner Douglass North (*Institutions, Institutional Change and Economic Performance*) has argued that the inability of societies to achieve low transaction costs is perhaps the most important cause of economic stagnation in the 'Third World'. One reason for high transaction costs, that is, the costs of doing business, is the inability of state institutions to protect rights and enforce agreements. Other reasons include the inability to maintain currency stability, and to provide proper communications and other infrastructure, commercial codes, fair taxation regimes, and flexible labour markets.

An efficient legal system (at least one that operates in a free market economy) thus requires more than functioning courts that are free from political interference. A proper system requires up-to-date company laws that define how business is capitalized, as well as a range of other laws that regulate commercial activity. Good governance, however, requires that a balance be struck between the need to regulate and the need to free business activity from constraints that stifle and inhibit economic activity.

Most Caribbean countries have judicial systems that are reasonably independent of the executive. Most, however, have a great deal of outdated company legislation and laws that restrict competition in a number of critical areas. We note, however, that Jamaica, Barbados and Trinidad either have updated or are in the process of updating their company laws, and the same holds for competition policies. Jamaica, for example, introduced the Fair Competition Act in 1993 and one is being prepared for Trinidad and Tobago.

Good Governance and the Media

A media that is free and uncontrolled by political executives or by private monopolists is vital to good governance, which requires a multidirectional flow of information to help decision makers and affected groups in civil society make and react quickly and meaningfully to policy issues. A free and investigative press, which does not fear being shut down or deprived of licences or that its reporters would be harassed or even killed, serves to discourage some types of corrupt or arbitrary behaviour, if only because its existence forces wrongdoers to count the costs of possible disclosure (Respondación III 1996). The existence of a fearless media which is unafraid to challenge established institutions and powerful individuals also helps to empower elements in civil society that wish to promote accountability and transparency.

While the region has had a reasonably good record of media freedom, there have been and there continue to be political elites who seek to intimidate the media, if not muzzle it completely. Such efforts were made in Grenada under both Eric Gairy and the People's Revolutionary Government; in Guyana under Forbes Burnham; in Antigua and Barbuda; and in Trinidad and Tobago, both in the 1970–73 period and in 1996–97. The recent Green Paper on media law (Ministry of the Attorney General 1997), which was published for comment by the Government of Trinidad and Tobago, has given grave cause for concern throughout the region, particularly since it is linked to statements made by key members of the government that attacked the media in general and impugned the integrity of publishers and editors. The prime minister of Trinidad and Tobago and other ministers accused the media of seeking to "beat into submission" or "overthrow" the United National Congress government as it had allegedly done in the case of other governments (*Trinidad Express,* 9 June 1997). While the Green Paper disclaimed any intent to muzzle the media and indeed proposed introducing a comprehensive press and broadcasting act (which would enhance media freedom by redefining the laws of libel, defamation, contempt of Parliament or of court for refusing to disclose sources of information), it also talked about giving the government the power to "punish or stop media behaviour which imperils national security or undermines the democratic fabric". Other bothersome but seemingly well-meaning proposals were:

1. Journalists and newspapers shall endeavour to highlight and promote activities of the State and the public which aim at national unity, solidarity, integrity of Trinidad and Tobago, and economic and social progress.

2. Journalists and newspapers shall avoid publication of reports and comments which tend to promote tensions likely to lead to civil disorder, meeting or rebellion.

3. Journalists and newspapers shall ensure that information disseminated is factual. No fact shall be distorted nor information known to be false or not believed to be true shall be published.

4. No sensational or tendentious reports of speculative nature shall be published. Any report or comment found to be inaccurate shall be rectified by prominent publication. (Ministry of the Attorney General 1997: 26–27)

Thus, while much in the Green Paper pointed to a recognition that a free media is vital to a free democratic society, there was also much to alert those who believe, rightly or wrongly, that another hidden agenda was being served, namely, the anxiety on the part of the United National Congress government to 'police the press' and coerce it into becoming a sympathetic organ for the new regime.

Whither Good Governance in the Caribbean?

What then are the prospects for refashioning and re-engineering good govern-ance in the Caribbean? What are the prospects for democratic renewal? Who is correct: the optimists who see light at the end of the tunnel of economic reform or the declinists who see irreversible economic pauperization and a return to the atavism of the 'state of nature'? Given what we know about the dramatic manner in which the changes taking place in the global economy are impacting on the small fragile economies of the region, what we are likely to see in the short run is a progressive loss of jobs in the manufacturing sector, a persistent leakage of capital, a decline in the quality of the educational, social and legal services offered the citizenry, growing alienation among the youth, a growing coarseness in the social order, a dramatic decline in the number of persons who are members of or participate meaningfully in trade unions and mass political parties, increased political cynicism, and a sustained disaffection with the process of voting as a result of the inability of parties to convince supporters that it makes much difference whether they support party A, B or C. All over the Caribbean, one can find evidence of disappearing or somnolent party groups and decreasing turnout at national and local elections. Party groups generally only come alive when there is patronage to dispense or when the likelihood of its availability exists.

The culture of civil discourse, which used to obtain among political elites once the political battles were ritualistically fought out, is also becoming a thing of the past. Politics has now become 'war by other means'. The same obtains in sports, including cricket which was once a gentleman's game, and in music, where the dancehall culture now rules supreme among black youth, if not all youth, in the region. The ghettos of the region are also rapidly becoming states within states which pay little heed to the polite norms of civil society. Elements from these shanty states ignore the police service or refuse to cooperate with it, execute or intimidate state witnesses, bribe or suborn officers of the police, the magistracy and the judiciary or terrorize businessmen who are required to pay what they call 'coward taxes'.[9]

Brian Meeks has written plaintively of the decline of political order in Jamaica, a country that, according to the United Nations Development Programme's *Human Development Report* (1993), had the greatest fall of living of any country in the world, with the exception of Romania. Jamaica, he notes, was once characterized by the existence of one of the tightest, most impermeable and consistent two-party systems in the hemisphere. That system, he observes, was underwritten in the 1960s and 1970s by a number of features "including clientelism, extreme Westminster centralization of power, the absence of an effective back bench, the exclusion of third parties and the absence of a strong independent civil society" (Meeks 1996: 127). The pattern of politics that obtained has begun to shift, as evidenced by the exhaustion of the two-party cycle and its replacement by one- instead of two-term governments.

The principal reasons for the change in the character of Jamaican politics, according to Meeks, has been the erosion of the resource base available to successive governments that enabled them to be effective patrons distributing largesse to needy clients. The main factor accelerating this erosion has been the International Monetary Fund–inspired structural adjustment agreements that have significantly reduced the size of government and consequently its effective role in the wider society. Other factors include the retirement of charismatic leaders from the political arena (the Manleys, Bustamante), the collapse of traditional support for the two traditional political parties, the decline in voter turnout at elections, fraudulent overvoting in certain constituencies, and the growth of social and economic contestation in several areas of the society, all of which have led to the decline of the power of Jamaicans ruling classes.

The points of contestation include that of language where there is a day-to-day battle for dominance between English as the lingua franca and Jamaican Creole; that of dress and popular fashion where daring unconventional modes do battle in the dancehalls and elsewhere with the more sober dress of uptown society; that of music, where a rift has emerged between 'classical' forms of music and the loud, violent and debased rhythms and lyrics of dancehall music. Meeks (1996: 132) also observes a general decline in the civility as evidenced by an unwillingness to queue, or to respect people's rights to their property or even life:

[T]he economic crisis, the collapse of the political project, the growing psychological independence of the subordinate classes and the shelving of social leadership by the middle classes are the conditions under which a moment of hegemonic dissolution has emerged. The glue which held Jamaica together is in the process of terminal meltdown. (201)

What is the likely outcome of this social contest? There is the possibility that no group would prevail and that one might end up with "the common ruin of the contending classes", to use a term coined by Marx and Engels. In Meeks's view, the answer to the question as to which element would ultimately prevail is not predetermined, but "the clues to its possible direction are to be found on the outskirts of Montego Bay, next to the pristine Blue Hole of Portland and in the throbbing dance halls of Kingston and every town in Jamaica on Saturday night" (1996: 132).

Mark Figueroa (1996: 2–3, 15) has also commented on the proliferation of garrison constituencies based on 'tribes' in which the gunman is the boss, and the impact of this phenomenon on party voting and other kinds of social and economic behaviour in urban Jamaica:

The garrison phenomenon has become a major threat to the exercising of the rights associated with universal adult suffrage. Universal suffrage is based on the principle of the individual casting a vote by the secret ballot. There are vast areas of urban Jamaica where this principle has been openly violated. What we need to focus on is the fact that in compromising the vote and the related political processes, a vast array of social and legal norms have also been compromised. Indeed, the point has now been reached, in many areas of Jamaica life, where illegality as a norm is probably at least on par with legality. What we need to emphasize is that the garrison phenomenon has left its mark on the entire texture of Jamaican politics, society and culture and has, in addition, had a significant impact on the prospects for economic development . . .

The garrison is, in its extreme form, a totalitarian social space in which the lives of those who live within its boundaries are effectively controlled. Indeed, the core garrison exhibits an element of extraterritoriality; they are states within a state. The Jamaican state has no authority or power except in as far as its forces are able to invade in the form of police and military raids. In the core garrisons, disputes have been settled, matters tried, offenders sentenced and punished, all without reference to the institutions of the Jamaican state. (2–3, 15)

Figueroa also remarks that "the casual observer might be fooled into thinking of Jamaica as a model Westminster system in operation. Looking closer, it is clear that this is not so" (10). The late Carl Stone also lamented the fact that the gun had become a critical instrument in the political process in Jamaica. To quote Stone:

[W]hat we have seen in Jamaica is a shift from a society from where you regulate behaviour through norms and values to a situation where you regulate behaviour through force . . . and the threat of force. We have legitimized purveyors of violence . . . It is a mistake to see politics as isolated . . . We have legitimized the power brokers. (Stone cited in Figueroa 1996: 23)

Trevor Munroe (1996) has likewise lamented the growing alienation of the people of the region, which is reflected in the decline in voter turnout and the erosion of the 'historically favourable political culture' that was inherited together with formal independence. He notes that "the average turnout across the region so far in this decade appears lower than that of forty years ago when adult suffrage and democratic elections were new to the Caribbean and popular involvement relatively limited" (16).

Munroe also notes that structural changes in the economy have given rise to massive layoffs, downsizing, currency devaluations, all of which have served to pauperize workers and undermine the trade union movement, which was one of the most vital institutions in civil society. Munroe has observed that although there have been calls for reform, much of it has fallen on deaf ears since the politicians invariably have a vested interest in the existing system. Such change as has taken place has been largely cosmetic. He notes, however, that even though there are developments that have served to disempower the people economically and politically, the media remains largely free in most of the region. Radio and television talk shows have also begun to proliferate, and these shows help many to ventilate their rage at or support for one policy or another. As he writes,

the picture that therefore presents itself is one in which the people of the Commonwealth Caribbean retain commitment to the values of freedom and justice. Indeed, the democratic character of civil society, nurtured by a relatively independent media, facilitated by a self-confident generation of post colonial youth, and reflected in the growth of nongovernmental organizations (NGOs), is being strengthened. At the same time, nonparticipation in elections and alienation from established political parties and state authorities have grown as socioeconomic inequities, official corruption, and social decay deepen. The people's loyalty to democratic governance in the Commonwealth Caribbean is being severely tested. (Munroe 1996: 20)

Havelock Brewster, an executive director of the Inter-American Development Bank, introduced the concept of 'social capital' to the discussion as to what is taking place in the region. Brewster commented unfavourably about Jamaica, which he describes as a society where the inherited social capital is being progressively dissipated. Barbados, in his view, has done much more to maintain that valuable resource (Brewster 1996: 3).

Barry Chevannes, Horace Levy and their co-researchers have also produced a chilling report (*They Cry Respect,* 1996) about the growth of political anarchy and violence in the inner cities of Jamaica. As Chevannes et al. write,

the stable peasant communities on which Jamaica's political leaders before, during, and after the great work of Jamaica Welfare tried to forge a nation, are being swept away in volatile city ghettos . . . There is a general feeling among ghetto residents that instead of helping to alleviate distress and poverty 'politics mash up everything'. Politics brought in its wake, guns, drugs and the don, the stigmatising of rival warring communities, premature death and unemployment . . . The politician by introducing the gun, employing the don and dividing up the areas is responsible for the current violence. The political dimension of the violence (under which criminal elements always 'hid') may have shrunk, but the gang violence now prevailing is not some brand new creation: it has emerged from the *cocoon spun by its political predecessor.* (1996: 38; emphasis in original)

They also note that, as is the case elsewhere in the Caribbean, the problem is aggravated by the fact that the old authority figures in the community no longer command respect – the member of Parliament, the police, parents, teachers and elder folk generally. The migration of many parents has also served to add to the problem. There is thus a leadership vacuum which is not being filled by social workers and other persons representing the state and nongovernmental organizations or other agencies that Jamaicans traditionally respect. The gap, unfortunately, is being filled by youngsters with guns:

The gap has manifestly been filled by peer group forces and pressures, to a large extent now those of corner gangs and their leadership. The authoritarian tradition evoked a demand for what is called 'strong leaders', often only another name for those willing and able to use force. The example of its legal use by the police had always been there. As soon as guns became easily available – with drugs and their quick wealth providing both means and reward – the youth with a gun, on every corner, offered an answer to the demand. In a context of prolonged unemployment and unrelieved poverty, this appears to many males as the only way to gain respect and status. To the woman the same context offers only dependence on the man (often the gunman, who has the greatest status), with the early pregnancies and subsequent domestic strife to which this often leads.

What we are witnessing in these inner-city communities – in the gangsterism and intra-community partitions, restricted movement and external stigma, teenaged gunmen and teenage pregnancies, 'secret war' and pervasive violence, along with a value system which exalts 'badness', the dependence of the woman, brandname clothes and even a flashy funeral! – has most if not all the features of a *descent into anarchy*. The extent to which violence and *death dominate the consciousness* of the people in these communities, even if, as is the case, the statistics they offer are exaggerated, confirms the point. A spiral of decay is touching bottom, with answers to the question 'What next?' not reassuring. (Chevannes et al. 1996: 39; emphasis in original)

Chevannes et al. ask what could be done to end the "devouring cycle of poverty and violence" that has enervated the occupants of these stigmatized communities and deprives them of the respect they crave and the opportunities to earn a livelihood without having to resort to hustling and criminal behaviour. Their answer is concerted community action that would mediate between warring communities. In sum, action is needed to end the isolation that now exists between the 'two Jamaicans'. As they put it, "what is needed is community building, community participation and community control without which [other transferred resources] will fall on stony ground" (40).

It is worth emphasizing that what is taking place in the ghettos and garrison areas of Jamaica, Port of Spain and, increasingly, in equivalent enclaves elsewhere are Caribbean versions of what one now finds in almost every country. In these areas, coercive power, once the monopoly of the state, has now passed to local or international drug dons, cartels, tribal warlords, praetorian elites, mafias, fundamentalists or sectarian religious groups and other alternative centres of power, which have effectively displaced weak and fragile central governments. Inhabitants of these 'shanty' or 'bazaar' states obey the local political leader or gang leader in return for jobs, utility services, security, protection and access to the proceeds of criminal activity. These sources of alternative income and security have become highly valued, given the inability of the central state to provide the basic needs of the citizenry on a sustained basis. As Herbert Gayle (1995: 6) observes:

The gang can go to a site and get jobs for all but a single person without political or other contacts might not be able to do so. The gang is also involved in drugs – the sale of ganja and sometimes cocaine – and thus able to buy guns. The result is often loyalty to the gang above loyalty to friend or family, and threat to or execution of informers who threaten the safety of the 'mother and life blood' which the gang now becomes. It is therefore common to find not only political divisions in these communities but those representing lines drawn by such gangs as described above. For these economic reasons sometimes combined with political ones, as well as activities of disrespect or provocation by gang members, they begin to war with each other. The guns become extremely important, and many youths get out of control. There is also no political leader to make peace since "a no him buy mi shot fi mi gun". The war divides the community into pieces and its members, especially the males, are now 'under siege'.

The process of the withering away of the state is of course not peculiar to the Third World. It is, however, most fully developed in these states. Somalia, Haiti, Liberia, Sierra Leone, Beirut, Sudan, Uganda, Rwanda, Zaire, Burundi, the Balkans and Pakistan are examples of the phenomena being discussed (Kaplan 1994). In these areas, prolonged war, massive migration, disease, unchecked population growth, illegal cross-border trading and movements of stateless capital, resource depletion and environmental degradation have led to the virtual disappearance of the nation state and its replacement by unarticulated crazy-quilt clusters of neofeudal power which owe no allegiance to any central political system. The emasculation of the state has served to change both the nature of war and of crime (Ryan 1990b: 4–12).

While it is true that in this 'posthistory' or 'postideological' era dictatorships have fallen and elected officials have replaced them in many parts of the world, much of the touted democracy is formalistic and not deeply entrenched. Ethnic politics has also reared its ugly head in areas where it is assumed to have been tamed (Huntington 1996). Standards of civic and moral conduct have been falling even in older democracies such as those in the United States, Great Britain and France.

Tony Blair, prime minister of Great Britain, has talked about the need for "democratic renewal" in Great Britain, which he claims is in "the second age of democracy". To quote Blair:

Changing the way we govern, and not just changing our government, is no longer an optional extra for Britain. So low is popular esteem for politicians and the system we operate that there is now little authority for us to use unless and until we first succeed in regaining it.

For three decades the standing of Britain's constitution has been declining. Barely a third of the people now declare themselves satisfied with their system of government. Parliament's very *raison d'etre* is to express and redress popular grievances. When it has itself become the focus of those grievances, it is obliged to act. (*Economist*, 14 September 1996)

Blair notes that the problem has become more urgent with the collapse of the grand ideologies of left and right which often elevated ends at the expense of means. "Pre-occupation with grand projects of social and economic reconstruction displaced the democratic requirement for consent and respect for rights . . . and to a steady accretion of power to ministers" (*Economist*, 14

September 1996). The problems of governance currently being faced by Britain, and indeed by other European states, have their counterparts in the Caribbean islands, which are of course much less well endowed economically than they are.

The question, then, is whether these states can muster the resources to reverse the social and institutional decay that is manifest, and rebuild the social capital that is required to sustain good governance. As the United Nations Development Programme's "Strategy Paper on Governance" (1995) warned:

[I]t is easier to erode than to create institutional or social capital. It is more difficult and time-consuming to build trust, confidence, norms of respect, responsible behaviour and motivated staff, than to destroy confidence, motivation and ethics, which can happen rapidly. Social capital can be eroded by a weak, corrupt or divided government, whether democratically elected or not. A weak civil society which is unable to exercise accountability from below may also allow a democratically elected government to degenerate into abuse of power and privilege. Similarly, civil strife or insensitive external interference can easily destroy social capital. The exaggerated emphasis in many third world countries on the transfer of physical and financial capital, as well as technical assistance, has had a disruptive impact on the existing social capital, as witnessed by the erosion of traditional norms and values in the wake of 'modernization'. The fact that social capital can easily be eroded poses a considerable risk for interventions in this area. (19)

The Charter of Civil Society

CARICOM member states have responded to this crisis of governance in the region by enacting the Charter of Civil Society on 17 January 1997. The charter, which was recommended by the West Indian Commission, chaired by Sir Shridath Ramphal in 1992 (Ryan 1996), recognized the need to enhance public confidence in governance if the loyalty of the people was to be reinforced. The charter seeks, *inter alia,*

to ensure continuing respect for internationally recognized civil, political, economic, social and cultural rights; to uphold the right of the people to make political choices; to promote, foster and maintain racial harmony and freedom of religion and to respect and strengthen the fundamental elements in civil society, and to implement all appropriate measures to ensure good governance which is just, open and accountable.

The enactment of the Charter of Civil Society in itself does not, however, do much to ensure that its terms are adhered to or given respect. Recognizing this, the charter document provides for reports to be compiled by national committees that advise the Conference of CARICOM Heads of Governments (through the secretary general) on measures adopted or progress achieved in compliance with the provisions of the charter. The committee is also expected to indicate and report on breaches of or noncompliance with the provisions of the charter attributed to the state or to one or more of the social partners. The committees are to consist of representatives of the state, other social partners, and other persons of high moral character or recognized competence in their respective fields of endeavour.

The author of this report is not aware that any national committee has as yet been appointed in any Caribbean country and it remains to be seen whether or not this initiative would yield any dividend that is meaningful. My fear is that it would take more than agreement on the Charter of Civil Society to make democracy and good governance a reality. Like Munroe, I am concerned that given what is taking place in the economy and the society, the prospects for democratic "renewal are not encouraging, at least not in the short run". As he writes, "coalitions . . . of forces with an interest in the preservation and deepening of Caribbean democracy are emerging, but much too slowly to prevent further short-run decay in the system and to provide increasingly alienated populations with any significant hope" (1996: 21).

Enhancing the Social Environment that Sustains Good Governance

Saying all this does not mean that nothing could or should be attempted to slow down, and in some cases possibly reverse, the institutional decay evident in the political process in the Caribbean. For a start, the multinational financial institutions and other agencies that have become an integral part of the political process in the region must be made to recognize that, while necessary, free and fair elections are not sufficient in themselves for the establishment of democracy, and that there is an underlying social reality that has to be addressed if democracy is to be secured over time.

A number of recommendations have been made as to what ought to be done to strengthen the economies of the region and increase their competitiveness in a number of niche areas particularly in the service sector. Henry Gill (1996), for example, has identified a number of specific areas that need to be given emphasis: assistance in enhancing capacity for international trade negotiations that require reciprocity, assistance in helping to bring into being the CARI-COM single market, in developing the informatics and education sectors and programmes of support for young entrepreneurs. Also stressed is the need to improve the system of regional governance. These are all important initiatives which are deserving of support. The initiatives will, however, yield little if the social environment that they require for proper incubation is not in place. In the final analysis, good governance is the prerequisite for the successful achievement of any meaningful programme of economic reform rather than the other way around. This view is also increasingly being endorsed by the World Bank, the Inter-American Development Bank and other international agencies.

The pervasive assumption in the region that the Westminster/Whitehall model of governance is the ideal one for us to copy needs to be questioned.[10] To be sure, that model has much to recommend it; but it clearly works best in societies that are striated along class rather than along ethnic lines. It also works best where there is a reasonably high standard of living and a more equitable distribution of the social product and the burdens of taxation. It likewise functions best where the legitimacy of the basic institutions is not in contestation and where there is broad agreement on the fundamentals of social and developmental policy (Lewis 1969). Finally, it functions best where there is civic concern but no fear on the part of the citizenry that a change in the outcome of an election would be absolutely disastrous for their welfare or make the critical difference between eating and starving.

The health and stability of a modern democratic state depends not only on the viability of its political institutions and its capacity to implement policy (that is, the hardware of the system) but on the attitudes and dispositions of the citizenry (that is, 'affect' that they have for the system and its decision-making procedures and the regard that they have for the key decision makers). If the general citizenry or significant parts thereof feel that their symbolic and other identities are not mirrored in the system, or feel that they can not affect outcomes by their actions, then that system is unlikely to attract the loyalty required for sustainability. As one political commentator puts it aptly:

[T]he integrity of a democratic political system depends on the desire of its citizens to participate in the political process in order to promote the public good and hold political authorities accountable; their willingness to show self-restraint and exercise personal responsibility in their economic demands, and in personal choices which affect their health and the environment; and their sense of justice and commitment to a fair distribution of resources. Without citizens who possess these qualities, the ability of liberal societies to function successfully progressively diminishes. (Kimlicka 1995: 175)

Our analysis of Caribbean societies thus far indicates that there is need to be concerned that while there are many who continue to be civic minded and who act to give effect to their commitment, the numbers doing so seem not to be significant enough to offset the loss of those who have withdrawn affect from the system. While there will always be haemorrhaging of civic commitment, the trick is to ensure that the system is being replenished with adequate positive material and human resources. This, then, is one of the tasks that now confront Caribbean society.

Given this, there is need for national and regional agencies as well as the multinational financial institutions to channel resources to assist nongovernmental organizations and state institutions, the energies of which are directed towards empowering civil society and building greater social trust and social capital therein (Fukuyama 1995). One of the principal targets for such activity should be groups that seek to rebuild communities generally and youth groups in particular. While we have made a number of critical statements about youth in general, clearly they do not embrace all members of the younger age cohorts. A considerable number of them in fact continue to subscribe to what might be called mainstream norms as opposed to those that might be characterized as countercultural. Resources should be directed to such groups to encourage them to participate in school and extra-school activities designed to stimulate civic awareness and competence. In sum, the provision of funds for safety nets and enterprise support (Youth Training and Employment Participation Programme and Youth Enterprise Support System) should be supplemented by funds for enhancing the social environment in which these programmes are located. Some of this is already being done; but given the severity of the crisis described above, much more needs to be attempted in order to avert further social and political decay. One needs to actively seek out organized community groups that might serve as vehicles for this effort at reconstruction. Where no such groups exist, efforts should be made to encourage their emergence. Focus also needs to be put on the principle of subsidiarity, that is, enhanced reliance on local nongovernmental organizations and local government bodies as copartners in the development process. As Neville Duncan (1996) advises, "local government is a critical dimension of a reformed system of governance and hence its development is urgent" (3).

Another area in which energy and resources need to be focused is consensus building on fundamental issues. Given all that we have said about politics in small societies, this would be a difficult project. We take note, however, of the case of Barbados where in the face of an economic crisis relating to the value of the currency, the major stakeholders – the government, the private sector and the unions – fashioned a protocol that governs prices and the allocation of national income to private and public sector workers linked to increases in productivity. The institutionalization of such a system has led to a dramatic reduction in industrial unrest. "Jamaica with ten times the labour force of Barbados manages to lose an average nearly thirty-seven times more work days a year due to strikes than Barbados" (Brewster 1996: 4). Barbados need not be the exception to our 'iron rule' about the contentiousness of politics in small Caribbean societies.

Caribbean societies need to put in place arrangements that predispose critical elites to come to some agreement as to what are the fundamentals about which there should be all-party agreement and the issues where division is permissible. The basic pillars of the economy (for example, tourism, energy, negotiations with multinationals, foreign policy) should be among the areas put beyond partisanship. We note that the governments of Trinidad and Tobago, St Lucia, Guyana, and Jamaica have all initiated national dialogues on the subject of consensus building. The multinational financial institutions should, for example, as a condition of the assistance they provide, insist that all critical elites, rather than just the government in power, buy into pro-grammes of assistance that commit the society (even if only in principle), since one would wish to ensure that such programmes do not become the object of division and disagreement within the national community. It may well be that these conditionalities might provide the catalyst needed to encourage consensus on the things that really matter.

Funding agencies might thus wish to commit resources that would assist in this process of consensus building wherein all stakeholders would come to appreciate that in the things that matter they should all be 'winners'. This assistance might take the form of providing resource persons and seed money for workshops or national consultations that bring together political and economic elites to discuss the long-term economic needs of the society and seek to engineer agreement as to what should be the most appropriate strategy for achieving agreed-upon national goals.

It might not always be possible to obtain full agreement, and one would have to allow for the games that politicians play as they seek to emphasize what distinguishes them from their rivals. But there is reason to believe that the changes that have taken place in the world economy have narrowed the ideological options available to contending elites in Caribbean society, and that, with a bit of help from external agencies, all-party consensus could be achieved on the things that matter.

Notes

1. Professor Gladstone Mills and others have argued that the concept of the neutral public servant is difficult to institutionalize in the Commonwealth Caribbean, especially when parties that come to office do not share the same ideological beliefs as their predecessors. Mills argued that what is required are civil servants who would be committed but who would, nevertheless, not be sycophants. While they should obviously avoid 'foot-dragging' on schemes, they should, at the same time, question where questioning appears appropriate, indicate the implications of proposed policies rather than behaving as time servers mesmerized by proximity to the aura of power. Mills notes that the problem of neutrality is not unique to small states but has also come under scrutiny in great Britain and Canada. Cf. also Nunes 1990.

2. Edwin Jones (1992) has drawn attention to some of the dysfunctional consequences of the use of these parallel expatriate bureaucracies in Jamaica: "With recent times, certain Commonwealth Caribbean public sectors, especially Jamaica's, have been installing parallel bureaucracies of expatriates mainly as a condition imposed by international technical bureaucracies (example IMF) in their recent regimes of 'structural adjustment' programmes. Representatives of this parallel bureaucracy attract better salaries, are lodged in crucial centres of decision leadership and enjoy other concession not available to the local civil service and has weakened its probity, as evidenced in the growing incidence of thefts, absenteeism, 'moonlighting' and underproduction in the public sector" (39). Both the Jamaican and Barbadian governments have raised objections to the attempt with the multilateral agencies to micromanage the policy-making and implementation process.

3. The former prime minister of St Lucia, John Compton, warned trade unions and opposition parties that their protests and demands for wage increases threatened to plunge the island into crisis inviting the "chilly embrace of the IMF" (*Trinidad Guardian,* 8 May 1995). There were similar street protests in Barbados in 1994 and, of course, in Trinidad and Tobago in 1990.

4. The World Bank reported (April 1995) that everyday, 750 million men, women and children go hungry, especially in poor countries, and that if current trends continue, there would be 1.3 billion people living in poverty by the year 2000. The report, "Strategy for Reducing Poverty and Hunger", concedes that to reduce hunger effectively, it is essential to tackle poverty. "Human hunger . . . is avoidable." It also conceded that when "so called structural adjustment programmes were implemented, little attention was initially paid to their effects on the poor". In its 1995 *World Development Report,* the World Bank indicated an intention to shift emphasis away from economic liberalism and deregulation and to highlight the developing world's needs for strong trade unions and greater equality. It notes that massive inequality – far from being the inevitable by-product of market economics – represents a barrier to rising prosperity and growth.

5. The Referendum Party in Great Britain and the 'eurosceptics' have expressed strong concerns about the loss of sovereignty that would follow upon the full incorporation of Britain into what they call a "federal European superstate" (*Times,* 10 January 1997).

6. Edwin Jones (1992: 41) also adverted to the relationship between the brain drain and maladministration in Jamaica. Jones noted that since 1976, Jamaica was losing an average of thirty top administrators annually to the private sector and international agencies. The public servants were attracted by the pull of better terms and conditions of service, as well as by push factors such as dissatisfaction with civil service work norms and worsening domestic condition.

7. Paul Streeten (1993) argues that social intimacy among key decision makers allows for the amicable resolution of problems which in other systems might give rise to resistance and conflict. He concedes, however, that "if leaders or groups are at logger heads in a small country, this can present a more severe obstacle than it would in a large country where they can be more easily be replaced" (200).

8. Cf. Benedict 1967.

9. Several state witnesses were eliminated by criminal elements in Trinidad and Tobago in 1994. In Jamaica, ghetto communities have lost confidence in the police and often undertake to accuse, try and execute those whom they deem guilty of crimes that affect their community negatively.

10. The newly elected prime minister of Trinidad and Tobago, Basdeo Panday, has been urging the people of the country to abandon the adversarial Westminster formula and find an alternative model that is better suited to the plural nature of the society. As he observes, "The Westminster System has done terrible things to Africa. The system is not written in concrete. It was designed for Westminster; but in Trinidad and Tobago, we have a plural society with antecedents and problems. Surely we should find a system that is indigenous to our own make up" (*Trinidad Express,* 11 December 1995).

    The former prime minister of St Lucia, Dr Vaughan Lewis, also used the concept of national consensus to urge the people of St Lucia to abandon the suicidal course upon which they are currently engaged which he warns could "destroy the banana industry and the economy in general" (see *Trinidad Guardian,* 9 April 1996).

References

Bagehot. 1995. "Roundheads and cavaliers". *Economist,* 21 January.

Barrett, Ina. 1986. "Administrative problems of small states with particular reference to the states of the Eastern Caribbean". *Social and Economic Studies* 35, no. 1.

Benedict, Burton. 1967. "Sociological aspects of smallness". In *Problems of Smaller Territories,* edited by B. Benedict. London: University of London.

Benedict, Burton. 1993. "The special problems of small countries". *World Development* 21, no. 2.

Booth, Cathy. 1996. "Caribbean blizzard". *Time,* 26 February.

Brewster, Havelock. 1996. "Social capital and development: Reflections on Barbados and Jamaica". Mimeo.

Carter, Richard. 1997. *Youth in the Organization of Eastern Caribbean States: The Grenada Study.* Cave Hill, Barbados: Institute of Social and Economic Research.

Charter for Civil Society. Annex VI to Rep. 97/7/4 SCMLA.

Chevannes, Barry, et al. 1996. *The Cry Respect: Urban Violence and Poverty in Jamaica.* Kingston, Jamaica: Centre for Population, Community and Social Change, University of the West Indies.

Chossudovsky, Michael. 1994. "Global impoverishment in the IMF World Bank economic medicine". *Third World Resurgence,* no. 49 (September).

DeLabastide, Michael. 1995. "Address of the chief justice at the opening of the 1995–1996 Law Term". Port of Spain, Trinidad. Mimeo.

Dominguez, Jorge. 1993. "The Caribbean question: Why has liberal democracy (surprisingly) flourished?" In *Democracy in the Caribbean,* edited by J. Dominguez, R. Pastor and D. Worrell. Baltimore: Johns Hopkins University Press.

Dominguez, Jorge, Robert Pastor, and De Lisle Worrell, eds. 1993. *Democracy in the Caribbean.* Baltimore: Johns Hopkins University Press.

Duncan, Neville. 1996. "Foundations of a new model of governance". Mimeo.

ECLAC (Economic Commission for Latin America and the Caribbean). 1993. "Poverty issues and poverty alleviation in the Caribbean". Paper presented at a meeting of Caribbean Working Group on Social Development, Port of Spain, 25–26 November.

Emmanuel, Patrick. 1976. "Independence and viability: Elements of analysis". In *Size, Self-Determination and International Relations: The Caribbean,* edited by Vaughan Lewis. Kingston, Jamaica: Institute of Social and Economic Research.

Farrugia, Charles. 1993. "The special working environment of senior administrators in small states". *World Development* 21, no. 2.

Figueroa, Mark. 1996. "Garrison communities in Jamaica 1962–1993: Their growth and impact on political culture". Mimeo, University of the West Indies, Mona.

Fukuyama, Francis. 1995. "Social capital and the global economy" *Foreign Affairs* 74, no. 5.

Gayle, Herbert. 1995. "The effects of poverty and violence on inner city males". Mimeo, University of the West Indies, Mona.

Gill, Henry. 1996. *Rethinking the UNDP is Caribbean Regional* Programme. N.p.

Gonzales, Ralph. 1993. "Controls on the civil service in the Commonwealth Caribbean". In *Issues and Problems in Caribbean Public Administration,* edited by Selwyn Ryan and Deryck Brown. St Augustine, Trinidad: Institute of Social and Economic Research.

Grindle, Merilee. 1997. *Challenging the State Crisis and Innovation in Latin America.* Cambridge: Cambridge University Press.

Gurley, Dennis, 1992. "Report of the review team appointed by Cabinet to advise on systems to reduce existing delays in the administration of justice". The Republic of Trinidad and Tobago. Typescript.

Harewood, Jack, and Ralph Henry. 1985. *Inequality in a PostColonial Society: Trinidad and Tobago, 1956–1985. UWI,* St Augustine, Trinidad: Institute of Social and Economic Research.

Henry, Ralph, and Juliet Melville. "Poverty revisited: Trinidad and Tobago in the late 1980s". Paper presented at Regional Conference on New Directions in Caribbean Social Policy. Hugh Wooding Law School, University of the West Indies, St Augustine, 28–31 March.

Hill, Anthony. 1994. "Symposium on human development". Jamaica Pegasus Hotel, Kingston, Jamaica, 21–24 July. Mimeo.

Huntington, Samuel. 1996. *The Clash of Civilisations and the Remaking of World Order.* New York: Simon and Schuster.

Jones, Edwin. 1971. *Small States and Territories.* United Nations Institute for Training and Research. New York: Arno Press.

Jones, Edwin. 1992. "Maladministration and corruption: Some Caribbean realities". In *Issues and Problems in Caribbean Public Administration,* edited by Selwyn Ryan and Deryck Brown. St Augustine, Trinidad: Institute of Social and Economic Research.

Kaplan, Robert. 1994. "The coming anarchy". *Atlantic Monthly.*

Kimlicka, Will. 1995. *Multicultural Citizenship.* London: Oxford University Press.

Lewis, Arthur. 1969. *Politics in West Africa.* London: Oxford University Press.

Lewis, Linden. 1995. "Dismantling the welfare state, the celebration of the market and the crisis of civil society in the Caribbean". Paper presented at the twentieth conference of the Caribbean Studies Association. Willemstad, Curaçao, 22–27 May.

Lewis, Linden, and Richard Carrer. 1995. *Essays on Youth in the Caribbean.* Cave Hill, Barbados: Institute of Social and Economic Research.

Maingot, Anthony. 1994a. "Confronting corruption in the hemisphere: A sociological perspective". *Latin American Studies and World Affairs* 36, no. 3.

Maingot, Anthony. 1994b. *The United States and the Caribbean.* London: Macmillan.

Maingot, Anthony. 1995. "Offshore secrecy centers and the necessary role of states: Bucking Committee to Examine the Rising Incidence of Crime in the Country and Make Recommendations". *Journal of Inter-American Studies and World Affairs* 37, no. 4.

Meeks, Brian. 1996. *Radical Caribbean: From Black Power to Abu Bakr.* Kingston, Jamaica: The Press, University of the West Indies.

Munroe, Trevor. 1996. "Caribbean democracy: Decay or renewal". *CARICOM Perspective,* no. 66 (June).

Nunes, Frances. 1990. "The nonsense of neutrality". In *A Reader in Public Policy and Administration.* Kingston, Jamaica: Institute of Social and Economic Research.

Panday, Basdeo. 1993. "Financial and economic scrutiny". *Parliamentarian: Journal of the Parliaments of the Commonwealth* (January).

Parris, Carl D. 1996. "A limited sovereignty for Caribbean states?" Institute of International Relations, University of the West Indies, St Augustine. Mimeo.

Planning Institute of Jamaica. 1994. *Estimates of Poverty in Jamaica, 1989–1993.* Kingston, Jamaica: Planning Institute of Jamaica.

Respondación III. 1996. Third Inter-American Conference on the Problems of Fraud and Corruption in Government. Final Report.

Rothwax, Harold. 1996. *Guilty: The Collapse of Criminal Justice.* New York: Random House.

Ryan, Selwyn. 1989. *The Disillusioned Electorate.* Port of Spain, Trinidad: Inprint.

Ryan, Selwyn. 1990a. *The Pursuit of Honour: The Life and Times of H.O.B. Wooding.* St Augustine, Trinidad: Institute of Social and Economic Research.

Ryan, Selwyn. 1990b. "The Caribbean state in the twenty-first century". *Caribbean Affairs* 3, no. 4.

Ryan, Selwyn. 1992. *The Muslimeen Grab for Power.* Port of Spain, Trinidad: Inprint.

Ryan, Selwyn. 1996. *Democratic Governance and the Social Condition in the Anglophone Caribbean.* New York: United Nations Development Programme.

St Bernard, Godfrey. 1996. *The Social Forces and Youth in Trinidad and Tobago.* St Augustine, Trinidad: Institute of Social and Economic Research.

Sterling, C. 1984. *The Time of the Assassins.* New York, New York: Holt & Co.

Sterling, C. 1990. *Octopus.* New York: W.W. Norton.

Sterling, C. 1994. *Thieves World.* New York: Simon and Schuster.

Streeten, P. 1993. "The special problems of small countries". *World Development* 21, no. 2.

Tanzi, Vito. 1995. "Corruption, governmental activities and markets". *Finance and Development* (December).

Taylor, Charles. 1971. *Small States and Territories.* United Nations Institute for Training and Research. New York: Arno Press.

Theodore, Michael. 1994. *Law: The Air We Breathe. A Look at Law and the Legal System in the Commonwealth Caribbean.* San Juan, Trinidad: Caribbean Legal Publications.

Trinidad and Tobago. 1995. *National Report.* Port of Spain: Government Printery.

Trinidad and Tobago. Ministry of the Attorney General. 1997. *Towards A Free and Responsible Media: Green Paper.* Port of Spain: Government Printery.

Trinidad and Tobago Chamber of Commerce. 1987. "Report of the trend". Mimeo.

UNDP (United Nations Development Programme). 1993. *Human Development Index.*

UNDP. 1995. "Strategy paper on governance". Mimeo.

Washington, Sally. 1996. *OECD Observer,* no. 199 (April–May).

West Indian Commission. 1992. *Time for Action: Report of the West Indian Commission.* Bridgetown, Barbados: West Indian Commission.

World Bank. 1995. *Trinidad and Tobago: Poverty and Unemployment in an Oil-Based Economy.* Washington: World Bank.

World Bank. 1997. *The State in a Changing World '97.* New York: Oxford University Press.

5

Rethinking Democracy in the Postnationalist State

PERCY C. HINTZEN

Introduction

While teaching a course on development during a sabbatical year spent at the University of Guyana in 1993, I was struck by the unquestioned and uncritical support expressed by my students for the programme of economic recovery fashioned by the Guyanese government to satisfy the terms of 'stabilization' and 'structural adjustment' imposed by multilateral and bilateral lending institutions, particularly the International Monetary Fund (IMF) and the World Bank. This was during a period of endemic economic crisis that had lasted at least one and a half decades and had intensified considerably to the point where the country was ranked as the second poorest in the Western Hemisphere after Haiti. The support and optimism of the students came at a time when the Institute of Development Studies at the university was documenting dramatic drops in incomes over the last decade and poverty rates that were estimated as high as 86 percent by some international agencies (see Institute of Development Studies 1993: 5–17). An economic recovery programme, begun in 1985 to satisfy conditions stipulated by the IMF and World Bank, had become fully operational by 1986. Its implementation had been accompanied by the intensification of poverty, economic insecurity and economic crisis. It seemed contrary to my own logic that university students familiar with the critical literature on development and experiencing the throes of economic crisis would accept, unquestionably, an economic programme that had little to show in terms of actual results in the improvement of *their own* lives and opportunities. I came to the conclusion that an analysis of the real 'objective' conditions of these students and of the population at large offered very little by way of explanation for their support of policies that were arguably detrimental to their own economic well-being.

Clearly, this uncritical support for structural adjustment by students at the University of Guyana could hardly be explained with reference to 'objective social facts'. Unquestionably, the students in my class viewed structural adjustment from the perspective of understandings that had little to do with extant economic consequences. Structural adjustment was 'understood' to be a desirable policy. From this perspective, structural adjustment is not merely a complex of policies whose implementation comes with consequences that can be analysed. It must be analysed in terms of its meaning to those who participate in what sociologists call social action.

The attitudes I observed to the complex of development policy known as structural adjustment were at the heart of the problem that has taken centre stage in my intellectual inquiry: Why are relations of domination and conditions of economic exploitation that are little different, and sometimes more severe, than those suffered under colonialism understood and interpreted differently in the postcolonial era? What explains the universal predisposition of those who engaged in and supported anticolonial struggles to accept the conditions of postcolonial repression and exploitation? The answer seemed to rest in the idea and meaning of nationalism, which has acted to transform understandings of conditions that are, in the eyes of the objective social scientist, identical. Nationalism, it seems, has acted to change understandings of who one is and of what is normal and desirable.

Nationalism in the West Indies, as elsewhere, had a specific meaning. It was an assertion of the right to self-determination manifested in the replacement of the colonial elite in positions of power and authority by their former colonized subjects. The right to self-determination was not asserted in a vacuum. It had, as its objective, the need for the assertion of equality. Implicit was the claim that the colonial condition of inequality and white superiority was artificial and imposed. Once removed, a 'natural state' of equality would assert itself. The task in the postcolonial era was to remove the legacies of colonialism that act as impediments to equality. The goal was to replicate the conditions of the colonizers in postcolonial reality. The argument will be made that anticolonial nationalism contains an inherent dialectical logic that leads not to less inequality but more, not to more self-determination but less. At the same time, the conditions of inequality and dependency become subject to different interpretations. This is precisely what I was observing among the students in Guyana.

In this manner, nationalism becomes transformative. Once the condition of equality becomes asserted in the postcolonial context, everything associated with colonial inequality is rendered irrelevant and subject to different interpretations, irrespective of the objective conditions. What once was exploitation becomes sacrifice. What was domination becomes functional organization. What was privilege becomes reward. What was discrimination becomes strategic allocation. These transformations are explained by the logic of equality embedded in the meaning of nationalism. Presuppositions of postcolonial equality become the force driving predispositions toward the acceptance of conditions of extreme inequality.

This is not to say that conditions of inequality become irrelevant and unrecognized. Rather, the context within which inequality becomes relevant is shifted from the national to the international. While anticolonial nationalism is directed at the elimination of colonial inequality, the quest of postcolonial nationalism is for equal status among the international community of nation states. Postcolonial elites are able to employ this national quest to explain their privilege. It is a privilege accorded to them as a 'modernizing elite'.

Once the privilege of the modernizing elites is normalized and legitimized, it can be employed to break out of nationalist constraints and for ensconcement into a metropolitan reality. This is one way in which nationalist interests become replaced by global and metropolitan interests. Another way pertains to the international level. International public policy, under the guise of promoting national economic and political development, employs the nationalist quest for equality to eviscerate any objective claim to self-determination. The quest for national 'development' is at the heart of international public policies of structural adjustment. Development, in turn, comes to be considered as the sole basis of equality with the formerly colonial metropole.

If what is outlined above is true, then why do these conditions come to be accepted as desirable? The question is pertinent because the undermining of national self-determination and sovereignty and the increases in inequality and external exploitation are the very conditions that sparked, sustained, and fed anticolonial nationalism. The explanation lies in differences in conceptual understandings brought about by nationalist discourse. Understandings are shaped by idea complexes that can change over time and that can produce profoundly different and even conflicting interpretations of social realities that may appear, objectively, to be identical. This, it will be argued, was the case when colonialism was replaced by nationalism as the driving force in the understandings of formerly colonized populations. Second, understandings are shaped by the participatory experiences of social actors. The two are integrally linked.

The intention is to examine constructs of identity and legitimacy contained in nationalist discourse. Constructs of identity pertain to understandings of who one is and where one belongs in relation to others. Constructs of legitimacy pertain to what is the normative ideal in social organization. Analysis will focus on nationalism and its implications for identity and legitimacy in the postcolonial reality of the English-speaking West Indies.

The Contours of Postimperialism

"Postimperialism," writes David Becker (1987: 51) "signifies *transnational* class domination on a global scale" exemplified by the production and repro-duction of "an international bourgeois class" (emphasis mine). The latter comprises "members of [a] 'corporate international bourgeoisie' . . . united by mutual interests transcending those expressed through the states whose pass-ports they happen to carry". If we accept this postimperialist reality of the modern world, then the possibility for democracy must be fully rejected, barring a fundamental social transformation. Yet, the *illusion* of democratic participation permeates the consciousness of those in the very regions of the world where domination and exploitation by an international bourgeois class is most embedded and most pervasive.

The English-speaking West Indies ranks, consistently, among the very top in conventional indices of democracy. Yet its territories constitute, arguably, the most penetrated and exploited by global capital. Indeed, as creations of Europe's colonial enterprise, they enjoy an ontogenetic link to global capital which is integral and inseparable. If we accept the Marxist notion of the state as the institutional form in which the social power of the bourgeois class is constituted and exercised and its interests expressed (albeit as universal or general interests), then the sheer impossibility of a democratic postcolonial transformation becomes evident.

What accounts, therefore, for this collective and almost universal consensus of 'democracy' in the postcolonial practice of the English-speaking West Indies? The explanation rests in the centrality of notions of territoriality in West Indian self-conceptualizations. Such notions serve to camouflage the deep embeddedness of each of the territories in the global reality out of which they were socially constructed and without which they would cease to exist, at least in their present constitution. These conceptions of territory make sense for a number of reasons, not least of which is their reflection in the geomorphology of the region and in the almost unique history of each of the small islands and the few mainland countries.

Discussion here is confined to the eleven island territories and the two small mainland countries that have, together, organized themselves into a Caribbean Community and Common Market (CARICOM). Guyana, the largest in land area, is a mere 83,044 square miles with a population of less than 760,000. It is the only English-speaking country in South America. Belize, the second of the mainland territories, enjoys a similar official linguistic distinction in Central America, even though half of its population is Spanish-speaking. Its history is unique, even for Latin America. Anything resembling an institutionalized colonial administration in Belize had to await the late eighteenth century for its emergence. The island territories are similarly diverse in size and history. While Barbados enjoyed untrammelled and uninterrupted British sovereignty from its beginnings in the seventeenth century, most of the other islands changed hands (some more frequently than others) with the winds of historical fortune of the various European contenders for colonial possession. Jamaica, with its nearly two and a half million people, is the largest and most populous of the islands, at 4,244 square miles. It passed from Spanish to British colonial control in the mid seventeenth century, remaining a British colony for over three hundred years. It is the only CARICOM member of the Greater Antilles group, separated from the rest by distances of several hundred miles. Trinidad, the second largest of the islands, came under British colonial rule after capture from Spain in 1797. Its history as a slave economy began only in the mid eighteenth century. The rest of the group are single and multi-island territories with only two (Dominica and St Lucia) exceeding 200 square miles in size. Apart from Barbados, with a population of 250,000, only St Lucia (136,000 people) and St Vincent (115,000 people) have populations that exceed 100,000. The population of St Lucia and Dominica speak, for the most part, a variant of French Creole, reflecting the influence of their colonial past. In Trinidad, on the other hand, the influence of the country's Spanish colonial heritage is everywhere. This influence is tempered by the pervasive presence of French planters and by the relative recency of its history of African slavery, giving the country much more of an African flavour among that group than in most other countries. Moreover, the largest segment of the populations of Trinidad and Guyana are Hindu and Muslim descendants of indentured labour from South Asia (India and Pakistan). CARICOM countries also enjoy a great degree of economic diversity, with Trinidad (oil and gas), Guyana and Jamaica (bauxite) as significant producers of minerals. There are differences in agricultural production with the cultivation of sugar, bananas, citrus, rice and spices spread among the various territories as well as differential emphasis on tourism in their economies. Manufacturing enjoys varied degrees of importance in the gross domestic products of the territories.

In other words, there is not much to cement a sense of 'oneness' among the CARICOM territories. Their economic, cultural and historical differences serve to reinforce their natural physical insular isolation and their separation by vast stretches of water. The sense of territoriality that all these have engendered has acted to hide the rooting of these political economies in a globalized reality. It has provided meaning to the nationalist struggle and has laid the foundation for the illusion of postcolonial democracy. With the image of national community confined to territorial and insular space, global actors have come to be understood as being outside the realm of democratic discourse. Their actions and behaviour are not accountable to the will of the people. At the same time, it is these very global actors, more than anyone else, whose social power is constituted in the state, whose interests are represented as universal, and whose class privilege is protected by law. Thus, the image of democracy is preserved, supported by a governing elite playing musical chairs in the occupancy of elective office. This gives substance to their claims of democratic governance.

Sovereignty, Development and Hegemony

At the core of the nationalist project was the quest for equality. From the inception, it was the project of a nascent elite. Equality, for the latter, was unrealizable under a colonial condition that depended upon the discourse of racial difference for its legitimation. This discourse necessitated a challenge to the ideology of white supremacy as the linchpin of colonial order. Thus, the struggle for racial equality had to become represented as the *universal* or *general* will. This is not to argue that racial equality is unimportant. However, the challenge to racial inequality cannot be separated from its social ontology (in this case, the construct of colonial plantation exploitation). When thus separated, the quest for equality, *qua racial equality*, cannot but serve to hide the manner in which social power is actually constituted. Indeed, and this is true for West Indian nationalism, it can act to legitimize the constitution of social power, however exploitative and repressive. Unlike those of colonialism, conditions of postcolonial exploitation and repression need not depend upon a discourse of racial inequality. When the former is challenged exclusively on the grounds of white supremacy, the fundamentals of exploitation and repression remain and become legitimized.

Anticolonial nationalism had to be represented as the 'general will'. Thus, the terrain of colonialism had to be contested not merely or exclusively from the position in which the constellation of interests of the nascent elite was located. Colonialism was a 'field of contestation' in which all social actors participated. In other words, it was a "set of objective historical relations between positions anchored in certain forms of power" that were the object of perpetual contestation (Bourdieu and Waquant 1992: 16). Thus, any challenge to colonialism, when directed against the colonial elite, could easily have been constructed as a universal challenge. With anticolonial nationalism, it was the interests of an emergent elite from the middle strata of colonial society that came to be represented as the universal will. This nascent elite, objectively constrained by colonialism, came to 'hegemonize' mass support and bring such support into equilibrium under its 'party leadership' (see Chatterjee 1986). Antonio Gramsci's conceptualization of hegemony applies particularly to this nationalist project. In a field of contestation, such as colonialism, various social groups:

come into confrontation and conflict, until only one of them, or at least a single combination of them, tends to prevail, to gain the upper hand, to propagate itself throughout society – bringing about not only a unison of economic and political aims, but also intellectual and moral unity, posing all the questions around which struggle rages not on a corporate but 'universal' plane, and thus creating the hegemony of the fundamental social group over a series of subordinate groups ... The development and expansion of the particular group are conceived of, and presented, as being the motor force of a universal expansion, of a development of all the 'national' energies. In other words, the dominant group is coordinated concretely with the general interests of the subordinate groups. (Gramsci 1971: 181–82)

Under the nationalist project, the interests of the subordinate groups came to be coordinated with those of the nascent elite through a discourse of equality. The institutions organized and controlled by the nascent elite became, in the nationalist transformation, the instruments of such equality.

Nationalist discourse had, at its core, ideas of sovereignty and development. The latter spoke to the objective conditions of colonial exploitation, that is, the expropriation of surpluses by the colonial metropole and its use to support colonial privilege. The trust of nationalism was the national appropriation of these surpluses. It was a discourse of modernity which effectively precluded any attempt to explain conditions of poverty and immiseration by demystifying capital. According to this logic of developmentalism, explanations for these conditions lie in the fact that control of capital is not located in the 'national' arena where it can be allocated in the 'national' interest. Sovereignty thus becomes, in part, the 'sovereign' right to exercise control (as opposed to ownership) over the conditions that govern capital accumulation. Sovereignty, in this nationalist construction, becomes the claimed right to dictate and determine the laws and policies of capital accumulation *in the sovereign territory*. In this manner, development can be represented as a resolution of the economic crisis of colonialism. To the extent that this crisis was universal, nationalist development can make legitimate claims as representing the universal will. In the West Indies, the crisis of colonial capitalism was particularly evident in the 1930s. It stemmed partly from a generalized crisis of capitalism and partly from increasingly successful contestations of white supremacy upon which colonial legitimacy rested. The crisis sparked mass working class mobilization and rioting. The nationalist movement was built on the backs of such mobilization.

The objective conditions for the nationalist challenge were laid in the changing technical and social conditions of colonial capitalist production. They emerged in the shift to the Crown Colony system and the replacement of the local merchant plantocracy by absentee owners and corporations based in the colonial metropole. This shift severed many of the organic links between those who owned capital and officially engaged in the exercise of power, on the one hand, and groups with legitimate 'national' credentials, on the other. The introduction of more capital-intensive forms of plantation production, urbanization, the growth of an urban working class, and the increasing bureaucratization of economic and political organization acted, *inter alia,* to erode the objective conditions that sustained and supported colonial discourses of difference. With a growing expatriate ownership, claims that economic production benefited territorial interests could no longer be sustained because of the association of the 'general will' with the will of those with organic links to the geographically defined territory. Without organic links to the territory, those who exercised economic and political power lost their ability to represent themselves legitimately as the embodiment of universal or general will. In this manner, colonialism began to suffer a crisis of legitimacy.

Sovereignty, realized through constitutional independence, resolves this crisis by transferring authorial power to a group with organic links to the territory. For the former colonial territories, sovereignty became a symbolic manifestation of equality as the newly independent states began to participate in the international system of nations. Sovereignty came to represent the general will to be free and equal with the state as agent. It allows the exercise of free choice by the state in new relations established between the former colonial territories and extraterritorial actors.

It was mass support that allowed the aspiring elite to ascend to political power, breaking the barriers of colonial exclusivity – both political and social. Hegemonization of the subordinate groupings, under the terms suggested earlier by Gramsci, was the precondition for the generalization of elite interests as the universal will. This was accomplished through incorporation of diverse movements of protests, including trade unions, ethnic and cultural organizations, and other politicized voluntary organizations into the nationalist political parties. These movements were the organizational expressions of groups with the most legitimate claims to the 'territory'. They were, at the same time, the expressions of the will of those whom they represented and for whom they spoke. With the adoption of variants of the Westminister model of parliamentary democracy, nationalist political parties became incorporated into the state. As a result, mass organization, representing the national will, became integrally, though symbolically, identified with the postcolonial state. With nationalist transformation, the latter came to be understood, universally, as the "motor force of a universal expansion, of a development of all the national energies" (Gramsci 1971: 181). As such, the interests of the now emergent elite came to be understood as national interests.

Almost universally, the newly emergent elite leadership emerged from educated factions of the middle strata. This group of leaders emerged victorious in the contested field of colonialism. As actors in the colonial "field of struggle", their goal was the transformation of the "structure of objective relations" (that is, of power) in efforts to "improve their position and to impose a new principle of hierarchization" most favourable to their own interests (Bourdieu and

Waquant 1992: 101). In the process, they employed their social, cultural and symbolic capital to impose their own organizational rationality on the institutional expressions of the collective will. Their 'leadership' was legitimized as the sole means for contestation of colonial authority rooted, as it was, in a discourse of white supremacy. In other words, the nationalist political organizations, headed by middle strata elites, came to be represented as the only legitimate challenge to the organizational rationality of the colonial state and to white supremacy and as incorporating the universal will. The organizational rationality of the middle class brought with it the promise of a sovereign state and the guarantee of 'development'.

Formal organization of the proletarian and peasant groupings established and cemented relations of affinity among professionals, intellectuals and nonproletarian wage and salaried workers on the one hand, and the proletarian and peasant lower classes on the other. The process was uneven both within and across territories. It fed upon proletarian mobilization, with intellectuals and professionals successfully incorporating lower class movements of protest into organized trade union and, later, into protonationalist political parties. To lower strata demands for racial and economic justice were added the demands of the middle strata for national sovereignty and power.

Thus, with the introduction of self-government and, later, with the granting of independence, popular organizations of nationalist struggle came to be symbolically included into the governing structures of the state. In this manner, the state became synonymous with national will in popular consciousness. Its area of jurisdiction came to be linked, firmly, with the insular territories of the region. It is important to emphasize the purely symbolic nature of this incorporation. The state is nothing more than a "set of objective, historical relations between positions anchored in certain forms of power" (Bourdieu and Waquant 1992: 16). It is differentiated by its ultimate relationship to *political power*, by its claim to authoritative decision making over all activities in all other fields and over the rules that regulate such activities, by its claim to jurisdictional authority over a specified territory and over all its inhabitants, and by the use of the rule of law as a mechanism to protect the social power of the interests embodied in its constitution (see Bourdieu and Waquant 1992: 100). The interests represented and protected by the state stem from the relative positions of power and principles of hierarchization evident in the objective relations among occupants of "positions of force" (Bourdieu and Waquant 1992: 101). As a field of struggle, the principles of hierarchization are in constant flux as occupants seek to safeguard or improve their positions.

This is precisely what occurred in the transformation from the colonial to the postcolonial state.

The definition of the state as a field of contestation allows for the incorporation in analysis of 'extraterritorial' actors. The criterion of inclusion becomes participation in the objective, historical relations that constitute the 'field' of state behaviour as earlier defined. Determining the hierarchy of authoritative decision making, the hierarchy of jurisdictional authority, and how the rule of law is fashioned and implemented are the methodological prerequisites in any attempt to map the field of the state. Naturally, the field is in constant flux. At the same time, certain overall historical patterns might be observed in the West Indies.

It is evident that, under colonialism, the most powerful social actors in the field of the state were extraterritorial representatives of the colonial power. This was particularly true of the era of Crown Colony government and less so when local merchant-plantocracies employed their control of the purse and local assemblies in order to gain and maintain hierarchical power. The situation after the postcolonial transformation became much more complicated within the context of contemporary forms of globalization.

The basis for a change in the technical and social conditions of global capital was laid in the early seventies. An inflationary explosion that followed the first oil shock of 1973–74 had profound effects upon the economies of the South. For the oil-importing countries among them, it produced a doubling of (import) commodity prices, a quadrupling of oil prices, and a 43 percent increase in their imports (by value). This was followed by an international recession in 1975–76 that severely depressed the prices and export volumes of these southern economies (see Girvan 1984: 169). The consequences of the second oil shock of 1979–80 were even more devastating. Once again the economies of the industrialized North were rocked by recession while international oil prices skyrocketed. Foreign exchange surpluses from oil-exporting countries that were lodged in Eurocurrency markets became increasingly inaccessible and, in 1982, credit windows were shut to many of these countries. Rocked by severe economic crises, many turned to the IMF as the agency of first resort for balance of payments supports.

IMF assistance to these beleaguered countries came with the upper-credit-tranche conditionalities in stabilization programmes that were later formalized, with the participation of the World Bank, into what are now known as structural adjustment programmes. Under programmes of stabilization, phased drawings on lines of credit established by the IMF are dictated by a country's performance in the achievement of usually quantitative monetary targets established in standby arrangements (see Dell 1984: 163–66). Structural adjustment programmes, established with the cooperation of the World Bank, proceeded from the conditionalities derived from such arrangements. To these are added stringent conditions of access to loans, investment funds, and aid specified and stipulated in the form of targets set primarily by the IMF, the World Bank and US funding agencies. These include: (1) strong curbs on domestic demand through credit contraction; (2) the lowering of state expenditures aimed at reducing public sector deficits, particularly through cuts in subsidies and in health, education, and welfare allocations; (3) revenue increases through tax reform programmes that increase personal income taxes and through reorganization of income tax administration; (4) currency devaluations; (5) programmes of export promotion; (6) programmes of economic and trade liberalization; (7) support for foreign investors involving granting of liberal concessions (including tax holidays and elimination of tariffs on imported inputs) and investments in infrastructural supports; and (8) the bringing of domestic prices in line with world market prices (see Bienen and Waterbury 1992: 376–85).

These new conditions of access to international economic resources have become the linchpin for the insertion of agents of the new globalized capital into the field of the state. Such conditions are very much in keeping with the need to transform the character of peripheral capitalist production as a precondition for effective functioning of the new form of globalization. In the West Indies, the process was helped by a change in the dynamic structure of the state through policies of direct interventionism by the United States. This became most evident after the election of Ronald Reagan in 1980. Interventionist policies included direct support for political leaders with neoconservative agendas. It also entailed efforts aimed at demobilizing groups, neutralizing political leaders and destabilizing governments that opposed the new conservative agenda.

Jamaica under the government of Michael Manley had come to typify the social conditions of peripheral capitalism of the 1960s and 1970s. It was the first to suffer the consequences of changes in the international economic and political environment. Even before the election of Ronald Reagan, the country had to bear the brunt of political and economic destabilization efforts. This was during a period when President Jimmy Carter's dovish approach in international affairs was coming under increasing attack by a resurgent conservative movement organized around Ronald Reagan's bid for the presidency.

The ensuing economic crisis, produced by the combined effects of international recession and US interventionism, forced Manley to agree to upper-credit-tranche conditionalities in standby arrangements for balance of payments supports with the IMF (see Girvan 1984; Manley 1982: 149–203). Thus, by employing the economic resources at its disposal and resources of violence and destabilization, the United States was able to secure the insertion of agents of multilateral financial institutions in the field of state contestation in Jamaica. The power resources of domestic actors with formal ties to global capital were also increased considerably. This resulted from the active support provided by the United States. Such supported was funnelled to the political opposition, led by neoconservative Edward Seaga, who had long demanded compliance with the new agenda of structural adjustment. His party, the Jamaica Labour Party had become the stronghold of globalized domestic capital. US policies of interventionism and support, more than anything else, were responsible for the election of that party to power in December 1980 (see Manley 1982: passim).

There is an essential link between programmes of structural adjustment and international interventionism of the type described above. The former entails a dissolution of the nationalist elite alliance of professionals, intellectuals, and nonproletarian wage and salary workers whose agents had ascended in the hierarchy of power relations that constituted the postindependent state. It also entails the dissolution of the welfarist structure of statist organization as the form that best catered to the interests of these actors. Such a dissolution creates the conditions for a respecification of 'national interests' in ways that become coordinated with the interests of global capital. This respecification satisfies, perfectly, the changing demands of international manufacturing and international finance capital. The groundwork for such a transformation of the state is laid by programmes of international political and economic intervention and particularly by structural adjustment interventions. They also take the form of strategic political support for local agents of international capital, intense efforts to oppose those whose interests are in conflict with the demands of global capital, and, of course, direct and indirect (low intensity) military intervention.

This "neoconservative transformation" brings in its wake a change in the "pattern of political and social power" (Bienen and Waterbury 1992: 382). The change is institutionalized in and through the state. It is necessitated by the conflicting demands of international manufacturing and finance capital on the one hand and of the welfarist social formations of the period of early nationalism on the other. The new interventionism that undergirds the neoconservative transformation is called forth by the changing structure of international capital. In its reconstituted form, high mobility provides capital with the means of escape from national contexts that are unfavourable. This mobility is accompanied by the development of a highly integrated global system of manufacturing creating, in its wake, a single global labour market. There is also a process of disaggregation of manufacturing where production is broken up into highly specialized component parts. Production and assembly are undertaken in multiple territorial locations. Different components of the final product are manufactured and final assembly undertaken in different territories and regions. These may be located considerable distances away from major markets. The consequences of all this is the increasing autonomy of capital. In its reformulated state, international manufacturing and finance capital are separated increasingly from dependence upon the means of any single state to create, protect and maintain the social conditions of exploitation.[1] One effect of the new autonomy of capital is to weaken the power of those in the field of state struggle who have any degree of hostility to the interests of global capital. A second is to ensure that the agents of global capital are located in the upper echelons of the power hierarchy of the state. In this manner, the interests of international capital come to be increasingly embodied in the national state. Domestic groups whose interests coincide with internationalized capital move into positions of ascendancy. Their economic power becomes enhanced with spin-off opportunities in the domestic economy provided by international capitalist penetration.[2]

In the process of its reformulation, many domestic actors in the state are sloughed off. This becomes reflected in state policy. The new internationalization and its related programme of structural adjustment produce drastic reductions in the public wage bill, achieved through the lowering of real wages (through, for example, delinking them from inflation). They also produce contractions in employment in the public sector achieved through the firing of public employees. These are accompanied by drastic reductions in public sector perquisites. The casting aside of public sector bureaucrats reflect the reduction in power of the non-capital-owning segment of the nonproletarian salaried class whose interests are vested in the 'public welfare industry'. Their loss of power is reflected also in their inability to stop the divestment of public assets to the private sector and the complete elimination of many of the remaining public enterprises, and in their inability to prevail against cuts in consumer subsidies and in state-provided services, including health, education, welfare and social security (Bienen and Waterbury 1992: 382–86). During the era of early nationalism, these were the bases of elite reproduction.

The relative positions of other domestic actors in the field of state contestation are affected equally and as profoundly. Agents of import-substitution industry, faced with their own relative decline in the power hierarchy of the state, are unable to prevail against escalating costs of foreign and domestic inputs and against competition from relatively cheap imports. Such competition is enhanced by a sophisticated internationally orchestrated advertising campaign. They are also unable to affect state action against declining domestic demand stemming from the ongoing and intensifying effects of a recessionary crisis that results directly from the new globalization.

Additionally, there is a restructuring of the power hierarchy among the governing institutions of the state. The power of political parties, represented in the state through its legislative bodies, suffer significant declines. This comes in the wake of the increasing power of the central executive as a result of its direct and institutionalized links with international financial institutions through programmes of structural adjustment and with global capital directly. The cadre of leaders in politically significant voluntary organizations, represented in political parties, find themselves locked out of the corridors of state power altogether. Their access to state resources becomes severely limited. It is upon such access that their elite status relies. Access provides them with the opportunity to satisfy their accumulative interests, to cater to the interests of the groups that they represent, and to deliver patronage as a basis of maintaining and enhancing their political power.

The penetration of global agents into the state also affects the relative positions of professional, technical and managerial groupings. They are displaced not merely by the economic transformations that are occurring but by the increasing employment of international consultants and experts funded by multilateral and bilateral agencies. Many are forced to migrate to the industrialized North, attracted by lucrative offers that contribute to a significant escalation of the phenomenon known as the 'brain drain'.

In the reformulation of the state, there is a constriction in the power and presence of groups who ascended to elite status in the anticolonial nationalist struggle. What remains in the new formulation is a political executive that is highly dependent upon international intervention (including military) for its power. This executive is joined by a group of technical experts involved in international negotiations with private and public sector international financial institutions (bilateral and multilateral). These negotiations involve setting the terms of structural adjustment. The executive is also joined in the hierarchy of state power by a managerial elite engaged in the task of neoconservative transformation as well as by a new grouping of merchants involved in importation and wholesale and retail activities. More importantly, it is joined by a new group of local industrialists engaged in export-oriented and export processing activity "producing orders on a subcontracting basis for trading and manufacturing firms based in" the industrialized economies (Crow et al. 1988). Tied to the international system of manufacturing as subcontractors, the latter undertake the labour-intensive parts of the disaggregated system of international manufacturing. They exploit low costs of production and low wages and salaries in their own peripheral political economies.

The neoconservative transformation forces groups with little or no participation in the power relations of the state into newly emerging extraterritorial global forms of behaviour. Already mentioned are patterns of international migration in the form of a brain drain. Such patterns become manifest also among proletarian workers and the semiproletarian peasantry who must rely heavily upon their own efforts to secure access to international resources, directly and indirectly. Many seek legal and illegal means of migration abroad. Those who remain become heavily reliant upon remittances transferred from abroad by legal and illegal migrants. Others become increasingly reliant upon small-scale, semi-legal or illegal activities in the informal sector, servicing the needs of the new domestic and international elites. Typically, the informal sector incorporates an enormous amount of nonconventional activities, including petty trade, smuggling, gambling, thieving, outworking, personal services and the like. Most important in the West Indies is involvement in the local and international drug trade and in male and female prostitution. These activities are directly associated with the tourist industry. In the formal sector, the displacement of the organized male labour force is matched by the employment of women in export-oriented activities as part of a process of global feminization of labour. The increasing use of women workers is accompanied by a weakening of income and employment security (see Standing 1992). There is also an intensification of women's participation in the informal sector.

In the Caribbean, structural adjustment and neoconservative transformation have been accompanied by the development of export-oriented activities in specially erected industrial parks and export processing zones. Domestic agriculture has plummeted and there has been an increasing emphasis upon the exports of traditional agricultural commodities. There has also been a heavy emphasis on tourism.[3]

Increasingly, the power hierarchy in the field of state contestations comes to be dominated by those national and global actors who are absorbed, directly or indirectly, in the international system of manufacturing and finance. This absorption derives, more and more, from their technical and managerial competence. This is true, even of industrialist investors in the system of global manufacturing. These investors must themselves possess technical or managerial competence or must be in a position to hire those who do to organize and run their businesses. Those with the requisite technical or managerial skills thus become part of an international elite with unrestricted means of geographical and even sectoral mobility.[4] Thus, the commitment of those at the apex of power to any one nation state is weakened as they seek opportunities to enhance their power and accumulation internationally. Domestic investors are constantly on the lookout to expand their operations overseas and, if need be, to relocate when conditions prove unfavourable. Many members of this technical and managerial elite, located in the public sector, are constantly on the move seeking the privileges and perquisites, ultimately, of employment in multilateral agencies with its limitless access to foreign exchange.

Thus, the interests of this new elite become linked firmly to sectors of the political economy that cater to the demands of international finance and manufacturing. The interests of domestic sectors of activity not so linked become increasingly neglected in the new constellation of state power. To fill the gap, there is a growing reliance upon nongovernmental organizations. These cater to the needs of those who have been discarded by the state. They cater, also, to the needs of those who never were or are no longer formally or fully integrated into the new system of globalized capital. This does not mean freedom from the authorial power of the state. As they increase in importance, there is an intensification of the process of co-optation of nongovernmental organizations by local and foreign state actors, by international capital, and by international financial institutions (McAfee 1991: 217–19). Indeed, as state functions become more exclusively tied to international capital, there is pressure for transferring the tasks of reproduction of labour and of the functions of control and regimentation to the nongovernmental organizations. This serves to relieve governments "pressed by economic constraints and structural adjustment conditionalities" to reduce spending on health, education, welfare and social security (McAfee 1991: 217). Nongovernmental organizations fill in the breach as persons become displaced from wage-earning activities and as real wages become significantly depressed. They are frequently encouraged to take over functions abandoned by the welfare state using resources raised outside of the public sector and, not infrequently, derived from the efforts of the local communities that they service.

Development, Equality and Legitimacy

How, in this neoconservative transformation, do the interests of this new form of global capital come to be represented as the general will, in spite of the evidence of intense and growing immiseration? The answer lies in the embeddedness of discourses of equality in nationalist ideology. Anticolonial nationalism was, first and foremost, an expression of the general will for equality. This expression was transformed by petit bourgeois ideology into demands for sovereignty and development. In the international system of nations, sovereignty was acquired when those with claims to an organic connection to the territory gained control of the governing institutions of the state. Full equality cannot be successfully realized, however, until the material conditions of the metropole come to be replicated in the territories under the jurisdiction of the newly independent states. Industry and the consumptive styles of Europe and North America were the pervasive symbols of white supremacy. Equality in the postindependence era demands a developmental transformation to forms of industrial production and consumption typical of the metropolitan North.

The ideology of development, embedded in nationalist discourse, came with the promise of its power to transform 'underdeveloped' political economies into developed (that is, metropolitanized) ones. As agents of modernization, the emergent national elite has been able to assert its exclusive and paramount role in 'developmental transformation'. In the West Indies, development gained additional legitimizing force because of the roots of the nationalist movement in the economic crisis of the 1930s. Nationalism came with the promise of an end to such crisis.

Thus, as an ideology, development contributed to the legitimization of the authorial power of the new elite by transforming this elite into its agents. The claims of this elite to power are enhanced by possession by its members of the technical, managerial, and bureaucratic skills considered to be the prerequisites for developmental transformation. As general will, development has come to be firmly identified with the state. It is to be effected through the incorporation of developmental planning into state function (see Hintzen 1995b and Lewis 1949). The symbolic power of such incorporation rests in its significance for the realization of true and full equality by the territorial population. Such equality comes with the material life conditions and productive technology of western Europe and North America that development brings in its wake. It is in this manner that the ideology of development comes to constitute a legitimacy construct. It justifies the authorial power of managers, professionals, technicians and bureaucrats who possess the skills, capacities, credentials and education needed for developmental planning and for its implementation (see Hintzen 1993). International global capital brings in its wake these trappings of development. Those participating in its field of activity begin to resemble the white population of the metropole. It is left for those located outside of its realm to devise strategies that secure their incorporation. Equality, it appears, is within reach, only for the want of trying. With its promise, the illusion of consensual democracy is maintained.

Notes

1. This analysis is taken directly from Harris 1987: 187–203.
2. For example, the need for military intervention that engenders an increase in military spending with spin-off benefits for the domestic political economy. In the United States, this was accomplished through deficit spending. While it was justified in cold war terms, the new military technology and the buildup of forces have been employed in peripheral political economies, particularly in the Gulf region (against Iraq and Iran), in Lebanon, in Grenada and in Panama.
3. The full programme of structural adjustment is thoroughly discussed in McAfee 1991.
4. These elements in the social and cultural order are identified by Weaver (1991) as characteristics and conditions of the 'monopoly capitalist' phase of industrial development. This phase corresponds to the process of internationalization of manufacturing and finance capital here identified.

References

Althusser, L. 1971. *Lenin and Philosophy and Other Essays.* Translated by Ben Brewster. New York: Monthly Review Press.

Amin, S. 1976. *Unequal Development: An Essay on the Social Formations of Peripheral Capitalism.* Translated by Brian Pierce. New York: Monthly Review Press.

Ashley, R.K. 1984. "The poverty of neorealism". *International Organization* 32, no. 2 (Spring).

Becker, D. 1987. "Development, democracy and dependency in Latin America: A postimperialist view". In *Postimperialism: International Capitalism and Development in the Late Twentieth Century,* edited by D. Becker, J. Frieden, S. Schatz and R. Sklar. Boulder: Lynne Rienner.

Becker, D., J. Frieden, S. Schatz, and R. Sklar. 1987. *Postimperialism: International Capitalism and Development in the Late Twentieth Century.* Boulder: Lynne Rienner.

Best, Lloyd. 1968. "The mechanism of plantation type economies: Outlines of a model of pure plantation economy". *Social and Economic Studies* 17, no. 3 (September).

Bienen, H. and Waterbury, J. 1992. "The political economy of privatization in developing countries". In *The Political Economy of Development and Underdevelopment,* 5th ed., edited by C. Wilber and K. Jameson. New York: McGraw-Hill.

Bourdieu, P., and L. Waquant. 1992. *An Invitation to Reflexive Sociology.* Chicago: University of Chicago Press.

Chatterjee, P. 1986. *Nationalist Thought and the Colonial World: Derivative Discourses.* New York: United Nations University.

Crow, B., et al. 1988. *Survival and Change in the Third World.* New York: Oxford University Press.

Drakakis-Smith, D. 1992. *Pacific Asia.* London: Routledge.

Dell, S. 1984. "Stabilization: The political economy of overkill". In *The Political Economy of Development and Underdevelopment,* 3d ed., edited by C. Wilber. New York: Random House.

Galli, R.E. 1991a. *Rethinking the Third World.* New York: Crane Russak.

Galli, R.E. 1991b, "Winners and losers in development and antidevelopment theory". In *Rethinking the Third World,* edited by R.E. Galli. New York: Crane Russak.

Girvan, N. 1984. "Swallowing the IMF medicine in the 'seventies' ". In *The Political Economy of Development and Underdevelopment,* edited by C.K. Wilber. New York: Random House.

Gramsci, A. 1971. *Selections from the Prison Notebooks.* London: Lawrence and Wishart.

Harris, N. 1987. *The End of the Third World.* Harmondsworth: Penguin.

Hintzen, P.C. 1989a. *The Costs of Regime Survival.* Cambridge: Cambridge University Press.

Hintzen, P.C. 1989b. "Pluralism and power: Racial politics and middle class domination in LDCs". Paper presented at conference on Pluralism in the Late Twentieth Century. Port of Spain, Trinidad, 7–9 December.

Hintzen, P.C. 1993a. "Democracy and middle class domination in the West Indies". In *Democracy in the West Indies,* edited by C. Edie. Boulder: Westview.

Hintzen, P.C. 1995. "Structural adjustment and the new international middle class". *Transition* 24 (February).

Hintzen, P.C. and Premdas, R. 1982. "Coercion and control in political change". *Journal of Inter-American Studies and World Affairs* 24, no. 3 (August).

Institute of Development Studies. 1993. *Poverty in Guyana: Finding Solutions.* Georgetown, Guyana: Transition.

Kothari, R. 1978. *India.* Boston: Little Brown and Co.

Lewis, W.A. 1949. "The industrialization of the British West Indies". *Caribbean Economic Review* 1.

McAfee, K. 1991. *Storm Signals.* London: Zed Books in association with Oxfam America.

Manley, M. 1982. *Jamaica: Struggle in the Periphery.* London: Third World Media.

Pryor, F. 1986. *Revolutionary Grenada: A Study in Political Economy.* Westport: Praeger.

Rudebeck, L. 1991. "Conditions of people's development in postcolonial Africa". In *Rethinking the Third World,* edited by R.E. Galli. New York: Crane Russack.

Segal, R. 1992. " 'Race' and 'colour' in pre-independence Trinidad and Tobago". In *Trinidad Ethnicity,* edited by K.A. Yelvington. London: Macmillan.

Standing, G. 1992. "Global feminization through flexible labor". In *The Political Economy of Development and Underdevelopment,* edited by C. Wilber and K. Jameson. New York: McGraw-Hill.

Weaver, F.S. 1991. "Toward an historical understanding of industrial development". In *Rethinking the Third World,* edited by R.E. Galli. New York: Crane Russak.

PART 2

Conjunctures

6

Reconsidering the Role of the Middle Class in Caribbean Politics

R U P E R T   L E W I S

Politics in the Caribbean, as anywhere else, is about power, and power

is about the capacity of social agents, agencies and institutions to maintain or transform their social or physical environment. It is about the resources which underpin this capacity and about the forces that shape and determine its exercise. Accordingly, politics is characterized as a universal dimension of human life, independent of any specific 'site' or set of institutions. At the other end of the spectrum are conceptions of politics linked more directly to the state. (Held 1991: 5)

Politics in this definition recognizes both the site of the state as well as other sites that are independent of the range of state institutions that we associate with political activities. The necessary preoccupation with the state, which is the site of middle class elite mobilization of the people, should not make us ignore the fact that the mass of the population conducts political activities quite independent of and without reference to the state. This does not mean that they are indifferent to the state and government but it means that just as there is an informal economy there is also informal politics. Just as there is a dynamic cultural life that has emerged from grass-roots Jamaica that now is a subculture of world culture, there is a corresponding set of political values, energies and activities that the middle and upper classes ignore at their peril. My focus is on a more specific area of the politics of the black middle class and black entrepreneurship in the Caribbean at the end of the twentieth century.

For most of our history, politics in the Caribbean has been colonial politics. It is only recently that we can speak of politics outside of that framework. Postcolonial politics in the English-speaking Caribbean is a recent affair as most of the territories secured political independence between the 1960s and the 1980s.[1] But Haiti has been independent for nearly two hundred years and Cuba since the start of the twentieth century and their political history prefigures that of the English-speaking Caribbean. Despite these varied contexts, it has consistently been the role of the middle classes to take control of the state by either evolutionary or revolutionary means. My comments therefore focus on the need to reconsider the role of the middle class in Caribbean politics.

On the one hand, the radicalized sections of the middle class have provided the leadership for the Cuban Revolution and later on the Nicaraguan and Grenadian revolutions of 1979.[2] Since the 1920s, with the spread of German, Russian and British socialist ideas concerning the dominant role of the party in the state, the significant role of the state in the economic sector, socialist internationalism and other adaptations of social-democratic and Leninist ideas to the region, their conceptions have run their ideological course. Thus the Left's rethinking the role of the state and of political parties is currently taking place in a radically different environment, one shaped by the end of communism in Europe and the redivision of the world into powerful economic blocs and the technological changes that have revolutionized production. On the other hand, the macoute politics of sections of the Haitian middle class has been politically discredited, and finds support principally among right-wing forces in the United States and in the Caribbean. But in economic terms, this mulatto and black political group has had a predatory relationship with the Haitian state since the nineteenth century, as well as with foreign capital, and is still poised to be a principal actor in a post-Aristide Haiti, though for the time being it may be unable to collaborate with government and the army in the exercise of arbitrary political power and thuggery.

In the case of Cuba, the legalization of the dollar, the growth of the tourism sector, and opportunities for Cuban lawyers and consultants to work with international businesses are creating a new middle class that is already privileged relative to the rest of the population.[3] This process will be enhanced by further economic liberalization in Cuba and the lifting of the US embargo. The racial stratification of this new middle class will be an interesting phenomenon to watch especially in the light of Cuba's racial history. A recent study, entitled *Cuba in Transition,* noted that

Black Cubans know they would suffer most from the loss of free government education and health care, and they are well aware that those in exile who might seek to reestablish their former lifestyle are white. Compounding these fears is the historical memory of the negative role the United States played in the struggle of Cuban blacks against slavery. While racism is still prevalent in Cuba (though more than 50% of the population is black, virtually no black Cubans occupy high posts in the current regime), the material gap between nonelite whites and nonelite blacks is far less pronounced in socialist Cuba than it was in earlier times. (Gunn 1993: 44)

Castro's generation has made its contribution to the battle against racial discrimination in Cuba as well as to the cause of South African liberation. But the assessment of race in Cuban society inside Cuba has been a tricky matter marked by denial among those who argued that there was no longer a racial problem. Evaluation of this dimension of Cuban politics remains the subject of controversy. The debate between Carlos Moore and other black Cuban critics of his book *Castro, the Blacks, and Africa* (1988), such as Pedro Perez Sarduy (1993), raises key issues missing from the current debate about political options in Cuba.[4] It is to be noted that Moore's interpretation of Cuban history was severely attacked by the white Cuban community in Miami while he was teaching at Florida International University in the mid 1980s.[5] The racial implications of the economic and political transition underway in Cuba is of critical importance and the rest of the English-speaking Caribbean, particularly black Jamaicans, have to find a way of raising it on the agenda at the same time that one opposes the American economic embargo.

The achievement of political independence in Jamaica and Trinidad and Tobago in 1962 effected no immediate change in the economic structures of colonial society but it did change the political institutions by ushering in the system of parliamentary democracy. The result of this was that the creole (locally born) white oligarchy and foreign corporations ran the economy and black and brown representatives occupied Parliament. The traditional economic elite minority has responded in its own way to Caribbean nationalism over the past fifty years. While it retains cohesion through kinship ties,[6] its companies have gone public and raise money through share subscriptions. The economic elite further sponsors a wide range of sporting and social projects and is careful about its public profiles even if in private it retains much of the old negative attitudes and paternalism towards black people. On the other hand, modernization of its businesses has involved the recruitment of nonfamily members to its boards and the expanding managerial apparatus for these enterprises has required better-skilled managers, accountants, bankers and other professionals, who have been drawn from the black middle class. Servicing these businesses is a growing white-collar working class with a high percentage of women workers. In the case of Jamaica, the traditional economic elite has expanded in the area of financial and insurance services. It also maintains considerable influence in the political process through the provision of finance to political party campaigns and networking with the political elite. These are some of the principal changes that the traditional elite has negotiated in the political life of the region since universal adult suffrage in Jamaica in 1944 and Trinidad and Tobago in 1946.

A white Barbadian, Robert Goddard, put his own interpretation of the attitude of sections of the white Barbadian business group towards the black Barbadian middle class in the following way:

It is too easily left out of the historical record that the Barbadian whites of today shared essentially the same economic experience as that of the blacks. The Barbadian whites of today are not those who dominated the politics and economy of the island during 300 years of colonialism. Instead they came as indentured servants, eking out a marginal existence for centuries. The famous planter names of the past – Alleyne, Barrow, Haynes – now belong to the descendants of their former slaves, not to present-day whites. Even the white plantocrats of 30 years ago – the Leacocks, Piles, Challenors – are relatively scarce. In their place have appeared C.O. Williams and his brother Ralph, the Goddards, David Seale and other businessmen who made their fortunes in recent decades, parallelling the success of the black professional-political class that emerged over the same period. Even the much-criticised networking among white businessmen finds a parallel among black professional-politicians. (Goddard 1993: 14)

I was very happy to read this frank piece by a white West Indian. The history of old 'plantation' and new money within the Barbadian and Caribbean merchant-capitalist class is an interesting aspect of recent economic and political history, and the relationship between the latter group and the black professional-political class is an important feature of postcolonial politics about which no serious research has been done.

At the same time the emergent black entrepreneurial middle classes, whose asset has largely been education, are negotiating their entry into the business class. This is so because it was not through the traditional private sector but rather the public sector that the middle class experienced rapid growth as the

English-speaking Caribbean emerged from colonialism into independence. This middle class has had largely administrative, political, teaching and legal experiences, not risk-taking economic experiences. The expansion of the black middle class is a direct result of the changes since the 1930s. In his summary of social mobility research done by the late Derek Gordon, Don Robotham pointed out that

the Jamaican middle-class and the black part of it in particular, has experienced enormous upward social mobility into the middle and upper classes between 1943 and 1984. Over those 40 years he was able to demonstrate that the higher managerial and professional group, from being 20 per cent black in 1943 became 42% black by 1984. (Robotham 1993: 13a)

Since the contraction of the state sector in the 1980s, sections of the black Jamaican middle class have been moving into entrepreneurial activity and away from bureaucratic, educational and regulatory spheres that were their traditional domain. But this embryonic development still takes place in a context "where the major locally owned financial, manufacturing, distribution and service companies are controlled mainly by . . . 23 prominent and strategic ethnic minority family interests" (Stone 1994: 260). In Trinidad and Guyana (Asian) Indian business growth has outstripped African initiatives, and in many of the English-speaking Caribbean islands there is no significant black business development to speak of.

The black political elite in Trinidad and Guyana did not have any perspective regarding the integration of blacks into the business class but emphasized the role of the state in economic development. The result was that the black middle class, which emerged from the peasantry, abandoned the land and positioned themselves in politics, the bureaucracy, the judicial system, the military and police, and the professions as the colonial state was changed.[7] This was not the case with Asian Caribbean populations whose foreparents had been recruited from India and China as indentured labour in the nineteenth century. They retained land, owned retail stores and saw the professions less as status-giving occupations and more as ways of accumulating capital. In their book *Sharks and Sardines: Blacks in Business in Trinidad and Tobago* Selwyn Ryan and Lou Anne Barclay conclude that

while there are several thousand black businessmen and women in the country, very few can be described as big. Most are in survival ventures, micro enterprises and professional operations. Our own search located about a dozen who might be deemed significant. Perhaps only three of the latter would be included in a list of the one hundred most successful businessmen in Trinidad and Tobago. In the post-1970 era, a significant number of blacks abandoned salaried employment in the private and public sector and ventured out into a variety of businesses, especially consultancies and construction. The petroleum driven boom years 1974–82 saw many of them prospering, and it appeared that some might make significant breakthroughs and become established in the world of trade and commerce and give economic meaning to the concept of black power. The windfall gains were not sustained, however, and blacks remain on the periphery of the business world. (Ryan and Barclay 1992: 201)

At the end of the twentieth century the entrepreneurial sectors of the Asian Caribbean communities are thriving relative to their counterparts in the African Caribbean populations. One should nevertheless remember that the bulk of the Asian Caribbean populations remain small farmers and workers and the success of a small section of the group does not reflect its overall welfare.

In recent years, therefore, a section of the West Indian middle classes has been extending its base from the state and bureaucracy, in the case of Jamaican blacks, and from the land, in the case of Indo-Trinidadians and Indo-Guy-anese, and are now positioning themselves to participate not only in the managerial area of the private sector but in finance, insurance, banking and manufacture. Interestingly, some of the black middle class, known as 'asphalt farmers', are finding their way back to the land as entrepreneurs, enticed by the opportunities for agricultural exports and foreign exchange earnings. The emergence of an entrepreneurial group from the middle classes is an important development in efforts to change the minority ethnic domination of the Jamaican and other Caribbean economies.

The composition of the middle classes is also being changed from below. A recent study of the impact of International Monetary Fund and World Bank policies on the Jamaican middle classes over the past seventeen years suggested that

there have been changes in the social composition of the middle class. This newly composed middle-class is made up of the traditional middle class which has managed to maintain its position in spite of the changes brought about by structural adjustment, as well as a newly emerging middle class. This newly emerging middle class is made up of artisans, blue-collar workers and merchants who benefited from the structural adjustment policies designed to expand the private sector and encourage entrepreneurial activities. These changes in social stratification represent a potentially conflicting situation in which attitudes towards traditional social status, values and norms are apt to lose their traditional significance. (Brown 1994: 103)

The social composition of the middle class has also been changing as a result of the impact of the informal economy in the region, the size and scope of which is greater than that of the formal economy in some territories. In the case of Haiti, for example, it is said that the informal economy contributes 93 percent of Haiti's income and in Guyana it is 66 percent. It is estimated that between 30 percent and 50 percent of all employment in the Caribbean is in the informal sector (see Gittens 1994). This development is a response to failed traditional private sector and state-managed economic policies as well as to developments in the world economy. What interests us here is that this has been another source for the emergence of the middle class and the political elite that is quite distinct from the path of education. The middle class is therefore experiencing radical changes and is no longer drawn principally from the civil service, teaching and the liberal professions. The main developments relate to growth in the Asian Caribbean entrepreneurial middle class in Trinidad and Guyana as well as the changing composition of the Jamaican middle class.

We have not yet started to examine the political implications of the changes in the social composition of the middle class. The hope I have is that there will be greater possibility over the next twenty years for the creation of an entrepreneurial class that breaks with the history of minority entrepreneurial domination with its racist attitudes, its lack of vision for the society as a whole and its rootedness in a colonial mentality. I do not accept the view that this development simply means the integration of a few into the dominant class and that global capital will subordinate it and make it play the game on the local terrain as it has always been played.

The impact of disinvestment in the region, structural adjustment policies, the rapidly changing technical basis of late twentieth century production systems, the emergence of megablocs and global free trade put considerable strain on the Caribbean private sector. Caribbean economies remain dependent on preferences in Europe and parity in the North American Free Trade Agreement (NAFTA). Anthony Gomes, director of the Jamaica Chamber of Commerce, put the anxieties of regional business interests in the following way:

This month it was learnt that the US administration, under political pressure, had withdrawn the CBI [Caribbean Basin Initiative] Parity Bill from GATT [General Agreement on Tariffs and Trade] implementing legislation, leaving Jamaica without any parity benefits at all, and the apparel industry in a very vulnerable position. These developments give credence to the strong reservations held by many Caribbean businessmen about the whole concept of NAFTA, its impact on the region, and the Government's approach to negotiations with the US administration . . . Philip Nassief, one of the Caribbean's leading entrepreneurs, is one such businessman with strong reservations about lowering the Common External Tariff (CET) to 20 percent by 1998 on the recommendation of the US . . . [According to Nassief] "They themselves have massive subsidies in their own agricultural sectors. That will destroy our agricultural and manufacturing base, reduce our foreign-exchange earnings, and create massive unemployment." Nassief's fears are so strong that he has executed that major shift, which to survive may eventually face many of us – that is the move into services. It is reported that this month Dominica Coconut Products will be sold to the US giant Colgate-Palmolive for an eight-figure US currency price, and Nassief will move into tourism. (Gomes 1994: 6, 8)

Much of what underlies the 1992 *Time for Action: The Report of the West Indian Commission* was a rather late wake-up call to these changes and it summoned the political will of the region to try to build a wider union in the form of the Association of Caribbean States. The fact is that the international economic environment will likely wipe away much of what we now have in agriculture and manufacturing. The only area of confidence about which most Caribbean governments speak is tourism.

Two volumes edited by Hilbourne Watson, *The Caribbean in the Global Political Economy* (1994) and a special issue of the journal *Twenty-first Century Policy Review*, "Human Resources and Institutional Requirements for Global Adjustments: Strategies for the Caribbean", pose sharply the significance the technical challenges arising from export competitiveness in the 1990s, whether it is in agriculture, manufacturing or the wide range of information and data processing services. Watson writes that

The main factors that have weakened Caribbean exports are the near hegemony of circulation over production; guaranteed markets that also distort the allocation of resources; changes in consumer tastes; net (negative) transfer of resources from the area; high energy cost, and especially intensive technological restructuring. If wage costs are high in the region, the way to compensate for this factor is to develop the productivity of labour via technological restructuring. (1994: 85)

Another economist, Donald Harris, in his essay "The Jamaican Economy in the Twenty-first Century: Challenges to Development and Requirements of a Response" (1994), concluded with a discussion on entrepreneurship, defining it as "the capacity to coordinate finance, investment, and technology, for carrying out production and marketing of products, while also bearing the risks involved in so doing" (35).

Entrepreneurship requires a technical as well as a social transformation in the production systems and relations among our investor/managers and workers that are not present in the Caribbean workplace. It also requires, as the West Indian Commission report indicates, an educational revolution in the Caribbean. The data on the probability of a young West Indian entering university in the English-speaking Caribbean is in most cases less than three in one hundred (West Indian Commission 1994: 185–87). It also challenges us to integrate research and development and production. But more importantly, from my point of view, it requires "the process of change to facilitate the development of black entrepreneurs in the core areas of the economy" (Watson 1994: 74). There has got to be a conscious decision by more black people to take this route and for Caribbean governments to support this shift that is already underway. While I have given up, to some extent, on my generation, there is a real change in this direction among young people born in the 1970s and 1980s.

The role of the middle classes has preoccupied Caribbean social philosophers from C.L.R. James and Nobel Prize economist Arthur Lewis to the current generation of social scientists. Their assessments provide differing but valuable perspectives from which to approach this problem in the mid 1990s. While Lewis saw the West Indian middle classes as being in the vanguard of Caribbean political modernization, James (1962) saw them in a somewhat rearguard position and wrote:

Our West Indian middle classes are for the most part coloured people of some education in a formerly slave society. That means that for racial and historical reasons they are today excluded from those circles which are in control of big industry, commerce and finance. They are almost as much excluded from large-scale agriculture, sugar for example . . . Thus they as a class of people have no knowledge or experience of the productive forces of the country . . . Thus the class has been and is excluded from the centres of economic life, they have no actual political experience, they have no political tradition. (131)

For James the middle class politicians did not emerge from the mass struggles of the 1930s but were beneficiaries of the social and political breach created in colonial society. This breach enabled the educated middle class to come into their own in politics and end the political monopoly of the British Colonial Office, the planters and merchants. The process whereby a new group of mediators arose from within the middle class, together with the role of the British Colonial Office, Washington and the local ruling class in allowing some leaders to emerge and others to be crushed, is one of the little-studied areas of

Caribbean political life. By the achievement of universal adult suffrage in 1944 in Jamaica, and in other territories later on, the middle classes were able to develop political vehicles in which they were firmly in the driving seat and competed over mass followerships. But democracy could not be limited to this. James posited the political dilemma of the middle classes very well when he pointed out that

> democracy is not a carefully doled out concession that rulers make to people, but an inherent part of their conceptions of themselves, a possession which they exercise and defend because they cannot conceive of existence without it. Not only in the West Indies is there no sign of this. The political leaders, instead of being its ardent advocates, are its bitterest enemies. (121)

James "repudiated in unambiguous terms the false and dangerous conception that we have been so educated by the British that the instinct for democracy is established among us".[8] On the contrary, he felt that the "tendency to naked power and naked brutality, the result of West Indian historical development, is here all around us" (122).

James (1962) argued that "The great danger in the whole of the West Indies is that no class in the West Indies has ever been able to make the conception of democracy an integral part of its existence" (1962: 123). The profound significance of this statement is that it applies to all social classes. The upper classes in the Caribbean are now not as open in their contempt for the mass of the population as before but the ideological core of class and racial prejudices remains intact and has been transmitted down the generations. It has not been fractured by the few desertions of individuals who have turned their back on the world view and lifestyle associated with their class and racial origins. Certainly no one is a prisoner of their class origins. Those who have risen to upper class status from the grass roots seem to have a tendency to assimilate very quickly the more negative features of the traditional upper classes long before they have consolidated an economic base. On the other hand, among the lower socioeconomic groupings there is still too great an acceptance of ideas of inherent inferiority and a belief that 'nothing black nuh good'.

C.L.R. James' conception of democracy and its possibilities in the West Indies in the 1960s remains a valid guide theoretically but needs to be updated. The focus on classes has to be complemented by reference to race and gender experience in politics. The political evolution of the black middle class in Jamaican politics in both the Jamaica Labour Party and the People's National Party has been determined by a history of black subordination to light-skinned players. There is unfortunately no study of the mechanisms of control employed in Jamaican political parties over the past fifty years. In Trinidad and Guyana political experience is assessed in relation to racial polarization between Africans and Indians and not only the class factor. The alternatives to racial politics are types of political coalitions that can point in the direction of transracial politics. One has to take into account the implications of racial history in the Caribbean in considering democracy. James is right, however, in pointing to the fact that the middle class politician of either African or Indian origin has, by and large, been unable to overcome the divisive legacy of race, class and gender oppression. But Indian and African, mestizo[9] and white, male and female West Indian politicians "know they have to win the election. But after that the only type of government and social relations that they know is that of power and subordination" (James 1962: 124).

By the 1970s when Walter Rodney examined the political stewardship of this class he was pessimistic about its prospects and, its socialist rhetoric of the 1970s notwithstanding, he was scathing in his denunciation of its rule (see Rodney 1974). Rodney (1974) pointed out that "In the Caribbean, the most significant of the set of internal and external socio-economic contradictions which shape neo-colonial politics are those that derive from the consolidation of the petty-bourgeoisie as a class around the state" (15). Rodney's use of the term 'petty-bourgeoisie' is interchangeable with the middle class as C.L.R. James uses it to refer to an intermediary grouping that is in the administrative, educational, legal and civil service areas of Caribbean society. The political monopoly of the Afro-Guyanese middle class over the state apparatus from the mid 1960s to 1992 was well exemplified in Guyana through the doctrine of party paramountcy of the late President Forbes Burnham. The doctrine subordinated the state to a type of personalized dictatorship that was run by cadres drawn principally, though not exclusively, from the African ethnic group. In the case of Jamaica the middle class politicians wrote a constitution that ensured no third party would be able to compete electorally. It gave enormous powers to the prime minister, enshrined the British sovereign as the head of the state and, while providing for the legal recognition of the fundamental rights and freedoms of the population, it qualified these by permitting considerable power to the state to abrogate them.

Although Caribbean political institutions are dominated by the middle classes, the impact of the multilateral institutions, such as the International Monetary Fund, the World Bank and the US Agency for International Development, is considerable in determining what the state does and does not do and how it runs its economy. But democratic elections remain an important lever against those social classes that would like to turn back the clock to arbitrary forms of minority power or military rule.

The middle class in the English-speaking Caribbean by and large continue to use the state in ways that are familiar in the Third World. The middle class manages resources under the close eye of international agencies, it appropriates some through the divestment programmes as well as through contracts, and it seeks to reallocate resources to ensure re-election. The problem is that with the decline of resources for partisan reallocation it is more expensive to bribe the electorate. Moreover regional electorates have become more critical of politicians.

In the context of the plantation economic history of the region the embourgeoisification of a section of the middle class which is underway throughout the Caribbean is an important development. As important as this change is, given our historical evolution, it by no means guarantees democratic conduct. These socioeconomic changes take place in the context of growing inequalities that condition the relationship between the social classes. Social and economic inequalities are most sharply expressed in the years since independence in the creation of a small black upper class in Jamaica and a significant middle income grouping on the one hand and the rapid expansion of a black underclass in both urban and rural Jamaica.[10] The negative implications of this development such as the growth in crime, the expansion of slums, the impoverishment of children and the elderly tell only a part of the story. The positive dimension of this underclass since the 1930s has been the emergence of the social movement of Rastafarianism, and its contribution to Caribbean religious forms, social thought, epistemology and culture. The Rastafarian movement and its contribution to Caribbean society has been documented by a number of Caribbean scholars including Barry Chevannes (1995). Rastafarianism has provided an important basis for the renewal of Jamaican popular music forms and by the end of the twentieth century Bob Marley's name is interchangeable with Jamaica to millions of people throughout the world.

The popular Lavalas movement of the Haitian poor in the 1980s and 1990s overthrew the thirty-year-old dictatorship and challenges the middle class to a new social, political and economic partnership. The relationship between the emergent entrepreneurial middle class and the underclass is a critical question, for the latter group has been the source for a variety of creative small businesses and artisan undertakings. The relationship between the entrepreneurial middle class and its workers is structured within the framework of current industrial relations practices and institutions. But there is no framework for the relationship between the black middle class and the underclasses functioning in the informal economy to develop outside of partisan politics. That political relationship is characterized by sterile dependency and political subordination, as is evident in the garrison constituencies of the urban poor communities or welfarism. The healthy and expanded collaboration between these sectors is an issue that is central to any discussion of the future of black entrepreneurship in the Caribbean and ought to be more openly discussed in national politics.

No programme for the modernization of Caribbean economies can succeed without being led by an entrepreneurial group with national and regional roots that is technically and socially equipped to lead the region. The relationship between the state and this entrepreneurial group is one of the most important issues on the agenda. My hope is that it will be possible to forge in this group a sense of commitment to itself and the region that has been lacking in its economic ancestors. I cannot see this being done only on the basis of economics. Other factors, such as the racial history, culture, religion and ethics of the region must enter into play on an equal basis in the effort to influence the values of the new entrants into the power elite and to help transform its attitude to the subordinate classes.

There is a fairly high level of integration among the middle class political elite in the English-speaking Caribbean that has been cemented by the role of the University of the West Indies, the meetings of the Caribbean Community and now the wider Association of Caribbean States, in addition to the informal sharing of experience in dealing with multilateral institutions. The group has gained in political experience and in confidence and has grown in sophistication in their conduct of global political relations. Part of their role ought to be to foster the emergence of a black entrepreneurial elite at the same time that they seek to modernize the workforce and raise the levels of health, literacy and living standards in the region through national policies.

These developments take place in a period of growing social differentation, enrichment and impoverishment, scepticism and cynicism about politics. In order to ensure that the social interests of the majority of the people are given priority, intellectuals in the Caribbean have an important role to play in identifying, explaining and bringing the changed global situation and relevant national issues on to national agendas. At the same time, there is need to learn from the bottom up about people's responses to the current situation and their own ideas about how to proceed. This involves work within traditional institutions such as parties and trade unions, the church and community organizations, as well as with the new generation of nongovernmental organizations and the growing number of urban gangs and crews[11] to which many talented youth are attached. The political parties, trade unions, professional, economic and civic organizations, as well as the parliamentary-democratic systems in the English-speaking Caribbean have been run by the middle classes who, as in the case of the Haitian and Cuban revolutions, have benefited from popular struggles.

Most of the region's radical leadership originated in the middle class or by professional training acquired middle class social status. By the Left I mean that broad spectrum of people who have been involved in efforts at social and economic transformation from Fidel Castro to Michael Manley and Cheddi Jagan to Jean-Bertrand Aristide. The end of century redivision of the world into global economic blocs, the post–Cold War economic and political relations, the fall of communism in Europe, the impoverishment of Cuba, the manner in which the Grenada Revolution self-destructed, political defeats, imprisonment and death have taken a toll on the traditional Left of the 1960s and 1970s. The Left has had to mature, to adjust and to work in the context of the new realities of the world at the end of the twentieth century. And so, to a lesser extent, has the regional Right who find that with the end of the cold war their trump card role as vigorous opponents of communism can no longer guarantee them client status for foreign aid or allow them to rule in arbitrary ways, as has been the case in Haiti. Neither the Right nor the Left can conceive of itself in its cold war garb. The political delinking of Caribbean politics from its cold war moorings offers new opportunities for re-examining Caribbean politics afresh.

In this context the embourgeoisification of sections of the middle classes is one important development that requires deeper thought, research and analysis. The tendency within the region has been for the Left to write off the middle classes except for those persons who were ideologically sympathetic to left-wing movements. However, a cursory look at Caribbean politics indicates that as a result of any wave of social upheaval, mass protest or revolutionary transition new forces from the middle strata arise to implement and direct alternative policies in the process of institutionalizing change. There needs to be a keener sense of how this middle class is changing, what is its capacity to move from a political/administrative class to a serious entrepreneurial group and what are the corresponding political conceptions given this transition. The African American philosopher Cornel West (1988) was trying to grapple with this issue when he wrote: "There surely are no reasons to rest emancipatory hopes on the black petite bourgeoisie, but to abandon it entirely is premature and unwarranted" (66). In this period of transition in the Caribbean this is one of the most important questions because it goes to the heart of the character of our production, social and political relations.

Notes

1. The independent states are: Antigua/Barbuda 1981, Bahamas 1973, Barbados 1966, Belize 1981, Cuba 1902, Dominica 1978, Dominican Republic 1865, Grenada 1974, Guyana 1966, Haiti 1804, Jamaica 1962, St Kitts and Nevis 1983, St Lucia 1977, St Vincent and the Grenadines 1979, Suriname 1975, Trinidad and Tobago 1962. The associated states are Aruba, French Guiana, Guadeloupe, Martinique, Netherlands Antilles. The dependencies are Anguilla, Bermuda, British Virgin Islands, Cayman Islands, Montserrat, Turks and Caicos Islands, US Virgin Islands (see Knight 1993).

2. See Meeks 1993 for his discussion of postcolonial revolutions from the middle.

3. This point was made and substantiated by Tony Bogues in a paper on Cuba at a staff seminar in the Department of Government, University of the West Indies, Jamaica, 13 October 1994.

4. See McGarrity and Cardenas 1995.

5. See "Heresy or history: Teachings on Cuban racism still outrage exile community", *Miami Herald* circa early December 1990. Undated photocopy sent to me by Lazaro Gonzalez of Miami, Florida.

6. For an important study of the elite families of modern Jamaica see Douglass (1992). See also an article by Goddard (1993) that provides a response from a white Barbadian to black nationalism in the postcolonial era. Goddard compares networking among white businessmen to political networking among black politicians.

7. See Selwyn Ryan (1992) for a very pessimistic view of black business in Trinidad and Tobago.

8. Hence we have the ridiculous calculation of democracy in the Caribbean being calculated on the basis of the year in the seventeenth or eighteenth centuries when particular islands became possessions of Britain and developed white representative government. What is more appropriate is the time from which the adult members of the population become enfranchised.

9. Mestizo in Belize refers to the mixture of Native American and Spanish.

10. For an important article see Portes, Itzigsohn and Dore-Cabral 1994.

11. See Ritch 1994 for a listing of gangs and crews in political constituencies in Kingston and St Andrew.

References

Brown, Lynette. 1994. "Crisis adjustment and social change: The middle class under adjustment". In *Consequences of Structural Adjustment: A Review of the Jamaican Experience*, edited by Elsie Le Franc. Kingston, Jamaica: Canoe Press.

Chevannes, Barry. 1995. *Rastafari: Roots and Ideology*. Kingston, Jamaica: The Press University of the West Indies.

Douglass, Lisa. 1992. *The Power of Sentiment: Love, Hierarchy, and the Jamaican Family Elite*. Boulder: Westview Press.

Gittens, Julius. 1994. "A mixed balance sheet for Caribbean women". *Gleaner*, 30 August.

Goddard, Robert. 1993. "Last at bat? White West Indians face the challenge of black nationalism". *Trinidad and Tobago Review*, September.

Gomes, Anthony. 1994. "The dawn of disillusionment". *Daily Gleaner*, 10 November.

Gunn, Gillian. 1993. *Cuba in Transition: Options for US Policy*. New York: The Twentieth Century Fund Press.

Harris, Donald. 1994. "The Jamaican economy in the twenty-first century: Challenges to development and requirements of a response". In *Jamaica: Preparing for the Twenty-first Century*. Kingston, Jamaica: Ian Randle Publishers.

James, C.L.R. 1962. *Party Politics in the West Indies*. San Juan: Vedic Enterprises.

Knight, Franklin. 1993. "The societies of the Caribbean since independence". In *Democracy in the Caribbean: Political, Economic and Social Perspectives*, edited by J. Dominguez, Pastor and Worrell. Baltimore: Johns Hopkins University Press.

McGarrity, Gayle, and Osvaldo Cardenas. 1995. "Cuba". In *No Longer Invisible: Afro-Latin Today*, edited by Minority Rights Group. London: Minority Rights Publications.

Meeks, Brian. 1993. *Caribbean Revolutions and Revolutionary Theory: An Assessment of Cuba, Nicaragua and Grenada*. Warwick Caribbean Studies Series. London: Macmillan Caribbean.

Moore, Carlos. 1988. *Castro, the Blacks, and Africa*. Los Angeles: Center for Afro-American Studies.

Portes, Alejandro, Jose Itzigsohn, and Carlos Dore-Cabral. 1994. "Urbanization in the Caribbean Basin: Social change during the years of the crisis". *Latin American Research Review* 29, no. 2.

Ritch, Dawn. 1994. "PNP outguns JLP". *Sunday Gleaner*, 11 December.

Robotham, Don. 1993. "Growth of the black middle class". *Sunday Gleaner*, 5 September.

Rodney, Walter. 1974. "Contemporary political trends in the English-speaking Caribbean". *Black Scholar*, September.

Ryan, Selwyn, and Lou Anne Barclay. 1992. *Sharks and Sardines: Blacks in Business in Trinidad and Tobago*. St Augustine, Trinidad: Institute of Social and Economic Research.

Sarduy, Pedro Perez, and Jean Stubbs. 1993. *Afrocuba: An Anthology of Cuban Writing on Race, Politics and Culture*. Melbourne: Ocean Press.

Stone, Carl. 1994 [1988]. "Race and economic power in Jamaica". In *Garvey: His Work and Impact,* edited by R. Lewis and P. Bryan. Reprint, Trenton: Africa World Press.

Watson, Hilbourne. 1994. "Global restructuring and the prospects for Caribbean competitiveness, with a case study from Jamaica". In *The Caribbean in the Global Political Economy,* edited by H. Watson. Boulder: Lynne Rienner.

West, Cornel. 1988. *Prophetic Fragments.* Michigan and Trenton: William B. Eerdmans Publishing and Africa World Press.

West Indian Commission. 1992. *Time for Action: Report of the West Indian Commission.* Bridgetown, Barbados: West Indian Commission.

West Indian Commission. 1994. "Human resource development". *Twenty-first Century Policy Review* 2, nos. 1–2 (Spring).

7

The Contestation of Race in Barbadian Society and the Camouflage of Conservatism

LINDEN LEWIS

Barbados has always been ruled by fear. There was no black man of my generation, irrespective of class or occupation, who was not afraid of white people. There was no black boss who did not see it as his role to intimidate his black subordinates: and to do so on behalf of white power. This legacy of fear, created and nourished by an ideology of racism, has never been overcome to this day.

    – George Lamming

Barbados is the most easterly island in the Caribbean. Despite its small size, it is only 166 square miles, it is one of the most densely populated islands of the region, with a current population of 266,000. The indigenous people on the island appeared to have migrated from South America and to have settled in the island before the advent of the Europeans. In 1625 the British established a claim on the island. Two years later England established a colonial settlement there.

    Barbados has an exceptionally high rate of literacy – believed to be some-where around 98 percent. Its infrastructural development is excellent, and it finds itself in a position to boast of its accomplishments in housing, health, education and public utilities, and in the areas of tourism development, sugar production and the export of high quality rum. Barbadians pride themselves on being a model of stability and prudent management, perhaps even to the point of arrogance. However, a changing social and economic climate, domestically and regionally, and the increasing threat of further marginalization in the global economy of the future served to activate previously repressed discourses on race during the late 1980s and early 1990s.

My purpose here is to examine the nature of the manifestation of this discourse, to examine its forms of representation in terms of class and gender, to tease out the implications of these developments, and to provide some context for understanding their emergence in this conjuncture. In the process, it is hoped that some insights might be provided with respect to addressing the areas of neglect to which such a discourse obviously points. The analysis of these phenomena covers the period from 1988 to 1991. It was in 1988 that one of the most serious recent attempts at contestation of racial domination of the corporate structure occurred. A sustained popular discourse ensued. However, by 1990 this discourse had begun to lose some of its poignancy. By 1991 the discourse on race in Barbados had once again entered a stage of remission, from which it has shown no sign of becoming activated in the immediate future.

The Genealogy of the Race Problem

Barbados is a little South Africa of the past. But certainly, racism is a highly denied realism in Barbados
— Mighty Gabby

The disjuncture between the racial composition of the island and the distribution of wealth is critical to an understanding of the nature of the present problem. Barbados is a society with a 92 percent black and a 3.2 percent white population (1990 population census). The other racial groups are individually less than 1 percent of the population. The economic strength and, by extension, the political influence of whites in Barbados far exceed their numerical representation.

Part of the reason for this economic dominance of whites is the historical legacy of colonial rule. Sugar production constituted the main economic base of the island at the time. A history of limited absentee proprietorship on the island served to consolidate plantation owners into a racial plantocratic class.

Ownership of land by individuals living permanently on the island therefore created and reproduced a powerful white planter class, which in turn accumulated and consolidated wealth in this class and within this racial group. Over the years this pattern has been carefully maintained and is structurally integrated into the political economy of the island. The net result is that this system of inequality has been ideologically articulated so convincingly as to be regarded as normative and acceptable to the ruling class and even to some who do not share in the economic spoils.

Whites, though a numerical minority, are clearly dominant socially and economically. The historical domination of whites during colonialism has left a legacy of accumulated capital upon which succeeding generations have been able to build. Expatriate whites intermarried with local whites and solidified their economic interests. Those who returned to the metropole, sold their interests to other whites – the only people who had the requisite financial means to purchase. Barrow and Green (1979) and Karch (1981) have documented the extent of interlocking directorates and white intramarital bonds that continue to secure white domination over the economy. White local ownership of resources tends to reside in such areas as construction, agricultural production, particularly in large-scale plantation agriculture and in dairy farming, insurance, import/export trading, and other forms of commercial retailing operations. Very little has changed since these publications that substantially affects the pattern of ownership in Barbados. The implication of this economic domination is that it has produced a very powerful correlation between race and class, in which the majority of local whites have consolidated and diversified their economic interests without too heavy a reliance on their connections with metropolitan capital. Indeed, the consolidation of resources in the hands of the white minority population has continued while substantive economic participation at this level by other racial or ethnic groups in the society has remained less representative.

It is fairly well known that whites in Barbados control the economic levers of the country. They remain the major players in all sectors of the economy. Whites control the retailing and merchandising trade. They exercise economic hegemony largely on the basis of merchant capital, which is the predominant form of capital in the country. In the agricultural sector, whites dominate the sugar cane industry, are major livestock owners, and are equally influential in vegetable and dairy farming. Though a number of hotels in the country are foreign owned, local whites own and control a significant number of those that are Barbadian owned. The pre-eminence of whites in the construction industry is incontestable. The extent of influence of this section of the population is truly remarkable.

[T]his economic oligarchy retains great influence in (for example) employment, wage levels, price fixing, economic diversification and growth – all of which relate directly to national political objectives and constitute highly sensitive areas of the country's development. The potential for the exercise of power to protect and promote their narrow sectional interests continues to be enormous and, in crucial national economic policy decisions, virtually unchecked and limitless. (Barrow 1988: 107)

Until the mid 1970s whites exercised almost total monopoly control of the print media in the country, except for some small presses and occasional newspapers with limited circulation. In addition, whites are strategically placed on state and parastatal boards and other important decision-making bodies in the country. In a small country with limited resource endowment, this kind of control by a white minority is indeed a source of the deepest concern for those who must share the same social and political space.

At the social level, whites have only relatively recently given up privileged access to housing. There were places in Barbados where blacks did not live – some parts of the parish of St James on the west coast, certain parts of St Michael, such as Pine Road, Belleville and Strathclyde, and in Christ Church such areas as Maxwell and Marine Gardens. In the field of education there were schools that were established for the benefit of whites but no longer have a place in the society. There are still some schools on the island that remain the preferred choice of white Barbadian parents for their children, for example, St Winifred's and St Gabriel's. However, while white children predominate at these schools, they are joined by their middle class black peers with whom they may or may not interact.

With respect to leisure activity, whites have enjoyed exclusive tennis, cricket, football, swimming and water polo clubs up until as recently as twenty years ago in some sports. Though for the more recent manifestations of white privilege there were no legal instruments limiting participation by blacks, the latter were made to feel sufficiently alienated as to forego consideration of membership. Herein lies one of the keys to understanding racial stratification and the discourse on race in Barbados. The social practice of this system of racial stratification is based on a form of segregation that is not legally enforced but is widely socially adhered to on the island. This latter point will be addressed in more detail subsequently; suffice it to reflect on the musings of Barbados' top calypsonian, the Mighty Gabby:

They [white people] are racist. They really are. All the sports they used to take part in before, once they began to realize that black people begin to play and they cannot dominate any longer, they stop playing it. They were very good in hockey, we start to beat them, they done wid dat. They were very good at swimming and water polo, we start to beat them . . . and I could call the things, Seafarers began to beat Tarpons and Snappers and dem, they done. In the hockey, Pickwick had a hockey team and then Empire and dem begin to beat them, they done. In squash, they had a squash team and then Eddy Grant and Rudy [Goodridge] . . . began to beat them, they done. They not many of them playing squash now, you understand? Anything . . . lawn tennis . . . they were very dominant, the little black boys like Tyrone Mapp and them begin to beat them, they done. Right? Everything . . . They used to go in the George Challenor Stand, black Barbadians began to get middle class salaries, and began to become members, you don't find many of them in the George Challenor Stand no more at cricket, they done. They're racist! (Personal interview with the author, 25 March 1997)

The above comment represents a very perceptive and not often articulated position about the retreat of white Barbadians from certain aspects of the social life of the country. This retreat is of course not a general retreat by whites from the economic or political sectors of the country; rather, it is the withdrawal from participation in those activities that bring whites into contact with blacks. In this sense, it is more of a distancing than a retreat.

There have been changes along the way, many of them emerging after 30 November 1966 – the postindependence period. Many blacks have gained social mobility largely through education. They are represented among the professions, in education and in middle management positions. There are fewer blacks in businesses of comparable size to those of whites. There are some who, because of limited financial resources, establish small businesses where the economic fortunes are often volatile. Though all small business persons are not black, 'small business' is often used as a synonym for black business in Barbados.

Some in Barbados have argued that the progress of black Barbadians is frequently overlooked. They cite in their defence the presence of a few very successful black property owners or business persons. Indeed, one caller to a popular call-in radio programme, in arguing what he considered to be the proof of black social mobility, informed the host that he was in a position to name five successful black businessmen. The myopia of such an assertion notwithstanding, the comment raises the spectre of the possibility that there will always be a few who will defy the odds and become successful. That we are able to identify with such precision these 'success' stories suggests that they are fewer in number relative to the general tendency.

Perhaps the single most misleading factor of the system of race relations in Barbados is the governance of the country by a black elite. Whites controlled the political apparatuses of state through the Legislative Council, the House of Assembly, the old vestry system[1] and other statutory boards from 1639 until around the time of independence in 1966. A break in this political hegemony occurred in 1937 with the rise of labour militancy and mass political mobilization which were sweeping across the entire Caribbean. The other reason for the political decline of whites in Barbados is a recognition of the winds of change that were blowing in the island, and more particularly the achievement of universal adult suffrage in 1951. Historian Trevor Marshall noted, however, that the decline of whites in Parliament occurred between 1948 and 1951 (Marshall 1990b: 11).

The fact of black occupation of positions of high visibility creates the illusion among those less familiar with the country, and also among less careful local observers, that those who govern represent the class interests and occupy the class location of the mass of black Barbadians. One can argue that political representation is fetishized by the conjuncture of the skin colour and class origin of elected officials who share similar characteristics to those of the majority of Barbadians. However, this phenomenal form obscures the class alignment and class interests of the black elite. The black political elite constitutes an integral part of the ruling class. In the administration of the apparatuses of the state, they provide an invaluable service for the reproduction of a system in which there is white domination but which also provides them with a privileged space. Indeed, it is precisely for reasons associated with reproducing themselves that the black political elite, quite apart from contesting the racial order, may vigorously defend the status quo to the extent that it continues to serve their own narrow class interest and project. The black political elite, however, represents a subordinate position within the wider ruling class, since it is largely without a material base in capital, and has had to rely on education as its principal vehicle of social mobility.

Unlike the white fraction of this ruling class, the black political elite did not gain its social mobility on the basis of inherited economic resources but via the acquisition of knowledge through education. This latter fraction of the ruling class, therefore, has had to be far more dependent on the state for its social reproduction than the white fraction of the same class. In short, given the absence of any deep roots in capital, the black elite has had to manipulate the apparatuses of state to reproduce, maintain and consolidate its position of power in Barbadian society. A black Barbadian elite may indeed have mastered what George Lamming called "the rituals of parliamentary procedure", but they have been unable to secure similar pre-eminence in the economic life of the country, despite their numerical strength. They possess some power but are at times themselves deluded by distorted notions of their own relative autonomy. Indeed, some have argued that whites conceded political control to blacks in preference to control over the economy as a political compromise for racial peace. This argument is essentially superficial in that it ignores the political struggles waged by the mass of black Barbadians to accomplish the gains they have made over the years. It also fails to recognize the resistance of whites, at every step of the way, in order to maintain the status quo.

In the latter half of the 1980s a black middle stratum of professionals and academics, as distinct from the black political elite, began articulating a counterhegemonic discourse on race which directly, perhaps less subtly than in the past, challenged white economic control of the island. This is not to say that in the past there have been no challenges to white domination; the history of the country is replete with examples of such contestation (see Belle 1974; Beckles 1984, 1989). However, this renewed challenge was much broader in scope – capturing the imagination of the national consciousness – and much more sustained than previously. It was a determination to move beyond tokenism and to begin to empower blacks through what had become known as 'economic enfranchisement'. This counterhegemonic discourse sought to challenge white economic control and to implement a process of economic democratization. The counterhegemonic discourse was articulated by a core of middle class, black professionals and university lecturers, whose particular challenge to white economic domination is discussed in some detail subsequently.

The Conceptual Framework

Theorizing about race in the Caribbean has tended to revolve around a few specific perspectives concentrated on such countries as Guyana, Jamaica, and Trinidad and Tobago. Admittedly, these countries demonstrate more racial and ethnic diversity than the other territories of the region. In addition, given the history and social and economic dynamics, overt racial conflict has occurred and is more likely to occur in any one of these countries than in Barbados.

For a long time, cultural pluralism dominated theoretical discourses on race in the Caribbean. This perspective, which argues a case for different sections of a community living side by side but never really interacting, was first proposed by J.S. Furnivall (1948) and articulated in the Caribbean by M.G. Smith (1965). There is a general corpus of literature, some of it influenced by cultural pluralism, that specifically addresses the issue of social stratification "as a form of social differentiation in which social groups (social classes) are differentiated in terms of status within a hierarchically arranged social order" (Braithwaite 1971: 95). For Smith (1965), cultural pluralism refers to societies that are culturally split and governed by a dominant demographic minority "whose peculiar social structure and political conditions set them apart" (29). This conceptualization is in turn quite similar to that of Lowenthal (1972), who advanced the case for a convergence of three basic elements: class hierarchy, social pluralism and cultural pluralism, which result in a pyramidal structure reflecting these elements (1972). Though cultural pluralism provides some insight into the social structure of the Caribbean at one level, its major defect lay in its insensitivity to the framework of the convergence of capitalism and race and the ways in which they affect the context of the theory. Mills (1987) goes a step further by arguing that M.G. Smith was very much opposed to any attempt to recast the theory of cultural pluralism "in terms of class and class stratification" (72). Despite its shortcomings, however, the plural model, along with the plantation and creole models, remains among the most developed sociological paradigms in the Caribbean.

Partly as a result of its own logic, and partly in reaction to the above-cited literature on race, there emerged a more radical alternative theoretical framework. Among its proponents are Campbell (1973), who articulates a radical materialist approach influenced by black nationalism. In addition, Post (1984), another writer of this genre, employs a new left and specifically Althusserian perspective. Other Caribbean scholars, such as Pierre-Charles (1980) and Munroe (1988), offer more traditional Marxist explanations, while Hall (1980) provides a Gramscian interpretation. Girvan's (1988) contribution to theorizing about race in the Caribbean is perhaps a more moderately leftist analysis, which is influenced by black nationalist sentiments. The common thread among these writers is the willingness to locate theoretically the role of colonialism in structuring the discourse on race. These authors are also concerned with examining carefully the impact of class, and in some cases colour (see Forsythe 1975), on race and the social structure. Their approach comes out of an emphasis on political economy that attaches primary importance to material circumstances of different racial groups, and exploitation and dispossession of these groups through political, economic and ideological forces.

There is a prevailing tendency within race-relations theory to view race as important only in terms of the intensity of conflict. In Barbados, perhaps given the absence of frequent overt conflict, research on race is largely undeveloped relative to neighbouring islands mentioned earlier. Much of the material that deals with race relations on the island is historical in orientation (see, for example, Mack 1967; Ligon 1970; Poyer 1971; Schomburgk 1971; Sheppard 1977; Handler 1974; Watson 1979; Karch 1977, 1981; and Beckles 1984, 1990). Building on the work of Belle (1974) and Karch (1977), Barrow and Green (1979) examined the difficulties faced by small business people, and the extent to which the corporate economy of Barbados is structured by race at the level of ownership. Basically, many of these studies, particularly the earlier ones, chronicle and comment on specific historical moments in which race assumes crucial significance. However, they do not provide the analytical and historiographical insights to illuminate the phenomenon of race relations in Barbados.

In recent years researchers have shown much more interest in studying race relations in Barbados, thanks largely to the counterhegemonic discourse that developed. Hilary Beckles, professor of history at the University of the West Indies and political activist, was one of the chief architects of this counterhegemonic discourse. He has written a number of popular and academic pieces on various aspects of the democratic restructuring of the island (see Beckles 1984, 1988, 1989, 1991a, 1991b, 1991c). Other observers of the impact of race in Barbados include Layne (1979, 1990), whose concern was with the interplay of race, education and development. He focused on the ways in which education was constituted along racial lines and how that feature influenced the socialization and internalization processes in the maintenance of the status quo. Watson (1990, 1991) also joined the discourse on race, drawing attention to the contradictions associated with the black middle class (both the black political elite and the more general middle stratum). He identified the profound paralysis of this stratum, members of which would prefer the discourse to end, since they assume that such a dialogue undermines their very tenuous position. Watson argued that the black middle class interest in maintaining the status quo is in part due to the belief that to 'stay the course' would result in some benefits from the dominant group, which presumably rewards the loyal and the well behaved. To articulate a concern for racial justice is to risk the withdrawal of such inheritances. The discourse on race in Barbados directly challenged this viewpoint. Marshall (1990a) also contributed a useful, though more traditionally instrumentalist, analysis of the nature of white power and privilege in Barbados.

The perspective employed in this paper is based on a political economy approach and examines the impact of economic crisis on the social configuration of the island. This approach also seeks to explore the extent to which race class and gender intersect. In addition, the perspective incorporates the Gramscian concept of hegemony as an analytical tool for understanding the degree of success of white domination and for helping to explain the evolutionary development of the counterhegemonic discourse on race in Barbados.

By hegemony Gramsci was referring to the domination of one class over another or others, not merely through force but through social, political and ideological indoctrination in order to achieve consent. This feature is made possible by virtue of the ability of the dominant class to transcend its immediate class interests (that is, its corporatist orientation) and to exercise a particular quality of leadership. The dominant class is prepared to make concessions to the dominated classes, providing that the long-term interests of the former are not challenged or undermined. Gramsci designates this site of the negotiation of leadership and consent as the social bloc.

The social bloc represents the terrain upon which the basis of the social order rests, and within which the hegemony of the dominant class is negotiated and renegotiated (see Gramsci 1980; Anderson 1976–77). One of the hypotheses of this chapter, therefore, is that whites in Barbados exercise a number of hegemonic influences over the black middle and working classes. However, in various historical conjunctures and for a variety of reasons, black middle (the general middle stratum as distinct from the black fraction of the ruling class) and working class Barbadians have contested this domination, mediating the hegemony of the white fraction of the ruling class. This challenge to hegemony is what is described in the paper as a counterhegemonic discourse. As Terdiman (1985) noted, no hegemonic or dominant discourse is unaffected by contestation: "A counter-discourse is counter-discourse because it presupposes the hegemony of its Other. It projects a division of the social space, and seeks to segregate itself in order to prosecute its critique" (185). The counterhegemonic discourse is an oppositional current whose challenges to the status quo run the full gamut of resistance from radical structural transformation to specific reforms of the system. In short, the counterhegemonic discourse "designates the generalized impulse . . . to pass beyond fixity, beyond closure" (343).

The Significance of the Conjuncture

Observers of the politics of race in Barbados may indeed ask what was there about the time under examination that made the issue of race so central, so noticeable. Those in neighbouring islands have even jokingly remarked that the racial and political ferment of the 1960s had only then reached Barbados. Even some observers from outside of the region, such as Ronald Segal, felt moved to comment on this situation. Segal (1996) asserted that the Black Power movement that permeated the African diaspora of the sixties "did little but rustle across the island until recently. Then, having abated elsewhere, it began blowing in Barbados against the emplacements of white business dominance" (294). Indeed, many in the Caribbean least expect social unrest or crisis to occur in Barbados. They see the island as a model of stability brought on by a widely perceived 'Englishness' of character.

John Hearne, the late Jamaican writer, in a stunningly unsophisticated and incredibly sexist article, described the Barbadian as a "problem" and as "English in a way that the rest of us are not" (1967: 6). Hearne, in a most peculiar social observation, concluded that the island of Barbados was, "the most un-West Indian of the islands" (7). In a parting invective, Hearne using the interpretative voice, presumably of other Caribbean people, suggested that, "In the climate of 'Southern' attitudes you [the Barbadians] are the 'Yankees' " (9).

Though openly critical of what he perceived as the English imprint on the Barbadian character, Hearne (1967) argued that Barbadians should not feel ashamed of their 'Englishness', because "It is a source of real psychic strength" (8). Perhaps the latter remark reveals more about Hearne's own ambivalence about British character and culture than it does with respect to any objective condition of Barbadian society. There are therefore some such as Hearne who are prepared to offer the above banalities to a much more complex and nuanced situation operating below the surface of the social landscape. However, such assessments demonstrate a failure to comprehend the social ontology of Barbadian society, the true nature of the persistence of a problem, or to appreciate the machinations of a crisis or, indeed, to understand the extent to which resistance can become incorporated by the hegemonic project of the dominant racial or economic order.

Hearne and Segal both refer to an apocryphal telegram, which was presumably sent to London from Barbados in response to the start of the Boer War of 1899, that allegedly stated: "Go ahead England, 'Little England' is behind you" (there are several variations on the wording of this message). Segal (1996) notes: "Apocryphal or not, the story says something of how seriously Bajans take themselves" (289). However, Hearne (1967) concluded from the alleged message that "it probably reflected, faithfully, the sentiments of every Barbadian, black or white" (8). What is remarkable about both these comments is that they are insensitive to or oblivious of the historical context. Even if one were to assume that the message had actually been sent, given the period (the end of the nineteenth century), how representative would such views have been of Barbadians and Barbadian society? This period, it should be noted, is a mere sixty-one years after emancipation. The colonial administration would have been firmly ensconced, and the mass of black Barbadians would only become enfranchised by the middle of the twentieth century. In short, all such a message could have told us is that the British, who were indisputably in control of the island, wanted to register their allegiance to the Crown and to confirm their identification with the British state irrespective of their location. It was a symbolic declaration of British nationalism. It is therefore a leap of logic to impute that such a sentiment as suggested in this alleged message could have been representative of all Barbadians and could continue to characterize Barbadian attitudes and behaviour.

Those who have lived in and observed Barbados over the years would recognize that the 'race problem' is one of long standing. In different historical moments it has manifested itself in one way or another, explicitly at times and more subtly in others. As Etienne Balibar has noted in another context: "Though it [racism] experiences fluctuations, though the tendency comes and goes, it never disappears from the social scene, or at least it remains waiting in the wings" (Balibar and Wallerstein 1991: 218–19).

Given the ebb and flow of crisis and resistance, it is important to the observer that certain occurrences be contextualized as part of an ongoing discourse on race. The early resistance of African slaves in Barbados has to be seen as the beginning of that process of economic and racial struggle. These struggles were waged not only against the physical horrors of plantation slavery but also against the hegemony of the minority white ruling class. The origin of this resistance is rooted, therefore, in the colonial struggles of slaves who fought and won their freedom from white oppression. The labour disturbances of 1937 were a continuation of the struggle for bread and justice. However, this resistance was not about extricating one's self from slavery but about demanding better terms and conditions of work in the postemancipation period. This was a liberation from what could be described as 'wage slavery'. This struggle also had racial underpinnings, in so far as it was waged against a white landowning and employing class.

The resistance to white domination was perhaps more readily observed in the popularity of Marcus Garvey's Universal Negro Improvement Association (UNIA) from the 1920s to about the early 1940s, where there were reportedly some eleven branches of the movement. The resistance contained in the participation of the UNIA, though part of the evolutionary chain of protest and contestation, was infused by somewhat different influences. The class struggle became secondary to the race issue in this instance. Such an orientation is consistent with the philosophy of black nationalism, of which UNIA was an important exemplar. The focus of the UNIA was on black upliftment, black economic empowerment, separatism, and a positive orientation to Africa and things African.

Though the 1960s would appear to some to have passed unnoticed in Barbados, it does not mean that political mobilization around race was nonexistent. There was, for example, the formation of a black nationalist and radically Marxist group – the People's Progressive Movement (PPM), founded in 1965 – which included such people as Leroy Harewood, Glenroy Straughn, Calvin Alleyne, John Connell and Robert 'Bobby' Clarke. The political philosophy of the PPM was a curious mixture of black nationalism and Marxism. According to Clarke (1983–84: 7), the son of Bobby Clarke, all of the leaders of the PPM were members of the Caribbean Socialist Union in Britain. This group used to publish a newspaper called the *Black Star,* named after the shipping line bought by Marcus Garvey's UNIA. The *Black Star* became the ideological mouthpiece of the group, openly chastising the government of the day – the administration of the late Errol Barrow – of adopting anti–working class positions. The *Black Star* declared war on poverty, poor working and living conditions, as well as racism and discrimination (Clarke 1983–84: 10). The *Black Star* encountered a number of problems from the state for the duration of its existence. Indeed, many of its members were constantly harassed. More importantly, the actions of the state with respect to the obstacles it presented for the PPM and the *Black Star,* represent one of the forms of suppressing the discourse on race in Barbados. However, while PPM was busy trying to raise the consciousness of the black masses, the government of the day was creating as much distance between the nascent Black Power movement and itself. In a pamphlet, Harewood (1968) commented on the government's reaction to the articulation of Black Power sentiments in Barbados: "Recently a group of politicians bitterly attacked the concept [of black power], and declared 'it has no place in Barbados . . . it originated in places like Montgomery, Alabama and Rhodesia, where the blacks were not allowed to be seen with whites' " (4). The foregoing represents a rather puzzling comment made by someone who has lived in Barbados for any length of time. In Barbados one is hard pressed to recall occasions when blacks and whites come together, when they socialize. Blacks and whites live separate existences. Hence to assert that there is no need for Black Power because the situation in Barbados is a lot different from those places where the concept first gained currency represents a certain lack of racial consciousness or awareness, not to mention a lack of theoretical clarity about the meaning of the term 'Black Power'.

Harewood also noted that "another politician said that 'Barbados already had Black Power' " (1968: 4). Harewood was not the only puzzled person observing the behaviour of the government on this issue. Writing about ethnic group relations in Barbados and Grenada, Henriques and Manyoni (1977) concluded:

Ironically, Black Power is also strenuously resisted and rejected by black politicians who see it as a threat to their own status notwithstanding that they claim to represent the masses. The most telling evidence supporting this assertion is that, in 1970, when the Barbados Government introduced a Bill severely to proscribe the activities of Black Power advocates, not a single political party or politician was prepared to oppose the Bill on behalf of the movement, and the Bill had an easy passage. (77–78)

This characterization overstates the case somewhat, in that there were objections raised in some quarters including that of an Opposition parliamentarian who noted that the Public Order Act was designed presumably to protect and preserve the public order but that the government had not produced any evidence to suggest that it had been 'disturbed' (Belle 1974: 152). Much of the objection to the Public Order Act stemmed from political partisanship and tended to focus on the encroachment on civil rights. Not much was articulated in defence of the advocacy of the idea of Black Power. Henriques and Manyoni continued: "Even the mightily proletarian Barbados Workers' Union supported the Bill and denounced Black Power publicly" (78).

The response of the trade union in this regard is typical of the ideological position that this organization held with respect to the way it interacted with corporate power in Barbados:

Much of the nature of the Barbadian labour movement can be explained with reference to the character of its leaders. As spokesmen for the black working class, they sought access to the system as it existed. There was no blueprint for restructuring and resource redistribution; merely a programme for alleviating the conditions of the poor within the established political and economic framework. (Barrow 1988: 98)

Here, then, is an example of how the race discourse is suppressed at the political level. In fact, with the introduction of the Public Order Act in 1970, referred to above, the government effectively suppressed the discourse. The passage of the Public Order Act prohibited individuals from engaging in any serious discourse on race for fear of being construed as inciting racial conflict and tension, or of being arrested for making inflammatory speeches. Consistent with the suppression of the discourse on race, the government in the 1970s allowed Black Power activist Kwame Touré (formerly Stokely Carmichael) to enter the island but did not allow him to make any public speeches.

The control and suppression, from time to time, of the discourse on race in Barbados in its discursive form is part of what David Theo Goldberg (1994) described as the field of racialized discourse. The field of racialized discourse refers to the articulation, one might add, the manipulation of the ways in which the material conditions of a racial group intersect with ideological conceptions. In the case of Barbados, the racial order is protected by the state and is maintained and reproduced by the vested interests of the white ruling fraction. However, it is often defended by some who may or may not benefit from the status quo but who unconsciously articulate what they have thoroughly internalized through years of socialization. The net result of an understanding of this field of racialized discourse is a preoccupation – which is of course never absolute, as we shall see – with stability above acts of contestation. Indeed, the practice of black elected officials being careful not to ruffle the feathers of the white fraction of the ruling class has a long history in Barbados. Brereton (1989) points to the case of the late Grantley Adams, former premiere of Barbados and prime minister of the West Indian Federation, who in the 1950s "felt impelled to threaten the passage of antidiscrimination laws when Barbados's chances of becoming the capital of the Federation of the West Indies was harmed by the belief, reflected in the report of the Federal Capital Site Commission, that open racial discrimination existed in the island" (93). During his long political life, Adams, it should be noted, could hardly have been accused of the practice of progressive politics. For reasons discussed earlier, Adams' behaviour is not surprising, and in some ways confirms much of what George Lamming is quoted as saying about black deference to whites at the beginning of this essay.

In addition to the forms of suppression of the discourse attempted both by the state and in civil society, one could summarize the remainder of such manifestations in the following way: (1) by appeals to the national economic interest – too much 'race talk' would scare away the tourists, who are so vital to the economic health of the nation; (2) by appeals to religion – race has no place in a Christian society and 'all are equal in God's sight'; (3) by appeals to social stability – those countries in the Caribbean in which there is public airing of the race issue (namely, Guyana and Trinidad and Tobago) have experienced serious racial conflict and violence; (4) by ostracism and labelling. The most effective weapon in the arsenal of suppression of the discourse on race has been ostracism and labelling of individuals as rabble-rousers and Marxists/communists if they decide to contest the system of race relations. It should be pointed out that, to date, the only person to be charged under the Public Order Act is Bobby Clarke, of the PPM, mentioned earlier.

The race discourse remained dormant for some time after the collapse of the PPM in 1971. The PPM folded partly through political frustration and exhaustion and partly through the attrition of its key members. By this time the political harassment of the group had taken its toll also. Moreover, the PPM folded because it had failed to create a mass appeal for itself. The limited appeal of the PPM is explainable partly in terms of what appeared at the time to be the actions of an extremist group.

During the late 1960s and early 1970s a well-known activist, Elombé Mottley, in the crucible of the Black Power movement and ferment in the United States and the Caribbean, began articulating a pragmatic form of Black Power. This effort was a combination of political mobilization around the issue of race, as well as an attempt to challenge the operation of the economic structure of some of the major companies in the island. In this intervention, the class project had once again given way to a 'race first' philosophy, even if the latter had not displaced the former completely. The Barbados Light and Power company was one such business that Mottley targeted for rate reductions. As essentially a one-man crusader, his success was at best limited. Mottley was arguably more successful in his cultural efforts, having established a cultural foundation called Yoruba House. Yoruba House was a small theatre that became well known for its staging of dramatic performances, for hosting lectures and debates and other cultural events, many of which celebrated the African heritage of the majority population.

It became clear, subsequently, that Mottley's interventions were the prelude to the launching of his own political career. In spite of this, however, the forays into the discourse on race had served to fill the political void of radical politics left open by the PPM in the evolution of resistance to white domination in the island. What is noteworthy of Mottley was that he managed to garner a reasonable amount of popular support for his efforts. Mottley's championing of the cause of the poor, in terms of challenging the rates charged for public utilities, for example, has always resonated among the poor and the economically marginal groups. Mottley later became involved in the Barbados Mutual affair, which will be discussed subsequently.

In 1973 a small group of mostly artists and university graduates formed an organization called Manjak.[2] Manjak was the name of the group and the newspaper they published. Manjak seemed generally interested in providing some insight and direction to the political climate of ideas of the day. It challenged white economic control through its pages, demanding an end to planter-merchant domination of the economy. It also began to develop a critique of capitalism. The group was perhaps more marginal than others of its kind. From its inception to its eventual decline in 1976, Manjak made no serious effort to mobilize popular support. It seemed to have been content with its 'political study group' status. Some of the ideas generated from the group were shared with a small section of the community through its newspaper. In various issues of its newspaper, Manjak called for a takeover of the distribution sector of the economy, for a programme of nationalization, a change in the ownership structure of the economy, and on several occasions, it argued the case for political and electoral reform (see Clarke 1983–84).

As to the shifting emphasis on race and class in this process of resistance, Manjak's contribution to the discourse fell more to the side of the latter. Given the political climate of the day, one did not anticipate a bright future for this movement. By 1976 the political mood of the country had shifted decidedly to the right with the coming into office of the late J.M.G.M. 'Tom' Adams, son of Grantley Adams referred to earlier, and his Barbados Labour Party. Tom Adams' tenure in office was characterized by a climate of intolerance and hostility to radical and progressive politics in Barbados. However, Manjak had not made things any easier for its survival by remaining faceless and distant from the Barbadian working class. In the end this strategy backfired, imploding on Manjak. Clarke (1983–84) summarized their demise with the following perceptive comment: "Manjak addressed everyone and no one in particular and ultimately, Manjak was itself largely unknown" (25).

One of the most insurgent and contestatory currents of counterdiscursive practice in Barbados is evident in the presence and articulation of a Rastafarian philosophy. This religious phenomenon has become so widespread that it is easy to overlook the nature of the interruption it represents for white ruling class hegemony in the Barbadian context. Rastafari, as a religious culture, contests every aspect of white rule, from its economic manifestation to its exaltation of European values, particularly the religious ones. It represents a definitive repudiation of images, representations, practices and cosmologies that are European, while valorizing things African. In 1974 Rastafari manifested a visible presence in Barbados for the first time (see Lewis 1977). Ever since then, the number of Rastafarians has grown in a country where the principal religious expression is that of Anglicanism.

Economically, Rastafarians have operated in the informal economy, resuscitating the leather craft industry. They are also active among health food store owners as well as vegetarian commercial and cooperative operations. Rastafarians are also musicians, artists, writers, painters and teachers, each occupation in its own way representing its particular brand of Rastafarian resistance. For the most part, however, Rastafarians opt to critique the status quo while remaining largely outside of its operation. Convinced of the incorrigibility of Babylon (white Western society and its value system), Rastafarians view the idea of meaningful change occurring from within the system as improbable, hence their withdrawal. It is this withdrawal, then, that often obscures the contribution of Rastafari to the counterhegemonic discourse. What should be noted, however, is that since its emergence in the Barbadian context, Rastafari has represented by far the most sustained and consistent challenge to white ruling class hegemony in the island.

Two additional points should be made in relation to the suppression of the discourse on race and to the nature of the counterhegemonic project chronicled above. First, given the general tendency to suppress the discourse on race, any attempt to interrogate this suppression becomes necessarily transgressive and subversive. Hence, when the counterhegemonic discourse seems to revolve around an individual or small group, such an occasion may in fact be an indication of the extent of the crystallization of the collective frustrations of a people. Moreover, as Gramsci (1980: 54–55) pointed out, the resistance of subaltern social groups is, of necessity, fragmented and episodic. Gramsci's position is unequivocal when he notes: "Subaltern groups are always subject to the activity of ruling groups, even when they rebel and rise up: only 'permanent' victory breaks their subordination, and that not immediately" (55).

A related point is that people who are dominated or repressed often, though not always, welcome certain forms of resistance. However, while welcoming a counterhegemonic discourse, they may not always be in a position to demonstrate their support in a concrete way because of fear of political victimization, economic recrimination or social isolation. In the context of a rather small society such considerations loom large. Lamming's comments about Barbados being ruled by fear once again resonate in this regard. The fear of losing the security of a government job, or the fear of appearing to be too sympathetic toward racial issues while in the employ of white capital, could indeed become politically immobilizing. To use the Caribbean expression, then, there may be "more to the mortar than the pestle", that is, popular support may not be immediately forthcoming for some forms of resistance, but it may exist at the subterranean level, within the mystical shell of apparent Barbadian political conservatism. Having so commented, one should hasten to add that the question of popular support has long been a source of political frustration for progressive political practice in Barbados as well as in other Caribbean islands. Such a problem will only be transcended with the creation of new modalities of intervention.

Furthermore, the contribution of migration to the development of a counterhegemonic discourse needs to be seriously interrogated in the Barbadian context. Many of the protagonists of the early efforts to resist white domination, as chronicled above, have all spent time in North America or Europe. So too have the leaders of the recent counterhegemonic discourse. It may very well be that those who migrate and are exposed to different levels of intensity of racism are more inclined, and in some ways better prepared, to contest these issues of race and class upon their return to the island. This is certainly the case in other Caribbean islands as well. The point here is not that people who remain in the country are themselves incapable of such contestation. Rather, it is merely a point that argues that those who remain in the island become more tolerant and accepting of the status quo because they have been more than likely incorporated into the hegemonic project of the white ruling class.

The Location of Hegemony

Gramsci initially distinguished between the site of hegemony in the state as opposed to within civil society. Gramsci's earlier formulation articulated the case for hegemony as operating within the context of civil society, while coercion, or what he called "direct domination", emanated from the state (see

Anderson 1976–77). Gramsci modified this formulation to indicate the combination of force and coercion in both the state and in civil society. This latter formulation is more in tune with Barbadian social and political reality.

The site of white ruling class hegemony in Barbados is the corporate economy, the schools, the church, in the editorial pages of both local newspapers and in other forms of popular discourse. It is indeed at the level of the ideological apparatuses of the state, namely the school, the church, and so on, and within popular discourses in the press that the historic valorization of whiteness, which is the legacy of slavery and colonialism, has often been reproduced. It is within these spaces that tolerance and acceptance of the status quo are nurtured (see Lewis 1990a for a discussion of the discursive practices of the race discourse in Barbados). Moreover, the executive arm of the state, that is, government, also becomes a site of hegemony for the white ruling class fraction, in so far as many black elected officials pander to and defend the interests of this same white ruling section. They, more than others, fully understand the extent of the control that Barbadian whites have over the economy and the extent to which they (the white ruling class) can exact compliance. Moreover, these black elected officials see their destinies, their political careers and their tenuous affiliation to the ruling class tied to the interests of the white ruling class fraction in Barbados.

Gramsci argued that it was ironic that the full maturing of a democracy tended to enhance the success of the hegemonic project. By this he meant that coercion was not a viable or acceptable option in the context of a fully functioning democracy. In the case of Barbados, belief in the democratic ideal also facilitates the efficacy of the hegemonic project in a way that, for example, the dictatorial Burnham regime of Guyana, the Gairy regime of Grenada or the Duvalier regime in Haiti could never have allowed. The latter regimes' coercive rule and control over the ideological state apparatuses had not, and could not have been, conducive to the hegemonic project. Indeed, as members of the ruling classes they all relied on coercion and intimidation to maintain their rule.

White domination in Barbados has been so deeply ingrained in the socialization process of the culture, beginning in slavery and colonialism, that a significant degree of acceptance and internalization of the status quo of the system of race relations in the country is inevitable. However, hegemony like coercion is not an absolute phenomenon. Implied in the notion of hegemony is a certain dialectical dimension. As has been shown in this chapter, there has been a history of resistance to this hegemony, if only at the margins of

Barbadian society. This resistance, then, is the foundation of the counter-hegemonic discourse on race in Barbados, in its various incarnations. This counterhegemonic discourse may not always have been adequately theorized or worked out but it has always held a revolutionary potential in its grasp.

It should also be pointed out that the counterhegemonic discourse has demonstrated a philosophical and ideological tension between race and class issues in its formulations. The ideas of black nationalism and 'race first' concerns are juxtaposed, or uneasily wedded to, some form of Marxist or socialist practice. This is an understandable tension but need not be a paralysing or debilitating one, given the race/class nexus of the political economy of the island. It is noteworthy, therefore, that this tension, though present in the most recent discourse on race, weighed more heavily in the direction of a populist black nationalist agenda. The most recent discourse on race has its genesis in the mid to late 1980s and represented the latest manifestation of this problem of long standing.

Aspects of the Most Recent Crisis

There were some features of the conjuncture that help to shape the trajectory of the most recent discourse on race in Barbados. Not all of these influences are local, some are in fact regional, while others are international. Afro-Barbadians, like other Afro-Caribbean people, have always had an interest in the plight of blacks in the diaspora. The historical experience of slavery has created this organic link among the descendants of Africa. Through the advances of modern technology, Afro-Barbadians, as well as other Afro-Caribbean people, have become even more aware of the plight of their brothers and sisters in other parts of the world. The global interest in the fate of other blacks in the diaspora is no doubt influenced by the viewing of such programmes as *South Africa Now* and *For the People* – an Afrocentric and historically focused programme produced by North Carolina Educational Television – both shown weekly in Barbados in the early 1990s. This awareness should not be discounted in an analysis of the articulation of a counterhegemonic discourse in Barbados. The discourse on race in Barbados, after all, occurred at a time of international racial tension. The upsurge of racism and racial violence in the United States and Europe generated a heightened sense of consciousness among racial and ethnic minorities in general. The continuing strategies of exclusion and control of immigrant groups on the part of many European states, along with what

Anthias described as "a potential growth in the wake of the 1992 Single European Act of a 'white European' identity" (Anthias and Yuval-Davis 1992: 427), combined to militate against Caribbean people living in Europe. The destabilization of Caribbean communities of the diaspora has important implications not only for those immediate communities but the extended families in the Caribbean who desperately depend on their remittances. To the extent that these are the real concrete concerns of Caribbean people at home and abroad would suggest that the global context is an important location of any attempt to understand the local manifestations of the real. It is part of what Cornel West (1993) called a "growing black international consciousness". Afro-Barbadians are no less concerned as black people.

In addition, many relatives and friends of Barbadians now live as migrants in these affected countries. Some five million Caribbean people live in North America. In Europe, another million Caribbean people have become 'deterritorialized', with just over half residing in the United Kingdom, while the remaining half is divided roughly between France and the Netherlands (see Lewis 1993). Indeed, the heightening of racial consciousness had reverberated around the Caribbean with the reopening of similar discourses on race in Montserrat, Guyana, Jamaica, and Trinidad and Tobago. Many political observers noted that the general elections held in Guyana (October 1992) and Trinidad and Tobago (December 1991) were characterized by strict voting along racial lines. Though the West Indian Commission report did not address the issue of race directly, it concluded that there were "creative tensions that still exist in the Region in its urgent effort to come to terms with its polyethnicity" (West Indian Commission 1992: 290). The occurrence of increasing racial consciousness in Barbados and the upsurge in racial tension regionally and internationally may not have been entirely fortuitous.

There is another level at which race continues to form an organic link among black people, and this is with regard to economic marginalization. As the technological revolution guides the world economy into the twenty-first century, black people in general must face the cold reality of their economic marginalization, irrespective of whether they are in the centre or the periphery. Walter Rodney (1975) reflected on this problem many years ago when he asserted: "There is nothing with which poverty coincides so absolutely as with the colour black – small or large population, hot or cold climates, rich or poor in natural resources – poverty cuts across all of these factors in order to find black people" (19). Fifteen years later the then Zaïrean minister of defence, Kamanda wa Kamanda, in an address to the Constituent Assembly of the

Institute of the Black Peoples in Burkina Faso, reiterated the concerns that Rodney raised. In observing that blacks were "the poorest of the poor, the most excluded of the excluded, the most marginalized of the marginal", he advanced the case for solidarity of black peoples "in a world experiencing global change in which Black people are the least integrated" (transcript of the address, 7–10 April 1990). Such a realization is both global and local and would be likely to strike a responsive chord among the majority of black Barbadians who remain poor and disadvantaged.

In addition to the foregoing, one could argue that the most recent discourse on race in Barbados emerged out of specific challenges to white monopoly control of the economy, in combination with a deepening economic crisis. One of these challenges came from Donald (Don) Blackman, who in 1988 was a government minister responsible for transportation and works in the then ruling Democratic Labour Party. Blackman was well known for his pan-Africanist views and his left of centre politics. Blackman, who had spoken repeatedly of 'white shadows' – the real political power behind the decision-making process in the country, became embroiled in national controversy over the awarding of a particular government contract.

In May 1988 an award of a contract for the rehabilitation of Highway 2A was made to a small black-owned construction company – Rayside Asphalt Company Limited – instead of a big white-owned company – C.O. Williams Construction Company Limited. It should be pointed out that C.O. Williams Construction had made what was believed to be a lower bid for the contract. The sitting minister of transportation and works at the time, Don Blackman, is reported to have made a number of comments in the House of Assembly concerning the awarding of the above-mentioned contract. Blackman argued that, given the history of ownership patterns in the country and the way in which economic participation was racialized, the time had come in Barbados for a policy of redressing imbalances in order to enhance economic justice.

It should be noted that C.O. Williams (familiarly known to Barbadians as 'Cow Williams') was at the time chairman of the Barbados Dairy Industries. He is also the owner and managing director of C.O. Williams Construction, C.O. Williams Electrical, C.O. Williams Farms and C.O. Williams Asphalt and Quarries Limited. For many years he had been the beneficiary of many government contracts, some of which themselves have been the source of controversy. In this instance, however, Williams cried reverse racism and took the minister and the government to court. Williams was granted leave to go to the High Court to seek a declaration that the award by the minister or the

Cabinet of Barbados, or both, was contrary to law. In February 1989, however, the chief justice, Sir Denys Williams, discontinued the case against Blackman, claiming that he had no case to answer. The chief justice claimed that according to the financial administration and audit financial rules, it was the Special Tenders Committee that had the statutory power of making recommendations and the minister of finance had the power of accepting or rejecting them. Where the minister of finance did not accept a recommendation, the Cabinet had the statutory power of making a final decision (see Civil Appeal No. 6/89, 24). Blackman therefore had no statutory power with respect to the awarding of the contract, hence the chief justice instructed that the case against him be dismissed but ruled that legal action could however be continued against the attorney general. The High Court, the Court of Appeal and the Privy Council all agreed that Blackman had no statutory power in this regard and that whatever he may have said in the House of Assembly could not be used in support of Williams' case. Williams nevertheless appealed this ruling.

In 1993 C.O. Williams Construction took their case to the Court of Appeal, the grounds of appeal being based on the performance of the minister of transportation and works, which was alleged to be motivated by prejudice and bias and influenced by irrelevant consideration (see Civil Appeal No. 6/89, 24). C.O. Williams Construction also claimed they had lost the benefit of the contract and the profit therefrom, which was estimated at $900,000, the cost of special damages with interest. The Court of Appeal upheld the decision of the High Court, at which point Williams proceeded to the Privy Council in London to have his case resolved. Finally, on 17 November 1994 the Privy Council overturned the decision of the Court of Appeal. It ruled that the decision of the Cabinet of Barbados made in 1988 was reviewable by judges in Barbados. This new ruling paved the way for the High Court to review the decision of the government to award the contract, which it granted to Rayside Asphalt Company instead of C.O. Williams Construction.

Williams felt vindicated by the decision of the Privy Council. He reflected on this after the decision: "All of us at C.O. Williams Construction are delighted that we are 100 percent vindicated and that the integrity and the truthfulness of our company has been totally vindicated and has been legally reinstated to its former, and I think always, outstanding moral position" (*Weekend Nation*, 13 November 1994, 3A). In the interim, the 1994 general elections ushered in a new administration to govern the affairs of the country. The Barbados Labour Party constituted the government and one of C.O. Williams' attorneys, David Simmons, QC, was sworn in as the attorney general. After six years of litigation and an estimated $300,000 in attorneys fees, the new Barbados Labour Party administration considered an out-of-court settlement. After three years of serious negotiations, the Government of Barbados agreed to pay C.O. Williams Construction approximately $1.3 million to settle in full the court action which began in 1988. The government also agreed to pay all of the firm's estimated $400,000 in legal fees associated with taking its case to the High Court, Court of Appeal and the London Privy Council (see Maynard 1996: 1)

C.O. Williams used the above case to make a very powerful point: the racial and economic order can not be changed without sustained and spirited resistance from those who currently benefit from the present order of things. Moreover, this was an exercise in muscle flexing, calculated to discourage any further attempt at reordering the system. Williams' tenacity was predicated not merely on what he perceived to be a violation of principle but basically on the fact that he possessed the requisite material resources necessary to counter this threat to the established legal and social norm, from the High Court and Court of Appeal in Barbados all the way to the Privy Council in London. What also became apparent in this entire legal drama is that C.O. Williams clearly understood the ways in which the law consolidated the interests of the class he represented. He further understood how legal principles reproduced social and economic hierarchies. As Mindie Lazarus-Black (1994) admirably points out: "[the] law always encodes a history of power. Law is a place where power is invented, negotiated, distributed, and consumed" (10).

Some have argued that had the previous Democratic Labour Party government been more forthcoming about what amounts to a new policy of affirmative action, there might have been more sympathy for the actions taken. It is debatable whether such a policy would have been any more welcome than it was, given the resistance to the appearance of the idea in the aforementioned. This event set the stage for a sustained debate over race and economic power in Barbados which took centre stage in both daily newspapers and on the call-in radio programmes for the next few months.

The second major challenge to white economic hegemony also occurred in 1988, involving the Barbados Mutual Life Assurance Society (BMLAS) and its policyholders. The Barbados Mutual was founded in 1840 and essentially functioned as a financial backer to the plantation and other agricultural interests on the island. "The BMLAS is owned by the policy holders, the majority of whom are black and lower middle class; yet, it has remained firmly controlled by the white corporate elite (and its few non-white appendages) since the mid-19th century" (Beckles 1989: 8). A group of concerned policy-holders, all of whom were black, led by Hilary Beckles, launched a challenge to the exclusionary policy of the BMLAS. Their initial goal was to be instru-mental in placing progressive and conscious black directors on the board of the BMLAS to break the white domination at this high corporate level. Second, the Barbados Mutual was seen as a good test case. Since it controlled so much capital and had so much influence on the agrocommercial elite, it was felt that a victory on this front could open new horizons for blacks in corporate Barbados. This challenge was fiercely resisted and resulted in all kinds of efforts by the BMLAS to maintain the status quo. Some of these efforts included what amounted to 'busing in' of old white policyholders from the northernmost and southernmost parishes of the island to vote at the annual general meeting. One should note that some of these individuals were not even interested in voting in this highly charged board election but were politically motivated to do so by BMLAS officials and their agents.

The initial effort to place two or three black directors from among the Association of Concerned Policyholders (ACP) failed to achieve its immediate objective. Hilary Beckles, who was the chief protagonist in this challenge to white economic control, chronicled the failure of the effort of the ACP. He noted that BMLAS officials attempted to discredit their campaign in many ways. One such effort was a full page advertisement in the local newspaper whose headline read: "*Vote For Confidence And Stability* placed above pictures of the three white candidates. The message which many policy holders believed was conveyed here was that you had to be part of this elite grouping in order to serve well your own Mutual Society" (Beckles 1989: 98; emphasis in original).

The attempt to discredit the challenge of the ACP extended to the familiar technique of labelling these candidates communists and worse. Beckles noted that the black middle class also failed to support their campaign, perhaps feeling that they (the black middle class) and not newcomers such as the ACP candidates should inherit the mantle of benefits. "They played into the hands of the white power structure whose representatives knew that once the blacks were divided every which way, their rule was secure" (Beckles 1989: 99). Finally, there were those who questioned the reputation and managerial credentials of the ACP candidates even though, as Beckles pointed out, "No one publicly questioned the reputation of the incumbent directors." However, the ACP effort ultimately succeeded in raising the racial and political con-sciousness of not only the BMLAS policyholders and its board but also the rest of corporate Barbados and the wider population.

The second effort by the ACP the following year was also unsuccessful. The reason for the ACP defeat the second time around had some of the resonances of the first effort, except that the voter turnout was very low and further militated against the corporate challenge. This time, however, it indirectly resulted in the election to the board of directors of two blacks, who were not members of the ACP but who were more acceptable to the BMLAS. Beckles was initially dismissive of the two black candidates who were elected, maintaining that they had stood on the backs of those who had initiated the struggle and by appealing to 'the oppressors' had been assisted in being elected. He nevertheless reflected more soberly:

But all along we had said that our task was helping our people to open doors and raise ceilings. This we did at The Mutual, and the fact that we ended with two persons hand-picked by The Mutual for reasons best known only to themselves, might be irrelevant at this stage in the struggle. (Beckles 1989: 192–93)

Some in Barbados have argued that as a result of the ACP mobilization around the issue of economic inclusion, other businesses had seriously re-examined their corporate policies in an effort to pre-empt the controversy of the BMLAS.

In addition to the insights of Beckles, the protagonist and participant, concerning the reasons for the two unsuccessful bids to create changes in the corporate economy of Barbados, one should make the following observations. Part of the problem of the economic enfranchisement movement was its failure to spell out its objectives more clearly. There was only some vague talk of using the BMLAS case as the hub and that a successful move on that organization would make subsequent interventions more realizable. The movement needed to have a series of coordinated projects working simultaneously so that there was some continuity of the struggle. Instead, with the last defeat of the ACP the movement went into hibernation.

Second, there was a need for a more comprehensive programme of empowerment of people, of which women and the youth should have been an integral part. Such a programme should have articulated a clear agenda for restructuring the society, not just tinkering with reforms. Coalition politics would have been critical to such an agenda. A counterhegemonic discourse must also appeal not just to the interests of the marginalized but must make serious efforts to incorporate them more than as the collective recipients of some generalized ideal. The ACP was basically a middle class group, the progressive politics of some of its members notwithstanding. Lastly, if such a movement was to retain its credibility as a democratic movement, then its leadership structure should have reflected such. A challenge as important as the one waged by the economic democracy movement should not have been allowed to suffer from any cult of the personality, irrespective of the charismatic appeal of any one individual. The Caribbean working class has had a history of disappointment going down this road. Despite some of the very positive aspects of the counterhegemonic project of the economic enfranchisement movement, there were still some of these issues that plagued them and were, in one form or the other, responsible for its ultimate demise.

Accompanying the challenges described above, and perhaps even giving life to them, was a serious and continuing economic crisis in the country. The discourse on race emerged in a conjuncture that was and continues to be characterized by a deepening of the economic crisis. This crisis exacerbated and brought to the fore race, class and gender problems. In a letter to Michael Camdessus, the managing director of the International Monetary Fund, the prime minister of Barbados, Erskine Sandiford, outlined some of his country's economic woes. He noted that the gross domestic product fell by 3 percent in 1990 and continued to contract in 1991. This position is in contrast to that of 1986–89 where average real growth was 3.7 percent per year. Sandiford acknowledged a decline in tourism earnings, which was accompanied by a sharp increase in amortization payments, which in turn was caused by heavy commercial borrowing in the 1980s and an unhealthy fiscal position. The prime minister's letter further noted a shift in the external current account from 'virtual balance' in 1989 to a deficit of 2 percent of gross domestic product in 1990. Net international reserves declined by US$47 million. Central government deficit widened from 0.8 percent of gross domestic product in 1989/90 to 7.3 percent in 1990/91. Given the uncertain economic situation, there had been little growth in private sector credit, while ceilings had been imposed on consumer credit from 1989 (for full text of the prime minister's letter see the *Weekend Nation*, 1 November 1991). Added to this already grim picture was an unemployment rate of 25 percent.

The cumulative effect of this economic crisis was social strain and anxiety. As the competition for scarce resources increased, many tensions and old antagonisms that lay below the surface of the social structure tended to emerge and re-emerge in various forms. This counterhegemonic discourse, then, was only one particular expression of a corpus of responses to the general crisis of the economy and society. In contesting white domination of the board of directors of the BMLAS, the counterhegemonic discourse was raising the moral and ethical issue of distributive justice in corporate Barbados. It is an issue that was framed in terms of the negation of black participation at the highest level of economic decision making in corporate Barbados and the need for a policy of inclusion.

Some Important Omissions of the Race Discourse

In the most recent discourse on race in Barbados there were some important lacunae that deserved more attention than they had so far received. Nothing was said about the existence of poor white Barbadians, nor was there any serious discussion or analysis of the gendered nature of race.

Barbadian Poor Whites

They [poor whites] get separate somehow from the other whites an' nobody notice them, black or white.

They get cut off from their own somehow, an' they got to go on livin' in the same land but as if their skin in make no difference. 'Tis why they call them Poor Whites. 'Tis the only place in these parts he say you see white people doin' all kind o' nasty low-down work, an' the Poor Whites as a class he say is worse off than the poor blacks. (Lamming 1979: 186)

The poor whites in Barbados represent an anomaly. They defy the generally recognized race/class nexus of Caribbean social stratification. Though possessing the phenotypic characteristic of whiteness they experience neither the privilege normally associated with this racial type nor do they possess the material resources of the class of whites who dominate the economy. This segment of the white population therefore experiences a different articulation of race and social class from economically dominant whites:

In Barbadoes [sic], where the whites, although so much diminished, still form a numerous body, the condition of the lowest class of them is described by observers just before emancipation as very degraded; without property, and raised by their colour above the debasement of labour, they were said to subsist in a great measure of charity, administered not unfrequently by the negroes [sic] themselves. (Merivale 1967: 83)

Poor whites can also be found in other Caribbean islands, such as Martinique, Grenada, St Thomas, Virgin Islands and the Bahamas, in similar social circumstances. In fact, the poor whites in Barbados are usually thought of as being at the lowest rung of the social ladder. The contempt with which the wider black population views the poor whites is evident in the epithets used in relation to this group. They are called 'red legs' – a term that, according to the folklore, was used to describe the colour of their skin that was exposed to the sunlight. Other names include 'ecky becky', 'poor backra' and 'backra johnny'. The word 'backra' is believed to have come from a West African word 'buckra' which means white man. In Barbados 'backra johnny' literally means 'back row johnny' or the white man in the back row – this is in reference to the specific location of the seating arrangement of the poor whites in church (Simmons 1976: 15). Simmons captured this race/class/religious conflation vividly when he wrote:

Ecclesiastical stratification was a straight reflection of secular stratification. The Church house on Sunday reflected the daily organization of the social hierarchy – white planters in the pews closest to the altar, if not to salvation; then the white petite bourgeoisie (plantation functionaries such as overseers, book-keepers, etc.); then the black petite bourgeoisie (the local schoolmasters, civil servants, etc.) then the black folk; and in the pews closest to the door, the Red Legs – poor white johnnies in the back row. (15)

The poor whites in Barbados are the descendants of the Scottish, Irish and Welsh who were brought to Barbados as servants by the English. They became known as Christian servants by the time of the arrival of the African slaves. Some of these poor whites were in fact sent to Barbados because they were considered outcasts and, in essence, exiled to the island as an alternative to punishment at home. Some also arrived during the eighteenth century as indentured servants. Beckles (1988) argues that the origin of the poor white problematic situation in Barbados is to be understood in the context of colonial sugar production in which white indentured labour was undermined and replaced by African slave labour (1). In addition, Beckles pointed to a contradiction in this colonial production, which is indeed typical within capitalism:

Although, in planter political ideology, the principle of 'race first' was clearly articulated, it was not dogmatically applied at the lower levels of society, unless the integrity of the entire structure was endangered. That is, planter elitism was not offended, but confirmed, by the white working class's degeneration into a culture of poverty on the periphery of the plantations. (7)

The economic and numerical status of the poor whites declined even further over the years, to the point of embarrassment of their more affluent counterparts. As a result, poor relief efforts were implemented to arrest the decline of this section of the population. Schools were established for the specific education of the poor whites. Such well-known schools in Barbados as the Alleyne School in St Andrew, founded by Sir John Gay Alleyne, Boys' and Girls' Foundation Schools in Christ Church, financed from the estate of Francis Williams, and the Haynes Memorial School were all specifically established to address the needs of poor whites. Today there are few poor whites to be found at these schools since having opened their doors to the wider black population. The Young Men's Progressive Club, established during the 1920s, was a social and community-based organization that was also intended to provide for the recreational needs of the poor whites in Barbados.

These efforts were largely unsuccessful. The poor whites did not embrace the educational opportunities with quite the fervour as had been hoped. Some managed to emigrate, mostly to North America – more specifically to the Carolinas. Some did seize the opportunity to gain mobility through education, and a few, through entrepreneurial skill, have become very successful business persons. C.O. Williams (mentioned earlier) and his brother Ralph, and John Goddard, of Goddard Enterprises, are among the best-known examples of this phenomenon. Most poor whites, however, remain among the poorest, least educated, largely invisible group in the country.

In this classic case of status anguish, the poor whites are unable to bridge the distance created between themselves and the rich Barbadian whites by virtue of serious social class differences. Conversely, they have chosen not to align themselves with the black majority, maintaining a deluded notion of superiority presumably conferred upon them by their white skins – a belief that seems to bear little relevance to their objective material conditions. Their efforts to remain 'pure' have led to inbreeding and its attendant medical problems. Commenting on the poor whites of the Caribbean, Gordon Lewis (1968) observed that their: "anomalous position as lower class economically but upper class in race and culture drove them, understandably, into their present-day closed communities, and whose members exhibit, as the price for their attitude, a high degree of consanguine degeneracy" (19). Today there are fewer than four hundred poor white families in Barbados. They represent a group on the brink of extinction.

One important reason why this group of poor whites did not become part of the race discourse in Barbados is that they are not part of the white hegemonic fraction of the ruling class. They have no material resources that make them important oppositional forces in the black economic struggle for inclusion. If the struggle were purely a racial one, then the poor whites would have been expected to figure in it at some level. That they were essentially marginal to the discourse suggests the existence of the articulation of both a race and class struggle taking place on the island, even though it may not always be so articulated. In a very dramatic way also, the marginalization of the poor whites to the race discourse demonstrates that there is an intersection between race and class, as Stuart Hall (1980) noted:

Race is thus, also, the modality in which class is 'lived', the medium through which class relations are experienced, the form in which it is appropriated and 'fought through'. This has consequences for the whole class, not specifically for its 'racially defined' segment. It has consequences in terms of the internal fractioning and division within the working class which, among other ways, are articulated in part through race. (341)

Privileged but Powerless

Though not occupying the same class location, white Barbadian women share a similar inability to exercise influence as do the majority of poor white males and females. They too were not central to the discourse on race in the period under examination. Though they enjoy all of the privileges conferred upon them by skin colour, they are similarly denied access to the real exercise of power. In this regard, patriarchal power demonstrably supersedes racial affinities.

White upper class women find themselves in a classic contradictory location. They face the difficult choice of contesting white patriarchal power, and risking the loss of privilege associated with control of the material resources exercised by their men folk, or maintaining the status quo. It would seem as though few choose the former option. Indeed, few actually have a real choice, being essentially controlled and oppressed by their men folk.

It should be pointed out that white Barbadian males have always reserved the 'right' to establish sexual relationships with black women, sometimes fathering children from these unions, though seldom marrying these black women. This covert attraction for black women by white men is part of what Young (1995) describes as the sexual economy of desire (90). Given their economic and social power in the country, it is quite 'normal' for white men to desire black women without incurring any social opprobrium about sexual degeneracy. Indeed, it is well known at the popular level in Barbados that some very prominent white Barbadian males have developed quite a desire for black female intimacy. White women, on the other hand, have always been protected from black men, often out of fear of racial desecration and hybridization. Much of this fear is premised on the pathologizing of black male sexuality, which has historically been constructed, particularly by whites, to be unquenchable and uncontrollable. Young, for example, refers to the fear of Jamaican planters who felt that the freeing of the slaves would bring about sexual pandemonium between white women and black men (145). Such pathology says as much about the fear that some white males have toward black male sexuality as it does about the amount of trust and fidelity conferred on white female sexuality in this regard.

Gordon Lewis (1983) notes that in "American society, money 'talks'; in Caribbean society, money 'whitens' " (10). This aphorism is not generally true of Barbadian society. Money, education or social standing never relieves the Barbadian black male or female of social stigma. White women in Barbados who marry black men are almost always expatriates from Canada, the United States, the United Kingdom or Europe – they are rarely Barbadian born. Immanuel Wallerstein (1990), writing in a different context, offers some pertinent insights on the matter of 'shielding' of the women of the dominant group:

The dominated racial group, because it is said to be more self-indulgent, is thereby thought more aggressive sexually (and more pan-sexual as well). The males of the dominated group therefore represent a threat to the females of the dominant group who, although women and not men, are somehow more 'self-controlled' than the males of the dominated group. But since they are nonetheless physically weaker, because they are women, they therefore require the active physical protection of the males of the dominant group. (44)

This form of socialization of white Barbadian women is so rigid that the few who defy the racial strictures do so with considerable loss of social status and often experience social isolation. The social and political divisions are so sharply drawn that in many ways they preclude meaningful dialogue and solidarity between black and white women in Barbados. Within this culturally determined space, therefore, the white Barbadian woman becomes an invisible, depoliticized and largely untheorized subject.

The Indian Community

Next to the poor whites the only other minority of relative significance are the Indians. These are immigrants from the subcontinent of India and their descendants. After the emancipation of slavery in 1838 in the former British

Caribbean, plantation owners in such countries as Guyana and Trinidad and Tobago supplemented their labour force with indentured labour from India, Portugal and China. This historical event accounts for the presence of Indians and the other ethnic groups in those various countries. Since Barbados was such a small country, however, it never experienced the same labour shortages as its bigger neighbours, hence it never employed indentured labourers. The Indians in Barbados, then, came after the period of indentureship without specific contractual arrangements.

The early Indians appear to have arrived in Barbados during 1919 and the early 1920s. This period immediately precedes the beginning of the Great Depression. At this time, many Indians were leaving the subcontinent to take up residence in other parts of the Commonwealth, in the hope of a brighter economic future. Most of those who migrated were merchant traders. They went to various parts of Africa, Canada, England and to the Caribbean. As they arrived in Barbados and were able to consolidate themselves, they brought their relatives to live with them. Hence the establishment of Indian families and, ultimately, the formation of an Indian community in the country.

The Indian population is very small, numbering less than 1 percent of the population (1,879 according to the 1990 census). Perhaps for religious, cultural and even racial reasons, Indians in Barbados have largely isolated themselves in certain parts of the country, mainly in some parts of the urban area. Their participation in the social and political life of the country is marginal, except that it is widely believed that they financially support both the government of the day and the opposition, in an effort to be always in tune with the main political currents.

Although the size of the Indian population in Barbados does not permit too vocal an opposition to blacks (this feature is not the same as in Trinidad and Tobago and Guyana, where the number of Indians is far greater), there are episodic conflicts between Indians and blacks, usually over conditions of work – Indians employ some blacks in small stores and garment factories – and over other business and cultural practices. Some Afro-Barbadians are also wary of the fact that though Indians are 'latecomers', they seem to have made significant strides in business. There is also the feeling in some quarters that the Indians' advancement is less threatening to white economic hegemony, given the size of this segment of the population, and therefore more acceptable. Hence the apparent inroads made by Indians in Barbados into the commercial and business community will continue to be a source of tension between the blacks and Indians. One gets a sense of the unease that black Barbadians have for Indians from a poem, provocatively called "Truth", written by Bruce St John (1982):[3]

De coolie tekin' over	You lie! You lie!
I say de coolie tekin' over!	You lie! You lie!
Dem strong in Guyana!	You lie! You lie!
Strong in Trinidad! You lie!	You lie!
Dem coming in Buhbadus	You lie! You lie!

The sentiment is greatly exaggerated here by St John to make the point about the perceived threat of some for what they believe to be the potential impact of the Indian community on the Barbadian economic landscape. He also points to the cultural differences between the two groups when he notes:

Coolie root back in India!	You lie! You lie!
Nigger root up in heaven!	You lie! You lie!
You does sell clot' in heaven?	You lie! You lie!
You does rent house in heaven?	You lie! You lie!
You does buy store in heaven?	You lie! You lie!
Uh lie? Uh lie?	You lie! You lie!

St John employs the familiar African call-and-response format to signal what he perceived at the time as misgivings and apprehensions over the presence and economic advancement of Indians, emanating from some sections of the Barbadian society. St John's poem captures the xenophobia and the fears of cultural contamination, if not dilution, which some Barbadians feel toward the Indian community. He very cleverly juxtaposes the perception of the acquisitive character of the Indian with the presumed other-worldly orientation of some blacks, perhaps intending to reorder the priorities of the latter. Moreover, toward the end of the poem, he raises the idea that in waging a struggle against whites, blacks may overlook the advances made by Indians. This latter point, though greatly exaggerated, perhaps suggests the popular feeling that the black/Indian tension is a potential source of serious racial conflict.

Though there are no published poems or calypsos, or other artistic expression known to this author, that convey an anti-black position emanating from the Indian community, the oral communication of such views is not unknown. Among some sections of the Indian community in Barbados, there is a notion of 'pak', which seems to embrace some conception of purity (see Hanoomansingh 1994: 334). There is therefore a reluctance by some Muslims in Barbados to interact with people who are non-'pak'. Hanoomansingh (1994) informs us that impurity of people could result from such practices as alcohol consumption, particular toilet habits, eating pork and not bathing after engaging in sexual intercourse (334). How some Muslims monitor the hygiene, sexual and eating habits of their own members, let alone people with whom they have limited interaction, boggles the imagination. Whatever the foundation of 'pak', it amounts to a mere rationalization in religious and cultural terms for separatist practices by some sections of the Indian community in Barbados.

Hanoomansingh (1994) notes that members of both the Muslim and Gujarati[4] communities condemn what they perceive as sexual promiscuity in Barbadian society (334). One gets the impression here that Hanoomansingh is referring exclusively to Barbadians of African descent at this point. Nevertheless, such a condemnation by some segments of the Indian community constitutes an attempt to pathologize 'non-Indian' Barbadian sexuality. The pathologizing of the sexuality of one racial or ethnic group by another is always overdetermined by racism at some level and constructed on stereotypes of the Other. In dealing with the social interaction of Indians in Barbadian society, unfortunately Hanoomansingh does not explore this dimension in his work.

A source of tension has emerged in the economic arena between Indians and blacks who operate in Swan Street – a commercial avenue in the heart of the city. Indians who had long established their small businesses on that street are now forced to share their commercial space with black vendors who operate in the informal sector and set up their stalls in front of the stores of the Indians. The Indian merchants claim that the black vendors hamper their business because the stalls block the access of their customers to the stores. There is also a feeling, which is articulated at the popular level, that erecting the stalls in front of the Indian business establishments may be politically motivated, if not encouraged, as a way to drive the Indian businessmen out of Swan Street. There is little to suggest an end to this conflict. Angry words have been expressed on both sides over this matter.

It is therefore worthy of note that whatever apprehensions and fears exist about the Indian population by the black population, they did not form an immediate part of the discourse on race. Part of the reason for this absence of dialogue on the Indian racial presence is that there exists within the national/popular consciousness a recognition that, irrespective of the business success of Indians in Barbados, they are still subordinated, as are their black male and female counterparts, to the hegemony of the white minority in whose ambit resides the real locus of power.

A Question of Colour

As in other parts of the Caribbean, colour gradation within the black community occupies an important place in the system of racial stratification. Colour distinctions among black Barbadians further demonstrate the heterogeneous nature of this section of the population. This chapter has already addressed the class differences among blacks and will be addressing the gender differences subsequently. The issue of colour, at least in the past, has tended to complicate the problem of race. Colour distinctions in the Caribbean manifest themselves in descriptive categories, so that blacks can be classified as 'light skin', 'dark skin', 'brown skin', 'high brown', 'yellow', 'red', 'grey-goose' and 'snuffy'. Each category represents close approximations to, or racial and therefore social distances from, conceptions of whiteness. The Barbadian journalist, poet and playwright Jeannette Layne-Clark (1993) humorously captures these nuances of colour gradation when she observed:

> From 'brown-skin', yuh movin'-up
> To 'red', 'high-brown' an' 'clear' . . .
> Wuh does separate dem t'ree shades
> Is de quality o' de hair!
> (21)

Moreover, as Michel-Rolph Trouillot (1990) points out:

'color' categories refer to many more aspects of phenotype than skin color alone, even when their etymology seems to indicate an exclusively epidermic referent. Epidermic shade remains crucial but skin texture and depth of skin tone, hair color and appearance, and facial features also figure in any categorization. (112)

The dominant ideology concerning these colonially constructed categories is that the closer to white you were, the more privilege you received. In other words, colour conferred what Trouillot (1990) described as "epidermic capital" on some individuals (123). These distinctions meant that at certain historical periods, namely, in the preindependence period in Barbados, lighter complex-ioned blacks were allowed to inhabit some of the spaces vacated by whites. This was particularly the case during the 1960s when rising nationalist sentiments in concert with emerging notions of Black Power combined to contest employment practices in the urban corporate environment. The response to such contestations was to replace white faces with 'light, bright, or damned near white' ones. Darker skinned blacks could not hope to get jobs in highly visible positions such as in retail services, banks, hotels, and front offices. Indeed, up to the present time, certain retail outlets, particularly those that sell cosmetics and other skin-care products, still exhibit a decided hiring preference for lighter complexioned women.

Despite the prevailing notions and practice of greater privilege for those of lighter complexion within the black community, there was also a less well articulated but present counterideational viewpoint that vigorously affirmed the dignity and beauty of darker pigmentation. This affirmation of the beauty of blackness was seen in the lyrics of the calypsonian Houdini in his song "Sweet Like a Honey Bee", in which he sang the line: "The blacker the woman the sweeter she be" (see Rohlehr 1990: 243). There is also a poem by Nicholas Guillén, entitled "Mulata", in which he asserts:

If the truth be told,
Miss High Brown:
I'm crazy for my coal black gal
and have no use for the likes of you.
(Cited in Kutzinski 1993: 170)

Guillén may very well have been working out some other issues related to race and racial mixing in this poem, but the expression of desire here resonates among those who did not totally subscribe to idea of the inherent superiority of people of lighter complexion. There were also those who believed Marcus Garvey, Edward Blyden and Hubert Harrison when they advanced an argument that privileged the purity of the African blood that ran through their veins and made them superior. There were also those who, since 1957, had followed the preaching and teachings of Archbishop Granville Williams of the Sons of God Apostolic Baptist Church, the most devoutly African-oriented cleric and church community the country has ever produced. At the height of the Black Power movement, the idea that black was indeed beautiful resonated among the darker complexioned Barbadian populace, building on similar sentiments to those mentioned above. In fact, there were times when lighter skinned blacks were regarded as suspect in matters of deliberation of racial issues of the day, given the sentiments of the Black Power philosophy.

These distinctions among blacks, however, served the obvious purpose of dividing the black community by diverting their attention from the dominant white community. It was a strategy born of the ideology of racism of the plantation, which made fine distinctions about the colour of the offspring of the sexual liaisons of slave masters and slaves and those who were not the products of interracial relationships. Nurtured in slavery, the strategy was reproduced in the preindependent society and persisted in postindependent Barbados. Given its articulation by whites to maintain their own dominance through division, the distinctions have been internalized and rearticulated by the black community in their quest to wrest some advantages, however minimal, from a system that marginalizes them and subjects them to Weberian notions of social closure.

In summary, then, it is worth noting that colour distinctions among black Barbadians are a function of the wider and more established system of racism, and can not be separated from it. It is a legacy that has been reproduced by blacks themselves but that has essentially been imposed on that community by the ideology of white racism. In contemporary Barbadian society, colour distinctions are not now as prominent a form of stratification as they used to be. In the context of the discourse on race in Barbados, colour distinctions within the black community become less meaningful since these artificial distinctions make no impact in terms of the distribution of power and valued resources in society.

Women and Race

The other significant omission from the discourse on race in Barbados was that issues affecting women or issues pertaining to women did not figure prominently. There were few female voices heard in this struggle, but this is not to say that women are a silent majority in Barbados. Women have been instrumental in getting the laws pertaining to the issue of domicile for spouses, common-law unions and family violence, changed or introduced. Barbadian women have also mobilized successfully around the issues of health and reproductive freedom. Women have also politicized the issues of gender in the wider society, either in terms of academic research or in terms of popular discourse.

Though at least three black women became involved in the effort to reconstitute the BMLAS board, alluded to earlier, their participation did not revolve around gendered notions of race. Their involvement had more to do with the issue of economic enfranchisement in the strictest sense. Attorney-at-law Donna Symmonds, a member of the ACP, to her credit, addressed the issue of health insurance coverage appropriate to women's needs – a fact conveyed in nine lines of Beckles' (1989: 94) two-hundred-page book on the BMLAS affair. Yet Symmonds' intervention did not tie the race discourse to a gender discourse.

The general failure to articulate a gendered notion of race warrants some examination. Wallerstein's comments (1990) on the relationship between race and gender are worth citing here:

Whereas a purely racist ideology might occasionally fail to persuade, the ideologues can find their clinching argument by adding the sexist overtones. So we hear arguments that the dominant group is more rational, more disciplined, more hard-working, more self-controlled, more independent, while the dominated group is more emotional, more self-indulgent, more lazy, more artistic, more dependent. And this is of course the same set of characteristics that sexist ideology claims distinguish men from women. (44)

Indeed, much of the imagery described by Wallerstein became a part of the description of the behaviour and attitudes of blacks and whites in the discourse on race in Barbados (see Lewis 1990a for details). The impact of race is differentially felt by women, who experience the double burden of racial and patriarchal injustice. Women also occupy different class positions which affect their ability to cope with their material circumstances. When there have been slight openings in the white-controlled economy of the island, it has been mostly black men who have been able to seize the opportunities for advancement. Women in general are still largely locked out of the major decision-making processes in the country. Indeed, in the sphere of influence of blacks – the political arena – it is mainly men who preside over this public domain. The current Parliament has only three elected female representatives out of twenty-seven. For most of the period since independence, there have seldom been more than two women sitting as elected representatives in Parliament.

The failure to articulate a gendered notion of race as it relates to women is associated with a historical disjuncture between these two concepts in Barbados and perhaps even in the rest of the region. Writing about this disjuncture, Cuales (1988) observed:

As regards the Caribbean, it may be suggested that gender and class have at most established a 'visiting relationship', that is a union without obligations or commitments such as those legalized by marriage. Considering the practice of gender relations in this region, perhaps this is the kind of relationship that some of us are most comfortable with. (120–21)

Cuales became more specific in her comments about the dissonance created between race and gender when she remarked:

Among women who have joined the ranks of conscious agents in the class struggle, few have taken action with regard to gender inequality in society. At the same time, organizations, groups and individuals who have taken up the battle against gender subordination, have not always manifested a class consciousness leading to their engagement in any form of class struggle. (121)

Despite this disjuncture, however, black women were expected to close ranks behind the race question even though their specific concerns were not addressed in the discourse.

Part of the explanation for the failure to merge the race and gender struggles of the discourse may lie in the class background of the men and women involved in the economic enfranchisement movement. As middle and upper middle class individuals, their preoccupation was essentially with a bourgeois objective, that of corporate participation. This is an objective that is not within the grasp of working class people, and especially not easily attainable for working class women. The latter are often preoccupied with issues of unemployment or deplorable working conditions in garment factories, sexual harassment (particularly for domestic workers), nonpayment of child support and juggling scarce resources to make ends meet. Another part of the explanation also has to do with the fact that many of those in the economic enfranchisement movement were black males who were not exactly well known for their advocacy of, sympathies toward or interest in issues concerning the empowerment of women.

Lastly, despite the overwhelming patriarchal nature of the discourse on race in Barbados, it does appear as though women, both within and outside the movement, who have been outspoken on other important issues of gender did not seize the opportunity to gain political mileage out of this issue of economic enfranchisement. The context may not have been conducive to feminist politicizing. This is hardly ever the case. However, it is incumbent on men and women – in this instance, those who were in the throes of this particular struggle especially – to ensure that such connections as those between race and gender be made. Having stated the above, one also has to interpret the event as a missed opportunity for men to build bridges and to foster strategic alliances with the feminist movement in Barbados. Perhaps the economic enfranchisement movement could have mobilized even more support had its agenda appealed to issues affecting women and broader working class issues.

The presence of a female candidate for election to the board of directors of the BMLAS from among the ACP was not sufficient. Indeed, at a time when women in Barbados were being blamed for many things – from the neglect of their parental responsibility because of their participation in the labour force to the poor performance of young boys at school because of the overwhelming presence of female teachers – it would have been quite appropriate to demonstrate the link between the racial and gender struggles (see Lewis 1990b for discussion of such a crisis). To be charitable, therefore, the absence of a gendered notion of race opens for discussion whether the fight for economic justice had been and continues to be a fight among black and white men for the control of the economy.

Black Nationalism and Cultural Revival

At a public meeting at the Clement Payne Centre in Bridgetown in 1990, Martin Cadogan, a devout pan-Africanist, noted: "it [the collapse of the Soviet Union and the Eastern bloc] means therefore that the socialists and the communists have lost, and the nationalists and the Garveyites have won – that's what it means. Because race is the ultimate element of this earth" (Transcript of the public forum, 1990). Cadogan may have difficulty proving his thesis but it is indeed the kind of argument that emerges out of the context of a strict black nationalist position. Though the economic enfranchisement movement articulated a much more sophisticated position than that of Cadogan, it was still largely a black nationalist movement. Its aim was merely to place blacks in areas where whites had traditionally dominated. Behind the scenes, the leaders of this movement had claimed allegiance to an undefined socialist orientation, but this was never publicly articulated.

Observers of social and economic struggles similar to those taking place in Barbados would note the general tendency of such movements to embrace a black nationalist philosophy. Part of the reason for this orientation is the populist essence of this philosophy. The appeal to the most common experiences of oppression and exclusion would always strike a responsive chord among the dispossessed. Hence black nationalism becomes the vehicle through which racial consciousness is asserted and articulated. Note the concern of the late black nationalist, Leroy Harewood: "Our struggle really, is not only a struggle for bread – although that is a high priority. Our struggle, to me, has always been, a struggle for bread and a struggle for the rebuilding of the African of the black man's psyche" (Transcript of the public forum, Clement Payne Centre, 1990).

At a certain level Harewood's point is well taken. He was concurring with what Malcolm X in another context called the need for 'psychic conversion' – a concept revived in the work of Cornel West (1993). Psychic conversion is a call for the restoration of dignity and self-affirmation of black peoples. This affirmation is not mediated by considerations of white approval or influenced by white standards. Such a call becomes an important step in the liberation of black Barbadians who have been so affected by white domination. The hegemonic power of whites in Barbados is another part of the explanation of the containment of racially overt, national conflict in the island. Moreover, given the relative autonomy of the various practices – social, economic, political and ideological – from the social structure, it is possible that the hegemonic racial faction can so influence the social system as to displace conflicts in one level while simultaneously avoiding a general crisis at the other levels of social practice.

To return to the articulation of black nationalism however, the counter-hegemonic discourse had indeed begun to address some of the very concerns of Harewood cited above. It had generated in some quarters a historical interest among some black Barbadians that was in some ways unprecedented. For some time, there had been celebrations of certain African events. These events have been associated in some form or fashion with one or the other of the groups who organized around the counterhegemonic project discussed earlier. However, with increasing historical consciousness at the popular level, these celebrations acquired a new significance and a broader appeal. This was seen in the resurgence of things African, the celebration of African Civilization Day, African Liberation Day, the independence of Ghana, the establishment of the Pan-African Association of Barbados, and countless public fora on issues revolving around race. In this regard, Hilary Beckles and the Department of History at the University of the West Indies, Cave Hill, Barbados, were undoubtedly the architects of the new historical awareness. They were responsible for sponsoring a number of public symposia on a variety of historical concerns.

The recurrence of the black nationalist orientation in the history of resistance in Barbados may in part be due to the society's opposition to radical politics of the Marxist or socialist variety. This opposition is deeply rooted in the political culture of the society. To circumvent this opposition, therefore, resistance seems to take the form of a black nationalist position that is capable of interpellating black disenfranchised subjects without unduly threatening the capitalist framework. The black nationalist struggle is one of advancing a case for the inclusion of blacks in the economic life of the country – that is, blacks need some or more of the economic pie. It is not a philosophy of complete structural overhaul. It is, in the end, essentially reformist.

To date, the white fraction of the ruling class, secure in its hegemony, has tended to ignore the challenges of black nationalists, considering them to be marginal and allowing their efforts to burn themselves out. This most recent black nationalist challenge perhaps gained more of the attention of the ruling class, but like previous contestations of similar genre, it too flickered, exhausted itself and died.

One of the problems with black nationalism is that though it is an important first step in the struggle for liberation, it often sees this initial step as an end in itself. This first step is important in terms of the value of self-affirmation that black nationalism offers, and herein lies one of its main appeals to the broad masses of oppressed black people throughout the world. Self-affirma- tion of 'black goodness' is a necessary but not insufficient condition of liberation from oppression. In a 1993 address at Princeton University, Stuart Hall pointed to another limitation of black nationalism when he noted that such a paradigm assumes an unalterable historical construction of race. Indeed, some have argued that white racism and black nationalism inhabit the same ideological space (Mills 1987: 100). Mills perceptively comments on the following observation about race relations in the Carib- bean. He argues, "being white in the Caribbean means, above all, not being black. Thus the ideas and values that develop in this so-called 'cultural section' will be permeated by necessity of defining itself against its despised and feared opposite" (100). Mills' remarks resonate of Gramsci's comments cited earlier about subaltern groups being subject to the activity of ruling groups, even when the former rebel. Among other reasons, therefore, the valorization of blackness in the context of the struggle for racial justice helps to explain why such a counterdiscourse tends to situate itself within a black nationalist framework.

Given its nationalist preoccupations, the leadership of the counter- hegemonic movement hardly recognized its problems extended beyond the confines of Barbados. It rarely acknowledged the connection between the small country of Barbados and its peripheral participation in the world economy. Herein lies its quintessential limitation. Watson (1991) reflected on this in his initial work on Barbados when he argued:

188 / New Caribbean Thought

While the economic barriers to black advancement are connected to race, they may also be a function of the limits of the agro-commercial model of capital accumulation: in other words, it is necessary to investigate the degree to which economic specializations in Barbados reinforce the semi-industrial character of the economy and impede the development of opportunities for building social links between the black professional and technical middle strata and white capitalists and creating a critical mass of talent and capital, resources that make technological and economic change possible. (10)

To date, these issues have not been addressed in any satisfactory manner. The race discourse in Barbados, therefore, has not yet begun to transcend this black nationalist stage or to situate the struggle in the broader context of social class and gender relations. Nor has this discourse recognized the link between itself and the global struggle and status of blacks. The counterhegemonic discourse has not yet been able to recognize the contingency of this struggle and its concerns with those of the relationship of the economic link of the country to global capitalism. Unless such an adjustment had taken place, the economic enfranchisement movement was destined to stagnate in its own narrow mindedness. In the end, the loss of momentum of the economic enfranchisement movement was testimony to the limitation of the black nationalist strategy. It was a strategy which had come to the end of its course.

What of the Future?

It has been a sometimes bitter but mostly healthy discourse on race so far in the island. However, the time has come to move beyond the rhetoric and to embark on an alternative path. There are times when one has to face the reality that not all conflicts are resolvable. There should be no illusions that all of the problems attendant to the Barbadian situation can be addressed successfully or easily. Given the disparity of economic resources between blacks and whites, it is easy to say that more egalitarian alternatives should be forthcoming. This is somewhat unrealistic. It fails to understand the capitalist project; capitalism is not about sharing equally. The alternative strategy, then, is not to expect that capitalism will yield greater equality but to create within the system greater opportunities for disadvantaged people.

Part of the process of providing more opportunities for disadvantaged people is to empower them. The concept of empowerment is becoming hackneyed in the literature on development, but there remains considerable revolutionary potential locked away in this notion. By empowering people, one means genuinely consulting with them to ascertain their goals and aspirations; involving them intellectually and pragmatically in decisions that affect their lives; providing them with the knowledge, information and skills to make intelligent decisions about their future; and fashioning an alternative that not only comes from them but is in harmony with the environment within which they find themselves. Evidently, this involves consulting with people more often than once every five years. Indeed, such an alternative need not wait for governments to get involved. People working together could achieve this alternative, and they are proving that they are capable of so doing within the context of nongovernmental organizations all around the world. One should hasten to say, however, that the nongovernmental organizations should not be allowed to carry the burden of the world on their backs and should always seek to bring the strength of the state to work to their advantage.

Having invoked the relationship of the state, one should also hasten to explain the class forces at work in this arrangement. In the final analysis, the ruling class that controls the state is concerned with its own survival. Though it is prepared to make certain concessions to the working class, it will not jeopardize its position to create an alternative structure that will reduce its power. Given its contested nature, it is naive to rely on the state in Barbados to redress imbalances of a historical and economic nature. In the first place, the state, in the broadest sense of the word, is strategically controlled by precisely those forces that would want to stymie the process of change. Second, the executive branch of the state, that is, government, even if it possessed the will to do so, was at the time in no position to attempt anything as ambitious as redressing imbalances. It was, after all, in the middle of the biggest fiscal crisis of its history which threatened its political survival, given the limited prospects for relief at the time.

Given the difficulty that black businesses face with respect to satisfying criteria of credit-worthiness of the commercial banks, alternative sources of revenue should be developed. For some time now, the credit unions in Barbados have been accumulating significant economic resources. They have acted as an alternative to the commercial banks for many working class Barbadians in terms of obtaining loans. There are some within the credit union movement who have called for a relaxation of the laws controlling their operations so as to provide seed money or venture capital to its members to start small and medium-sized businesses. At the moment, most of the loans of the credit union go to purchase consumer durables and are not invested in productive activity. One way of providing more opportunity for blacks in Barbados could be to explore this option of financing and to tap its potential.

Economically marginalized, increasing numbers of Barbadian blacks survive in the informal economic structure. In Barbados, no other racial group has a visible presence in this sector, which in itself is an indication of the economic status of blacks *vis-à-vis* other racial groups. Conceived in the bowels of the contradictions of capitalism and uneven development, the informal sector relieves the pressures and frustrations built up from unemployment and lack of growth in the main sectors of the economy. Though admittedly some fare relatively well in this sector, the majority merely ekes out a living. The long-term survival of economically marginal groups therefore demands that the root causes of the social and economic forces that created the informal sector in the first place be addressed and ultimately transcended. Such considerations would, of necessity, require a much more thoroughgoing structural transformation than is suggested by recent efforts at contestation.

The reality of all that has been suggested so far is lost if there is no serious attempt at transformation of the society. As Hilbourne Watson (1991) has suggested, such transformation requires a break with the previous and dominant form of accumulation, that of merchant capital. In a global economy, merchant capital – the kind of capital that creates its surplus through buying and selling – is perhaps a necessary but not sufficient condition for economic development. It is hardly the foundation upon which to build a model of accumulation. Merchant capital has essentially run its course in Barbados. In Barbados the time has come to move economic activity away from its heavy dependence on the sphere of circulation of capital and more toward the operation of the circuit of production. Barbados has to face this realization which requires restructuring of the economy and the setting of new national objectives that will often transcend race.

Finally, if there is to be any change in Barbados at all, people in the working class will have to keep up the political mobilization and pressure on the forces that retard their progress. Power does not concede without a struggle. It is important that the issues of economic injustice be kept in the forefront and that those in positions of privilege be responsive to these demands – it is in their best interest to so do. More importantly, working class people must be central to this struggle. It was Gramsci who had offered the wise counsel that the most effective way to proceed in the process of political struggles is for a class to succeed in elaborating and establishing its own organic intellectuals. The time has come for the real organic intellectuals to emerge from among the folk and from within organizations dedicated to pursuing their interests. Space has to be created for ordinary men and women, who normally bear the brunt of the economic and political hardships, to become involved in setting the agenda for the future of Barbados.

Notes

The author would like to thank the following people whose critical comments on an earlier draft of this chapter were much appreciated: John Campbell, Nigel Bolland, Mark Alleyne, Winston James, Hilbourne Watson, Meenakshi Ponnuswami, Glynis Carr and Charles Sackrey. They too must share in the blame for failing to identify any shortcomings of this chapter. Earlier versions of the chapter have also benefited from feedback from the World Anglican Encounter, held in Bahïa, Brazil, the Faculty Colloquium and the Postcolonial Theory Group at Bucknell University, Pennsylvania, and from the Society for Caribbean Studies Annual Conference, held at St Stephen's House, Oxford University.

1. The vestry system refers to the municipal and parochial structure of local government that preceded central administration. The vestry looked after the maintenance of public roads, poor relief, and repair and maintenance of churches.
2. Manjack is the name given to a type of coal that was mined in Barbados up until the 1920s.
3. I am indebted to Denis Sardinha of the University of the West Indies, Cave Hill, Barbados, for locating this poem for me at short notice.
4. The Sindhis and Gujarati are the two principal Indian ethnic groups living in Barbados (see Hanoomansingh 1994 for details).

References

Anderson, Perry. 1976–77. "The antinomies of Antonio Gramsci". *New Left Review* 100.

Anthias, Floya, and Nira Yuval-Davis. 1992. *Racialized Boundaries: Race, Nation, Gender, Colour and Class and the Anti-racist Struggle*. London: Routledge.

Balibar, Etienne, and Immanuel Wallerstein. 1991. *Race, Nation, Class: Ambiguous Identities*. London: Verso.

Barbados. Supreme Court. Civil Appeal No. 6/89, 1992–1993.

Barrow, Christine. 1988. "Ownership and control of resources in Barbados: 1834 to the present". *Social and Economic Studies* 32, no. 3.

Barrow, Christine, and J.E. Green. 1979. *Small Business in Barbados: A Case of Survival.* Cave Hill, Barbados: Institute of Social and Economic Research.

Beckles, Hilary. 1984. *Black Rebellion in Barbados: The Struggle Against Slavery, 1627–1838.* Bridgetown, Barbados: Carib Research and Publication.

Beckles, Hilary. 1988. "Black over white: The 'poor white' problem in Barbados slave society". *Immigrants and Minorities* 7, no. 1.

Beckles, Hilary. 1989. *Corporate Power in Barbados – The Mutual Affair: Economic Injustice in a Political Democracy.* Bridgetown, Barbados: Caribbean Graphics.

Beckles, Hilary. 1990. *A History of Barbados: From Amerindian Settlement to Nation-State.* New York: Cambridge University Press.

Beckles, Hilary. 1991a. "Economic enfranchisement: How the black Bajan missed out". Part 1. *New Bajan,* July.

Beckles, Hilary. 1991b. "Economic disenfranchisement: The children of 1937". Part 2. *New Bajan,* August.

Beckles, Hilary. 1991c. "Economic disenfranchisement: Search for self-sustained economic growth". *New Bajan,* September.

Belle, George. 1974. "The political economy of Barbados 1937–1946, 1966–1972". MSc thesis, Department of Political Science, University of the West Indies, Mona.

Braithwaite, Lloyd. 1971. "Social stratification and cultural pluralism". In *Peoples and Cultures of the Caribbean,* edited by M. Horowitz. New York: The Natural History Press.

Brereton, Bridget. 1989. "Society and culture in the Caribbean: The British and French West Indies, 1870–1980". In *The Modern Caribbean,* edited by F.W. Knight and C.A. Palmer. Chapel Hill: University of North Carolina Press.

Campbell, Horace. 1973. "Jamaica: The myth of economic development and racial tranquillity". *Black Scholar* 4, no. 5.

Clarke, Russell W. 1983–84. "The historical development of the political Left in Barbados since 1920s". Research paper, Faculty of Arts, University of the West Indies, Cave Hill, Barbados.

Cuales, Sonia. 1988. "Some theoretical considerations on social class, class consciousness and gender consciousness". *Gender and Caribbean Development,* edited by P. Mohammed and C. Shepherd. Kingston, Jamaica: Women and Development Studies Project, University of the West Indies.

Forsythe, Dennis. 1975. "Race, colour and class in the British West Indies". In *The Commonwealth Caribbean into the Seventies,* edited by A.W. Singham. Montreal: Centre for Developing Area Studies, McGill University.

Furnivall, J.S. 1948. *Colonial Policy and Practice: Burma and Netherlands India.* Cambridge: Cambridge University Press.

Girvan, Norman. 1988. "The political economy of race in the Americas: The historical context of Garveyism". In *Garvey: His Work and Impact,* edited by R. Lewis and P. Bryan. Kingston, Jamaica: Institute of Social and Economic Research.

Goldberg, David, Theo. 1994. *Racist Culture: Philosophy and Politics of Meaning*. Oxford: Blackwell Publishers.

Gramsci, Antonio. 1980. *Selections From the Prison Notebooks*. New York: International Publishers.

Hall, Stuart. 1980. "Race, articulation and societies structured in dominance". In *Sociological Theories: Race and Colonialism*. London: UNESCO.

Handler, Jerome. 1974. *The Unappropriated People: Freedmen in the Slave Society of Barbados*. Baltimore: Johns Hopkins University Press, 1974.

Hanoomansingh, Peter. 1994. "Beyond profit and capital: The Sindhis and Gujaratis of Barbados". In *Entrepreneurship in the Caribbean: Culture, Structure, Conjuncture*, edited by S. Ryan and T. Stewart. St Augustine, Trinidad: Institute of Social and Economic Research.

Harewood, Leroy. 1968. *Black Powerlessness in Barbados*. Pamphlet. Barbados.

Hearne, John. 1967. "What the Barbadian means to me". Barbados Independence Issue. *New World* 3, nos. 1 and 2.

Henriques, Fernando, and Joseph Manyoni. 1977. "Ethnic group relations in Barbados and Grenada". In *Race and Class in Post-Colonial Society: A Study of Ethnic Group Relations in the English-speaking Caribbean, Bolivia, Chile and Mexico*. London: UNESCO.

Karch, Cecilia. 1977. *Changes in Barbadian Social Structure, 1860–1977*. Cave Hill, Barbados: Institute of Social and Economic Research.

Karch, Cecilia. 1981. "The growth of the corporate economy in Barbados: Class/race factors, 1890–1977". *Contemporary Caribbean: A Sociological Reader*, volume 1, edited by S. Craig. Port of Spain, Trinidad: The College Press.

Kutzinski, Vera M. 1993. *Sugar's Secrets: Race and Erotics of Cuban Nationalism*. Charlottesville: University Press of Virginia.

Lamming, George. 1979 [1953]. *In the Castle of My Skin*. Reprint, London: Longman Drumbeat.

Lamming, George. 1992. "Barbados: The heart of the crisis". *Trinidad and Tobago Review* 13, no. 12.

Layne, Anthony. 1979. "Race, class and development in Barbados". *Caribbean Quarterly* 25, nos. 1 and 2.

Layne, Anthony. 1990. "Racial injustice and national development in post-colonial Barbados". *Bulletin of Eastern Caribbean Affairs* 15, no. 6.

Layne-Clark, Jeannette. 1993. *Bajan Badinage*. Barbados: Impact Production.

Lazarus-Black, Mindie. 1994. *Legitimate Acts and Illegal Encounters: Law and Society in Antigua and Barbuda*. Washington: Smithsonian Institution.

Lewis, Gordon. 1968. *The Growth of the Modern West Indies*. New York: Monthly Review Press.

Lewis, Gordon. 1983. *Main Currents in Caribbean Thought: The Historical Evolution of Caribbean Society in its Ideological Aspects, 1492–1900*. Baltimore: Johns Hopkins University Press.

Lewis, Linden. 1977. "Rastafarianism and its implications for Barbados". Parts 1 and 2. *Advocate-News,* 21–22 October.

Lewis, Linden. 1990a. "The politics of race in Barbados". *Bulletin of Eastern Caribbean Affairs* 15, no. 6.

Lewis, Linden. 1990b. "Are Caribbean men in crisis? An economic and social dilemma". *Caribbean Affairs* 3, no. 3.

Lewis, Linden. 1993. "European integration, Caribbean regionalism and the future of the working class". *Twenty-first Century Policy Review* 2, nos. 1 and 2 (Spring).

Ligon, Richard. 1970 [1657]. *A True and Exact History of the Island of Barbadoes.* Reprint, London: Frank Cass.

Lowenthal, David. 1972. *West Indian Societies.* London: Oxford University Press.

Mack, Raymond. 1967. "Race, class and power in Barbados". In *The Democratic Revolution in the West Indies: Studies in Nationalism, Leadership and the Belief of Progress,* edited by W. Bell. Massachusetts: Schenkman Publishing.

Marshall, Trevor. 1990a. "The whites in perspective". *New Bajan,* July.

Marshall, Trevor. 1990b. "Whites out of politics: A 'quiet revolution' in Barbados". *New Bajan,* August.

Maynard, Tim. 1996. "Cow's $ 1. 3M". *Daily Nation,* 26 March.

Merivale, Herman. 1967 [1841–42]. *Lectures on Colonization and Colonies.* Reprint, New York: August M. Kelley Publishers.

Mills, Charles. 1987. "Race and class: Conflicting or reconcilable paradigms?" *Social and Economic Studies* 36, no. 2.

Munroe, Trevor. 1988. "The left and the question of race in Jamaica". In *Garvey: His Work and Impact,* edited by R. Lewis and P. Bryan. Kingston, Jamaica: Institute of Social and Economic Research.

Pierre-Charles, Gerard. 1980. "Racialism and sociological theories". *Sociological Theories: Race and Colonialism.* London: UNESCO.

Post, Ken. 1984. "Class, race and culture in the Caribbean: Some speculations on theory". Typescript. Institute of Social Sciences, The Hague.

Poyer, John. 1971 [1808]. *The history of Barbados from the first discovery of the island in 1605 till the accession of Lord Seaforth, 1801.* Reprint, London: Frank Cass.

Rodney, Walter. 1975. *The Groundings with My Brothers.* London: Bogle-L'Ouverture.

Rohlehr, Gordon. 1990. *Calypso and Society in Pre-Independence Trinidad.* Port of Spain, Trinidad: Gordon Rohlehr.

Schomburgk, Robert. 1971 [1848]. *The History of Barbados.* London: Frank Cass.

Segal, Ronald. 1996. *The Black Diaspora.* New York: Noonday Press.

Sheppard, Jill. 1977. *The 'Redlegs' of Barbados: Their Origins and History.* New York: KTO Press.

Simmons, Peter. 1976. "Red legs": Class and color contradictions in Barbados". *Studies in Comparative International Development* 11, no. 1 (Spring).

Smith, M.G. 1965. *The Plural Society in the British West Indies.* Berkeley: University of California Press.

Smith, M.G. 1984. *Culture, Race and Class in the Commonwealth Caribbean.* Kingston, Jamaica: Department of Extra-Mural Studies, University of the West Indies.

St John, Bruce. 1982. "Truth". *Bumbatuk* 1. Barbados: Cedar Press.

Terdiman, Richard. 1985. *Discourse/Counter-discourse: The Theory and Practice of Symbolic Resistance in Nineteenth Century France.* Ithaca: Cornell University Press.

West Indian Commission. 1992. *Time For Action: The Report of the West Indian Commission.* Bridgetown, Barbados: West Indian Commission.

Trouillot, Michel-Rolph. 1990. *Haiti, State Against Nation: The Origins and Legacy of Duvalierism.* New York: Monthly Review Press.

Wallerstein, Immanuel. 1990. "Culture as the ideological battleground of the modern world system". In *Global Culture: Nationalism, Globalization and Modernity,* edited by Mike Featherstone. London: Sage.

Watson, Hilbourne. 1990. "Beyond ideology: The question of the black middle class in Barbados". *Bulletin of Eastern Caribbean Affairs* 15, no. 6.

Watson, Hilbourne. 1991. "Global restructuring and Merchant Capital: The limits of black nationalism and economic democracy in Barbados". Draft research proposal. Department of Political Science, Howard University.

Watson, Karl. 1979. *The Civilised Island: A Social History 1750–1816.* Bridgetown, Barbados: Caribbean Graphics.

Young, Robert. 1995. *Colonial Desire: Hybridity in Theory, Culture and Race.* London: Routledge.

8

Conceptualizing 'Difference' in Caribbean Feminist Theory

RHODA REDDOCK

The concept of 'difference' has emerged as a significant one in contemporary social theory. Whereas for the most part this has been the result of the increasing influence of poststructuralist and postmodernist thought, in feminist scholarship this was predated by the black feminist critique of what they saw as white feminism. It is also interesting that this concept assumed importance at a time when conflicts based on differences of various kinds, in particular ethnicity and religion, have become the main loci of war and intergroup violence in many parts of the world.

The emergence of the concept of 'difference' and related terms, such as diversity, have presented a major epistemological challenge to larger world views and projects based on attempts to create collectivized subjects or imagined communities (Anderson 1991) such as nation states, social groups and unified classes. As such, therefore, overarching projects, such as the socialist project, which sought to organize based on the collective subject of the worker, and feminist projects, which sought to organize based on the collective subject of the woman, have come in for serious challenge.

The Black Feminist Critique

As noted before, one of earliest challenges to mainstream feminist theory as it emerged in the North in the 1960s and 1970s was the black feminist critique. This emerged from a strong feeling among black feminists in the United States and the United Kingdom in particular of being excluded from a generalized discourse about women as well as from the discourse about blacks. In their classic 1977 statement, "A Black Feminist Statement", a group of black US feminists known as the Combahee River Collective (1983) stated, among other things, that:

A black feminist presence has evolved most obviously in connection with the second wave of the American women's movement beginning in the late 1960s. Black, other Third World and working women have been involved in the feminist movement from its start, but both outside reactionary forces and racism and elitism within the movement itself have served to obscure our participation. In 1973 Black feminists, primarily located in New York, felt the necessity of forming a separate Black feminist group. This became the National Black Feminist Organization (NBFO). (14)

The main focus of the black feminist critique was the invisibility/absence/erasure of black women from the feminist discourse. For example, the popular early analogy between 'blacks' and 'women' denied the existence of black women with experiences that differed from those of black men and white women. One of the earliest writings on this was Audre Lorde's "Open Letter to Mary Daly" (1983), where she expressed the pain she felt at not seeing her experience expressed in Daly's then most recent book *Gyn/Ecology*.

Black women also accused white women of refusing to examine the effects white racism had on the experiences of black women. In highlighting sexism and ignoring racism, white feminists were denying an important factor in configuring the experience of black women as well as not exploring their own complicity along with white men in this process. From very early, therefore, the situation of the black woman in the United States was described as being one of double jeopardy, where their life chances were determined both by race and sex. In later years this was expanded to include class as it was realized that the structuring of race in the United States was such that class had been 'raced' and 'gendered' so that an understanding of black women's situation had to consider the difficult economic situation in which most of them found themselves. The black feminist critique also raised the issue of class to mainly middle class feminists, contrasting the economic circumstances and work-life experiences of both groups.

The focus on difference at this time was couched in terms of discriminations and jeopardies as each factor was the cause of a different set of disadvantages. Whereas these three multiple jeopardies, later joined by sexual orientation, were initially seen as additive, Patricia Hill-Collins (1988), in her conceptualization of *multiple jeopardies,* saw these discriminations as not simply additive but as multiplicative, in that each discrimination multiplies the impact of the other. For example, racism is multiplied by sexism which in turn is multiplied by classism and so on. She explains: "The importance of any one factor in explaining black women's circumstances thus varies depending on the particular aspect of our lives under consideration and the reference groups to whom we are compared" (48). Furthermore, this she rejects as "monism": "any political claim that one particular domination precipitates all really important oppressions" (51).

Postmodernism

In recent times this black feminist concern with difference has received a fillip from the popularization of poststructuralist and postmodernist discourses, particularly in their challenge of hegemonic universals and their understanding of power as a dispersed phenomenon. For example, the work of Jean-Jacques Lyotard, who challenged the role of hegemonic metanarratives that serve to silence and deny competing discourses through the creation of overarching and totalizing universals, and that of Michel Foucault, who questioned the false power of hegemonic knowledges and the institutionalized structures that sought to control the creation and dissemination of knowledge, have influenced the black feminist discourse. Foucault also stresses the need to critique existing understandings of power as overriding and dominant and calls on us to see power in various forms and in social relations where we would not have seen it before. Finally, Jacques Derrida questions the Western tradition of constructing knowledge in binary opposites where the first term is the signifier of the Other and where the second term is defined in opposition or in contrast to the first; for example, white/black, unity/diversity, man/woman. He calls for a deconstruction of these controlling systems of meaning and for the opening up of new ways of understanding difference, and the specificities of its historical, social and cultural construction in ways that do not lead us into new essentialisms.

According to Jane Parpart (1993), while postmodernism has been received with mixed responses from various tendencies within feminism, it has served to strengthen the arguments long put forward by black feminists in the North. She notes:

Black and Native women in North America and Europe have become increasingly vocal about their unique problems, and the need to incorporate race and culture as well as class and gender into feminist analysis. While minority feminists have been arguing for a long time for a racially and ethnically specific feminism. (443)

For many black feminists, mainstream (that is, white) feminism had created an essentialized woman, one based on the experience of mainly white middle class women of the North. This model ignored the fact that black women had had a different experience. This approach is expanded on by bell hooks (1992), who in opening up a discourse on black postmodernism sees its utility not only in the de-essentializing of woman per se but, further, in a de-essentializing of blackness through a recognition that there may be different ways of being authentically black. In addition, this approach heightens the recognition, often ignored by early black feminists, that the black experience has not been singular. Increasingly today, differences in class within the black community have meant that the experiences of black women could be vastly different.

Deconstructing Blackness

The term 'black' has always been a problematic one, the main problem being its emergence within the modernist era as an oppositional term for white and the differential meanings that it has had in different contexts. For example, whereas in the United States the word 'black' referred specifically to the descendants of African slaves or any other person who had the slightest trace of African ancestry, in Europe in general and Britain in particular the word 'black' was used as a political oppositional term to encompass a wide range of racialized groups. In the words of Avtah Brah (1996):

The concept 'black' now emerges as a specifically political term embracing African-Caribbean and South Asian peoples. It constitutes a political subject inscribing politics of resistance against colour-centred racisms. The term was adopted by the emerging coalitions amongst African-Caribbean and South Asian organisations and activists in the late 1960s and 1970s. They were influenced by the way that the Black Power movement in the USA, which had turned the concept 'black' on its head, divested it of its pejorative connotations in racialised discourses and transformed it into a confident expression of an assertive group identity. The Black Power movement urged black Americans to construe the 'black community' not as a matter of geography but rather in terms of the global African diaspora. Eschewing 'chromatism' – the basis of differentiation amongst blacks according to lighter or darker tone of skin – 'black' became a political colour to be claimed with pride against colour-based racisms. The African-Caribbean and South Asian activists in Britain borrowed the term from the Black Power movement to foster a rejection of chromatism amongst those defined as 'coloured people' in Britain. (Brah 1996: 97)

While for almost two decades the term 'black' served as a useful unifying mechanism through which South Asian and African Caribbean activists were able to make successful demands upon the British state, this term has come under increasing attack. According to Brah, ethnicist scholars have argued that the term 'black' in Black Power ideology referred specifically to the historical experience of people of sub-Saharan African descent, and was designed primarily for them. When applied to South Asians, the term black did not have the same cultural meanings, such as those associated with black music, and so was relevant to South Asians in a political sense only (Brah 1996).

The argument about the term 'black' has been echoed in the Caribbean as well. Well into the 1980s the nascent Hindu Women's Organization questioned the use of the term 'black' to refer to Caribbean people of Indian ancestry. They too argued that 'black' had a meaning and relevance to people of African descent that it did not have for Indians and so was a hegemonic concept that denied the specificity of the Indian Caribbean experience (Reddock 1993). While the British critics suggested the replacement of the term 'black' by Indian or Asian, the Caribbean activists initially called for the term 'brown' then later for Indian Caribbean, a term that stressed the cultural and historical specificities of that group.

While Brah argues that the term does not necessarily have to be defined in essentialist terms, and can have different political and cultural meanings in different contexts, we have a situation where African diaspora feminists, after decades of arguing against a erasure of their specific experience, are being cast in a similar position in relation to South Asian identities. What is clear is that the existing and now hegemonic discourse of race, class and gender that developed in the North is inadequate to deal with the differing complexities of the Third World. But then again, it is possible that the overarching dominance of the white audience in the North has overshadowed the very real differences that exist among women of colour there.

In the last two decades, since the end of the cold war and the disappointment in the promise of modernization and socialism, there has been an upsurge of small- and large-scale conflicts based on ethnic and religious differences. While the politics of difference quite correctly directs us to the social, cultural and political marginalization of groups by dominant and hegemonic practices and discourses, the violence that accompanies much of this conflict has particular consequences for women.

Women are subject to some of the worst physical and emotional violence in open conflict situations, including rape and forced pregnancy. Women are often called upon to wear the 'ethnic markers' of their community resulting in calls for 'returns' to the veil, to 'family' or other symbols of female subordination. This has become particularly important under circumstances of economic liberalization experienced in the South, as structural adjustment policies that limit the availability of already scarce resources are introduced.

It is imperative, therefore, that women's movements tackle head-on the issue of difference, exploring its complexities of empowerment and oppression in ways that open it up for debate. In this way, women can themselves assess the situation and chart a way forward.

Difference in Caribbean Discourses

Issues of race and class and later ethnicity have been central to Caribbean postcolonial discourse. Yet for the most part, the black feminist critique of the United States and Britain did not find an echo in the Caribbean. This dissonance was most strongly reflected in the critique of black feminism by Trinidadian Gemma Tang Nain (1991), who characterized it as follows:

We in the Caribbean are no strangers to racism, having experienced some of its most extreme manifestations during slavery and for some time after its abolition. However, given the numerical advantage of persons of African descent in the region, it has been possible since the end of colonial rule, and particularly since the 1970s, to weaken the hold of racism. White men (both local and foreign) may still control the economies of the region but black men have achieved political power and do exercise considerable control over the public sector. To the extent then that power changed hands, it went from white men to black men; women did not feature in that equation. Caribbean women therefore have not found it necessary to differentiate feminism into 'black' and 'white'. (1)

In conclusion, Tang Nain argued for a change from the label 'black feminism' to antiracist or socialist feminism as a more acceptable alternative. The former term she saw as divisive and based on a narrow understanding of feminism. This article was important as it is one of the only documents that provides a clear critique of black feminism from the perspective of a woman of colour. At the same time, however, her paper failed to draw reference to the issues of race and difference within the Caribbean itself.

Contextualizing the Caribbean

The Caribbean is a diverse area comprising the islands of the Caribbean archipelago, the Guianas in South America (Cayenne, Guyana, and Suriname), and Belize in Central America. This region is ethnically diverse due to its tumultuous history of conquest, genocide, slavery, indentured or contract labour, and various migrations, forced and voluntary, over its history.

In all of this, the African-descended population comprises the largest single grouping, although this too differs from country to country. For example, in Guyana descendants of Indian indentured labourers are the largest group, and in Cuba and Puerto Rico a significant population of European descendants still exists. There are also descendants of the indigenous peoples, Chinese, Lebanese and a range of Europeans. Additionally, ethnic intermixtures of various permutations abound, some forming new groupings of their own. The Caribbean, therefore, in common with many postcolonial societies, is an extremely heterogeneous region.

For decades, in spite of the numerical dominance of the African-descended population, anti-African discrimination and racism was rampant throughout the region. This was accompanied by a well-established self-denial among many of these peoples and a rejection of Africa and 'Africanness' in many instances. However, interestingly, this denial of Africa was often combined with a strong sense of resistance against discrimination and racism. Although strong African-consciousness movements developed at various points through-out the history of the region, it was not until the Black Power movements of the 1970s that a true reclamation of an African identity could be said to have been experienced in the region. In the words of Rawwida Baksh-Soodeen (1993):

The post-colonial discourse which emerged since the independence movement of the 1960s and 1970s in the humanities and social sciences, the literary, fine and theatre arts and the field of journalism have all been attempts to grapple with the experience of colonialism from an anti-imperialist framework which included the perspectives of race and class . . . In the Caribbean then, the discourse has been one of reclaiming identity. The reclaimed identity, however, has been predominantly African. (25)

This is not surprising as the Caribbean, possibly excluding parts of the Hispanic Caribbean, is a primarily creole space, and one where major struggles took place (and still take place) for the valorization of African-derived languages, lifestyles and cultural forms. The term 'creole' here is derived from the work of Edward Kamau Brathwaite in his essay "Contradictory Omens". In this essay he defines the process of 'creolization', the creation of creole society as taking place through the forced acculturation of Africans to European norms and behaviours, the inadvertent assimilation of Europeans to African norms and the unconscious and reciprocal interculturation of one to the other (Brathwaite 1977: 11). This process he saw as resulting in a new cultural creation – a creole society, comprising a continuum of cultural and linguistic forms ranging from the prestigious and more accepted Euro-Creole forms to the more despised and often hidden Afro-Creole or folk forms.

In Trinidad and Tobago, Guyana, and Suriname, Indians comprise a much larger proportion of the population than in other parts of the region. As latecomers, however, they were never totally integrated into the dominant creole cultural paradigm. In recent times, however, due to a strong Indian identity movement and the increasing economic and political power of the Indian community, this is changing. This identity movement has included cultural nationalist tendencies as well as religious fundamentalist movements of Hindus and Moslems. All this has served to place the issue of difference squarely on the table.

Toward a Caribbean Theory of Difference

As this chapter is an exploratory one, I shall seek to analyse how some of the feminist scholars of the region have sought to deal with the difficult issue of difference.

One of the first Caribbean scholars to introduce the concept of difference was V. Eudine Barriteau-Foster in her article "The Construct of a Postmodernist Feminist Theory for Caribbean Social Science Research" (1992). In this article she sees liberal and socialist-feminist analyses as of limited relevance to the experiences of Caribbean women because of their grounding in assumptions of the Enlightenment. For example, she argues that socialist analyses constructed women essentially as victims and so ignored ways in which they daily resist and participate in actions aimed at changing their lives. In proposing a new Caribbean theory, Barriteau-Foster posits the contours of such a theory as a space "filled by operationalising gender, class, race, sexual identity and political action within the Caribbean context" (17). She continues, "The theory views all past generalizations of Caribbean woman as 'subject to scrutiny and change', available for revision unless they can meet the requirements of this new construct" (17). In applying this new theoretical approach, however, the author did not really go beyond earlier understandings of the experiences of Caribbean women. While noting that "Black women's experiences of race in the Caribbean differs from that of black women in North America" (25), this paper, probably because of the parts of the region on which it was based, lost an opportunity to more fully explore the complexities of difference in the Caribbean feminist context.

A clearer beginning to the discourse on difference in the Caribbean is provided by feminist scholar and activist Rawwida Baksh-Soodeen. This is probably understandable as her location as an Indo-Caribbean woman of Muslim background contributes to her sensitivity to the subject. In a 1992 paper, she notes in passing the difficulties for Indian feminists in circumstances of communal and ethnic tension to openly admit to and denounce the patriarchal practices within their community. Later, in "Is There an International Feminism?" (1993), she develops her ideas further, noting that in the emerging discourse on Caribbean feminism in the 1970s and 1980s, the discussions on race almost exclusively concentrated on the African Caribbean experience within the postcolonial context.

Baksh-Soodeen (1993) noted, for example, that in Caribbean feminist historiography (with one major exception), studies of family and slavery had concentrated on issues of matrifocality, female-headed households and so-called male marginality, all issues that contrasted greatly with the Indian Caribbean experience. This discourse she characterized as "Afrocentric":

[W]hat this means is that feminist analyses of Caribbean society have tended to focus on the black and coloured population and creole culture. Hence the lower-class family is always discussed in terms of the female-headed household despite the fact that among Indians (in societies with significant Indian populations) the lower-class family shows forms ranging from the Indian joint family, the three generation extended family and the female-headed household. (26)

In the main, this is a correct analysis although not yet understood by feminist scholars in all parts of the region. But the weaknesses in this analysis could also be explained by the absence of Indian women themselves as writers of those analyses. As soon as this changed, the discourse also changed. My main criticism of this argument, however, would be her choice of the word Afrocentric, for this gives an incorrect understanding of the mainstream discourse. Indeed, Afrocentrism is also a minority discourse within the region; the majority of African descendants have more of a creole consciousness than an Afrocentric one.

This view of a creole consciousness is supported by Rishee Thakur in his review essay "Orientalism Revisited" (1993), where he comments that

[c]omplaints of the essential Afrocentric character of the Caribbean functions along the same lines. As with the 'Indo-Caribbean' it is not certain what Afrocentric means other than the fact that the Governments and major institutions of the Caribbean are dominated by Afro-Caribbeans.[1] But there is really nothing Afrocentric in that, if Afrocentric means traditions and practices that have their roots in Africa and were reconstituted in a post-slavery Caribbean. What is at issue is who gets to manage the post-colonial settlement, codified and organised around the creolised ideals of an Anglo-Christian tradition, Westminster and all. (13)

Baksh-Soodeen continues, however, to note that the issue of racial difference within the Caribbean feminist movement is quite distinct from that of the United States and Europe. In the postcolonial situation the African population has had some degree of political if not economic control. As a result, she notes, the bitterness characteristic of interethnic relations among feminists in North America and the United Kingdom is not as characteristic of the Caribbean region. She posits that in spite of the real cultural differences among feminists of different ethnic and religious groupings, the larger tradition of anticolonial struggle, based on the commonalities within the different experiences of the plantation, slavery and indentureship, provides a common point from which to collaborate. This tradition also facilitates links to wider social movements, such as trade unions, Left political parties and other social movements, creating a greater possibility for a multicultural feminist platform.

A third contribution to this discussion is put forward by another Trinidad Indian woman of Muslim background, Patricia Mohammed. In her doctoral dissertation "A Social History of Post-Migrant Indians in Trinidad from 1917–1947: A Gender Perspective" (1994), Mohammed is able to use her concrete analysis of gender relations in Trinidad society. Mohammed's thesis traces the processes through which former indentured immigrants adapted to freedom and settlement in Trinidad in the three decades after immigration. She paints a picture of this period of Indians as a despised and despising minority seeking to establish themselves in an alien and hostile environment. A hostility, she argues, based not like today on sexual rivalry or scarcity of jobs but on antagonism to perceived racial and cultural differences on both sides.

Mohammed (1994) argues quite convincingly for a system of competing patriarchies operating simultaneously. The dominant white patriarchy, which at that time controlled state power as it existed then; a 'creole' patriarchy, emerging from among the African and mixed groups; and an Indian patriarchy at the lowest end of the ladder, which sought to consolidate and reconstruct the patriarchal traditions of India (30–32). In her own words:

> Thus the patriarchal context as it existed in Trinidad in 1917 was that of a competition among males of different racial groups, each jostling for power of one sort or the other – economic, political, social status and so on. In the face of a hegemonic control by the white group and another kind of dominance by the 'creole' population, the contestation was both a definition of masculinity between men of different races, and for Indian men to retrieve a ruptured patriarchy from the ravages of indentureship and thus be better placed to compete in this patriarchal race. This required a consolidation of the patriarchal system brought from India. (32)

As with many groups, symbols of women's subordination became markers of ethnic differentiation. Mohammed argues that in the hostile environment of the Caribbean, Indian women colluded with their men in the reconstruction of a Caribbean Indian patriarchal system. At the same time, where possible, they negotiated privately for spaces within which to manoeuvre.

Mohammed's analysis is useful as it helps us to conceptualize the difficulties of difference for feminist scholars and activists in postcolonial and ethnically differentiated societies, where loyalty to a competing patriarchy often influences the ways in which we are able to articulate the wider struggle. Mohammed posits a situation where women, in the name of community, collude consciously or unconsciously in their own subordination, even as they negotiate with it, in situations where symbols of women's subordination become markers of group identity. This was true of the Black Power and black consciousness movements of the 1970s and still contributes to some ambivalence among some Afro-Caribbean women activists in the region today.

Thus men's competing and conflicting relations with other men affect their relations with women, which in turn affect their relations with other women.

It brings to mind the ways in which struggles for identity and nation are always couched in masculinist language often referring to restoring a 'manhood' of some sort.

At another level altogether, Honor Ford-Smith's oral testimony, "Grandma's Estate", in SISTREN and Ford-Smith's *Lionheart Gal* (1986), provides yet another example of the conceptualization of difference in Caribbean feminist thinking. In that collection, her use of Standard English at once distinguishes that piece from the others (written, at Ford-Smith's insistence to the publishers, in the language of the authors, Jamaican 'creole'). In the very first line she identifies herself as the offspring of a brown woman and a white man, differentiating herself by class and colour from the other contributors in the text. In this article she also chronicles her African grandmother's quest to get rid of their blackness through her children and her children's children, with the end result being that Ford-Smith herself is, for all intents and purposes, a white Jamaican. But like other women in that text, Ford-Smith fights the battles of race, class and gender that are part and parcel of life in the postcolonial Caribbean, in her specific case exploring the contradictory locations of persons such as herself in the evolving realities of the region (SISTREN and Ford-Smith 1986: 177–97). Ford-Smith's work raises the issue of white Caribbean feminists, their conflictual situation within the postcolonial struggle for identity and their positioning within the Caribbean women's movement.

For my own part as an Afro-Caribbean feminist activist/scholar, I was acutely aware of the differences between myself and Indo-Caribbean women. This difference was, to me, both a real difference and a constructed difference. It served to maintain cultural spaces through which men could maintain control over 'their' women and also alternate their behaviours towards women of different groups according to the ethnic stereotypes. It was my experience, for example, that African and Indian women were constantly being defined in opposition to each other, Indian women were or are what African women were or are not. This, within the ethnic contestations and configurations of our society, served to narrow the options and spaces available to the women concerned.

It was for this reason, therefore, that in my own historical research begun some years ago, my efforts at understanding the experiences of Indian women was as important to me as was my understanding of African women. Not simply because it was politically correct to do so but because our differences had in some way contributed to what we had now been constructed to be. In other words, it was impossible to know myself if I did not know my Other/s.

In conceptualizing a theory of difference for the Caribbean, therefore, it is not enough simply to celebrate diversity. We need to isolate the ways in which the constructed differences have contributed to how we have conceptualized ourselves. Difference in the Caribbean therefore can be a mechanism for showing interconnectedness. The long-term project of a feminist understanding of difference would not be simply to come to terms with the other but rather to understand the other within ourselves as we have in many ways been defined in opposition and in relation to each other.

In this sense, I find the work of Patricia Mohammed particularly enlightening as it suggests that feminist conceptualizations of difference need to be quite different from masculinist ones. They should also be conceptualizations that highlight our interconnectedness as well as our separateness and that, most importantly, provide the basis for collective social action, a reality that I believe we have gone some way in achieving in the Caribbean.

Note

1. That was until recently. Both Guyana and Trinidad and Tobago now have Indian prime ministers and predominantly Indian Cabinets.

References

Anderson, Benedict. 1991. *Imagined Communities: Reflections on The Origin and Spread of Nationalism*. Revised edition. London: Verso.

Baksh-Soodeen, Rawwida. 1992. "Indo-Caribbean women: The contradictions of continuity and change". Mimeo.

Baksh-Soodeen, Rawwida. 1993. "Is there an international feminism?" *Alternative Approach*, Summer.

Barriteau-Foster, V. Eudine. 1992. "The construct of a postmodernist feminist theory for Caribbean social science research". *Social and Economic Studies* 41, no. 2.

Brah, Avtar. 1996. *Cartographies of Diaspora: Contesting Identities*. London: Routledge.

Brathwaite, Edward Kamau. 1977. *Contradictory Omens: Cultural Diversity and Integration in the Caribbean*. Kingston, Jamaica: Savacou Publications.

Combahee River Collective. 1983. "A black feminist statement". In *This Bridge Called My Back: Writings by Radical Women of Color*, edited by C. Moraga and G. Anzaldua. New York: Kitchen Table Press.

Hill-Collins, Patricia. 1988. *Black Feminist Thought: Knowledge, Consciousness and the Politics of Empowerment*. Boston: Unwin Hyman.

hooks, bell. 1992. *Black Looks: Race and Representation*. Boston: Southend Press.

Lorde, Audre. 1983. "An open letter to Mary Daly". In *This Bridge Called My Back: Writings by Radical Women of Color*, edited by C. Moraga and G. Anzaldua. New York: Kitchen Table Press.

Mohammed, Patricia. 1994. "A social history of post-migrant Indians in Trinidad 1917–1947". PhD diss., Institute of Social Studies, The Hague.

Parpart, Jane. 1993. "Who is the 'Other'? A postmodern feminist critique of women and development theory and practice". *Development and Change* 24, no. 3 (July).

Reddock, Rhoda. 1993. "Primacy of gender in race and class". In *Race, Class and Gender in the Future of the Caribbean*, edited by J.E. Greene. Kingston, Jamaica: Institute of Social and Economic Research.

Reddock, Rhoda. 1994. *Women, Labour and Politics in Trinidad and Tobago: A History*. London: Zed Books.

Tang Nain, Gemma. 1991. "Black women, sexism and racism: Black or antiracist feminism". *Feminist Review*, no. 37 (Spring).

Thakur, Rishee. 1993. "Orientalism revisited". *Caribbean Affairs* 16, no. 2.

SISTREN, with Honor Ford-Smith, ed. 1986. *Lionheart Gal: Life Histories of Jamaican Women*. London: Women's Press.

9

Rethinking Power
Political Subordination in Jamaica

OBIKA GRAY

The dialectic of oppressive state power, and opposition to it, remains a compelling subject for political analysis. Recent studies of this phenomenon have emphasized the ability of socially marginal and disadvantaged groups to constrain power holders in ways they find hard to suppress.[1] Although mainstream social science has traditionally had little interest in this theme of power from below, increasing attention is being given to the subject of the social power of the urban poor and to their relations with contemporary states. It has become more apparent that the social actions of the poor are politically relevant and these actions are increasingly being examined for their political import.

Among the studies that focus on the poor and their relations with the powerful are those that call attention to their fugitive and evasive tactics. Such studies have emphasized unorthodox strategies of marginal groups who appear to rely less on direct violence and overt rebellion in challenging political authorities than on 'hidden' forms of opposition, ranging from dissimulation, evasion, smuggling and theft to the ridiculing of power by gossip, character assassination and biting popular song. Still other studies have emphasized not only the critique of power by these tactics but also how the rejection of a bourgeois, civic morality in favour of the cultivation of an identity of radical otherness has empowered stigmatized groups. These reports argue that such strategies and renegade forms of opposition secure for the poor the status, honour and respect an exploitative society has denied them (see Cooper 1994).

Other analysts in this tradition have also commented on outlawry and crime as forms of political defiance. These analysts do not reject the importance of covert actions of the poor, but they go beyond an emphasis on fugitive acts to emphasize overt, defiant, and extralegal forms of contesting power. These forms are seen as having little to do with organized or revolutionary action. Rather, they are regarded as representing collective, autonomous acts of empowerment, which strike a blow against an oppressive and unjust system by resorting to predation, criminality, banditry and other forms of social outlawry. Commentators on these forms of social action in contexts of marginality and unequal power note their political relevance and insist that they be viewed as part of the evidence of political response to social oppression by disadvantaged groups (see, for example, Crummey 1986). While consider-able disputes and controversies attend these formulations and there are ques-tions of whether crime and outlawry should be regarded as 'political' or 'emancipatory', it is undeniable that the states dealing with these issues have taken notice of them, recognize their political relevance, and have been attempting to crush them.[2]

The fluorescence of unorganized renegade behaviours, the resort to non-bourgeois identities and the formation of rebellious moral communities on the part of disadvantaged urban groups in contemporary states are increasingly matters of urgent concern for such states. Rebellious cultures of the urban poor, and their acts of defiance, pose for states the problem of political legitimacy, the challenge of ideological dominance and social control, and the predicament of securing obedience to law and official morality. These challenges become especially acute in contexts where the state is nominally democratic and is concerned not to be seen as contravening the rule of law.

At the same time, the expansion of these rebellious cultures in various societies opens up other interesting issues. These issues include identifying the social bases for the cultural formation of rebellious cultures of the urban poor; locating the processes involved in the construction of their identities; assessing the contents and political resonance of their moral culture; evaluating the rules for joining the moral community of the alienated poor; and determining the effects these rebel cultures of the urban poor have on political systems and on social and cultural change. These issues suggest the need to pay greater attention to the politics and social actions of the urban poor. Because of their growing demographic, social and political importance in both industrialized and underdeveloped societies, the urban poor cannot be easily dismissed as irrelevant to the politics of these societies. Despite serious problems involved in studying such groups, and notwithstanding the tremendous handicaps that confront them in their encounters with states, the urban poor have a political life and a moral economy whose contours require closer examination than they have received so far.

Disadvantaged groups, while lacking political power and denied the traditional resources of their social betters, do have resources they can deploy in social conflicts. The forms such responses take, however, should not be reduced to a simple continuum that goes from mere resignation to their unequal status, to sudden violent outbursts against it. Between these two extremes there exists a vast terrain on which myriad forms of resistance to domination are enacted. Recent studies have examined some of these forms and identified their significance for the persistence of domination and hegemony. Despite their differing emphases, such studies share a basic conclusion that, whatever power states or ruling groups might exercise, hegemony is never total. The dominated have the capacity to resist and often find the means to elude power, constrain its effects on them, bargain with it and adapt it to conform to some of their needs.[3] Disadvantaged groups exhibit a social power that can be identified and examined for its compulsion on power and for its impact on social change.

In light of these considerations, this chapter revisits the issue of state power in postcolonial Jamaica. It offers a revision of the identity of that power, examines the forms of opposition it, and discusses the political meaning of responses to this power among rebellious, socially mobilized tributaries of the urban poor in Jamaica.

Rethinking Power and Subordination in Jamaica

Conceptions of the identity of the Jamaican state have emphasized its paternal and authoritarian qualities. The late and influential political scientist Carl Stone, for example, has shown how clientelism, linked to a competitive electoral system, produced a faction-ridden and violent political system (see Stone 1986). His emphasis on political patronage and its dynamics offers a revealing anatomy of the postcolonial Jamaican political order. His analysis shows how that order combines authoritarian, democratic, paternalist and populist features to hold together a class-divided society.

In Stone's analysis, unequal class relations in Jamaica are addressed through a combination of patronage, multiclass party alliances and strategic use of violence to quell popular opposition. For him, state power in Jamaica is pre-emptive, invasive, monopolistic and coercive. But he also argues that this power is flexible, adaptive, and it is one that retains significant democratic content. As Stone (1986) observes,

the real strength of the Jamaican parliamentary system is clearly to be found in the resourcefulness of the party leaders that have shown over the years a remarkable capacity for adapting to the changing moods and trends of the political community . . . Democracy will continue to grow in strength in spite of foreboding Marxist predictions about political collapse. (189)

In this view, power is not only adaptive to shifting political trends in Jamaican society but it is also exercised democratically. Similarly, when Stone turns to the analysis of popular protest, he maintains that, despite a capacity for creating 'disturbances' and some turbulence in the social order, the protests of the rebellious urban poor "do not amount to any real threat to political stability in Jamaica and have become incorporated into the turbulent process of often violent interparty contestations for power and popular support" (194).

This formulation of the character of state power and opposition to it is insightful. Yet as I will argue, it is in need of revision in two substantive ways. First, the claim that democracy is the dominant, defining feature of Jamaican politics needs to be revised to take account of contrary practices that have been in the ascendancy and indicate a decisive mutation in the political identity of the Jamaican state. Second, Stone's estimation of the significance of the politics of the rebellious urban poor must be reconsidered. Rebel cultures of the urban poor and their defiant protests have not succeeded in toppling power holders, and the radical claims of the poor on the society have often been integrated into the processes of the Jamaican political system. However, underestimating the significance of the urban poor on the Jamaican political scene, ignoring their increasing accumulation of social power, and slighting the definite compulsion they exercise on relations of power would be as unfortunate an error as overestimating the capacity of the poor to challenge power and to unilaterally determine the terms and conditions of their lives.

Notwithstanding these demurrals, Stone's analysis of state power in Jamaica is extremely persuasive for its emphasis on the adaptive and flexible character of power. The specificity of this form of power is its protean, mutating, and flexible identity. The identity of Jamaican state power goes beyond mere

214 / New Caribbean Thought

clientelism; that power is not reducible to its democratic features; nor is it to be identified with sheer authoritarianism and the unchecked use of force – all features exhibited by this state. The expression of state power in Jamaica is not shaped solely by formal institutional inheritances such as electoral activity or the rule of law. Nor, again, is it purely autocratic and brutally repressive. Rather, this form of power appears to be a flexible ensemble of all these contradictory components. State power in Jamaica can simultaneously be predatory and populist; violent and paternal; democratic and viciously abusive of human rights, depending on the exigencies of the political situation.

Moreover, unlike some forms of clientelism, which are purely prohibitive, repressive and generative of a supine dependency among the disadvantaged, political rule in Jamaica cedes significant social space, limited political influence and a palpable cultural agency to clients and supplicants from the urban lower class. Rather than being 'totalitarian' and cruelly disempowering, the strategy of power in Jamaica grafts itself onto existing structures of autonomy and patterns of community culture among the poor and permits them a modicum of independence. Despite this adaptation, power in Jamaica nonetheless feeds on, and assimilates, cultural structures of the urban poor and adapts them to its protean form of rule. In this respect the Jamaican state is parasitic rather than overtly destructive in its political relations with the poor and in its approach to existing cultural structures in urban poor communities. Unlike 'traditional' forms of power that attempt to establish a sharp divide between the forms of the culture of the people and the culture of the ruling class, parasitic rule reproduces the hegemony of the latter by appropriating aspects of popular culture and blurring, even collapsing, the boundaries between antagonistic cultural forms of the poor and those of their nemesis in the class system.

Despite the contrary implications that can be drawn from Stone's analysis of the Jamaican political order, his observation that the political system is essentially democratic conflicts with his other assessments, which called attention to the illiberal character of state power.[4] Stone's repeated claim that stable democratic rule thrives despite widespread party-sponsored electoral fraud, massive party and state violence against the poor, and ever-expanding official corruption and resort to blatantly illegality is untenable.

It may be argued that while 'electoralism' persists, albeit in a highly compromised form, and though the pluralism of the Jamaican two-party cartel remains durable, the outstanding feature of the Jamaican political order is not to be found in its democratic credentials. On the contrary, it is not so much that Jamaican democracy survives and flourishes as that a predatory state that increasingly corrupts and violates existing democratic attributes has flowered into maturity, particularly after 1972.

Rather than the factional, embattled, but thriving democracy depicted by Stone, we need to revise that perspective to emphasize that political rule in Jamaica is exercised through a mutating, opportunistic system that willy-nilly incorporates antagonistic norms and practices, several of which are hostile to the ones it publicly defends and selectively enforces. The implications of this mutation for the political identity of the system itself go beyond the fact of mere turbulence amidst democratic control. These considerations invite a reassessment that asks whether the democratic elements in the ensemble have been supplanted by predatory, violent and illegal forms of rule.

Such considerations raise the question as to whether the Jamaican state should not be more accurately identified as a violent, parasitic entity that retains some democratic features. It can be argued that violent, parasitic rule is now ascendant over liberal democratic rule. Evidence from the past thirty years confirms an erosion of democratic practices in Jamaica as the state has increasingly resorted to political victimization, violence and illegality as methods of political rule. At the same time, official corruption persists and appears to be expanding in recent years.

In the past two decades, certainly, it may be argued that the balance between official respect for democracy, on the one hand, and the resort to force and official illegalities, on the other, has been tipped decidedly in favour of the latter. This mutation into a violent parasitic state does not mean that the democratic content of the system has been totally eliminated; it does mean, however, that it has increasingly lost its vigour; that the forces that have traditionally defended democratic values are retreating from the political scene; and that this 'democratic' state has increasingly found it necessary to turn to violence, political criminality, countermarkets and other forms of official illegality. In light of these developments in a mutating political practice, descriptions of the Jamaican political system as unambiguously democratic are woefully inadequate in describing the complex realities involving the uses of power in that country over the past three decades. In contrast, therefore, to the relatively benign and optimistic interpretations of democracy in Jamaica, the mutation of the political order into the dominance of parasitic and predatory rule should be grasped.

One unmistakable feature of this state is its shifting definition of law, morality and crime. Despite an official rhetoric of 'law and order' and affirmations of allegiance to democratic values, established parties and their agents have systematically contravened law, order and democracy in the quest for political dominance. In specific conjunctures, what is regarded by the state as 'criminal', 'illegal', and 'morally right' gets redefined as acceptable or unacceptable depending on the exigencies faced by rival parties and competing interests. Thus at one moment, criminal gunmen are defended by state agents as untouchable heroic protectors of their ghetto neighbourhoods, while in a subsequent period they may be regarded as social pariahs to be hunted down and summarily killed by the state. At one moment, official morality may converge with a popular morality that demands protection from the state, while at the next moment, state morality changes and comes into conflict with notions of social justice in popular moral culture. Likewise, at one point in time, the supplicancy of the poor for material benefits and handouts is stoutly affirmed and defended by state agents as morally just; however, as political relations between antagonistic classes change, these same supplicants are denounced by their patrons as succumbing to an alleged 'freeness mentality' that identifies them, in the eyes of the state, as indolent freeloaders and moral bankrupts.

This shifting definition of propriety, morality and law extends to a variety of phenomena including land seizures by the poor, the violent conduct of the police, the enactment of special agreements to favour corporate interests, and the appropriation of public funds to meet the demands of favoured political clients at the top and bottom of the class structure. Contradictory and ambiguous official orientations on the lawfulness of these processes, and the stunting of independent criticism of such activities in the society, capture the ongoing mutation of the Jamaican state away from its nominal liberal-constitutional identity and into parasitism.

This variable definition of law, morality and crime not only confirms the adaptability of the state to changing circumstances but it also shows the capacity of the state to escape its nominal democratic political identity and its ability to develop new repertoires of control in a disintegrating and volatile environment. As the Jamaican state moves back and forth across the border between the legal and the illegal, between the shadow economy and the formal economy, and between reliance on constitutionally mandated security forces and dependence on private, party-linked militias, it becomes something new in the process.

This new identity is its parasitism. Parasitic rule in Jamaica is the form that state power takes as dominant classes attempt to extend their political power, control a fragmented society, manage dependence in the world system, and expunge rebellious challenges from below. Yet the exercise of parasitic rule is neither essentially 'for' the rich nor 'against' the poor. Parasitic rule is not based on alien models of power; nor is it so slavish to foreign interests that it ignores local political realities. Indeed, because parasitic rule explicitly draws on indigenous sociopolitical tendencies, it is typically experienced as culturally familiar, and even as representative of national-popular traditions, by those over whom it rules.

Similarly, parasitic rule does not employ state power in favour of 'order' against 'disorder'; it does not valorize legal-democratic measures over illegal-mercenary tactics in political contestations; nor is it reluctant to embrace both the rule of law and the subversion of that law in making public policy. Rather than making such distinctions as a method of establishing itself as a lawful and legitimate power, parasitic rule blurs the political boundaries between the formal-constitutional and the covert-illegal; it exploits political antinomies and employs them as repertoires to secure its own power. Parasitic rule deploys and integrates antinomies to secure its control of Jamaican society. In this respect, parasitic rule is Janus-faced in its simultaneous adoption of constitutionalism and dictatorial predation.

Likewise, parasitic rule does not expunge all forms of opposition to its sway. Dissent within the rebellious cultures of the intelligentsia and the urban poor have typically encountered the solicitude of the Jamaican state. It does so by domesticating, canalizing and feeding on elite and popular dissidence to reproduce its dominance. Thus state agents in Jamaica are solicitous of the rebellious cultures of the urban poor and the intelligentsia, and in reproducing dominant class power, they have consistently put to use the outlawry of the one and the ideological antagonism of the other.

I am sympathetic to views that assert that state agents in Jamaica are facing a crisis of political authority; that they are experiencing uncertain moral leadership and encountering a marked disequilibrium in the social relations between classes. A palpable expression of this crisis has been a growing deflation in the authority of the state. Since political independence there have been major defections from the moral community constructed by creole nationalist leaders, and defiant tributaries of the urban poor have fashioned rival structures of social power which seriously compete with state power.

These developments are evidence of erosion of the moral and cultural leadership of historically dominant classes. The widespread flaunting of laws among all classes, the incapacity of the state in the face of rising crime rates, and the increasing capacity of disadvantaged groups who seem able to 'govern' the politico-cultural identity of the society highlight a decisive shift in the social balance of power from the early postcolonial years.

But despite this threat to the existing mechanisms of control, and notwithstanding the inflation in the social power of the urban poor, the Jamaican state may not be in its last stages of decline. It retains a significant capacity for self-renewal. But this recuperation is not necessarily due to its law-abiding and democratic tendencies. Rather, the state owes its recuperative power in large part to its ubiquity in strategic social spaces; its punishing violence against challengers; its capacity for invading non-state arenas of power relations and throttling potential opposition there; and its remarkable ability to maintain elite consensus.

That the Jamaican state may not be able to curtail all political dissidence or that it seems to be increasingly overwhelmed by the maturation of economic and social crises is not necessarily confirmation that it has lost complete control of the society. While parasitic rule is certainly an index of growing social crisis and unravelling social relations, the sway of parasitic rule is not an absence of political control. Burgeoning economic crises, high levels of factionalism, increasing social violence and spiralling crime rates have done little to loosen the grip of the two-party cartel in Jamaica or to shatter elite unity. Political control has not ceased with either growing social conflicts or mounting challenges to dominant class power. On the contrary, dominant class power exerts its control in this unstable and turbulent environment. Parasitic rule may be seen, then, as a particular form of political management amidst crises in peripheral societies within the global system. Parasitism may be an unflattering form of power, and it may be inimical to the liberal sensibility. However, it should be seen as an identifiable form of managing power in contexts of underdevelopment and peripheralization in the world system.

The dilation of parasitic rule across moral boundaries and its straddling of political oppositions are evident, for example, in the approach of the parasitic state to crime. Rather than retreat from predation in the face of growing public disillusionment and cynicism about its provocation of partisan violence, and its inability to stem violent crime, predatory rule in Jamaica assimilates public concerns about crime to its own discourse and uses these concerns to reproduce its power. Hence, both the inability to curb violent crime and public knowledge of the complicit role of the state in fomenting partisan political violence become means for pursuing even more extralegal and politically suspect measures to achieve public order!

Contrary, then, to claims that see this type of state as being in its last throes of control, parasitic rule may be regarded as not so much an expression of a collapsing state, weakened by social disintegration, but as a form of state that establishes its identity in these unstable, volatile contexts and tries to turn this social and economic unravelling to political advantage. In this sense, parasitic rule should properly be regarded as a political strategy that state agents employ in contexts of underdevelopment where existing structures of control are no longer able to maintain dominant group needs.

Parasitism is a method of political management, of maintaining domination in contexts where a peripheral society is in crisis and where neither the labouring class nor propertied groups have the capacity to exert their unchallenged dominance over the state apparatus. Parasitism emerges in contexts of underdevelopment and peripheralization where state agents are pressed to forge strategies of control 'independent' of the major classes, in order to maintain social cohesion and class dominance. In these contexts, both constitutionalism and official outlawry become repertoires of power.

It should be noted, of course, that predation may be a strategy available to both powerful and subordinate groups. However, the specificity of state predation in Jamaica is that it represents an institutionalized form of political control, whose means and resources are far greater than those that most disadvantaged groups can muster. Predation by the state is also different from the predation of social groups because, unlike them, the predatory actions of the state often carry with them the imprimatur of legitimacy and the stamp of official authority.

Thus, while predation is a strategy to which contending classes may resort, state parasitism is a protean form of power in the peripheral states of the world system. Here the state not only adapts itself to the political field and absorbs social tendencies there but it moves beyond this accommodation to provoke those tendencies, moulding and exploiting their sharp antinomies as a means of political control. By extending its political grip at the nexus of political antinomies, parasitic rule brings an inventive, generic strategy to political management in the Third World.

One such antinomy over which this state exerts leverage relates to the historical clash between the social customs and material condition of the urban poor and those of the middle class and propertied groups. In Jamaica the clash of class cultures has expressed itself primarily as a struggle for equal identity evident in a conflict between the allegiance of the poor to a demeaned black nationality, and the commitment of the better-off classes to a multiracial or

Europeanist identity in the first decade of independence. In terms of material issues, the conflict between classes has been expressed largely in terms of demands by the poor for peace, jobs, social justice and a living wage, which have been denied them. In relating to these antinomies, the predatory Jamaican state has done more than merely to go on the defensive. Instead, it has adopted an active, formative approach by moulding and shaping these contradictions. The parasitic state has used both populism and patron clientelism to address these antinomies. The ability of the Jamaican parasitic state to mould contradictions is evident in its harnessing of the rebel cultures of the urban lower class to the state's agenda of domesticating, disorganizing and demobilizing the rebellious poor by means of a crucifying political partisanship.

The Jamaican state has not fled from the antagonistic, rebellious customs of the urban poor. To the contrary, it has absorbed and used them to form the rival and warring 'protonations' of the political parties. Acting much like communal factions, poor partisans of the two-party system have been slaughtering each other in political battles for more than fifty years. Party leaders in their quest for political power have actively promoted that slaughter. Hence, the antinomy between a dominant-class antagonistic defiance among tributaries of the rebellious poor, on the one hand, and the state's commitment to the reproduction of unequal class relations and a discriminatory party system, on the other, is addressed by harnessing rebel cultures of the poor to party politics. The result has been that carriers of that rebellious culture have been transformed into protonational tribal communities engaged in murderous conflicts with each other. By a risky but inventive strategy, then, parasitic rule has shaped a troubling political antinomy and shaped it into a form of social domination in Jamaica.

Punitive violence by security forces, official corruption and party solicitation of the outlawry of the poor therefore represent more than just the seamy side of Jamaican democracy. They are inventive means of social domination. But such extralegal 'political border crossings' coexist in an unstable unity with some attention to the rule of law, concern for excessive corruption, and official respect for the achievements of champions of the poor, such as Marcus Garvey and Bob Marley.

Yet, rather than a failure or debility of the Jamaican political system, these political border crossings, and moulding of antinomies, define the essential identity of the Jamaican political order. This parasitism, with its transgressive character, is the identity of the Jamaican state, and it has defined sociopolitical relations in the country for more than fifty years.

Contesting Parasitism: The Social Power of the Urban Poor

Because state parasitism is the form that power takes in Jamaica, it is not surprising that the poor have developed unique responses to it. These responses show that power is not a zero-sum relationship but, rather, a field of action nested in complex relationships involving mutual dependencies, bargaining and trade offs between protagonists. The dynamics of this relationship give to each of the protagonists a potential leverage on the other that can produce a compulsion and constraint on their actions. This constraint alters the capacity of each actor to exercise unchecked influence and limits their efforts to unilaterally secure important group needs.

I argue that the urban poor have exercised such a leverage on parasitic state power and that this compulsion on the powerful has not been exercised through an ideologically coherent, elite-led and politically organized frontal assault on the state from below. Rather, the social power of the urban poor has expressed itself through autonomous, small, persistent and cumulative acts of individual and group empowerment, both inside and outside the state apparatus. The array of these small acts of empowerment and the compulsion they exert on the society and on power holders are referred to here as the social power of the urban poor.

As the previous discussion of parasitic rule has shown, this form of power is simultaneously repressive and solicitous in its relations with the poor. It is not surprising, therefore, that the poor exhibit contradictory responses to it: complicitly engaged with power and defiantly rejecting its predation. Despite being ensnared in the web of parasitic rule, mobilized contingents of the urban poor have nonetheless accumulated significant social power and have used it to alter power relations.

This capacity for compulsion has allowed tributaries of the urban poor, particularly the lumpenproletariat, to influence the politics of the parasitic state. It has permitted them to jockey with the powerful for political spoils; to constrain policy choices of state agents; to bargain with them for benefits; to contest ideological efforts to fully integrate them into the bourgeois-moral community fashioned by creole nationalist leaders; and to exert a pervasive influence on the cultural identity of Jamaican society. This accumulation of social power by contingents of the urban poor since the late 1950s has not only entailed an alteration in the balance of power between classes but it has also produced a reshaping of the social identity of the urban lower class, stimulating in its members a lively consciousness of social inequality and a potent sense of their capacity to challenge the state.

This insistence on the agency and political relevance of a historically disadvantaged group in Jamaica need not romanticize them. Acknowledging their leverage on power only highlights the fact that the poor are not marionettes in the hands of the powerful, and they are not a powerless group, merely to be moulded and manipulated by rulers. It is apparent that the poor are capable of fighting back in their own way, and that they at times may even capture the powerful in a shifting and a complex relationship of mutual dependence and antagonism.

Recognizing this display of social power does not therefore imply that the urban poor hold advanced political views, have a coherent social project, or possess a sophisticated perspective of either the structure of domination or of the outlines of an alternative society. A few socially conscious members and contingents from the ranks of the poor may indeed exhibit this capacity as a function of the spontaneous consciousness of the group. But to berate the poor for lacking attributes usually associated with the intellectual class is to demand that downtrodden groups exhibit an ideological coherence not seen even among more advantaged members of Jamaican society.

The political behaviour of the poor therefore shows a similar complication and heterogeneity evident among other groups. Thus, while some contingents of the urban poor may respond enthusiastically to populist regimes and their redistributionist policies, others from their ranks rally, just as fervently, to the appeals of conservative, procapitalist parties that oppose policies that make levies on propertied groups. The claim here is not that the poor are agents with an uncomplicated outlook on power or that they possess a capacity to represent their needs through self-organization. Rather, the concern here is that these renegade forms of popular social action are politically relevant.

Our perspective is therefore not unmindful of the deeply conflicted moral and social outlook of the urban poor. Nor am I unaware of the severe handicaps that limit the poor and downtrodden in urban Jamaica. Commentators on their plight rightly call our attention to their lack of traditional political resources, absence of bureaucratic know-how and exclusion from official networks of political influence. As one observer remarked of the Jamaican poor:

[t]he average citizen in most communities lacks the information, the organizational connection, the resources and the necessary channels of representation to solve simple problems, to pressure the bureaucracy into conceding just demands, to ensure that he or

she is not taken advantage of by more privilege [*sic*] interests, and to provide a vehicle by which individuals with common problems can put minds and hands together to work them out rather than await the never never promises of politicians. (Stone 1978: 10)

Such handicaps are a real hindrance to the ability of the urban poor to alter their circumstances, and class and social divisions within this group aggravate these obstacles.

These debilities are made worse by contradictory tendencies within an uneven popular moral culture. That moral culture reflects the often volatile social relations in which the socially mobilized poor are enmeshed and exhibits the contradictory customs of the diverse strata that make up the ranks of the urban poor. The latter include myriad categories, and while it is possible to identify several strata and categories of the urban poor, as in the description of the five important strata below, it should be remembered that social reality is more complex, with its overlapping social categories, protean occupational identities, and dynamic moral cultures defined as much by relations of culture as by relations of production.

Within the ranks of Jamaica's unemployed urban poor are the following:

1. Those who stoutly reject what they regard as the 'slave wages' paid to the poor, and who turn to petty hustling, street trading and other self-supporting entrepreneurial pursuits as various as artinsanry, street vending and popular singing.
2. Those who fall into the ranks of the militant lumpenproletariat and who turn to crime and predation, drug dealing and social banditry.
3. Those who attach themselves to the political apparatus to become its fanatical supporters, its militia members, 'political badmen', constituency enforcers and nibbling supplicants of the state's largesse.
4. That broad strata of the striving, working poor, who see themselves as representing the law-abiding, 'respectable poor' with aspirations of upward mobility, and ambitions for self and community recovery.
5. That contingent within the lowest rungs of the working poor who retain a tenuous attachment to the wage nexus. Within this contingent are the barmaids, menial workers in the service sector, those hiring themselves out as domestics, gardeners, casual labourers and others working in myriad jobs for which it was necessary to pass a law establishing a national minimum wage.

Given this heterogeneous social composition, complex location within the production process and contradictory relationship to political power, the identity of a moral culture among the urban poor is necessarily complicated. It is well known, for example, that defiant antisystem sensibilities compete with the complicit involvement of the urban poor with predatory power. The group also exhibits norms, both law abiding and outlaw in character, that link them to a wider set of social values in Jamaican society. Communal sentiments and norms of mutuality within the ranks of the poor are articulated with powerful tendencies toward social cannibalism and with beggar-thy-neighbour strategies, particularly in times of extreme need. Though the poor may be badly victimized by parasitic rule, many within their ranks have nonetheless preyed on their kith and kin in the urban ghetto.

Alternatively, socially militant strata of the poor using renegade tactics have directed their hostility against predatory power. Such acts of defiance have won sympathy from other contingents of the poor who morally underwrite these acts of 'uncivil' anti-dominant-class outlawry. Alienation, anger and deep frustration with the conditions of their lives cause many among the poor to lend tacit and active moral support to the defiant ones among them.

Still, it should be remembered that when this antisystem alienation collapses into violent crime, murder and theft from the hardworking poor, it might also elicit harsh retaliation and biting moral disapproval. Many among the poor, especially the 'respectable' and working strata, are outraged by this criminal behaviour, are embarrassed by its occurrence within their community and unqualifiedly reject the abandonment of what is seen as a violation of an older moral standard among the community of the poor.

These scandalized contingents of the urban poor find such outlaw structures of defiance 'disgraceful', and regard them as a transgression of an older community standard of dignity that is marked by hard work, uplift and sacrifice. These contingents of the poor reject the criminal extremism of their marauding peers; they are threatened by it and inveigh, as militantly as their social betters, against a descent into rapacious and anomic behaviours that target hapless members of the society, whether poor or well to do.

These contrasting dispositions highlight the protean nature of popular moral culture with its simultaneous possession of defiant, opposition practices and restraining moral sensibilities borrowed from a wider system of shared values in Jamaican society. These dispositions indicate not only that the poor are capable of resorting to crimes against each other and their social betters but that they are not immune to the wider network of norms and values in Jamaica. This network of values has become increasingly complex since the 1970s and has been characterized by an erosion of the disciplinary moral leadership of creole nationalists and their allies, and by the expansion of predation, aggressive violence and rejection of public authority among all groups.

It is not surprising, therefore, that the moral culture of the urban poor reflects tendencies within this shared political culture. That culture includes: aggressive personal dispositions and resort to violence as a means of resolving disputes and securing advantages; intense individualism and self-seeking; status consciousness and preoccupation with consumer materialism as measures of achievement and social recognition; a pragmatic orientation to political life with 'necessity' and short-run advantage as operative principles rather than any sustained commitment to radical politics or to utopian ideologies; and a deeply ambiguous disposition toward black consciousness as the basis for the civilization-identity of the Jamaican people.

Thus, contrary to views that hold that the social actions and moral sensibility of the rebellious poor are outside the pale of Jamaican culture, these wider traditions in which the poor participate show that what the rebellious poor do politically ought not to be regarded as moral aberrations inflicted upon a 'civilized' society by a criminal, barbaric class. Rather, much of what the rebellious poor do, and the moral sentiments they exhibit, should be regarded, in part, as expressions of the banal, 'everyday' attributes of a widely shared social sensibility in late twentieth century Jamaica.

Notwithstanding these shared traditions, the customs of the urban poor, and the politics of this group are not all identical to those of other social classes. Distinctive group experiences, peculiar to the urban poor, do separate them from other classes and give their customs a specificity of their own. The role of the dispossessed group in production, and their material circumstances and social experiences, inform their political dispositions and moral sensibilities, setting the urban poor apart from other classes and strata within the Jamaican social structure.

Part of the distinctive social identity of the urban poor is closely related to their tenuous relationship to the system of production and to its inability to provide employment for job seekers from the poorer classes. A historic and persisting feature of the Jamaican economy has been the chronic unemployment and underemployment of urban unskilled labour and the casualization of these castaways from the ranks of the employed labour force. Joblessness, economic insecurity and poverty have been the lot of generations of the urban poor, and this condition of chronic economic deprivation and marginality is shared by few other classes in the urban milieu.

Nor do the more advantaged groups participate in the acute experience of being unhoused in urban Jamaica. While many among the urban poor do find shelter with modern facilities and public amenities, the lot of the vast majority of the poor is one of homelessness, lack of privacy and inadequate shelter. Where better-off social classes can speak meaningfully of living in 'homes', the poorer urban classes have long been housed in decrepit, substandard dwellings, in crowded tenement yards and in baleful shanty towns. The absence in many of the poorest slums of public amenities, such as piped water, electricity, modern sewage and drainage systems, makes these areas not only a hazard to the health of residents but also identifies such slums as breeding grounds of resentment and sites of social desperation.

The deprived material conditions in which the poor live, and the social relations that flow from being poor, unemployed and black in a race- and class-conscious society, have inevitably spawned rebellious social dispositions and antagonistic moral responses far more bitter among the urban poor than among other deprived groups. In Jamaica the unequal and discriminatory social relations provoke such acute responses. Among the most notorious of these are the following:

1. The predatory reach of the state into poor communities where residents become captive populations confined to constituencies and 'protected' by party-linked militias.
2. Political victimization and denial of work and benefits to the poor on the basis of their political affiliation.
3. Imposition of humiliating social stigmas and the persistence of economic discrimination by employers on the basis of class, status and residence.
4. The targeting of rebellious contingents of the urban poor for harsh state violence, cultural inferiorization, discriminatory application of penal codes and even summary executions by security forces.
5. The persistent articulation of a social ideology that identifies the unemployed among the urban poor as a debased, uncivilized and criminal class because of their poverty, rebelliousness, low social status and cultural orientations.

Alienated Cultures of the Urban Poor and the Predicament of the Parasitic State

Over the years, these unequal relations and other social determinants have provoked hostility among the poor, producing in them a rebellious sensibility.

Commentators who have remarked, for example, on the pioneering dissident role and importance of the Rastafarians in Jamaica have captured an important expression of this defiance. Less attention has been given, however, to other contingents of the poor, to their contribution to the social power of the group, or to the social linkages and networks of influence within the heterogeneous 'society of the poor' in urban Jamaica.

This society has spawned unique customs and practices, networks of influence, distinct repertoires of resistance, and a pantheon of heroic figures. The society of the urban poor has thrown up identifiable, alienated and socially mobilized contingents who share, in different degrees, relations of conflict and cooperation with the parasitic state and with a culturally inferiorizing society. The most notable among these alienated and socially mobilized contingents are

1. Legendary political sentries in poor communities who are armed, connected to and shielded by rival political parties.
2. Heroic 'Robin Hood' figures with primitive political agendas for subverting the state through hit-and-run tactics.
3. A self-helping entrepreneurial stratum, defiantly assertive of its right to dignity and protective of its niche in urban petty trading and street vending.
4. A picaresque lumpenproletariat subsisting on petty crime, predation, and engaging in opportunistic forays into politics during volatile periods of social conflict.
5. Bandit gangs and their flamboyant leaders thriving on the expansion of the gun, drug and contraband trade, and using part of the largesse from crime as bases of patronage, power and influence in poor communities.
6. Contingents of jobless youth and allied politicized strata in ghetto communities who resort to spontaneous political demonstrations, riotous acts and recurrent bids for social respect, personal dignity, and autonomy from parasitic state power and a culturally dismissive society.
7. Outriders of cultural defiance and moral tribunes of the urban poor whose ideological appeals through popular song, music and oral-kinetic dramaturgy critique power and rally the poor to subvert the moral grip of the society, while urging them to demand the right to equal identity, social justice and freedom to enjoy the aesthetic pleasures of a nonbourgeois identity.

As the foregoing distinctions imply, the social identity of these important contingents of the mobilized poor is powerfully influenced by the group's insertion in complex political, economic and cultural relations. Such ties typically involve unequal relations of power, which impel the poor to sometimes adopt defensive postures of self-protection and self-help.

But the urban poor are also involved in a process of cultural self-construction. The seven contingents identified above have been decisive in the process of the cultural self-formation of the alienated and socially mobilized urban poor. These contingents have not only been a defiant vanguard, often opposed to the authority of the parasitic state, but they have also been pacesetters in establishing the political and moral foundations for an oppositional political culture among the urban poor. Indeed, they have been the leading agents of an anti-dominant-class morality evident among the poor. These tributaries have helped fashion rival structures of power; developed models of community rallying based on natal community loyalty; carried out seizures of strategic social spaces; and established the dramaturgic and aesthetic bases of a dissident cultural consciousness.

These leading forces within urban rebel cultures in Jamaica have, over the years, provided the ranks of the poor with a compelling politico-cultural tutelage. This pedagogy by the poor on behalf of those who are 'politically poor' provides repertoires for acquiring a dissident consciousness; it offers apprenticeships in social outlawry and gives lessons in how to win social respect and constrain politicians. These tribunes issue summonses for recruits to join the oppositional moral community; they call on the poor to share in solidarities and commitments; and they demand allegiance to a martial, combative social identity.

In the aftermath of the enervation of the Rastafarian movement of the 1960s, and in the wake of the decline of elite radicalism in the 1980s, these alienated cultures of the urban poor, with their antisystem, 'uncivil', outlaw dispositions, have assumed the task of social opposition to persistent state predation. Their rejection of the civilized identity proffered by creole nationalists; their recurrent demands for work and social respect; their bold bids for social justice and peace in their communities; as well as their complicit involvement with predatory power all highlight the agony and dilemmas of the urban poor.

Their dilemma arises from the fact that urban dispossessed groups are 'politically poor' in terms of traditional resources and must turn to alternative means to achieve political influence. Socially marginalized and deficient in the resources held by better-off groups, the urban poor have developed compensatory repertoires of defiance whose combination produced, over time, an increase in their social power. As the foregoing has shown, that power is evident in the fluorescence of independent initiatives; in the checkmating of state strategies; in seizures of strategic social spaces; and in the near-monopoly of a small vanguard over definitions of urban lower class identities. This social power of the urban poor is now increasingly, if reluctantly, being recognized.

The predicament of the poor, however, is that their status as social outcasts acts as a constraint on their capacity to transcend stigmas assigned to a downtrodden group. This status of the mobilized poor as social pariahs has been both the source of a remarkable inventiveness and a condition for an equally stunning group suppression and collective immolation.

Moreover, because of a political imagination that has seemingly linked middle and upper class social power with unredeemable corruption, political venality and chronic victimization of the poor, political defiance within these mobilized tributaries of the poor has come to assume a problematic form: rebellious outlawry, deep suspicion of middle class politics and an abiding rejection of bourgeois norms of respectability.

In these terms, it is apparent that the social power of the poor is contradictory and ambiguous. In Jamaica's predatory, violent and levy-imposing social environment, forms of subordinate-class social power have become bases of group autonomy, honour and identity. At the same time, however, the context of predation, and the conflictual relations spawned by it have also provoked responses that hobble the poor, made them into complicit challengers to power and induced in them self-destructive cultural reflexes.

Put in other terms, the predicament of the mobilized urban poor is that the very forms of their social power, which act as powerful constraints on dominant groups, are themselves bases of subordinate group cannibalism and self-suppression. Their social power has altered the dynamics of power relations, but not always in ways that permit the urban poor to unilaterally dictate outcomes to the power holders. Paradoxically, then, the urban lower class – the most rebellious and feared social stratum in postcolonial Jamaica and nemesis of the powerful – finds itself in a checkmated situation, anchored in the very marginality that gave it a purchase on power.

Such debilities of the poor are matched, however, by predicaments of the predatory state. As this state absorbs social contradictions and becomes both a leading agent in the unravelling of social relations as well as an agent of cohesion, it too is beset by its own contradictions. The predicament of the predatory Jamaican state is that the measures that secure its dominance and sustain the cohesion of the society – clientelist party rule, punitive violence and elite unity – become the very sources that threaten the erosion of its power. As the parasitic state and its agents move into the shadow economy, violate democratic practices with impunity, protect fearsome gunmen, and foment a crucifying political violence in which the poor become cannon fodder and the well-to-do fear for their physical safety from violence and crime, a legitimization crisis ensues and state agents' hold on power become increasingly tenuous.

Recurrent attempts to surmount this dilemma, however, seem only to compound the problem. Repeat announcements of harsh crime eradication programmes appear ineffective as they provoke party factionalism, distress civil libertarians, and alienate the poor whose neighbourhoods become the targets in combating crime and political violence. Similarly, official denials of state involvement in political violence and ties to political gunmen and the parties' subsequent signing of peace truces to quell violence earn politicians the cynicism of the poor and the unease of middle class and corporate backers of the state. In both instances the generic strategy of combining both 'order' and 'disorder' entangle the state in continued predicaments. The loss of authority by the state requires measures to arrest this loss. However, such measures to stem the state's weakening hold over economic processes and social relations, while crucial to the reproduction of parasitic power, are themselves sources of hegemonic decline.

Thus, on the one hand, the perception of growing disorder and unravelling of social relations produced by this strategy impel the state to devise even bolder strategies involving risky political border crossings. On the other hand, these measures, in all their apparent contradiction, provoke dominant-class disgust with what appears to be a foundering state that cannot maintain order, achieve legitimacy or solve economic problems. In recent years, this flailing, often panic-ridden, use of force, the incapacity of the state to redress urgent economic problems, and the parties' resort to convenient pacts of peace to maintain class unity disclose both the durability and the crisis of the parasitic state.

Notes

1. For a discussion of this dialectic see, for example, Scott 1985 and Bayart 1993.
2. For a discussion of the political significance of new social movements in the Third World, see Amin 1993.
3. For a review of political domination in Africa see Fatton 1992.
4. Stone's political journalism in the *Daily Gleaner* in the 1970s and 1980s typically called attention to the violent and undemocratic character of the Jamaican state.

References

Amin, Samir. 1993. "Social movements at the periphery". In *New Social Movements in the South,* edited by P. Wignaraja. Atlantic Highlands, NJ: Zed Books.

Bayart, Jean-Francois. 1993. *The State in Africa.* New York: Longman.

Cooper, Carolyn. 1994. *Noises in the Blood.* New York: Heinemann.

Crummey, Donald. 1986. *Banditry, Rebellion and Social Protest in Africa.* London: Heinemann.

Fatton, Robert Jr. 1992. *Predatory Rule: State and Civil Society in Africa.* Boulder: Lynne Rienner.

Scott, James C. 1985. *Weapons of the Weak.* New Haven: Yale University Press.

Stone, Carl. 1978. "Community councils". *Daily Gleaner,* 6 December.

Stone, Carl. 1986. *Class, State, and Democracy in Jamaica.* New York: Praeger.

Wignaraja, Ponna, ed. 1993. *New Social Movements in the South.* Atlantic Highlands, NJ: Zed Books.

10

The Emergence of a Caribbean Iconography in the Evolution of Identity

PATRICIA MOHAMMED

The first illustrations in this essay are photographs of painted imagery found in 1998 on the walls of two buildings in Jamaica.[1] Figure 10.1, titled for my convenience *World's End*, was taken from the wall of Dr Ian Sangster's brewery in Gordon Town, Jamaica, on a winding road that leads up to Blue Mountain. The brewery is one of the sites to which bus tours of tourists are taken each week to sample and purchase the various liquor products produced by Sangster. Figure 10.2, titled *Rastaman Lion,* was photographed from the wall of a small shop selling liquor and groceries in Great Bay, St Elizabeth, a little fishing village on the south coast of Jamaica. There is no thoroughfare through Great Bay. This little shop was off the main road, on a narrow, picturesque side street that led to the dead end of the village. Who painted these scenes is not important here. What is interesting is that they represent the shared sensibility of the painters, and those who commissioned them, about an image of Jamaica, its political and social history, its people and their landscape.

World's End, which was probably commissioned by Sangster, represents a mood or idea of Jamaica which is sold in his products – as described on the bottle of one of these: "An exotic blend of the finest aged golden rum and smooth dairy cream, creating a magical taste of the Caribbean." Sangster is a

Figure 10.1 *World's End*

Scotsman, a trained scientist, who settled in Jamaica and embarked on the manufacture of a range of liquor, using Jamaican produce. The range is successfully marketed worldwide and is of some fame in Jamaica itself, both for its packaging and its quality. What is remarkable about this range is that the packaging of the product draws on the ideas of a colonized eighteenth and nineteenth century Jamaica, as does the illustration *World's End*, one of two in a similar genre that decorate the outer wall of the shop in which the products are sold. In *World's End*, two dark chocolate-skinned ladies sit on the side of a country road, selling their goods to passers-by. The colours of their dresses, their baskets, the tree trunks and foliage are rich and vibrant, the contrasting white on black against the bodies of the women, within a oval-shaped simulated rope frame, replicating, if you like, the delicate European miniature on the rude walls of a weather-exposed building. This image does not interrupt an ongoing narrative of Jamaica's history. It is a pastoral extract, an idyllic setting displaying the exotic image of a colonized peoples.[2]

The second image, *Rastaman Lion*, is a twentieth century masculine image, a political shifting of lens. If you hypothetically place a male instead of one of the female figures in *World's End* and contrast this mental image of a black man in the quasi–nineteenth century illustration with the one presented on the rudely constructed walls of this village shop, they are separated by

Figure 10.2 *Rastaman Lion,* Ras Clarence 'Guilty' Williams, Great Bay, Jamaica

revolutions of both thought and deed. *Rastaman Lion* represents the Con-
quering Lion of Judah, the result of Garveyism of the 1920s and 1930s, the
later Rastafarianism of the 1950s and 1960s, and the musical glamour and
messages of Bob Marley and Peter Tosh in the 1970s, a new invention of the
black Caribbean male removed from slavery and metaphorically reinvented.
The new image resonates with a pan-African one – the lion, the master of the
jungle, who controls and is in control, both of his tribe and his space. This
totemic image of human head on animal body is an old and powerful one, and
a particularly relevant one for a people who were wrested out of Africa. The
Sphinx of Egypt is perhaps one of the most well known and widely reproduced
images in the world today. The hair, a biblical symbol of Samson-like strength,
is superimposed onto the magnificent mane of the lion, thus retaining a shared
symbol of patriarchy while identifying a sign of otherness. The symbolic
importance of the hair and its links to Africa are substantiated in the work of
both Warner-Lewis (1993) and Chevannes (1995). The reshaping of the image
of masculinity has been a necessary one for black masculinity damaged by the
enslavement of African peoples outside of the African continent. This perhaps
explains its appeal to black men, not only in Jamaica but elsewhere.

Where are such images derived from? How much are we involved in the fashioning of these images that represent us? Who fashions them and to what purpose? How have they evolved over time, and what do they represent to the people who absorb them? What is the relationship between the image produced and reproduced over time and the visual icon it begins to represent of the place and the people of a society? How is all of this linked to the evolution of identities – how we think of and define ourselves in relation to others?

Identity is constructed in relative terms and,[3] in general, in hierarchical ones. We determine masculinity in opposition to femininity, ethnic/racial identity both in relation and in opposition to other groups. Class identities are configured as specific behaviours of upper against lower, bourgeois against proletariat, and the sum of these national or regional identities are valorized in relation and in opposition to other societies and other cultures. Identities are not only conveyed through verbal declarations and polemics. They are continuously constructed through the mental and visual images we conceive and produce. We either reinforce recurrent imagery, if it is representative of common perceptions or beliefs, or we reconfigure it to suit the political and social moment. For each individual or group within a society, this process is an ongoing one – the process itself dependent on the circumstances that allow the creation of new identities. At the same time, the sum of individual or group identities cumulates to a collective ensemble, a set of identities that describe or define a geographical space, or the peoples within it, at a particular historical moment. Some of these images may be competing ones because they are being presented by different groups with varied life experiences and therefore different mental images of the same society.

The definition of self or society is often, if not always, linked to a similar process taking place in the mind of the Other. For instance, with respect to gender identity, masculinity is constructed and reconstructed in relation to other masculinities and in relation to and opposition from femininity. Nationalist or regional identification also follows a parallel logic. The impact of Europe 'discovering and creating' a new world of the Americas was the subject of intense fascination for European scholars and artists. That this discovery had repercussions within Europe, and the way it continued and continues to define itself in relation to the Americas, has traditionally received less attention. In *The Old World and the New 1492–1650*, J.H. Elliot (1970) fractures the universalizing Eurocentric conception of history and examines instead the impact of the discovery of the 'New World' on Europe itself. Elliot concludes that "The attempt of one society to comprehend another, inevitably forces it to reappraise itself" (14). An understanding of identity creation, through any medium, forces an interrogation of oneself in relation to how one is perceived by others, consequently sharpening the lens of how one defines oneself.

This chapter is deliberately exploratory, and extremely selective in its approach, at this formative stage of research. It attempts several related tasks and the political project that it aims at is fuelled by several concerns. At this point, it is a series of ideas cobbled together with inconclusive findings and apparent disconnections. The approach is to first find a grammar through which visual imagery can be interrogated in the Caribbean, thus directly and indirectly contributing to the discourse of art history in the Caribbean.[4] This grammar includes a decoding of the visual alongside the historical and social text – an intertextuality that is itself problematic in the study of iconography. On the one hand, the technical conventions of an art form, and the aesthetics thus derived, have an internal integrity (Bucher 1981). On the other, the narrative function of the art employs the image as its base and thus allows for interrogation by the viewer or explanation by its creator. The idea of a visual grammar brings to mind that words and the messages they convey have developed along parallel lines in the creation of identity, with language providing the medium through which the visual is being interpreted. There is an ongoing sense in which the project of linguistic discovery has been continuously undertaken through literary fiction and linguistic studies in the Caribbean, some examples being J.J. Thomas's *The Theory and Practice of Creole Grammar* (first published in 1869) and Richard Allsopp's recently published *Dictionary of Caribbean English Usage* (1996).[5] There has also been a visual representation at work, the narrative of which remains to be decoded.

In suggesting that there is an emerging set of symbols, I want to speculate that these represent a Caribbean iconography that contains external messages and internal contestations of society, culture, nation state, ethnicity, masculinity and femininity – in short, the bases of identity creation of an evolving history of the Caribbean. That this history is a relatively young one must be appreciated. Our visual and literary imagery are recent compared to those found in ancient Greek mythology. For instance, in *Lysistrata,* written by Aristophanes (*c.* 450–*c.* 385 BC), a contemporary feminist theme of women sexually denying themselves to their husbands until they make peace was examined in Greek drama. Plays such as this provide thematic confluences with contemporary drama. In contrast, in "Tropic Zone" Derek Walcott (1984) remarks somewhat cynically on the youthfulness of our memories in the Caribbean: "Whenever a thought can go back seventy years, / there is hope for tradition in these tropical zones" (v). This is not to say that the subterranean layers of our cultures and the marked absence of artefacts or visual imagery do not invite excavation. In a historical examination of the evolution of art in Britain, Andrew Graham-Dixon (1996) argues: "Nothing tells us more about British culture than the gaping holes punched into the fabric of the past by those radical, muscular acts of censorship and abolition which lie at the heart of the history of British art" (14). His reference was to the violence of iconoclastic acts of destruction brought on by the radical leaders of the new Protestant church from 1534 who were "determined opponents of all Roman Catholic rituals and imagery" (16).[6] A similar act of vandalism from various quarters was wrought in the emergent Caribbean culture. Colonization did not facilitate or encourage the indigenous art forms, which were largely eradicated, making way for the European lens through which the societies were looked at and, consequently, the way in which the immigrant groups who comprised the society began to look at themselves.[7] The truth is also that these layers are to be uncovered in the cultural graveyards of the societies from which many contemporary Caribbean peoples have themselves been derived or in those of their colonizers.

In investigating a history that spans roughly five hundred years, I limit my own inquiry to the medium of painting, focusing specifically on the work of a few painters from the eighteenth century onwards. This is not to negate the value and importance of the sculpture, artefacts and domestic objects of the pre-Hispanic and later centuries of discovery and colonization in the shaping of iconography. Of the latter, Veerle Poupeye (1998) has pointed out that "these utilitarian art forms are telling – the Jamaican pottery tradition that originated on the plantations, for instance, combines Taino, West African, Spanish and English influences and represents a graphic record of the island's complex cultural history" (29). The larger project, which this short essay merely introduces, anticipates the examination of the evidence that remains of such artefacts to assess their importance and value in informing present-day aesthetics. I focus here on the medium of painting as it is perhaps more accessible as a symbolic form and because it lends itself to reproduction in other media, for example, in advertising and labelling of products, thus enhancing its symbolic importance in identity creation. Perhaps the same can be attributed to the mass of tourist art produced in the region, a product of individual creativity as much as it is stimulated by the demand for such art.

A project such as this requires not only an explanation of its parameters but some of the reasons for undertaking such a task. It presents a challenge to historians, as we continue to write history, to employ such images as do exist more pertinently and, in doing so, to examine how they also inform our mental images of ourselves as we reinvent the history of Caribbean society. James Walvin (1996) has pointed out, for instance, that a host of graphic images of slave sufferings drawn by William Blake and later by William Turner and others, recur in modern scholarship "as support for a textual argument. Yet such images were themselves politically shaped and directed." Walvin observes that it is not the incorrectness of the image that is being called into question, rather that they "form a corpus of historical data which is itself disputed ground" (5). The paintings and sketches that have described the Caribbean in the eighteenth and nineteenth centuries have, in general, been used unproblematically. In examining the image, the disputed terrain of artistic production in terms of style, purpose for painting, the artist's own sentiments as well as the political concerns that led to the emergence of the artistic text in the period also need to be clearly established.[8]

The history of the West Indies or the Caribbean has unfolded through orthodox historiography as a history of discovery, colonization and settlement, a record of legendary abuses and forms of oppression, comprising constitutional and political reforms, all circumscribed by the economic demands of warring imperial nations and declining agricultural and industrial ventures. Social history added names and personalities to the characters who made this history also one of resistance, revolution and change. Women's history has been added to this recovery of invisible players in historical passages. More recently, the task of engendering history has been tallied to the ongoing list of challenges to historiography. Engendering history can take, and has obviously taken, many forms.

In the Caribbean and elsewhere, there is at present a valuable body of historical writing on gender.[9] One of the major problems of engendering history is a methodological one, in the sense that the data on gender tends to be more elusive. Gender recurs in history as metaphor rather than as concrete causality or fact. It is unrealistic to expect the records of the distant past to render up material that is gender sensitive. The present consciousness of gender inequality that has come into being now did not inform the past recorders of events. The visual recorders of events or landscapes, however, were not indifferent to the people who made or inhabited these. The idea of examining the meaning of gender through painting occurred to me several years ago when I saw the exhibition of Agostino Brunias's paintings on loan to the Barbados Museum, many of which contained images of men and women. "These pictures of . . . faces are small miracles, like stills snipped from a lost film of the past. Although they seem to speak in a whisper they are revolutionary. They teach a new and radical way of seeing" (Graham-Dixon 1996: 63). Finally, the primary political aim of this project is to focus new lenses on the Caribbean and thus to find new ways of seeing, writing and thinking about the evolution of the Caribbean.

Invention of the Caribbean in the New World: Views from Without

Peter Hulme's book *Colonial Encounters* (1986) provides a useful preface to a visual definition and interpretation of Caribbean iconography. Hulme draws on visual representations where these are available, but he concentrates on a textual analysis of myths that have emerged and fed the discourse of the colonial encounter between the Old World and the new prior to 1796. Several of these myths grafted on to reality have contributed immensely to the perception of the Caribbean as it is interpreted to this day. Another body of work, several hundred copperplate engravings, illustrating the Europeans' Great Voyages of discovery were published between 1590 and 1634 by the de Bry family. According to Bucher (1981), these illustrated texts

relate the conquest of the Americas from the venture of Columbus to the English and Dutch settlements in the early seventeenth century. The illustrations offered, then, a kind of pictorial reportage on the New World and its inhabitants to the Europeans, as well as the eventful story of the changing relations between the conquerors and the Amerindians and among the invaders themselves (English, French, Spanish, Dutch and so forth). (xiii)

I draw on both these impressive bodies of research and others culled from various texts in order to demonstrate the interpretation of the Americas before such images were actually produced from within.

Mythological interpretations derived from classic literary imagery are as compelling, if not more so, than the early visual images. The encounters between Columbus and the Caribs, and the association of Caribs as cannibals or eaters of human flesh, lead to the mythological depiction of the early Caribbean as savage territory to be civilized by a more highly developed culture. The construction of the temperament and customs of the indigenous peoples of the Caribbean as tribal opposites leads naturally to the notion that one is a more deadly and intrusive species – the Caribs, who are being challenged by the civilized Old World colonizers, having themselves appropriated the lands forcibly from the 'peaceful' Arawaks. The fictional characters of Shakespeare's *Tempest* – Prospero, Caliban and Miranda – are never fully located in the Caribbean but the association of the incident appears to have been based on reports of a shipwreck in the uninhabited island of Bermuda.[10] In *The Tempest* itself, the "Bermoothes" describes the fierce winds that rage and cause the tempest. The result of this encounter is that the seafaring European comes into contact with the native, but there is no recognition of Caliban's claim to original sovereignty: "This island's mine, by Sycorax my mother which thou taks't from me." His name is an anagram of and thus locates him near enough to the 'Cannibal'. He is depicted as a grotesque, untrustworthy and savage character who can be easily enslaved. For Prospero, the island becomes "merely an interlude, a neutral ground between extirpation and resumption of power" (Hulme 1986: 124), while both Caliban and Ariel, the original inhabitants, are servants to the will of the newcomers.

Robinson Crusoe and Man Friday reinforce the original myth of human-eating savages, Friday being the character saved and taught by the shipwrecked Crusoe. Another reading of this text is important here. Robinson Crusoe is a product of the Enlightenment and the novel itself, written from the point of view of first-person narrator, embodies the values and ideas that evolved in European civilization during the period. The process of 'enlightenment' also required that knowledge be recorded and categorized, so there was great curiosity about the customs and habits of other lands and the need to record the 'peculiar' customs of others. Paintings also became a means by which people, customs and habits were recorded. Crusoe establishes his character in relation to the speechlessness of Friday (Descartes's "*Cogito, ergo sum*"), thereby privileging immediately one culture over the other. Crusoe is a temporary interloper, economic necessity forces him to remain and consolidate, economic individualism drives his purpose – "I came, I saw, I conquered" – and he moves on, having civilized his Man Friday, the original butler and manservant of the islands.

A less well-known myth is that of Inkle and Yarico, the archetypal love story of the Caribbean: the native girl who 'succours' the shipwrecked Englishman, Inkle. A period of mutual love obtains, when he is dependent on her for survival on the island. He is rescued by an English ship and she travels with him from her island for he promises a continued love story in his country. Returning to English territory, Inkle realizes that he has lost both time and money during

Figure 10.3: *America, c.* 1600, engraving by Jan van de Straat

his stay with Yarico and so sells her into slavery to recover his losses, despite the fact that she carries his child.

These myths and original tales are founded on part truth and part fiction, no doubt, but more crucial for my purposes here is that these encounters between the fifteenth and eighteenth centuries, and the evolution of these myths, create a much more deep-rooted and convenient fiction and ideology. There is a taken-for-grantedness about the power relations between the discoverer and the discovered, an assumption of nonexistence before discovery, and an implicit belief in the superiority of the finder.

Some visual images support these messages of cannibalism or naivete, others expand the contradiction and complexity of the early encounter between the Old World and the new. One early image, an engraving by Jan van de Straat (Stradanus) entitled *America, circa* 1600 (Figure 10.3), consistent with the existing graphic conventions, allegorizes the new continent as a woman. She is unclothed, primitive, while the conqueror, male by definition, approaches with the symbol of invention in his left hand and the flag, which when planted claims ownership of the territory and its peoples. The sexual dimension of the encounter with Vespucci Amerigo is both visually and linguistically explicit according to Hulme's (1986) reading of the illustration, her invitation being

Bucher 1981: plate 6

Figure 10.4 *Zemi worship among the Arawak of Hispaniola,* illustration
from de Bry's *Great Voyages* published between 1590 and 1634

a open outstretched hand to the newcomer, while the staff and flagpole can no
doubt be interpreted as the metaphoric masculinity of the conqueror.

In the sixteenth century, when the de Bry series on the Great Voyages was
published, the images were based on drawings by talented artists, some of
whom had been attached to expeditions as cartographers. Theodor de Bry drew
on the originals to produce the copperplate engravings. Bucher explains that
although some of the material depicted in the copperplate engravings was
faithful to the interpretations of the original artists, De Bry appears to have
taken artistic licence with the original interpretations of text and images by
those who had travelled. Part 4 of these illustrations, *Benzoni's Voyages to the
Spanish Colonies* (1594), and part 5, *Epic of the Conquistadors,* comprise a total
of sixty-one plates, each of them depicting various scenes of conquest or notable
events, such as *Forth voyage of Columbus, battle in Jamaica against Francisco
Poraz,* or one that is illustrated in Bucher's *Icon and Conquest* (1981) and

reproduced here as Figure 10.4, *Zemi worship among the Arawak of Hispaniola.* Of this illustration, Bucher writes:

De Bry rigs out the inhabitants of Hispaniola – thus of the Arawak group – in the garb of the Peruvian Inca: the *lauytu* or *lyawo,* the vicuna-wool turban wrapped around the head several times, topped off by the *mascapayacha,* a kind of semicircular miter of birds feathers, and a sleeveless short tunic. As explorers had brought back no iconographic models or information, de Bry obviously uses all the iconographic material available at the time. (17)

Bucher deals at length with the perceptions and misrepresentations of physical traits and features at the end of the sixteenth century, indicating that pictorial depictions lag behind the descriptions found in the explorers, some-times very detailed narratives. The early iconography that emerges from external sources confused territorial and cultural differences between the various Amerindian and Indian populations. For clarity to emerge, one must explore the text and deconstruct the image to arrive at a more accurate picture of the physical characteristics and habits of the original populations of the Caribbean. The construction of beauty as defined by the Old World already confronts the newcomer, as these definitions of beauty, however misguided, appear to be derived from a simple aesthetic formula – the familiar was beautiful. The unfamiliar or unknown, if it did not match the criteria by which one group had defined beauty, was, by extension, ugly. Descriptions of both the Indian and Negro celebrate the bodies rather than the facial characteristics. The human body, apart from differences in skin colour between one group and the next, tends to follow fairly recognizable features. Durer writes that there are only

two species of mankind, whites and negroes, in these a difference of a kind can be observed as between them and ourselves. Negro faces are seldom beautiful because of their very flat noses and thick lips . . . Howbeit, I have seen some amongst them whose whole bodies have been so well built and handsome otherwise that I never beheld finer figures, nor can I conceive how they might be bettered, so excellent were their arms and all their parts. (cited in Holt 1957: 324–25)

Bucher (1981) notes that this same dichotomy of body and face is found in the perceptions of the Amerindian physical features, with the narrators noting that "their faces are seldom beautiful" but the body can be perfect (33). In the illustrations that have emerged of these early settlers of these islands, we thus have conflicting images and representations, whether of their cannibalistic tendencies or their physical features. For instance, the illustration of a meeting

Figure 10.5: *An Indian Cacique of the Island of Cuba addressing Columbus concerning a future state*

between Columbus and the Indian population of the island of Cuba, contained in Bryan Edwards' *The History, Civil and Commercial, of the British Colonies of the West Indies* (first published in 1793) is depicted in Figure 10.5. There is little differentiation between the facial characteristics or skin colour of both of the groups represented here, other than one is clothed while the other semi-unclothed. The nudity or semi-nudity of the native group, especially that of its women, becomes a signifier of civilized over the uncivilized.

Edwards 1801

Figure 10.6a *The Voyage of the Sable Venus from Angola to the West Indies*

The image of the Negro in the West Indies could not have received much early attention as the African slave trade to the Caribbean did not begin until the sixteenth century. A few of the images which I have on hand provide a reference point for the archetypes of blackness we begin to see by the eighteenth century. At the same time, such portrayals also demonstrate the transfer of iconographic messages from one geographical and cultural space to another.

Two very popular images are depicted in Figures 10.6a, 10.6b and 10.7. Figure 10.6a, *The Voyage of the Sable Venus from Angola to the West Indies,* included as an illustration in Edwards' book, is a highly allegorized interpretation of the traumatic journey taken by slave women and men across the Atlantic; in my reading, it is an attempt to make more palatable the crudity of the slave trade.[11] The child sprites, called *putti,* were conventional characters in Renaissance paintings accompanying and

Figure 10.6b *The Birth of Venus,* Sandro Botticelli

Figure 10.7 *Europe supported by Africa and America*

giving religious significance and credibility to the figures they surrounded. On the left, Neptune (God of the Sea) holds the Union Jack, while two dolphins in the forefront pull the shell/boat that carries the Sable Venus. This image is a pastiche of the original and famous Botticelli painting of 1485, *The Birth of Venus* (Figure 10.6b),[12] using a standard iconographic device of substituting a black woman for the woman of European descent. Barbara Bush (1990) writes on the depiction of the black woman as the "Sable Queen" that it was "one of the more pleasant contemporary images of the black woman. Part of the white male mythology, it reflected a common and often near-obsessional interest in the 'exotic charms' of African woman-hood" (7). Figure 10.7, possibly of later origin, similarly invokes woman as symbol of nation. Here the centred female figure, lightest of hue, is coyly partially clothed. The more crucial message of this image is the symbolic interpretation of the interdependence between the three continents – Europe, Africa and America – through colonization and the slave trade. Both the iconographic imagery and the messages persist and shift as we examine eighteenth and nineteenth century painting from the region itself.

Painting *En Pleiner* in the Caribbean: Views From Within

Many images and material depicting scenes and events of the Caribbean in the eighteenth and nineteenth centuries have been published and the number is continuously growing. This selection is meant to illustrate the increasing artistic production emanating from the region at that time. In her recently published *Caribbean Art* (1998), Veerle Poupeye records monuments in Jamaica and Barbados by John Bacon (1709–87), John Flaxman (1755–1826) and Sir Francis Chantrey (1781–1841), itinerant European artists who travelled with the largely absentee West Indian plantocracy to the region or were commissioned to work in Europe itself. She observes of this genre of production that "[t]his Creole elite aspired to a 'metropolitan' lifestyle and was wealthy enough to patronize the arts" (29). In the Hispanic Caribbean, with a more settled creole elite, there emerged the first significant Caribbean artists, who catered to the appetites of the elite population's desire for religious art, portraits and, rarely, landscapes. Not many of the Caribbean-born artists were exposed to European training, but they were exposed to the influences by the art that "trickled down to the colonies" (30). Among these were the Cuban painters José Nicholás de Escalera (1734–1804), Juan del Río (born *c.* 1748) and Vincent Escobar (1762–1834), and the Puerto Rican José Campeche (1751–1809). While this chapter does not deal with the style or images produced by all of these artists identified, it is useful to identify the fact that among those cited from Cuba, Campeche was the coloured son of a black slave who had bought his own freedom and that Escobar was described as a mestizo. Poupeye points out that even though such men did not interact socially on an equal footing with the white elite, they could nonetheless take up professions such as painting and sculpture (32).

Among the other artists identified, some of whom were European artists who had travelled to the Caribbean during the eighteenth and nineteenth centuries, are to be found Agostino Brunias (1730–96), who came as the personal painter of Sir William Young (first appointed British governor of Dominica) and who painted mainly in the smaller Windward Islands of the Caribbean and George Robertson (1748–88), who came to Jamaica in 1773 under the patronage of the Jamaican planter-historian William Beckford. Also well known is the series by James Hakewell, who produced twenty-one full-colour plates entitled *A Picturesque Tour of the Island of Jamaica* (1825), and the work of German nationalist Alexander von Humboldt (1769–1859), who visited Cuba in 1800. Several nineteenth century European artists of note were born in the Caribbean, among these Theodore Chasseriau (1819–56) and Camille Pisarro (1831–1903).

Apart from Agostino Brunias, whose work I shall return to in more depth, three nineteenth century artists have come to my attention as their work provides both a record and measure of documentation of customs and physical types in the region. Among these were Jewish-descended Isaac Mendes Belisario (*c.* 1795/96–*c.* 1849), the first known Jamaican artist; Victor Patricia Landaluze (born 1825) who came to Cuba from Madrid in 1852; and Michel Jean Cazabon (1813–?), born in Trinidad to Spanish and French parents.

Many of these painters worked primarily in oils, the medium most popular in the eighteenth century. Oil painting refers to more than a technique; it defines an art form.

The art of any period tends to serve the ideological interests of the ruling class. If we were simply saying that European art between 1500 and 1900 served the interests of the successive ruling classes, all of whom depended in different ways on the new power of capital, we should not be saying anything new. What is being proposed is . . . that a way of seeing the world which was ultimately determined by new attitudes to property and exchange, found its visual expression in the oil painting. Oil painting did to appearances what capital did to social relations. It reduced everything to the equality of objects. (Berger 1974: 86–87)

In the emergence of Caribbean painting, not only does this apply to the oil painting but also to the lithographic reproductions, pen and ink sketches and watercolours that were commissioned or bought by the propertied classes. The customs, habits and physical characteristics of the local population came under the interpretation of the painter who found in the propertied class willing customers for their stylized characterization and records.

My argument is that while partially fulfilling the original intention of the medium and classical styles as visual recorders of the society, these painters, now located in the 'New World', only partially represented nature and reality as they actually saw it. They also took some of the licence allowed the artist and created imaginary or inventive icons or narratives. As with analyses of the literary text, the subtext has to be peeled away, layer by layer. The Caribbean landscape and peoples recorded by these painters must be viewed as a palimpsest. The underlayer has been partially or completely erased to make room for another text.[13] For instance, Poupeye (1998) observes that "Brunias did not focus on the landscape or portraits of the colonial and Creole elite, instead he painted the black slaves, the free coloureds and the St. Vincent Carib in picturesque scenes closer to the rococo *fêtes galantes* than the real colonial life", while Landaluze is "the best-known Cuban exponent of costumbrino, the documentation of picturesque customs and physical types – a significant trend in Latin American painting and literature during the nineteenth century" (32–39).

The work of such artists is important to grasp for other reasons. Sketches from original paintings were being used in the eighteenth and nineteenth centuries in publications abroad and these visual grammars were invoked to support the ideas of both abolitionists as well as apologists for slavery and colonialism. James Walvin (1996) supports this point. He comments that the cult of the British print was firmly established in the eighteenth century by William Hogarth's social satires, which captured the imagination of the increasingly leisured middle class. Prints were well on their way to becoming a favourite and accessible form of domestic decoration by the eighteenth century and blossomed into a lucrative commercial market predating the rise of British abolition. "But that movement," writes Walvin, "and its related commercial interests, soon appreciated that here was a perfect combination of political and commercial interests; pictures of anti-slavery could make profits and advance the anti-slavery cause" (9).

For the first time, therefore, the sketches illustrating the Caribbean began to be drawn from paintings that were carried out by artists working in the region. For example, the engravings of Agostino Brunias's paintings were used as illustrations in Edwards' *The History, Civil and Commercial, of the British Colonies in the West Indies.* Michel Jean Cazabon became a contributor to the *Illustrated London News,* depicting *The Water Riots of October 1, 1849; The Trial of the Rioters in the Courthouse of Port of Spain* of 10 November 1849 and *The Great Fire at Port of Spain,* 7 March 1850 (MacLean 1986: 22). An engraving by one Milton Prior, *Water Street, Georgetown,* was published in the *Illustrated London News* on 28 April 1888. With the increase in localized publishing activity over the last few decades, there has also been widespread use of many of the works of these painters and graphic artists within the Caribbean itself, but this may not serve any other useful purpose than relieving the density of the text or adding to the atmospheric quality of the content. The subtext of the painting and the iconographic image it perpetuates may very well be a misplaced or indifferent one. For example, in his analysis of Hogarth's blacks, David Dabydeen (1987) observes that while many critics have commented on the elaborate narrative structure of Hogarth's work, "at the fact that each detail within a particular work is purposefully placed to yield specific meaning or to create a specific effect, no detail being gratuitous or accidental . . . no attempt has been made to place Hogarth's blacks in the narrative contexts in which they occur" (9). He notes that the black man (and woman) are as invisible in English social history as they are in English art history. The project of defining an iconography therefore attempts to make visible some of the other discourses that they raise, particularly that of an emerging sense of identity that progresses with time.

Reinventing the Caribbean Gaze: Decoding the Visual Narrative

I concentrate here on a small selection from the work of two of the painters cited above to demonstrate the way in which the visual text can be approached and some insights which may emerge.

Agostino Brunias was born in Italy. He was a student at the Academia de San Luca. An oil painting by him was exhibited in Rome as early as 1752. In 1756 he met the Scottish architect Robert Adam who was on a grand tour of Europe and who employed Brunias as draughtsman, along with other young artists, for his study of the magnificent ruins of Italy. Impressed by his work, in 1758 Adam encouraged Brunias to travel back to London with him, temporarily converting him into an architect, although he also completed paintings to ornament the interiors of some of the famous buildings designed by Adam in England. By 1762, however, Brunias appeared to have quitted his mentor and is recorded as residing in Broad Street, Carnaby Market, London, and participating in prestigious exhibitions at the Free Society of Artists. Brunias did not arrive in the West Indies until 1770, when he accompanied Sir William Young, on his appointment as the first British governor to the island of Dominica, as his personal artist. Brunias left Dominica for England a few years after the governor's departure in 1773, but he returned after a short stay in England and lived in Dominica until his death.[14] The records of the Catholic archbishop in Roseau have the original burial certificate of Agostino Brunias, which authenticates that he died on 2 April 1796 in Dominica and was buried in the Catholic cemetery, the site of the existing Roseau Cathedral (Pereira 1992: 9). In total, he would have spent roughly twenty-five years in the West Indies.

Christie's of London (1994) describes Brunias's pictures as having "much in common with the engrossing and theatrical work of English painters steeped in academic and classical tradition who travelled to the New World and the South Seas in the second half of the eighteenth century" (43). Brunias worked in the tradition of painters who introduced *verite ethnographique* into the art

Figure 10.8 *Pacification of the Maroon Negroes*, Agostino Brunias

of painting. The presence of Agostino Brunias in the West Indies and his depictions of West Indians scenes are linked to the ascendancy of Sir William Young to the post of first governor of Dominica. Brunias is recorded as having exhibited two drawings "after nature" at the Society of Arts in London, submitted "From the West Indies" in 1770, the very first year he accompanied Young to Dominica. He had previously exhibited landscapes at the Free

Society of Artists in 1762 and 1763, and together with his connections to architect William Chambers, he would have developed a reputation as an artist in London. In this way, his submissions from the West Indies would have been brought to the attention of the English art and publishing world, and thus engravings after his paintings would be used to illustrate Edwards' *History*.

The facts available on Brunias's life suggest conclusively that he arrived in the Caribbean in 1770, had never visited Jamaica, and that his travels in the West Indies were limited to the islands of St Vincent, Dominica, St Christopher and Barbados. Figure 10.8, *Pacification of the Maroon Negroes*, is used by Edwards (1801) to illustrate an event that took place in 1738 in Jamaica, before Brunias himself was born: "Governor Trelawny by the advice of the principal gentlemen of the island, proposed overtures of peace with the Maroon chiefs. Both parties were now grown heartily wearied out with this tedious conflict" (311). The illustration used by Edwards is an engraving after an original painting owned by Sir William Young and drawn from the life by Brunias. It depicts an apparently peaceful, almost happy settlement of differences between the British and the Maroons. Through the trick of composition, the light from the northwestern sky leads the eye straight to the seated figure, the central English 'chief' whose vision is connected to one of the group of black men, another of whom is kneeling in a postulant position. Guns and weapons are laid to rest in full sight of each other. The title suggests the taming of a group of recalcitrant outlaws through negotiation, a process that did not in fact take place in St Vincent from which the original was drawn. The Black Carib chief Chatoyer was shot in 1795 and five thousand Garinagu or Black Caribs were put on boats and sent across the Caribbean towards the Yucatan peninsula. Two thousand survived and landed on the island of Roatan, some moving on to the Spanish Honduran main, others to British Honduras, now named Belize, where ironically, they were again to live under British rule.[15]

In 1763 Sir William Young was appointed to head a commission of enquiry into St Vincent. The Treaty of Paris had given England control of the last remaining land in the Caribbean suitable for plantation, the best land being found in the island of St Vincent. Unfortunately for the English, St Vincent was occupied on the windward side by the Black Carib population who were granted this land through a treaty made with the French in 1700. The English did not take this previous treaty seriously and Young's commission sought to discredit the claims of the Caribs to this property. A history of how the Caribs came by this land was recorded by Young himself:

The Negroes, or Black Charaibs (as they have been termed of late years) are descendants from the cargo of an African slave ship, bound from the Bite of Benin to Barbadoes, and wrecked, about the year 1675, on the coast of Bequia, a small island about two leagues to the south of St. Vincent's.

The Charaibs, accustomed to fish in the narrow channel, soon discovered these Negroes, and finding them in great distress for provisions, and particularly for water, with which Bequia was ill supplied, they had little difficulty in inveigling them into their canoes, and transporting them across the narrow channel to St. Vincent's where they made slaves of them and set them to work. These Negroes were of a warlike Moco tribe from Africa and soon proved restive and indocile servant to the less robust natives of the western ocean. (Hulme 1986: 246)

According to Young's account, the blacks attempted a massacre of the Caribs. In the ensuing insurrection, they escaped to the mountains of the northeast where they joined forces with other runaways and shipwrecked African refugees and formed nation, "now known by the name of Black Charaibes: a title themselves arrogated, when entering into contest with their ancient masters". Young's account was presented to justify the British retrieval of the lands that were wrested from the Caribs, the true owners who had been wrongfully dispossessed. Interestingly, this was not done with a view to returning the land to its rightful owners, merely to provide a rationale for the usurpation by the British. The Caribs, or Charaibes, in this mythologized or real narrative of Young, are cast as the "less robust natives of the western ocean, innocent and pacific victims of black usurpation, an uncanny repetition, down to the linguistic borrowing of the supposed relationship, three centuries earlier, of Carib to Arawak" (Hulme 1986: 246). The first task of an iconography of the Caribbean is to demystify the manifest narrative of the sketch or painting in order to establish its accuracy in Caribbean historical reference, while at the same time drawing attention to its aesthetic value and contribution to informing ideas of the more obscure layers of Caribbean history, and of Caribbean art history.

Despite the obvious romanticization or explicit misrepresentation for political motives of the subject, Brunias's depictions of the Red and Black Caribs are vital contributions in the absence of other images that bring this layer of Caribbean history to life. What is also interesting is that unlike the imaginary depiction of De Bry's (Figure 10.4, *Zemi Worship*) or that in Figure 10.5, *An Indian Cacique of the Island of Cuba addressing Columbus concerning a future state*, the engravings after the painting of Brunias's *A Family of Charaibes*

Figure 10.9 *A family of Charaibes drawn from the Life in the Island of St Vincent,*
Agostino Brunias

drawn from the Life in the Island of St Vincent (Figure 10.9) and another (not
illustrated here), entitled *Chatoyer the Chief of the Black Charaibes in St Vincent
and his five Wives,* are more likely to be representative of the dress and detail
of Carib life on the island. Certainly, these images are often invoked to discuss
the origins of the Garifuna peoples, some of whom still live in St Vincent and
others who live in communities in Belize.[16]

The work of Brunias clearly represents an important record of life in the
Lesser Antilles. His collected works reveal that he became primarily a figure
painter in the West Indies, concentrating on the new culture of the mulatto,

Figure 10.10 *The West Indian Washer Woman,* Agostino Brunias

born from the mixture of European, African and Carib races. In such paintings as *The Fruit Market at St Vincent, St Vincent Villagers merry making* and *A Negro Festival drawn from Nature in the Island of St Vincent,* as well as others such as *Free Natives of the West Indies* and *The Barbados Mulatto Girl,* there is sufficient recurrence of detail of dress, posture, landscape and activity to invite an iconographic reading. In his oil paintings, stylized and inaccurate though they may be, there is a sense of the gender, class and race relations that typified the evolution of creole society. It is likely that in many of these there is a transposition of a European aesthetic and artistic form and composition into Caribbean life, most obvious, for example, in his *West Indian Washer Woman, c.* 1779 (Figure 10.10). Here the central figure is clearly the mulatto woman, already establishing the desired notions of femininity and beauty that had emerged in creole society. Comparing this to Figure 10.7, *Europe supported by Africa and America,* in Brunias's poetry, the black handmaidens on either side of the mulatto woman complete the triad, replacing the brown and black women on either side of the white. In this, a conventional composition for balance, the mulatto woman is already given centre stage, a technique also employed in *The Barbados Mulatto Girl* cited above.

The facts surrounding the biography and work of Isaac Mendes Belisario are not clear. Valerie Facey[17] and Jacqueline Ranston have been working for a number of years on discovering the obscure details of his life and work and have situated Jamaica as his birthplace in 1795 or 1796, contrary to other published information which estimated his birth in 1792 or 1793 in England. He is of Jewish stock, as evidenced by Jacob A.P.M. Andrade's *Record of the Jews in Jamaica* (1941). Facey and Ranston have identified his mother as Esther Lindo, a member of the Jewish community in Jamaica. They place his death at 1849 in London.

Belisario describes his style in the preface to the subscribers of the first folio of his sketches made available in Jamaica. He describes his work as "Nothing extenuate nor set down in malice", "drawn after nature and in lithography", and he promises that he

purposes to furnish but 'Sketches of Character' steering clear of Caricature: nature in her ordinary form alone, having been the source from whence all the original drawings were derived, and however amusing her accidental deviations from that course of moulding the human shape, may prove to the admirers of the ludicrous, it behoves not an Artist in this instance, to lend himself to the portraying of deformity.

While a definitive chronology of Belisario's life and work is still currently being researched, it is perhaps accurate enough to say that he was trained in England in the classical style of portraiture and landscape. The method of lithography allowed the artist to reproduce original copies from one painting and thus made them more accessible to the purchaser. For his twelve sketches that depicted characters from the Jonkonnu festival, as well as other 'types' in the island, Belisario had consolidated a list of 165 top-ranking persons in the island as subscribers. Heading this list of subscribers was "His Excellency Sir Lionel Smith, Governor of the Island", "The Most Notable the Marquis of Sligo", "The Right Reverend the Lord Bishop", and others of the professional or planter class. It is an interesting if not a crucial point that of the 165 listed subscribers, only one was a female, a Miss Swayne.

Figure 10.11 *Milkwoman, Kingston, Jamaica,* Isaac Mendes Belisario

The record of sketches that Belisario left must be analysed not only as requirements of the school in which he was trained but also in terms of what his patrons or potential buyers considered worthy subjects to be painted. This fact might account for the way in which his work reflects neither abject poverty nor distress. Unlike others who had recorded the indignities and cruelty of slavery and colonial society, Belisario's work appears almost indifferent to some aspects of social existence in pre- and postemancipation society. This is

Figure 10.12 *Lovey, alias Liverpool,* Isaac Mendes Belisario

particularly evident in the almost facile presentations of social situations or characters of the period. Figures 10.11 and 10.12 illustrate two of these sketches produced by Belisario: *Milkwoman, Kingston, Jamaica* (Figure 10.11) and *Lovey, alias Liverpool* (Figure 10.12)

Along with the sketches, Belisario provides a picturesque description of all the characters he has portrayed. Of *Milkwoman,* he writes:

What a striking difference exists in many respects, between the rosy-cheeked milkmaid of London, and this, her sable sister of the milky-way of Kingston – in dress, manner and complexion how dissimilar! The yoke and large tin pails of the former, give place to the bowl and small tin pans of the latter, and by this mode of carrying the same on her head, her hands are left more at liberty. We are of the opinion, the habit also tends greatly to produce the remarkably erect position of Negroes generally, for from their youth they are so trained to sustain weights.

Many coloured persons, as well as free Negroes living at short distances from towns or villages, find it to their advantage to supply the inhabitants with goats' milk, which being richer than that of the cow, is therefore preferred by most families. A small flock of these animals becomes very profitable to the owner at a moderate expense for food, their wandering disposition leading them to it.

The damsel depicted may be considered as on her way from the Pen to town, at an early hour of the morning to supply her customers: her head is closely enveloped in a handkerchief to protect it from the 'cole' (cold) as she would be pleased to term the balmy, and refreshing air before sunrise, than which nothing can be more delightful. The Blacks are universally a chilly race, and are never so well content as under the enjoyment of the sun's rays at his meridian height, which accounts for such a seeming contradiction in their feeling on this subject. Divested of the encumbrance of shoes and stockings, and with dress of a convenient walking length, the Milkmaid of Jamaica travels along at a rapid rate, and beguiles the way with snatches of songs, in a style peculiarly her own; arrived in town, she announces herself with "See me da ya wid de milk" (Here I am with the milk).

The character Lovey is described in Belisario's hand as follows:

Few residents in Kingston, we conceive, are wholly unacquainted with the tender name, as least, of this vender of bouquets . . . [W]e annex his portrait, in which, it must be confessed, there exist no pretensions whatever to *loveliness;* yet, wanting as our quaint-looking model is in personal appearance, he still possesses sufficient tact to arrest the attention of the Fair admirers of flowers, and has, for the last thirty years, diligently, and successfully, disposed of the produce of his Master's garden, situated in the vicinity of Kingston, in cultivation of which he likewise assists. As a means of increasing his own store, he nightly dances two wooden puppets, facetiously styled by him, Captain and Mrs. Jones. A small gratuity from the public usually rewards him for such performance, which is accompanied with songs of his own composition; his receipts in more prosperous times, have frequently amounted to ten shillings per night.

It may be remarked in this instance, as of most of the other "Cries of Kingston", that an air of pleasantry characterises his manner and tone of voice, differing widely from the doleful strain, and depressed figure of the same class of persons in England. The Lightheartedness of the *former* may, in a great measure, be attributed to their firm reliance on receiving ample means of support, at the hands of their Master, whilst the *latter*, are wholly dependent on their daily exertions to obtain food, which many, furnishes a precarious subsistence. The wants of a Negro in a tropical climate are few, are supplied with facility in this ever-productive, and beautiful Island, affording him decided advantages over his transatlantic brethren.

Lovey is an apprentice, a native of Congo in Africa, and about fifty-one years of age, he was there called 'Kangga' but in 1803 was baptised here by a Catholic Priest, as Louis; for reasons only known to himself, he has however, for several years assumed the appellation of *Lovey (*The name of Liverpool was given him by his Master, the motive for which does not appear). He is a shrewd, intelligent, kindhearted, and industrious fellow, and although no subscriber to the regulations of a 'Temperance Society' enjoys such excellent health, as scarcely to have five days' illness during the last twenty-seven years. Of good living he is remarkably fond, and seldom fails to gratify his taste in that respect. (Belisario 1837)

The idea of happy-go-lucky natives, unencumbered by the demands of property or propriety, cheerfully engaged in making a day's living, is textually mythologized, providing symbols for future art forms to build on to characterize the black/Caribbean personality. In both instances it is striking that each of the characters is compared to their counterpart in London, the reference point for creole society being the metropole.[18] Both the sketches and their verbal characterizations are explicit, needing little additional interpretation. Belisario's image of the milkwoman does not tamper with the classic depiction of black femininity also portrayed in Figure 10.1, *World's End.* Between Belisario's *Lovey* and *Rastaman Lion* (Figure 10.2), there is a distinctive shift, as noted previously, signalling a more authoritative and strident figure of masculinity. Of iconographic significance, a feature that recurs in Figures 10.2, 10.3, 10.5 and 10.6 is the flag carried by the male figures. Like the male discoverers before, *Rastaman Lion,* the bearer of the flag, is given the task of naming, after the country or sovereign he represents, and laying claim to that space. Thus the flag is a signifier of masculinity itself, and in the case of *Rastaman Lion,* it is an important symbol that clearly has to be invoked in the reclamation of black male identity and geographical space.

How a shift begins to take place in the way Caribbean people have defined themselves and how they have been defined by others needs to be systematically examined through the plethora of iconographic images that have emerged over the last two centuries. There is much scope for examining these images at comparative and differentiated levels across the territories in order to arrive at the icons of identity that they produce for the region. This chapter has merely sketched the promise of such a project and the possibilities of a method for such an enquiry.

Notes

1. My purpose here is not to enter a critique of the paintings as artistic production but to examine the symbols they represent. This may include some analysis of composition and technique, but I do not pretend to be well versed in these matters.
2. I am grateful for the assistance of my husband Rex Dixon, a notable expatriate painter who has settled in the Caribbean. Having had a European training and now long exposure to the Caribbean, his observations are invaluable in the writing of this chapter.
3. Anthony Cohen (1985) notes on the idea of community that this is formulated when members of a group of people have something in common with each other, which distinguishes them significantly from members of other groups. Community and therefore identity seem to imply simultaneously similarity and difference. The word therefore suggests a relational idea, the opposition of one community to others and to other social entities.
4. While there are no doubt other valuable other texts on art history in the region, many of these are not now known to me. The recent work by Veerle Poupeye (1998) is one of the first of its genre written in the English-speaking Caribbean and is a welcome and useful resource.
5. Also included here would be other studies such as Rawwida Baksh-Soodeen 1995 and Antonio Gaztambide-Geigel 1996.
6. Graham-Dixon (1996) points out that Henry VIII, determined to divorce Catherine of Aragon despite the disapproval of the pope, repudiated papal authority and rejected the Roman Catholic faith. He dissolved the monasteries and founded the Church of England, a vastly more austere form of Christianity. The radical new leaders of the new Protestant church were vigorous and determined opponents of all Roman Catholic rituals and imagery, and under their direction, thousands and thousands of religious artworks were burned and destroyed, emptying the cathedrals and churches of Scotland, England and Wales of sculptures, paintings and stained glass (16).
7. The absence of indigenous arts forms, including a sense of colour and design and styles of painting that each group brought with them, is very obvious even among the later groups of migrants. It occurred to me in my research on Indians in Trinidad and elsewhere in the Caribbean that the aesthetic had undergone a radical shift: flourescent pink and green nylons were used for dress as opposed to hand-woven naturally dyed

cottons which produced the rich green and pink colour tones and patterns traditionally worn. Only where a particular group of artisans came as a caste – for instance, jewellers or potters – did this art form persist.

8. It is useful to point out as well that painting and sculpture preceded photography and motion pictures, which today have revolutionized our global perceptions and interpretations of different societies and different cultures. It was not until the development of a dry-plate process in 1871 that the method we are more familiar with today was made possible by William Henry Fox Talbot in England. For the most part, the painters whose work will be examined here predated the age of mass-produced photography.

9. In the Caribbean the pioneering work of Lucille Mair, later Hilary Beckles, Rhoda Reddock, Barbara Bush, Verene Shepherd, Bridget Brereton, among many others, and my own work on Indians in Trinidad may describe this listing.

10. Hulme (1986) notes that there are close verbal parallels between parts of *The Tempest* and what have become known as the Bermuda Pamphlets, a series of documents pertains to the shipwreck of the *Sea-Venture* and the salvation of its crew in 1610.

11. I need to locate the actual date in which this image was commissioned and by whom to be more precise on how it must be read.

12. This Renaissance painting was commissioned by the Medici. Botticelli made the goddess, emerging full grown from a seashell, more ethereal than sensual, and he placed the figures in the arrangement usual for the baptism of Christ. The original painting is in the Uffizi Gallery in Florence.

13. The use of palimpsest here is analogous to its usage by Salman Rushdie in *The Moor's Last Sigh*. In this book Rushdie invokes, through the metaphor of painting and the method of palimpsest, the layers of history behind contemporary ethnic, caste and gender relations in India and the connections between this history and global political and economic concerns.

14. Facts elicited from a pamphlet on the work of Agostino Brunias, prepared by the Barbados Museum and Art Gallery, n.d.

15. These details were extracted from the video entitled *The Garifuna Journey: A First Voice Testimony Celebrating the Resiliency of the Garifuna People and Their Traditions,* a documentary by Andrea Leland and Kathy L. Berger, Leland/Berger Productions, United States, 1998.

16. In the above cited video, the lithographs from Brunias paintings on the Red and Black Caribs are the chief sources used for illustrating a visual record of the Garifuna origin.

17. Valerie Facey is owner and publisher of the Mill Press, Jamaica. This press is republishing a volume on Belisario's sketches along with new information on his life and work as part of the Jamaica Old Masters series.

18. Nonetheless, these optimistic renditions must be embraced despite my search for the subtext. To reduce a people at any moment in history to pure victimhood produces an equally destructive discourse. Somewhere between fictional portrayal and reality, there lies a truth.

References

Allsopp, Richard. 1996. *A Dictionary of Caribbean Usage*. Oxford: Oxford University Press.

Andrade, Jacob A.P.M. 1941. *A Record of the Jews in Jamaica: From the English Conquest to the Present Time*. Kingston, Jamaica: The Jamaica Times.

Baksh-Soodeen, Rawwida. 1995. "A historical perspective on the lexicon of the Trinidadian English". PhD diss., University of the West Indies, St Augustine.

Belisario, Isaac. 1837. *Sketches of Character*. Kingston, Jamaica.

Berger, John. 1972. *Ways of Seeing*. London: British Broadcasting Corporation and Penguin Books.

Bucher, Bernadette. 1981. *Icon and Conquest: A Structural Analysis of the Illustrations of de Bry's Great Voyages*. Chicago: University of Chicago Press.

Bush, Barbara. 1990. *Slave Women in Caribbean Society, 1650–1838*. Kingston, Jamaica: Heinemann.

Chevannes, Barry. 1995. *Rastafari: Roots and Ideology*. Kingston, Jamaica: The Press, University of the West Indies.

Cohen, Anthony. 1985. *The Symbolic Construction of Community*. Tavistock: London.

Dabydeen, David. 1987. *Hogarth's Blacks: Images of Blacks in Eighteenth Century English Art*. Manchester: Manchester University Press.

Edwards, Bryan. 1801. *The History, Civil and Commercial, of the British Colonies in the West Indies*. London.

Elliot, J.H. 1970. *The Old World and the New 1492–1650*. Cambridge: Cambridge University Press.

Gaztambide-Geigel, Antonio. 1996. "The invention of the Caribbean in the twentieth century". Paper presented to the twenty-eighth annual conference of the Association of Caribbean Historians. Barbados.

Graham-Dixon, Andrew. 1996. *A History of British Art*. London: BBC Books.

Hall, Neville. 1984. "Maritime Maroons: Grand marronage from the Danish West Indies". Paper presented to the sixteenth annual conference of the Association of Caribbean Historians. Barbados.

Hogg, Peter. 1979. *Slavery: The Afro-American Experience*. London: British Library.

Holt, Elizabeth G. 1957. A *Documentary History of Art*. New York: Doubleday.

Hulme, Peter. 1986. *Colonial Encounters*. London: Methuen.

MacLean, Geoffrey. 1986. *An Illustrated Biography of Trinidad's Nineteenth Century Painter Michel Jean Cazabon*. Port of Spain, Trinidad: Aquarela Galleries.

Pereira, Mark. 1992. *Agostino Brunias (1730)–1796*. Port of Spain, Trinidad: Gallery 101.

Poupeye, Veerle. 1998. *Caribbean Art*. London: Thames and Hudson.

Rushdie, Salman. 1997. *The Moor's Last Sigh*. New York: Pantheon.

Scott, Michael. *Tom Cringle's Log*. London: George Routledge and Sons.

Shakespeare, William. 1958. *The Tempest*. Arden edition. Edited by Frank Kermode. London: Routledge.

Sheridan, Richard B. 1994. *An Economic History of the British West Indies 1623–1775.* Kingston, Jamaica: Canoe Press.

Walcott, Derek. 1984. *Midsummer.* New York: Farrar, Straus and Giroux.

Walvin, James. 1996. "Looking at slavery: The iconography of slavery". Paper presented to the twenty-eighth annual conference of the Association of Caribbean Historians. Barbados.

Warner-Lewis, Maureen. 1993. "African continuities in the Rastafari belief system". *Caribbean Quarterly* 39, nos. 3 and 4.

Zendegui, Guillermo de. 1975 "Landaluze: Painter of nineteenth century Cuba". *Americas* 27, no. 9 (September).

11

A Scuffling of Islands

The Dream and Reality of Caribbean Unity in Poetry and Song

GORDON ROHLEHR

Roseau to Montego Bay

The name of this chapter is meant to suggest the link between economic necessity, the desperate struggle to survive ('scuffling') and the insular conflicts ('scuffling' in another sense of the word) that have attended all efforts at Caribbean integration. This chapter contends that calypsonians and poets have always been aware of both types of scuffle and undertakes an account of their commentaries from the Roseau Conference of October 1932 into the 1990s. Calypsonians had from the turn of the century monitored the movement of the islands away from nominated and towards representative government, and they were among the first West Indian artists to promote the idea of Federation as a means towards this end. Poets such as Louise Bennett, Eric Roach and Derek Walcott had all shared in the dream of a unified West Indies. In the case of Roach and Walcott, anger and disillusionment felt at the break-up of the West Indian Federation in 1961 darkened their portrayals of the postindependence era.

Atilla's "Expedite Federation" (1933) was his response to the Roseau Conference where representatives from Trinidad, Barbados, Grenada, St Vincent, St Lucia, Dominica, Antigua, St Kitts and Montserrat "met for the purpose of recording a concerted demand for Federation, backed by some practical plan" (Mordecai 1968: 22). Atilla's calypso was a clarion call to "lethárgic West Indians" to overcome the geographical barrier of distance and form a federation that would be the first step towards a dominion within the British Empire, similar to those of Canada, Australia, New Zealand and South Africa. Such dominions, he noted, had "parliaments and governments of their own" even though they paid "their allegiance to the British throne", so that it was possible to reconcile the reality of one's colonial status with the ideal of full internal self-government. Such self-determination Atilla viewed as a prerequisite to freedom "from the bondage of economic misery", a phrase that located the Roseau Conference in the context of the Great Depression of 1929 whose full effect was being felt in the West Indies during the 1930s.

"Expedite Federation" was a powerful statement of a dream of regional "stability and unity" as well as of a longing felt by Caribbean people for "a permanent place in world history" and a seat "in the conferences of the world" (Quevedo 1983: 121–22). As an articulated dream this calypso offered hope, faith, cliché and slogan – "United we stand, divided we fall / We must succeed, yes, one and all" – but no guidelines as to how unity in political administration, stability in social affairs or freedom from economic dependence, hunger and the current depression were going to be achieved by the mere act of wishing a West Indies Federation into existence. The divisions between dream and reality, which opened out as the Roseau Conference progressed, proved to be paradigmatic and prophetic of what was to occur in future efforts towards regional unity or cooperation.

The federal dream flowered in the latter half of the 1930s, nurtured by the emergence of a militant labour movement and the spate of violent disturbances that occurred in 1935 (St Kitts, Trinidad, British Guiana, St Vincent, St Lucia), 1937 (Trinidad, Barbados) and 1938 (Jamaica). The leaders of labour intensified the gospel that the pathway towards political and economic liberation lay in regional cooperation. One calypso, the Growling Tiger's prize-winning "Advice to West Indians" (1939) indirectly captures the connection between burgeoning trade unionism and the federal idea. Tiger promotes not the notion of a West Indies Federation but that of an aroused West Indian working class that has become conscientized into the wisdom of joining the labour movement.

> I am advising every worker as a West Indian
> To be careful and join a labour union
> It's the only way you can achieve your right

And to stop the oppressive hands of might
And allow your progressive march to be an inspiration
To the rising generation
(Rohlehr 1966)

Tiger advises the West Indian working class to develop values of unity, worker solidarity and fidelity to the labour movement, broad objectives that transcend the notion of Caribbean integration.

Postponed by World War II, formal discussion of Federation resurfaced in a September 1945 meeting of the Caribbean Labour Congress in Port of Spain and the Montego Bay Conference of 1947. Atilla the Hun, who monitored the Montego Bay Conference from reports in the local press, identifies the issues of self-government and dominion status as the central concerns of the conference. His focus in the calypso "Montego Bay Conference" is, however, not on those issues but on the theatre of the occasion:

Nearly every West Indian politician
Went to discuss Federation
The *Gleaner* said that Manley was eloquent
Crawford and Gomes were magnificent
But William Alexander Bustamante
Was the real hero of Montego Bay
(Quevedo 1983: 130)

Bustamante, according to Atilla, spoke "eloquently and brilliantly", demanding "self-government for Jamaica / And he wanted to be the first Governor". Admiring the brilliance and the charisma of Bustamante's "intriguing personality", Atilla fails to recognize the ambiguity of his two stances: (1) that a Federation of mendicant states was doomed to failure and (2) that Federation was acceptable only as a prelude to full self-government for Jamaica.

The 1950s

All the great dreaming and creeping doubt that surrounded the idea of Federation, surface in the calypsos and poems of the 1950s. The first of these, Lord Beginner's (Egbert Moore) "Federation" (1951), was probably inspired by the recommendations of the Standing Closer Association Committee (October 1949), though, like Atilla's "Montego Bay Conference", it gives no hint of the complexity of the recommendations or the divergent positions of which reconciliation needed to be sought. "Federation" sets the mood for the decade: one of boundless optimism that signals the trust that these grass-roots poets feel for the black or brown certificated or self-made intellectuals who dominated the politics of that transitional decade.

Beginner names Trinidad, Barbados, Jamaica and British Guiana as the "big four" on whose natural resources – Trinidad's oil and asphalt, British Guiana's gold and diamonds, Barbados's sugar, and Jamaica's soil – the federal economy will be constituted. Apart from the fact that British Guiana was, even then, suspicious of the federal idea, it was precisely on the particular issue of natural resources that West Indian territories – none of whom controlled these resources – were and would continue to be most insular and intransigent.

The calypsos and poems that grow out of the 1953 and 1956 deliberations, tend to be more cautious, apprehensive and even sceptical. There is still considerable euphoria in, say, King Fighter's calypso on Federation, where full confidence is placed in leaders who were even then locked in grim debate:

> Barbados have Grantley Adams
> Trinidad have the great Doctor Williams
> Jamaica have Norman Manley
> And BG have a great great man like me
> We should join together and form a plan
> I can't understand
> Why we can't reap the fruits of Federation[1]

But there are also several indications that all is not well. The Roaring Lion, for example, describes the sentiments that led to his composition of "West Indians Get Together" (or "Federation"):

News of the Federation of the West Indies reached me in London; needless to say that my blood pressure went up instantly with joy in my heart. But my spirit was soon daunted by adverse rumours making the rounds between West Indians. I thought for a moment that it couldn't be true that all the leaders in the area were so insular in their outlook as to defeat the purpose of the dream they were having for years, just when the dream was about to come true. I doubted it, but, alas! It was true. So I made my observation and advice in this song.

"West Indians Get Together"
(Federation)

> I am warning you islanders in the West
> To get together and do your best

Amend your differences if you please
And fight for the good of the West Indies

Chorus
West Indians, I beg you be wise
West Indians, please open your eyes
West Indians, before it's too late
Call your leaders together and federate.

This is no time for bickering
Political squabble or mudslinging
Politicians, be sensible, please
And build the prestige of the West Indies

Marryshow, I beg you, be wise
Bustamante and Gomes, open your eyes
Adams and Jagan ere its too late
Use your commonsense and please federate
(De Leon 1988: 159–60)

There is no evidence that West Indian leaders, with their minds locked on the hard realities of designing a constitution capable of satisfying the special interests of so many tiny island-worlds, either listened to the 'orations' of calypsonians or read poetry. Mordecai (1968) does, however, bear witness to the extraordinary impact of Beryl McBurnie on a deadlocked Conference on Freedom of Movement that was held in Trinidad in March 1955.

The deadlock which threatened on the first day seemed miraculously to disappear under the influence of a flow of Trinidad hospitality described as 'lethal', of elaborate entertainment – staged by the celebrated Miss Beryl McBurnie and her troupe of dancers, and of the decision of the Trinidad Government to relax restrictions immediately on fifty-three categories of working migrants. (48)

Theodore Sealey of the *Sunday Gleaner,* reviewing the show, noted that after the performance

peers and prime ministers, politicians and public servants caught the spirit of the maracas and the steel band in what must have been the most celebrated evening of riotous fun in the history of the West Indies . . .

. . . Tomorrow in the Federation Conference, many a delegate will be humming the tunes. They will never forget the evening. No one could. (Ahye 1983: 44)[2]

It is, no doubt, occasions such as this that have inscribed in many Trinidadian minds the notion that there is no barrier that cannot be surmounted by calypso, pan and breakaway mas. Even the hardheaded Chalkdust has contributed to this particular myth when in "Carnival Is the Answer" (1989) he offers steelband, calypso and carnival as the solution to the serious problems of Afghanistan, Iran, El Salvador, Nicaragua, Pretoria, Russia and Lebanon. There in 1955 McBurnie had performed the dream of Federation within that deadlocked theatre of political debate, and the impact was extraordinary.

McBurnie and the Little Carib Company were invited to perform at Jamaica's celebration later in 1955 of three hundred years of British rule. "The Company presented 10 shows during the three week stay in Jamaica and got a chance to forge some valuable links", including a reunion with the Ivy Baxter Dance Company of Jamaica, whom they had met three years before in Puerto Rico while attending the Caribbean Festival in 1952 (Ahye 1983: 52–53). Louise Bennett's "Free Movement" celebrates this moment as one of epiphanic self-revelation: Caribbean peoples open up themselves to each other's gaze and thus illustrate possibilities for the Federation that the region's men of words cannot previously have imagined.

> Dem dance de Tambo Bamboo, an
> De Bacanal dem prance
> Me never see movement more free
> Dan Trinidadian dance.
>
> Me watch Trinidad carrins awns
> An baps me understan
> How dem teck 'freedom of movement'
> An confuse federation
>
> Me sey Massi me Massa
> Trinidad noh ordinary
> Dem chat gains Freedom of Movement
> But a so dem movement free!
>
> But Trinidadian deed gwine fine dem out
> As sure as fate
> Wen McBurnie dancin movement
> Meck West Indies federate!
>
> (Bennett 1966: 164–65)

McBurnie's ability to communicate and break down barriers, her Legba role as pointer who clears the pathway at the beginning of a ceremony, is contrasted with the "speaky-spoky" of the statesmen of the region, most of whom are out of touch with the vernacular consciousness of the common folk of the region whom they seek to federate.

Bennett's reductive laughter in poems such as "Big Wuds", "Free Movement" and "Capital Site" is, like all such satire, partly an evasion of the seriousness of the issue. Trinidad's apprehension that free movement would mean an uncontrollable traffic of job-seeking immigrants was, given that country's history since emancipation, well founded. It is, however, precisely this history that Atilla invokes to remind Trinidad's delegates at the deliberations of March 1955 of the contribution that immigrants have made to culture, civil life, commerce, industry, and the health and legal services in Trinidad.

> The whole question of Federation
> Is meeting with misinterpretation
> The question is freedom of movement
> And the right of settlement
> Because the whole thing to me is stupidity
> Because we have Federation already
>
> Mr Justice Duke is a Demerarian
> Justice Comacho he is a St Lucian
> Your Legal Draughtsman is a Antiguan
> And your Attorney General is a Barbadian

Atilla continues in a later stanza:

> In every office of the Government
> In every avenue of employment
> In every Government institution
> They're holding administrative position
> Your Director of Agriculture is a Barbadian
> Your currency expert is a Vincentian
> And I can tell you here openly
> They even control the Press in this colony
> (Quevedo 1983: 156–57)

Atilla, himself of Venezuelan ancestry, recognizes the free flux of people as having been central to the emerging identity of Trinidad. His calypso admonishes Courtenay Hannays and Albert Gomes – both of whom were long time connoisseurs of calypso – to recognize the great positives that have grown out of the concourse and admixture of peoples and cease trying to reverse or control a process that has given the nation its shape.

Federation, 1958

After the Federation was inaugurated with all due pomp and ceremony on
Friday 3 January 1958, three singers, Kitchener, Sparrow and Bomber, chronicled the joy of the occasion, which was hailed as the fulfilment of a dream of
nearly three decades. The fact that Federation was inaugurated at the beginning
of the eight-week Carnival season was, of course, not lost on Kitchener who,
though living in Manchester, England, was, even then, an inveterate celebrant
of the annual masquerade, who used to send home some of the most attractive
calypsos to vie for Road March honours. Kitchener's "Federation" was a call
to celebration.

> This is Federation
> What a big occasion
> Now we are united
> And can't be divided
> With this little combination
> Soon we will declare a nation
>
> Oh bacchanal, play carnival
> So everybody let's be social
> Jump around and play carnival
> Oh bacchanal, play carnival

Kitchener names many of the islands and includes British Honduras (Belize)
and British Guiana who opted out of Federation and Bermuda, which was not
considered by the British to be West Indian. The very names of the islands, as
in Derek Walcott's "A Sea-Chantey" of the same period, become magical in
this act of celebration and in this moment of dreaming the great dream.

Sparrow's "We All Is One" or "Federation" (1958), a similar sort of calypso,
was ironically, like Kitchener's, a description of the event and a call to
celebration taking place from a vantage point of two or three thousand miles'
distance: Kitchener was in Manchester and Sparrow in New York. Sparrow
celebrates a union that has been achieved despite the negative stereotypes that
each island has in the past, even during the federal negotiations, been prepared
to promote of its neighbours.

> Well is big Federation
> For a new little nation
> On this occasion
> We should have a big celebration

So Tom, Dick and Harry
Let us drink and be merry
Don't wait for tomorrow
Everybody sing now with Sparrow

Chorus
Whether you're a damn Trinidadian
We all is one
If they say you're a smart Barbadian
We all is one
Get away from me you greedy Grenadian
We all is one
I don't care if you're a bad Jamaican
We all is one
Let us join together and love one another
We all is one
If you born New York and your parents West Indian
We all is one

British Guiana, severely divided within itself, stayed out of the federal experiment, much to the chagrin of its own calypsonian King Fighter, who was a federalist to his very core. In 1957 King Fighter and Lord Coffee had both been allowed to compete in the Trinidad Calypso Monarch Competition, and it is with this memory of a cultural acceptance that transcended insular nationalism that Fighter in "Warn BG" (1958) castigates his native land. Fighter begs immigration officials in Trinidad to put pressure on Guyanese immigrants, or even travellers passing through the country. Arguing for the isolation and ostracizing of Guyanese from the rest of the Caribbean community, Fighter is willing to undergo such moral isolation himself.

Aye, aye British Guiana
This is your own King Fighter
Ah hope you paying attention
Listen to my conversation
Ah want you to understand
That this is Federation
So ah begging you, please
Wake up and join with the West Indies

Fighter feels that of all the Caribbean territories British Guiana is the one that possesses an extensive land base which grossly underpopulated, she is powerless to develop.

> BG is a big wide area
> The mainland of South America
> And the thing that really worry me
> It has about sixty people, you see
> They must be keeping the colony
> For a burial industry
> Ah don't know what to say
> But they getting me fed up day after day

Fighter's exasperation over Guyana's refusal to join the Federation is matched only by Louise Bennett's at the contestation between Trinidad, Barbados and Jamaica over the issue of where the capital site is to be located. Trinidad gains the site but is powerless to deliver Chaguaramas for the capital. The Chaguaramas issue is the Federation's first lesson on the real limits within which it can operate. This is not, however, how Louise Bennett sees it:

> Trinidad confuse bout Capital Site
> Me noh bizniz wid dem biznis
> But monkey should know weh him gwine put him tail
> Before order trouziz
>
> Look how dem struggle strain an strive
> So till de votin' grant i_____
> Den wanti-wanti tun geti-geti
> But geti-geti noh wanti!

Remembering the fierceness of the debates about the site, Bennett acridly comments that the new nation seems to be more interested in the capital site than in the Federation itself. As with her pun in "Big Wuds" about the island being on an "up word trend", she plays with the ideas of 'capital' (head, headquarters, splendid) and site (spot, location also 'sight'). The site/sight pun implies that there is an absence of vision (sight) at the very head (capital) of the Federation.

> The plot was tick, de riddle hard
> De darkness wouldn' light_____
> De islands all look capital
> But some don't got noh site!

This leads the narrator to consider a number of modest proposals for a moving capital sited on a plane, or kite or, best of all, a ship named *Capital Site*.

> Some people sey fe buil a plane
> Some sey fe buil a kite,

Some sey fe buil a ship an
Give it name "Capital Site"

Den launch de ship or fly de plane
Or put de kite to flight
An every islan dat it stop
Will have Capital Site.
                    (Bennett 1966: 166–67)

Louise Bennett had now experienced two aspects of Trinidad. Beryl McBurnie's visit in 1955 and her subsequent lecture tour to Jamaica for several months in 1957 had introduced the northern Caribbean to the elation, gaiety and marvellously affirmative *joie de vivre* of Trinidad's artists. McBurnie's vision was wide, encompassing the ancestral roots of the various races – African, Indian, Chinese, European, Native Caribbean – whose coming together in the crucible of Caribbean history had engendered the unique and multifaceted collective identity of the region. It was through McBurnie that the region glimpsed its cultural potential as a federated nation. Jeff Henry, a member of McBurnie's Little Carib Theatre who accompanied her on her lecture tour "was co-opted to train dancers and to choreograph for a pantomime, 'Busha Bluebeard' ", a work in which the author, Louise Bennett, performed the leading role (Ahye 1983: 46).

The other side of Trinidad, one that elicited the anger, sadness and exasperation of "Capital Site", was the carnivalesque foolishness of its politicians and statesmen performing in their own alternative theatres of Absurdity and Egotism. After flaying such performance in her most sarcastic tone, Bennett's persona finally abandons her mask of sweet, wise and bitter fool, to offer a desperate prayer – "Lawd help the Federation" – for a Federation that even before it has begun seems to have adopted the style of failure. Ironically, at the very moment of McBurnie's lecture tour, that most fruitful interface between Jamaica and Trinidad, while Bennett is perceiving Chaguaramas as an omen of coming disaster, Mc Burnie's Little Carib Theatre is staging "Diwi-Jhal", a show "influenced by the Federal themes such as 'Miss Capital Site', a dance which highlighted the charms of Trinidad and Tobago which was chosen for the capital site of the West Indies" (Ahye 1983: 47).

Sparrow's "The Base" (1958) presents the face-saving position that Dr Eric Williams eventually adopted on Chaguaramas, which is that Young, the British governor at the time of the agreement in 1941, never approved of and did not sign the document by which Chaguaramas was leased to the United States for ninety-nine years in exchange for fifty ageing destroyers. What Williams omitted was that the agreement had been signed over the head of Governor Young by the king himself who, presumably, had the sovereign right to dispose of his property in whatever way best served the interests of imperialism. Acting as if he were already the prime minister of an independent state, Williams seized on Chaguaramas as the issue that he hoped would catalyse the nascent nationalist movement in Trinidad and Tobago. In the process, he constructed his own image of a knowledgeable, courageous and outspoken champion of the rights of the small state, ground between the millstones of two rival but interdependent imperialisms: British and American.

Referendum: The End Um

The obsequies of the Federation can be heard in Lord Laro's "Referendum" (1961/62), Sparrow's "Federation" (1962) and Louise Bennett's "Dear Departed Federation" (1961/62). These three commentaries are finely and appropriately balanced, both in terms of their mood and content and in terms of the situation of the three commentators. Louise Bennett and Sparrow look out from their respective vantage points: Jamaica, the northernmost and largest, and Trinidad and Tobago, the southernmost islands of the Federation. These two territories had come to represent the mighty polar opposites in every issue. Barbados, via the federal prime minister, Sir Grantley Adams, tried vainly to hold the centre by imposing his own shaky authoritarianism between northern and southern egotisms and nationalist ambitions in constant and complex contestation.

Laro was a Tobagonian calypsonian who had served in the West India Regiment in Jamaica, and who was therefore in Jamaica during the referendum campaign. His "Referendum" is a strictly descriptive documentary calypso: whose narrator speaks with the authority of impartial, nonjudgemental witness about what he has seen and heard during the referendum campaign of 1961. It dramatizes the stark simplicity of Bustamante's appeal to the tribal public via the single repeated watchword: "Freedom". Employing the traditional litanic 'call-and-response' structure of the old stick-fighting chants, a structure that has always signified the rooted belonging of shaman, priest, chantwel, warner, calypsonian or batonnier to a fiercely loyal and partisan 'folk' community, Laro illustrates both Bustamante's instinctive understanding of the tribal mind and his demagogue's skill in manipulating it.

For the Referendum . . . Freedom
Is the talk all around . . . Freedom
Anywhere you pass . . . Freedom
You could hear a loudspeaker blast . . . Freedom
Busta say Federation
Ain't good for the country
But I getting a different view
When I listen Norman Manley

Chorus
Busta bawling: "No, No, No Federation, No!"
But when I listen Manley he ain't shouting so.
All his supporters with 'Federation' sign on their chest
And if you hear them: "Yes, Yes, Yes Federation, Yes.

I went Busta meeting . . . Freedom
Everyone was bawling . . . Freedom
Bungo drum was playing . . . Freedom
Then he started speaking . . . Freedom
"If Jamaica join the Federation,
All the small islanders will come and flock up the land"

On the radio every time . . . Freedom
On the *Gleaner* headline . . . Freedom
People in the street
You could hear them shouting when they meet . . . Freedom
Manley say is our last chance
Jamaicans use all yuh brain
Cause this opportunity might never come back again

Narrative sequencing of incident suggests here that the Bustamante call for "Freedom" and representation of Federation as the biggest obstacle in the path of Jamaican independence spreads outwards in waves from his meetings to the radio, press and population at large, until there is almost no need for Bustamante to make the call, so spontaneous and automatic has the response become. In the face of this spontaneity, Manley's appeal to reason simply peters out into the final diminuendo of the chorus of his supporters, whose "Yes, Yes, Yes Federation, Yes" is indistinguishable from lamentation.

Louise Bennett's "Dear Departed Federation" (1966: 168–69) constitutes a humbled descent from the moral high horse of "Capital Site", when it was Trinidad's nationalistic self-centredness that seemed to be jeopardizing the Federation. Now, two years later, the centre of dissent has shifted to Jamaica, Louise's native land and one of Trinidad's chief rivals in the bid for the capital site. A greater effort is discernible in "Dear Departed Federation" to achieve a balance between according blame, passing judgement, suggesting the need for understanding and broad sympathy, and begging for forgiveness.

Blame and judgement are suggested in the description of the referendum as "murderation" and "mutilation". Clearly a tragic error of choice on Manley's part, the referendum has turned out to be "a heavy blow", a dreadful act of violence that has not only murdered the Federation, but atrociously dismembered its corpse, placing it beyond anyone's recognition. Responsibility for such atrocity is squarely placed on Jamaica's communal shoulders, the "we" of the poem whose narrator can find no fault in the federal idea and muses on the irony that the relatively tiny islands of the West Indies should have found it more difficult to federate than people inhabiting vast continental land masses.

The narrator, having accorded blame and accepted responsibility, next appeals for understanding and sympathy. The very smallness of the island spaces amplifies "boderation"; that is, bothersome problems, differences, fears, insecurities, frustration and intolerance. Jamaica's fears that a strong federal government will mean a diminution of national autonomy, and that as the largest and least underdeveloped island she will have to bear the economic burdens of her smaller less-developed partners, are, appropriately, not spelled out in the poem. They are, rather, represented in broad, vague, abstract terms – "big confusion", "heap o' boderation", "Jamaica contribution", "final constitution" – the very "big wuds", that is, that confused the sceptical folk-narrator, who five years earlier commented sardonically on the rhetoric of the 1956 London conference. It is precisely because the issues of Federation had never been clearly explained to the common folk in a language that they could understand that Bustamante, who understood and could communicate in the vernacular register better than anyone else, was so successful in promoting secession by playing on vague popular fears. All he needed to do was to concretize all that was vaguely understood and feared into one monstrous enemy figure: Federation, and conversely to summarize all the vaguely glimpsed avenues of deliverance into the single slogan: "Freedom".

Sparrow's "Federation" is the opposite in mood, tone and message to Bennett's elegy or eulogy. Preceding the two 'Solomon' calypsos, "Solomon" and "Get to Hell Outa Here", by three years, "Federation" is Sparrow's last unequivocal vindication of the politics and policies of Dr Williams in the final year of colonialism. Postindependence calypsos will first be euphoric (for example, "Model Nation" and "Grenada Must Join") then, increasingly, critical and deeply protesting as Trinidad encounters the difficulty of constructing national identity in the decade after independence. "Federation" condemns Jamaica for the failure of the Federation, but absolves Trinidad and Dr Williams of all blame for their subsequent and even more abrupt withdrawal from the experiment. Jamaica, who at least tested her leaders' misgivings about Federation in a national referendum, is condemned for having behaved "like a blasted traitor"; Trinidad, who simply departed by its premier's autocratic decree, is portrayed as the abused victim of treachery. There is no room for Louise Bennett's euphemism in this open expression of anger. Jamaica's behaviour has been secretive and shocking. Why, asks Sparrow, did they not speak before? Why was there no openness between the Jamaican antagonists, Manley and Bustamante, and Trinidad's premier, Dr Williams? Why was there no north/south dialogue between Federation's Big Two?

Sparrow, in fact, suggests an answer to his own questions when he outlines a sequence of events from the rivalry of the two countries over the capital site to the referendum and Jamaica's secession.

> When they didn't get the Capital Site
> That nearly cause big fight
> When Sir Grantley Adams took up his post
> That even make things worse
> They bawling: "We ain't want no Bajan Premier."
> "Trinidad can't be capital for here!"
> So the grumbling went on and on
> To a big Referendum

If this description of the process of disintegration is accurate, then it is clear that Jamaica had from the start both signalled and spoken about her misgivings. So, indeed, had Trinidad and all the other islands. Viewed from the vantage point of hindsight, the real question is not why the Federation ended, but why it started at all. Sparrow, intent on indicting Jamaica alone, and in the electric forum of the 1962 Dimanche Gras Calypso Monarch finals, asks the crucial questions about Jamaica alone.

> . . . if they know they didn't want Federation
> If they know they didn't want to unite as one and only one
> Ah say to tell the Doctor you not in favour
> Don't behave like a blasted traitor
> How the devil you mean you ain't federating no more?

Unlike "Dear Departed Federation", Sparrow's "Federation" does not attempt to understand Jamaica's position. It rather dismisses that position as incomprehensible and a betrayal of "the Doctor". Jamaica has, through her untimely withdrawal, jeopardized the regional movement towards independence: "Independence was at their door / Why they didn't speak before?"

Did Sparrow at this late stage (March 1962), five months before both culprits – Jamaica and Trinidad – gained independence, believe in that axiom of the thirties, forties and fifties that Federation was to be the only pathway towards dominion status or independence? He may have; yet by the final stanza, in which he brutally sums up his thoughts about Federation, he seems pretty certain that even with the Federation dead, some of the islands will achieve independence on their own. It may well have been that Jamaica sensed, or had secret foreword of that possibility and thus seceded from the Federation with full expectation that independence would be granted. It may also be that Trinidad had precisely the same expectation, hence her own o'er-hasty departure after Jamaica's secession.

Such possibilities are only hinted at in Sparrow's final stanza.

Federation boil down to simply this:
Is dog eat dog and survival of the fittest.
Everybody fighting for independence singularly
Trinidad, for instance
We goin' get it too, so don't bother
But I find we should all be together
Not separated as we are
Because of Jamaica

According to Sparrow's analysis here, the entire region has failed because its politics has not matured beyond the Darwinian level of savage bestial survivalism. Federation was, therefore, no more than a dialogue or dogfight between equally fierce pot-hounds. The "efforts and energy" of the region's leaders have been squandered by their inability to transcend insular concerns. Sparrow seems, however, to be reluctant to include the equally canine Trinidad, in his blanket condemnation of this region of dogs.

Right now it's only a memory
We failed miserably
Some say we shouldn't help part it
But is Jamaica what start it.

If Louise Bennett holds out a rather wan hope for dialogue and alliance in the indefinite future, Sparrow, his dream of "we-all-is-one" shattered, realistically bids adieu to the whole federal enterprise and sets his sights on independence for Trinidad and Tobago as a separate and autonomous state. Bennett, meanwhile, shocked at the suddenness – "Biff, Referandum! Buff, Election! / Baps, Independence drop pon we" ("Jamaica Elevate", 1966: 174) – and saddened by the manner in which Jamaica becomes independent, greets the independence moment with a mixture of careful hope and muted scepticism.

The Aftermath: The 1960s

The idea of a united Caribbean nation and related notions of a Caribbean identity, culture and aesthetic did not die with the collapse of the West Indian Federation. The intensity of the federal dream; the exposure of Caribbean people, however briefly, to each other during the years of Federation; the expansion of the University College of the West Indies as a regional institution; the formation of the Caribbean Artists' Movement in the late 1960s and the New World Movement in the same period; and the success of the West Indies cricket team under Worrell and Sobers all served to keep the Caribbean dream alive into the 1970s. And, of course, West Indian literature grew and became magnificent throughout the 1960s and beyond. Consider this short list: Wilson Harris's *The Guyana Quartet;* Derek Walcott's *In a Green Night, The Castaway, The Gulf, Dream on Monkey Mountain and Other Plays;* Edward Brathwaite's *The Arrivants;* George Lamming's *Of Age and Innocence, Season of Adventure, Water with Berries, Natives of My Person;* V.S. Naipaul's *A House for Mr Biswas, The Middle Passage, An Area of Darkness, The Mimic Men;* much of Samuel Selvon and John Hearne; Earl Lovelace's *While Gods Are Falling* and *The Schoolmaster;* and Jean Rhys's *Wide Sargasso Sea;* all falling within a fifteen-year span between the final negotiations of 1956 and the first years of the 1970s.

Carifesta 1972 was the dream reborn in the least likely of places: Guyana, which had stayed outside of the Federation and withdrawn from University College of the West Indies between 1961 and 1962. Yet it was, perhaps, precisely this sense of being isolated outside of the West Indian tragicomedy of Federation, that had bred in Guyana that terrible hunger for location in a wider regional entity. As it turned out, Guyana calmly redefined the Caribbean to include not only the francophone and Hispanic territories, but also Suriname, Belize, the Bahamas, Brazil, Venezuela, Mexico, Peru and Chile. Nowhere else in the Caribbean has such phenomenal dreaming ever been manifest. And Guyana was, as Trinidad was to become before the salvation of the oil-dollar windfall engendered by the Organization of Petroleum Exporting Countries in 1974, on the brink of a bankruptcy from which she has not yet recovered.

If Carifesta '72 represented the dream in its full magnificence and improbability, crisis of one sort or another was the constant reality that the region faced in the postfederal years. The first theatre of crisis was Guyana 1962 to 1964, a horrendous period when the fissures between ethnicities widened into chasms and the country was torn in a catastrophe of civil war, murder, arson and rape. Then there was Trinidad in 1970 with its army mutiny and profoundly traumatic Black Power marches, followed by the 'guerrilla' activity and the gun-downs of the first half of the 1970s. The crisis shifted to Grenada between 1979 and 1983 and back to Trinidad in 1990. All the while, Jamaica, as its rudie, reggae, ragga and dancehall music amply illustrates, was living through such a relay of crises that the term seems to have lost its meaning there. Like Carifesta, each crisis has affected the region's construction of its identity by simultaneously crushing the dream and intensifying the need for some vast transcendent dreaming. So in the face of J\$38 to US\$1 in Jamaica and G\$135 to US\$1 in Guyana, our singers and writers are dreaming Haiti.

The contribution of the University of the West Indies to the maintenance of the dream has been immense. The New World Movement, emerging out of the ashes of the West Indian Federation, derived its regional flavour from the University of the West Indies. For West Indian lecturers and students at the University of the West Indies in the late 1950s and early 1960s, the Caribbean as a region became a slowly emerging reality. Hence it was that students from throughout the region joined Norman Manley's referendum campaign in an attempt to explain the idea of Federation to as many people as they could. As the decade of the 1960s wore on, there was a noticeable phenomenon: key West Indian academics would make their intellectual and political contributions in territories other than their own: Lloyd Best, William Demas, Edwin Carrington, Norman Girvan and Alistair McIntyre in Guyana; Clive Thomas, Havelock Brewster, Vaughan Lewis, Kamau Brathwaite and Maureen Warner in Jamaica; Patrick Emmanuel, Bill Riviere, Lewis Bobb and Eric St Cyr in Trinidad and Tobago.

What this meant was that a West Indies had in the 1960s come into being for the academic that had little meaning for the political directorate of each 'independent' microstate. Inevitably, the politicians from Jamaica in the north to Trinidad and Tobago in the south reacted with suspicion, withholding a passport here, barring entry there, refusing work permits everywhere and kicking out this victim or that as the necessity for scapegoating demanded. The political lampoonist of *Public Opinion* on 5 April 1964 satirized the Jamaican (and wider Caribbean) tendency to stigmatize political concern on the part of the academic as 'communist subversion'.

> Subversives are hiding at Mona
> Avenging the death of the Fed.
> We'd better confess that the U is a mess
> Colour it red.
>
> The country is seething for action,
> Resenting inaction and spite.
> When the only work done is for those whose side won
> Paint our sepulchre white.
> . . . .
> Our image is faceless and formless
> We've only our own selves to thank
> If our soul has been sold, be it black, green or gold
> Colour us blank.
>   ("Sybil's Colouring Book", 7)

The achievement of the New World Movement, in this era of growing political hostility towards the academic, was to keep alive the idea of regionalism; to set about the business of providing a language for the analysis of regional problems; to begin the journey towards a definition of a Caribbean aesthetic and to publish a journal of high intellectual quality often in the midst of a demoralized or a scandal-mongering press. Like the Federation, New World eventually disintegrated on the hard rock of indigence. It lost its regional character, too, as each intellectual headed for home and the necessity for self-definition within the national state. Somewhere, the New World dream would smoulder – it is certainly alive in the *Trinidad and Tobago Review* – but the movement itself has not existed for many years.

The 1970s

The 1970s began with the Black Power 'revolution' in Trinidad, which was itself a signal of the economic straits through which the entire archipelago was passing at the time. The euphoria of Guyana's assumption of republican status coincided almost exactly with the eruption of Black Power demonstrations in next-door Trinidad. Since the point of crisis was located in Trinidad and Tobago, there was no time for complacent looking out on the desperation or folly of any other Caribbean state. The early part of the 1970s, a period when near bankruptcy led to the resignation of Dr Eric Williams from the government and the People's National Movement in September 1973, was preoccupied with introspection. What strikes one about the music of the Roaring Seventies is not its anger but its sadness and brooding introspection.[3]

Eric, Eric and Derek

Older heads such as Eric Roach and Derek Walcott were not at all cheered by what had happened to the federal dream, and they tended to vent their rage in criticism of the cultural performance of Eric Williams' five regimes since 1956. The best example of the disillusionment of the poets of the 1950s could be seen in the change that had come over the work of Eric Roach between the time of Federation and 1974 when he committed suicide. Born in 1914, Roach was eighteen in 1932 and forty-four in 1958. He had thus lived through the entire federal dream, from its inception to its brief realization and its dissolution in 1961. If speaking with the voice of the archipelago in its dream of dominion status he recognized the Caribbean person as the seriously damaged product of a violent and squalid history ("I Am the Archipelago", Roach 1992: 128–29)[4], he yet felt that hope lay neither in the insularity and isolation of each small voice nor in escape "from sun to snow, to bitter cities . . . the hostile and exploding zones" ("Love Over-grows a Rock", Roach 1992: 127). Hope lay, rather, in transcending insularity through a shared regional identity and dream.

> . . . So, from my private hillock
> In Atlantic I join cry:
> Come, seine the archipelago;
> Disdain the sea; gather the islands' hills
> Into the blue horizons of our love.
>
> ("Love Over-grows a Rock", Roach 1992: 127)

After the dissolution of the Federation, independence became for Roach merely a jagged fragment of the greater dream of a regional dominion. The rhetoric of black nationalism, fanned into flame by the North American civil rights and Black Power movements of the 1960s, which ran concurrently with the early years of West Indian independence, had, by the late 1960s, overwhelmed the founding words of the national anthem and the national motto.

It is significant that Trinidad's national anthem had originally been composed as an anthem of the West Indian Federation, hence the lines "Side by side we stand / Islands of the blue Caribbean Sea". By 1970 the cry was not for discipline, tolerance and production or for a mutual aspiration and achievement but for power to the people, 'the people' meaning black people; and 'black', despite all attempts to associate the term with the multiethnic working class and the attractiveness of the slogan "Africans and Indians Unite", was in 1970 most emotive as a synonym for the diasporan African.

Having lost the dream of Federation and grown wary of the rhetoric of independence, Roach rejected the new language of old-time Garveyism with a virulent scorn: "This veteran of griefs, betrayals, shames / snarls in the ancestral void" ("Hard Drought", in Brown, Morris and Rohlehr 1989: 75). The present (1970) is depicted as "ancestral void" because Roach regards independence as a betrayal of the fervent protests and faith of the 1930s. The superman of the 1950s, Williams, turns out to be "not ours but history's ruin/ his homing instincts back to barracoons / and slave plantations". Thus it is with bitterness that Roach in "Hard Drought" addresses the youthful shamans of the Black Power movement:

> Don't mock me about dreams
> I am too old
> Don't sneer of prophecies
> count me among the numberless dead
> this grisly century
> I've eaten so much history that I belch
> boloms of years to come.
>   (in Brown, Morris and Rohlehr 1989: 74–75)

One can discern the shattered dream in all of the post-1970 poems, as well as the utter helplessness and hopelessness, the conviction that nothing is to be done, the terror that the region has exhausted its possibilities:

> Ah brother, what's to do?
> Acres of shanty town in Port of Spain
> dungle in Kingston town
> beyond the boundary of hope,
> outside the furthest reaches of our love,
> flyblown as offal rotting in the sun
> while the rich bore their souls with orgies
> and power hoards guns, grenades,

bull pistles and tear gas against its doom.
Gord brudder, what to do?
Jeesas! Gord brudder!
Wha' de arse to do?
                    ("Littering the Earth's Centre", Roach 1992: 203)

Note how the expansive federal vision of "the blue horizons of our love" becomes the shrunken closed and crowded perspective of the slum, an immediate 'close-up' of terrifying decay, stasis and imminent explosive break-up. Strangely, this vision that is so immediately in front of the eye is also "beyond the boundary of hope / outside the furthest reaches of our love". The allusion to C.L.R. James' *Beyond a Boundary* may well be meant to suggest Roach's abandonment of hope in James' faith in the power of the masses to direct their own affairs. James, whose analysis of social situations throughout the years used to carry a prescriptive section entitled "What to Do" is being asked by the desperately sceptical Roach for a formula to heal these times: "Gord, brudder, What to do?" Of course, Roach may also be asking the question of a seemingly helpless deity, or of the numerous messiahs of the street, his equally emasculated and powerless 'brudder' men.

At the moment of Roach's death (1974) Trinidad, through the instrumentality of the Organization of Petroleum Exporting Countries' cartel, found herself suddenly performing in a bright new masquerade that promised to render equally irrelevant the bitterly recriminatory rhetoric of black nationalism, the more doctrinaire rigidity of the Marxists, and the anthem-and-flag enthusiasm of those who could still remember independence. The rest of the decade was thick with calypsos and poems that sought to chart the meaning of the oil-windfall of dollars and to marvel at the new life that it made possible. Calypsos such as Valentino's "Dis Place Nice" (1975) Chalkdust's "Three Blind Mice" (1976), "Trinidad Money" (1979); Swallow's "Trinidad the Godfather" (1979); King Austin's "Progress" (1980); and Shorty's "Money Is No Problem" (1979) were typical of the latter half of the 1970s. So too was the harshly retrospective vision of the two decades since Federation, the years of independence, that one begins to discern in Derek Walcott's poems and plays: "The Spoiler's Return" (1980/81), "The Schooner *Flight*" (1977), "The Star-Apple Kingdom" (1977), *Remembrance* (1980), and *In a Fine Castle* (1970), later rewritten and renamed *The Last Carnival* (1986).

The portraits of Williams and Trinidad in the era of the petro-dollar were seldom flattering. Derek Walcott's Shabine, narrator of the long monologue "The Schooner *Flight*", has to escape the corruption of Trinidad, "the Limers'

Republic", and journey through madness, nightmare, guilt, history's holocaust, and a storm that is both meteorological and psychological, before he can regain the innocence and moral wholeness that lie beyond experience, and, like a priest, bless the archipelago. The dream is regained, the word purged of madness, bile and vituperation. But the poet who, like Roach, has seen too many betrayals, now prefers the single lamp of his own vision and the solitude of his own inner space, even as his craft fares forward.

"A Sea Change" (1980) is shorter and more taut. The name derives from the song that Ariel sings to Ferdinand in Shakespeare's *The Tempest* but implies the very opposite to the redemptive transformation that was Shakespeare's theme in all of his late plays. In "A Sea Change" it is the islands themselves, the once idealized green mountains and bays of the federated archipelago, that have undergone transformation "into something rich and strange": the playgrounds of the metropolitan rich. All the richness is on one side, all the estrangement on the other. "A Sea Change" is of the same spirit as "In the Virgins" (1976) and "Parades, Parades" (1976): those dry but enraged meditations on islands that have lost their innocence – 'virgins' despoiled of their virginity – whose politicians, losing their eyes, have nothing to offer besides an empty self-aggrandizing authoritarianism, deepening corruption and a tourism-based economy that erodes and degrades indigenous lifestyles. These poems are also a reaction to the already significant and still-growing shadow of American military, economic, materialistic and cultural presence in the archipelago.

As a man of the 1950s and the poet whose historical epic *Drums and Colours* occupied a privileged space in the Festival of Arts that marked the opening of the Federation in January 1958, Walcott can still remember less desperate and more gracious times. So in "A Sea Change" he assumes the persona of a hapless tourist, lured to these pitiable shores by the deception of the tourist brochure and shocked at the reality he encounters:

> Islands hissing in rain,
> light rain and governments falling.
> Follow, through cloud, again,
> the bittern's lonely calling.

> Can this be the right place?
> These islands of the blest
> cheap package tours replaced
> by politics, rain, unrest?
>   (Walcott 1981: 19)

Here the persona may be Walcott himself, seeking still some area of innocence, some fragment of his lost dream, but finding, as ever, the snake's hissing voice punctuating the politics of each make-believe, tottering government in "these islands of the blest".

In "The Spoiler's Return" (1981: 53–60) Walcott abandons this mask of Marquesian satire for the dead cold eyes of the anaconda. The calypsonian Spoiler died in December 1960, less than a year before the Federation broke up. The two decades that he has been dead, or rather living in a hell that is far better organized than Port of Spain which resembles it in many other respects, have for the most part been years of independence. The returned Spoiler is on a mission to reveal a hellish truth that is the reality of postindependence life. He is placed high on a bridge in Laventille, that is above both city and the distant Caroni plains; above too, the Gulf and the Caribbean Sea.

His vision, indeed, wanders from an overview of the archipelago where the terse images are those of sharks voraciously trying to devour their own shadows and the homelier one of crabs scrambling in vain over each others' backs to escape from the proverbial crab-barrel. These are images of absurdly futile greed and individualism and they are used to describe the activity of a new generation of leaders who have changed nothing "but colour and attire".

Spoiler's fixed macajuel stare is at its most severe when it focuses on Trinidad under the spell of its "oil-bloated economy". The criticism here is that Trinidad has found itself in a position to fulfil some of the objectives of the old federal dream, but is too corrupt or too disorganized or simply too uncompassionate or too self-centred and self-righteous to either bother to help its neighbours, or helping, to do so without a patronizing smugness. It breaks Spoiler's heart "to see them line up, pitch-oil tin in hand: / each independent, oil forsaken island".

The word "independent" is, of course, laden with the snake's venemous sarcasm. Here, the situation of Chalkdust's "Three Blind Mice" or Explainer's "Charity Begins at Home" is re-entered with a depth of bitterness that, with the possible exception of Delamo's "Apocalypse" (1981), "Sodom and Gomorrah" (1983) and "Armageddon" (1984) did not take up residence in calypso until the late 1980s and early 1990s, with Sugar Aloes and Watchman:

> some begging bold as brass, some coming meeker,
> but from Jamaica to poor Dominica
> we make them know they begging, every loan
> we send them is like blood squeezed out of stone
> and giving gives us back the right to laugh

that we couldn't see we own black people starve
and, more we give, more we congratulate
we-self on our own self-sufficient state.

Interestingly enough, Swallow, a calypsonian from Antigua, was that very
year singing "Trinidad the Godfather" (1980), which offers a far more balanced
vision than that of Spoiler's fixed negative snake's stare. Not concerned with
avenging the death of the Federation, Swallow admits that it is humiliating
and painful to have to beg, but commends Trinidad for the 'substantiable' (*sic*)
loans that she has been giving to clients, some of whom "borrow and borrow
and don't pay back". He notes that Trinidad's loans are often made at the
expense of neglecting Trinidad's own domestic interests. That was certainly
true, and constituted the main grouse of Explainer's "Charity Begins at Home".

Spoiler, however, is still imbued with a nostalgia for the federal dream.

Around the time I dead it wasn't so,
we sang the Commonwealth of caiso
we was in chains, but chains made us unite
now who have, good for them, and who blight, blight.

There is something idyllic about Spoiler's comparison of contemporary time
with what transpired twenty years earlier. There was no time during the federal
negotiations when there wasn't quarrelling, suspicion, a constant scuffling of
islands, and a tendency towards insularity and fragmentation. The fear of the
more developed islands, that free movement of the citizens of the region would
open doors on a flood of hungry mendicants, suggests that even in Spoiler's
time the motto was "who have, good for them, and who blight, blight". Blakie,
who in "Send Them Back" sang with relish about Trinidad's policemen
brutalizing Grenadian immigrants during the 1950s – Spoilers's idyllic time –
was still on the same theme well into the 1970s when he sang "Send Them
Back to They Land". There was a dream of Federation and there were many
idealists who dreamed the dream with deep intensity. But there was no idyllic
time when the dream was truly lived.

Black Power to Grenada

Dr Williams, seemingly as disillusioned as those who blamed him for their
own disillusionment, withdrew from attending Heads of Government meetings after abandoning his plans for an alumina smelter plant, and the team of

Ken Corsbie and Marc Matthews composed their song "Who Put the Rift in CARIFTA". Later in the 1970s, when CARICOM replaced CARIFTA, Chalkdust's "CARICOM" (1979) and Stalin's "Caribbean Unity" (1979) offered different interpretations of the concept of a Caribbean Community. According to Chalkdust, CARICOM provides the West Indies with an opportunity to make amends for the failure of the Federation nearly two decades before:

> Mr Gairy, come here Mr Gairy
> The Federation all you done waste down
> So now you have a chance
> To mend the mistakes we made
> And strengthen and balance
> Our Caribbean lands and trade

Such strengthening and balancing require positive steps towards attaining some of the goals of the old Federation, such as free movement of people, labour, skills; a common regional tariff structure with preferential rates for Caribbean products; a common CARICOM currency, or at very least, common acceptance of the various national currencies; a strong reliable regional airline; a barter system to help the smaller, poorer territories; either a common ideology or tolerance for a plurality of ideologies; a common education and examinations system; dialogue among leaders and spokespersons for the region with the aim of establishing consensus on how the region is to be represented in international fora.

The boldness with which Chalkdust calls the leaders out is a sign of the authority that he imagines himself to have won after a decade of jousting against the policies and performance of Dr Williams. It is a daring extension of the privileged space of the tent and the fool's licence of the calypsonian. Stalin, no less a warner than Chalkdust, dismisses the very premise on which the new regional movement is based. Confusing the sequence of CARIFTA and CARICOM, Stalin implies that it hardly matters, since both of these institutions confine themselves to matters of commerce rather than to people and culture. Like Chalkdust, he sings with the memory of Federation in his bones and addresses his sermon to "Mister West Indian Politician":

> You try with a Federation
> The whole thing end in confusion
> CARICOM and then CARIFTA
> But somehow I smelling disaster
> Mister West Indian Politician

You went to big institution
How come you can't unite seven million?
When a West Indian unity
I know is very easy
If you only rap to your people and tell them like me

Chorus
Dem is one race
De Caribbean Man
From de same place
De Caribbean Man
That make the same trip
De Caribbean Man
On the same ship
De Caribbean Man
So we must push one common intention
For a better life in the region
For we woman
And we children
Dat must be the ambition of the Caribbean Man
De Caribbean Man, De Caribbean Man

Herein then lies the difference between Stalin's approach to regionalism and that of Chalkdust. Chalkdust belongs to a more recent version of the class of intellectuals from which political leadership in the Caribbean has traditionally derived: the up-from-slavery "talented tenth" of Booker T. Washington and W.E.B. Du Bois, in whose inherent right to leadership and responsibility to lead Trinidad's Eric Williams (1956) also believed. Stalin sings as a spokesperson for the presumably 'untalented' 90 percent of the people or, at least, the African-ancestored segment of the untalented ninety, and his first objective in addressing "Mister West Indian Politician [who] went to big institution" is really to call into question the legitimacy and fitness for rule of this class of people. When in "Run Something"/"Piece o de Action" (1976) he claims the right to address Dr Williams (Mr Divider) on the basis of "man talking to man", he is not claiming – as Chalkdust sometimes does – to belong to the same class of intellectuals and 'leaders' as Williams but to possess alternative knowledge, skills and experience rooted in his status and struggle as a man from the working class. It is on these alternative skills and this grounded knowledge and rooted experience, as much as on the intellectual brilliance, manipulative dexterity and civic responsibility of the talented tenth, that the performance of government and the construction of nationhood depends.

Stalin, who began singing calypsos in 1964, was fifteen years old when the People's National Movement came to power and twenty when the Federation disintegrated, twenty-one when Trinidad and Tobago became independent and twenty-nine when the neo-Garveyism of the Black Power movement resurfaced to provide an entire generation of lost, disillusioned and largely unemployed 'black' (that is, African-ancestored mainly, though there were Indian youth involved in the movement) youth with an ideology that seemed to provide them with historical context, political purpose and a basis for coherence. That Black Power's new-Garveyism was viewed with positive alarm by both the governing black intelligentsia and the self-appointed spokespersons for the East Indian masses is a well-documented fact. It is, however, what Stalin brought to his penetrating calypsos about patronage and clientelism ("Run Something" [1976], "Breakdown Party" [1980]); class, labour, struggle and persistent poverty ("Make Them All Right" [1983], "Nothing Ain't Strange" [1975]); African consciousness ("Martin Luther King" [1969], "No Other Man" [1971], "The All Season Man" [1979], "Black Star Liner" [1979], "Caribbean Unity" [1979]); culture and national identity ("Steelband Gone" [1973], "Play One" [1979], "Mr Pan Maker" [1987], "De Jam" [1978/1980]); patriotism ("Sing for the Land" [1985], "We Can Make It If We Try" [1987]); the family ("Caribbean Unity" [1979], "No Woman" [1986], "Stay Giving Praises" [1981]); the Caribbean ("Caribbean Unity" [1979], "Isms Schisms" [1985], "Cry to the Caribbean" [1992]).

By 1979 when Stalin won the national Calypso Monarch competition with "Caribbean Unity", he had already become noted for a wide range of themes, all of which grew out of his deep concern for class, country, family and the African ethos in which he was grounded. In 1963 he had sung "United Africa" and "One Nation Together", a choice of themes that gave early indication of how Stalin would orient himself in the future. His critique of the intellectuals in power and those seeking office ("More Times" [1979]), "Vampire Year" [1981], "Breakdown Party" [1980]) was foreshadowed by his earlier "De Ole Talk" (1974).

> More courthouse in dis country
> De jail hiring more turnkey
> St Anns want nurses daily
> Bigger and bigger cemetery
> Take a look in these places you sure to see
> Poor people in de majority
> So tell dem politician gimme a break
> Is de talk we can't take

Like Louise Bennett in "Big Wuds" (1956), Stalin perceives the intellectuals as men of words, 'ole talkers' who are impotent to bring about change for the better or stop things from disintegrating.

> Plenty talk and no action
> From priest down to politician
> Brother, all ah dem ha solution
> To bring happiness to de poor man.

"Caribbean Unity" (1979) simply continues the critique by citing as examples of the failure of the class of intellectuals the Federation and CARIFTA, and predicting the failure of the newly established CARICOM. Stalin's diagnosis of past failures and prognosis for future ones reveal a disconnection of the planners, movers and shakers from the majority of Caribbean people, an emphasis on purely commercial concerns and an indifference to the necessity for cultural unification. Such unification, according to Stalin, needs to be grounded in a people's awareness of a common history of transportation and struggle, and in a "common intention" to work "for a better life in the region / for we women and we children".

Stalin then pointed to Rastafarianism as an example of the sort of common historical consciousness that he had in mind as the foundation upon which the new Caribbean man and nation would be founded. Rastafarianism had almost overnight become a trans-Caribbean movement. Its phenomenal expansion pointed to the presence of a dialogue taking place at the very roots of Caribbean societies, which showed that the people understood the meaning of Caribbean unity at deeper levels than "dem politicians".

"Caribbean Unity" was attacked by Indian academics on the grounds that it was sexist (it spoke of a Caribbean man as the actor in reconstructing Caribbean society and seemed to erase the women) and racist (it spoke as if only one race, the Africans, had made the trip across the Middle Passage. It thus excluded the contribution of all other races, particularly that of Asiatics, who saw themselves as having been alienated and marginalized from the centre of nationalist discourse and political activity in Trinidad.)5 Stalin defended his Garveyite stance in an interview with Brother Resistance (Roy Lewis).

> If you look at Caribbean unity yuh go see dat de heaviest ting dat ever happen, even tho de whole action wasn't on a specific emphasis on de Caribbean, was when Bro. Marcus Garvey was around . . . No one say, when Garvey around, had anything to do wid who is Vincentian, Grenadian, or who is Trinidadian, but de whole Caribbean was togedda. All Bro. Garvey do was to give de man he identification jus tell de man who he really is. (Lewis 1981: 89–90)

In addition to this declaration of ground, Stalin reminded a Trinidad and Tobago Television discussion panel that, as far as he could remember from his teenage days, the people who had been most prominent in their promotion of the idea of Caribbean unity – Norman Manley, Grantley Adams, Eric Williams, T. Albert Marryshow – had not been Indians but were African ancestored.

"Caribbean Unity" and the debate it engendered illustrated that one of the issues that had beriddled the West Indian federal negotiations, that of ethnic and cultural pluralism and the political division based on such pluralism, was alive and well eighteen years after the break-up of the Federation. Written large or shouted loud in the Caribbean unity debate was the older Indo-Caribbean fear of absorption in a greater Afro-Caribbean solidarity. African Caribbean calypsonians who promote such notions of black solidarity and consciousness are perceived as dangerous even when, like Stalin, they advocate healthy notions such as the need for black males to assume responsibility for improving the lives and circumstances of their families. In the context of ethnic contestation, such advice is dangerous because it strengthens 'the enemy' and destroys the negative stereotyping through which blacks, particularly calypsonians, have traditionally been represented.

The controversy strengthened Stalin, whose work during the 1980s became even more deeply rooted in its two grounds: African consciousness and pan-Trinidadian, pan-Caribbean patriotism. The debate had, nevertheless, reopened the question of whether there could ever be a viable political Federation of so many units, some of which were so deeply divided within themselves along lines of ethnicity, or class, or even (as in postindependence Jamaica) political party tribalism.

The notion of a common African ancestry, derided by John Hearne and Vidia Naipaul as being merely "the sentimental camaraderie of skin" (Naipaul 1962: 84), and rejected, often scornfully by non-African West Indians as being inapplicable to them, has nonetheless remained quite strong among calypsonians. One thinks of those two anthems on the Haitian tragedy, David Rudder's "Haiti" (1988) and Ronald Boo Hinkson's "Down to the Bone" (1992), which female calypsonian Cheryl so hauntingly renders. "Down to the Bone" is, like "Haiti", a direct appeal to African consciousness:

So every time a Haitian mourn
Is a Black man mourn
And every time a Haitian drown
Is a Black man drown
Every time a Haitian cry

Is a Black man cry
And every time a Haitian die
Is a Black man die
Soften up your heart of stone
The Haitian is Black people down to the bone.

"Down to the Bone" is equally Afrocentric in its reading of international politics and economics as the steady consolidation of 'the white race':

the white race always sticking together
even after war they helping each other
that we must learn
or else we burn
So keeping Haiti alive
we make sure the whole Black race survive

In "Haiti" Rudder sings to increase awareness of the debt the Caribbean people owe to the Haitian Revolution as a major catalyst to emancipation and whatever freedom followed thereafter. He questions the meaning of a black consciousness that advocates freedom in South Africa while remaining oblivious to the Haitian cause:

Many hands reached out to St Georges
And are still reaching out
And to frightened, foolish men of Pretoria
We still scream and shout
We came together in song
To steady the horn of Africa
But the papaloa come and the babyloa go
And still we don't seem to care

Chorus
Haiti I'm sorry
We've misunderstood you
One day we'll turn our heads
And look inside you
Haiti I'm sorry
Haiti I'm sorry
One day we'll turn our heads
Restore your glory

Like Hearne and Naipaul, Rudder questions sentimental black nationalism; but unlike them, his aim is to clarify and affirm a more genuine and meaningful solidarity of Africans at home and abroad. Thus he sings:

When there is anguish in Port-au-Prince
Dont you know it's still Africa crying?
We are outing fires in far away places
When our neighbours are burning
The middle passage is gone, so how come
Overcrowded boats still haunt our lives?
I refuse to believe that we good people
Will forever turn our hearts and our eyes
. . . away

This is a powerful invocation of the idea of pan-African solidarity. Rudder soon after dedicates an entire album to the anti-apartheid struggle. Concern for Africa is counterpointed by a deep sense of the Caribbean as a region. Rudder's "Rally Round the West Indies" (1988) has become an unofficial anthem for the cricket-playing islands. "Caribbean Party" (1993), "Here Come the West Indies" (1994), "Cuba" (1994) and "One Caribbean" (1994) all indicate the enduring possibilities for a reconciliation of pan-Africanist and pan-Caribbeanist sentiment.

There is a similar two- or three-dimensionality about Valentino's work between the mid 1970s and the 1990s. Rooted like Stalin in Black Power consciousness, Valentino early declares the necessity for interethnic boarding on the basis of mutual class interests. Liberation, he declares, can only come if Trinidadians "forget the 'nigger' and the 'coolie' grouse" and realize that they "belong to the same old house". "Dis Place Nice" (1975) focuses on Trinidad in the grips of wildcat commercial expansion and predicts a coming revolution of trouble, fire and fighting. "Namesake" (1975) compares the two Erics, Gairy and Williams, accusing them both of employing state terrorism to reinforce their now uncertain grip on power. "Ah Wo" (1980) is his reaction to the 1979 Grenada Revolution, his prediction that its spirit will spread throughout the Little Eight. Grenada (1979) is the uprising of the people he had dreamed of since Trinidad (1970) and predicted in "Dis Place Nice" (1975).

In his ironically named "No Revolution" (1971), Valentino equates blackness with an heritage of unrewarded or inadequately recompensed labour:

Is black blood, black sweat and black tears
But is white profits
Cause all through the years
Is the white man who reaping the benefits.

The Black Power uprising was enacted not for the purpose of 'revolution' but to free the black worker from all forms of oppression.

Because the fight was against racial prejudice
The imperialists, the capitalists
Yet some ignorant people they talk bout communism.
(Valentino 1996: 12)

This vision of blackness as inadequately recompensed labour will be re-peated in Chalkdust's powerful "Grandfather's Back Pay" (1985). It expands Black Power beyond Afrocentricity towards a politics of the international proletariat and establishes the basis for those later efforts that calypsonians were to make in the decade between 1975 and 1985, to rekindle the spirit of Caribbean integration by appealing to either pan-Africanist or socialist senti-ment. In a few cases, these two bodies of ideology merged into each other; at other times they were perceived as distinct and divergent.

Born in Grenada, Valentino interpreted the Grenada Revolution as a symbol of the fulfilment of a regional quest for freedom that has been taking place since enslavement and is the very essence of Caribbean history. In "Free Grenada" (1980) he gives his interpretation of the previous year's events:

Thirteenth of March, Tuesday, 1979
Will remain in every Grenadian mind
Was the day the people made their motion
And the nation supported the Revolution
Like how L'Overture free up Haiti
And Castro free Cuba
On that Tuesday
Maurice Bishop free Grenada
(Valentino 1996: 7)

The concept of a people's revolution now takes precedence over all others as the main inspiring idea that can rekindle the ancient federal dream of 'one Caribbean'. Valentino's location of revolution at the centre of a reconfigured Caribbean history is in the tradition of C.L.R. James' *The Black Jacobins* and, not so obviously, of Derek Walcott's *Drums and Colours* which, beginning with Columbus and Raleigh, ends with Toussaint and George William Gordon.

Valentino's bitterness and sadness at the self-destruction of the Grenada Revolution in 1983 matches that of Walcott and Roach after the dissolution of the Federation. In "Saga of the PRA" (1984) he accuses Austin and Coard of having turned "a dream into a nightmare", "orchestrated a crucifixion" and reversed revolutionary process.

Like all you start the third World War
And brought a colonial disaster
On an oppressed people
Forwarding out of that struggle
Hudson Austin and Bernard Coard
These consequences you cannot afford
Was it Russia, Cuba or America
That made you commit such a great crime
By turning back the hands of time?
Betray the Nation
And turn back the Revolution.
       (Valentino 1996: 7)

Again one observes the agonizing transition from dream to nightmarish reality with the poet awakening from the idyllic mental landscape that he has constructed around some central axis or *poteau mitan:* Federation, cultural interface, black nationalism, ethnic solidarity, a proletarian international or Caribbean revolution. The reality to which Valentino now awakens is that of latter-day cold war politics, for which Grenada had become the most fantastic and improbable theatre. He lists the disintegration of CARICOM as one of the disastrous consequences of the failure of Grenada.

The Democrats and the Socialists
Republicans and the Communists
They had the world confused
With so much of different views
George Chambers say was an invasion
Eugenia Charles say "rescue mission"
Bernard Coard so dumb
He mash up the CARICOM
The comrade put water in we eye
By making way for the CBI.
       (Valentino 1996: 7)

Valentino represents Reagan's Caribbean Basin Initiative as the next phase, after the defeat of the Grenada Revolution, in the entrenchment of American imperialism in what he terms the leaking basin of the Caribbean. "Down with the CBI" (1983) was composed and sung several months before the actual break-up of the revolution, but it already contains an ominous note of the inevitability of an American intervention. In a direct address to Reagan, Valentino accuses:

You trying to get at Cuba
So you picking on Grenada
Spreading false propaganda
You're a destabilizer
Your military manoeuvres
In our territorial areas
Like you waiting to pull the trigger
As you did on Argentina

At this juncture, Valentino recognizes two choices for the Caribbean: passive surrender to a new era of subservience and abject dependency on America and a renewed drive towards Caribbean integration.

What we need in the Caribbean
Is a powerful federation
We need to be united
And not divided
But you divide Latin America
And you deal with Jamaica
And Dominica under your command
Since Eugenia Tom fell inside your plan

You aim to control our resources
And direct our economy
But stay off Caribbean courses
With your modern day piracy
The leaders in the region
Should come under one union
Cause this Basin Initiative
Is not imperative
                    (Valentino 1996: 7–8)

This may sound like Atilla's "Expedite Federation" (1933), but fifty years have elapsed since 1933 and the options open to the Caribbean have not apparently changed much. It is still a choice between hanging together and hanging separately, even though the status of the victims and identity of the imperial hangman may both have changed.

Black Stalin, Valentino's 'blood brother' of the mid 1970s, records his own reactions to the Grenada crisis in "Isms Schisms" (1985). An entire year separates this calypso from Valentino's "Saga of the PRA" and Stalin has therefore had the time to compose a balanced, sober but equally resolute response to the tragic turn of events. What Stalin says he learns from Grenada is a profound mistrust of ideology.

> They teach me: Capital-, Social-, or Communism
> Is the same gun head all o' dem on
> And from the time you team up with them
> Like Grenada you straight on the losing end

Superpower cold war politics, based as it is on the concept of a balance of terror, is inevitably a politics of violence. Client states entangled in such politics may find themselves becoming the theatres of a strife that is really irrelevant to their own concerns and detrimental to their welfare.

> One ism with a gun telling you to vote
> One say "Don't vote" with a gun at your throat
> They saving all their arms and ammo for me
> And sending their wheat for their enemy

Stalin recoils from this Orwellian situation in which two equally cynical power blocs settle their ideological differences in a war for the resources of the underdeveloped world that seldom involves any direct military encounter of the superpowers on their own soil. Indeed, far from actually fighting each other, capitalists and communists have worked out grounds for amicable dialogue and humane exchange between themselves. America sends wheat to starving Russia and the cosmonauts of both countries exchange greetings in space, even as the client nations attached to both blocs are required to observe the most proper masquerade of ideological hostility.

Like Boo Hinkson in "Down to the Bone", Stalin suggests that for the Caucasian nations, ideology serves the primary interest of white supremacism:

> Rescue mission to help Grenadians
> Rescue mission to Afghanistan
> Rescue mission going the world over
> But no rescue mission to South Africa

South Africa, at the time the worst example of racist and undemocratic tyrannical rule in the world, is pressured via economic sanctions, not military intervention; an option reserved for non-Caucasian transgressors against 'democracy'. Recognizing the meaninglessness of ideology in a world dominated by economic and ethnic pragmatism, Stalin calls for his own version of the new world order.

> The time is ripe right now more than ever
> For man to sit down and write the new order
> Where man would respect a man as a man
> And not through colour and superior weapon

When we must be equal, righteous and fair
And realize the earth is for all to share
And to his fellow man always be true
But until the day come, hear what I go do

What he will do is "to stay away from them isms" whose ultimate consequence is death or deep impoverishment.

These Islands Now

If Stalin in "Isms Schisms" ends with a prescription that tells the Caribbean people what they must avoid until the dawning of the new age, Rudder's "Rally Round the West Indies" (1987) is more positively prescriptive in advising them on what they need to affirm. That calypso is indeed about cricket; but cricket becomes, as in C.L.R. James' *Beyond a Boundary,* whose title Rudder invokes, much more than a game. It becomes a manifestation of the spirit, potential and human excellence of the West Indian people, the perception of which had inspired and ignited the original dream of Federation. It is no mistake that the cyclic rise, fall and rebirth of West Indian cricket are compared with the ebb and flow of the Haitian Revolution:

. . . when the Toussaints go
The Dessalines come
We've lost the battle
But will win the war

Towards the end of "Rally Round the West Indies", just to make sure that his listeners recognize that cricket is a metaphor for much more, Rudder explains:

This is not just cricket
This goes beyond the boundary
It's up to you and me to make sure that they fail
Soon we'll have to take a side
Or be lost in the rubble
In a divided world that don't need islands no more
Are we doomed forever to be at someone's mercy?
Little keys can open mighty doors.

If Stalin advises Caribbean people and states to seek such neutral spaces as might exist between hotly or coldly warring ideologies, Rudder warns them that they will be forced to choose, "to take a side . . . in a divided world that don't need islands no more". The 'side' that he prompts them to take is their own. The West Indies' team has provided them with an example of what that side should be, demonstrating what skilled West Indians, imbued with a collective sense of their own revolutionary history and potential, can achieve.

Early in the decade of the 1980s, Chalkdust, reacting to the cultural and economic penetration of Trinidad and the Caribbean by the United States, concludes that "the Caribbean belong to Uncle Sam". Many calypsos of the decade chronicle the steady erasure of anything like a Caribbean consciousness by American values, lifestyles, goods and services that are as mindlessly absorbed by Caribbean people as they are resolutely marketed by American capitalism. Merchant, employing the metaphor of the fête, celebrates the emergence of a unified Caribbean consciousness and aesthetic in "Caribbean Connection" (1988), four years after Valentino employs the self-same metaphor in "Trini Gone Through", his unremittingly negative portrayal of an "irresponsible and lazy nation", "running last in their work ethics", "only conscious of money", "petty, jealous", "heading in the wrong direction", "sinking in corruption", "on a hopeless trip / Rocking a sinking ship".

Chalkdust, with slightly more laughter but considerable acerbity, fills out the portrait next year with "Rum Mania" (1985). Local, regional or international crisis means nothing to the devil-may-care carousing Trini. "While Guyanese smuggling gold in their bum / All day all night Trini drinking their rum". Similarly, "While Yankee soldiers eating Grenadian plum", the Trinidadian remains in a nirvana of blissful intoxication. The fête is again associated with mindlessness, and it is this absence of 'mind' that has made it easy for America to fill the vacuum left by the departure of the British imperialist. A sense of the Caribbean is erased in direct proportion to the Americanization of the region.

Reflecting on the "Roaring Seventies", Valentino laments the ease with which the entire era seems to have faded from people's memory.

> But Trini have this funny funny way of forgetting
> Their history to dem like it don't mean nothing
> The history that went down here in the 1970s
> As though it never was today in the 80s
> But don't care how much they try to tarnish these historic memories
> I will always remember the Roaring 70s
>> (Valentino 1996: 9)

While he resolves to remember, Valentino recognizes his society to be a nation of amnesiacs and wonders whether the rebels of the 1970s "gave their lives for a hopeless cause". While this question is asked mainly about Trinidad, foremost on Valentino's mind was Grenada; so the question of memory or amnesia as equal and opposite attitudes towards historical trauma is being implicitly asked of the wider Caribbean region. How can a region that wilfully denies its own heroic effort, that negates and erases even its immediate past, survive? How will it generate a dream, an idea, or an ideal that is worth the sacrifices that will have to be made? Valentino holds out no hope in this regard. He ends, rather, with a vision of the region's recolonization:

> Looking through that era
> Well I see changes develop politically
> Who leave this party and join that party
> And who stole all the oil money
> I see conscious black men and women
> In the 80s crumble and bend
> And the nation gone right back to Europe
> On a Western trend.
> (Valentino 1996: 9)

Chalkdust's "Sea Water and Sand" (1986) counterpoints Valentino's "Trini Gone Through" of the same year. It acknowledges that the region has redesigned its mechanisms for measuring human and national worth. Caribbean countries are now literally measuring each other according to what their dollar is worth in US currency. The devaluation of the once proud Jamaican dollar to the north and the struggling Guyanese dollar to the south, is received by those who imagine themselves to be more wealthy with loud laughter and ribald mockery instead of dread and sadness.

"Sea Water and Sand" questions the wisdom of such laughter, unmasks the same old insularity in each leader, and warns the region that "unless there is cooperation / All o' dem on the same road to destruction". In typical Chalkdust style, the persona cites numerous examples of insular and arrogant behaviour, beginning with the false confidence that Barbados and Dominica have invested in their status as the favourite mendicant client states of Washington and London; continuing with Trinidad's tariff barriers against CARICOM products and immigration restrictions against Grenadian refugees; Antigua's blockage of the British West Indies Airlines' bid to become the regional carrier; and the failure of regional leaders to implement treaties that they have signed. Ingratiating themselves with America, and prostituting themselves to earn whatever handouts they can acquire from the United States, the islands neglect their most crucial necessity: that of maintaining meaningful contact, discourse and exchange with each other. Foreign exchange replaces local human interface.

Dreamers of the dream of Caribbean unity are not deterred from their dreaming merely because of the grimness of social and economic reality that surrounds them. There is no greater realist than David Rudder, whose chants in "Another Day in Paradise" (1995) or the "Madman's Rant" (1996) are the most harrowing chronicles of social disintegration. Yet there is also no deeper dreamer, as his "One Caribbean" (1994) proves:

> We got so little on our own but as a region we can face tomorrow
> Athletes and artists have shown the way
> And from our roots of resistance and old suffering we can rise through this sorrow
> We're much too bright in spirit not to find a better day
> But in this New World all the time we have this common crisis
> For debts won't die away and social tension's on the rise
> From Havana to Georgetown oh the danger, the danger is spreading
> It's time for a common front, it's time that we realize

I am saying:

> One Caribbean, One Caribbean
> One heart together in a changing world
> One Caribbean, One Caribbean
> One love, one heart, one soul
> Reaching for a common goal.

Again the dream, the call. It will not take time. The region has had time. It will require, as Rudder senses when he assumes the role of shaman, chanter and exhorter, magic. Hence the invocation of the "one love / one heart" spirit of Bob Marley. Hence the long wild chant, at times in fragmented French and Spanish as well as English, with which the Caribbean people are invited to join hands across the water. Hence, too, the final attestation of faith: "We're coming together", though this is nowhere visible, as the hard-nosed realists illustrate in their grim songs.

Notes

1. Words quoted from memory.
2. Quotation taken from Theodore Sealey, *Sunday Gleaner,* 20 March 1955.
3. Over twenty years after 1970, Zeno Constance reconstructed the events of the decade through its calypsos in a calypso-opera entitled *De Roaring Seventies.*
4. "I Am the Archipelago" in Roach 1992: 128–29. (Poem originally published in 1957.)
5. For a detailed account of the controversy see Deosaran 1992: 317–70.

References

Ahye, Molly. 1983. *Cradle of Caribbean Dance: Beryl McBurnie and the Little Carib Theatre.* Port of Spain, Trinidad: Heritage Cultures.

Bennett, Louise. 1966. *Jamaica Labrish.* Kingston, Jamaica: Sangster's Book Stores.

Brown, Stuart, Mervyn Morris, and Gordon Rohlehr, eds. 1989. *Voiceprint: Oral and Related Poetry from the Caribbean.* London: Longman.

De Leon, Raphael. 1988. *Calypso: From France to Trinidad, 800 Years of History.* Port of Spain, Trinidad: Raphael De Leon.

Deosaran, Ramesh. 1992. *Sociology Psychology in the Caribbean Directions for Theory and Research.* Port of Spain, Trinidad: Longman.

Lewis, Roy [Brother Resistance]. c. 1981. "De Black Stalin". Caribbean Studies thesis, University of the West Indies, St Augustine Trinidad.

Mordecai, John. 1968. *The West Indies: The Federal Negotiations.* London: George Allen and Unwin.

Naipaul, Vidia. 1962. *The Middle Passage.* London: André Deutsch.

Quevedo, Raymond. 1983. *Atilla's Kaiso: A Short History of Trinidad's Calypso.* Port of Spain, Trinidad: Hera Quevedo.

Roach, Eric. 1992. *The Flowering Rock: Collected Poems 1938–1974.* Leeds: Peepal Tree Books.

Walcott, Derek. 1981. *The Fortunate Traveller.* New York: Farrar, Straus, Giroux.

Williams, Eric. 1956. *Federation: Two Public Lectures.* Port of Spain, Trinidad: The College Press.

Brother Valentino [Emrold Phillip]. 1996. *Life is a Stage: The Complete Calypsos of Brother Valentino, Anthony Emrold Phillip 1971–1996,* edited by Zeno Obi Constance. Port of Spain, Trinidad: Emrold Phillip.

PART 3

Critique

12

Caribbean Diversity and Ideological Conformism
The Crisis of Marxism in the English-speaking Caribbean

FOLKE LINDAHL

> Marxism has been the greatest fantasy of our century. It was a dream offering the prospect of a society of perfect unity, in which all human aspirations would be fulfilled and all values reconciled.
> — Leszek Kolakowski

It is probably too early to seriously assess or to draw any far-reaching conclusions concerning the intellectual impact on the Caribbean of the crisis of both theoretical and practical Marxism in the post–cold war world, but it is certainly appropriate to initiate a critical discussion of some problems that have already emerged as a result of this crisis. In fact, the demise of Marxism as a practical force in politics in large parts of the world is merely the most recent development of what historically could be seen as a much longer illness that slowly worsened over the past two decades. Theoretically, Marxism was in trouble much before the current last gasps, but it is only in the past few years that the symptoms of this early weakness have become more visible.[1]

In this brief reflection, I merely want to initiate a discussion of some obvious elements of the decline and possible fall of Marxism as an ideology in the Caribbean. Although this essay will be largely critical in tone, it should be stated from the outset that there is no doubt that Marxism has contributed valuable perspectives and analyses of Caribbean society and politics over the last century or so. However, it has been a two-edged sword; on the one hand, providing moments of illuminating insights with important practical political consequences and, on the other, displaying areas of blindness and, to put it mildly, less impressive politics.

On the positive side, there is now an intellectual heritage that can be described as both informed and inspired by a broad Marxist tradition, a heritage that is distinctly Caribbean and at the same time firmly planted in a Western, if not global, Marxist discourse. At its best, this legacy is highly original and impressive in both scope and depth. I am here thinking of the works of writers and scholars such as C.L.R. James, Gordon Lewis, Eric Williams and Walter Rodney. They – and others – are already solid and permanent cornerstones in the Caribbean literary and intellectual pantheon. For this reason alone, Marxism is and will remain a lasting feature of Caribbean intellectual and political culture; for one thing, it will continue to inspire and influence new generations of writers and academics. However, it is worth querying the extent to which individuals such as C.L.R. James and Gordon Lewis have received their intellectual prominence due to their brilliance and talents as *original writers and critics* rather than as Marxist theorists or Marxist political analysts. In other words, as Marxism declines as a scientific theory of history and as time passes, their works will be read more and more as essential, path-breaking and monumental contributions to Caribbean social and political thought in general and less and less as specifically Marxist political tracts. The Marxist element will thus be treated as one of many possible sources of inspiration and as a framework that provides historical and political insights for understanding the past and the present. What it cannot be, from this angle, is a blueprint for political action or a 'correct' scientific theory of history. (Be that as it may, predictions of this kind are inherently flawed and without much significance; at the very least, this argument would require detailed analysis and discussions of particular works.)

The critical emphasis in this chapter will be on some of the more questionable assumptions and elements in Marxist theory. I will make my case with regard to two aspects of Caribbean Marxism that illustrate fundamental weaknesses in its ideological perspective and analysis: the overall historical–eschatological assumptions with their claims to universal truth that (over)determine the entire Marxist edifice, and the more specific but equally rigid categories and concepts that permeate all concrete investigations and analysis.

These two broad spheres of the Marxist perspective – the general framework and the concrete political economy categories – interact and influence each other in a manner that often makes concrete discussion and analysis both predictable and overly simplistic. There are of course striking exceptions to this 'rule', but as an analytical tool and political ideology, Marxism has become more of an obstacle to insightful analysis and productive political practice than a perceptive alternative approach to the various political and economic problems facing the Caribbean societies. And if we add to all this the pervasive discrepancy between the theoretical claims of Marxism and its rather dismal record in terms of political practice, we have completed the contours of the crisis.

In order not to fall into a futile ideological bickering between a Marxist and an anti-Marxist position, I try to develop a style of argument that is sceptical and questioning rather than condemning and dismissive. It is part of my contention that the current disenchantment with or withdrawal of support from both socialist projects and Marxist theory is best understood as a growing scepticism *vis-à-vis* the grand promises of Marxism and the unpersuasive categories with which it makes these utopian claims. A critical and deconstructive attitude towards the Marxist 'language game' or 'master code' might prove to be the most fruitful and promising approach. (It is worth noting that people's passions – including the passions of intellectuals – for equality and social justice have not suffered the same disillusionment and decline as Marxism and socialism. At the extension of the concerns in this chapterr lies the question of how and in what direction these passions can find a productive and fruitful outlet.)

In his interesting and concluding chapter of *The Poor and the Powerless,* Clive Thomas (1988) typically asserts that "production aimed at providing for the basic needs of the masses, in the first instance, implies a systematic, conscious, deliberate and planned attack on poverty". He then goes on to provide a set of objectives that can serve partly as a critique of what I interpret as Caribbean Marxism, but that also perpetuates a language and a cluster of 'myths' that themselves need to be questioned. Thomas rightly points out that the dilemma with this 'basic needs' approach is that it has had limited and questionable outcomes where they have been tried, for example, in Grenada under Bishop, in Jamaica under Manley and in Burnham's Guyana. In the latter, "the basic needs programme coincided with a period in which the real incomes of the masses actually fell" (356–57). Cuba is then given as a positive example of this approach, which in hindsight seems problematic.

The main problem here, from my perspective, is that the failure of a policy is not viewed as a possible flaw inherent in the policy but as a failure only in the implementation stage. There is no recognition of the built-in dilemma in trying to articulate "the basic needs of the masses" from the desks of intellectual planners and social scientists. To develop a "systematic, conscious, deliberate and planned attack on poverty" in order to satisfy the basic needs of the masses might very well involve assumptions about basic needs, the masses and planning that undermine even the thinnest notion of 'democracy', which for Thomas, after all is said, remains a desirable means and end for his ideal society. His commitment to democracy is expressed in another objective: "development also implies that work, politics and social organisations are based on democratising power in society and on the effective (as opposed to nominal) exercise of fundamental rights, such as those to free expressions and organisation, respect of an individual's privacy and the abolition of repression and torture". As if this is not enough, Thomas gives an even more ambitious definition of democratic practice: "The democratisation of power also implies the democratisation of all the decision-making structures in the society, from the level of the workplace and community right through to central government" (1988: 358). This hyperbolic rhetoric can only serve to obscure concrete political analysis and invite intellectual frustration on the level of both theory and policy articulation – to say nothing about the question of implementation.

Albeit in attractive and seductive language, what we have here is a range of problematic assertions that are dominant features in both socialist and Marxist ideologies. One does not have to push the interpretation very far in order to accuse this discourse of trying to have its cake and eat it too. The tone, style and content belong to two genres of political writing: one is purely utopian, that is, it describes a nonrealizable ideal, a no-place, as it were; the other is more dangerous in that it implies that a society can actually be harmonious, planned and democratic, all at the same time. Planning, individual rights, the needs of the masses and a total democratization of all levels of government combine to give the impression that these assertions contain no problems or contradictions. Admirable as Thomas's endorsement of individual rights and freedom of expression is – the Marxist tradition has never been particularly concerned with these 'liberal' rights – it poses a great dilemma for the rest of his value judgements.

First of all, once we recognize individual liberties, we also recognize conflicts, dissent, factions and, most importantly, limits to power and government. Second, we cannot have both a planned society and a completely democratized governmental structure (whatever that means). Democracy and individual rights, however we define them, must have room for both dissent and organized opposition, including (no, *especially*) opposition to governmental planning with its implied right to define the basic needs of the masses. Third, although appealing in its rhetoric, and persuasive in terms of the empirical reality of most Caribbean societies, the assertion about the basic needs of the masses does not hold up under scrutiny, I suspect: there are no clearly definable 'basic needs', and there are no homogeneous 'masses'. Both claims are inherently contestable as well as inherently political in content. When we speak of the masses as if we know what 'they' desire and need, we are engaged, at best, in wishful thinking and, at worst, in authoritarian metaphysics. 'The masses' – if the concept means anything – are of course both heterogeneous and pluralistic, and their needs are not to be assumed prior to politics but only *through* politics, hopefully a somewhat democratic and representative politics. Thomas's discussion of the masses, however, assumes that he knows what 'they' want, prior to politics. I take this latter assumption of knowing what people want as emblematic of Marxist ideology, whether it appeals to 'the masses', 'the people', or 'the proletariat'. Democracy is only endorsed as an afterthought, since the theory has already spelled out what the outcome is and should be.

On this last point, Thomas (1988) is unambiguously unclear, so to speak. He subordinates 'the state' to the will of the majority, if I interpret him correctly. "The interpretation of development advanced here is intended to subject the functioning of the state, as well as the development of the society as a whole, to what has been aptly termed the 'logic of the majority' " (361). He rightly wants the majority to make its own decision concerning, what I take to be, development projects. But his analysis still reads as if this majority wants something that Thomas too wants and already knows. This is confirmed in his linking the future development success of the Caribbean to "the survival and eventual success of the region's two major social experiments, Cuba and Nicaragua". He continues:

It is important to recognise that this view does not imply that Cuba, Nicaragua, or even a combination of the two, have to be accepted as future models for the poor and powerless to adopt, but rather that the survival of the *very notion of experimenting to build new Caribbean societies is indissolubly linked to the survival of the only two surviving experiments.* It provides, as it were, a regional alternative and, as such, must remain a high priority in any development thrust. (362; emphasis in original)

Whatever one's perspective is on these two experiments, one would hate to think that the future of the Caribbean is somehow linked to their 'success'. Fortunately, there is of course no objective or provable link in this manner; here Thomas is engaging in his own ideological politics. The quote nevertheless sheds some light on what he means by the "logic of the majority" in the previous paragraph. This is part and parcel of much of Marxist eschatology and metaphysics: there are laws of history; some societies are objectively more progressive than others; politics has an objectively correct goal or direction; the masses – the majority – of course, want this goal as well; this goal coincides with what Marxist intellectuals (or the leaders of 'the Party') think; and so on.

The fundamental weakness with this line of argument is its hidden (or not-so-hidden) epistemological dogmatism: that politics and history are pre-dictable (and logical) and that there is an objective criterion by which we can judge any particular historical moment and any particular society, and that, if the masses just know what is good for them, then there is only one correct judgement or decision. (Although this needs to be sorted out in more detail and depth, it is my argument that this type of discourse has become increasingly untenable in the last decade or so, both as a guide for politics and as a persuasive political theory.)

The dogmatic impression from this discussion of the two critical experiments is enhanced by Thomas's objectivistic claim concerning the need for a specific social transformation in the Caribbean. I will quote at length to illustrate the peculiar style of this teleological discourse:

Given the nature of the Caribbean economies, transforming them will inevitably be an extended social project. Nevertheless, it is still necessary (as part of the mobilising effort of the society) to incorporate, as early in the process as possible, a more or less definite *conception* of the main economic configurations of the economy the society is working to construct. Moreover, this conception should be elevated to the level of a *popular conception,* rather than simply remaining the possession of the economy's political leadership, technocrats and managers. Rooting the project in the popular culture is the only way of ensuring its success, of organising and promoting the development of a new social order.

Another reason for having a clear idea of the configurations of the economy under construction is that it provides a point of reference with which *to test and measure its performance and development. This is important since there are no purely technical tests of a process as profound as the transformation of an economy.* (Thomas 1988: 367; emphasis in original)

What happened to free speech and democratic procedures (on all governmental levels!) in this context? Here we have a case of science for the elite and ideology for the masses. One could construe (and only slightly misconstrue) this to imply that the "main economic configurations of the economy the society is working to construct" are neither subject to nor the result of democratic procedures; they are the product of the elites, and "the people" just need to be brought on board via the creation of a "popular conception" of these "configurations". This understanding of politics does not only mock democratic processes, it blatantly disregards social and political deliberations and account-ability, and reduces previously celebrated masses to an object that can be subjected to propaganda in the name of 'the need' for the transformation of the economy; a transformation that is presumably related to the two experi-ments of Cuba and Nicaragua.

Hopefully, I am not excessively caricaturing Thomas's position, although this is a case in which only the exaggeration is true, since it is easy to miss the ideological commitments in this neutral-sounding discourse. Suffice to say that this conceptualization is not compatible with liberal democracy as it has come to be understood in any of the versions of the Westminster model. To be sure, Thomas is not particularly enamoured with this model, but he is relatively silent on the *institutional* and *procedural* dimensions of his own alternative. In spite of his explicit endorsement of individual rights and liberties, he is not forthcoming with regard to their institutional protection and legal guarantees. His arguments, in spite of their apparent concreteness, remain relatively abstract and vague when it comes to legal and procedural implementation and realization. The criterion for his position above seems to be what Carl Stone (1991) outlines as a Marxist version of development: "the key criterion is whether development is moved toward socialism to ensure that these countries keep pace with the unfolding pattern of inevitable world historical develop-ment from capitalism to socialism" (294). That this criterion hinges on the persuasiveness of the teleological thesis concerning the inevitability of a certain historical path goes without saying. Regardless of what has been made of Marxism as a science, here we are moving in the realm of faith: once we lose faith in the laws of history, we can no longer be enchanted by this kind of language. By contrast, if the faith is present then the liberal rights and liberties and constitutional limits to power are viewed as trivial in comparison to the necessary unfolding of world history. Whatever the appropriate label for this Marxist model, it cannot be called 'democratic' if in the definition of the latter we include the inherent *uncertainty* and *unpredictability* that are entailed in a politics based on mass participation (however limited and sporadic) and (relatively) frequent elections of representatives belonging to competing factions or parties.

However, in recent years there have been notable and admirable shifts among radical (Marxist) intellectuals towards more appreciation and concern for so-called liberal rights and for procedural aspects of democratic government. Still, the concerns often appear as strategical and tactical manoeuvres rather than genuinely substantive commitments to the procedures and processes themselves. Trevor Munroe (1990: 1–25), in a highly self-critical re-evaluation of Marxist theory and practice in Jamaica, expresses this somewhat oscillating position. On the one hand, he clearly and unambiguously acknowledges and criticizes both the authoritarian tendency in most Marxism and the concomitant lack of appreciation for rights and procedures; he also shows an impressive respect for the growing complexity and pluralism of contemporary Jamaican society and culture.

There is, therefore, a definite relationship between the struggle against authoritarianism and for empowerment in civil society and the struggle to deepen and consolidate democracy in the state. The more complex and differentiated the society, the more manifold the points at which this struggle needs to be taken up. Correspondingly, the more numerous and varied are the activities, organizations, leaders and ideologies appropriate to this undertaking. Forcing, inducing, or manipulating homogeneity onto this heterogeneous complex both contradicts the goal of democracy and weakens the instruments of struggle. Equally, the leading role in this protracted effort cannot be legitimately decreed to belong to the working class or to any other sector. Such is determined in the course of the movement itself and, in any event, should not restrict the autonomy of other elements. (20–21)

All of this points in the direction of an open-ended and circumstantial attitude towards a democratic politics that can never be said to be 'correct' or definitive, if for no other reason than that it is exactly that: democratic, as opposed to authoritarian or vanguardistic. In other words, Munroe is defending a *political* position, not asserting a 'scientific' truth or a historical necessity. However, in the next paragraph Munroe almost falls back into a deterministic–historical mode of reasoning. Now, the commitment to democratic procedures and competitive elections are merely a strategic part in a much larger and ambitious historical (and necessary?) saga: "Radical democratization should be the precondition, the concomitant and the consequence of fundamental socio-political transformation" (21). What this fundamental transformation entails more concretely remains uncertain, but Munroe does identify a "growing dissatisfaction with the existing situation" in "many sectors of society", and he interprets this dissatisfaction as expressing "aspirations towards new qualities of *democracy, social justice, national development, public morality, and individual fulfilment*" (23; emphasis mine). Undoubtedly, these are areas of politics and society that *all* political parties or factions have some ideas about, and to a critical extent these huge contestable realms define the very space of politics. Munroe defines his own political programme in relation to these broad areas:

> It is around these five dimensions that the real strivings of the people are critiquing the system and that any new movement should seek to develop its basic programmatic platform. Extracting the platform, as it were, 'from below' must be our method, rather than imposing it 'from above'. Such will not yield any detailed blueprint for change but we should resist our 'natural' impatience with this fact. Focus on this method and on these dimensions will, however, facilitate formalizing as soon as appropriate a common framework for the more organized association of diverse groups, activities, ideologies, and leaders. (23)

Although still containing teleological remnants (or possibly merely a dose of wishful thinking), this is where Marxism virtually ends (as we have theoretically come to understand it) and liberal democratic politics begins. Whatever is left of an implied Marxism has now become one *political* perspective among many; no longer privileged for obscure and untenable epistemological and eschatological reasons, but merely a set of contestable arguments about how to perceive the central five dimensions that Munroe has identified as critical. Of course, the argument is still – like most political platforms – extremely vague on specifics and weak on implementation of concrete policies; it is nevertheless removed from both a metaphysical foundation and from the realm of blind faith.

One reason for the failure of Marxism in at least the English-speaking Caribbean must be partly attributed to the often-noted commitment by the people to a parliamentary system with its constitutional restraints and built-in limits to power. Grenada under Bishop and Guyana under Burnham (and Hoyte) are of course exceptions to this rule. Nevertheless, it is interesting and somewhat ironic that, in the final analysis, it is 'the people', through deeply rooted values and ideas about what is acceptable and legitimate government, who have contributed to the decline of Marxism in the region, and it is the failure of the Marxist rhetoric to appeal to this same 'people' that further weakens its impact in the Caribbean. However disillusioned and cynical about the various Westminster models and the particular governments, public opinion in English-speaking Caribbean is not particularly enamoured of the

Marxist model of politics and economics. And it is doubtful that one can imagine a scenario in the near future in which this antipathy would turn around. If Marxism survives, it will be, I predict, as an odd but surprisingly widespread doctrine among intellectuals and academics.

Carl Stone (1991) offers another interesting middle-ground view, possibly close to that of Munroe, somewhere in between Thomas's and my own position regarding the future of Marxism in the Caribbean. He too endorses the 'basic needs' economy as a socialist alternative to liberal capitalism. He sees it as "the only route by which socialism in the Caribbean can bring lasting and long-term improvements in the quality of life on the Caribbean poor and unemployed" (305). However, he thinks it unlikely that it stands a chance to be successful under current circumstances. A host of factors, plus the debacle in Grenada, has weakened the prospect for a Marxist alternative politics.

Development of a basic needs socialist economy requires a hegemonic, one-party state, a strong dominant Marxist ideology, and a mass party or movement with a highly developed capacity for mobilization and administration. Organizational weaknesses within Caribbean leftist parties; fratricidal contentions for power among ruthless, leftist, intelligentsia; low levels of organizational discipline; and weak leadership at the grass roots level, as in Grenada, all suggest that prospects for socialist development in this direction after Grenada are not very promising. (305)

Again, we see the ingredients that we encountered in Thomas's prose, but this time in a less teleological frame. History is not present with its inevitable path towards an already determined goal; all signs of determinism and inevitability are, in fact, absent. Instead, we have a context-specific assessment of the prospects of a particular kind of politics. Perhaps there is still a hint of the desirability of a Marxist approach, or should I say a hint of lament over its weak prospect, if not in the previous quote, in the article as a whole – but whatever it is, it is muted and barely implicit.

Subjective elements and human contingencies play a much larger role than objective laws of history in Stone's evaluation. To the weakness of the Marxist leadership and ideology, he adds a whole range of other factors, equally contextual and contingent, that mitigate against the possibility of a Marxist politics in the Caribbean:

The failure to consolidate power in Grenada and the murder of the regime's popular leader has left an indelible scar on the image of Marxist-oriented socialism. This has served to exacerbate the strong anti-communist political tendencies in the region, based on conservative and fundamentalist church influences, peasant values (which are skeptical of state ownership or control of productive assets), and the regional obsession with aping and aspiring to the mercantilist, acquisitive, and affluent life-style of North America. The penetration of the region by North American media, extensive networks of family connections with the North American mainland through migration, and strong social traditions that encourage excessive consumerism, individualism, private accumulation, and upward social mobility into middle-class life-styles all render the basic needs model incompatible with the value system of most Caribbean peoples. Cuban successes at transforming the quality of life among its people through the development of a basic-needs economy (albeit with extensive Eastern bloc help) has consequently not had the big impact many expected in promoting Marxist socialism in the Caribbean. (Stone 1991: 305–6)

Although here the lamenting tone is unmistakable, this is a penetrating summary of the social and political circumstances that undermine Marxism – and, incidentally, strengthen liberalism – as a viable ideology or political praxis for the region. We now find ourselves in the heterogeneous and diverse concrete Caribbean life-world. There is no longer any appeal to a unified people or proletariat; instead 'the masses' are presented as explicitly rejecting the models of both basic needs and socialism. The analysis points towards the post–cold war and post-Marxist situation. Present is still the appeal to Cuba as a model or example, but this time in a more disenchanted voice; today, the latter would be even more pessimistic, I suspect. Stone concludes his article with the following sentence: "The experience of Grenada, Jamaica, and Guyana has thus helped demystify socialism and ideology for the Caribbean" (308). All of these observations pertain to what we can call the external or circumstantial elements in the decline of Marxism in the Caribbean. It is significant that the very social and political milieu that Stone laments for its inhospitable reception of socialism is exactly the complex cement that promotes a liberal democratic society and politics. In other words, all the factors that are presented in a negative light in the quotation above can easily be reinterpreted as promoting a heterogeneous and valuable democratic culture, even under conditions of both economic hardship and social unrest.

What is virtually absent in Stone's treatment is an evaluation of the internal demise of Marxism, its weakness as a coherent ideology compatible with democracy; absent is also a discussion of its metaphysical foundations in an antifoundational and antimetaphysical epoch. Both Munroe's re-evaluation of Caribbean Marxism and Stone's pessimistic conclusions concerning a Marxist politics point precisely towards this post-Marxist, antiteleological and non-dogmatic political theory, but they do not themselves discuss or draw these conclusions.

These elements are addressed, however, in Brian Meeks's penetrating study, *Caribbean Revolutions and Revolutionary Theory* (1993). Again, Grenada provides a sobering lesson and experience in the shortcomings of a rigid Marxist approach to politics. In response to his own question of why the revolutionary government did not allow opposition parties to form, Meeks reflects:

> The only suggested answer as to why this was not done is to be found in Mandle's notion of paternalistic socialism, woven into a cumulative and available ideological context which, in the path of Chile and Jamaica, placed dogmatic emphasis on the need to be hard and decisive, together with the elevation of the leadership above the society, which endowed them with a sense of 'correctness' and infallibility. This blind and resolute adherence to a policy of 'heavy manners' long after it was required, served to alienate many people. (161)

The dogmatic premises of Marxism leads to a paternalistic and self-righteous political practice. The practical failure of the Grenadian revolution is a mirror of the failures of Marxism as theory and epistemology. "This inability to escape from a deeply-entrenched cumulative and available ideological context of Leninism and hierarchy and not the chimera of conspiracy was the critical element in the *denouement* of the revolution" (178). Meeks concludes his discussion of the Grenada situation with a list of what an alternative – and more successful – strategy might have included. Given the endless scorn of and constant attacks on liberal democracy by virtually all types of Marxists, it is certainly something of the cunning of history that Meeks's list reads like a basic lesson in liberal, constitutional, multiparty politics:

> a) the holding of general elections in 1980, open to the GNP [Grenada National Party], the GULP [Grenada United Labour Party] without Gairy and any other group openly engaged in violence; b) the proposal, popular discussion and passage of a new multi-party constitution, linked to a popular system of parish and zonal councils in which no single party would have hegemonic control, and including regular consultations such as the national budget debate as central elements; c) within the NJM [New Jewel Movement] itself, a return to an open tribune-like party, allowing wide membership, discussion and circulation of ideas including d) an established system of elections in the party, in which any candidate could stand on joint or single tickets; e) a statutory limitation on the length of tenure of the national leader, including, given the small island's limited human resources, the possibility of re-election after a term out of office. (178)

These elements are a healthy mix of liberal principles and circumstantial, pragmatic political considerations; the very opposite of twentieth century Marxism in theory and practice. Politics cannot be situated in a teleological frame, nor can a democratic politics ever be treated as certain or predetermined with regard to outcome or result. Liberal democratic politics is, in fact, characterized by radical uncertainty, indeterminacy, perpetual conflict and disharmony.

Grand appeals to laws of history; faith in emancipated human nature as an unfolding potentiality; faith in a harmonious conflict-free community; and faith in simplistic dichotomies such as bourgeois versus proletariat, imperial centres versus (neo)colonial peripheries, ignorant masses versus avant-garde leaders, and black versus white or, for that matter, white versus non-whites: all these metaphysical and eschatological commitments and beliefs have come under severe attacks in recent years and are incompatible with our postmodern, cosmopolitan, polyglot social and political realities. The Caribbean region is no exception; on the contrary, it embodies and exemplifies this cosmopolitan and multifarious late modern or postmodern social existence. No wonder the Marxist edifice is no longer a viable structure for organizing our thinking about politics and society.

What remains, however, is still the possibility and need for channelling the inevitable modern passions for *equality* and *social justice* in a productive political direction. In a democratic age, these passions will always make themselves felt and cry out for a political formulation and practice. That both 'equality' and 'social justice' are inherently ambiguous and open-ended code words must be recognized from the outset; no particular political practice or necessary political position follow from a passionate commitment to these vague markers. All that can be said is that this urge is extremely intense and inevitable (and sometimes dangerous) in all democratic cultures. With the Marxist ideology practically dead and gone, the possibility still exists for a radical democratic theory and politics to find a place inside a liberal Caribbean institutional structure. In order for such a theory and practice to generate a response among significant segments of the public, a different style and substance of intellectual political arguments have to emerge.

What has to disappear is the old Marxist-Leninist tendency towards "excessive faith in itself" and "ferocity towards opponents" (Blackburn 1991: x). A recognition of political uncertainty, a willingness to accept other points of view, as well as an acceptance of compromise and negotiation as an integral part of politics must all be genuine ingredients and commitments in this new democratic theory. This is a theory free from utopian and holistic conceptions, and it is one based on, as Bobbio (1991) argues in a different context,

recognition of the rights to liberty that are the first prerequisites of democracy – not, please note, of 'progressive' or popular democracy, or however else it might be called to distinguish and exalt it over our democracies, but precisely of the democracy that we can only call 'liberal' and which emerged and consolidated itself through the slow and arduous conquest of certain basic freedoms. (4)

By "basic freedoms" Bobbio means, above all, individual freedom (including the right to a fair trial according to clearly defined penal and judicial rules), freedom of the press and opinion, freedom of assembly, and freedom of association (including free trade unions and political parties). That these freedoms already exist and function relatively well in most English-speaking Caribbean nations requires radical intellectuals to move much closer to established everyday politics and power than Marxists ever did in the past. The current situation demands a reorientation towards such non-Marxists notions as limits to power, checks and balances, and separation of powers. As Miliband (1991) puts it, with reference to problems of authoritarianism in communist regimes:

To tackle these problems requires that attention be paid to some ancient propositions. Of these, none is more important than the proposition that only power can check power. Such checking power has to occur both within the state and from the outside. Within the state, it involves mechanisms which Communist regimes, to their immense detriment have spurned: the checking of the executive and the administration by an effective legislature; the independence of the judiciary; the strict and independent control of police powers; the curbing and control of official discretion. (14)

This is pragmatic and antimetaphysical politics inside a liberal, constitutional framework. If we add that this type of politics has to involve, especially in the Caribbean setting, serious concerns with crime, corruption, drugs, and governmental and administrative inefficiency – all problems that are potentially threatening to a democratic regime – we move even further away from abstract, holistic and totalistic political theorizing in the Marxist mode. No abstract intellectual theory can determine the direction of society or the outcome of politics; only slow, practical and tentative steps inside of established political institutions can promote productive and legitimate policies, and only an active, energetic and independent civil society can provide the mores and milieu for a dynamic democratic culture.

What Hans Magnus Enzenberger (1991) states about the new German society holds for the Caribbean as well:

Instead of hoping for salvation from a single forceful idea, people would rather put their trust in an infinitely complicated, self-correcting process, which not only knows progress, but also retreat, not only grabbing what one can get, but also restraint. It may be that such a way of walking lacks grace. Nature plays tricks, the human being stumbles; without a degree of chaos there can be no self-organization. (21)

Both politicians and intellectuals – especially radical theorists – should get used to the fact that "democracy is an open, productive, risky process which is self-organizing and which evades their control, if not their influence" (24). What the response will be to this new political challenge among radical Caribbean intellectuals is an interesting but open question.

Note

1. Leszek Kolakowski's three-volume work on the rise and decline of Marxism will probably turn out to be far more prophetic and influential than it looked at the time of publication. In spite of some rhetorical excesses, this work stands out as a most serious attempt at mapping the slow decline and ultimate death of Marxism as both a theoretical and practical force in the world. See especially the third volume, *The Breakdown* (Kolakowski, 1981).

References

Blackburn, Robin. 1991. Preface to *After the Fall: The Failure of Communism and the Future of Socialism*. London: Verso.

Blackburn, Robin, ed. 1991. *After the Fall: The Failure of Communism and the Future of Socialism*. London: Verso.

Bobbio, Norberto. 1991. "The upturned Utopia". In *After the Fall: The Failure of Communism and the Future of Socialism*, edited by R. Blackburn. London: Verso.

Enzenberger, Hans Magnus. "Ways of walking: A postscript to Utopia". In *After the Fall: The Failure of Communism and the Future of Socialism*, edited by R. Blackburn. London: Verso.

Kolakowski, Leszek. 1981. *Main Currents of Marxism*. Oxford: Oxford University Press.

Meeks, Brian. 1993. *Caribbean Revolutions and Revolutionary Theory: An Assessment of Cuba, Nicaragua and Grenada.* Warwick University Caribbean Studies Series. London: Macmillan.

Miliband, Ralph. 1991. "Reflections of the crisis of communist regimes". In *After the Fall: The Failure of Communism and the Future of Socialism,* edited by R. Blackburn. London: Verso.

Munroe, Trevor. 1990. *Jamaican Politics: A Marxist Perspective in Transition.* Kingston: Heinemann (Caribbean).

Stone, Carl. 1990. "Whither Caribbean socialism? Grenada, Jamaica, and Guyana in perspective". In *A Revolution Aborted: The Lessons of Grenada,* edited by Jorge Heine. Pittsburgh: University of Pittsburgh Press.

Thomas, Clive Y. 1988. *The Poor and the Powerless.* New York: Monthly Review Press.

13

Caribbean Marxism
After the Neoliberal and Linguistic Turns

PAGET HENRY

That Caribbean Marxism is in a state of crisis is a well-recognized fact. The collapse of socialist experiments in Grenada, Guyana and Jamaica, as well as in the Soviet Union and Eastern Europe have raised serious doubts about the viability of its praxis. These failures have given rise to several attempts at examination and criticism. For example, there is Carl Stone's (1990) social democratic assessment, Folke Lindahl's (1994) postmodern evaluation, Brian Meeks's (1994) insurrectionary reflections and David Scott's (1995) poststructuralist critique. Not surprisingly, the results of these analyses are quite divergent. Stone's doubts about the future of Caribbean Marxism derive from difficulties in its economic practice. Lindahl's rejection is based on postmodernist evaluations of problematic discursive totalizations such as 'the people', or Clive Thomas's "the logic of the majority". Scott's critique is based on a deconstructive reading of the concept of revolution which shows that its salience has evaporated in our time. In Meeks, concern is focused on the problem of structure and agency.

In this chapter, I undertake an analysis of Caribbean Marxism in the light of two developments that have affected it adversely. These developments I have called the neoliberal and linguistic turns. Like Stone, I will argue that the primary challenge confronting Caribbean Marxism is the 'higher cost' of its socialist practice in the globalized world created by the neoliberal turn. In contrast to Lindahl, I will argue against the appropriateness of a postmodern lens for an assessment of Caribbean Marxism. Lindahl uses its critical power as a one-directional instrument that sees only the problematic totalizations of Marxism. Those of postmodernism (relativism, nihilism, grand narratives, binary opposites, particulars) and liberalism ('the people', the state, rights, the individual) are not subjected to the same doses of postmodern scepticism.

Although more carefully argued, my analysis of the linguistic turn will show that Scott's poststructuralist critique makes some of the same errors as that of Lindahl. I will show that Scott's critique is of a type that can usefully be called subtextual. It is subtextual in the sense that it reads the fate of the concept of revolution in terms of the epistemic conditions that govern its textual elaboration. In my view, this is a reasonable suggestion. What is unreasonable is Scott's exclusion of all other factors that determine revolutions and the absolutizing of the epistemic factor. The episteme is elevated above the historical process in which he insists revolutions and other concepts must be immersed. From this monopoly position, epistemic readings then become criteria to which political theorizing must be subject. The fate of the latter is determined by the movement of epistemes without regard for explicitly political and sociological questions, which now become obsolete and illegitimate. At no time does Scott consider the possibility of a dialectical synthesis between these two levels of analysis. Rather, his position is one in which the epistemic displaces the political. Later, we will see that this is a persistent tendency in poststructuralist thought.

In contrast to this antagonistic relationship between the linguistic and political economy perspectives, I will argue for a more productive and dialectical relationship between the two. This will be a relationship in which episteme or sign decentres labour as much as labour decentres sign or episteme. My argument unfolds in four basic steps. First, I present a brief overview of Caribbean Marxism. Second, I examine the impact of the globalizing strategies of the neoliberal turn on both its theory and practice. Third, I critically assess the impact of four specific poststructuralist arguments: the dominance of the sign form, the 'empty space' of discursive totalizations, specular doubling and structural complicity. Fourth and finally, some conclusions about the future of Caribbean Marxism.

Caribbean Marxism: An Overview

The historic opposition between capitalism and socialism emerged in the early phases of European modernity. Particularly in its Marxist variant, socialism has always seen itself as an alternative to capitalism. Thus both the theory and praxis of Marxism have been closely associated with popular revolutions and upsurges against the contradictions and excesses of capitalism. The rise of Caribbean Marxism cannot be separated from the upsurges of Caribbean peoples against the racism and colonialism that Western capitalism imposed on them.

With the collapse of the Garvey movement in the late 1920s, the global struggles of African peoples against racism and colonialism took a decidedly labourist turn. It was in the course of this development that Caribbean Marxism was born, along with trade unions and mass political parties. At the intellectual level, the major statements of this early phase of Caribbean Marxism are to be found in the works of three Trinidadians: George Padmore, C.L.R. James and Eric Williams. In these three, the basic lines of socialist praxis in the region were effectively demonstrated. In the early Padmore, an orthodox Leninist practice emerged, in James a popular insurrectionary practice, and in Williams a social democratic one.

This shift toward a class or labourcentric orientation, did not eliminate the older pan-Africanist tradition and its practice of racial mobilization. Rather, the latter provided an important context in relation to which Caribbean Marxism would revise both classical and Leninist Marxism. This special role of race in Caribbean Marxism is clear in the work of Padmore, James and Williams. The reworking is even stronger in Frantz Fanon, the leading Caribbean Marxist theory of the next generation. Fanon's Marxism is a highly original mix that incorporated race theory, existentialism and psychoanalysis.

With the regaining of political independence, there was a shift in emphasis from resisting foreign capitalism to pushing local economic development. This emphasis on development raised the issue local capitalism. The consequences of this shift are most evident in the work of Arthur Lewis who moved from a pro-worker position in *Labour in the West Indies* (1939) to a pro-capitalist stance in his later works.

The failures and hardships produced by the pro-capitalist turn in the labourist tradition helped to set the stage for the next phase in the history of Caribbean Marxism. This phase was marked by the rise of the New World Group which produced Caribbean dependency theory. Among others, this group included Lloyd Best, George Beckford, Norman Girvan, Clive Thomas and James Millette. Caribbean dependency theory offered a radical critique of capitalism and advocated a social democratic practice that focused on changing the behaviour of multinational corporations.

Also emerging out of the upsurges that accompanied the crises of the Lewisian development model were three other distinct approaches to Marxism. The first was the fairly orthodox Leninist approach of Trevor Monroe and his Workers' Party of Jamaica, which found echoes in the People's Progressive Party of Cheddi Jagan. The second was the Marxism of Walter Rodney. Rodney's Marxism was distinguished by its efforts to link the problems of class and race in a way that addressed Indo-Caribbean concerns. His Marxism also had a strong influence on Clive Thomas, a figure in whom the New World and Rodney traditions meet (see Thomas 1988). Third and finally, we have the racially nuanced democratic socialism of Carl Stone. Stone's socialism centred around a basic needs strategy that is shared with that of Thomas (see Stone 1990).

The contemporary phase of Caribbean Marxism is distinguished by two important challenges: the first is the attempt to assimilate feminist critiques of the notions of wage labour that have been central to this tradition of thought. These critiques have suggested that, in spite of its universal form and gender-neutral appearance, the concept has a male bias which results in the systematic underrepresentation of the economic contributions of women. In this regard, the works of Paula Aymer (1997), Rhoda Reddock (1994), Patricia Moham-med (1997), Joycelyn Massiah (1986) and others come immediately to mind. The second challenge is the attempt at a process of critical self-examination in the wake of the collapse of the major socialist experiments in the region except for the case of Cuba. Particularly difficult for Caribbean Marxism has been the tragic collapse in Grenada and the economic crisis that overtook Michael Manley's democratic socialism. These attempts at rethinking can be seen in the works of Clive Thomas, Norman Girvan, Trevor Monroe, Brian Meeks and Hilbourne Watson.

This, in brief, is the field of Caribbean Marxism. It is a complex discursive field that allows for the taking up of quite varied positions. Thus a figure such as the well-known journalist and activist Tim Hector clearly inhabits the Jamesian space of this field. One such as Alex Dupuy occupies a space between Rodney and the New World Group. Much of my own work falls between the Jamesian and New World spaces.

What these varying position share is the discourse of the commodity that opens Marx's *Capital*, and more specifically its application to Caribbean labour power. The practice of class domination in capitalist societies is effected and legitimated through the commodification of labour. This domination is masked by the claim that, like all other commodities, labour power is bought by capital in a fair and equitable exchange. Consequently, there is no exploitation or unequal exchange. On the whole, Caribbean Marxism has rejected these claims and has sought to present counterdiscourses that make clear the unequal exchanges and practices of domination that surround the appropriation Caribbean labour by both local and foreign capital.

From this common point, the varying positions inside the field of Caribbean Marxism diverge on a number of points, two of which are particularly important. The first is: Just how central are the dynamics of labour as a commodity (compared to other factors of production) for the growth of capital, on the one hand, and the poverty of workers, on the other? The second is: To what extent do the contradictions arising from the representation and exploitation of labour as a commodity lead directly to a socialist alternative? On these points we find significant differences. Consequently, the impact of the neoliberal and poststructuralist turns will be different for the varying position within Caribbean Marxism.

The Neoliberal Turn

As the persistence and nature of the socialist alternative have depended upon the anticapitalist contents of popular upsurges, the persistence of capitalism has depended upon special periods of hegemonic self-assertion and creative restructuring. These strategic and re-creative moves have often been in response to socialist challenges and to internal or systemic crises of capital accumulation.

The neoliberal turn is one of these periods of hegemonic restructuring. It is the set of policies with which Western capitalism has responded to the call of the Third World for a new international economic order, and to economic challenges from the Pacific rim countries. Together, these challenges had created a global environment in which Western multinational corporations were losing their hegemonic and competitive edges. Commodity cartels such as the Organization of Petroleum Exporting Countries and the International Bauxite Association, and the rise of Asian textile, automobile and consumer electronics industries were sources of Western losses in hegemonic and competitive power. Steel, electronics, motorbikes and textiles were just some of the major industries that collapsed. The neoliberal turn is the set of corporate-driven initiatives aimed at reversing this trend.

Toward this end, Western corporate elites have been able to mobilize both liberal and conservative parties behind their reforms, creating, in effect, a new model of the corporate state out the earlier national security model. On the home front, these reforms have included lessening state regulation of capital, even of affirmative action guidelines; making capital more mobile; supporting it with supply-side incentives; weakening both unions and the enforcement of labour legislation; and reducing the support government gives to other classes and groups and the economic competition it gives to the private sector. On the international front, the initiatives have been oriented toward increasing Western access to Third World resources and markets, and rejecting the demands for a new economic order. Instead, the neoliberal turn has pushed for liberalization of Third World trading regimes, privatization of state assets, export promotion, wage cuts, and reductions in both the size and role of government in the economy. The implementation of these policies in the form of structural adjustment packages was facilitated by the worsening debt crisis and rising levels of political instability in Third World states. Hence the emergence of the International Monetary Fund and the World Bank as global financial policemen.

Within the economic spaces created by these policy shifts, Western corporations have been able to radically restructure themselves. Through mergers and acquisitions they have gotten larger. Through massive layoffs, wage cuts, new technology and the further globalizing of production, they have been able to dramatically cut labour costs. This reshuffling has resulted in three major sectoral changes in Western economies: the ballooning of the financial sector, and unprecedented expansions in both the retail and information processing sectors.

Particularly important for Caribbean Marxism is the rise and restructuring of the retail sector. Both the rise and restructuring of this sector were the results of responses to Asian competition in apparel and durable consumer production. In the United States, retail chains such as Sears and JC Penny got larger in the 1970s as they gobbled up smaller independent retailers. In the 1980s these enlarged chains became the objects of devastating competition from even larger discount chains, such as Wal-Mart and K-Mart, and a growing number of specialty stores, such as Montgomery Ward, that catered to high-income shoppers.

Because of the size of the markets they control, these super-chains have been better positioned to counter Asian competition in apparel and durable consumer goods than many older production companies. These giant chains have been able to contract out on unprecedented scales the production of these goods in Asia, the Caribbean and Mexico to counter the labour cost advantages of their Asian competitors. Thus we have a very important case of production being driven by the marketing and retail ends of these global commodity chains. It is the success of these 'buyer driven' strategies of the giant retail companies in meeting the Asian challenge that accounts for the rise of this sector (Gereffi 1994: 96–100).

The rapid expansion of the financial sector in the early 1980s was due primarily to the growing inability of Western industrial production to profitably absorb surplus capital. Hence the turn to investing profits in financial assets or privatized state enterprises. The phenomenal growth of speculative trading in foreign exchange, stocks, bonds and futures, loans to Third World governments, and corporate mergers were all indicative of the shift away from productive investment. The rise of the information-processing sector was a direct result of ongoing revolutions in communications and computer technologies, whose absorption by other sectors has spurred the growth of this sector.

The results of these changes in the organization of Western capitalism have been mixed. They have restored dynamism to the US economy, but have increased patterns of inequality in wealth and income. In Europe they have dampened economic dynamism, threatened the welfare state and have also increase economic inequalities. To the Japanese economy, these changes have brought a long period of stagnation. More recently, they have brought both collapse and stagnation to the South Korean and a number of other Asian economies. To the Caribbean, Africa and much of the Third World they have also brought stagnation, collapse and dramatic rises in levels of poverty. Whether it is Kingston, Georgetown or Accra, we can see those who have been discarded by structural adjustment trying to sell just about anything on the streets of these cities. Neoliberal reforms have produced a ballooning of African and Caribbean retail sectors of a very different sort. Let us take a closer look.

Caribbean Marxism and the Neoliberal Turn

Earlier I suggested that the theoretical core of Caribbean Marxism was its critical discourse on labour as a commodity. The three distinct forms of praxis associated with this body of thought have as their goals the ending of the class domination and surplus labour extraction that commodification masks, particularly in the case of working class. I also argued that the corporate restructuring of the neoliberal turn has made the production of large number of commodities more global in nature. Thus central to any assessment of the impact of this turn on Caribbean Marxism must include its consequences for the latter's commodity discourse and its socialist practices. I shall argue that the neoliberal turn confirms much of the theory while at the same time making the conditions for its practices more difficult.

Neoliberalism and Caribbean Labour Power

From the period of early colonization to the present, the peripheral function of the Caribbean has been that of a site for the reproduction of cheap, highly exploitable labour. On such sites the masks of commodification are often very thin. The unequal exchanges, the extraction of surplus, the repression and dehumanization that are generally concealed are here exposed in varying degrees to public viewing. This exposing of the violence of the commodity form is one way in which it has been affected by race. As Fanon noted, racial domination strives to other and exclude its subjugated masses and not to maximize surplus labour time. Its fulfilment is apartheid not capital accumulation. Thus, with the racist othering of black workers, it has been possible to relax the masking that usually hides the violence that commodifies labour. Gender adds a similar dynamic to the process of commodification, the full significance of which we are now realizing.

Despite its many restructurings, the production of Caribbean labour as a cheap commodity has remained the item of exchange by which Western capitalism has defined the peripheral role of the region. It is this highly exploitable labour power, rather than the specific commodities that it produces, that continues to generate external interest and to determine the specific places that we occupy in the ever more global production networks of Western capitalism. Thus, whether it was the plantations of the mercantile and competitive phases or the bauxite and tourist industries of the monopoly phase, our primary role in these production networks has been the supplying of labour. Girvan's analysis of the bauxite industry in Jamaica showed that the primary benefits to the Jamaican economy were payments to labour and taxes to the government (Girvan 1971: 39–74). Much the same could be said of the tourist industry (Henry 1985: 121–36). Thus from a developmental view of

Caribbean economies, it is labour and not bauxite or satisfied tourists that we are really exporting.

This stark reality, that for Western capitalism Caribbean economies are, at bottom, labour-exporting economies, was indeed masked by the mode of commodification that came with the bauxite and tourist industries. The flurry of industrial activity together with the impact of trade unions created the impression that regional economies were industrializing and diversifying their output; that through significant percentages of value added they were exporting more than just labour; and that the peripheral function of the region had changed. However, with the neoliberal turn, this masking of the real peripheral role of Caribbean economies has been shattered by the competitive pressure that current modes of commodification must absorb.

Earlier, we saw that neoliberal restructuring produced important sectoral shifts and new forms of corporate organization in Western economies. The latter has emphasized flexibility, resulting in shifts towards subcontracting and away from earlier levels of emphasis on vertically integrated corporate structures. These subcontracting arrangements are designed to catch the cheaper labour of the semiperipheral and peripheral areas by shifting greater proportions of the production process to them. Hence the growth and greater visibility of global production networks in which semiperipheral and peripheral labour is being incorporated under the more competitive conditions created by the neoliberal turn.

In the Caribbean the changes in the mode of commodification can be clearly seen in the garment factories that increasingly 'source' the US apparel industry (and hence the new retail sector) through subcontracted production. The dramatic rise of the Caribbean clothing industry since the early 1980s can be linked directly to the response of US clothing manufacturers and retailers to the Asian challenge. The various bilateral agreements between the United States and the Caribbean such as 807 and super 807 are clearly protectionist measures, which at the same time give US capitalists access to Caribbean labour. By combining this labour with their inputs and technology, American businessmen have been able to retain their market shares by re-exporting the finished products back to the United States. In this way, they have been able to counter the lower labour costs of their Asian competitors. Not surprisingly, the bulk of these investments have gone to Haiti and the Dominican Republic where labour is cheapest. Jamaica and Costa Rica come in third and fourth.

However, it is not just American clothing producers who are making use of Caribbean labour in this new competitive game; it is also the Asian producers.

In all of these territories, substantial segments of this industry are Asian owned. By relocating to the Caribbean, Asian producers have been able to circumvent US quota restrictions placed on their countries. This has been the Asian countermove to the US response. Our involvement in this game is clearly the good location and the low cost of our labour.

As in the case of Girvan's analysis of the bauxite industry, a close examination of the clothing industry suggests that regional economies are unlikely to develop as a result of the growth of this industry. Because its competitive pressures require higher and more restrictive rates and conditions of labour exploitation, Caribbean economies are likely to derive much less from this industry.

In his study of the Jamaican clothing industry, Keith Nurse (1995: 195–227) has shown that its potential as a leading sector is not very great as presently organized. The Jamaican clothing industry shows very few signs of generating significant backward and forward linkages. Further, it generates little or no transfers of technology, low levels of value added and only moderate amounts of foreign exchange. In contrast to bauxite, Nurse shows the labour-intensive nature of the industry and, hence, the importance of low labour costs for profit margins. Thus, even more than tourism or bauxite, the primary benefits from this industry will accrue through payments to labour. This is particularly the case as these firms operate in export processing zones and are therefore exempt from major taxes. This outcome should really reinforce the labour-exporting nature of Caribbean economies, and their limited peripheral roles. Consequently, it would be a mistake to view this industry as a case of the export-oriented industrialization that is supposedly the key to Asian success.

Similar patterns of more exploitative commodification can also be seen in Caribbean agriculture, where traditional staples are being replaced by the production of off-season fruits and vegetables for the US market. Laura Raynolds' study of these industries in the Dominican Republic shows the primary role of labour in these industries as well as the extent to which they have been using subcontracting practices (Raynolds 1994: 143–61). It is still too early to say what the impact of the information processing industries will be on the region. Studies of these, such as the one in Barbados, need to be done before we can assess their potential. However, from the cases of clothing and agriculture we can conclude that Caribbean labour is being incorporated through a commodity framework that is more exploitative than the framework of the bauxite and tourist industries. This higher level of exploitation together with the impact of structural adjustment programmes can only mean rising levels of immiseration in the region. Hence the growth of informal activity, street vending in particular, and the overcrowding of the retail sector.

These outcomes of the neoliberal turn do not in any way undermine or invalidate the commodity discourse of Caribbean Marxism. On the contrary, they have increased the relevance of this discourse. More than before, Caribbean workers need a critical discourse that exposes the unequal exchanges concealed by the current commodification of their labour. As long as these masked, exploitative arrangements persist, the theory of Caribbean Marxism will always be relevant.

Neoliberalism and Socialist Practices

If the impact of the neoliberal turn on Caribbean Marxist theory has been to increase it relevance, the impact on its praxis has been to make it much more difficult. This is indeed a paradoxical outcome. However, it is one that derives from the introduction of the power factor into the implementing of this theory. Between structural adjustment and the semi-peripheralization of former socialist countries, the neoliberal turn has been accompanied by dramatic increases in institutional power for the advanced capitalist societies. These increases have occurred both at home and abroad.

Although the difficulties created by these increases in capitalist power have affected all forms of socialist practice in the region, it should be clear that they affect some more than others. The negative affects have probably been greatest for the Leninists, then for the popular insurrectionists and, finally, the social democrats. For the latter, the June 1997 elections in France, which brought the socialists to power, and the October 1998 elections in Germany have been important barometers for the future.

Despite the differences in their praxis, there are some common elements around which there has been considerable consensus. First, that the limited benefits from peripheral industries, such as clothing, point to the need for a more nationally oriented economic strategy, which would increase local control and root production more securely in local demand. Such a strategy has been given its most comprehensive and elegant formulation by Clive Thomas (1974). Caribbean Marxists have argued that only such a strategy can put an end to the peripherally structured strategies of development that we have been repeating, and in which we never get beyond the exporting of labour. Thus, in addition to the commodity discourse, the negative developmental impact of the neoliberal turn has brightly illumined the relevance of Marxist development strategies. This illumination has made it clear that dependence is a major problem that neoliberal strategies are compounding by making the peripherally functioning sectors of the economy lead the growth process. Hence the need for a development strategy in which the nonperipheral sectors lead the growth process. A second common element in the praxis of Caribbean Marxism has been the need for some measure of central planning that would result in more equitable distributions of the economic surplus. These concerns can be found throughout the tradition, whether it is James, Thomas, Girvan or Meeks. Third and finally, Caribbean Marxists have been committed to ending the exploitation and commodification of Caribbean labour through structures of empowerment and self-organization such as self-managed enterprises or organizations that encourage popular participation.

Implementing all of the above will now be more difficult because of the politico-economic context that neoliberal reforms have created. Three things in particular stand out: (1) the new role assigned to the state; (2) the deepening and widening of the institutionalization of market competition; and (3) the increased technological minimum required for effective competition.

With the new American corporate state as the model, the pressure is increasing on countries whose political economies diverge too far from this norm. All of the above socialist strategies presuppose a strong interventionist state, and hence a political economy that is very different from the American model. The preference of the Left has been for a workers' or a worker-oriented state rather than a corporate one. The strengths of these workers' states are different in the three traditions of practice. It is strongest in the Leninist tradition and weakest among the social democrats.

In the work of Monroe (1990: 1–20), we can see the struggles of the Leninist tradition with the problems of authoritarianism. In both the popular insurrectionist and social democratic traditions, these problems have been much less central. The works of James, Thomas and Manley in particular make clear breaks with authoritarian models of socialist practice. Thus Lindahl's critique of Thomas really misses the mark, unless his point is that liberalism, and not participatory formations, represents the maximum measure of democracy attainable. Further, Lindahl never critically examines the authoritarian aspects and expressions of liberalism in region, and their possible roots in sources shared with authoritarian socialism. Thus the question of the management of power and the democratic organization of the state in the popular insurrectionary and democratic socialist traditions are poorly represented, and not sufficiently distinguished from the authoritarian tradition. Of these three socialist state formations, only the democratic socialist ones are likely to thrive during the lifespan of the neoliberal turn. Today, it is only the latter that has a chance of surviving without debilitating pressures from capitalist states. For the other two, the conditions are extremely adverse. So it is only those elements in the socialist agenda that social democrats affirm that can remain in place or be implemented.

Even more devastating for a socialist practice is the increase in the level to which economies all over the world are being marketized. This rise must impose greater limits on the scope and exclusivity of central planning as an organizing principle of socialist economies. Global markets have clearly become forces that socialist economies cannot ignore. Further, given the practical difficulties that Eastern Europe and the Soviet Union experience with central planning, its limits and real capabilities must be reassessed. If Alec Nove is right, the experiences of China, Eastern Europe and the Soviet Union all suggest that there are overwhelming difficulties associated with the attempt to plan an entire economy, at least at our present levels of planning capability. Consequently, long before the socialist collapse and current levels of marketization, he vigorously argued for reforms that would have marketized substantial portions of these economies. He suggests a mutual dependence between plan and market such that the two cannot be absolutely separated (Nove 1983: 68–81).

In the Caribbean, planning capabilities have been significantly less than they were in the Soviet Union and Eastern Europe. At the same time, levels of external dependence on the advanced capitalist countries have been much higher. Given these two facts, it should come as no surprise that socialist experiments in Grenada, Jamaica and Guyana never moved to fully or predominantly planned economies. On the contrary, the market remained the dominant organizing principle in these economies. In the present period, the power and global scope of the market is even greater than it was at the time of these experiments. Thus, whatever the next major round of anticapitalist upsurges may bring to the region, it will be harder to pursue socialist strategies that exclude the market.

Along with restructuring the state and expanding global markets, the neoliberal turn has further increased the significance of technology as a factor of production. Like the market, technology imposes its own organizational imperatives on societies. These are often indifferent to or opposed to the redistributive and egalitarian goals of socialism. With the further globalizing of markets, appropriate technologies are determined less by national criteria and more by international ones. This external technological pressure can only make central planning more difficult. Insulating open economies such as ours from these pressures will only become more difficult under present circumstances. In other words, local control over this factor of production is likely to lessen, thus making planning and, hence, redistribution more difficult.

These three factors that have come with the neoliberal turn will force a serious rethinking of the praxis of Caribbean Marxism. In the area of politics, Leninist and popular insurrectionary approaches will encounter great resistance and little support. In development strategies, structural transformation has been limited to the possibilities of occupying higher value-added positions in production networks such as clothing and agriculture than the labour-supplying positions we now fill. In central planning and redistribution, options are again severely restricted. Hence the need for rethinking the practicalities, technicalities and the power dynamics of socialist practice in the region. In particular, new ways of mobilizing popular power and reorganizing the postcolonial state must be explored.

Language and Caribbean Marxism

In addition to these adverse changes in the objective situation of Caribbean Marxism, the linguistic turn in European philosophy has confronted this discourse with adverse changes in the subjective and ideological conditions of its practice. Here we cannot escape the question of how a shift in European philosophy has been able to affect Caribbean Marxism in this way. In truth, it is quite similar to the way in which the reorganization of the American retail sector has affected Caribbean labour. Both are explained by underlying patterns of dependence. In this case, it is philosophical rather than economic. This philosophical dependence has been particularly strong in areas such epistemology, ontology and philosophies of the self. Thus the labourist/productivist notion of the self in Caribbean Marxism derives from the rationalism of the European Enlightenment period. It is these Enlightenment conceptions of the self that the linguistic turn, particularly in its poststructuralist variant, have been deconstructing. Hence the implications for the subjective foundations of Caribbean Marxism.

More specifically, the poststructuralist turn to linguistic explanations of human behaviour have produced one set of arguments that challenge the commodity discourse of Caribbean Marxism, and three that challenge the viability of its socialist praxis. The argument against the commodity discourse is one that suggests that the consumption of commodities as signs has displaced in importance their production as commodities. The first of the arguments against a socialist praxis is that of the inauthentic or delusional nature of such discursively totalized projections. The second, is that of specular doubling, while the third rests on the assumption of a structural (semiolinguistic) complicity between contested and contesting discourses. Because of the ways in which these argument undermine the agency of subjects such as the Marxian revolutionary, their concerted effect has been to foster a subjective mood of postmodern malaise and an ideological outlook from which revolutionary transformation appears impossible.

However, I shall argue that, in themselves, none of these arguments are as prohibitive as poststructuralists often suggest. First, some of them are not really new and echo themes that have been stated less deterministically by Caribbean poeticists such as Wilson Harris and Sylvia Wynter. Indeed, had Caribbean Marxism drawn its conception of the self from this poeticist tradition, the linguistic turn would have affected us very differently. I will begin my response with a brief overview the linguistic turn and then examine each of these arguments separately.

The Linguistic Turn

The linguistic turn refers to a major shift in the relationship between language and the disciplines of the humanities and social sciences. In these disciplines, language was for a long time seen largely as an instrument or medium of communication for the thinking ego. With the change in relations, language ceased being the neutral communicative medium that it was thought to be. Thus, we can describe the linguistic turn as the gradual releasing of language from imprisonment in its communicative role as modern cultural systems become more internally differentiated. Freed from these communicative restrictions, language has emerged as a distinct domain of human self-formation, with distinctly linguistic explanations of human behaviour that have fundamentally altered the relations between language and the established disciplines.

Both the structuralist and poststructuralist versions of the linguistic turn emphasize the unconscious enmeshment of human subjects in the semiotic aspects of the languages we speak. In other words, to speak a language is to be inscribed in the system of binary oppositions (male/female, right/wrong), their hierarchical ordering and functioning that make the language possible. It is the names, categories, codings and meanings that the system of binaries imposes on our social interactions that give language the capacity explain human behaviour. In these explanations, it is the dynamic movements of signifiers, the textualities woven by their semiotic play that is crucial. They are the explanatory competitors of the economic and political structures of Marxist discourses.

In the early phases of the linguistic turn, the tensions with Marxism were not particularly severe, as the works of V.N. Volosinov (1973), Louis Althusser (1979), Pierre Bourdieu (1977) and the early writing of Jean Baudrillard (1981) suggest. Those that did exist, centred around humanist notions of the subject that Marx inherited from the Enlightenment. For Marx, the central activity of the subject was his or her capacity to labour, that is, to transform subjective desires into objective realities. This creative/productivist view of the subject clearly concealed the constitutive powers of language that the linguistic turn has uncovered; hence the existence of mild tensions, as in the case of Althusser.

However, with the passage of time, and particularly the collapse of the May 1968 student/worker insurrection in France, relations turned more opposi-tional. This collapse was the occasion for a major disengagement of French intellectuals from Marxism. Former Maoists turned 'New Philosophers', such as Bernard-Henri Levy, Christian Jambet and Guy Lardreau, all made their dramatic exits. In doing so, some turned to religion, others to themes in poststructuralist thought that were contained in the published works of Jacques Lacan, Michel Foucault and Jacques Derrida. More recently, in *Spectres of Marx*, Derrida attempted to reassert some of the closer ties with Marxism, largely in response to excesses of the neoliberal turn.

The Commodity versus The Sign

In the poststructuralist literature, the commodity discourse of Marxism is most directly challenged in the work of Baudrillard, who counterposes the sign to the commodity. Baudrillard's argument for the hegemony of the sign form rests on the claim that the production and consumption of signs has taken primacy over material production in contemporary capitalism. Consumption is no longer the appropriating of a commodity for the satisfaction of a need:

"It is not defined by the food we eat, the clothes we wear, the cars we drive, . . . but in the organization of all this as signifying substance" (Baudrillard 1988: 22). To become "an object of consumption, the object must become a sign" in a larger system of objects that have also become signs. Baudrillard then goes on to suggest that consumption is a "systematic act of the manipulating of signs" (22).

This imposition of the sign form transforms not only material commodities but also the subjective commodity of human labour power. It transforms the identity of the Marxian subject, which has been defined in terms of the commodification of its capacity to labour. From the self-acting commodity, the subject becomes the self-manipulating sign. Because this shift inscribes the subject in a consumptive discourse of the sign, Baudrillard speaks of a new humanism, the semiotic humanism of consumption.

In other poststructuralists, such as Foucault, Derrida and Roland Barthes, semiolinguistic analyses examine the self in relation to textual and knowledge production rather than consumption. Writing and knowledge production become crucial sites for re-examining the agency and creativity of Enlightenment conceptions of the subject, such as those of Marx. The result is a much more radical displacing of everyday, action-oriented models of the subject than in the case of Baudrillard.

In these theorists, the author or subject is displaced as the real creator of texts or systems knowledge, or both, and is replaced by the unconscious combinatory activities of linguistic binaries, the founding analogies and metaphors of pre-reflective epistemes. The subject does not make these epistemes that structure and make possible his or her textual or knowledge production. On the contrary, it is the subject that is made by the dynamic activity of these epistemic spaces. The subject inhabits these spaces and carries the signatures of their internal structures which are seen as independent of human consciousness. From this subtextual perspective, the self appears radically decentred and its agency severely compromised. It is similar to the quantum or subatomic perspective from which the solid objects of everyday life appear to be primarily empty space. David Scott's deconstructive analysis of the concept of revolution takes this approach. From the subdiscursive level of the episteme, very little of the everyday solidity of the concept remains. It is this quantum or subtextual view of the solid, unified self that results in its more radical displacement.

In general terms, poststructuralism's subtextual view of the self leads to major differences with the Marxian labourist/productivist model of the self. The latter is seen as a solid view of the self that ignores its own subtextual dimensions. This in turn leads to the rejection of a number of Marxian claims regarding the self: first, the claim that the self is the centre of its own actions and experiences; second, that the primary activities of the self are productive and transformative; third, that the creative elements in its primary activities are of its own making; fourth and finally, that the self becomes an authentic historical agent when through practical action it causes something new, such as socialism, to appear. These are all everyday, solid appearances that turn out to be primarily 'empty spaces' when viewed from the subtextual perspective of poststructuralism. I will have more to say on this general perspective, but for now we return to Baudrillard's critique.

Is Baudrillard's claim regarding the hegemony of consumption correct for our region? I do not think it is. I am not even sure that it is correct for the advanced capitalist societies. There can be no denying the increase in importance of consumption that Baudrillard has attempted to theorize. However, I think he overstates his case, and in so doing, he prematurely announces the death of production. The competitive and productivist nature of the economic battle between the United States and the Asian countries shows production and its global reorganization to be at the heart of neoliberal restructuring. Further, the attempts to revitalize the US industrial base and not let a pure consumer society emerge as a result of foreign competition, show the continuing importance of production.

If the shift to consumption is questionable in the case of the advanced societies, it is even more so in the case of peripheral economies such as ours. Everything I have argued for in regard to the impact of the neoliberal turn on Caribbean economies works against Baudrillard's claim. These arguments clearly suggest that production and a more exploitative commodification of labour will be increasingly important for the region. Thus Baudrillard's suggestion that we shift our conception of the subject from *homo faber* to *homo significans* is not one that is likely to advance our understanding of the new challenges confronting Caribbean labour.

In most other Third World countries, such a shift is certainly not the reality. The heated debates in China over the commodification of Chinese labour power, occasioned by the labour reforms of the 1980s, demonstrate very clearly the dominant role of production in peripheral and semi-peripheral economies (Lee 1997). As China continues to capitalize its economy and redefine its relation to global capitalism, we can expect this role of production to grow, as it will have the largest and cheapest supplies of labour on the global market.

These two cases suggest that the preponderance of consumption becomes a possible claim only when the global and polarized nature of capitalist production is overlooked. By focusing on the French case, Baudrillard is indeed able to make a plausible case for the hegemony of consumption. However, this plausibility declines sharply when the global and polarized (varyingly exploitative) nature of capitalist production is taken into account. This preponderance of production, even through increasingly located in the periphery, points to the dependence of consumption on production.

Further, this dependence helps to explain the rather forced nature of Baudrillard's linguistic analogies. Commodities are more than signs and cannot be reduced to their semiotic dimensions. In Marx's commodity discourse, the semiotic elements are quite clear. Commodities are represented by their exchange value or their prices. The price is thus an important signifier in the representation, production and exchange of commodities. Consequently, the behaviour of the signifiers of commodities, exactly how and what they represent constitute an important semiotic dimension of the Marxian commodity discourse.

However, the order of this discourse is not determined by the set of general rules that govern the algebra of prices and other signifiers in this discourse. These formal semiotic processes are subject to an instrumental/productivist logic that systematically restrains and orders the constitutive and disseminative play of these signifiers. Thus the textuality of the Marxian commodity discourse cannot be reduced to the play or manipulation of signifiers. This textuality is necessarily shaped by feedback relations with productive activities in concrete factories which impose instrumental, profit-oriented constraints on it. Precisely this instrumental limiting of semiotic play allows it to critically reflect the situation of workers. It is this nonlinguistic, productivist element that embarrasses Baudrillard's linguistic/consumptionist reading. But despite such excesses, there can be no going back to the old conception of the relationship between language and the subject. The constitutive and behaviour-determining powers of language must become an integral part of Caribbean Marxism.

Discursive Totalities: The Subtextual View

Unlike the critique of production that affected the theory of Caribbean Marxism, our remaining three poststructuralist critiques regarding discursive totalities, specular doubling and structural complicity all affect its practice. In particular, they focus on the capacity for practical action required for the realization of its socialist alternative. By practical as opposed to technical action, I am referring to the principled (ethical or political) actions of individuals that are oriented towards achieving a goal or bringing about a change.

Given poststructuralism's subtextual view of the self, it should come as no surprise that it takes a similar view of closely related discursive formations, such as universals, closed systems of thought, teleologies, and transformative totalizations such as historicism, humanism or socialism. These formations have all been objects of deconstructive critiques and declared primarily 'empty space' from this quantum perspective. Thus it is the apparent fullness and solidity of discursive totalities rather than the superior power of the opposition that misguide practical action and severely compromise its effectiveness.

Given the preference for difference, discursive totalities, like all other constructions of sameness or identity, are suspect for the poststructuralist. The unity and coherence that these totalizations offer are seen as forced and hence both oppressive and illusory. They are discursively produced or forged with the aid of metaphorical and analogical tricks that establish equalities and identities between things that are unequal and different. For example, are the identities among the workers of the world over established by the Marxian notion of commodified labour real or illusory? Are there not real differences, such as race and gender, that such a universal category suppresses? Thus, discursive totalities can only be false totalities as they generate identities and equalities through the unacknowledged suppression of real differences. For the poststructuralist, all such universalistic or totalized constructions are discursively authoritarian, and hence should be deconstructed and the suppressed differences given their play at the price of the totalized formation.

The fatal dependence of practical action on such problematic totalities is clearly demonstrated in the work of François Lyotard, Lindahl and Scott. As noted earlier, practical action needs not only strategic information but also a legitimating and transformative vision. For Lyotard practical action derives this vision from problematic totalizations such as the movement toward socialism, the dialectics of spirit, the emancipation of the rational or the working subject. Both Lindahl and Scott share Lyotard's view that these are all false totalizations, grand narratives that cannot deliver the alternatives they promise. They cannot because the images of equality, unity and reconciliation that they offer are not genuine but misleading. As opposed to being real, they are the discursive effects produced by a masking of semiotic difference. For

Lyotard and Lindahl, the mark of our postmodern period is precisely an incredulity toward such grand narratives. With this incredulity, the viability of practical action (particularly revolutionary action) collapses, giving way to a mood of *fin de siècle* or to the reign of strategic and technocratic action.

As in the case of Baudrillard, I think Lyotard, Lindahl and Scott overstate their cases against totalizing strategies. First, the problematic nature of discursive totalization is a well-recognized fact. This recognition is very clear in work of Sartre (1968: 85–181), James (1980: 34) and Fanon (1967: 12–13), to mention a few. Sartre analysed the existential conditions that made totalizations problematic, James examined the social conditions, and Fanon brought both of them together dialectically.

Second, what these individuals recognized that our poststructuralist critics have overlooked is that, unlike semiotic or interpretive action, both strategic and political action function quite well and sometimes require problematic totalizations in which real difference have been suppressed. This oversight is particularly evident in the case of Scott, who 'normalizes' interpretation in this instance in the same manner that he criticizes sociologists. In fact, the world of everyday life, its interactions, the everyday selves and linguistic analogies that poststructuralists project all require such problematic totalizations. To resist neoliberal reforms or to struggle against capitalism does not require a subtextual epistemic knowledge of all the difference and semiotic play suppressed by the strategic and practical stand taken in order to engage in these struggles. Some of this subtextual knowledge can be usefully integrated into these strategic positions but cannot replace them on the level of everyday interaction. The epistemic or semiotic microdynamics of interpretive action cannot be superimposed on the strategic and practical activities of political action at the everyday level of parties, states and economies. Quantum physicists know that walls are primarily empty space, but they still use doors. Similarly, the empty subtextual appearance of capitalism or socialism does not mean that we can walk through the former and replace the latter with social criticism or liberalism.

Third and finally, to be consistent, our poststructuralist critics would have to abandon all forms of argumentation since even those they employ make use of analogical and metaphorical strategies for establishing instances of sameness or identity. The provisional eliminating of real differences is basic to human forms of argumentation. As we saw in the case of Baudrillard, the identity between commodities established by his concept of the sign rests on a rather forced analogy between language and consumption. In short, even poststructuralist critiques make use of totalizing strategies. The current resurgence in both James and Fanon studies in this high period of poststructuralism points very directly to the resilience of the dialectical solutions they gave to the problematic nature of discursive totalities. On this point, they anticipated the poststructuralist critique.

Political Action: In the Grip of Specular Doubling

The phenomenon of specular doubling takes us from the subtextual world of semiotic play to the libidinal world of desire. This is of course the world of the Freudian unconscious that has been given a structuralist facelift by Lacan. Critiques of political action that made use of specular doubling were very prominent among 'New Philosophers' such as Bernard-Henri Levy. The road travelled by Regis Debray from *Revolution in the Revolution* to *The Critique of Political Reason* certainly crossed the avenue of specular doubling. We also find these critiques in poststructuralist figures such as Julia Kristeva (1984) and Hélène Cixous (Cixous and Clements 1986).

By specular doubling Lacan is referring to certain prelinguistic and narcissistic patterns of self–other identification that are really misidentifications. These misidentifications are in principle quite similar to the ones we encountered in the case of discursive totalities. Here the misidentification affects the self rather than a discursive formation. By splitting or dividing the self, this false identification will leave it severely incapacitated. This incapacitation of the self will in turn condemn its practical actions to a tragic fate of Sisyphean repetition.

The errors in the misidentifications that ground specular doubling are precisely their inability to recognize and handle the differences that remain despite the identity posited between self and Other. If a child identifies with his or her father, then an absolute identity requires the elimination of all differences that are not consistent with image of the father, or vice versa. The nonrational or counterfactual elements in these misidentifications derive from the primary narcissism of the subject. This mode of self-identification through the internalizing of the Other is both internally contradictory and self-alienating. It leaves the ego divided; it becomes a specular double as it is both itself and another. This *intrasubjective* impasse becomes the code for the specular doubling of *intersubjective* activity. Under the weight of this coding, practical action is condemned to its tragic fate.

Particularly fatal for revolutionary or transformative action are the specular identifications that we make with others who will later be adversaries. Action against such an Other will be ambivalent and internally contradictory as the ego must be divided in this instance. To resist such an Other, the ego must also resist itself. To support this Other is also to support itself. Thus deliberate attempts to defeat such adversaries are likely to end in failure or, even worse, the reproduction of the adversary one is trying to overthrow. Specular doubling thus traps practical action in a tautological circle of abortive repetition that condemns the revolutionary to reproduce the very order that he or she is trying to overthrow. Hence Lacan's reference to "the revolutionary of today who does not recognize his ideals in the results of his acts" (1953: 12).

This portrait of political action is extremely problematic as it traps the political actor in the impasses of early stages of ego development. First, as in the case of the subtextual critique of discursive totalities, there is a level-specific problem with this specular, subpersonal view of the political activist. Through a one-sided quantum shift in perspective, the concrete historical actions of the activist are evaporated and made to disappear. The autonomy and integrity (limited as they are) of the ego's capacity for political action is eclipsed by a subpersonal view of its formative dynamics that is unable to adequately grasp the realities of the everyday level. Consequently, the problem is a level-specific one: To what extent are the apparent solidity and capabilities of the everyday ego determined by stadial ego-genetic problems such as specular doubling or an Oedipal complex?

These 'hard' features of the ego cannot be wholly determined by such psychological conflicts as they are also shaped by cultural traditions, institutions and other sociological factors. In other words, arguments of specular doubling make two problematic assumptions: (1) that the capacity for everyday political action is wholly or overwhelmingly determined by stadial conflicts in the process of ego formation, particularly the narcissistic ones that arise in Lacan's imaginary stage; and (2) that effective political action requires activists to be free of stadial conflicts and related divisions. These are, I think the conditions for spiritual action. For as Kierkegaard has reminded us, purity of heart is to will one thing. Such unity, I am sure, would improve the ethical quality of political action and hence must recognized and encouraged as such. However, it is not a precondition for successful battles against the injustices and exploitations that plague our world. What these struggles require is that we can say, with Fanon: today I will take in hand my narcissism and my psychoexistential complexes.

Second, arguments that approach political action via its conditioning by ego-formative processes are not new. They are standard in psychology and European existential philosophy. Further, throughout this text we have discussed many arguments from the Afro-Caribbean philosophical tradition. Consequently, the real issue here is how are these psychoexistential dynamics to be brought into mutually critical and dialectical relationships with the social factors that also help to determine the reality of everyday egos and their interactions.

For Caribbean Marxists, the best response to this issue is still that of Fanon (1967). He deals directly with the problem of specular doubling in his examination of the pathological misidentifications made by Jean Veneuse and Mayotte Capecia in *Black Skin, White Masks*. The latter case in particular has become a heated issue in recent feminist scholarship (see Sharpley-Whiting 1998). In both, the specular double of the ego is clearly the white colonizer. Hence their anticolonial activities take the form of whitening themselves through the specific seeking of white lovers, and thus reproducing the colonial order. Despite such tragic realities inherent in the colonial situation, Fanon was still able to declare his belief in love, political action and revolutionary transformation. Such commitments are possible because the misidentifications that ground specular doubling are not all-determining. Fanon's dialectical weavings between this narcissistic/prelinguistic level and the everyday personal level of political action does the latter more justice than those of Lacan or those of his appropriators.

Finally, the historical record of political action reveals more successes than the abortive and circular view of specular doubling would suggest. One can certainly think of cases that fit this cycle of repetition. In Antigua, the dramatic way in which Prime Minister George Walter, after such an aggressive struggle against Vere Bird, came to resemble the man he replaced is certainly grist for the Lacanian mill. It is quite conceivable that Walter misidentified with the neocolonialism that Bird had created in ways that were similar to the misidentifications of Veneuse and Capecia with the colonial order. However, in spite of this disturbing outcome, the movement led by Walter brought something new to the historical stage in Antigua. It deepened Antiguan democracy (Henry 1985: 121–27). Similarly, in spite of their premature collapse the Afro-American civil rights movement did succeed in ending social apartheid, and the student movement succeeded in changing American attitudes toward gender and the environment. Finally, the original and influential heritage that Lacan himself has left behind shows quite clearly that the repetitive logic of specular doubling is not all-determining.

Political Action and Structural Complicity

Perhaps the most recognizable political feature of poststructuralism is the way in which it has legitimated the relocating of oppositional action from the political to the cultural arena. In the world of Africana thought, the work of Cornel West, Henry Louis Gates, Sylvia Wynter, Stuart Hall, David Scott, Paul Gilroy, V.Y. Mudimbe and Homi Bhabha in different ways all register this shift away from party to cultural politics. According to West (1983), the

distinctive features of the new cultural politics of difference are to trash the monolithic and homogeneous in the name of diversity, multiplicity and heterogeneity; to reject the abstract, general and universal in the light of the concrete, specific and particular; and to historicize, contextualize and pluralize by highlighting the contingent, provisional, variable, tentative, shifting and changing. (3)

In short, it is a subtextual approach to politics that focuses more on the power relations that are inscribed in images, identities and discursive formations and less on organized institutional structures.

Behind this emphasis on cultural politics are two important differences with Marxist practices. The first is a capillary conception of power, which sees it as extending beyond the state and the party and into the interstices of society via the languages spoken by its members. In the hierarchical structure of the binary oppositions of the latter is a political order that languages reproduce and transmit. This political order is the primary focus of the new cultural politics of difference as opposed to the order of parties, elections and corporate elites.

The turn away from the latter order is linked to a second argument. From the subtextual perspective, organized politics appears as semiotically structured where it is not 'empty space.' Its oppositional aspects in particular, such as government versus opposition, appear to be governed by a complicity that affects all semiolinguistic binaries. This semiotic complicity is such that binaries can suppress or oppose one another, recombine in different ways but never absolutely separate. They are eternal pairs whose perpetual play is a necessary condition for semiolinguistic representation. On the level of every-day discourse and action, these semiotic conditions impose their fateful complicity on the dynamics between contesting and contested discourses. Thus oppositional political binaries, such as socialism and capitalism, are viewed as being caught in this structural stalemate, whose repetitive outcomes are similar to those of specular doubling.

Consequently, the goal of the socialist or anticolonial revolutionary is a semiotically prohibited possibility as radical or absolute separations are barred. Given this binary impasse in which organized socialist politics is caught, the way out is to subvert the dominant signifier without aiming for a final overthrow. Within the complicities of this strategy, the political order of languages, as manifested in identities, images and discourses, becomes the crucial site of political work.

This linguistic displacing of organized politics is particularly clear in the case of the French Left. In the work of Cixous, Kristeva, Barthes and Derrida we see this transference of revolutionary activity to the realm of language. Cixous declares writing to be the place "that is not obliged to reproduce the system" (Cixous and Clements 1986: 42). In the Caribbean, Scott's replacement of revolution with a writerly social criticism reflects this trend. On the whole, this turn to language and writing is reminiscent of the religious displacement of the organized politics of the Garvey movement by the more spiritual and discursive politics of the Rastafarians.

This shift to the linguistic realm is particularly clear in Barthes. In his work, we can see the use of intermediary deconstructive strategies to circumvent the repetitive logic of structural complicity without a frontal attack on particular binaries. Rather than the political arena, the revolution will now to occur in language. Barthes locates himself in the linguistic space between capitalism and authoritarian socialism. From this position, he rejects the unified languages of both for a third that would be outside of the complicity that has governed the relations between the opposing pair. That is, he will attempt to write the socialist revolution in a language in which it will be possible to think outside of the logics of both the commodity and the centralized political resource, as well as outside of the coercive strategies inherent in everyday linguistic discourses. A plural, disseminative textuality became the house and symbol of the revolution. This textual pluralism was seen as different from liberal pluralism, because of its break with monolithic and centralized notions of power (Barthes 1978).

With regard to these and other arguments based on structural complicity, I have three comments. First, as in the case of specular doubling, they are often overstated to the point of semiolinguistic determinism. The autonomy of the political disappears under the weight of its semiotic coding. Even political strategies are now semiotically determined. This overstating often rests in part on an isolated, analytic deploying of language rather than a dialectical one that brings it into mutually decentring relations with other determinants of political action. Of course, such a centred and essentialized posture (neostructuralism) is precisely what poststructuralists have sought to deconstruct in other modes of thought.

Second, the turn to the micropolitical order of language, which we must welcome, cannot be seen as an alternative to organized party politics that focuses on the problems of state power. If it is viewed in this way, it becomes a dishonest retreat. Despite the snares of structural complicity, the problem of state power must be addressed strategically and in organizational terms. If it is not, micropolitics becomes either an alibi or is itself trapped in an equally fatal complicity with the macrostructures of state power.

Third, the real contribution of arguments of structural complicity to Marxist praxis will remain inaccessible if the above two issues are not resolved in a more satisfactory manner. As in the case of specular doubling, these arguments can be useful in dissecting some of the hidden constraints on political action that can cause it to fail. These would be good but level specific contributions. However, when such arguments transform failures into absolute barriers, they become counterproductive. The activist is then forced to examine what exactly is behind such overreactions.

The Future of Caribbean Marxism

If the above assessments of neoliberalism and poststructuralism are correct, then the current situation of Caribbean Marxism is indeed a difficult one. It is sandwiched between the offences that have been launched by these two movements, and hence is on the defensive. The first has adversely changed the material conditions of its practice, while the second has done the same on the subjective and ideological levels.

To reverse the shift in material conditions, Caribbean Marxism will require a new mandate from popular insurrectionary activity. This activity must be innovative and strong enough to change neoliberal and postmodern outlooks, as well as their economic and political agendas. These popular upsurges will have to bring new and strong anticapitalist images to the fore, as well as new symbols and discourses of equality, freedom and cooperation. The future of socialism rests heavily on the specific contents that will emerge from the insurrectionary activities of the future. If the creative responses currently taking shape in the imagination of the Caribbean masses are no longer reflected in the socialist mirror, then it will indeed be time to move on. However, this new consciousness can only be known through some outward expression or manifestation. Without this, it is difficult to imagine the reinvigorating of Caribbean socialism.

Assuming the return of such popular infusions of power and legitimacy, there will of course be the new problems of higher levels of technology and market competition. The extent to which central planning can and should be undertaken in this new international environment has to be carefully reassessed. The credibility of a revitalized socialist economics will depend on this, particularly when groups will again seek state protection from the market. More than capitalism and socialism themselves, market and plan appear to be governed by a complementary complicity that is in need of closer examination. The involvement of one in the life of the other certainly echoes that of the eternal pairs of semiotics. We cannot overlook the excesses and inefficiencies of state action and state leadership that contributed to the neoliberal turn. This global loss of faith in state-led collective action must be recovered. Thus, in relation to the adverse conditions created by the neoliberal turn, socialist practice can only be restored through popular upsurges that are capable of empowering and legitimating a new socialist political economy in which market and plan complement one another.

With regard to the poststructuralist offensive, the ground to be covered is more subjective and ideological. An adequate response will require greater philosophical autonomy on the part of Caribbean Marxism, particularly in basic areas such as ontology, epistemology and the philosophy of the self. Unless we can speak for ourselves and draw on our own experiences in these matters our response to the poststructuralist challenge will be inadequate. If my assessment of this challenge is correct, then at least four important conclusions can be drawn.

First, poststructuralism has introduced a subtextual, subpersonal, semiolinguistic perspective that yields very different views of basic concepts used by Marxism, such as the self, history universals and discursive totalizations. I have tried to show that, despite its epochal self-presentation, it is a partial perspective with level-specific contributions to make. As long as this perspective is not deployed as an erasing of the 'solidities' of the everyday world, there is much in it that can be dialectically incorporated into Marxism. Thus in considering the nature and status of important Marxian universals, such as class, the proletariat and commodified labour, the deconstructive insights of this subtextual perspective can most definitely be enriching.

Second, although they were often presented as decisive, the arguments based on the problematic nature of discursive totalities, specular doubling and structural complicity have not really produced absolute barriers to successful revolutionary action. Hence we must reject the postmodern mood that has been created by the attempts to absolutize these arguments. Such attempts lead to what Lewis Gordon (1997) has called "political nihilism" (92). This we must avoid at all costs.

Third, there is an important lesson to be learned from the poststructuralist relocating of revolutionary activity to the domain of language. It may represent a temporary or strategic retreat that preserves the revolutionary impulse in what appears to be a dormant or inactive period. Preserved in this way it could again leave the safety of this linguistic haven and attempt to change the world.

Fourth and finally, the poststructuralist critique raised no barriers to new popular insurrectionary activity. Thus our analysis can only conclude with a call for Caribbean Marxism to revise and restructure itself in the creative ways that James and Fanon did. However, in this undertaking we must be guided by the writings that fill the pages of popular insurrectionary activity.

References

Althusser, Louis. 1979. *For Marx*. London: Verso.

Aymer, Paula. 1997. *Uprooted Women*. Westport: Greenwood Press.

Barthes, Roland. 1978. *The Pleasure of the Text*. New York: Hill and Wang.

Baudrillard, Jean. 1981. *For a Critique of the Political Economy of the Sign*. St Louis: Telos Press.

Baudrillard, Jean. 1988. *Jean Baudrillard: Selected Writings*, edited by Mark Poster. Stanford: Stanford University Press.

Bourdieu, Pierre, and Jean-Claude Passeron. 1977. *Reproduction*. London: Sage.

Cixous, Hélène, and Catherine Clements. 1986. *The Newly Born Woman*. Minneapolis: University of Minnesota Press.

Fanon, Frantz. 1967. *Black Skin, White Masks*. New York: Grove Press.

Gereffi, Gary. 1994. "The organization of buyer-driven global commodity chains: How US retailers shape overseas production networks". In *Commodity Chains and Global Capitalism*, edited by G. Gereffi and N. Korzeniewiz. Westport: Praeger.

Girvan, Norman. 1971. *Foreign Capital and Economic Underdevelopment in Jamaica*. Kingston, Jamaica: Institute of Social and Economic Research.

Gordon, Lewis. 1997. *Her Majesty's Other Children*. Lanham: Rowman and Littlefield.

Henry, Paget. 1985. *Peripheral Capitalism and Underdevelopment in Antigua*. New Brunswick, NJ: Transaction Books.

James, C.L.R. 1980. *Notes on Dialectics.* London: Allison and Busby.

Kristeva, Julia. 1984. *Revolution in Poetic Language.* New York: Columbia University Press.

Lacan, Jacques. 1953. "Some reflections on the ego". *International Journal of Psycho-Analysis* 34.

Lee, Jung-Hee. 1997. "Government and urban labor reforms in post-Mao China (1978–95)". PhD diss., Department of Sociology, Brown University.

Lewis, W. Arthur. 1939. *Labour in the West Indies: The Birth of a Workers' Movement.* London: V. Gollancz and the Fabian Society.

Lindahl, Folke. 1994, "Caribbean diversity and ideological conformism: The crisis of Marxism in the English-speaking Caribbean". *Social and Economic Studies* 43, no. 3 (September).

Massiah, Joycelin. 1986. "Women in the Caribbean", Parts 1 and 2. *Social and Economic Studies* 35, nos. 2 and 3 (June and September).

Meeks, Brian. 1994. "Re-reading *The Black Jacobins*: James, the dialectic and revolutionary conjuncture". *Social and Economic Studies* 43, no. 3 (September).

Mohammed, Patricia. 1997. "Midnight's children and the legacy of nationalism". *Small Axe,* no. 2.

Munroe, Trevor. 1990. *Jamaican Politics: A Marxist Perspective in Transition.* Kingston, Jamaica: Heinemann (Caribbean).

Nove, Alec. 1983. *The Economics of Feasible Socialism.* London: George Allen and Unwin.

Nurse, Keith. 1995. "The developmental efficacy of the export-oriented clothing industry: The Jamaican case". *Social and Economic Studies* 44, nos. 2 and 3 (September).

Raynolds, Laura. 1994. "Institutionalizing flexibility: A comparative analysis of forest and post-forest models of Third World agro-export production". In *Commodity Chains and Global Capitalism,* edited by G. Gereffi and N. Korzeniewiz. Westport: Praeger.

Reddock, Rhoda. 1994. *Women, Labour and Politics in Trinidad and Tobago.* Kingston, Jamaica: Ian Randle Publishers.

Sartre, Jean-Paul. 1968. *Search for a Method.* New York: Vintage.

Scott, David. 1995. "Revolution/theory/modernity: Notes on the cognitive-political crisis of our time". *Social and Economic Studies* 44, nos. 2 and 3 (September).

Sharpley-Whiting, T. Denean. 1998. *Frantz Fanon: Conflicts and Feminism.* New York: Rowman and Littlefield Publishers.

Stone, Carl. 1990. "Whither Caribbean socialism? Grenada, Jamaica, and Guyana in perspective". In *A Revolution Aborted: The Lessons of Grenada,* edited by Jorge Heine. Pittsburgh: University of Pittsburgh Press.

Thomas, Clive Y. 1974. *Dependence and Transformation: The Economics of the Transition to Socialism.* New York: Monthly Review Press.

Thomas, Clive Y. 1988. *The Poor and the Powerless.* New York: Monthly Review Press.

Volosinov, V.N. 1973. *Marxism and the Philosophy of Language.* Cambridge, Mass.: Harvard University Press.

West, Cornel. 1993. *Keeping Faith.* New York: Routledge.

14

Themes in Liberalism, Modernity, Marxism, Postmodernism and Beyond

HILBOURNE WATSON

An Interpretation and Critique of "Re-Reading *The Black Jacobins*"

A special issue of the journal *Social and Economic Studies* (43, no. 3 [September 1994]) was devoted to a theme of New Directions in Caribbean Thought. One of those essays, "Re-reading *The Black Jacobins*: James, the Dialectic and the Revolutionary Conjuncture", by Brian Meeks (1994) raises a number of issues about the problematic(s) of Marxism, with special reference to C.L.R. James' *The Black Jacobins,* a landmark study of the Haitian (Saint Domingue) Revolution. Meeks uses the essay not only to 'reread' James' classic study but also to announce his break with Marxism and to indicate a transition into what seems like an unspecified postmodernism. While one's rejection of a theoretical, epistemological and ideological position may signal an appreciation of the partisan and contingent nature of all knowledge, it may not necessarily lead into a "new direction in . . . thought", because a new direction in thought may not necessarily announce a contribution to new knowledge.

I do not set out in this article to limit myself to a critique of the main arguments found in Meeks's article, though I develop my argument with

356/ New Caribbean Thought

Meeks's thesis prominently in view. I will weave themes on modernity, liberalism, Marxism, and postmodernism into my analysis. Meeks used to be a member of the now defunct Workers' Party of Jamaica (WPJ); the WPJ had embraced a pro-Soviet outlook that was equated with Marxism. Neither the former USSR nor the WPJ made any specific theoretical or epistemological distinction between their outlook and that of Marx, though the USSR saw itself as heir to Lenin's legacy. The USSR and the WPJ collapsed during the late 1980s. Meeks is not the only former member of the defunct WPJ to have repudiated his Marxist politics and ideology.

What I will say about Meeks's rethinking and rereading of Marxism unfolds at a number of levels. I do not begin by summarizing Meeks's argument; I work through his assertions by weaving his major arguments into my text. I attempt to deal with Meeks's arguments on their own terms as they relate to claims of Marxism, but I want to go much further and address critical issues in Marxist thought that Meeks leaves unaddressed. Since Meeks relies on C.L.R. James' *The Black Jacobins* to present his break with Marxism, and since he cites studies by traditional liberal and conservative academics to refute certain Marxist claims, it is not improbable that Meeks sees himself inverting his earlier outlook by going back to the future through academic liberalism. I will address this claim as I discuss the relationship between Meeks's own interpretation of "Jamesian Marxism" and non-Marxist theoretical and epistemological perspectives. I argue that Meeks's understanding of Marxism bears a Hegelian cast such that the 'new direction' seems less than new, and it reflects a traditional (Cartesian) pluralist bent. There is a point to be made that postmodernism extends the theoretic and ideological spaces of liberalism through a radical deconstructionist pluralism (see Castoriadis 1992).

There are obvious divergences among the historical, theoretical and episte-mological problems in Marxism and the arguments posed by Meeks about Marxism's strategic problems. Meeks does not differentiate among different tendencies within Marxism; he settles for a reductionist concept of Marxism. I will focus on the terms of his inquiry with special reference to historical determination, agency and structure (structuralism) in the historical process (including productive forces and production relations, economism, democracy, freedom, the state and other untheorized concepts), and a number of counterfactual (hindsight) arguments about how the actions of leaders of the Haitian Revolution determined the prospects of Haiti in the Western Hemisphere since 1804.

Rereading a major study such as *The Black Jacobins* can be very useful, especially when the project of rereading makes a creative contribution by revealing the theoretical or epistemological weaknesses in the original study. Given Meeks's interest in charting new directions in Caribbean thought, one should expect to find creative contributions to theory, knowledge and ideology in his essay. I want to suggest that Meeks's criticisms of Marxism have long been a fixture in liberal discourse and they are a staple in Marxological and Marxisant criticisms of Marxism.

It is problematic to reread *The Black Jacobins* without looking at James' argument on dialectics, where he traced the development of two strategic concepts of the universal abstract and the universal concrete, along lines of Enlightenment rationalism. The concept of the universal abstract is an embedded, structuring principle and a presupposition of the entire 'Enlightenment project' of modernity: the concept of the universal abstract holds the status of a historical continuity or universalism that unfolds along a predetermined course that flows from mythical Greco-Roman genealogical origins of the 'West'. Meeks does not confront this problem that informs James' own presuppositions. This is a major omission given that historical materialism emerged in confrontation with bourgeois sociology (see Therborn 1975). Meeks simply attributes to Marxism all the problems he has with *The Black Jacobins,* without referencing any degree to which James might have modified his position at any subsequent point. I will argue that what might be called 'strategic problems' in, say, 'classical Marxism' are of a different nature, scope and substance than Meeks indicates. Meeks does not attempt to distinguish between weaknesses in Marxism, such as its failure to pursue seminal issues it raises and its failure(s) to understand and account for strategic issues around, say, the agency/structure problematic.

On Historical Determination and the Autonomous Individual

Meeks mentions five objectives he intended to pursue in connection with *The Black Jacobins.* Meeks did not address each of those objectives in any careful or consistent manner. He devoted most of his attention to one such objective – historical determination – that he considers to be a confirmation of a rigid 'faceless determinism' in Marxism, and which he detects in *The Black Jacobins.* I begin with historical determination for two reasons: first, historical determination is central in Marxism, and second, Meeks uses this concept to build a straw man around which he centres his criticism: this makes it easy for him to demolish the straw man. Meeks (1994) discusses historical determination under his notion of faceless determinism. His entry point is that Marx and Engels show "glaring silences on questions of the state, politics and historical analysis" (78–79). This point is neither accurate nor original. Most of Marx's popular pamphlets were written to simplify complexities of history, society and theory for the explicit purpose of making those complexities readily accessible to the fledgling working class groups (for example, the League of the Just) on whose behalf documents such as *The Manifesto of the Communist Party* had been written. Commonplace liberal criticisms of Marx's popular writings seldom face this fact, possibly because critics are opposed to bringing knowledge to the masses; but I would not identify Meeks with such a tendency.

My concept of historical determination begins with the idea that human nature is neither presocial nor precivil. I do not attribute the origins of human nature to any metaphysical alienation or determination. I locate the origins of human nature within the social world of the "instituting ground power of society" (Castoriadis 1991: 151). This instituting ground power is like the magma on which the social is formed at a very early point. From this angle, historical determination acquires a different meaning. Meeks's idea of historical determination is grounded in notions of the so-called autonomous individual and autonomous self. These notions are integral to the ideological requirements and reproduction of the existential aspects of anarchical capitalism. Liberal ideology favours Cartesian 'theoretical humanism' (see Cullenberg 1996), with its anxiety and predisposition to treat all parts of phenomena and the social world as autonomous: each part is taken to be independent of the whole, and the totality is assumed to acquire its integrity from the confluence of individual parts. This obvious functionalist pluralism is what informs Meeks's view of the autonomous individual and the self as a form of an ontological and irreducible 'spiritual essence' in itself. All individuals in the real world exist within a context that is bounded by history, politics and time. The development of the individual and the 'self' is subject to the limitations of the "politics of time" (Osborne 1995). Liberal concepts of individual identity, including notions of one's unmediated relationship with 'God', are really metaphysical, precivil notions that invent mythical origins of history: these notions act as their own archaic originary and telos.

In large measure, academic and intellectual liberalism embrace the presuppositions about human nature that are found in the precivil, Lockeian (state of nature) individual as the fountainhead of power, freedom and democracy.

The precivil individual is a contradiction in terms, much like a subject without subjectivity. Seldom is it appreciated that the individual in the state of nature was merely a working concept with Hobbes and Locke, though Locke tended to reify the precivil being. Liberalism pretends that individual freedom is a natural predisposition among certain humans whose genealogy lies in the West (see Wolf 1982; Patterson 1991). The precivil individual predates the meta-physical alienation of precapitalism and the economistic (market) alienation of bourgeois capitalist society. As such, the precivil individual is an imaginary that straddles the archaic (metaphysical) traditions that treated reality as a concrete totalization and the modern Cartesian traditions that view social totality as the sum of the parts. The former embraces the notion of a universal community under one God; the latter separates the secular from the theological world in the transition to modernity. Rationalism and economistic alienation are the bedrock of the latter perspective, and capitalism is its material and social base; the individual is the basic unit of analysis and measure of things. In reality, neither the individual nor the self can be autonomous of the historical process. Humans are agents who build structures and institutions: neither the individ-ual nor the structure absolutely predetermines the other. Notions of the autonomous individual and the autonomous self constitute essentialisms.

In Meeks's conception of historical determination in Marxism there is no evidence of any interest in pursuing Marx's understanding of dialectics. Marx's historical determination is grounded in a dialectical relationship between real historical individuals and the social world those same individuals produce and reproduce: individuals humanize the world consciously through the social relations that they enter. These social relations signal the dialectical process in which the socialization of human nature takes place as an unending process that has no precivil originary. Marx appreciated that the ends of politics should be consistent with the dialectics of humanization, and meaningful concepts of autonomy should be aware of this fact. Marx did not fetishize any irreducible ontology of ahistorical individuals-in-general. The world that humans make takes on a sociohistorical concreteness that is never reducible to the whims and fancies of this or that individual-in-general. Ideologies that rest on the primacy of the individual-in-general invent the autonomous self as an abstraction that hovers in permanent flight in the 'spirit world' outside the social forms. History is then set at the mercy of this fictive entity, becoming posthistory along the way. Meeks's concept of the individual and the autonomous self comes very close to this fictive notion, and he runs the risk of employing Enlightenment rationality as a type of 'character structure' through which to overturn historical determination, without resolving the tension reason and science built up between nature and emotion, and between knowledge and subjectivity.

By appearing to locate individuals outside their history, and thereby rupturing any interdependence between the two, Meeks appears to reiterate the Hobbesian tenet of a world of individuals at war with itself or themselves. Into this world he has imported a Hegelian 'objective idealist' view in which psychological 'spiritual essence' exists independently of matter. I challenge Meeks to demonstrate, outside of commonplace liberal excess, that there is a dichotomy in any serious reading of Marx with respect to "determination by agency or by productive forces". Classical Marxism addressed these issues, even though it might not have pursued them to the logical conclusion. Marx understood reality as complex and heterogeneous. He rejected the Cartesian principle that was embraced by Kant and other Enlightenment figures; and his historical materialism introduced a rupture into the dominant Enlightenment themes that were common in his time (Therborn 1975; Resnick and Wolff 1996: 185–88).

Meeks's argument about the relationship between "democracy and the relevance of Marxism . . . for human emancipation" (1994: 81) trivializes this important theme. Democracy remains an untheorized concept in Meeks's argument, for he does not confront the social nature of agency and how it is constructed in Western political thought. This is evident in how he treats the struggles of the Haitian slaves for liberty, a liberty that contrasted with the property rights of the slave owners whose own social reproduction was contingent on being able to alienate the surplus value produced by the slaves to reproduce private property in the means of production. This was a class relation that was grounded in power, violence, knowledge systems, values and materiality. Meeks's individual threatens to obfuscate the historical connections between rights, liberty and private property. His position is akin to that of Femia (1993), who argues that the Achilles heel in Marxism is its failure to come to terms with the irreducible ontology of the individual. Femia's individual is also a precivil metaphysical entity endowed with a primitive ontology that has roots in timeless history. Femia and Meeks would have to account for why the philosophical and political significance of individual ontology has changed through historical time: for example, they would have to account for, say, Plato's conceptions of the individual in relation to the state, and they would have to clarify the liberal bourgeois construct of the individual who developed in modernity, accounting for why thinkers such as Hobbes, Locke, Rousseau, Kant and Marx developed their interpretations of the nature and role of the individual in history. Why does the individual actor become so central after the rise of capitalism and why did the fetishization and reification of the individual become so pivotal during and after the bourgeois revolutions? Meeks makes no connection between the primacy of the individual and the rise of capitalism, with its peculiar economistic alienation that works through market relations, embedded in money, law and bureaucracy, to fetishize individualism through the process of separation with its Cartesian motif.

Marx did not force the individual back into the integument of the ancient system, much like the leaders of the French Revolution and their Haitian counterparts seemed bent on doing. Conceptually, Marx tried to liberate the historical individual of the bourgeois epoch from that integument by demonstrating a sophisticated understanding of the relationship between the individual and the social system. Marx saw readily that the bourgeois order invents the abstract universality in which to displace and reconfigure the precivil individual who had been constrained by absolutism. This abstract universality puts the social integrity of the social being at war with the abstract identity of isolated individuals. This contradiction is at the heart of the perversion and alienation that private property represents: this perversion is the foundation of the theory of formal political equality coincident with the reality of material and social inequality. It structures the logic of historical necessity as economistic/market alienation. Marx also understood how this alienation participated in the destruction of the metaphysical 'concrete totalization' that preceded the bourgeois epoch. Machiavelli, Hobbes, Locke and a number of other early modern thinkers who devoted themselves to the analysis of complex issues at the intersection of premodernity and modernity — issues such as the formation of the modern state, rights, and the nature and forms of secular power — contributed to these debates that surged in the transition from the tributary (feudal) orders to capitalism.

On a related note, Lindahl argues that Alexis de Tocqueville's concept of democracy offers a fittingly appropriate alternative to Marxism and socialism in the contemporary Caribbean. Lindahl is mistaken. We know that de Tocqueville embraced classical liberalism and he was wrong in suggesting that the liberal (bourgeois) state has a democratic nature (see Manent 1994). No state can have a democratic nature, for democracy is a historical form of political power. Such a flawed notion derives from Cartesian anxiety and the functionalist predisposition that grows up inside liberalism. The notion that the bourgeois state possesses a democratic nature comes from essentializing the individual as the rational source of sovereign power: this peculiar power does not possess a nature but it has rational functions. Montesquieu went further in suggesting that the power of the liberal democratic state knows how to check itself. This is pure liberal flourish and excess. Lindahl (1994) compounds the first error of liberal excess with a second mistake in arguing that democracy is a self-organizing system that takes a long time to mature. While Meeks does not explicitly embrace Lindahl's errors about the nature of the state and democracy, he does not distance himself from them: there is nothing in Meeks's introduction to that special issue of *Social and Economic Studies* in which Lindahl's argument on democracy appears to suggest any critical reaction to this argument. It is perplexing to find Lindahl advancing this dated classical democratic theory to the Caribbean masses as the alternative to Marxism at this juncture. What are Caribbean masses to do with this classical liberal Enlightenment flourish? Why does Lindahl want to reinvent classical democratic theory as an extension of a Eurocentric universalism, under the guise that it is still good for the Caribbean, when the West has long passed over it? Tocquevillianism serves in the United States as a legitimatizing and mediating principle in the imaginary of modern democratic thought.

de Tocqueville's thesis is the thesis of the politics of representation under petit bourgeois forms of largely agrarian (frontier) capitalism. de Tocqueville embraced the notion that early nineteenth century Americans were "truculently free" in a social system that was based on large-scale slavery, open oppression, genocide and everyday violence to secure the economic basis of capital accumulation. de Tocqueville also embraced the theory of the individual autonomy from whom the slaves were separated. Even if the slaves were considered as individuals, they were still largely excluded from full humanity. This was easy to do, because the individualist impulse in early American democratic thought invented competition subjects as marketized entities who could separate the self from the conditions in which those individuals reproduced themselves: these subjects could negate their own subjectivity, like all Cartesian beings. de Tocqueville was fetishizing petit bourgeois individualism at the borderlands of frontier capitalism.

Lindahl would have to account for de Tocqueville's view of American democracy, represented by autonomous individuals, with the strategy of the violent, expansionist American state that used genocide to liquidate the 'Indians' by destroying their ecological balance, killing the buffalo and the crops that constituted their food line. The particular relationship between the genocidal mania and the imperatives of primitive accumulation in the early American republic was grounded in the negative sociability and negative freedom of bourgeois culture. There is a clear connection between ecological disaster, cultural strangulation, genocidal practices and the truculently free American civil society of Meeks's autonomous individuals: the autonomous individuals who made up America then and now also gave us three legitimatizing myths about American exceptionalism, invincibility and manifest destiny. Cartesian 'theoretical humanism' paves the way for the compartmentalization of social reality as the preferred way to separate the self from guilt or any necessity for atonement for crimes against humanity or nature. This allows Meeks's autonomous individuals to engage in debauchery, greed, destruction and other excesses of passion: ecological destruction could be defined as the price of progress; capital accumulation as the progress of freedom's primary vocation; commodity fetishism as postmodern self-actualization; and expending wage labour as natural alienation. Psychoanalysis functions as the flagship therapeutic discipline that medicalizes the economic and social excesses of capitalism by dehistoricizing them and diagnosing them as by-products of human nature (see O'Neill 1995) or the 'natural' alienation/anarchy of the social system, or both. Individual autonomy becomes the highest form of self-realization, for there is no collective emancipation, only individual autonomy within necessity. Meeks does not explore the implications of the negative sociability of his autonomous individuals.

Historical Determination, Civil Society and Social Relations

With respect to the Haitian Revolution, Meeks does not seem comfortable with the historical evidence that privileges history; he appears to be on the boundaries of posthistory and the antiphilosophy of history, a position that seems to resonate with Foucauldian and Lyotardian notions that reject philosophy and the metanarratives of the Enlightenment (see Foucault 1977; Lyotard 1984; and Wilding 1995).

A civil society made up of autonomous individuals who act outside of history cannot be posited in opposition to Marxist homogeneity. The space inhabited by autonomous individuals is the only space open to such a notion of ahistorical individuals. Preoccupation with identity politics encourages an autonomous civil society as the site of the lived experiences of people-in-general who have never encountered history. States, productive forces and production relations inhabit spaces alien to civil society in posthistorical theories, for this is the arena of subjects without subjectivity. These ludic spaces contain fetishized civil society with untheorized, precivil origins. It would be necessary to compare the civil society that preceded the rise of capitalism with the bourgeois forms of civil society in order to avoid the mistaken impression that the real origins of civil society are coterminous with the transition to capitalism in Europe. What is integral to capital's restlessness and its need to reproduce itself and accumulate is the historical necessity to revolutionize the productive forces to the point where the same productive forces are in constant conflict with the social base of capital and capitalist society. The productive forces–production relations problematic in capitalism simply cannot be punctuated in a dichotomous relationship of agency to productive forces. This problematic expresses a relationship that is shaped and reproduced through the alienation of social labour. It is not evident in Meeks's argument that bourgeois society is a particular type of historical society, known as marketized, competition society, with a predisposition to equate itself with society-in-general.

A more critical reading of bourgeois civil society would show that it

is determined by the subjectless economic process of valorization and accumulation, reproduced by the generalized structures of commodity production and exchange and the income seeking activities of competition subjects in competitive society regulated by the market. The state is particularized as the social subject legitimated to intervene in, and thence negate, the subjectless processes of civil society in pursuit of what it conceives as the general interest. The existence of the state is grounded first by its positing right as law . . . and secondly by its legitimation in the will of its citizens. (Reuten and Williams 1989: 175)

Civil society under capitalism is commodity society, marketized society, society of competition subjects, pursuing rational self-interests in their individuated beings: it is class society in its gendered, ethnicized, racialized, polarized forms, torn by class contradictions that are mediated by the state. Meeks tears civil society from the broader social process and contradictions in capitalism. He singles out individual agency and dehistoricizes and essentializes it as though agency can ever be an ahistorical category. Meeks fetishizes the reality that "social structures shape and are shaped by individual subjects in a continuous dialectic" (Resnick and Wolff 1996: 186). He introduces an unnecessary humanist-structuralist dichotomy, which reinforces a Cartesian-Hegelian tension that contradicts the social basis of all identities. Meeks is reaching for an identity politics for which the autonomous individual serves as primitive of social explanation or unit of analysis.

Agency is historical; historical processes are conjunctural; human agency operates within conjunctural and heterogeneous social spaces. The thrust of

Meeks's argument reduces heterogeneity to semblances of pulverized, autonomous ontologies. Meeks appears to conflate separation with heterogeneity. It is necessary to appreciate that functionality does not create agency: we have to start from the nature of agency rather than from the functions of agency. The multiplicitous and heterogeneous basis of agency demonstrates that human actors are integral members of the complex yet fragmented and heterogeneous totality (Callari and Ruccio 1996: 22–23). Meeks essentializes individual agency and imposes a closure through which the individual is reduced to an archaic agency. This is unwarranted in that theories of the primacy of the individual must account for how individuals enter and participate in social systems, since it is impossible for thinking to be independent of socially heterogeneous processes. Heterogeneity and autonomy are not interchangeable, nor do they share common boundaries.

Opposition to historicization leads to the dismissal of facticity, a tendency that is fashionable in posthistorical relativism. Marx understood the historical basis of knowledge; for him, people make history and act it out. We can change history as we make it; we can end prehistory and move on to the real history in which humans really achieve their universality. To do this, we must first overthrow alienation in all its social forms, including the national state; but we simply cannot get outside history. The needs of the emerging bourgeoisie and its struggle to set itself up as the new ruling class reinforced the separation of the individual from society and separated coercion from the economic and labour processes. Capitalism and bourgeois culture need a theory of the primacy of the individual because the market is the site where all social identities are pulverized as part of the commodity reproduction system: What better way to secure the sway of capital than to equate the individual with the logic of freedom and the market with the site where freedom truly expresses itself? Social pulverization is part of the process through which social alienation is reproduced. Under capitalism, workers sell labour power as individuals and not as a single undifferentiated social class. Similarly, each capitalist comes to the market as an individual bearer of means of production, leaving social class identity behind, so to speak. This is a figment of methodological atomism.

The market keeps and preserves individual identity and autonomy around the separation of the unity of the twofold nature of the value contained in commodities. Money advances social alienation as the grand mediator of exchange value. In the break-up of the tributary (feudal) system there occurred the separation of the individual from the state, of the state from society, and of state and individuals from the economy. The legal, formal abolition of political inequality was integral to this process. Simultaneously, the very violent and bloody process reflected the unity of coercion, capital and the state. The capital–labour relation is a class relation of unity-in-contradiction. It is not possible to analyse civil society outside this reality (see Tilly 1990). There is a tendency to treat the process of separation as the consolidation of democracy-in-general, with the unsavoury effect of externalizing contradictions.

The inequality problem as a problem of the estrangement and alienation of labour was eventually displaced inside the market under the impetus of law and money and externalized from the sphere of politics. Inequality assumed the form of an extension of 'natural' alienation. The immediate effect was to shield the class interests of the bourgeoisie from unnecessary political exposure. These class interests are essentialized and reduced to self-interests to reinforce the myth of the individual as a sovereign actor who is at once the source of power. Individual interests could be separated from politics just as the individual was separated from the state, politics and society. Government could be made purely administrative; the market could be reinvented free from state interference; and the model could be made to work harmoniously through the logic of 'social physics', to which neoclassical economics has reduced itself.

The depoliticization of the state and individual interests could be invented on the scaffolding of bureaucratic, administrative techniques and mediated by a disinterested state that miraculously gets its power from the same autonomous individuals. This is ludic theory that invents a subject without subjectivity, who can stand apart from class, productive forces and social relations: this is the space inhabited by the alienated self of autonomous individuals. All attempts to elide the social contradictions of capitalism can accomplish little more than to reduce democracy to radical pluralism. Meeks has to be reminded that the questions of democracy and historical determination are inextricably linked.

So far, I have used my critique of Meeks's concept of the autonomous individual to reveal the problems I detect in his argument on historical determination and democracy. It is necessary to elaborate on democracy. Democracy is a particular historical way of organizing political power in the modern national state; democracy's modern roots are sown in the political, economic and social struggles that formed around certain types of social, economic and other contradictions in society. Democracy cannot be reduced to a rationalizing learning process, any more than the economy can be reduced to a set of psychological signals and drives that determine how competition subjects pursue 'self-interests'. There is no way to reduce democracy to a fully worked-out 'self-organizing system' that is prepackaged to go. Meeks finds relief in returning to ideological views of democracy put forward by men such as F.A. Hayek and Robert Nozick, who reduce democracy to an essentialism in which the market is the telos of its own subjectless process. Meeks's autonomous individuals seem to be captives of this imaginary.

Milton Friedman, like Hayek, was insistent about the relationship between marketized individuals and the imperatives of economized 'democratic' civil society. Hayek and Friedman insisted that it is dangerous to let autonomous individuals (such as those of Meeks) in civil society assert their social and political civil rights over primary economic property (that is, the primary civil rights) rights of capitalists. Hayek is frequently cited to validate structural adjustment, liberalization and privatization, and the expansion of the base of the primitive culture of negative freedom (see Watson 1995: 113–16). There are ample lessons to learn from why the freedom of individual capitalist entrepreneurs is always equated with the freedom of people-in-general who have never owned means of production. The problem with Hayek's argument is that it is grounded in psychobabble about how private property is the prerequisite for the development of all human personality; it seems that some special humans can decipher this precondition in their recourse to a certain universal reason. This is a sly way to generalize from the property rights of the few to the abstract equality of the many who have never had private property in the means of production.

I share Orlando Patterson's argument that since "valuing freedom is not part of the natural human condition" but, rather, a cultural invention, the West "must be scrutinized and explained for its . . . peculiar commitment to this value" (Patterson 1991: xi). But the trick lies in the content of this value called freedom. This was the value Europe had to carry to the rest of the world under the ponderous weight of the 'white man's burden'; the United States has supplanted Europe, shouldering it under manifest destiny. A great deal of blood has been spilled securing this most universal of all metavalues. Neither Locke nor his followers managed to demonstrate how the precivil, autonomous individual, with his irreducible ontology, managed such a leap out of the state of nature into the political society. Yet ideological commitment to this ludic premise remains, for it plays a key legitimatizing function in bourgeois ideology.

There remains a very strong temptation to misrepresent 'sovereignal freedom' by equating it with the metaphysical 'spiritual' quality of the modern bourgeois state in the West: Christian metaphysics in Western culture mediates social relations of domination and exploitation under bourgeois rule by shifting the material and temporal base of the state into a mystical realm of 'One nation under God'. This metaphysical alienation is captured in notions such as God the King, Sovereign, Shepherd, Provider, Rock of Ages, and all the other attributions and cultural insignia of power that secular rulers assert for themselves (see Nicholls 1992). This produces the contradictory effect of mystifying the secular ruler while also humanizing and demystifying the godhead. Evidence shows that the origin of the godhead started out first as a material embodiment in the social existence of societies, long before it became a symbolic representation of power and authority removed from the lives of real people to constitute a mystical force. It has also been secularized in the state and associated with claims about absolute right and repression: all freedom is historical or it is nothing at all.

Productive Forces and Production Relations: Democracy, Economism and the Politics of Representation

Productive forces and relations of production are historical and contingent; as such, they change on an ongoing basis. Any intelligent discussion of democracy must begin with democracy as a problematic construct. Such a discussion must be grounded in an intellectual consciousness and awareness of the difference between abstract universality, in which bourgeois ideology must locate humans, and the concrete universality this bourgeois ideology must suture at the level of formalism. It is necessary to bring the tension between agency and the productive forces face to face with the two universalities of the abstract and the concrete (Meeks 1994: 81). States and political societies that develop around specific historical forms of power relations cannot be neutral. There is a tendency to depoliticize democracy by ignoring or discarding its nature and starting with its functions, much like the habit of depoliticizing the state by deriving the power it exercises from fictive sovereign individuals. This is a design to accomplish the impossible of rendering power nonpolitical. Montesquieu tried to do precisely this by hiding power from politics so as to alienate its true political nature (see Manent 1994). This explains why there is a tendency for many academics to reduce the role of coercion, domination, inequality, and the construction and usurpation of power to externalities and by-products of human nature in general. The social physics that informs neoclassical economics is notorious in this regard.

The agency–productive forces problematic as depicted by Meeks negates the social form of the existence of the capital–wage labour relation as a perverted form of class-divided social existence, and it sets social relations outside class relations in class society. Class relations and class society are bifurcated and set at variance with historical reality. The effect is to fetishize social relations and pervert them by negating the social nature of the individual. The net effect is to elide the abolition of historical alienation. Private property as capital in the means of production is the social form of the alienation of labour. This alienated labour must reproduce itself and capital. This makes it absolutely necessary for there to be a political economy in which capital can legitimately enforce domination over alienated labour that continues to live and reproduce itself as a 'factor of production', as a mere resource and an input, cut away from its social content. Meeks does not come to terms with the fact that private property is the specific form of the existence of alienated labour. For all practical purposes, the concept of the social individual is consistent with social reality as a heterogeneous, unstable reality, but it does not embrace the fetishized notion of any autonomous individual or self. The fact is that the social individual appears as an autonomous being in bourgeois society because of the process of alienation. Meeks's case for a new direction in Caribbean thought ought not to abandon this seminal issue, since revealing it lies at the heart of all efforts to develop a theory of emancipation for Caribbean people.

The key question, then, revolves around how Meeks's autonomous individual encourages or participates in the movement from alienation towards emancipation. This is problematic in that intellectual labour is no less alienated than manual labour, and the fragmented social and technical conditions in which intellectual labour reproduces itself are not conducive to discerning this contradiction. But neither history nor philosophy can be negated except through realization beyond necessity. True, individuals make their own history; in so doing they construct their world behind their own backs, as it were. The social practice of power works with a vengeance through and against individuals who contribute to social practice as social change. It is only when we see human individuals as subjects with a purpose and not as a resource that we can move thought beyond the forms of alienation and thereby demystify the alienated individual that Meeks tends to celebrate as the real autonomous being (see Bonefeld 1995: 205–7).

A close reading of *Struggle*, the ideological organ of the former WPJ, tends to show a much closer affinity between the WPJ and Sovietism than with Marx's Marxism. There seems to be little to gain from haunting the ghost of systems that claimed to have lived by Marx's tenets. The Soviet system imagined and practised their version of socialism as the inversion of capitalism. The Soviets went very far in constructing a system much like capitalism without capitalists and the private market. How those who have built social systems in the name of Marxism have fared in relation to 'democracy' is a concrete historical matter. These contradictions cannot be resolved or displaced by exhorting anti-Marxist themes about the end of history. It seems there may be more than a simple coincidence between Meeks's new perspective on Francis Fukuyama and Trevor Munroe's celebratory review of Samuel Huntington's recent book on the clash of civilizations (see Munroe 1994).

Meeks implies that major tectonic shifts such as the collapse of the USSR and minor developments such as the collapse of the WPJ offer proof that capitalism and liberal democracy have defeated history. This is neoliberal flourish. The reality is that liberal democracy has been around for a very limited time; it is practised in a limited number of countries, especially the ones that have employed violence and domination to take control of the world's resources in the name of doctrines of private property, individual freedom and justice. The role of the market and alienated labour under historical capitalism are specific matters that demand concrete analysis. They cannot be treated in any general discussion about the power of democracy or its universal ideas. Alienation is a historical contingency. Furthermore, the crisis of the national state model demands close analysis. It is not acceptable to elide this critical issue by folding it into politically correct notions about the death of Marxism.

Meeks does not deal with the fact that the politically correct notion of the death of Marxism constitutes a theoretic closure. The disappearance of the WPJ, the destruction of the former People's Revolutionary Government (PRG) in Grenada, and the collapse of the 1970s' social democratic strategies of the People's National Party (PNP) in Jamaica simply will not serve to defend Meeks's claims against Marxism. Is there life after capitalism? Neither the WPJ nor the PRG ever matured beyond petit bourgeois notions of the noncapitalist path to development, a notion that worked well with Soviet realpolitik in the realist imaginary of spheres of influence and the balance of power. The PNP was consistently anti-Marxist and anticommunist. Meeks would have to demonstrate the original contributions to Marxism that have been left by the

WPJ based on Jamaica's experience in the Caribbean. The WPJ ideology never developed any autonomy from Sovietism (see Campbell 1994).

Democracy, as it is practised in various countries today, is not an aberration from any ideal type of a democratic model. The West offers itself as such a genealogical model of democracy, and this is what Meeks seems to accept. Democracy is conditioned by the class struggle. This is precisely why contending social forces have to be sufficiently vigilant to push back the borders of any democratic experiment all the time. The condition of democracy depends on the balance of social forces in society. To imply, as Meeks does, that there is a universal democracy-in-general is to block theoretical development by advancing a structuring essentialism. Democratic struggles are like continuous plebiscites. Views of democracy that ignore the problematic concept and process it represents become essentialist, and they have the effect of making defeatism more comfortable to tolerate.

There is a bigger issue of the relationship between defeatism and the politics of representation. In liberal democracies the politics of representation serves to negate the politics of participation, due to the class nature of democracy and capitalism. Meeks's autonomous individual fits neatly with the politics of representation; this may be why he does not pay any attention to the dialectic between a politics of representation and a participatory politics. Meeks equates representation with participation in the electoral process. This idea of democracy, which remains untheorized in Meeks's essay, converges with political representation that begins with the populist notion that power flows from the people as a mass of undifferentiated individuals. Bourgeois democracy is self-consciously limited within a logic of representation that starts from the premise of its own finiteness and closure, and this predisposes its own idealism and its essentialism.

Classical Marxism, Productive Forces, Alienation and Postmodernism

The Marxist conception of the productive forces accounts for real people with production experiences, professional training, technical skills and other capabilities that facilitate social development. The alienation of labour stamps this process; the alienation of labour is necessary for the reproduction of private property as capital. This legitimizes private property in the means of production and sanctions rightful property income along with the psychobabble about

how possessing private property is the necessary prerequisite for the development of the human personality. The politics of representation is the politics
of necessity grounded in social alienation.

I argue that it is necessary to abandon Cartesian formalism and structural
functionalism to overcome the structuralist contrivance that dichotomizes the
productive forces and the production relations. Capital is an integral part of
the social relations of production; labour is another integral part and so is the
state. To appreciate this fact is to begin to move towards dismantling the habit
of reducing totalization to an essentialism. It is impossible to escape essentializing concepts. Marxist materialists would essentialize in strategic, contingent
ways; Cartesian modernists would essentialize as absolute necessity; postmodernists would deny that they essentialize because they deconstruct and leave
debris strewn across the intellectual landscape. The habit of essentializing the
individual leads to essentializing the state, the market and other processes. This
is the point at which all social relations between people become relations
between things. Meeks's analysis of productive forces and relations of production tends in this direction, for it is trapped in a mere sensuous and reductionist
materiality and physicality of agency and productive forces (Callari and Ruccio
1996: 24–26).

Meeks's insistence that religion, the state and historical analysis are glaringly
deficient in Marx's writings (1994: 78) draws on what is commonplace in
Marxisant criticism. Callari and Ruccio (1996) have raised a number of
important arguments about the "strategic problems in Classical Marxism"
(41). It is far more helpful to concentrate on the theoretical implications of
the strategic problems in Marxism than to restate criticisms about glaring
deficiencies. Callari and Ruccio discuss the strategic problems of classical
Marxism in relation to

its construction of the social space in essentially homogeneous terms and its historical
teleology. These two aspects of Marxist discourse . . . reinforce one another. On the one
hand, the vision of the process of historical transformation as fundamentally a process of
transformation of class relations depended on a prior analytical operation that exhausted
the social space in a structure of purely economic relations; on the other hand, the very
ability to analytically reduce the social space to this structure itself depended on a
philosophy of history, a teleology, the profession of a certainty that the transformation/abo-
lition of class relations and the rational organization of production would also entail the
transformation/abolition of all nonclass forms of oppression. (41)

Still, the contributions of Marxism set it apart from Cartesianism and the Hegelian objective idealism. There is space for serious engagement, analysis and intellectual critique within the spaces of critical Marxism. I suggest there is a far more fruitful path to take by looking at Marxist materialism beyond simple matter that is understood in terms of the economy or the physical world, and one that eschews any telos or originating subject that grounds idealist notions of knowledge. I am thinking of a materialism that is radically disposed to the questioning of everything existing, following Marx's own disposition and method (Callari and Ruccio 1996: 23–26). This materialism refuses to settle for deconstructing the world to the point of leaving empty vessels strewn across the intellectual vista.

It is not difficult to generate criticisms of Marxism that announce the irrelevance or death of Marxism in politically correct ways. There remains the serious matter of how to get over the historical necessity capitalism has imposed under the mantle of the national state. There are acute problems of capitalist oppression and exploitation that Marxism continues to account for. It is impossible to abandon Marxism not only because of the "concreteness of the class dimensions of struggles that still punctuate the world . . . but also for discursive and philosophical reasons" (Callari and Ruccio 1996: 27). Nor is there any intelligent grounds on which to make a case for a complete break between modernity and postmodernity, unless one wants to posit "the conditions for an uncontested restoration of bourgeois modernism". The truth is that "the survival of the critical, destabilizing effects associated with postmodernism requires a continuing Marxist presence" (Callari and Ruccio 1996: 27–28).

Callari and Ruccio (1996), who are quite illuminating on the contributions and contradictions of postmodernism, make very explicit the insipid basis of superficial Marxisant criticism. They argue that

it is true that postmodern discourse moves on a multidimensional and fragmented social space and recognizes (and participates in producing) a plurality of irreducible subjects and identities, and while it is also true that postmodernism rejects in principle any closure, any suturing of the social space, it also happens in practice that postmodern discourses cannot avoid importing at some unanalyzed level, suturing concepts from the universe of modernist discourse. One such concept is the 'economy', which . . . when used in an untheorized fashion can serve to reintroduce, however unintentionally or unconsciously, the very suturing operation that postmodern injunctions tend to proscribe. Other such concepts are democracy, rights; equality, justice, that in their bourgeois forms amount to little more than masked universalisms that introduce the spaces of insipid representation understood as reified identities beyond affirmation and negotiation and renegotiation. (27–28; see also Bonefeld 1995: 205–7; Wilding 1995)

Progress is a historical construct. The market seductively misrepresents itself as a subjectless process in which individuals pursue their self-interest as competition subjects, mediated by a depoliticized, administrative state (Reuten and Williams 1989). Popular notions of autonomous individuals or selves who are unconstrained by class relations and other social contradictions are fetishized reflections that pander to the ways money, law, bureaucracy and commodity processes make defeatism and accommodationism more accept-able. The commodification of culture and everyday life engenders a ubiquitous cultural pluralism and flexibilization of thought that immobilizes the imagi-nation. No matter how seductive this "pauper soup of liberalism" (see Casto-riadis 1991: 242) may be, it simply cannot negate the fundamental capitalist social process.

Materialist Dialectics of the Haitian Revolution: The Counterfactual 'What If'

Marx's historical materialism emerged in frontal opposition to bourgeois sociology and the 'Enlightenment project' (Therborn 1975). This point bears on the argument Meeks advances in his descriptive summary about the role of Toussaint L'Ouverture in the Haitian Revolution. Toussaint appreciated the necessity of abolishing slavery, but he also understood the necessity of preserv-ing economic exploitation as a form of historical alienation: this is where Toussaint's notions of necessity and freedom intersected. The intersection of necessity and freedom is the site where agency and productive forces live out their dialectical interconnectedness in class societies. The Haitian Revolution was not about abolishing economic and social exploitation: rather, its project was ending the alienation of labour power in servitude. Some of the leaders of the revolution already owned private property and some of them had risen to high positions in the coercive areas of the state. They were interested in making the slaves free to sell labour power by separating direct coercion from the economy. Their notion of freedom had nothing to do with creating an autonomous self; rather, they were in pursuit of a historical form of freedom as necessity. The problem arises when we fetishize and reify freedom won under the bourgeois revolution as freedom-in-general. Callari and Ruccio (1996) point out that postmodernists use untheorized concepts such as autonomy, the economy, democracy, freedom and justice. These untheorized concepts are strewn across the landscape of bourgeois intellectual culture, which pretends to separate itself from the contradictory process of social change as well as from the construction of social identities and "particular forms of perception and agency" (23).

Toussaint L'Ouverture was interested in abolishing one type of exploitation based on slavery and replacing it with a more recent type of exploitation based on wage labour and the abolition of formal political inequality: along the way his project would necessitate the separation of coercion from the economy and the labour process. This is where the tension between abstract and concrete universality became evident in the Haitian Revolution. Naturally, the French state, Toussaint and the other leaders had their own views; the slaves had a very different view that was bound to put them in conflict with those who had to exploit them in order to reproduce themselves as owners of the means of production. Even if the slaves had no view of freedom other than full freedom beyond necessity such as comes with the abolition of exploitation, oppression and inequality, the fact remains that the revolution could only have survived in a world based on different forms of exploitation.

The broad goals of the Haitian slaves were revolutionary in the way that the French Revolution embraced Enlightenment principles grounded in the rule of necessity: these very principles were designed to deepen the separation of state from society, of the economy from state and society, of the individual from the state and society, and to organize bourgeois property relations in order to make peasants and urban workers free to sell labour power. This project lies at the heart of bourgeois democracy, and therefore capitalist democracy has to be grounded in domination and necessity. This was the way to institutionalize and strengthen the bourgeois revolutions with their new property rights, laws, and other socioeconomic and political bases, including the separation of coercion from society and the economy and the socialization of the doctrine of the 'Right of Man' from which women were excluded, except generically under men. The nationalization of society was also integral to this project. It was about reconstructing the state, the productive forces and social relations of production beyond mere sensuousness, physicality and materiality. The crisis of the Reign of Terror that befell the revolution under Robespierre and the revolutionaries had certain parallels in the Haitian Revolution. Toussaint and the Saint Domingue revolutionaries appeared as individual actors, seemingly outside the concrete social relations of production within the revolution. At the existential level, the individual identities of the revolutionary actors appeared to have been limited by the individuated side of their social consciousness, but their particularistic identities were integral to their social being as agency. It is therefore unacceptable to dichotomize the dialectic of agency and structure the way Meeks does on this seminal issue.

Meeks would have to demonstrate a more developed appreciation of the development of civil society in the bourgeois revolution. Marx had a profound understanding that capitalism was a very important moment along the historical development of human civilization. He understood the rupture that had been taking place between theological metaphysics, as old-fashioned alienation, and bourgeois rationality, as modern economistic alienation. Marx grasped the limitations of the culture of negative freedom (see Patterson 1991) that is so fundamental to generalizing the abstract universality in bourgeois society. Ruling class ideas do not acquire absolute dominance or sway. This is why we must understand the partisan disposition in all theories of society. The bourgeoisie appreciates the necessity of inventing 'national interest' as an extension of the universalization of specific class interests. This is accomplished always as an unstable and contingent achievement. Getting to this point involves the nationalization of society as a prerequisite for the construction of national interests: here, society is that mass of individuals who are disconnected from deeper social identities such as class identity or gender identity. When social identities are constructed on a scaffolding of 'difference', and when dangerous nationalist barriers are set up to cement those barriers, difference can be made into a high or low order to validate violence by the few against the many along national or ethnic lines in the same way bourgeois culture, the national state and capital have divided the modern world to privilege capital accumulation. We must be clear about how the national is invented and constructed out of the particulars. The class struggle is at the centre of this process, and civil society is the unspecified, undifferentiated mass that is refashioned out of prenational social and ethnic fragments, vernaculars, and other components (see Reuten and Williams 1989; Smith 1991).

Marx saw how the development of civil society beyond the bounds of 'absolutism' was carried forward by the generalized individualist impulse of the bourgeoisie through the new forms of capitalist private property, money, law and the market. It was through these specific mechanisms that the social process was restructured. The claims of 'absolute right' and claims of 'divine' rulership were abolished in bloody struggles along the way. It was through the overthrow of absolute right that the concept and reality of a modern political economy, with its new political culture, new value system, ideologies and a new state formation process, could develop. Both the modern state and a new individual came into relief in the market system, masquerading as the ghost of history – the autonomous individual-in-general becoming the source of power that would gird the loins of the same modern state. The ideological ruse of assigning to this individual a set of precivil virtues was not lost on Marx. The Haitian Revolution was a piercing scream for a new type of civil society to be born to release these same concrete, historical, individual impulses: necessity hijacked freedom. The formation of the Haitian state in the revolutionary process soon exposed the contradictions and instabilities of this process (see Trouillot 1990; Dupuy 1989).

It is true the American War of Independence and the French Revolution pointed the way forward in the development of modern concepts of citizenship and national identity and the articulation of the principle of individual rights, but this was done under bourgeois dominance. Meeks seems to miss the point that it is Enlightenment ideology that universalizes and dehistoricizes this process. It is absolutely necessary to defetishize concepts of bourgeois rights, freedoms, and such. The bourgeoisie did not grant rights to anyone; the bourgeoisie had to engage in protracted struggle before it could win the rights it got and take control of the state and dominate labour and society. The French Revolution also revealed the contradictions that *Fraternité, Liberté, Egalité* posed for gender relations and women in particular. The revolution's own concepts of citizenship and individual rights and the social processes in which they were embedded were circumscribed by the inherent limitations of the bourgeois variant of the culture of negative freedom, particularly as it applied to women. The consciousness of the revolution had a very limited notion of the social construction and political determination of gender relations, and rights of peasants, workers, colonized peoples and other groups. The French Revolution did not create an inclusive gender strategy: the development of national institutions on a logic of national inclusiveness is what girds the ideology of equity, which is the best that the bourgeoisie can advance as a substitute for substantive equality. After all, if persons must possess private property in the means of production to acquire a real personality, and if they must accept that alienation in the labour process is a natural thing as opposed to a historical relation of exploitation, what else is there left for the masses but to succumb to the fate of substantive inequality? Hence, we see that capitalism and bourgeois democracy reproduce themselves in the culture of negative freedom as social alienation. Yet the bourgeoisie must invent a theory of social equality. Meeks abandons the critique of the bourgeois social forms.

Marx was very clear that the real human universality is nothing less than "a dialectical totality that preserves the previous achievements of civil society" towards the abolition of that type of civil society (Avineri 1978: 190). The problematic of the French Revolution, from the perspective of the proletariat, rested in the fact that it was mainly a political revolution that contained the seeds of a social revolution that remained an incomplete revolution because the "political sphere cannot . . . impose itself on civil society unless civil society has already developed within itself the elements that make this . . . unnecessary . . . [and] politics by itself is impotent" (Avineri 1978: 194). This point exposes the inadequacies of Meeks's argument about autonomous individuals in relation to agency and structure. The Jacobins did not grasp this reality, so that when they tried to impose the political sphere upon civil society by subsuming "all the spheres of private life under a political universality abstracted from its concrete conditions" (Avineri 1978: 193), they created a vacuum between political power and the prevailing socioeconomic conditions. Marx's point was that the merely political revolution is nothing but the ultimate radicalization of the dichotomy between the particular and the universal; it finally proves that merely political universality is illusory, since it makes it clear that the state can realize its universality only by disregarding the particularistic content of civil society and by abstracting from it. Such a one-sided universality does not constitute a synthesis that incorporates and overcomes particularism (Avineri 1978: 194; from Marx and Engels, *Selected Works*, 1: 362).

Marx summarized his views on Jacobinism in the following terms:

Robespierre . . . and their party fell because they confused the ancient, realistic and democratic republic based on real slavery with the modern spiritualist democratic representative state which is based on emancipated slavery, with civil society. What a terrible mistake it is to have to recognize and sanction in the Rights of Man modern civil society, the society of industry, of universal competition, of private interest freely following its aims, of anarchy, of self-alienated natural and spiritual individuality, and yet subsequently to annul the manifestation of the life of that society in separate individuals and at the same time to wish to model the political head of the society after the fashion of the ancients . . . Terror wished to sacrifice [civil society] to an ancient form of political life. (quoted in Avineri 1978: 191; from Marx and Engels, *The Holy Family* [Moscow 1956])

Here we see how the bourgeois revolution, as an incomplete revolution, set free a particular type of civil society from the prison of the political sphere; it also deepened the separation of the economy and the market from the political sphere where coercion is grounded: displacement is a form of preservation. In the process, produced within this form of historical liberation was a new tension between civil society and the new national state, "which institutionalizes the alienation of man from his universality" (Avineri 1978: 185; see Marx 1963: 27–29). Broadly, the bourgeois revolutions advanced the separation of the economy and civil society from the state, intensified the consolidation of the material and juridical basis of individual rights (civil and political rights), gave the bourgeoisie the freedom it needed to develop the market and institutionalize the wage labour–capital relation, through which coercion was separated from the market and the economy, in a very formal way. But this liberation from direct subjugation to the 'absolutist' state produced two new forms of linked identities: the bourgeois state became the symbol of separation-in-unity with the fusion of nation and state into the nation state: the nation state facilitated the identity of unity-in-separation or collective identity (Reuten and Williams 1989). The new ruling class could thus represent its particularistic interests as the general interest.

In *The German Ideology*, Marx clarified how a new ruling class in the making comes to

represent its interests as the common interest of all members of society, put in an ideal form; . . . it will give its ideas the form of universality . . . the class making a revolution appears from the very start, merely because it is opposed to a class, not as a class but as the representation of the whole society; it appears as the whole mass of society confronting the one ruling class . . . Every new ruling class achieves its hegemony only on a broader basis than that of the class ruling previously, in return for which the opposition of the non-ruling class against the new ruling class develops all the more sharply and profoundly. (Quoted in James 1947: 5)

Clearly, the notion of civil society inhabiting a purely private space is a deeply flawed one; but such a notion is necessary to bourgeois rule, which thrives upon social individuation and fragmentation. The modernist and postmodernist forms of bourgeois ideology idealize and fetishize this fragmentation, partly by treating concepts of freedom, the individual and autonomy in untheorized and essentialist ways. Many of them would rather forget about capitalism by equating it with a so-called totalizing concept, much in keeping with liberal excess and market prejudice. Individual rights cannot secure individual autonomy under class rule. Liberalism sees the development of these rights flowing from the unction of nature in the teleological guise of the consciousness of God in the world, conditioned by the instrumentality of the beneficent state, empowered by sovereign individuals. Liberalism retraces its steps through historical up-time to engage in a certain historical necromancy in which it bases this claim in Christianity which had "established universality in its most abstract form" (James 1947: 2).

Meeks has confused autonomy with separation as 'theoretical humanism' after the manner of Descartes (see Cullenberg 1996). Meeks's eagerness to dismiss historical materialism forces him to ignore important arguments. He ignores the fact that James put the Haitian Revolution in its proper context in the Enlightenment, capitalism and classical liberalism, thereby situating Toussaint within the same context where he belongs. One may reject any grand narrative from history, but one cannot displace history. Toussaint's social background out of Africa had something to do with how he related to the slaves, both in wanting to free them from slavery and to keep them subordinated to economistic alienation as necessity. I see nothing in Toussaint's African 'chieftain' social origins that made him an economic leveller. There is little doubt the class interests with which he identified had something to do with his ambiguous way of relating to the French slave order in Haiti (Meeks 1994: 96, n. 57).

James never hid his own unreconstructed Enlightenment intellectualism. But James was far more honest in his understanding about culture and ideology and how these shaped his own identity than many of those who want to claim him for black nationalism, Marxism, or any fashionable trend. I see nothing in the social practices of Toussaint, Dessalines, Moises, Hedouville or other leaders of the Haitian Revolution to suggest that blackness defined their human nature or their way of thinking. Those men were not united in a common African origin for they did not come out of Africa; they came from different places on the continent of Africa, Africa having been a colonial construct. Nor did they share a common position in spite of their broadly common experience with slavery and European oppression. Capitalist slavery, wage labour and their connection with modernity and imperial domination influenced the development of their consciousness in Haiti. The freedom they sought was a contingent freedom, as those men had a stake in the former slaves selling labour power on the plantations. The values of the Enlightenment were grounded in modernity, commodification, wage labour and capital accumulation by any means necessary. The dialectical side of this reality was that the slaves were constantly struggling to decommodify their existence. Still, numerous academics of the Enlightenment treat wage labour as free-labour-in-general, so as to elide the centrality of commodification as necessity.

People are always "intervening in history" (Meeks 1994: 97, n. 61). Yet it is not clear what this means. I suppose it takes autonomous individuals to intervene in history outside of their class and other identities. Since people make history, it seems strange to find them intervening where they are all the time. How can we intelligently account for intervention without an understanding of the centrality of Cartesian humanism in the separation of individuals from the state, the state from the economy, and so on, as though the social relations of production and civil society freely decide to hang apart? To say the capitalist state intervenes in the capitalist economy is like saying that the state is not a part of the social relations of production. What is the basis of treating the division of labour as the nature of the social relations of production? Notions of state autonomization are the result of the rigid separation of state from economy and of the reduction of economic life to sensuous and material processes (see Callari and Ruccio 1996: 43). Why is it necessary to suggest that the separation of economy from state and society is the instituting ground power of society? Is this not to say that what is necessary for capital to secure its self-movement is that which guarantees democracy?

The bourgeois state has to act as a sort of social capitalist to protect the entire capitalist order from itself in ways that no single capitalist can do. The anarchy of capitalist production always threatens the system; this is partly why the bourgeoisie needs the state to protect the bourgeoisie from the bourgeoisie and the system from its excesses. The individual autonomy argument is little more than everyday pluralism functioning as a radical postmodernist stance against a backdrop of untheorized concepts about autonomy and freedom. A recognition of the fact that heterogeneous, historical social spaces have long been occupied by social beings is central to grasping the basic fact that

production relations were never separated from social relations that were culturally and politically constituted. It is only in the modern world, the bourgeois world, that the economy comes to have a formal and separate existence; it is only in this modern world that the social space comes to be constructed in the homogeneous terms of a logic of production – or consumption, of a distribution of quantities of homogeneously produced wealth. In accordance with this conception, we can read in Marx's value concepts not expressions of how an immanently posed logic of production (of the division of labor) manifests itself, but a reference to the acts of *violence* through which bourgeois rationality seeks to impose its order upon the multitude of communities it touches, a reference to the homogenizing tendencies of this order, a reference to the maneuvers through which bourgeois modernity seeks to cut through the materiality/difference of communities (and of the world of nature) and attempts to subject them to the rational calculus of economic necessity. (Callari and Ruccio 1996: 43; emphasis in original))

The above passage on the historicity of separation and particular social relations of production demonstrates that rhetoric about economism in Marx's treatment of capitalism is mere liberal excess and disappointment over the exposure of the universalist claims of the Enlightenment. It also exposes the poverty of postmodernist claims about capitalism as a totalizing category. This claim may also be a cover for disappointment. Callari and Ruccio have forced a critical view of the sensuous psychological disposition. As one determinant of ideological consciousness, social psychology comes to us like the Hegelian spiritual essence that needs no social embodiment, much like the monotheistic godhead. It is like the precivil, primitive identity that anticipates time and history, capable of standing as its own telos. When Meeks argues that it takes a "leap of faith" to rely on the "materialist determinant" (1994: 98, n. 61), he is merely reading things backward without making a serious effort to theorize the subject of his inquiry. The fact is that Meeks's own reading of the materialist determinant falls at the intersection of Cartesian humanism and Hegelian spiritual essence. The problem with it is that it lacks a clear appreciation of the meaning of Marxist materialist dialectics.

The Cartesian humanism in Meeks's orientation reinforces methodological atomism. In this view, there is no integral, heterogeneous totality because causality is believed to emanate from the independent parts. The logical conclusion is that "causes are separate from effects, causes being the properties of subjects and effects the properties of objects" (Cullenberg 1996: 129; see also 127–28, 135). This way of ordering relationships between power, truth and knowledge in society invents the autonomous individual or self as a sovereign subject and makes it the precivil "primitive of social explanation" (Cullenberg 1996: 129). In contrast with Cartesian positivism is the Hegelian totality of spiritual essence that can stand within and without any origin or subject, while producing its origin and subject through its own telos. Meeks has yet to overcome the Hegelian predisposition that he equates with Marxist materialism and the Cartesian anxiety that serves as his surrogate pluralism. Hegel contradicted himself when he rejected "every philosophy of Origin and . . . Subject, whether rationalist, empiricist or transcendental", while simultaneously accepting a "concept of a telos guiding history". Hegel moved from identifying Being with Nothingness and to projecting "this into the end of a telos which in return creates, within its own process, its own origin and its own Subject" (Althusser 1975: 180; in Cullenberg 1996: 136).

In contrast, Marxist materialism is a "dialectical totality" (see Wilson 1991) that "neither reduces the parts to an expression of the whole, as does the Hegelian totality, nor the whole to an aggregation of its independently constituted parts, as does the Cartesian totality. Instead the Marxist totality is conceived to be totally nonessentialist as the parts . . . mutually constitute one another" (Cullenberg 1996: 136). Marx was fully aware of the nature and process of economistic alienation in capital, and he could trace the 'inner connections' of phenomena as the defining moment of his dialectical methodology (Wilson 1991). Marx could see how stressing the surface manifestations of reality could mislead the unsuspecting observer because the "crudity and lack of comprehension lies precisely in *the fact* that organically coherent factors are brought into a haphazard relation with one another, into a purely speculative connection" (Marx 1986: 26; in Burnham 1995: 96). In the Marxist materialism as dialectical methodology, externality and structure are "replaced by dialectical categories of process and contradictory internal relationships" (Burnham 1995: 96; see Callari and Ruccio 1996; emphasis mine).

Clearly, James constructed Toussaint's social position in relation to Toussaint's and his (James') own position on the Enlightenment. Intellectuals (Meeks 1994: 98, n. 63) are a category within the social division of labour; they are not a social class. Gramsci made an important contribution to the clarification of this very point in his discussion of the role and functions of organic intellectuals. Intellectuals may float from side to side on issues in relation to their location, position, aims and interests. They have no special reason to support the workers or peasants, though they too are workers and may not know it. The dominant class can shape ideas and values via religion, education, control over the labour process, the media, the means of coercion, politics, the state, and so on. The question of scepticism about intellectuals is an important one. The workers and peasants in Marx's time were broadly without much formal education; the ruling classes were deeply sceptical about the possibility of educating the masses; there was as yet no commitment to liberal 'democratic' values and practices as far as the role of the 'masses' was concerned; there was much fear, hostility and hatred toward popular society.

Meeks (1994) contends that the 'subsoil'–agency relationship in Marx is mechanistic (94). He argues that James gives "agents . . . room to act

independently and autonomously" (94). If one accepts the social determination of human nature, the argument changes fundamentally; if one recognizes
and appreciates that liberalism has to privilege an abstract universality of all
humans in order to negate prospects for their real and effective social and
material equality, it also changes the interpretation. Failure to understand this
point tends to reinforce the pluralist reading of the relationship between agency
and structure: this is the real 'mechanistic' view. The same problem about
agency and structure crops up again in relation to the argument about the
"primacy of agency" (99). The real problem is not that Marxism never got
around to theoretical questions about politics, subject–agent formation and
such. Classical Marxism engaged these and other very important issues but did
not transcend the bourgeois (Hegelian) frameworks it was struggling to leave
behind. This is where the strongest hold of Hegelianism on classical Marxism
was registered and where functionalism came to influence aspects of the
ideological consciousness of Marxism. My basic point, then, is that Meeks's
argument about the positivist view is one-sided, for it is not a convincing or
accurate argument about the failures of Marxism but a recognition of a certain
incompleteness and inadequacies in relation to "theories of agency and subjectivity and of politics . . . [and] the heterogeneities of the processes of subject-
agent formation . . . [and] adequate theories of subjectivity and of politics"
(Callari and Ruccio 1996: 14).

Yet a more strategic focus on these issues might advance theoretical analysis
beyond any preoccupation with treating the failures of social democracy in
neocolonial situations, such as typified the PRG or the PNP as evidence of the
mechanical view of Marxism on the fundamental questions of agency and
subjectivity. To cite the PRG and the PNP amounts to ideological overreach.
Meeks assigns far too much credit to Maurice Bishop and the Grenada
revolutionaries in relation to revolutionary Marxism. As such, Meeks's argument does not help us to understand why Bishop and the PRG acted the way
they did when they took power in the concrete conditions inside Grenada.
Why did the PRG have to implement foreign aid (so-called noncapitalist)
development between 1979 and 1983? Did not Marx advise the French
Communards in the Paris Commune of the folly and adventurism of their
actions? Did Marx ever tell the Communards that the productive forces had
willed them to storm the Bastille?

Social phenomena are always overdetermined; there is no single factor, such
as agency, that predisposes social change to go in any given direction. Overdetermination is a dialectical concept that moves analysis beyond irreducibility

as pluralism and mechanistic notions of cause–effect relationships. This is why I am sceptical about what Meeks (1994) means when he says James gives "agents . . . room to act independently and autonomously" (94) since he locates independent and autonomous action within a psychological privileging of voluntarism that locates individual initiative in some Archimedean originary.

When capitalists seek to reproduce themselves as capitalists in a liberal democratic context this dictates certain conditions: they have to possess and use the means of production as capital; they must be able to pursue growth strategies defined in terms of accumulation and legitimated on the ideology of modernization and progress; they have to be able to take control of the state – while declaring democracy and equal rights and justice for all – in order to dominate and subordinate those whose labour power yields up surplus labour; they must ground this practice of domination and subordination in an abstract universality that is based in formal political equality (in which the state no longer enforces formal political inequality and where coercion is separated from the economy); and there must be an administrative apparatus situated in relation to technical rationality to mediate the social relations. Meeks's untheorized notion of autonomy does not come to terms with any of these imperatives; instead, it is a notion that embraces theoretical (Cartesian) humanism as its own ideological principle.

Speculation and the Counterfactual

The problems deepen when Meeks discusses the 'what ifs' in relation to alternative paths Toussaint might or should have taken to produce radically different outcomes for the Haitian Revolution. It is difficult to see how Meeks (1994: 100) can rely on the purely speculative argument about 'what *if*' in relation to Hedouville's actions. Meeks would have to retrace his steps through the history of the French Revolution and its role in the making of modern France. Rereading does not legitimatize a rejection of historical evidence on grounds that history is fictive. Such an argument trivializes history and fictionalizes reality: the point is that all theories of knowledge are partisan, but partisanship should not be equated with relativism. Several factors have to be accounted for in the making of the modern French nation and several other factors, including the state and the nationalization of French society, should be accounted for as well.

Trouillot (1990) reminds us that less than 40 percent of the total population of France spoke or understood French in 1789. Smith (1991) notes that concepts such as

autonomy, identity, national genius, authenticity, unity, fraternity form an interrelated language of discourse that has its expressive ceremonials and symbols [such as] . . . flags, anthems, parades, coinage, oaths, war memorials, ceremonies of remembrance of the national dead . . . frontiers, as well as more hidden aspects, such as . . . military codes . . . and ways of acting and feeling that are shared by the members of the historical community. (77)

My point is that the concept of 'revolutionary France' must be discussed with reference to the complex and contradictory process of nation formation in the time of the revolutionary transformations. The French Revolution was revolutionary in relation to the *ancien régime* it overthrew in 1789. We know the revolution brought forward all the economic, political, gender, class, geographical and other contradictions that could not be resolved in the abstract universality that was depicted in *Fraternité, Liberté, Egalité*. The revolution did not make Frenchmen into the autonomous and independent agents in the unproblematic ways Meeks suggests. What the revolution did was to make people in France free in a contingent way so that bourgeois power could be asserted in state, economy, society and beyond. It was in this soil that particular ideas of specific historical forms of democratic power could emerge (Callari and Ruccio 1996: 41). The revolution displaced and preserved a number of contradictions by trying to bury them in the abstract universality: the Reign of Terror demonstrated that displacement is not resolution.

There is no validity to the counterfactual claim that Toussaint's lack of conciliation toward the French (Meeks 1994: 101) influenced or determined the future place of Haiti in the New World. Such an argument stretches history, facts and faith, and it depoliticizes history. Is it necessary to invent this myth to excuse such an unproblematic reading of European and American imperialism in their excesses against Haiti? Is it necessary to invent such reasoning to inform an anti-Marxist reply to the Marxism of C.L.R. James and the failure of Marxism to liberate autonomous agency? The Enlightenment had written off Africans as falling outside real history and civilization. Europeans possessed, according to the genealogical principle of the Enlightenment, a natural inclination to freedom; this myth is commonplace in Hegel's spiritual essence, which is a genealogical claim for European superiority.

The United States and the European powers were deeply opposed to blacks in the Caribbean or Africa governing themselves. The policy of the United States on Haiti and the Hispanic Caribbean colonies and Brazil was heavily influenced by the racist myth of the 'Africanization scare', which the very colonial powers had invented as part of their ideological apparatus to justify oppression in defence of capitalism and certain forms of white privilege. During the Haitian Revolution, US Congress actively debated the potential embarrassment from "niggers speaking French" in Haiti and functioning as diplomats in the 'civilized' capitals of the world. Just imagine the implications of such a development for the myth of white racial and intellectual superiority! Many slave states in the United States were frantic about the prospects of a black republic such as Haiti coming to power anywhere in the New World. A good number of American slave holders talked about annexing Brazil to save New World slavery and capitalism, and some of them emigrated to Brazil at the time of the American Civil War, ostensibly to secure Brazil against a slave revolution. They were committed to white mythologies that were (and are) central to capitalism which began its history in blood, infamy, oppression and exploitation.

Meeks's argument that the Haitian Revolution should not have beheaded LeClerc's army seems to imply two sets of military rules, one for French colonialism and one for the struggling Haitian slaves. We know what fates befell individual slaves who challenged their masters in Caribbean societies. What fate do we think would have befallen the slaves had they laid down their arms in front of LeClerc? Meeks should explain why Britain, who wanted to demolish France's presence in the Caribbean, set aside her differences with France when Haitian slaves took up arms in alliance with the other social forces in Haiti who saw abolition in their interest. By implying that the death of large numbers of Frenchmen was the cause of Haiti becoming a pariah is empirically and theoretically vacuous. Why were the French forces despatched to Haiti?

Is Meeks on safe ground to argue that agency fell victim to 'sub-soil' (structure)? How was Toussaint to read LeClerc's ambitions and the motives of Napoleon? What were the options that were open to the Haitians in the Western Hemisphere? Should Toussaint and the revolutionaries have expected the new national state of Haiti to be treated with the 'fairness' other national states were receiving? Meeks pays no attention to the dialectic of national state formation in the world, yet such consideration is absolutely necessary to fill out the argument on this score of Haiti's options at the turn of the nineteenth century. How did Marxism shape the process of the Haitian revolution? What role did Marxism play in the formation of dominant ideas in France at the turn of the nineteenth century? We know that British forces killed many colonists at the time of the American War of Independence, and many British forces were destroyed by the American colonists. Did these developments prevent the United States from gaining diplomatic recognition by Britain? What was the connection between US recognition of Haiti (after more than fifty years of independence), the American Civil War, and the implications for a black revolt in the United States? Was there an untheorized African peculiarity that prevented Toussaint from thinking with his colour rather than with his imagination? Who is to blame: the slaves or James who seemed to have put negative ideas in Toussaint's head ex post facto? How could Toussaint have put the unfolding of the nation-state system and international relations in the world and the Western Hemisphere ahead of the challenges he faced? Is not the national state form a contingent form in world historical time? How does agency relate to 'sub-soil' in this context? It seems agency is constrained by historical forces after all.

In effect, to argue that a conciliatory Toussaint would have allowed "Haiti to enter the new century not so much as an international pariah but as a legitimate part of the family of Latin American states" (Meeks 1994: 100) is to turn reality on its head. This argument sets up the counterfactual as historical surrogate. Did the Haitian Revolution promote the numerous invasions of Latin American and Caribbean countries by the United States since the nineteenth century? How do we account for the genocide the United States had already initiated against the indigenous 'Indians' in the battle to take away their lands? How do we account for the genocide Spanish and Portuguese Catholics carried out (with the crucifix as standard bearer) against indigenous peoples in South America around the same time? We know of the genocidal acts by the Spaniards against the defenceless, indigenous peoples of the Caribbean islands as early as the 1540s, as described by Friar Bartolomé de Las Casas in *The Devastation of the Indies*. But why bother with all this boring history when it is so much easier to deconstruct old books?

Let us extend the counterfactual logic: What *if* the Vietnamese had not liquidated at least ten thousand French imperial troops at Dien Bien Phu in 1954? Could it mean that approximately fifty-eight thousand Americans would not have been killed in the Vietnam War, and Vietnam would have been made an integral part of the nation states of Southeast Asia? What *if* the French had learned from the experience in Haiti after sixty thousand of France's best soldiers were destroyed and decided against colonizing parts of

Africa and Indochina? It would be interesting to hear about the forces at work in shaping the relationship between agency and structure in France's behaviour: Was it autonomous agency, material forces of capitalist accumulation, Enlightenment hubris, or what?

Horace Campbell (1994) has made an insightful argument about the relationship of the former Workers' Liberation League and the WPJ to Soviet Marxism. The Workers' Liberation League and WPJ turned to Sovietism at the very moment of the deepening decrepitude and crisis of the Soviet system in the postwar years. It may yet be fashionable to deconstruct the 'grand narratives' of the Enlightenment and leave empty vessels clanking in orgies of neotonous (authorial) assassination. This is one side of the crisis of modernity. The crisis of philosophy is integral to the deeper social and societal crises. There is much to Cornelius Castoriadis's (1992) assertion that postmodernism is the "pauper soup of liberalism". This syndrome of "downcast eyes" in French intellectual thought (Jay 1995) can be repackaged for distribution across the ideological, fetishized, commodified academic markets.

It has also become fashionable to deconstruct and elide power (see Weber 1995) by medicalizing sociology and bourgeois society's social ills (see O'Neill 1995). Many postmodernists are suspicious of any rigorous reading of social categories such as class, class relations, capitalism and the like (due, no doubt, to their 'totalizing', and essentializing characteristics). Wedded to Freud and Talcott Parsons, the medicalized sociology and the psychoanalytic rendering of the real ills of bourgeois society puts the therapeutic disciplines on a firmer footing by providing the necessary sanitized interpretations of the schizophrenic ontologies of history (O'Neill 1995). It thus becomes much easier for the state, the psychoanalysts and other experts from the 'therapeutic' disciplines to define the real schizophrenia across the plateaus of capitalism. Meeks's treatment of what he sees as the strategic problems of Marxism amounts to an instalment to forms of displacement that reinforce these schizophrenias.

Conclusion

The political and ideological practices with which Meeks was associated in Jamaica were grounded in the working assumption that socialism was and is the inversion of capitalism. Meeks seems to have come full circle by returning to capitalism as its own reinversion. There is no evidence in Meeks's criticism of Marxism that reality is a complex process of overdetermination. Meeks does not raise any new or challenging questions for Marxism in "Re-reading *The Black Jacobins*"; he settled for restating liberal Marxisant criticisms. I have attempted to show that by recognizing that there are structural problems in Marxism and raising these questions and problems in a creative way moves the critique of Marxism beyond empty theoretical closures about the irrelevance or death of Marxism. The strategic problems of Marxism cannot be resolved by returning to the theoretical humanism of Descartes or the spiritual essence of Hegel that came into Marxism from the outset. I have shown how the theories of the abstract universality seduce us into equating historical forms of economistic alienation with a natural condition. This seduction extends to inventing and theorizing the formalistic, homogeneous spaces that were imported into Marxism. Modernity and postmodernity exist in an integral relationship. Caribbean social science theory has not been helpful in identifying the problems of Marxism or moving discourse beyond the limitations of Marxism. Our understanding of theoretical and epistemological problems arising from the discourse on historical determination, structuralism, democracy, freedom and other themes covered in Meeks's article has not been enhanced. I have shown that Lindahl's notion of democracy as a self-organizing system and process is extreme, counterfactual and atheoretical. Lindahl' s argument also constitutes a closure on the theoretical development of democratic theory.

The reasons that Marxism has occupied a marginal space in Commonwealth Caribbean social science intellectual culture as well as in electoral politics, working class politics, trade unions and class struggles are at variance with the assertions made by Lindahl (1994) that the Caribbean people are naturally ill-disposed towards Marxism and naturally disposed to democracy as a 'self-organizing' system. The lives of the masses have been filled with metaphysical ideas about life, death and the future. Slavery, racism and religion have imposed notions of suffering, representation, redemption and deliverance that were grounded in the negation of a radical, materialist self-consciousness. The movement along radical and revolutionary options after World War II had to confront the American cold war offensive. The British Caribbean as a whole, the Cuban Revolution, and the Dominican Republic after 1965 all provide instructive experiences that confound Lindahl's arguments about democracy. All such efforts in the Caribbean were designed to develop democratic institutions through negative reinforcement, given the legacy of colonialism and the heavy hand of US imperialism. Lindahl would have to theorize the historicity of Caribbean reality and abandon the attempts to impose theoretical closure on Caribbean social theory. Meeks's 'new directions' argument reinforces hostility towards revolutionary theory; it is this that makes his argument both disturbing and problematic in the post–cold war. What is needed is a frontal and thoughtful critique in the post–cold war age of global neoliberalism that seeks to impose the harsh discipline of the market on the masses in the service of global capital accumulation.

The struggles initiated by the Black Jacobins in Haiti were integral to the long historical struggles by slaves, peasants and workers against historical forms of commodification and sustained oppression. Meeks seems to have come to the point that there is or can be no emancipation outside capitalism. Global capitalism engenders its dialectical process in strategies for decommodification. The attempts by the French and their allies to dethrone and strangle the Haitian Revolution are linked to contemporary economic, political and intellectual struggles to reinforce commodification. Capitalism remains inherently class based, exploitative and oppressive, and Marxism keeps us honest and aware of the necessity to struggle against this system.

In the final analysis, Meeks's autonomous agency is a plea for an identity politics that asserts the primacy of methodological individualism as a closure and a conservative attack on the future that does nothing to aid us in understanding the "concreteness of the class dimensions of struggles that still punctuate the world" (Callari and Ruccio 1996: 27). In going back to the future, Meeks genuflects to a postmodernist bias that reinforces bourgeois modernism as hegemony and undermines postmodernism's own "critical, destabilizing effects" that necessarily require "a continuing Marxist presence" (Callari and Ruccio 1996: 27–28). In part, the postmodernist critique of modernity sees no necessary connection between their critique and the historical necessity to liberate the human spirit and social relations from the control of capital and capitalism. This outlook is ideological and political; it makes defeatism and cynicism more tolerable. This separation has a way of destroying the theoretical bases of the unity of liberty and equality to the advantage of equity, given that liberty is equated first with the freedom to possess the means of production as capital. The concept of the autonomous individual flourishes in the theory of rights as liberty. Meeks is not sensitive to these issues in his analysis, and that is why negative freedom stalks his criticism of historical materialism. Modernity and postmodernity simply do not constitute or occupy unbridgeable spaces; such an assertion amounts to a postmodernist teleological essentialism that reinforces bourgeois ideological hegemony and marginalizes the necessity of class and other social struggles. It is at best a plea for radical

392 / New Caribbean Thought

pluralism that treats market economism as natural alienation and privileges individual self-actualization as a form of existence in in-betweenity, which can be a very inhospitable site. Defeatism becomes all the more comfortable to endure when Marxism is declared dead and reduced to nostalgia. The postmodernist impression is that we are all consumed by technological determinism, cybernetics and the free market, which construct the boundaries and fault lines of discordance.

The most pressing factor is that, today, capital and intellectual relativism are unhappy with the

existing relations of exploitation, of capital's incapacity to subordinate the power of labour on which it depends. Despite appearances, the restless movement of capital is the clearest indication of the insubordination of labour. It is not the breaking of old patterns by money, not the form of the state, *nor postmodernist discourse,* which holds the key to the recovery of capitalist health, but the reorganization of exploitation, the restructured subjection of the power of labour to capital, and . . . it is not clear that capital has achieved this end. (Holloway 1995: 135; emphasis mine)

Capitalism cannot escape the limits of the politics of time, for time and history are inseparable, yet neither one is the simulacrum of the other. In the final analysis, Marx's materialism deals with the historical perversion of social forms in their representations as alienated, autonomous things that become the simulacra of alienated social relations: this is the disembodiment of the social-historical. Appreciation of the Marxist materialism does not require a leap of faith: it requires theoretical and historical understanding of the forms of historical perversion as contingency in which labour seems forever lost in the integument of capital. But on careful reflection we would not take this at face value, since it is this abstraction that capital would have us to receive as the end point of history. The end of history, the arrival of the autonomous individual and the death of Marxism inhabit the same homogeneous timeless space. It is ludic history! Neither events nor history can exist in homogeneous empty spaces after all.

References

Althusser, Louis. 1975. *Essays in Self-Criticism.* London: New Left Books.
Anderson, Perry. 1978. *Passages from Antiquity to Feudalism.* London: Verso.

Avineri, Shlomo. 1978. *Karl Marx: Social and Political Thought.* Cambridge: Cambridge University Press.

Bonefeld, Werner. 1995. "Capital as subject and the existence of labour". In *Emancipating Marx, Open Marxism* 3, edited by W. Bonefeld, R. Gunn, J. Holloway, and K. Psychopedis. London: Pluto Press.

Burnham, Peter. 1995. "Capital, crisis and the international state system". In *Global Capital, National State and the Politics of Money,* edited by W. Bonefeld and J. Holloway. New York: St Martin's Press.

Callari, A., and D. Ruccio. 1996. Introduction to *Postmodern Materialism and the Future of Marxist Theory: Essays in the Althusserian Tradition,* edited by A. Callari and D. Ruccio. Hanover: Wesleyan University Press.

Campbell, Horace. 1994. "Progressive politics and the Jamaican society at home and abroad". *Social and Economic Studies* 43, no. 3 (September).

Castoriadis, Cornelius. 1991. *Philosophy, Politics, Autonomy.* New York: Oxford University Press.

Castoriadis, Cornelius. 1992. "The theory of modernity and the problematic of democracy". In *Between Totalitarianism and Postmodernity,* edited by P. Beilarz, G. Robinson, and J Rundell. Cambridge, Mass.: Massachusetts Institute of Technology Press.

Cullenberg, Stephen. 1996. "Althusser and the decentering of the Marxist totality". In *Postmodern Materialism and the Future of Marxist Theory: Essays in the Althusserian Tradition,* edited by A. Callari and D. Ruccio. Hanover: Wesleyan University Press.

Derrida Jacques. 1993. *Spectres of Marx.* London: Routledge.

Dupuy, Alex. 1989. *Haiti in the World Economy: Class, Race and Underdevelopment since 1700.* Boulder: Westview Press.

Femia, Joseph. 1993. *Marxism and Democracy.* New York: Oxford University Press.

Foucault, Michel. 1977. *Language, Counter-Memory, Practice.* Ithaca: Cornell University Press.

Holloway, John. 1995. "Global capital and the national state". In *Global Capital, National State and the Politics of Money,* edited by W. Bonefeld and J. Holloway. New York: St Martin's Press.

James, C.L.R. 1947. *Dialectic of History.* Cambridge, Mass.: Radical America.

James, C.L.R. 1989. *The Black Jacobins: Toussaint L'Ouverture and the San Domingo Revolution.* New York: Vintage Books.

Jay, Martin. 1995. *Downcast Eyes: The Anti-Occularcentric Tendencies in French Intellectual Thought.* Los Angeles: University of California Press.

Lindahl, Folke. 1994. "Caribbean diversity and ideological conformism: The crisis of Marxism in the English-speaking Caribbean". *Social and Economic Studies* 43, no. 3 (September).

Lyotard, Jean François. 1984. *The Postmodern Condition: A Report on Knowledge.* Manchester: Manchester University Press.

Manent, Pierre. 1994. *An Intellectual History of Liberalism.* Translated by Rebecca Balinski; with a foreword by Jerrold Seigel. Princeton: Princeton University Press.

Marx, Karl. 1963. *Early Writings*. Edited by Tom Bottomore. London.

Marx, Karl. 1986 [1857]. *The Grundrisse* (MECW, vol. 28). London: Lawrence and Wishart.

Marx, Karl, and Friedrich Engels. 1965. *The German Ideology*. Revised English translation. London.

Meeks, Brian. 1994. "Re-reading *The Black Jacobins*: James, the dialectic and the revolutionary conjuncture". *Social and Economic Studies* 43, no. 3 (September).

Munroe, Trevor. 1994. Review of *The Third Wave: Democratization in the Late Twentieth Century*, by Samuel Huntington. *Social and Economic Studies* 43, no. 3 (September).

Nicholls, David. 1992. *Images of God and the State in the Nineteenth and Twentieth Centuries*. New York: Routledge.

O'Neill, John. 1995. *The Poverty of Postmodernism*. New York: Routledge.

Osborne, Peter. 1995. *The Politics of Time: Modernity and the Avant-Garde*. London: Verso.

Patterson, Orlando. 1991. *Freedom in the Making of Western Culture*. Volume 1. New York: Basic Books.

Resnick, Stephen, and R. Wolff. 1996. "The new Marxian political economy and the contribution of Althusser". In *Postmodern Materialism and the Future of Marxist Theory: Essays in the Althusserian Tradition*, edited by A. Callari and D. Ruccio. Hanover: Wesleyan University Press.

Reuten, Geert, and Michael Williams. 1989. *Value-Form and the State: The Tendencies of Accumulation and the Determination of Economic Policy in Capitalist Society*. London: Routledge.

Smith, Anthony D. 1991. *National Identity*. Reno: University of Nevada Press.

Therborn, Goran. 1975. *Science, Class and Society*. London: New Left Books.

Tilly, Charles. 1990. *Coercion, Capital and European States: AD 990–1992*. Cambridge: Blackwell.

Trouillot, Michel-Rolph. 1990. *Haiti: State Against Nation*. New York: Monthly Review Press.

Watson, Hilbourne. 1995. "Global powershift and the techno-paradigm shift: The end of geography, world market blocs and the Caribbean". In *Postintegration Development in the Caribbean*, edited by Maribel Aponte-Garcia and Carmen Gautier Mayoral. Rio Piedras: University of Puerto Rico Center for Social Research.

Weber, Cynthia. 1995. *Simulating Sovereignty: Intervention, the State and Symbolic Exchange*. Cambridge: Cambridge University Press.

Wilding, Adrian. 1995. "The complicity of posthistory". In *Emancipating Marx, Open Marxism 3*, edited by W. Bonefeld, R. Gunn, J. Holloway, and K. Psychopedis. London: Pluto Press.

Wilson, H.T. 1991. *Marx's Critical/Dialectical/Procedure*. London: Routledge.

Wolf, Eric. 1982 *Europe and the People without History*. Los Angeles: University of California Press.

15

New Light on Afro-Caribbean Social Mobility in New York City
A Critique of the Sowell Thesis

WINSTON JAMES

Going by some of the most influential texts on American immigration, one could easily come away with the notion that the Caribbean presence in the United States is a recent, at most a postwar, phenomenon. After all, Caribbean nationals and non-Europeans in general do not figure in Oscar Handlin's classic study, *The Uprooted* (1973). And they do not get so much as a mention in the best general study of American immigration, John Bodnar's *The Transplanted* (1985), despite the author's claim to comprehensiveness of coverage. Intentionally or unintentionally, the field of American immigration studies to this very day is riven with ethnocentrism, if not out and out racism. It is marked by a discernible filiopietistic streak: the historian of American immigration by and large writes about the ethnic group of which he or she is a part, and often uncritically. And so the Italian American historian writes about Italian immigration to the United States; the Jewish American historian writes about Jewish emigration from nineteenth century Germany or from Eastern Europe in the late nineteenth and early twentieth centuries; the Finnish American writes about the Finns; the Irish American about the Irish, and so on. Now, there is nothing intrinsically wrong with writing about the experience of one's own ethnic group. After all, if one does not do it, who will, and how? And the insider writing from within his or her own group often brings insights that most outsiders can never have, or can never be expected to have to the same degree. No, there is nothing wrong with this type of ethnic history, per se. But there are two problems with the way it is executed. First, there is the problem of the way in which the historian handles the relations between one ethnic group and other groups, and especially the relations between European immigrants and Afro-Americans. This is the area in which many of the ethnocentric biases and misleading and harmful silences come in. The other problem arises when the historian claims, or pretends, to be writing a general history of American immigration and in fact writes a history of, at best, only a few groups of immigrants. It is from reading these ostensibly general histories of American immigration that one will close each book believing that black people did not migrate to the United States before World War II, except as enslaved Africans directly from the continent.

Contrary to the claims and implications of these histories, the migration of black people, especially from the Caribbean to the United States, has been continuous, if uneven, since the seventeenth century. And the impact of this migration upon American society, and especially upon Afro-America, has been profound. Barbadian slaves had been taken by their British owners colonizing South Carolina during the seventeenth century, and earlier in the same century slaves from Barbados constituted an important portion of the black population of Virginia.[1] South Carolina was in fact developed by and in subservience to Barbadian interests, supplying beef, pork and lumber products to the island in exchange for sugar. Furthermore, it has been persuasively argued that South Carolina was, even in the eighteenth century, the dependent of little Barbados – "an island master". South Carolina, said Peter Wood (1974), was the "colony of a colony" (32–34; see also Greene 1987: passim). Little wonder, then, that the settlement was referred to in London as "Carolina in ye West Indies", for South Carolina was an integral member of the Caribbean universe of exchange and commerce. In the eighteenth century South Carolina extended and deepened its trading relations with other Caribbean colonies, with Jamaica surpassing Barbados as a market for its products in the late eighteenth century. Up to 1700 it is safe to assume that all the slaves in South Carolina came from the Caribbean and Barbados in particular. It has been estimated that between 15 and 20 percent of slaves to South Carolina in the eighteenth century came from the Caribbean (Littlefield 1990: 69–71). But the degree of intercourse between the two areas, as Jack P. Greene (1987) has forcefully argued, was enormous. And the significant influence of the Caribbean on South Carolina endures to this day.

But the pre–twentieth century Caribbean presence in the United States extends well beyond colonial Virginia and South Carolina. Prince Hall established black freemasonry in the United States and was a distinguished leader of black Boston during the eighteenth century. Up to the 1970s Hall was generally said to have been Barbadian, but modern scholarship expresses uncertainty as to precisely where he was in fact born (Kaplan and Kaplan 1989: 202–3).[2] But given the preponderance of Barbadian slaves in Boston in the early eighteenth century (Hall is believed to have been born around 1735), it is likely that he was in fact born on the island. Despite substantial black migration from the South, from Canada and from Europe, as late as 1860 one in five black Bostonians had been born in Barbados and other Caribbean islands (Horton 1993: 26–27).[3] The Caribbean population in the United States was relatively small during the nineteenth century, but it grew significantly after the Civil War. Indeed, the foreign-born black population, which was almost wholly Caribbean in origin, increased fivefold between 1850 and 1900, from 4,067 to 20,236 (Bureau of the Census 1918: 61). And distinguished Caribbean migrants populate the annals of nineteenth century Afro-America.

Denmark Vesey in 1822 organized in Charleston, South Carolina, what one authority accurately described as "the most elaborate insurrectionary project ever formed by American slaves". In "boldness of conception and thoroughness of organization there has been nothing to compare with it" (Higginson 1998: 107). The conspiracy was betrayed and Vesey, along with his co-conspirators, executed. Vesey was from the Virgin Islands.[4] John B. Russwurm of Jamaica, one of the early New World settlers of Liberia, was also one of the first three black people to graduate from an American college – Bowdoin College, Maine, in 1826.[5] In the spring of 1827, Russwurm, with his Afro-American colleague, Samuel E. Cornish, started *Freedom's Journal*, the first black newspaper published in the United States. Russwurm's compatriot, Peter Ogden, organized in New York City the first Odd-Fellows Lodge among the black population. Robert Brown Elliott, the brilliant fighter and orator of the Reconstruction era, claimed Jamaican parentage.[6] David Augustus Straker, a law partner of Elliott's, a fighter for civil rights, educationalist, journalist, chronicler of the dark, post-Reconstruction days, and a distinguished lawyer in his own right, was from Barbados (see Straker 1886, 1888, 1896, 1906; Hawkshawe 1974; Phillips 1981). Jan Earnst Matzeliger, the inventor of a revolutionary shoemaking machine, had migrated from Suriname. Edward Wilmot Blyden, a brilliant man and major contributor to the stream of black nationalist thought in America and abroad, was born in the Virgin Islands (Lynch 1970). William Henry Crogman, Latin and Greek scholar, former president of Clark College and one of the founders of the American Negro Academy, came from St Maarten. Bert Williams, the famous comedian, was born in Antigua. And at the beginning of the new century Robert Charles O'Hara Benjamin (1855–1900), journalist, editor, lawyer and writer was gunned down – shot in the back six times – in Lexington, Kentucky, because of his work of "uplifting the race", including writing and speaking out against lynching and defending the constitutional right of black people to vote. Benjamin had emigrated from St Kitts.[7] W.E.B. Du Bois (1868–1963), James Weldon Johnson (1871–1938), his brother Rosamond Johnson (1873–1954) and William Stanley Braithwaite (1878–1962) were among some of the most distinguished sons and daughters of these nineteenth century Caribbean immigrants to America.

A significant number of the nineteenth century migrants were skilled craftsmen, students, teachers, preachers, lawyers and doctors. Even more skewed in social origins than those who were to migrate to the United States in the twentieth century, these migrants gained a reputation that distorted Afro-America's perception of the Caribbean reality. For, as Hubert Harrison, another distinguished Caribbean migrant, observed, "It was taken for granted that every West Indian immigrant was a paragon of intelligence and a man of birth and breeding" (*Pittsburgh Courier*, 29 January 1927).[8]

What was new in the early twentieth century was, therefore, not the Caribbean presence itself, but the scale of it. The number of black people, and especially Caribbean people, who migrated to the United States increased dramatically, from a trickle of 412 in 1899 to a flood of 12,243 per year by 1924, the high point of the early black migration (see Tables 15.1, 15.2a and 15.2b).

From a population of 20,000 in 1900, the foreign-born black population in the United States had grown to almost 100,000 by 1930. Over 140,000 black immigrants – exclusive of black visitors or tourists – passed through the ports of America between 1899 and 1937. This occurred despite the viciously restrictive legislation of 1917, 1921 and 1924 – the figure for those admitted in 1925 was 95 percent below that for the previous year. It should also be noted that the increase occurred in spite of the economic and migratory reversals of the Depression 1930s, when more Caribbean people returned to the islands

Table 15.1 Black Immigrant Aliens Admitted and Black Emigrant Aliens Departed,
United States 1899–1937

Year[a]	Admitted	Departed	Net Admission
1899	412	n/a	n/a
1900	714	n/a	n/a
1901	594	n/a	n/a
1902	832	n/a	n/a
1903	2,174	n/a	n/a
1904	2,386	n/a	n/a
1905	3,598	n/a	n/a
1906	3,786	n/a	n/a
1907	5,235	n/a	n/a
1908	4,626	889	3,737
1909	4,307	1,104	3,203
1910	4,966	926	4,040
1911	6,721	913	5,808
1912	6,759	1,288	5,471
1913	6,634	1,671	4,963
1914	8,447	1,805	6,642
1915	5,660	1,644	4,016
1916	4,576	1,684	2,892
1917	7,971	1,497	6,474
1918	5,706	1,291	4,415
1919	5,823	976	4,847
1920	8,174	1,275	6,899
1921	9,873	1,807	8,066
1922	5,248	2,183	3,065
1923	7,554	1,525	6,029
1924	12,243	1,449	10,794
1925	791	1,094	-303
1926	894	865	29
1927	955	870	85
1928	956	789	167

Table continues

Table 15.1   Black Immigrant Aliens Admitted and Black Emigrant Aliens Departed,
United States 1899–1937

Year[a]	Admitted	Departed	Net Admission
1929	1,254	425	829
1930	1,806	776	1,030
1931	884	737	147
1932	183	811	-628
1933	84	1,058	-974
1934	178	604	-426
1935	246	597	-351
1936	272	502	-230
1937	275	433	-158
1899–1937	143,397	33,518[b]	85,731[b]

Note: 'African, black', is the term used by the Bureau of Immigration to describe these migrants
(Senate 1911: 100–101).
[a] Fiscal year, that is, year ending 30 June.
[b] These figures apply for the period 1908–37.
Source: Adapted from Department of Labor 1899–1937.

than entered the United States (see Table 15.1). Despite all this, the black
population of foreign origin and their American-born offspring grew from
55,000 in 1900 to 178,000 in 1930. The overwhelming majority of America's
black immigrants came from the Caribbean islands; over 80 percent of them
– if we include those of Caribbean origin coming from Central America –
between 1899 and 1932 (see Table 15.2b). During the peak years of migration,
1913 to 1924, the majority headed not only for the state of New York but also
for New York City, settling primarily in Manhattan and Brooklyn (see Figure
15.2). By 1930 almost a quarter of black Harlem was of Caribbean origin
(Osofsky 1971: 131).

This wave of black migration, it is true, was small in comparison to the
gigantic white one that rushed in from across the Atlantic, bringing southern
and eastern Europeans at the turn of the century in the millions. But it was
concentrated in the northeast and broke mainly on the shores of New York
City. So Caribbean nationals too, in tens of thousands, went through Ellis
Island; but you would hardly know this from the literature on, and the

Table 15.2a Black Immigrants by Region of Last Residence, 1899–1932

Year	Total	Caribbean		Central America		South America		British North America		Portuguese Atlantic (Cape Verde & Azores)		Others	
		Number	%	Number	%	Number	%	Number	%	Number	%	Number	%
1899	412	388	94.1	n/a	n/a	n/a	n/a	n/a	n/a	n/a	n/a	23	5.9
1900	714	703	98.4	n/a	n/a	n/a	n/a	n/a	n/a	n/a	n/a	11	1.6
1901	594	520	87.5	n/a	n/a	n/a	n/a	n/a	n/a	n/a	n/a	74	12.5
1902	832	805	96.7	n/a	n/a	n/a	n/a	n/a	n/a	n/a	n/a	27	3.3
1903	2,174	1,134	52.1	1.0	–	2	–	n/a	n/a	934	42.9	103	4.9
1904	2,386	1,762	73.9	3	–	25	1.0	5	–	439	18.4	152	6.4
1905	3,598	3,034	84.3	37	1.0	66	1.8	9	–	347	9.6	105	3.1
1906	3,786	3,018	79.7	91	2.4	43	1.1	57	1.5	301	8.0	276	7.3
1907	5,233	4,561	87.3	99	1.7	48	–	105	2.0	349	6.7	71	1.4
1908	4,626	3,563	77.0	116	2.5	77	1.7	102	2.2	705	15.2	63	1.4
1909	4,307	3,340	77.5	107	2.5	30	–	172	4.0	615	14.3	43	1.0
1910	4,966	3,769	75.9	120	2.4	38	–	212	4.3	778	15.7	49	–
1911	6,721	4,973	73.9	154	2.3	111	1.6	304	4.6	1,101	16.1	76	1.5
1912	6,759	4,885	72.2	245	3.6	94	1.4	329	4.8	1,103	16.3	103	1.7
1913	6,634	4,891	73.8	277	4.2	91	1.4	338	5.1	972	14.6	65	–
1914	8,447	5,724	67.7	348	4.1	111	1.3	342	4.1	1,711	20.2	211	3.6
1915	5,660	4,104	73.9	252	4.5	38	–	286	5.1	838	13.1	144	2.7

Table continues

Table 15.2a (cont'd) Black Immigrants by Region of Last Residence, 1899–1932

Year	Total Number	Caribbean		Central America		South America		British North America		Portuguese Atlantic (Cape Verde & Azores)		Others	
		Number	%	Number	%	Number	%	Number	%	Number	%	Number	%
1916	4,576	3,257	70.9	160	3.5	100	2.2	364	7.9	653	14.3	82	1.2
1917	7,971	5,769	72.3	662	7.9	135	1.7	409	5.1	940	11.8	96	1.2
1918	5,706	3,993	69.9	906	16.0	158	2.7	142	2.5	407	7.1	100	1.8
1919	5,823	4,027	69.2	799	13.7	268	4.6	274	4.7	329	5.6	126	2.2
1920	8,174	6,059	74.1	417	5.0	193	2.3	415	5.1	845	10.3	245	3.2
1921	9,873	7,046	71.4	543	5.5	197	1.9	414	4.2	1,364	13.8	309	3.2
1922	5,248	4,424	84.3	188	3.6	154	2.9	172	3.3	201	3.8	109	2.1
1923	7,554	6,580	87.1	254	3.4	171	2.2	292	3.3	164	2.5	138	1.5
1924	12,243	10,630	86.6	511	4.1	375	3.1	498	4.0	128	1.4	105	–
1925	791	308	38.9	174	22.0	47	5.7	224	28.3	13	1.6	25	3.5
1926	894	480	53.8	197	22.0	50	5.6	114	12.7	7	–	46	5.1
1927	955	581	60.1	125	13.1	53	5.9	153	16.0	2	–	41	4.7
1928	956	586	61.3	136	14.2	57	6.0	134	14.0	9	–	34	3.6
1929	1,254	803	64.0	169	13.5	89	7.1	123	9.8	8	–	62	5.0
1930	1,806	1,388	76.8	112	6.2	158	8.7	106	5.8	0	0	42	2.5
1931	884	674	76.2	77	8.7	61	6.8	30	3.4	9	1.0	33	3.9
1932	18.3	113	62.3	13	7.1	10	5.4	28	15.3	3	1.6	16	8.3

Source: Department of Labor 1899–1932.

Table 15.2b   Black Immigrants by Region of Last Residence, 1899–1932

		Caribbean		Central America		South America		British North America		Portuguese Atlantic (Cape Verde & Azores)		Others	
Year	Total	No.	%	No.	%	No.	%	No.	%	No.	%	No.	%
1899–1932	142,740	107,892	75.6	7,253	5.1	3,050	2.1	6,153	4.3	15,275	10.7	3,205	2.2

Source: Department of Labor 1899–1932.

iconography of, Ellis Island. Its impact upon the nation as a whole, and Afro-America in particular, was much greater than its size would first suggest. The members of this group, and their children, were to distinguish themselves in business, the professions, politics, sports and the arts. From this group came outstanding men and women such as Hubert Harrison, Marcus Garvey, Amy Jacques Garvey, Otto Huiswoud, Hugh Mulzac, Claude McKay, Eric Walrond, J.A. Rogers, W.A. Domingo, Claudia Jones, C.L.R. James, Oliver Cromwell Cox, George Padmore, Kenneth B. Clark, Maida Springer-Kemp, Richard B. Moore, James Watson, Hulan Jack, J. Raymond Jones and Sidney Poitier. In this group is Hubert Harrison, the person A. Philip Randolph aptly referred to as the "Father of Harlem Radicalism". Another, Marcus Garvey, was the founder of the largest black political organization in the United States, and the first and only genuinely pan-Africanist organization, which reached and moved people of African descent around the world; here, too, are leading black communists and socialists (Huiswoud, Briggs, Moore, Domingo, Claudia Jones, Mulzac), including a leading member of the American Trotskyist movement in the 1930s and 1940s (James); the first black sailor to earn a captain's licence in the United States (Mulzac); two of the most outstanding writers of the Harlem Renaissance (McKay and Walrond); the highest ranking black official in the Communist International in the 1930s (Padmore); the first black Manhattan borough president (Jack); the first black municipal judge in the state of New York (Watson); and also, we should not forget, the first black head of Tammany Hall (J. Raymond Jones).[9] It was this first wave of twentieth century black migrants to the United States that laid in place the institutional infrastructure of Afro-Caribbean life in New York City and elsewhere. By the 1930s it was claimed that a third of New York's black professionals, including doctors, dentists and lawyers, came from the ranks of Caribbean migrants, a figure well in excess of the group's weight within the black population of the city (Reid 1939: 121).[10] Furthermore, the Caribbean newcomers accounted for a disproportionately large number of black business-men and businesswomen in New York City. A study of the entries in *Who's Who in Colored America,* the definitive guide to Afro-America's elite at the time, covering the period 1915 to 1932, yielded a "disproportionately high" presence of black migrants. In 1930 only 0.8 percent of the black population of America was of foreign birth, yet 6 percent of those listed were migrants. Over 8 percent of the doctors, 4.5 percent of the lawyers, more than 14 percent of the businessmen, 4.5 percent of the clergymen, over 3 percent of the professors, and 4 percent of the writers/authors listed over the period were migrants (Walter and Ansheles 1977: 51–52; see also Malliet 1926: 351 and Smith 1933). No doubt the proportion would have been higher if the data included those of immigrant *descent,* instead of being confined to those of foreign birth. Among the sons and daughters of this first generation of Caribbean migrants were Malcolm X, Louis Farrakhan, Harry Belafonte, Colin Powell, St Clair Drake, Clifford Alexander, Cicely Tyson, Maida Springer Kemp, Vincent Harding, Robert Moses, Shirley Chisholm, Constance Baker Motley, Margaret Walker, Kareem Abdul-Jabbar, Audre Lorde, Michelle Wallace, Paule Marshall, Sonny Rollins, Rosa Guy, June Jordan and Lani Guinier.

The remarkably distinct socioeconomic profile of the Caribbean mi-grants is not in question. But the explanation of the trajectory of this first generation and their children has long been the subject of heated debate. Despite the heat generated by the debate over Caribbean social mobility in the United States, the first generation of twentieth century immigrants is the least studied and, not surprisingly, the least understood. Yet, as I shall show, a study of this generation of Caribbean migrants is crucial to a proper understanding of Afro-Caribbean socioeconomic trajectory in the United States. The remainder of this chapter shall accordingly concentrate on this group in order to shed new light upon their origins, status and social mobility in America.

Much of the controversy about Caribbean social mobility in the United States revolves around the work of the influential and conservative Afro-Ameri-can economist Thomas Sowell. Sowell is rightly described as a cultural deter-minist. To him, the 'success' of Afro-Caribbean nationals relative to Afro-Americans in the United States can wholly be explained by what he regards as cultural differences. In his influential essay "Three Black Histories" (1978), where he first developed these ideas, Sowell dismisses the suggestion that differences in the educational background between the two groups might be relevant. It is worth noting how he deals with this question. He writes:

Some people have attributed the West Indians' success either to superior education under the British system or to different treatment by white American employers. One way to test these theories would be to isolate *second generation* West Indians – those blacks born in the United States of West Indian–born parents, and therefore likely to have been educated in the United States and unlikely to have an accent that would enable a white employer to distinguish them from native blacks. A compilation of 1970 census data for second-generation West Indians in the New York City area showed them to *exceed* the socioeconomic status of other West Indians, as well as that of native blacks – and the United States population as a whole – in family income . . . education . . . and proportion in the professions. (44; emphasis in original)

There are a number of problems with this argument, but the main one is that it is a fairly obvious non sequitur. The fact that second-generation Caribbean nationals succeed in the United States does not, in itself, invalidate the claim that their parents might have enjoyed a better education than that of their Afro-American counterparts. On the contrary, the fact that the second generation succeeded to the extent Sowell suggests might very well have been an index, and indeed, as we shall see, largely was, of the relatively high quality of their parents' education.

He similarly dismisses the idea that selective migration might have had a role in explaining the characteristics of the migrants:

'Selective migration' has sometimes been offered as an explanation – assuming that the more able people migrate to the United States from the West Indies. However, this explanation also does not withstand scrutiny very well. The magnitude of the outmigration from the West Indies to various parts of the world is so great that 'selective' is hardly an appropriate description. (Sowell 1978: 45)

Of course, except for refugees in desperate flight, migrants, especially those to America, have always been self-selecting (Bodnar 1985: chap. 1; Borjas 1987). And this has been as true of those who came from the Caribbean as those who came from elsewhere. Even during the mass migrations to Panama and Cuba in the late nineteenth and early twentieth centuries, and that to Britain in the postwar years, those who left the islands were generally more skilled than those who remained. Sowell's bold claim, then, that the notion of selective migration does not withstand scrutiny very well, is itself in need of scrutiny. For if Sowell did, in good faith and with care, examine the evidence of selective migration, he could not have so readily dismissed it. A disturbing but not implausible reading of Sowell is that he *did* scrutinize the claim, but because it did not fit his conservative political agenda and preconceived ideas, he dismissed it. The claim withstood scrutiny, but it was politically unpalatable. The fact is that Sowell read and cited Ira Reid's book *The Negro Immigrant* (1939) that presented strong evidence about the selective nature of Caribbean migration to the United States. But Sowell utters not a word about this evidence; it was as if it did not exist.[11]

Why is the argument about selectivity so unacceptable and unpalatable to Sowell? It is because it dynamites and reduces his argument to rubble. For Sowell wants to argue, and does indeed argue, that, except for culture, the Caribbean nationals who entered the United States were essentially the same as the Afro-Americans that they met in New York City and elsewhere. Let me spell out the political logic of his argument: West Indians are black, West Indians succeed; Afro-Americans are also black, but Afro-Americans fail; ergo, Afro-American failure cannot be blamed on racism, because West Indians are also black, and yet they succeed. From this, Sowell (1978) makes the leap – the big leap – that West Indian success must be explained by the latter's superior culture. Likewise, Afro-American failure must be explained by this group's inferior culture. The desideratum of culture was the only difference. As he explains:

West Indians in the United States are significant not only because of their overrepresentation among prominent or successful blacks, but also because their very different background makes them a test case of the explanatory importance of color, as such, in analyzing socioeconomic progress in the American economy and society, as compared to the importance of the cultural tradition of the American Negro. (42)

He continues: "Color alone, or racism alone, is clearly not a sufficient explanation of income disparities within the black population or between the black and the white populations" (43). Of course no sensible person would argue that colour alone, or racism alone accounts for the position of Afro-Americans in the way in which Sowell posits the problem, that is, without taking into account the way in which racism *over time* (in fact, centuries) blighted the prospects of Afro-Americans. With their access to education denied or restricted, their property rights abridged, their access to skilled jobs and training blocked, Afro-Americans more than any other group in the United States have been disproportionately proletarianized. Thus in the contemporary period, the position of Afro-Americans within the class structure is perhaps as much a product of their historically forced proletarianization and *sub*proletarianization as it is the outcome of more immediate and current experiences of racial discrimination. In short, social class and race are necessary elements to a proper understanding of the plight of contemporary Afro-America.[12] True to form, Sowell pays no attention to the extent to which Afro-Caribbean social mobility in the United States was hindered by racism. That the black migrants succeeded to the extent that they did, does not mean, as Sowell suggests, that their path was not blocked by racism. One can only imagine how much further many of these highly skilled immigrants might have reached in an America without such racist restrictions.[13]

In his many subsequent renderings of this claim, Sowell's argument became simultaneously more nuanced and more crude. Thus, in his 1981 book, *Ethnic America,* Sowell acknowledges Reid's data on the distinctive occupational profile of the migrants, but in the same breath he dismisses them by claiming that "the occupational level of the early West Indian immigrants was not very different from that of the southern black migrants who arrived in the urban Northeast at about the same time". He presents no evidence, for there is none, to show that the difference was insignificant, and goes on to claim that "The contrast between the West Indians and American Negroes was not so much in their occupational backgrounds as in their behavior patterns" (219). Thus he makes one step forward and two steps back to the culturalist explanation.

In her comparative examination of the postwar Caribbean migration to Britain and the United States, Nancy Foner (1979) pointed out that not only was the occupational profiles of the two streams of migrants different (a larger proportion of those who migrated to New York than those who went to London had professional and skilled occupations before they left Jamaica) but that the environments into which they entered were also different. New York City, in marked contrast to London, provided a much larger, more concentrated – and, she could have added, more highly paid – black population that served as a market for goods and services of Caribbean business people. Noting that most black businesses in the United States depend upon black patronage, she went on to argue that Caribbean nationals in Britain were less likely to invest savings in small enterprises "because there are fewer West Indians in British cities than blacks in New York and other major American cities to furnish a market, because they are a minority in most boroughs and wards and because they fear that English whites might not patronize black businesses" (292).[14] In *Ethnic America,* Sowell cites Foner's article when he noted that "West Indians in England are not nearly as successful there, perhaps because of the absence of a larger non–West Indian black population to provide them with a constituency" (220). Of course, Sowell conveniently sidesteps Foner's point about the significantly different occupational profiles of Jamaicans going to London compared to those who went to New York City. But were he to have paused for a moment, he would have recognized that the implications for his cultural determinist argument were profound. Foner rightly points out that the culture of the Jamaicans who went to London was in no way different from the culture of their compatriots who went to New York, yet their socioeconomic trajectories took radically different directions in the two environments. Culture, per se, then, cannot explain the relative success of Jamaicans in New York City, as Sowell has argued.

In his 1984 book, *Civil Rights: Rhetoric or Reality?*, Sowell concedes that the migration to the United States might have been selective, but he still rated culture as the determining factor in the socioeconomic profile of Afro-Caribbean immigrants (77–79).[15] It is hard to imagine what evidence would prove sufficient for Thomas Sowell to abandon his cultural determinism. Furthermore, until his book *Race and Culture* (1994), Sowell never even bothered to attempt to define the term 'culture'. And in *Race and Culture* his conception of the term is incoherent and used inconsistently.[16] At times, in that book and elsewhere, he uses 'culture' in such a broad manner – skills, values, attitudes, receptiveness to new ideas (especially technologies), behaviour – that it explains virtually everything, and therefore nothing. At other times, he opportunistically and in an ad hoc way narrows the definition to score a point. What is clear, however, is that, despite his pretensions to the contrary, to Sowell culture is static, a constant, an independent variable, standing outside of the turmoil of history and change with stubborn immutability. As Stephen Steinberg (1985) suggests, Sowell sees cultures as the biologist sees genes. Steinberg goes on to say, fiercely, but with some justification, that "like the earlier practitioners of scientific racism, Sowell argues that action on the part of the state to eliminate poverty is not merely useless, but counterproductive, since it encourages idleness, immorality, and dependency" (71–72).[17] And when it comes to discussing the differences between Afro-Americans and Afro-Caribbean nationals, culture for Sowell means attitudes, values and behaviour.

There are some sound critiques of Sowell's comparison of Afro-Americans with Caribbean immigrants, most notably that of Reynolds Farley and Walter Allen in their book *The Color Line and the Quality of Life in America* (1989), and that of Stephen Steinberg in *The Ethnic Myth* (1989).[18] But to my mind, these are generally too defensive and not radical enough; that is, they do not go deep enough to the root of Sowell's argument and its weaknesses. They both concentrate on the post-1965 migration, making only slight reference to the earlier generation. They concentrate on the experience of the migrants in the United States, rather than examine *who* were the people who migrated from the Caribbean in the first place. Not only do they not examine the educational and occupational backgrounds of the first generation of Caribbean immigrants but, remarkably, despite an abundance of evidence supporting the selective character of the postwar migration, they never mobilize that evidence in their argument against Sowell. Both books seem far too preoccupied with asserting that Sowell overstates the relative success of Caribbean immigrants. They both succeed in doing so because Sowell *does* exaggerate the success of Caribbean nationals in America.[19] But in the end, criticism along these lines simply provides nuance. And I believe that the culturalist argument of Sowell needs to be uprooted, because it is so profoundly false, misleading and detrimental in its political consequences. Thus, Sowell escapes virtually unscathed despite the righteous passion and laudable aims of his adversaries. What I propose to do here, then, is to indicate some of the fundamental weaknesses of Sowell's work by looking at the background and trajectory of the first generation of Caribbean migrants and their children in America. By so doing the analysis can be more firmly anchored historically. And it is in his history – or rather lack of history – of Caribbean migration to the United States that Sowell is most deficient and vulnerable.

In a number of key respects, Caribbean migrants differed from most Afro-Americans. And we can concretely pinpoint the ways in which they did and show that these differences largely explain their distinct socioeconomic profiles and trajectories, without resort to the slippery and catch-all notion of culture as used by Sowell. The greater level of educational attainment of the black migrants when they entered America is one of these. "Those from the British West Indies," observed James Weldon Johnson in 1930, "average high in intelligence and efficiency." He noted that there was "practically no illiteracy among them, and many have a sound English common school education" (53). Indeed, as early as 1923, 98.6 percent of the migrants entering the country were literate and by 1932 this figure had risen to 99.0 percent. Only 1.1 percent of adult black migrants to America were illiterate for the period 1918 to 1932 (Reid 1939: 84–85; Department of Labor 1900–33) (see Table 15.3).

Table 15.3   Literacy of Black Immigrants, 1899–1932

Years	Adults Admitted	Literate		Semiliterate		Illiterate	
		Number	% of adults	Number	% of adults	Number	% of adults
1899–1910	30,177	24,444[a]	81.0	n/a	n/a	5,733	19.0
1911–17	42,593	35,341	83.0	145	0.3	7,107	16.7
1918–24	46,815	46,185	98.7	68	0.1	562	1.2
1925–32	6,284	6,250	99.5	3	–	31	0.5
1899–1932	125,869	112,220	89.1	216	0.2	13,433	10.7

Note: Between 1899 and 1917, adults were defined as those fourteen years and over; from 1918 to 1932, adults were defined as those sixteen and over. Literates are defined as those who could read and write; semiliterates, those who could read but not write; illiterates are those who could neither read nor write.
[a] Includes semiliterates.
Source: Department of Labor 1899–1933.

The fact that literacy was a general requirement for adults entering the United States under the 1917 immigration act helps to explain these high rates.[20] The general level of black immigrant literacy was, incidentally, lowered in the early years by the skewing effect of a large number of black Cape Verdeans entering the country at that time (see Table 15.2a) and who were far less literate than migrants from the Caribbean. Thus, while the general level of illiteracy for black immigrants entering the United States between 1899 and 1910 was 19 percent, that for black Cape Verdeans was 45.9 percent, almost two-and-a-half times the overall rate. Between 1911 and 1917 the illiteracy level dropped to 16.7 percent for entering black immigrants. But that of the Cape Verdeans increased to 48.5 percent. Not surprisingly, there was a clear correspondence between the proportion of immigrants from the Cape Verde Islands and the general level of black immigrant illiteracy. Thus, in 1914 when they made up 20.2 percent of black immigrants, the level of illiteracy was 23.1 percent. When in 1917 they made up 11.7 percent, the rate of black illiteracy fell to 9.2 percent.[21] As their numbers and proportion dramatically fell in the aftermath of the immigration acts of 1917 and 1924, so did the level of illiteracy.[22]

Further, included in this figure was a large number of labourers who migrated from the Bahamas to Florida, who were, in general, substantially less

Table 15.4 Illiteracy in the Population Twenty-one and Over, by Colour and Nativity for the United States, 1900–1930 (percentages)

Year	National	Black	White[a]		
			Native	Foreign born	All Whites
1900	12.0	51.7	5.3	13.3	7.3
1910	8.9	35.7	3.5	12.9	5.9
1920	7.1	27.4	2.4	13.7	5.0
1930	5.3	20.0	1.8	10.3	3.4

[a] Mexicans included with the white population in 1910 and 1920.
Source: Department of Commerce 1935: 232, Table 5.

literate than those who migrated to New York and elsewhere in the northeast.[23] Despite the downward pull that the presence of Cape Verdeans and Bahamians had on the black migrants' aggregate literacy figures, the overall level of literacy among the black migrants compared favourably with the levels for the United States. For in 1920 and 1930 the national levels of illiteracy for adults over 21 were 7.1 percent and 5.3 percent, respectively. The illiteracy rates for black American adults (twenty-one years and older) in 1920 and 1930 were 27.4 percent and 20.0 percent, respectively (see Table 15.4).

In the North, with better access to education, the level of illiteracy for Afro-Americans ten years old and over was 7 percent in 1920 and 4.7 percent in 1930. In New York state, the level of black illiteracy for those ten and older dropped from 5 percent in 1910 to 2.5 percent in 1930. For New York City, it had fallen even further, to 2.1 percent in 1930 (Department of Commerce 1935: Tables 15, 18, and 21, 235–37) (see Table 15.5).

Table 15.5 Illiteracy Rates of Black Population Ten and Over in New York City, 1890–1930 (percentages)

Year	New York City	Manhattan	Brooklyn
1890	15.0	n/a	n/a
1900	8.3	6.6[a]	11.1
1910	3.6	3.2	4.2
1920	2.1	1.8	2.9
1930	2.1	1.9	2.8

[a] Manhattan and Bronx boroughs.
Source: Department of Commerce 1918: 434, Table 31; 1935: 252, Table 35.

As dramatic as this progress was, the Afro-American rate of illiteracy in New York City was more than twice that of Caribbean immigrants entering the city over the period. Although literacy was defined one way in the United States and another in the British Caribbean, there is every indication that the Afro-American population in New York City was, by any measure, more literate than that of the islands. The profound asymmetry of the literacy profile of those in the islands and those who migrated to New York is easily explained: those who migrated to Manhattan came from the thin layer of the most literate of the Caribbean.

The illiteracy rate for white American adults (twenty-one years and older) in 1920 was 5 percent, which fell to 3.4 percent ten years later. When we disaggregate the white population into foreign born and native we find that the levels of illiteracy for the foreign born in 1920 was 13.7 percent and 10.3 percent in 1930. For the native-born whites the rates were 2.4 percent in 1920 and 1.8 percent in 1930 (see Table 15.4). As we have seen, only 1.1 percent of the black immigrants entering the United States between 1918 and 1932 were illiterate. The rates of illiteracy for those who actually entered the country in 1920 and 1930 were even lower: in 1920, less than 1 percent (0.86 percent) were illiterate and in 1930, less than half of one percent (0.41 percent) were illiterate.[24] In other words, the Afro-Caribbean migrants were not only more literate than Afro-Americans, they were more literate than white Americans, native as well as foreign born. That the rate of illiteracy (for those over ten) in Jamaica (the source of probably the majority of black migrants to the United States at the time) was as high as 34 percent in 1921 is highly significant (Department of Statistics 1984). And the fact that, as recently as 1946, the level of illiteracy in the British Caribbean was as high as 22 percent,[25] underlines, contrary to Sowell's assertions, the profoundly selective character of the Caribbean migration to the United States earlier in the century.

It is a sobering thought that in 1946 St Lucia had the highest rate of illiteracy (44.8 percent) in the British Caribbean. For in seeming contradiction to this fact, two of her children, who were both born when illiteracy on the island was even more widespread (W. Arthur Lewis in 1915, Derek Walcott in 1930), would become the first among the Caribbean sons and daughters of Africa to win the Nobel Prize for Economics (1979), and Literature (1993). How was this possible? Part of the explanation – and it is a big part – is that while the mass of black St Lucians were kept in ignorance, a few, such as Lewis and Walcott, received what Walcott in one of his poems called "a sound colonial education" (1977: 4), comparable to the best secondary education in the world.

They both attended the same and most prestigious secondary school on the island. And it is this uncommonly good education that laid the foundations for excellence. Significant, but not surprising, is the fact that both Lewis and Walcott became members, in the prime of life, of the Caribbean diaspora in the United States. For it has been the pattern since at least the nineteenth century, that the most highly educated black Caribbean nationals made their way to those shores in disproportionate numbers.

Even more important than their extraordinarily high rate of literacy is the fact that Caribbean migrants had a socioeconomic profile at radical variance with that of black America. From 1925 to the end of the 1930s farmers and agricultural workers, the largest occupational category among Afro-Americans, never formed more than 4 percent of their number. Although some 44.4 percent of black migrants had been labourers and servants during the period 1899–1931, and their numbers reached a peak of 51 percent for the period 1906–12, the proportion declined steadily thereafter. (Again, these figures are skewed by the large number of Cape Verdeans and Florida-bound Bahamians entering the country during these years.) It had fallen to 23 percent by the period 1927–31 (see Table 15.6a).

But the most remarkable feature of the socioeconomic profile of the early migrants is the high proportion of their number that held, in their country of origin, professional, white-collar and skilled jobs. Caribbean teachers and doctors, clerks and accountants, dressmakers and seamstresses, tailors and carpenters emigrated to the United States in disproportionately large numbers compared to their unskilled compatriots. From 32.4 percent in the period 1899–1905, the professional and skilled workers had increased to 43.2 percent of the migrating black adults for the years 1927–31. In marked contrast, 81.7 percent of Afro-Americans were employed in agriculture and domestic service in 1910, falling to 67.3 percent in 1920. Despite the gains made by Afro-Americans during the period of World War I and the great migration to the North during those years, by 1920 only 20 percent were classified as skilled (Greene and Woodson 1930: 204, 334). Between 1899 and 1931, 37.9 percent of the black immigrants with occupations were skilled (see Table 15.6b) and the proportion classified as professional was more than twice that for Afro-Americans.

In 1910 only 1.3 percent of Afro-Americans were employed in professional services; this rose only slightly, to 1.7 percent in 1920, reaching 2.5 percent in 1930 (Department of Commerce 1935: Table 7, 290; Greene and Woodson 1930: 204).[26] Among the black immigrants, the proportion of professionals

Table 15.6a Occupational Status of Black Immigrants, 1899–1931

Years	1899–1905		1906–12		1913–19		1920–26		1927–31		1899–1931	
Number Admitted	10,710		36,398		44,817		44,777		5,855		142,557	
Children	1,496		3,264		4,394		6,717		1,051		16,922	
Adults	**9,214**		**33,134**		**40,423**		**38,060**		**4,804**		**125,635**	
	Number	% of Adults	Number	% of Adults	Number	% of Adults	Number	% of Adults	Number	% of Adults	Number	% of Adults
Adults without Occup.	1,383	15.0	4,010	12.1	4,646	11.5	5,334	14.0	1,393	29.0	16,766	13.3
Adults with Occup.	7,831	85.0	29,124	87.9	35,777	88.5	32,726	86.0	3,411	71.0	108,869	86.7
Professional	**204**	**2.2**	**811**	**2.4**	**1,152**	**2.8**	**1,286**	**3.4**	**289**	**6.0**	**3,742**	**3.0**
Teachers	69	–	248	–	405	1.0	448	1.2	94	2.0	1,264	1.0
Physicians	11	–	31	–	36	–	36	–	16	–	130	–
Skilled	**2,787**	**30.2**	**9,552**	**28.8**	**13,291**	**32.9**	**13,802**	**36.3**	**1,789**	**37.2**	**41,221**	**32.8**
Carpenters & Joiners	234	2.5	940	2.8	1,643	4.1	1,574	4.1	120	2.5	4,511	3.6
Dressmakers & Seamstresses	298	3.2	2,773	8.4	4,493	11.1	4,645	12.2	632	13.2	12,841	10.2
Clerks & Accountants	182	2.0	777	2.3	1,236	3.0	1,563	4.1	320	6.7	4,078	3.2
Servants, Farm Laborers & Laborers	**3,804**	**41.3**	**16,901**	**51.0**	**18,801**	**46.5**	**15,150**	**39.8**	**1,106**	**23.0**	**55,820**	**44.4**

Source: Department of Labor 1899–1931.

Table 15.6b Distribution of Black Immigrants with Occupations, 1899–1931

Years	1899–1905		1906–12		1913–19		1920–26		1927–31		1899–1931	
Adults with Occupations	7,831		29,124		35,777		32,726		3,411		108,869	
	No.	%	No.	%	No.	%	No.	%	No.	%	No.	%
Professional	204	2.6	811	2.8	1,152	3.2	1,286	3.9	289	8.5	3,742	3.4
Skilled	2,787	35.6	9,552	32.8	13,291	37.1	13,802	42.2	1,789	52.4	41,221	37.9
Servants, Farm Laborers & Laborers	3,804	48.6	16,901	58.0	18,801	52.5	15,150	46.3	1,106	32.4	55,820	51.3

Source: Department of Labor 1899–1931.

entering the country rose significantly over the years – from 2.6 percent in 1899–1905, it reached 8.5 percent for the period 1927–31 (see Table 15.6b).

There is also corroborative evidence from the Caribbean itself, indicating the occupational characteristics of those who migrated to the United States in the early twentieth century. The president of the artisans' trade union in Jamaica claimed that his union collapsed largely because of the massive migration of its members, especially the most "zealous" ones (Eaton 1962).[27] The occupational distribution of the passengers on the New York City–bound boats from Port Antonio (Jamaica) and from Bridgetown (Barbados) did not reflect those of the societies they were leaving behind. Indeed, in 1927 a Barbadian migrant, Clyde Jemmott, lamented, albeit in the gloomy language of eugenics prevalent at the time, what he perceived to be the degenerative effect this prolonged selective migration had on his native land: "When you take away large numbers of the strong, able-bodied and healthful members of a community, then those who are economically among the middle-class, and finally those who are ambitious, progressive and far-sighted, you are practically skimming the cream from that Society" (4). According to Jemmott, the results for Barbados are

a preponderant increase in the mediocre members of the community because of their relative numbers and also because of the fact that those lowest down are the fastest breeders, a gradual weakening of the physical and mental vigor of the people, and a lessening in the number of those ambitious, progressive and far-seeing people without whom no Society can go ahead. (4)

Jemmott drew two conclusions. First, because of "favorable selection" the Caribbean migrant, including the Barbadian, in the United States is conceded to be one of "the most progressive elements in the community". And second, the Barbadian left at home, because of "adverse selection", is "self-satisfied, complacent, lethargic, not desirous of change; in other words, he is not progressive" (4). Similarly, in a 1921 memorial to the Colonial Office in London (PRO 1921), the Jamaica League, a black middle class pressure group, complained that the economic situation in the island was so bad that "Emigration has been proceeding at a rate which threatens to denude the Colony of its working force: the brains of the Island have been going to the United States and the brawn to Cuba to settle down and earn higher wages than they are able to earn in their homeland." Jamaica must then, have been an island of headless and limbless beings – a weird population of torsos. But note the distribution of brain and brawn: the United States gets the brain, Cuba the brawn.

Thus, when Ras Makonnen and his middle class Guyanese friends took a ship from Barbados to Oriente province in Cuba they were shocked at what they saw. According to Makonnen (1973: 58–60), the boat was met by "Spaniards swaggering up with their two pistols: '¡Vene Aqui!' they shouted as they began to get their twenty and thirty Negroes and put them into trucks to drive them off to the plantations. It seemed just like the old slave-pens," said Makonnen, "with these Spaniards examining this latest batch of slaves, and the Negro old-timers hanging around them, giving advice on which ones looked rebellious like the Coromante slaves." Born George Griffith, Makonnen was an old boy of Guyana's most prestigious secondary school, Queen's College, and a scion of one of that country's most respected black middle class families. He would have none of Oriente's disrespect and superexploitation. He called the captain of the ship and said to him: "What is this nonsense? We are not slaves, you know; we have a British passport marked student and we have a legitimate affair." Makonnen and his friends summoned the British consul, a Mr Black, and pointed out that their taking the cheap fare did not mean that they should become bondsmen on arrival. The group of Guyanese, finding the sugar fields and semibondage of Oriente uncongenial, made its way to the greener pastures of the United States, like similarly aspiring members of the Afro-Caribbean middle class at the time. In so doing, they left behind in Oriente their less well heeled, less educated, and more proletarianized British Caribbean compatriots to struggle on the sugar plantations of Cuba.

Like the Jamaica League, a St Kitts newspaper in 1903 similarly bemoaned "the continual exodus of our respectable people to the States and Canada" (*Saint Christopher Gazette and Charibbean* [sic] *Courier,* 14 September 1903). And on 21 June 1909, during a drought in Antigua, the *St Kitts Daily Express* reported that the labourers were heading for the Canal Zone in Panama and some for work on Mexican railroads, whereas the "middle-class young men and women" headed for the United States and Canada.[28] Crude though some of these formulations are, they point to a genuine pattern that many could not help but notice, and found alarming: the profoundly selective nature of the migration to America (in itself, as well as compared to places such as Cuba and Central America) and in particular to the disproportionate number of the highly skilled who left the islands for the United States.

Given the highly selective character of the flow from the Caribbean to the United States, it comes as no surprise that the occupational distribution of the migrants differed from that of black America, including even black New York, the most advanced black community in the nation at the time. Accordingly, a disproportionately high number of the black professional and business class of the United States was of Caribbean origin (Domingo 1925: 344–45; Reid 1939: 83–84). This pattern, as we have seen, was established in the nineteenth century and continued into the twentieth. In a survey of black craftsmen in New York carried out in 1906, it was found that almost 61 percent of the men who reported that they knew a trade came from the Caribbean. (At the time, Caribbean nationals made up less than 10 percent of the black population of the city.) While 51 percent of the Caribbean men surveyed were skilled, only 13 percent of their Afro-American counterparts were similarly trained (Tucker 1907: 549–50; Haynes 1912: 58). Another and more comprehensive survey, carried out in 1909 by the Columbia-trained black sociologist George Edmund Haynes, found that just under 22 percent of black businesses in New York City were run by Caribbean nationals. This exceeded by 12.4 percent the proportion of the black population that came from the Caribbean.[29] In other words, the proportion of the black businessmen that were of Caribbean origin was twice the proportion of the black population in the city that was born in the Caribbean (Haynes 1912: 100–101, 108).

The relatively skewed profile of the black migrant community was partly a result of the fact that, of those migrants who returned to the Caribbean, between two-thirds and three-quarters were classified as labourers, servants, and "miscellaneous" workers. The percentage of skilled and professional migrant workers returning home was considerably lower than that of unskilled

Table 15.7   Black Aliens Admitted Into and Departed From the United States by Selected
Occupation, 1908–1924

Occupation	Admitted	Departed	Departures as Percentage of Admissions
Professionals	2,951	424	14.4
Teachers	1,005	56	5.6
Skilled Workers	33,233	2,767	8.3
Seamstresses	6,650	269	4.0
Dressmakers	4,041	312	7.7
Carpenters and Joiners	3,826	271	7.1
Clerks and Accountants	3,348	471	14.1
Servants	22,204	2,961	13.3
Farm Labourers	12,338	5,022	40.7
Labourers	12,449	4,789	38.5

Source: Department of Labor 1908–1924.

workers. Between 1908 and 1924, for instance, only 5.6 percent of the black teachers (teachers were, by far, the largest category among the incoming black professionals) who emigrated to the United States returned to their country of origin. In marked contrast, 13.3 percent of servants, 38.5 percent of labourers, and over 40 percent of farm labourers did so. Skilled workers such as seamstresses, carpenters and joiners, as well as dressmakers returned in considerably smaller numbers than unskilled workers: the proportion of farm labourers returning to their country of origin was ten times that of seamstresses (see Table 15.7).[30]

In other words, the professional and skilled were both more likely than the unskilled to migrate to the United States in the first place and far more inclined to stay than unskilled islanders were. The socioeconomic profile of the Caribbean population in the United States was therefore marked by two selective patterns of movement: it was skewed on the way out in favour of the skilled and professional, and skewed on the way back in favour of the skilled and professional remaining in the United States. Both movements, then, increased the relative weight of the skilled and professional within the

Caribbean immigrant community in the United States. In net terms, black migrants from the higher rungs of the occupational ladder would constitute a greater proportion of the migrant population than the gross migration statistics would lead one to believe. Thus, without careful disaggregation, the true story remains unrevealed and untold.

Noteworthy, too, is the fact that many of those who remained built upon their education and augmented the skills that they had when they came to America. They attended night school; they acquired more qualifications. Not infrequently, Caribbean teachers became American doctors and lawyers. Both Harrison and Colón, two leading radical Caribbean intellectuals of the period, finished their secondary education in the United States. Huiswoud got trained as a printer. Petioni, from Trinidad, worked as an elevator operator to finance his medical studies at City College and Howard University. One government survey of immigrants in cities found in 1910 that next only to Russian Jews, of all the foreign-born, black migrants had the highest percentage of men sixteen years and older at school (Reid 1939: 196–97; Smith 1933; Senate 1910: 761, Table 34). Moreover, they did extremely well in their studies, generally much better than their Afro-American counterparts. In his 1934 study, *The Negro Professional Man and the Community,* the Afro-American historian Carter G. Woodson attributed this better educational performance of the Afro-Caribbean students to access to better schools in the islands. He was emphatic on this point:

In the case of those [students] coming from the West Indies . . . the elementary schools attended were at strategic points where thorough training was easily obtained. This had a telling effect in the advantage which these West Indian trained students have had over Negro medical students who have been handicapped by the lack of thorough training in the backward parts of this country. Several deans in medical schools, where Negroes especially have been trained, have thus testified. (83)

Evidently, Woodson had a mistaken and exaggerated view of the ready access to, and high quality of, education in the Caribbean. Nevertheless, in relative terms, Afro-Caribbean nationals generally had a better chance at getting an education than Afro-Americans, especially those – the overwhelming majority during this period – who lived in the Jim Crow South. The practice of energetically augmenting their educational qualification, of course, skewed the occupational distribution of Caribbean nationals even further.

The migrants from the Caribbean who entered America in the first three decades of the twentieth century were doubly exceptional: they were radically different in their socioeconomic and educational profile from those whom they had left behind in the islands; and they were radically different in their socioeconomic and educational profile from Afro-Americans in the new society. They were a new people, an ethnic group *sui generis,* whose uniqueness and complexity the adjective 'Caribbean' does not adequately capture. To be sure, they were from the Caribbean, but they came from a rather narrow band of Caribbean societies. They educated their children, and there is no mystery to the relative success of their progeny, for that has been the general historical pattern of American immigration: the second generation surpasses the first, and even the children of those born in the United States (Chiswick 1977). Some accumulated capital; and together they laid the foundations of Afro-Caribbean middle class America.

The relative success of these black immigrants in the United States cannot be explained solely or even primarily on the basis of culture. This is not to say that aspects of their culture did not play a role. I think that the Caribbean people's extraordinary obsession with acquiring education, and their tenacious belief in what its possession can yield, played a role, albeit a secondary one, in shaping their socioeconomic profile in America (James 1998: 78–80). But what is clear to me is that the ahistorical and mistaken conceptualization of culture as used by people such as Thomas Sowell to explain the upward social mobility of Caribbean people in the United States is, at best unconvincing and at worst dangerous and harmful mischief. What I have attempted to do here is to show that the social mobility of Afro-Caribbean nationals in the United States can be more convincingly explained through a materialist reading of the experience, without recourse to the notion of culture. And the argument – mistaken, shallow but remarkably influential and enduring – of Sowell and his right-wing followers, cheerleaders and paymasters should be exposed for what it is, and combatted for what it is, because it is untrue.

Notes

1. See, in particular, Wood 1974: passim; Greene 1987; Littlefield 1990; Morgan 1975: esp. 303–7, 327; Dunn 1976.
2. Cf. Horton (1993: 42), who declares that Hall was born in Bridgetown, Barbados in 1748.

3. In 1638, the first group of black slaves/servants were brought to Boston from the Caribbean, thus becoming the first black inhabitants of the city (Horton 1993: 25).

4. See Lofton 1964, which after more than three decades remains the most detailed and best analysis of the subject.

5. Recent scholarship goes against the accepted notion that Russwurm was the first black person to graduate from an American college. At least one authoritative source now suggests that he may have in fact been the third black person to so graduate, for "Edward Jones received his BA degree from Amherst College two weeks before Russwurm's graduation, and Alexander L. Twilight graduated from Middlebury College [Vermont] in 1823" (Contee, Sr 1982: 538). Cf. Woodson and Wesley 1972: 269–70. There is no scholarly biography of Russwurm, but see Brewer 1928.

6. Elliott claimed that he was born in Boston of Jamaican parents and attended school in England and Jamaica. His biographer, however, thinks he was probably born in Liverpool. But this in itself, given the strong and long connection between Liverpool and Jamaica, does not preclude Jamaican antecedents (Lamson 1973: esp. chap. 1).

7. Details on Benjamin are drawn from Simmons 1887: 991–94; Taylor 1982: 39–40; and in particular Wright 1990: 67, 296–97. Further details on the lives of many of those mentioned here may be gleaned from Simmons 1887; Logan and Winston 1982; Rogers 1972; Woodson and Wesley 1972. For Crogman's relation to the American Negro Academy, see Moss, Jr 1981.

8. See also William Ferris in *Pittsburgh Courier,* 28 January and 4 February 1928.

9. The early black radicals are discussed at length in James 1998.

10. Cf. Gutman 1976, where a radically different pattern of occupational distribution is given for 1925; see Tables A–41 and A–42, 512–14. Unfortunately, the reliability of Gutman's figures is called into question by his methodological silence: we are not given any information about how he arrived at these magnitudes. (Was there some kind of sampling involved? If so, what kind?) Nor, for that matter, are we even enlightened about the source of the raw data. He apparently used the New York state manuscript census, but he is explicit about this as a source only in relation to his figures for 1905 and the Tenderloin district of Manhattan (450–55).

11. Sowell, in his essay, cites Reid's book in no less than ten footnotes, but never once in relation to Reid's evidence on selective Caribbean migration to the United States.

12. This imbrication of race and class is powerfully and poignantly revealed by Wilson 1987 and 1997.

13. For evidence of such restrictions as they pertain to Caribbean immigrants, see Reid 1983; Model 1991; Butcher 1994; Waldinger 1996; and especially Holder 1998.

14. I can testify to the fact that a close relative, a first-rate mechanic, did not open his own business in a little town in Cheshire, northwestern England, where he lived, because his was, for many years, the only black family in the town. He thought that because of racism he would not get enough business to provide for his family. And so he worked for a white firm, believing – rightly, in my view – that his income was more secure as a skilled proletarian than as a small black businessman.

15. Compare Sowell 1983: 107.

16. See especially the preface and chap. 1.

17. Also see Darity, Jr and Williams 1985 for a fine critique of the human capital argument as explanation for the economic fortunes of Afro-Americans.

18. See especially chap. 12 in Farley and Allen 1989 and epilogue in Steinberg 1989.

19. Model (1991) and Butcher (1994) also take up this theme.

20. On top of the inevitable self-selection involved in the migration process, prospective immigrants were required, after 5 May 1917, to pass a literacy tests in order to be admitted to the country. The Burnett-Smith Immigration Act, which was passed on 5 February 1917, provided exemptions from literacy tests for adults joining close relatives, primarily husbands and wives, in the United States. Only 588 of the 52,968 (or 1.1 percent) black immigrants admitted between 1918 and 1931 were exempted under this provision. (Figures calculated from Department of Labor 1918–31.) On the execution and implementation of the tests, see Department of Labor 1917: xiv–xv. The literacy tests, thus, screened the black population that entered the United States. For the background to these tests see Jones 1960: 259ff.; Higham 1963: esp. 202–3.

21. Figures for Cape Verdean literacy rate come from Halter 1993: 48; for black immigrant literacy, calculations from Department of Labor 1900–33.

22. In fiscal year 1917, 940 black immigrants entered the United States from Cape Verde and the Azores, but in 1918, the first full year of the operation of literacy tests, the number fell to 407, a drop of 57 percent. The black migration from the Caribbean over the same period fell from 7,971 to 5,706 – a drop of 28 percent, or half that of the Cape Verdeans (see Table 15.2a).

23. The Bahamas, especially the Out Islands from which most of the immigrants to the United States came, had one of the worst educational systems in the Caribbean in the late nineteenth and early twentieth centuries. Unlike the rest of the British Caribbean, there was no government provision for secondary education until 1925. And as late as 1957 the percentage of primary school students who went on to receive secondary education was lower than that for Haiti. Coming from the most poorly educated populations of the Bahamas, they were less literate than the other migrants from the Caribbean entering the United States. Thus, according to Howard Johnson (1996), there is "extensive evidence indicating that the introduction of literacy test checked migration to Florida from the Bahamas" (197, n. 66). See Craton and Saunders 1998: 29–31, 179, 191–92, 203; and Johnson 1996: chap. 9. For a good comparative analysis of late nineteenth century education in the British Caribbean, also see Bacchus 1994. Johnson (1996: chap. 9) provides the most detailed analysis of the forces behind and pattern of Bahamian migration to Florida in the late nineteenth and early twentieth centuries, but also see Mohl 1987.

24. In 1920, of the 6,951 black adults admitted into the United States, 26 were semiliterate (could read but not write), and 60 were illiterate; in 1930, of the 1,457 who entered, 6 were illiterate and all the others could read and write (Department of Labor 1920, 1930).

25. It should be noted that although the mean for the region was 22 percent, there was great variation in the level between the territories. Barbados stood at one extreme, with

only 7.3 percent, while St Lucia stood at the other with 44.8 percent (Lowenthal 1957: Table 6, 468).

26. For a good analysis of the precariousness and challenges faced by Afro-American professionals at the time, see Woodson 1934.

27. For a fine discussion of the problems of artisans in early twentieth century Jamaica, see Brodber 1984: 125–29.

28. Both newspapers cited in Richardson 1983: 133.

29. This figure includes 2.1 percent from South America, most of whom, apparently, turned out to be Guyanese.

30. The fact that during this period, dressmakers and seamstresses in the Caribbean were hit hard by imported ready-to-wear clothing, and the breakthrough of Caribbean migrant women in the New York needle trades largely accounts for their low rate of return to the islands. See Reddock 1990: 89–125 and 1994: 85–88; Terborg-Penn 1985: 147–51.

References

Bacchus, M. Kazim. 1994. *Education as and for Legitimacy: Developments in West Indian Education Between 1846 and 1895.* Waterloo: Wilfrid Laurier University Press.

Bodnar, John. 1985. *The Transplanted: A History of Immigrants in Urban America.* Bloomington: Indiana University Press.

Borjas, George J. 1987. "Self-selection and the earnings of immigrants". *American Economic Review* 77, no. 4 (September).

Brewer, William M. 1928. "John Brown Russwurm". *Journal of Negro History* (January).

Brodber, Erna. 1984. "A second generation of freemen, 1907–1944". PhD diss., University of the West Indies.

Butcher, Kristin F. 1994. "Black immigrants in the United States: A comparison with native blacks and other immigrants". *Industrial and Labor Relations Review* 47, no. 2 (January).

Chiswick, Barry R. 1977. "Sons of immigrants: Are they at earnings disadvantage?" *American Economic Review* 67, no. 1 (February).

Contee, Sr, Clarence G. 1982. "John Brown Russwurm". In *Dictionary of American Negro Biography,* edited by R. Logan and M. Winston. New York: Norton.

Craton, Michael, and Gail Saunders. 1998. *Islands in the Stream: A History of the Bahamian People, II – From the Ending of Slavery to the Twenty-First Century.* Athens: University of Georgia Press.

Darity, Jr, William A., and Rhonda M. Williams. 1985. "Peddlers forever? Culture, competition, and discrimination". *American Economic Review* 75, no. 3 (May).

Domingo, W.A. 1925. "Gift of the black tropics". In *The New Negro: An Interpretation,* edited by A. Locke. New York: Albert and Charles Boni.

Dunn, Richard. 1976. "The English sugar islands and the founding of South Carolina". In *Shaping Southern Society: The Colonial Experience,* edited by T.H. Breen. New York: Oxford University Press.

Eaton, George. 1962. "Trade union development in Jamaica". *Caribbean Quarterly* 3, nos. 1 and 2.

Farley, Reynolds, and Walter Allen. 1989. *The Color Line and the Quality of Life in America.* New York: Oxford University Press.

Foner, Nancy. 1979. "West Indians in New York City and London: A comparative analysis". *International Migration Review* 13, no. 2.

Foner, Nancy. 1983. *Jamaican Migrants: A Comparative Analysis of the New York and London Experience.* Working Paper no. 36. New York: Center for Latin American and Caribbean Studies, New York University.

Greene, Jack P. 1987. "Colonial South Carolina and the Caribbean connection". *South Carolina Historical Magazine* 88, no. 4 (October).

Greene, Lorenzo, and Carter G. Woodson. 1930. *The Negro Wage Earner.* Washington, DC: Association for the Study of Negro Life and History.

Gutman, Herbert G. 1976. *The Black Family in Slavery and Freedom, 1750–1925.* New York: Pantheon.

Halter, Marilyn. 1993. *Between Race and Ethnicity: Cape Verdean American Immigrants, 1860–1965.* Urbana: University of Illinois Press.

Handlin, Oscar. 1973 [1951]. *The Uprooted.* Reprint, Boston: Little, Brown and Company.

Hawkshawe, Dorothy. 1974. "David Augustus Straker, black lawyer and reconstruction politician, 1842–1908". PhD diss., Catholic University of America.

Haynes, George Edmund. 1912. *The Negro at Work in New York City: A Study in Economic Progress.* New York: Studies in History, Economics and Public Law, Columbia University.

Higginson, Thomas Wentworth. 1998 [1889]. *Black Rebellion: Five Slave Revolts.* Reprint, New York: Da Capo Press.

Higham, John. 1963. *Strangers in the Land: Patterns of American Nativism 1860–1925.* New York: Atheneum.

Holder, Calvin. 1998. "Making ends meet: West Indian economic adjustment in New York City, 1900–1952". *Wadabagei: A Journal of the Caribbean and its Diaspora* 1, no. 1 (Winter/Spring).

Horton, James. 1993. *Free People of Color: Inside the African American Community.* Washington, DC: Smithsonian Institution Press.

Jamaica. Department of Statistics. 1984. *Statistical Yearbook of Jamaica, 1982.* Kingston, Jamaica: Department of Statistics.

James, Winston. 1998. *Holding Aloft the Banner of Ethiopia: Caribbean Radicalism in Early Twentieth-Century America.* London: Verso.

Jemmott, Clyde. 1927. "Emigration and Barbados: Reflections". *West Indian–American,* November.

Johnson, Howard. 1996. *The Bahamas From Slavery to Servitude, 1783–1939.* Gainesville: University Press of Florida.

Johnson, James Weldon. 1930. *Black Manhattan.* New York: Knopf.

Jones, Maldwyn A. 1960. *American Immigration.* Chicago: University of Chicago Press.

Kaplan, Sidney, and Emma Nogrady Kaplan. 1989. *The Black Presence in the Era of the American Revolution,* rev. ed. Amherst: University of Massachusetts Press.

Lamson, Peggy. 1973. *The Glorious Failure: Black Congressman Robert Brown Elliott and the Reconstruction in South Carolina.* New York: Norton.

Littlefield, Daniel C. 1990. "The colonial slave trade to South Carolina: A profile". *South Carolina Historical Magazine* 91, no. 2 (April).

Lofton, John. 1964. *Insurrection in South Carolina: The Turbulent World of Denmark Vesey.* Yellow Springs, Ohio: Antioch Press.

Logan, Rayford, and Michael Winston, eds. 1982. *Dictionary of American Negro Biography.* New York: Norton.

Lowenthal, David. 1957. "The population of Barbados". *Social and Economic Studies* 6, no. 4.

Lynch, Hollis. 1970. *Edward Wilmot Blyden: Pan-Negro Patriot.* New York: Oxford University Press.

Makonnen, Ras. 1973. *Pan-Africanism From Within.* As recorded and edited by Kenneth King. Nairobi: Oxford University Press.

Malliet, A.M. Wendell. 1926. "Some prominent West Indians". *Opportunity,* November.

Model, Suzanne. 1991. "Caribbean immigrants: A black success story?" *International Migration Review* 25, no. 2.

Mohl, Raymond A. 1987. "Black immigrants: Bahamians in early twentieth-century Miami". *Florida Historical Quarterly* 65 no. 3 (January).

Morgan, Edmund. 1975. *American Slavery, American Freedom: The Ordeal of Colonial Virginia.* New York: Norton.

Moss, Jr, Alfred A. 1981. *The American Negro Academy: Voice of the Talented Tenth.* Baton Rouge: Louisiana State University Press.

Osofsky, Gilbert. 1971. *Harlem: The Making of a Ghetto,* 2d. ed. New York: Harper and Row.

Phillips, Glenn O. 1981. "The response of a West Indian activist: D.A. Straker, 1842–1908". *Journal of Negro History* 66, no. 2 (Summer).

Reddock, Rhoda. 1990. "Women and garment production in Trinidad and Tobago 1900–1960". *Social and Economic Studies* 39, no. 1 (March).

Reddock, Rhoda. 1994. *Women, Labour and Politics in Trinidad and Tobago: A History.* London: Zed Books.

Reid, Ira. 1939. *The Negro Immigrant: His Background, Characteristics and Social Adjustment, 1899–1937.* New York: Columbia University Press.

Richardson, Bonham C. 1983. *Caribbean Migrants: Environment and Human Survival on St Kitts and Nevis.* Knoxville: University of Tennessee Press.

Rogers, J.A. 1972 [1947]. *World's Great Men of Color.* Reprint, New York: Collier Books 1972.

Simmons, William J. 1887. *Men of Mark: Eminent, Progressive and Rising.* Cleveland: Geo. M. Rewell and Co.

Smith, Alfred E. 1933. "West Indian on the campus". *Opportunity,* August.

Sowell, Thomas. 1978. "Three black histories". In *Essays and Data on American Ethnic Groups,* edited by T. Sowell. New York: The Urban Institute.

Sowell, Thomas. 1981. *Ethnic America: A History.* New York: Basic Books.

Sowell, Thomas. 1983. *The Economics and Politics of Race: An International Perspective.* New York: William Morrow.

Sowell, Thomas. 1984. *Civil Rights: Rhetoric or Reality?* New York: William Morrow.

Sowell, Thomas. 1994. *Race and Culture: A World View.* New York: Basic Books.

Steinberg, Stephen. 1985. "Human capital: A critique". *Review of Black Political Economy* 14, no. 1 (Summer).

Steinberg, Stephen. 1989. *The Ethnic Myth: Race, Ethnicity, and Class in America,* 2d ed. Boston: Beacon Press.

Straker, D. Augustus. 1886. *Reflections on the Life and Times of Toussaint L'Ouverture.* Columbus, SC.

Straker, D. Augustus. 1888. *The New South Investigated.* Detroit: Ferguson Company.

Straker, D. Augustus. 1896. *A Trip to the Windward Islands; or Then and Now.* Detroit: James H. Stone and Co.

Straker, D. Augustus. 1906. *Negro Suffrage in the South.* Detroit: D.A. Straker.

Taylor, Arnold H. 1982. "R[obert] C[harles] O['Hara] Benjamin". In *Dictionary of American Negro Biography,* edited by R. Logan and M. Winston. New York: Norton.

Terborg-Penn, Rosalyn. 1985. "Survival strategies among African-American women workers: A continuing process". In *Women, Work and Protest: A Century of US Women's Labor History,* edited by R. Milkman. Boston: Routledge and Kegan Paul.

Tucker, Helen. 1907. "Negro craftsmen in New York". *Southern Workman* 26, no. 10 (October).

United Kingdom. Public Record Office (PRO). 1921. Colonial Office 137/748, Dispatch 391. June.

US Bureau of the Census. 1918. *Negro Population of the United States, 1790–1915.* Washington, DC: Government Printing Office.

US Department of Commerce. 1935. *Negroes in the United States, 1920–1932.* Washington, DC: Government Printing Office.

US Department of Labor. Bureau of Immigration. 1900–33. *Annual Report of the Commissioner General of Immigration to the Secretary of Labor* [1899–1932]. Washington, DC: Government Printing Office.

US Senate. 1910. *Abstract of Reports of the Immigration Commission, with Conclusions and Recommendations and Views of the Minority.* 61st Cong., 3d sess. S. Doc. 747. Washington, DC: Government Printing Office.

US Senate. 1911. *Reports of the Immigration Commission: Dictionary of Races and Peoples.* 61st Congress, 3d Session. S. Doc. 662. Washington DC: Government Printing Office.

Walcott, Derek. 1977. *The Star-Apple Kingdom.* London: Jonathan Cape.

Waldinger, Roger. 1996. *Still the Promised City? African-Americans and New Immigrants in Postindustrial New York.* Cambridge, Mass.: Harvard University Press.

Walter, J.C., and J.L. Ansheles. 1977. "The role of the Caribbean immigrant in the Harlem Renaissance". *Afro-Americans in New York Life and History* 1, no. 1 (January).

Wilson, William Julius. 1987. *The Truly Disadvantaged: The Inner City, the Underclass, and Public Policy.* Chicago: University of Chicago Press.

Wilson, William Julius. 1997. *When Work Disappears: The World of the New Urban Poor.* New York: Knopf.

Wood, Peter. 1974. *Black Majority: Negroes in Colonial South Carolina from 1670 through the Stono Rebellion.* New York: Knopf.

Woodson, Carter G. 1934. *The Negro Professional Man and the Community.* Washington, DC: Association for the Study of Negro Life and History.

Woodson, Carter G., and Charles Wesley. 1972. *The Negro in Our History,* 12th ed. Washington, DC: Associated Publishers.

Wright, George C. 1990. *Racial Violence in Kentucky, 1865–1940: Lynchings, Mob Rule, and 'Legal Lynchings'.* Baton Rouge: Louisiana State University Press.

16

The Government of Freedom

DAVID SCOTT

Time is still waiting in the heart of the oldest lands
in spite of a victory
of man over slavery that seems more legendary than true.
And in the desert of culture
the wind or earthquake comes and tumbles
the patience of history, the tribe or woman who is forgotten
but remembers her own bitter love like a far distant sail
in the darkening west.

– Wilson Harris, "Spirit of the Labyrinth"

The Darkening West

Reading and writing after Michel Foucault, it is scarcely a controversial matter to assert that the investigation of the past ought to be connected to questions derived from the present. This, after all, is the now familiar idea of a history of the present. Such histories are concerned with destabilizing the seeming naturalness or inevitability of the present, to show the ways in which the present is in fact assembled contingently and heterogeneously. They are concerned, in short, to historicize the present, the better to enable us to act – and act *differently* – upon it. But while this Foucauldian idea may now be more or less axiomatic, what is still not often-enough thought through is that one implication of so understanding the theoretical project of historical (or genealogical) investigation is that alterations *in the present* we inhabit ought to urge us to alter the questions through which the past is made a resource for contemporary intellectual reflection. If, in other words, what we want the past to illuminate for us ought to be guided by the task of understanding the predicament in which we find ourselves, then as that predicament itself alters, what we ask the past to yield up to us has also to alter. Surely the project of writing histories of the present, if they are not to be merely academic exercises, ought to hang on some such focus on a *changing present.*

Now, clearly, one of the conceptual-ideological fields in which the Foucauldian exercise of writing histories of the present has been pursued with much sophistication in recent years is the field of the recharacterization of colonialism. This exercise has indeed constituted an important strategy in postcolonial criticism. Part of the critical point of these exercises, it is obvious enough, has been to demonstrate (against the claims of, say, liberal-rationalist historiographies or Eurocentric ones) the hegemonic persistence into the postcolonial present of aspects of colonialist discourse and practice. I do not doubt the importance of these moves; indeed, they have been enormously enabling in my own work (see Scott 1994). However, the protagonists of these revisionist efforts (myself included) have seemed to take it for granted that we already *know* under (or in relation to) what general description *of the present* these recharacterizations of the colonial past are supposed to perform their labour of criticism. So that while the supposed transparency of the colonial past is subjected to a searching scepticism, and meticulously scrutinized and deconstructed, the self-evidence of the postcolonial present is assumed, and it stands unexamined, indeed, unproblematized. One consequence of this, it seems to me, is that it always remains unclear exactly what demand in the present these historiographical strategies are being mobilized to meet; and, therefore, there is no way to judge whether in fact they are adequately doing so.

In the last decade or so, one of the questions that has acquired a new cognitive-political resonance and a new ideological salience for the present is that of freedom. Indeed, 'freedom' is one of the defining watch-words of the so-called new world order that, supposedly, has come into being with the end of the cold war. Freedom, so we are told, has finally, after a long and difficult ordeal in the struggle with its totalitarian adversaries of the Left and Right, assumed its proper place as the supreme value, acknowledged and unchallenged, not only in the local history of Western culture, but in the History of

Culture as such. The force of this story of our time is evident in the fact that it has reorganized the very context of cultural-historical and ethical-political debate; and in doing so, it has reorganized the old distinction between conservatives and radicals, between progressives and reactionaries. But even if we have to acknowledge the force of the historical claim that neoliberalism's freedom has hegemonized contemporary global politics, and even if we cannot now *not* write from within a present marked by this transformation, do we need to embrace it *normatively?* This is the question. For those of us who are sceptical of the claims of the protagonists of the 'liberal revolution' and of democracy's 'third wave' surely the present also exerts a counterdemand, namely the demand to problematize precisely the seeming transparency of these normalized claims to the self-evidence of freedom.[1]

On my reading of it, this is the challenge that Thomas Holt has taken up in his remarkable study of the problem of slave emancipation in colonial Jamaica. In the course of introducing this study, Holt (1992) reflects on the link between the historical matters that constitute the focal object of his investigation and the contemporary intellectual-political predicament that frames the conceptual problematic through which his questions emerge as visible questions of moment:

This study grew out of, is connected with, and was partly formed by the concerns of my historical present – the decade of the 1980s. That amazing decade began with the election of Ronald Reagan to the American presidency; it ended with the collapse of communism in Eastern Europe and the threat of its collapse in the Soviet Union itself. Reagan's simple and forceful message was that the best policy was to let the market govern social relations and that those who did not make it in modern America had only themselves to blame. Thus, while in contemporary usage Democrats claimed the liberal label, Reagan and his modern conservative allies took up many of the essential elements of the original nineteenth century liberalism, which differs from the so-called advanced liberalism of the late nineteenth century.

Reagan's seemingly new and fresh approach had a powerful appeal, especially to people looking for respectable ways to evade the failure of American society to satisfy the basic needs of large sectors of its population. It is not irrelevant to the composition of this book that the 1980s were a period when the gap between rich and poor grew wider and racial tensions and despair grew worse. At the same time, self-determination and free enterprise were conflated in public discourse, and democracy and capitalism became synonyms. (xviii–xix)

Holt's work is staged on this connection between slave emancipation and the *contemporary* predicament of freedom. It is the latter, in fact, that gives to the historical problem of the former its compelling significance.

As I understand him, Holt wants to make it impossible for us to buy the seeming transparency of contemporary liberalism's self-congratulatory story of freedom, particularly the claim that the 'free market' is the neutral space of impartiality and equality, especially for those – such as peoples of African descent in the New World – who have historically been objects of modern forms of systematic discrimination. He seeks to do this by exposing the contradiction – between freedom and constraint, between autonomy and authority – that, in his view, is internal to, and constitutive of, liberalism as such. For Holt, liberalism is not what it takes itself to be in its autobiography – that is, the unceasing extension of individual freedom. To the contrary, on his reading, the story of liberalism is the story of the simultaneous extension/containment and expansion/contraction of freedom. And what for him is illuminating about British slave emancipation is that, in it, the constitutive contradiction of liberalism stands out in sharp relief; and stands out, moreover, in the register of race.

In this chapter I want to examine the story Holt tells about the problem of black freedom in postemancipation Jamaica. I want to worry about the kind of historiographical project into which it is inserted – that is to say, the politico-theoretical demand in the postcolonial present to which it takes itself to be responding – and to consider whether the conception of freedom that supports Holt's argument is one with a continuing warrant, a continuing critical purchase in the postcolonial present. It is here that the whole question of what I will call the 'government' of freedom is to be posed. I will employ this Foucauldian notion to rethink our assumptions about 'freedom' and to urge a different conceptualization of 'the problem of freedom' in postemancipation Jamaica than the one urged by Holt. I should make it clear, however, that I do not intend in this exercise to offer even a partial rewriting of this postemancipation history. The labour I offer is of another kind, one both more and less than such a history might purport to be. What I intend to offer is a reconsidered conceptual terrain upon which that history might be written. It is more in the sense that it seeks to be a critical inquiry into the assumptions through which the claims of history are made intelligible; and it is less because it does not suppose itself to be a substitute for such a history but only a recurrently necessary preface to it.

I shall begin elsewhere, however, with a different telling of the story of slavery and freedom than the one Holt offers, though arguably one as concerned as his is with the present from which he writes, and one that crosses many of the same intellectual debates. I am thinking of the work of Orlando Patterson.

Freedom in the Autobiography of Western Culture

I do not believe that it is an exaggeration to say that Orlando Patterson has, over the course of an immensely productive career, been almost single-mindedly preoccupied with the problem – perhaps I should say, with the value – of freedom. One can trace, through all his major works (of both fiction and nonfiction), a relentless thematization of the value of freedom.[2] Recall, for example, the way he uses Albert Camus's *The Rebel* to stage the existential scenario with which he closes the otherwise academic prose of *The Sociology of Slavery* (1973). Patterson is endeavouring to explain how it is that slaves who had been born into slavery and who therefore had never known freedom (that is, creole slaves) could nevertheless have desired it so fervently as to give their lives for it. He has in mind, of course, the greatest of all slave rebellions in British colonial Jamaica, the so-called Christmas Rebellion of 1831/32 led by Sam Sharpe.

What then, accounted for the presence of this need which seems to survive under conditions which in every way conspire to smother it? Every rebellion, Camus has written, "tacitly invokes a value". This value is something embedded deep in the human soul, a value discovered as soon as a subject begins to reflect on himself through which he inevitably comes to the conclusion that "I must become free – that is, that my freedom must be won". In the final analysis it is the discovery of this universal value which justifies and stimulates the most tractable of slaves to rebel. (282–83)

On my reading of Orlando Patterson, everything follows from this central paradox: the paradox of the birth of the desire for freedom in the breast of the slave. All of his mature work has been an attempt to give a historical-sociological account – to form a theoretical understanding – of this animating paradox. Now, I do not myself agree with the argument Patterson develops. In my view, the story he ends up telling turns out to be an autobiographical account of Western culture's self-image of freedom. However, there is something of fundamental importance for us in the *itinerary* of Patterson's preoccupation, something that has to do with his pursuit of that question that animates him, the internal – dialectical – connection between slavery and freedom.

In order to get at his existentially defined question – How could a slave who had never known freedom nevertheless conjure up the desire for it, and formulate an idea of it? – Patterson feels constrained to pose and pursue a prior and more fundamental one, namely, What, in its essentials, is slavery? His second major book, *Slavery and Social Death* (1982), is the attempt to give an answer to this question. Slavery, he says, is to be defined as "a permanent, violent domination of natally alienated and generally dishonored persons" (13). But even as he pursued that question of the fundamental definition of slavery, the original question of freedom forced itself into his preoccupations.

It has been my objective to come to a definitive statement of the fundamental processes of slavery, to grasp its internal structure and the institutional patterns that support it. Throughout this work, however, the ghost of another concept has haunted my analysis . . . That is the problem of freedom. Beyond the socio-historical findings is the unsettling discovery that an ideal cherished in the West beyond all others emerged as a necessary consequence of the degradation of slavery and the effort to negate it. The first men and women to struggle for freedom, the first to think of themselves as free in the only meaningful sense of the term, were freedmen. And without slavery there would have been no freedmen.

We arrive at a strange and bewildering enigma: are we to esteem slavery for what it has wrought, or must we challenge our conception of freedom and the value we place upon it? (341–42)

Or as he put it at the beginning of the book that followed this one, *Freedom in the Making of Western Culture* (1991):

Originally, the problem I had set out to explore was the sociohistorical significance of that taken-for-granted tradition of slavery in the West. Armed with the weapons of the historical sociologist, I had gone in search of a man-killing wolf called slavery; to my dismay I kept finding the tracks of a lamb called freedom. A lamb that stared back at me, on our first furtive encounters in the foothills of the Western past, with strange, uninnocent eyes. Was I to believe that slavery was a lamb in wolf's clothing? Not with my past. And so I changed my quarry. Finding the sociohistorical roots of freedom, understanding its nature in time and context, became my goal. (xiii)

The project of this book is then an attempt to show the intimate interconnection between slavery and freedom as values, and the theoretical implications that follow from this. The basic argument in this book is that the value of freedom was historically generated out of the experience of slavery. People, he says, came to value freedom, "to construct it as a powerful shared vision of life, as a result of their experience of, and response to, slavery or its recombinant form, serfdom, in their roles as masters, slaves, and nonslaves" (xiii).

It seems to me that whether or not you are persuaded by the details of Orlando Patterson's argument, there is a significant achievement here. He has situated the institution and ideology of slavery in its widest possible sociohistorical context – not merely in the social history of capitalism, or of the West, but of humanity as such – and by so doing, he has helped to make the point that slavery anywhere cannot ever be taken as a merely marginal, local practice. So that those Jamaican slaves in Montpelier, St James, with whom he begins his scholarly career, can no longer be seen as isolated characters in a minor drama in a no-longer-consequential colony. For in his narrative they now take their place as central characters in the much larger story, the story of the rediscovery – out of their own historical conditions – of a fundamental transhistorical human value: the value of freedom. This is the scope of Patterson's existential humanism.

There is, too, a compelling moral at work here; namely, that our most cherished and elevated ideals are often born out of our most debased institutions and practices. Patterson is an unremitting dialectician. His project has been to gift to Hegel the benefit of a professional historical sociology.

The history of freedom and its handmaiden, slavery, has bruited in the open what we cannot stand to hear, that inhering in the good we defend with our lives is often the very evil we most abhor. In becoming the central value of its secular and religious life, freedom constituted the tragic, generative core of Western culture, the germ of its genius and all its grandeur, and the source of much of its perfidy and its crimes against humanity. On both the secular and religious levels, its separate elements remained yoked in continuous, creative tension within themselves, and with each other, each at once good and evil, bearing the dread mark of its birth and the glow of its possibilities. (Patterson 1991: 402)

But it is here that Patterson unfortunately joins the chorus of voices that take the West as a sort of historical plateau. "Individually liberating, socially energizing, and culturally generative, freedom is undeniably the source of Western intellectual mastery, the engine of its extraordinary creativity, and the open secret of the triumph of Western culture, in one form or another, over the other cultures of mankind" (403). But is this uncontroversially so? Whatever the virtues of Western culture – and no doubt there are such virtues – why are these to be taken uncritically as spelling out the best form of human flourishing? Leaving aside the large question whether we buy Patterson's account of Western freedom, what of other virtues sheltered by other forms of life, in other traditions of human society – the virtue of courage, say, of civic activism, of social justice, of self-government. Part of the problem with Patterson's argument, in other words, is that while it claims to be a historical sociology, what he is really doing is inscribing the story of slavery and freedom into a universal history. And this is why Thomas Holt's *The Problem of Freedom* provides a useful contrast.

Liberalism's Slave Emancipation

The Problem of Freedom is constructed as an intervention in the historiography of New World slave emancipation. It is, I think, an immensely important intervention. I want to say why I think this is so, and why also, in the end, I have a doubt about the *purchase* of the story he tells for the postcolonial conjuncture we inhabit.[3]

As we know, the question that has preoccupied modern historians concerned with the issue of slavery abolition in the British Caribbean is: What prompted the timing of its occurrence? Was the abolition of slavery the consequence of humanitarianism (the story of the rise, in the last decade and a half of the eighteenth century, of an organized abolitionism that captured the moral imagination of the British public and forced the hand of Parliament)? Or economics (the story that capitalism first encouraged slavery and then, when it began to impede further development, helped to destroy it)? Or slave resistance (the story that were it not for the radical agency of the slaves themselves, and especially the creole slave rebellions of the first decades of the nineteenth century – Barbados in 1816, Demerara in 1823, and Jamaica in 1831/32 – the British Parliament would not have acted when it did)? Or what combination among these, or balance between them, is responsible for the timing of freedom? There is now a whole multivolume archive of important historical work that addresses itself to the professional debate over these questions.[4] What interests me here, however, is not the empirical merit of one or another of these interpretive positions – how the historical evidence stacks up on one side as opposed to another – or whether (to use Collingwood's terms) the answers provided by one or another hermeneutic constitute logically appropriate answers to their underlying questions. Rather, what interests me is what I might call the political unconscious of the problem-space in which these interpretive apparatuses operate or operated. The question is not who got it right but what cognitive-political demand set the discursive conditions in which the interpretative questions as such were formulated, and whether or not this demand continues to exercise a legitimate claim on us. This is a *strategic* question. It is concerned with understanding the extent to which the questions in relation to which we have fashioned our practices of criticism continue to be questions worth having new answers to *in any given conjuncture.* When, for instance, in the 1930s and 1940s, respectively, C.L.R. James and Eric Williams challenged the hitherto hegemonic Whig story that British colonial slavery was brought down by William Wilberforce, Thomas Clarkson and the other 'Saints' sensitizing the British conscience to the evils of plantation slavery there was more at stake than the professional academic question of the proper weighing of the facts.[5] There was a crucial cultural-politics of the contemporary colonial present at stake. Both Williams and James were, in effect, writing nationalist, anticolonial histories: Williams, a liberal-nationalist history, and James a nationalist-liberationist one.[6]

In other words, the critical purchase of these antihumanitarianist versions of the story of slavery abolition has depended upon an anticolonial nationalist/liberationist demand. This is a demand to demonstrate the falseness of Europe's humanity (its hollow patronizing racism), and to set against that falseness the fullness and the legitimacy of the humanity of the colonized. The critical purchase of the anticolonial story has depended upon the nationalist/liberationist demand to secure the view that far from being the self-present agents of universal history that they took themselves to be, Europe was obliged by the hitherto denied agency of the slaves themselves to accede to a new history. In short, that story of resistance and heroism – of slaves making their own history – has been crucial to the self-image of the emergent new nations, the legitimacy and dignity of whose sovereignty has not had the historical privilege of self-evidence. My own suspicion, though, is that there is not much more that this particular story of resistance and agency can yield. This is because, in my view, the postcolonial present does not offer to us a problem-space shaped by a nationalist/liberationist demand.

Now, as I read him, Holt wants to displace the centrality of these animating questions: What are the true causes of abolition? What is the appropriate weight to give to economics, humanitarianism and slave resistance? While clearly sympathetic to the critique of Eurocentrism implied in Williams (and James too, I imagine, though he is not named in this connection), Holt wants to redirect our attention to another issue.[7] What he wants to understand is this: What forces shaped the British government policy maker's perception of the alternatives to slavery and of how to achieve those alternatives (Holt 1992: 28)? Not so much, then, what were the causes of abolition, as what went into the making of emancipation; not whether freedom was taken or given but what were the ideological materials out of which freedom was constructed. This shift alters the whole shape of the *kind* of social history of slave emancipation available to be written. Essentially, it enables Holt to frame a story with a different set of preoccupations – one that examines the moral and political assumptions that underpinned the design and implementation of the project of emancipation. And this in turn enables him to link the story of slave emancipation to the much larger story of liberalism; indeed, to deeply implicate the project of the one in the conceptual-institutional claims of the other. So the story of slave emancipation has now to be read as a central episode in the story of the social and political forms of modern power. Formulated in this way, of course, the story of race and freedom that shapes liberalism's slave emancipation can be connected to the story of race and freedom that shapes liberalism's present. I fully endorse this move. For me, however, the question is whether the *particular* story of liberalism Holt tells is the most adequate one for the present we inhabit. Or, to put it another way, whether in displacing the animating questions of an older radical-abolitionist problematic Holt manages to displace the nationalist/liberationist narrative in which they were posed.

The Problem of Freedom is the story of a slave emancipation conceived and delivered in liberalism's name. The 'liberal awakening'[8] of the first decades of the nineteenth century and its political victory in the Reform Act of 1832 constitute the discursive space in which the formal 'problem' of slave emancipation was given shape and articulated in colonialist discourse. Liberalism, in other words, provided the basic political and economic vocabulary – of rights, of individual autonomy, of interests, of the market, and so on – out of which the British colonial policy makers fashioned the Emancipation Act, and imagined the transformation of a slave economy and society into a free one.

Holt's story of British slave emancipation is framed by Eric Hobsbawm's famous concept of the 'dual revolutions' – economic and political, Industrial and French – that are the defining coordinates of the long European nineteenth century (see Hobsbawm 1962). The dual revolutions constitute the defining coordinates of the new conception of individual freedom that emerged in this period. Holt's concern here is to highlight the social and historical character of liberal freedom in two important senses: first, to suggest the historical novelty of the liberal idea of the individual, of a disembodied, self-possessed individual whose social relations were essentially contractual, entered into voluntarily on the basis of a rationally deduced self-interest; and second, to elaborate the internal paradox of liberal freedom. This paradox consists in the impossibility of reconciling economic and political freedoms. As Holt (1992) argues, capitalist society required for its justification formal equality in rights yet inherently generated class differences in effective rights, powers and possessions. As he puts it, freedom defined by capitalist market relations "inevitably produces unequal class relations which undermines the substantive freedom of most members of the society. On the other hand, the freedom defined by civil and political institutions – to the extent that society is democratic and egalitarian – must threaten an economic system based on inequality" (6). Consequently, he goes on, though theoretically conjoined, "the dual revolutions rushed down two separate, mutually incompatible courses: the economic demanded greater scope for individual expression; the political required greater constraint" (6). Holt's point here is that this contradiction is constitutive of liberalism; and the history of liberalism, on this view, is the history of the unfolding of this internal contradiction.

Now for Holt, this contradiction internal to liberalism is crucial to an understanding of British slave emancipation inasmuch as the dual revolution constituted the discursive frame within which the freedom of the slave was conceived. This is because the fundamental problem for British colonial policy makers and planters alike was how to simultaneously free the slaves and maintain the central features of the old social, economic and political order. The several proposed emancipation schemes – those of Henry Taylor, Henry Grey, James Stephen – tilted on this dilemma. On the one hand, they all, to one degree or another, defended the right of the ex-slave to formal legal equality and rights. As Holt (1992) says:

All four rejected racist interpretations of slave behavior and insisted that blacks shared the basic, innate traits of other human beings, that is, that all human beings could be motivated by self-interest and the desire for self-improvement. This was the mainspring of social action in a rationally ordered society. They were committed to laissez faire, though to differing degrees. Artificial and arbitrary constraints on the free exercise of self-interested behavior must be removed to ensure an efficient and productive economy. (50)

At the same time, however, since a ready supply of cheap, continuous labour was the overriding concern of the plantation economy, it was understood that essential elements of the social order and its power structure were to be maintained.

They would be free, but only after being resocialized to accept the internal discipline that ensured the survival of the existing social order. They would be free to bargain in the marketplace but not free to ignore the market. They would be free to pursue their own self-interest but not free to reject the cultural conditioning that defined what that self-interest should be. They would have opportunities for social mobility, but only after they learned their proper place. This at least was the intent of the British policymakers who framed and implemented emancipation. (53)

Holt's point, I think, is clear. British slave emancipation is organized around a certain economy: the problem of the extension and containment of freedom. On this account, British colonial policy toward Jamaica between 1838 and 1938 constitutes a series of departures, each of which sought simultaneously to extend and to contain freedom. So that, for instance, of the departures that came in the wake of the labour revolt of 1938, he writes:

But again, as in 1838, the policy and its ideological analogue sought to embed dependence within independence, to confine self-determination within vaguely defined, non-threatening limits. As in 1838, what was envisioned was a 'freedom' drained of the power of genuine self-determination: materially, a freedom stripped of control over basic material resources; ideologically, a freedom that internalized its own antithesis. After a century-long struggle for freedom, Afro-Jamaicans confronted new forces on new terrain, yet the fundamental structure of the contest – the combatants, the ideological content and discourse – remained much the same. (Holt 1992: xxv)

The success or failure of the liberal project of emancipation hangs on this tension. The problem of liberalism's freedom is that the freedoms it extends are invariably limited and are moreover 'drained' or 'stripped' of real content. And the moral point of the story is that slave emancipation failed, and that this failure was not fortuitous. To the contrary, as he says, this failure

was not so simple a matter as a wish by the powerful not to see it succeed, or errors of judgment or policy. Something was amiss in the very project of emancipation, in the very premises on which it was founded. And those premises appeared to be linked to its outcomes and to the extreme racism that followed in its wake in the late nineteenth century. (xix)

The problem of race in postemancipation Jamaica constitutes something of a limit to the promise of liberal freedom. For Holt, in fact, it is on the horns of race that the liberal project collapses.

I have a doubt about this story, however. It seems to me that whereas Holt has displaced the nationalist preoccupation with whether freedom was given or taken, he nevertheless reproduces a story about the ultimate failure of the liberal emancipation project to confer substantive freedoms. His concern, in effect, is to demonstrate the failure of a liberalism that gives freedom with one hand only to take it back with the other. Although his narrative eschews the liberal story of a steady unfolding of freedom, it nevertheless treats freedom as a normative horizon. I suspect, in other words, that his narrative harbours a progressivist faith and a liberationist desire: an eschatology that envisages freedom as an overcoming, as the other side of domination, or as an end of constraining determinations.[9] Now I am not against normative horizons per se, but my doubt is whether a story about slave emancipation told in terms of its success/failure and a story about freedom told in terms of extension/containment continues to offer the kind of critical purchase our postcolonial present demands. I wonder whether the anticolonial liberationist project of reading for the failure of liberalism (or, indeed, of the West more generally) continues to be the reading of the colonial past most crucial to a present in which the Marxist and nationalist languages, through which counterhorizons of freedom were defined and defended are no longer the options they used to be. I do not think that it is. These languages depended upon a *direction* of social emancipation and a conceptualization of sovereignty that are, at least, no longer clear. In my view, the postcolonial present demands a different story, one concerned less with the *ideological* dispute between liberalism and its adversaries and more with the illumination, in a more considered and systematic way, of the conceptual-institutional space created by the reorganizing project of modern power.

This is why the Foucauldian story of 'government' and its relation to modern power is useful. In his later work (as he turns his attention away from practices of modern sexuality to practices of modern politics), Foucault outlines a form of power – government – that, he suggests, is intimately tied to the history of liberalism or, more properly, tied to a history of liberal political reason. The distinction is a crucial one, because Foucault is not really interested in liberalism in the traditional sense of a political philosophy or a political ideology. As Graham Burchell (1996) has usefully summarized it, Foucault's approach to liberalism

consists in analyzing it from the point of view of governmental reason, that is from the point of view of the rationality of political government as an activity rather than as an institution. On this view, liberalism is not a theory, an ideology, a juridical philosophy of individual freedom, or any particular set of policies adopted by a government. (21)

Rather, it is a form of political reason, a political rationality. Foucault, in other words, is concerned with illuminating something else about liberalism besides its ideological function, something about its modes of problematization and style of reasoning, and something about its distinctive targets, spaces, technologies and modalities. And what is distinctive about the political reason of liberal government is that it constitutes a form of power that utilizes a range of strategies that support the civilizing project by shaping and governing the capacities, competencies and wills of the governed. Government, in other words, is about 'the conduct of conduct'.

Like Holt, I want to insist that freedom cannot be understood except in relation to power. But what interests me is not whether power negates freedom or empties it of real content but how freedom is positively *shaped* by power – the shaping quality of the power that comes to reconstruct, or make over, the lives of the ex-slaves. Because Foucault is interested in how power shapes conduct, how it actively creates conditions that oblige behaviour, freedom cannot appear as a desideratum, as what is left when restraint (that is, negative power) is lifted. Rather, what comes to be crucial is an understanding of the emergence of freedom as a central element in practices of rule – in effect, how freedom has emerged as the condition and ground of political government – and an understanding of the conditions within which certain practices of freedom have been possible – importantly, those that have to do with the shaping and regulation of autonomy and free choice, with the emergence, that is to say, of a 'responsibilized' liberty. As Nikolas Rose (1996) has put it, what is at stake in a Foucauldian understanding of liberal political reason is neither a matter of celebrating liberty (as a liberal might) nor of condemning it as an ideological fiction (as a Marxist might). What is at stake, rather, is understanding that

the freedom upon which liberal strategies of government depend, and which they instrumentalize in so many diverse ways, is no 'natural' property of political subjects, awaiting only the removal of constraints for it to flower forth in forms that will ensure the maximization of economic and social well-being. The practices of modern freedom have been constructed out of an arduous, haphazard and contingent concatenation of problematizations, strategies of government and techniques of regulation. This is not to say that our freedom is a sham. It is to say that the agonistic relation between liberty and government is an intrinsic part of what we have come to know as freedom. (61–62)

Reform and the Government of Ex-Slaves

How then to sketch the story of liberalism in postemancipation Jamaica from the point of view of governmentality? In other words, from the perspective of a liberalism understood not as an internally contradictory social and political philosophy or ideology but as a political rationality of rule, through what kinds of concepts would one think the history of the inscription of a liberal technology of government into the politico-institutional terrain of postemancipation Jamaica? This is what interests me.

The moral-political question that confronted the construction of liberal mentalities of government consisted in this: How to contrive a set of conditions such that the governed pursue ends that are only of value if pursued voluntarily? The liberal art of government depends, as Burchell (1996) suggests, upon the governed adopting "particular practical relations to themselves in the exercise of their freedom in appropriate ways". It thus depends upon an ensemble of governmental institutions that oblige or promote a *rational* and *responsible* self-conduct – "the promotion in the governed population of specific techniques of the self around such questions as, for example, saving and providentialism, the acquisition of ways of performing roles like father or mother, the development of habits of cleanliness, sobriety, fidelity, self-improvement, responsibility and so on" (26). In a word: reform. Central to the political rationality (and political vocabulary) of nineteenth century liberalism was the project of reform.

Now, 'reform' cannot be understood as merely the hoped-for end of liberal ideology and liberal policy, the naturalized horizon of a universal history. It is important to detach the problem of reform from the normative liberal-progressivist narrative in which it is typically located. Reform has to be understood as central to modern power, to modern forms of political rationality. In this sense, the problem of reform is connected to the construction of a certain kind of knowledge (a rationalist, universalist knowledge), a certain kind of division of social-institutional space (the secular/religious, state/civil society division), a certain kind of historical understanding (a teleological and progressivist history), and a certain kind of subject (a self-improving one). In other words, reform depends upon a 'norm of civilization'. Or to put it another way, reform produces the fundamental link, internal to liberal political reason, between liberty (as individual autonomy) and social and moral progress. And in the nineteenth century, it did so in the register of 'character'. As Stefan Collini (1985: 29–50) has suggested (and as Richard Bellamy [1992] has explored fruitfully in relation to J.S. Mill, T.H. Green, and L.T. Hobhouse), the problem of 'character' played a crucial role in Victorian political discourse.

Character was a central issue of liberal government. As a political rationality, what reform worked on was character. Individual liberty was crucial to the liberal project not so much because of its intrinsic value but because it was understood as a necessary condition for the reforming self-improvement of character. Understood in this way, it is not a matter of the constraints reform exercises on freedom or how much freedom is left over after reform but what kind of freedom reform positively seeks to shape. On this view, it is not reform that is central to freedom but individual freedom that is an indispensable condition of reform, that is a condition of the improving project of liberal reason. Read this way, the liberal project was not so much about freedom but about reform, not so much about liberty but about improvement.

Maurice Cowling (1990), the conservative critic of liberalism's self-image, has brought this out very nicely in his discussion of the work of J.S. Mill. As he says, the emphasis in Mill's "justification of freedom is neither on its intrinsic goodness nor on any belief man may have in its natural rightness, but on the fact that a free individual is more likely than an unfree one to contribute to the higher cultivation" (30). For Mill, in other words, contrary to normative readings of him (whether dismissive Marxist readings or congratulatory liberal ones), liberalism's claim on us is not derived from the intrinsic goodness of freedom but from the part freedom plays in what Norbert Elias would call "the civilizing process".

[Mill's] detailed delimitation of the power of society (and government) in relation to the individual is made, not in view of the natural right of individuals to be free, but from regard to the consequence to the general interest of imposing limitations on the exercise of social pressure to conform. For natural rights Mill had as much dislike as Bentham. Pursuit of individual liberty for Mill is not by itself and without regard to its consequences, a proper end of social action. Individuals must be left as free as possible from social pressure, not because they have a *right* to consideration of this sort, but because, if they are not left free, society may find it more difficult than otherwise to achieve the ends for which it exists. (Cowling 1990: 41)

And what are these 'ends'? They consist in the rational cultivation of secular truths.

The demand for liberty is not the assertion of a fundamentally binding end, but the designation of a means to the end – the end of allowing men to approach as close as possible to that highest of all pleasures which comes from mental cultivation of the closest approximation possible to knowledge of what is True. (Cowling 1990: 42)

Reform therefore depends upon a 'norm of civilization' and a division between those who are ready for citizenship and those who have to be *made ready* for it (blacks, women, the colonized, the working class). This is why it is no contradiction for Mill to declare in *On Liberty* (1978) that liberal principles only applied to "human beings in the maturity of their faculties", and therefore naturally excluded "those backward states of society in which the race itself was in its nonage". A paternalistic despotism was appropriate for them "provided the end be their improvement, and the means justified by actually effecting that end" (9–10). The point here, though, is not simply to dismiss Mill as a racist liberal but to grasp the political rationality at play in his argument.

From the point of view of governmentality, then, the story of slave emancipation has to be the story of the putting into place of the rationalities, institutions and apparatuses of reform (in this expanded sense of the term). It ought to be the story of how the liberal project sought to so alter the existing relations of power that power would no longer operate (primarily) directly upon the body in the service of extraction but would seek to operate upon character through the newly emerging space of the 'social' in order to construct a 'responsibilized' freedom or a rationalized self-conduct. This is not to denounce the freedom won by the slaves as a sham, or as insufficient, or as contradictory. Rather, it is to urge the writing of the history of the institutional spaces upon which that freedom depended; it is to write the history of the relations, conditions, discourses and practices that have shaped modern colonial freedom. It is to write the history of an alteration in the conditions of the lives of the slaves such that they would be obliged to perform their freedom not merely in the ways they chose but in 'appropriate' ways, such that they would be obliged (whether they liked it or not) to become modern, to exercise modern choices, and acquire modern habits and tastes.

This project of colonial reform itself, however, has also to be understood historically. Colonial liberalism, as Holt rightly argues, itself alters across the nineteenth century. Recall that a central episode in the story he tells about the dilemma of freedom in postemancipation Jamaica is that episode in which there is a shift in the ideological emphasis of colonial liberalism. This is a shift away from the Glenelg doctrine of the first decade of emancipation (a nonracist, civic egalitarian liberalism) to a more authoritarian, more paternalistic liberalism of the second half of the nineteenth century. On this account, the first decade of emancipation was governed by the optimistic liberal view that the freed people were to enjoy a substantive freedom: equal protection under the law, equal access to public institutions, the exercise of the franchise on the same property basis as whites. Moreover, references – implicit or explicit – to the race of the former slaves were to be expunged from colonial law. However, between the end of the first decade of emancipation and the middle decades of the second, there was a noticeable shift in colonial policy away from freedom and in the direction of constraint. And this constraint is articulated in terms of race. Colonial power is directed no longer at protecting the rights of freed people but at placing obstacles in the way of black political power. Over the course of these emancipation years freed people had demonstrated a desire to be their own freeholders and they had withdrawn their labour as far as possible from the control of the plantation. They were seeking, as Holt argues, not merely to be free labourers but to be a free people. For the colonial policy makers and for the planters, however, the refusal of the freed people to submit entirely to the plantation was interpreted as a regression to 'African barbarism'. As Holt (1992) writes:

These years, 1844–54, constitute a transitional era in British politics, colonial policy and racial ideology; changes in all these areas stimulated new approaches to the problem of freedom. The political dimensions of that problem for British policymakers paralleled the economic: how to reconcile freedom with coercion, or more specifically, how to structure a political system in the colonies nominally consistent with liberal democratic principles, while maintaining ultimate control over black political expression. (217)

This shift is crucial to the overall story because it illustrates the claims Holt wishes to make about liberalism; namely, the general claim about the constant tension between liberty and constraint, and the more specific claim that the racism that comes to define the later period was no anomaly but internal to the logic of liberalism. For Holt, the crucial story about race is that black power was thwarted, blocked and constrained. Like David Goldberg in his recent discussion of the relation between racism and modernity, the problem of racism is framed largely in terms of power's practice of exclusion/inclusion (see Goldberg 1993).

Without denying the importance of this story, I want to suggest that there may be another story about race in postemancipation that would be worth telling and that may have a more critical purchase on our present. This is the story of the relation between race and the rationalities of reform. In this story it is necessary to understand the following: How does reform, the relation between power, self-interest and character, come to depend upon a discourse of race? How was race inscribed into the social formation such that it comes to be central to self-fashioning in everyday life? What we need to understand is how – through what conceptual apparatuses and through what grids of social division – we have been produced (and have produced ourselves) as the sorts of *raced subjects* we are, with the sorts of raced self-understandings we possess.

It is this story that needs to be told. This is important for our present, it seems to me, because the contemporary postcolonial demand cannot simply be for inclusion into what colonialism has hitherto excluded us from (whether on the basis of race, class or gender), nor can it be a matter of denouncing colonialism's (despotic, paternalistic, racist) attitude towards us, but must be a demand to understand in more profound ways than we do the cognitive-political game of power (the mentalities of rule, the rationalities of government) into which we have historically been inserted, or in which we ourselves have – however misguidedly – sought so far to play in the free exercise of our postcolonial self-conduct. From where we stand today, the problem of freedom cannot be a problem of the more or less of it, of the extension or limiting of it, or of the illusion or truth of it. If I agree with Holt that the problem of slave emancipation in Jamaica can teach us something about the problem of freedom in the modern world, that lesson is not that we have not really got freedom yet or that the promise of that August emancipation has been a false one. Rather, it is simply this: that black freedom is a project, not a teleological movement in the direction of an already existing horizon. The issue today is not that we resisted colonialism or complied with it but how the epistemological/institutional terrain on which resistance/compliance could appear as options as such was historically constructed. The issue today is not what attitudes of liberationist defiance we have struck up but the senses in which the language through which those attitudes were constituted and its liberationist hopes embodied are governed by the normative assumptions of modernity.

To sum up: How to think a history of the postemancipation present, and with it the historical project of black freedom in the New World? This is the question. I have not endeavoured to actually rewrite such a history, of course, but only to think critically with a particularly instructive telling of it, that of Thomas Holt. What has interested me in large part has been the rhetorical economy of Holt's story of freedom, the conceptual protocols through which it is constructed – in a sense, the politics of the kind of story he thinks ought to be told about postemancipation Jamaica. I have suggested that what makes his story of special importance is not only its unsurpassed erudition and its deeply sympathetic narrative, but the connection he draws between the ideology of liberalism and the freedom of the ex-slaves. The importance of this connection hangs – as Holt himself well recognizes – on the relation between nineteenth century classical liberalism and late twentieth century neoliberalism; the connection hangs, in other words, on historicizing our present. The rhetorical thrust of Holt's story turns on the failure of liberal freedom, the inability of liberalism to overcome its constitutive contradiction, and in particular to its giving rise to and sheltering racism. As Holt tells it, the story of liberal freedom in postemancipation Jamaica is the story of the successive embattlement of freedom with its constituent unfreedoms.

I have offered the view that perhaps there is another story to be told about the problem of freedom in postemancipation Jamaica; namely, a story about an alteration in the political rationality of colonial rule, one in which a new rationality comes to be inscribed into the cognitive-institutional terrain of social and political life, in which power seeks to operate through the shaping of conduct rather than the shaping of bodies. The central category of this rationality is reform. Liberal freedom does not exist outside of the project – and the constitutive apparatuses and technologies – of reform. Liberal freedom depends upon constructing a relation between government and governed that obliges individuals to become the 'subjects of their lives', obliges them to exercise a responsible self-conduct, and this in turn depends precisely upon the 'character' that an improving reform seeks to bring into being. On this reading, the story of the relation between liberal reason and racism in mid to late nineteenth century Jamaica is not (or not only) a story about the *exclusion* of blacks from access to political power on the basis of 'race' but the story of the (re)organization of the rationalities, modalities and instrumentalities through which raced subjects (and raced bodies) were constituted as such, and through which the conduct of conduct could come to articulate itself in the register of race.

Notes

1. "Liberal revolution" is Bruce Ackerman's phrase (see Ackerman 1992); the idea of a "third wave" of democracy is Samuel Huntington's (see Huntington 1991).
2. His three works of fiction, *The Children of Sisyphus* (1974 [1964]), *An Absence of Ruins* (1967), and *Die the Long Day* (1972) centre on the dialectical tension between forms of unfreedom and the desire for freedom.
3. For one critical appreciation of Holt's book, which differs in some respects from mine, see Hall 1993: 229–32.
4. The literature is of course much too vast to list in full here, but see, in particular, the following that have been useful to me: Anstey 1968: 307–20; Drescher 1986; Davis 1975 and 1984; Blackburn 1989; and Walvin 1997.
5. I am referring of course to James, *The Black Jacobins* (1963 [1937]) and Williams, *Capitalism and Slavery* (1944). For an overall view of the debate over Williams' work, see Solow and Engerman 1987. On James' account, he was centrally involved in Williams' formulation of his argument. See "Interview with C.L.R. James" in Munroe and Sander 1972: 36–37.
6. This Jamesian theme of liberationist resistance would become more prominent from the late 1960s through to the 1980s. See, for instance, Craton 1982; Hart 1980–85.
7. It is perhaps W.E.B. Du Bois who is the nationalist/liberationist figure looming in the background of Holt's narrative.
8. The phrase is Elie Halevy's. See his useful history, *The Liberal Awakening* (1987 [1926]).
9. For some useful theoretical discussion see "Beyond Emancipation" in Laclau 1996.

References

Ackerman, Bruce. 1992. *The Future of Liberal Revolution.* New Haven: Yale University Press.

Anstey, Roger. 1968. "*Capitalism and Slavery:* A critique". *Economic History Review,* 2d ser., 21.

Bellamy, Richard. 1992. *Liberalism and Modern Society.* Philadelphia: Pennsylvania State University Press.

Blackburn, Robin. 1989. *The Overthrow of Colonial Slavery, 1776 to 1848.* New York: Verso.

Burchell, Graham. 1996. "Liberal government and techniques of the self". In *Foucault and Political Reason: Liberalism, Neo-Liberalism and Rationalities of Government,* edited by A. Barry, T. Osborne and N. Rose. Chicago: University of Chicago Press.

Collini, Stefan. 1985. "The idea of 'character' in Victorian political thought". *Transactions of the Royal Historical Society,* 5th ser., 35.

Cowling, Maurice. 1990. *Mill and Liberalism,* 2d ed. New York: Cambridge University Press.

Craton, Michael. 1982. *Testing the Chains: Resistance to Slavery in the British West Indies.* Ithaca: Cornell University Press.

Davis, David Brion. 1975. *The Problem of Slavery in Western Culture.* Ithaca: Cornell University Press.

Davis, David Brion. 1984. *Slavery and Human Progress.* New York: Oxford University Press.

Drescher, Seymour. 1986. *Capitalism and Antislavery: British Mobilization in Comparative Perspective.* London: Macmillan.

Goldberg, David. 1993. *Racist Culture: Philosophy and the Politics of Meaning.* Oxford: Blackwell.

Halevy, Elie. 1987 [1926]. *The Liberal Awakening (1815–1830).* Reprint, London: Ark Paperbacks.

Hall, Catherine. 1993. Review of *The Problem of Freedom,* by Thomas Holt. *Slavery and Abolition* 14, no. 1 (April).

Hart, Richard. 1980–85. *Slaves Who Abolished Slavery,* 2 vols. Kingston, Jamaica: Institute of Social and Economic Research.

Hobsbawm, Eric. 1962. *The Age of Revolution, 1789–1848.* New York: Mentor.

Holt, Thomas. 1992. *The Problem of Freedom: Race, Labor, and Politics in Jamaica and Britain, 1832–1938.* Baltimore: Johns Hopkins University Press.

Huntington, Samuel. 1991. *The Third Wave: Democratization in the Late Twentieth Century.* Norman, Oklahoma: University of Oklahoma Press.

James, C.L.R. 1963 [1937]. *The Black Jacobins.* Reprint, New York: Vintage.

Laclau, Ernesto. 1996. *Emancipation(s).* New York: Verso.

Mill, J.S. 1978 [1859]. *On Liberty.* Reprint, Indianapolis: Hackett.

Munroe, Ian, and Reinhard Sander, eds. 1972. *Kas Kas: Interviews with Three Caribbean Writers.* Austin: African and Afro-American Research Institute.

Patterson, Orlando. 1967. *An Absence of Ruins.* London: Hutchinson.

Patterson, Orlando. 1972. *Die the Long Day.* New York: William Morrow.

Patterson, Orlando. 1973. *The Sociology of Slavery.* Kingston, Jamaica: Sangster's Book Stores.

Patterson, Orlando. 1974 [1964]. *The Children of Sisyphus.* Kingston, Jamaica: Bolivar.

Patterson, Orlando. 1982. *Slavery and Social Death.* Cambridge, Mass.: Harvard University Press.

Patterson, Orlando. 1991. *Freedom in the Making of Western Culture.* London: I.B. Tauris.

Rose, Nikolas. 1996. "Governing 'advanced' liberal democracies". In *Foucault and Political Reason: Liberalism, Neo-Liberalism and Rationalities of Government,* edited by A. Barry, T. Osborne and N. Rose. Chicago: University of Chicago Press.

Scott, David. 1994. *Formations of Ritual: Colonial and Anthropological Discourses on the Sinhala Yaktovil.* Minneapolis: University of Minnesota Press.

Solow, Barbara, and Stanley Engerman, eds. 1987. *British Capitalism and Caribbean Slavery: The Legacy of Eric Williams.* New York: Cambridge University Press.

Walvin, James. 1997. *Questioning Slavery.* Kingston, Jamaica: Ian Randle Publishers.

Williams, Eric. 1944. *Capitalism and Slavery.* Chapel Hill: University of North Carolina Press.

PART 4

Construction

17

Caribbean and Latin American Development Theory and Policy

An Agenda for Deconstruction–Reconstruction

MARIBEL APONTE-GARCIA

Introduction: The Theoretical Vacuum

Caribbean and Latin American development theory is at a crossroads. After development studies entered into what was widely referred to as 'the impasse' in the 1980s, deconstruction permeated the field, doing away with many of the constructs that were once the axis of theoretical arguments (that is, mode of production, modernization, dependency, class) and with traditional policy prescriptions structured around import substitution and state intervention. Development studies merged into area studies (defined by geography or gender) or were subsumed in international economic issues such as debt, the informal economy, poverty and the environment, among others (Hoogvelt 1997). Meanwhile, neoliberalism and 'market economics' gained ascendancy and the focus of development policies shifted to structural adjustment, privatization, free trade and export-led growth.

Consequently, the Caribbean and Latin America were left with a theoretical vacuum concerning the formulation of production and development strategies suitable for the region. Today, decisions concerning development are shaped by the structural adjustment or neoliberal discourse, or both, and free trade agreements rather than by alternative proposals from within the region. This situation contrasts sharply with the rich theoretical legacy of the 1960s and 1970s when the construction of theory and policy proposals spurred the region on.

There have been three important exceptions to the lack of production and development proposals from within the region. One is the contribution of gender studies, which has focused on the feminization of poverty and on the ability of structural adjustment programmes to articulate a critique of these policies (Emeagwali 1995). A second is the contribution of neostructuralists, who have sought to articulate a proposal of 'development from within' by focusing on macroeconomic policies and on a change in production patterns with social equity (van der Borgh 1996; Sunkel 1993). A third is the contribution of works which focus on base communities and argue that alternative structures and organizations should be the focus of development policies (Lehman 1990; de Soto 1989; Portes and Schauffier 1993; Portes, Dore-Cabral and Landolt 1997). Interestingly, these exceptions have been articulated from within areas in development studies that grew as a reaction to the impasse of the 1980s (that is, gender studies, issues of debt, the informal economy and poverty) and benefited from the deconstructed notions of social actors and traditional organizations, including the state. However, although these works have made important contributions, they have not solved the theoretical vacuum concerning production and development strategies for the region because they have not articulated theoretical constructs of production and the firm linked to a development theory.

At present, Caribbean and Latin American academicians, government, entrepreneurs, managers, community development groups, nongovernmental organizations and civil society confront the urgent need of discussing the aforementioned theoretical vacuum for several reasons. First, because structural adjustment programmes and free trade agreements implemented thus far have failed to provide self-sustained economic growth with equity and have not ameliorated poverty and social deprivation. Second, because the old models – the capitalist model of industrialization by invitation and export promotion as well as the models of real existing socialism – and the old theoretical paradigms of management and economics are insufficient to construct development strategies in accordance with present needs. Third, because the discourse that presented development as a succession of progressive stages through which industrialization and economic growth occurred in the image of more developed countries has been deconstructed, invalidating the replication of development policies as an integral part of the process that sought to mirror economic development and progress.

Our challenge is to take up the deconstruction–reconstruction of theory that benefits from previous work, looks at new theoretical spaces and possibilities opening up within current discourses and debates and brings together new social actors (or old actors in new ways). If we avoid this process, policy proposals will reproduce the same theoretical limitations we are trying to overcome and will not be appropriate for meeting the challenges we now confront. This chapter is presented as an initial step taken in that direction.

An Agenda for Deconstruction–Reconstruction

There are four areas where we can both observe limitations of economic theory and replication of development policy. For each area, I will first state how a limitation of a concept of production and the firm in economic theory has influenced development policy, either historically or within the context of current regional integration. Then, an approach that would foster an alternative type of development is proposed. The four areas are: (1) macroeconomic policy unlinked to an analysis at the level of production; (2) the production versus markets discourse; (3) large-scale mass production as 'the way' to industrialize; and (4) development theory and the enterprise. The contents presented under each heading constitute excerpts of works that I have recently carried out or areas that I am currently researching.

Macroeconomic Policy Unlinked to an Analysis at the Level of Production[1]

Theoretical Limitation

Macroeconomic policy[2] has not been, in general terms, linked to a concept of production or, for that matter, to an analysis at the level of production; that is, a microeconomic analysis that would allow us to construct a development policy for targeted sectors and industries, based on the needs of enterprises.

Influence on Past Development Strategies

The three examples that follow illustrate how macroeconomic policy was formulated without a production-based focus.

The first example is the strategy of import-substitution industrialization proposed by Raul Prebisch and the Economic Commission for Latin America, in which the state would act both as a productive agent in the economy and as a protector formulating economic policies.[3] The state was, among other things, to attract foreign investment into Latin American industry, stimulate and orient national investment, adopt wage policies aimed at boosting effective demand, and protect the internal market. These policies attempted to overcome the internal and external obstacles to industrialization (Palma 1978: 881–924).

Import-substitution industrialization confronted several contradictions that served to undermine its capacity to stimulate development because macroeconomic policy was formulated without a production-based focus. For instance, the activity of the state in attracting foreign investment allowed foreign firms to locate themselves behind Latin American tariff walls and take advantage of liberal tax and investment incentives. The Economic Commission for Latin America lacked vision about the kind of production it wanted to stimulate and therefore could not foresee the relocation of foreign firms as a problem. The state allowed foreign firms to enter Latin American industry partly because local capital was scarce but also because the Economic Commission for Latin America envisioned that capitalist investment would trigger growth, regardless of whether this was achieved with local or foreign capital.

The relocation of foreign firms hindered the development of local firms and debilitated the formation of forward and backward linkages in Latin American economies. Local production did not prosper, in part because foreign firms, subsidized by government, imported capital goods and intermediate products. In general terms, when local firms did produce and sell intermediate goods to foreign firms, they did not gain control over design and technological knowledge. Consequently, they became dependent on the foreign subsidiaries.

The second example is the export promotion strategy pursued by Puerto Rico, which built an economic development strategy based on a fiscal policy that granted tax incentives to attract the relocation of foreign manufacturing firms to the island and on government spending that provided the infrastructure and the labour training that these enterprises required. This strategy was complemented by an element of international trade policy, that is, export promotion based on the duty-free trade relation between Puerto Rico and the United States.

Like the import-substitution strategy, the export-promotion strategy also lacked an analysis at the micro level that would inform the design of macroeconomic policy. This strategy – initially known as Operation Bootstrap – was based on the logic of the 'Industrialization by Invitation' model. It concentrated on foreign-capital attraction – because local capital was scarce – and export promotion – because the local market was then too small to absorb the consequent increase in production. Later, the initiative was reformulated to attract heavy industries, by combining fiscal policy and financial incentives based principally on Section 931 and subsequently on Section 936 of the Federal Internal Revenue Code.

In the same manner as the import-substitution strategy, it hindered the development of local firms and debilitated the formation of forward and backward linkages. Moreover, it created a dependency on federal transfer payments that supported both the displaced population and the government bureaucracy that were the results of the strategy.

The third example is CARICOM's strategy of regional integration. CARI-COM's strategy was built upon the critique by Caribbean economists of the outcome of the Industrialization by Invitation model. It was also built upon their analysis of the structural and functional dependency to which the Caribbean was subjected.

CARICOM proposed a strategy based on a regional programme that delineated three areas of cooperation: cooperation in trade and production; functional cooperation in noneconomic areas such as education, health, transport, communications, energy, meteorology, science and technology; and coordination of foreign policy (Samuel 1989; Deere et al. 1990: 137). Regional cooperation in these three areas would allow Caribbean countries to overcome the limitations that small size and functional dependency imposed on their economies. This strategy combined some elements of international trade (an integrated regional market with a common external tariff, and the phasing out of nontariff trade barriers); fiscal policy (coordinated fiscal stabilization policies); and industrial policy (establishing integrated production arrangements) (Samuel 1989).

CARICOM promoted regional integration in production, structured around local capital. In that sense, it differed from the other two examples stated above. However, as with the other two cases, the macroeconomic policies of CARICOM were not founded on a concept of production, even when the similar productive structures of member countries made such formulation necessary. Moreover, CARICOM did not conceptualize alternative forms of production. It viewed mass production as providing to its firms the scale economies that would allow them to decrease costs and enhance competitiveness in the regional economy. Instead of seeking alternative forms of production to solve the constraint of market size, it sought a regional market to solve the production constraint (that is, the utilization of mass-production methods and scale economies). These limitations affected the outcome of CARICOM's initiative. These three examples briefly illustrate how Caribbean and Latin American countries have failed to articulate macroeconomic policies that integrate the micro level of analysis centred on a production-based approach.

Alternative

The design of a macroeconomic policy that is conceptually linked to a microeconomic concept of production can be approached by constructing a strategic industrial policy that integrates the micro and macro levels of analysis. The concept of strategic industrial policy differs from the concept of industrial policy.[4] A strategic industrial policy targets and centres around strategic industrial sectors, that is, those where local or international competitiveness can be attained by applying effective organizational and production concepts and that can be expected to fuel future economic growth.[5] Strategic industrial policy combines elements of fiscal, financial and international trade policy to respond to and foster the development of these strategic sectors and industries.

Strategic industrial policy focuses on production. It seeks to establish a dynamic production concept in the enterprises, in the associations formed between enterprises and in the extra-firm agencies that comprise a sector or industry. It characterizes functions within the firm – design, technology, production, work organization, management systems – and also those outside the firm, including market – labour, supplies, finance, consumption – and nonmarket – government, enterprise associations – in a way that will serve to promote the development of the strategic sectors and industries (Best 1990). A sector may include various practices between firms and extra-firm agencies, such as commercial associations, educational and training facilities, joint marketing agreements, regulating commissions, each of which facilitates co-operation between enterprises.

By focusing on sectors, strategic industrial policy allows for distinctions, such as types of sectors and forms of coordination within and between sectors, that inform industrial policy. Then an industrial strategy may be designed to emphasize those elements of macroeconomic policy pertinent to the sector or industry. The instruments of strategic industrial policy may range from access to foreign capital, imports, technology and licensing all the way to access to domestic credit, influence upon credit assignment in public and private banks, a particular taxation structure, and the authorization to form cartels that can constitute forms to legitimate elements of cooperation. By recognizing differentiation of sectors and industries, policy can address the problems that are rooted in the specificity of sectors and industries and thus become effective (Best 1990).

This argument pretends to explore whether, given the disarticulated nature of macroeconomic policy with respect to a concept of production, a strategic industrial policy could potentially generate a growth process in less developed countries of the Caribbean as it has achieved elsewhere (Japan, Italy, the Netherlands, Germany, among others) (Best 1990; Johnson 1982; Sengenberger, Loveman and Piore 1990).

The Production Versus Markets Discourse

Theoretical Limitation

In general terms, economic development policy and strategy are approached from a market and not from a production perspective at the micro, macro and international levels of analysis. That is to say, a micro analysis of a sector or industry focuses on demand, supply and product prices rather than on production. Similarly, an analysis at the international level becomes a tale of demand, supply and product prices among different countries. Consequently, the market discourse also permeates the discussion about integration, as the next section explains.

Influence on Present Development Strategies[6]

As a development strategy, almost everyone talks about the need to integrate our economies soon, as if something inevitable were about to occur. However, the alternative has been posed mostly in terms of the integration of markets, leaving unquestioned our vision of the form production will assume within these agreements. The discussion about the integration process is stated – at the level of the market – in terms of the need of concretizing an outward-oriented integration. Integration, then, means inserting Caribbean and Latin American countries in the world economy liberalizing trade within commercial blocs but continuing to stimulate export promotion strategies of industrializa-

460 / New Caribbean Thought

tion based on subsidiaries from the United States and mass production. In
these analyses, discussion centres on the characteristics of the import-export
structure of each country; on how the elimination of tariff and nontariff
barriers that allow or obstruct the 'liberalized' flow of goods, services, people
and capital will impact those structures; and on how the gradual elimination
of tariffs, local content requirements and technical-sanitary measures will
stimulate export growth in different sectors.

The analysis at the level of production is almost always excluded from the
debate on outward-oriented integration. Therefore, the impact of a trade
agreement on Caribbean industries is evaluated in terms of whether countries'
exports increased. If there was an increase in exports, then the conclusion is
reached that Caribbean countries benefited from the trade agreement. The
analysis at the market level does not specify which type and size of firm, form
of production, work organization, type of investment, source of capital and
industrial structure characterized the sector and industry responsible for the
export growth. This type of analysis does not reveal the type of production –
mass production – or enterprise – subcontractor, subsidiary – around which
investment in Caribbean countries is articulated. Considerations about which
corporation elaborated the products and what implications this production
had for regional development are ignored. Therefore, if foreign corporations
were displacing local producers, hindering the development of competitive
potential and adversely affecting the region, this would not be registered in the
analyses at the level of the market.

Recent analyses of regional integration differ from those formulated in the
1960s. Then, when integration was discussed, an analysis at the market level
was linked to one at the level of production (although the concept of production was not really discussed). Analysts postulated an inward-oriented integration, accompanied by an import-substitution programme and complemented
by national and regional production processes based on local capital, as the
preferred alternative.

At present, although many analysts recognize the need for regional
complementarity of production, it is unclear how such complementarity
should be structured. For instance: Around which type of firm and production should it be articulated? What role should foreign and local capital play
in that process? As a consequence, it seems possible to conceptualize
complementarity based on the coproduction concept of foreign corporations in the Caribbean instead of around a coproduction scheme of local
enterprises.

The above considerations have hindered the construction of a production-based approach to economic development. The primary development alternative is an outward oriented integration based on a market-level approach. The problem is that regional integration of markets that do not question the scheme of production is not a solution for us. The Caribbean Basin Initiative II, the North American Free Trade Agreement or, for that matter, the proposed Initiative for the Americas will not solve our problems.

Alternative

We must carry out analyses at the level of production. This implies using the sector and industry as entry points in an analysis that considers, among other elements, industrial structure, firm type and size, production and work organization, type of investment, and source of capital. In the case of integration, these analyses must be located within a similar analysis of the sector and industry at the international level, within an analysis of the new forms of production and investment at the international level, and within an analysis of what the restructuring of world trade rules, institutions, agreements and blocs means for less developed countries.

For instance, an analysis of the Caribbean apparel industry must be approached at the sector level. Such perspective would then integrate analyses at the firm and at the international levels. Only in this manner can a strategy which allows for a definition of a strategic industrial policy be articulated. If the Caribbean industrial structure is dominated by US subsidiaries using mass production for export, then a sector strategy built around local producers must identify how to obtain competitiveness against these mass producers in production and organization in order to gain international market shares. In order to achieve this, one must analyse how the production and organization of firms that constitute the sector are structured. What are the advantages and disadvantages of the local firms in terms of performance, as demonstrated by financial, operational and market indicators? How could alternative forms of production and organization enable these local firms to overcome the disadvantages they face and gain a competitive advantage? What are the growth sectors at the international level, given the new trade agreements where these local firms could obtain increasing market shares? What organizational forms, in accordance with the new types of investment, would be most appropriate to facilitate penetrating these growth sectors? How does the Uruguay Round

Agreement on Textiles and Clothing affect the future of the industry and promote or hinder the development of these local firms?

This type of analysis is necessary because, in a world of economic and commercial blocs, the economies that do not have strong local enterprises capable of positioning themselves in the world market or of articulating coproduction and codevelopment agreements with US or European firms to gain access to the blocs will confront growing competition from foreign enterprises or alliances of international enterprises. Within this context, the fundamental problem for the Caribbean is that, in general terms, it does not have enough local 'world class' enterprises or the competitive capacity to establish joint ventures with US firms in the United States or European firms in Europe. Then, it has to wait on the decisions of foreign subsidiaries that can decide whether they will relocate their operations to Mexico, Europe or any other country, and on the US and European governments on extending or offering access to the blocs. But since neither of these two things depend on Caribbean decision-making power, we have to sit and wait for those who make the decisions.

Furthermore, the Caribbean has to wait on these decisions given a panorama where integration in asymmetrical conditions can create economic, social and political instability for less developed countries (as exemplified in the Mexican case), and integration of regional markets, where countries have similar production structures, can aggravate competition among members and between members and nonmembers (as exemplified in the Caribbean Basin Initiative–North American Free Trade Agreement debate for parity).

The construction of a production-based approach to economic development based on sector and industry analysis, and the articulation of a strategic industrial policy, would offer concrete alternatives for the Caribbean. We must use this type of analysis to explore, industry by industry, how to compete internationally. In sum, the development discourse must be deconstructed and reconstructed around a production approach.

Large-Scale Mass Production as 'The Way' to Industrialize

Theoretical Limitation

Large-scale mass production has been portrayed in development theory as 'the way' to industrialize. Mass production combines the principle of interchangeability (American System of Manufactures), the principle of flow and scientific management to produce economies of time (Best 1990).[7] It depends on high fixed-cost technology (Lazonick 1993) and on 'big business' (Best 1990).[8]

Because it represents the shortest road to development, development strategies have been structured around large-scale mass production technologies on the grounds that it is more efficient – cost minimizing – than other alternative types of production and that the utilization of mass production technologies is historically and technologically necessary to attain national economic development.

Influence on Development Theory

In Latin America and the Caribbean, macroeconomic policy design and economic development strategy formulation have not been explicitly linked to production. However, policy design and strategy formulation have relied implicitly on the concept of mass production.

Since the 1960s, Latin American and Caribbean theorists and government officials have advocated industrialization strategies based on import substitution and export promotion. These strategies had as a foundation that large-scale mass production was both more efficient than alternative types of production and it was a historical and technological necessity for national economic development. Conceptually, these notions rested on the neoclassical microeconomic and macroeconomic foundations of economic development theory.

The neoclassical microeconomic theory of production presents large-scale mass production as the most efficient form of production. The neoclassical macroeconomic theory of economic growth does not explicitly present a production concept because it approaches economic growth in terms of increases in capital stocks. To the extent that it incorporates the constructs of neoclassical microeconomic and macroeconomic theory, economic development theory reproduces the same limitations in its conceptualization of production.

Socialist economic theory does not question the productivist logic of large-scale mass production as the most efficient form of production either. Assuming the dichotomy between the market and centralized planning, it presents the latter as the ideal way to organize the process of production, consumption and distribution in a society. Debate concerning the logic of production concepts is ignored because, like its neoclassical counterpart, it assumes that this is a technical problem.

Alternative

We will need to deconstruct the arguments used in neoclassical microeconomic theory as well as those used in growth and development theory to justify mass production as efficient and technologically and historically necessary. We will also need to analyse current debates concerning alternative concepts of production.

To approach the deconstruction of the arguments used in microeconomics, we must include a discussion about how mass production is not necessarily efficient; internal economies of scale do not necessarily make large-scale mass production inherently efficient; external economies of scale can generate the benefits associated with internal economies of scale and this can be achieved without being inherently linked to a size specification; high-fixed cost technology is not inherently cost minimizing; large volumes of output associated with mass production do not necessarily minimize costs; those sources of internal economies of scale that depend on the internalization of business functions under big business can be articulated through external economies of scale; and technology is a historical and social construct (see Aponte 1995 for a detailed analysis of these arguments). To approach the deconstruction of the arguments used in growth and development theory, we must include a discussion of growth and development theory as a social and economic process founded on concepts of production and of the firm. To approach a discussion of current debates[9] on alternative production concepts, we must include a discussion of how flexible production, alternative types of production, such as variable-cost systems and external economies-of-scale systems (see Aponte 1995 for a detailed analysis of these arguments), and alternative types of firms and entrepreneurship can be used to articulate economic development strategies.

Development Theory and the Enterprise[10]

Theoretical Limitation

In Latin America and the Caribbean, development theory has relied mostly on the neoclassical theory of the firm and on traditional notions of a successful firm. This approach has precluded a consideration of alternative forms of entrepreneurship and enterprise that current debates point towards, including popular and informal ones, as elements within a formulation of development theory.

In neoclassical theory, the firm is considered as a function of production that transforms inputs into final products. Production participants (subjects) and their subjectivities do not form part of this vision. The absence of subjects and subjectivities negates a theoretical space for the concept of entrepreneur and entrepreneurship. The suppression of the subject implies that the role of beliefs and purpose in human behaviour are reduced to the pursuit of individual action and interests and that the entrepreneur, the managers and the workers can not be conceptualized as a source of innovative ideas (Best 1990).

Neoclassical economics cannot conceptualize the firm as an economic development agent. As it constructs its analysis around the notion of equilibrium, neoclassical theory suppresses the concept of organization in a marginalist analysis and negates the concept of structural change (Best 1990). By suppressing the subject and subjectivity and negating structural change, neoclassical theory impedes us to approach entrepreneurship as an organizational concept capable of generating structural change (that is, economic development). Furthermore, neoclassical economics establishes a dichotomy between market and coordination inside the firm. Consequently, those relations that cannot be located within those spaces cannot be adequately conceptualized. These include, among others, practices that relate the home and market spaces, those located within the informal economy, and those that structure interfirm relations of cooperation that cannot be approached through the dichotomy.

Just as neoclassical theory is insufficient to approach the topic of entrepreneurship, the understanding of what should be an adequate and traditional setup for an enterprise also becomes problematic. For instance, the large enterprise, with corporate ownership, mass production, Taylorist work organization and a hierarchical organizational scheme of several management levels is, without a doubt, a recognized form of 'adequate' traditional entrepreneurship. Similarly, the small enterprise, with family ownership, low barriers to entry (in terms of skills, capital and organization), labour-intensive production (and obsolete technology), low productivity, and operating in unregulated markets has been looked upon, until recently, as an anachronic and unproductive agent in economic development theory (Peattie 1980 quoted in Portes and Schauffier 1993).

However, the definition of what is an adequate setup cannot be constructed around a specification of size, ownership, organization of production and work, or organizational and institutional form. In sum, entrepreneurship can not be circumscribed to the neoclassical conceptualization or to the understanding of what constitutes an adequate setup for an enterprise.

Influence on Future Development Strategy

Debate on development theory and the concept of the firm is necessary in order to articulate entrepreneurial alternatives within an economic development policy. The concept of the firm is unlinked to the concept of economic development in development theory. However, economic policy in Latin America and the Caribbean has tended – until recently – to view large enterprises that are mass producers as the axis of development. This has been the case in capitalist as well as in socialist countries. For instance, capitalist Caribbean countries have emphasized the attraction of large mass producers, mostly subsidiaries of the United States, to assemble or elaborate export goods. Socialist Caribbean countries have emphasized large state enterprises, which function on similar production principles, as the axis of development.

At present, however, capitalist as well as socialist Caribbean countries confront processes of restructuring that force them to redefine the concept of the firm within their economic development strategies. These restructuring processes are generated partly by the new processes of economic integration that make necessary the promotion of world-class enterprises and partly by the need for a new type of entrepreneurial organization compatible with flexible production. (The process in Cuba is also prompted by the economic restructuring brought about by the disappearance of the economy subsidized by the former Soviet bloc.) Within the present situation, a space has been created for the small and medium enterprise as a generator of this development process. However, in order to conceptualize future dynamic forms, it is necessary to take off from the points of debate stated earlier.

Alternative

To approach the study of development economics and alternative enterprise, it is necessary to go beyond traditional notions of the firm and of the 'formal' economy. This approach would comprehend the subjects who articulate entrepreneurship from within traditional spaces (the formal economy), around institutionalized practices (formally established enterprises) or around traditional subjectivities (for example, family enterprises, proprietorships, small and medium enterprises). It would also have to include the subjects who articulate entrepreneurial initiatives from within alternative spaces (the home or the informal economy), around alternative practices (noninstitutionalized) or around different subjectivities (for example, communities) (see Aponte and Alvarez 1997).

Furthermore, development theory would need to incorporate concepts that would: (1) integrate notions of entrepreneurship, organizational theory, culture and the internal dynamics of the firm; (2) link form of organization and type of production with production performance; (3) present ideas on the innovative enterprise, the new virtual organization, the firm with decentralized structures and horizontal management, the firm with labour democracy, and green economics; (4) focus on structural changes and not in equilibrium processes (Best 1990); (5) establish relations among enterprises and spaces that transcend the dichotomy pointed out earlier; and (6) incorporate the informal economy.

Conclusion

This chapter has presented some reflections on four topics that would necessarily be part of the agenda for the deconstruction–reconstruction of Latin American and Caribbean development theory and policy. It has explored four areas where we can both observe limitations of economic theory and replication of development policy. For each area, I stated how a limitation of a concept of production or the firm in economic theory has influenced development policy, either historically or within the current regional integration context. I argued for alternative approaches in each of these four areas, in the spirit of the deconstruction–reconstruction of theory.

Notes

1. This is a condensed and updated version of some of the arguments put forth in Aponte and Alvarez 1999 and Aponte 1995.
2. Macroeconomic policy can be designed in four areas: fiscal, international trade, monetarist and financial, and industrial. Each one of the four areas of macroeconomic policy is founded on a theoretical approach and contains some instruments or tools of analysis that are used when implementing the formulation of economic policy.

3. The work of Raul Prebisch presented a critique of international trade theory and formulated an alternative economic policy – import substitution – founded on this critique and built on a Keynesian framework.

4. In general terms, industrial policy literature justifies governmental intervention to promote certain industries in situations where market failures, such as oligopoly or monopoly, external economies or public goods, natural monopolies, common access to environmental resources, imperfect markets, incomplete information, individual behaviour that is not optimizable and taxation schemes that do not propitiate efficiency exist (Krugman 1994). As such, this type of analysis is founded upon a neoclassical interpretation that limits the concept of industrial policy to a series of macroeconomic policies, such as tax concessions, participation in research and development, and so on, by which governments may attempt to correct such inefficiencies.

5. Other criteria, such as local added value, volume of employment created, potential future economic growth and so on, may be used to select targeted industries.

6. This is a condensed and updated version of the arguments presented in Aponte 1992: 6–7.

7. The American System of Manufactures combined the use of machine tools and precision instruments to produce interchangeable parts. The principle of flow reduced unit costs by increasing the speed and volume of throughput in a sequential machine layout. Scientific management reorganized the division of labour within the enterprise by separating the planning, which was the prerogative of managers, from the doing, which was the activity of workers (Best 1990; Marglin 1974). Scientific management increased the velocity of throughput and lowered unit labour costs in two complementary ways: first, by intensifying the speed at which workers could handle materials, and second, by decreasing the time for a product to be machined.

8. Big business created a multidivisional structure and a managerial hierarchy to coordinate production and distribution in diverse product lines scattered throughout multiple geographical areas and financed, through equity, the capital needs of large-scale operations. It paved the way for the appearance of the multidivisional corporation and the new managerial class.

9. These debates present some concepts that could serve to structure alternative forms of production in the Caribbean. For instance, flexible production has been applied successfully in Japan, the Asiatic tigers, Italy, and other European countries. Flexible production, as a form of production, offers some advantages for Caribbean countries. Among these advantages we have the following: production may be successful at volumes more attuned to the size limitation of the small economies of the Caribbean; and it is possible to innovate and design continuously, without having to invest large sums to acquire technology in order to compete in international markets. The alternative our countries confront is to articulate a new type of competition around flexible production, restructuring their concept of the enterprise.

10. Some of the ideas presented here are developed more fully in Aponte and Alvarez 1997.

References

Aponte, Maribel. 1992. "The run to integrate". *International Report* 10, no. 3 (November).

Aponte, Maribel. 1995. "Caribbean and Latin American economic development strategy: Theoretical deconstruction within the regional integration context". In *Postintegration Development in the Caribbean,* edited by Maribel Aponte and Carmen Gautier Mayoral. Rio Piedras: University of Puerto Rico Center for Social Research.

Aponte, Maribel, and Carlos Alvarez. 1997. "La empresariedad popular en Puerto Rico: Sujetos, gestiones, y espacios". Manuscript.

Aponte, Maribel and Carlos Alvarez. 1999. "Política industrial estratégica, producción y empresas en Puerto Rico". In *Futuro Económico de Puerto Rico: Antología de Ensayos del Proyecto Universitario Sobre el Futuro Económico de Puerto Rico,* comp. E. Martínez. Rio Piedras: Editorial de la Universidad de Puerto Rico.

Best, M. 1990. *The New Competition: Institutions of Industrial Restructuring.* Cambridge, Mass.: Harvard University Press.

de Soto, H. 1989. *The Other Path,* translated by June Abbot. New York: Harper and Row.

Deere, C., E. Melendez, P. Antropus, L. Bolles, and M. Rivera. 1990. *In the Shadows of the Sun: Caribbean Development.* Colorado: Boulder Press.

Emeagwali, G. 1995. *Women Pay the Price: Structural Adjustment in Africa and the Caribbean.* Trenton, NJ: Africa World Press.

Green, D. 1995. *Silent Revolution: the Rise of Market Economics in Latin America.* London: Cassell and Latin America Bureau.

Hoogvelt, A. 1997. *Globalization and the Postcolonial World: The New Political Economy of Development.* Baltimore: Johns Hopkins University Press.

Johnson, C. 1982. *MITI and the Japanese Miracle.* Stanford: Stanford University Press.

Krugman, Paul. 1994. *Economía Internacional, Teoría y Política,* 2d ed. Spain: McGraw Hill.

Krugman, P. 1996. *Pop Internationalism.* Cambridge, Mass.: Massachusetts Institute of Technology.

Lazonick, W. 1993. *Business Organization and the Myth of the Market Economy.* Cambridge: Cambridge University Press.

Lehmann, David. 1990. *Democracy and Development in Latin America.* Cambridge: Polity Press.

Marglin, S. 1974. "What do bosses do? The origins and functions of hierarchy in capitalist production". *Review of Radical Political Economics* 6 (Summer).

Palma, G. 1978. "Dependency: A formal theory of underdevelopment or a methodology for the analysis of concrete situations of underdevelopment?" *World Development* 6.

Portes, A., Carlos Dore-Cabral, and P. Landolt. 1997. *The Urban Caribbean: Transition to the New Global Economy.* Baltimore: Johns Hopkins University Press.

Portes, A., and R. Schauffier. 1993. "Competing perspectives on the Latin American informal economy". *Population and Development Review* 19 (March).

Pyke, F., and W. Sengenberger. 1992. *Industrial Districts and Local Economic Regeneration.* Geneva: International Institute for Labour Studies.

Samuel, W. 1989. "An assessment of the CARICOM integration experience". In *Development in Suspense,* edited by G. Beckford and N. Girvan. Kingston, Jamaica: Friedrich Ebert Siftung.

Sengenberger, W., G. Loveman, and M. Piore. 1990. *The Reemergence of Small Enterprises. Industrial Restructuring in Industrialised Countries.* Geneva: International Institute for Labour Studies.

Sunkel, Osvaldo, ed. 1993. *Development from Within: Toward a Neostructuralist Approach for Latin America.* Boulder: Lynne Rienner.

van der Borgh, C. 1996. "Una comparación de cuatro modelos contemporáneos de desarrollo en América Latina". *Revista ECA.*

18

Revisionist Ontologies
Theorizing White Supremacy

CHARLES W. MILLS

Political Philosophy and Race

The black philosopher (a small category)[1] or the black Caribbean philosopher (an even smaller one) in North American institutions faces a problematic and paradoxical situation. On the one hand, he or she (usually he) comes out of a history rich in issues and ideologies that would seem to cry out for philosophical investigation: race, culture, identity, existential crisis, pan-Africanism, Garveyism, Negritude, Rastafari. On the other hand, if he or she has been educated within the dominant Anglo-American analytic school, he or she has been trained in a tradition for which these issues are invisible.[2] Race has long been extensively discussed within political science, anthropology and sociology, of course; and in the last decade or so, with the challenge to the core curriculum, there has been an astonishing boom within cultural studies of the analysis of white-supremacist and colonial discourses, involving representations of nonwhites and the Third World. But philosophy, the 'queen of the sciences' in one famous formulation, is, for the most part, regally detached from this rainbowed multiculturalist bustle, gaze serenely fixed on the metaphysical distances, apparently contemplating what one writer tellingly, if maliciously, describes as "the unbearable whiteness of being" (Romano 1993). Even political philosophy, whose this-worldliness would seem to make it most congenial to discussions of the significance of race, has little to say on the subject. Most historical anthologies restrict their contents to the traditional European figures, and an otherwise excellent recent introduction to *Contemporary Political Philosophy* by one of the leading young scholars in the field is unfortunately typical in having no systematic analysis at all of race, though feminist theory gets a whole chapter (Kymlicka 1990).

So the result, especially for non-white Third Worlders teaching at white First World philosophy departments like myself, may often be an uncomfortable kind of dichotomization both in one's teaching and one's research projects. One teaches regular philosophy courses – and then, as I have done, one *also* teaches a course in Caribbean Studies, or in African American Philosophy. One publishes on 'respectable' subjects in established mainstream philosophy journals – and then one *also* pursues one's black or Third World research interests, destined for eventual publication in Caribbean journals and edited collections. There may even be, as in my own case, and in the case of an African friend of mine, a conscious adoption of a two-track policy, in which (at least for the first few years out of graduate school) 'black' publications are carefully paired with 'white' publications (1:1, or, for the more cautious, 1:2 or even 1:3). In effect, it is as if one always has a wary eye out for potential First World evaluators and referees, trying to assuage their concerns in advance: "I may seem to be doing some weird stuff on the side, but really, it's OK, because, as you can see, I *am* able to get into the journals you know on the subjects you recognize."

The question is, though: Why should this be necessary? Why should these black/Caribbean/Third World issues (see, for example, LaGuerre 1982) not be incorporable into a history of modern political philosophy course on Hobbes, Locke, Rousseau, Kant, Mill, Marx, or a contemporary thematic course that looks at contractarianism and communitarianism, welfare liberalism and *laissez-faire* libertarianism, at Rawls, Nozick, Walzer, Sandel? Why should there be this ghettoization of the Third World, as if it were really on a separate planet rather than being very much a part of one world interconnected with and foundationally shaped by the very region studied by First World theory? What exactly is it about the way political philosophy has developed that encourages this kind of intellectual segregation?

I think the problem in part involves a kind of exclusionary theoretical dynamic, in that the presuppositions of the world of mainstream theory offer no ready point of ingress, no conceptual entrée, for the issues of race and culture that typically preoccupy much of Third World theory. (The issues of Third World poverty and economic underdevelopment, on the other hand, *can* be handled – if the will exists – within the framework of discussions of international justice, through an expansion of moral concern beyond the boundaries of the First World nation state.) The assumptions are so different that one may seem to be caught between two heterogeneous intellectual universes, with no ready way of translating the concerns of the one across the boundaries of the other. And where racism in European thought *is* mentioned, the discussion is usually limited to the writings of marginal theorists such as Gobineau; the biases in the views of the central figures in the pantheon are not examined.

So typically, what one gets (in so far as any effort is made at all) is an attempt to piggyback the problem of race on to the body of respectable theory. For example, one looks at racism as a *violation* of the ideals of liberal individualist ideology, or one tries to *explain* race and racism within a Marxist paradigm. But race is still really an afterthought in such deployments, a category theoretically residual. That is, one is starting from a pre-existing conceptual framework – an overall characterization of the system ('constitutionalist liberal democracy', 'capitalism'), a set of large-scale and small-scale theories about how this system works, or should work, and an array of corresponding concepts – and then trying to articulate race to this framework.

Unsurprisingly, then, there is usually something unsatisfactory about these efforts. I want to propose an alternative approach as an innovation in political philosophy. Suppose instead we try something different and place race at the centre stage rather than at the wings of our theory. The idea here would be to follow in philosophy the example of those feminists of the 1970s once characterized as 'radical' (as against 'liberal' or 'Marxist') (Jaggar 1983), who – themselves inspired by the US black liberation movement – decided to put gender at the centre of their theorizing and appropriated the term 'patriarchy', correspondingly, to describe a system of male domination. So rather than starting from some other theory and then trying to smuggle in gender, one begins from the fact of gender subordination itself.

There are, of course, crucial disanalogies that need to be noted. For one thing, gender as a system of power has been seen by some as practically universal, and dates back, if not to the origins of the species, at least to an age thousands of years before our own time, whereas white domination is clearly a product of the modern period. Moreover, many radical feminists appeal to varieties of biological determinism to explain patriarchy and regard it as the source of all other oppressions, claims I would certainly not make for race. But with these and other caveats registered, it would still seem that one could fruitfully consider race itself as a political system. So we would treat this as a particular mode of domination, with its special norms for allocating benefits and burdens, rights and duties, its own ideology, and an internal logic at least semiautonomous, influencing law, culture and consciousness.

We could use the term 'white supremacy' to conceptualize this system. The term is currently employed in a much more restricted sense, for example, to describe the regimes of the American Old South and apartheid South Africa (Fredrickson 1981). But what I am suggesting is a more latitudinarian conception, encompassing de facto as well as de jure white privilege, that would refer more broadly to the European domination of the planet for the past several hundred years that has left us with the racialized distributions of economic, political and cultural power that we have today. We could call this global white supremacy (Kiernan 1981; Said 1993). And the idea would then be to locate *both* oppositional black/Third World theory *and* establishment white/First World theory in the conceptual space brought into being by recognizing this expanded political universe. From this perspective, I suggest, we would then be able to appreciate that black and Third World theory have characteristically been concerned to map the *whole* of this system, while mainstream theory has pre-eminently been focused on a very limited section of it, with the rest of the world either ignored or squeezed awkwardly into the categories developed for this restricted mapping.

Global White Supremacy as a Political System: Replies to Objections

Now this notion of global white supremacy may seem immediately problematic, so I want to go through some of the possible objections that might be raised to it.

First, there might be the friendly amendment that we already *have* a politico-economic term with the same approximate referent, in the form, say, of 'imperialism' or 'colonial capitalism'. But in the first place, of course, this is not true, because these terms are not usually taken to apply (apart from upholders of variants of the 'internal colonialism' thesis) to the *internal* politics of the white settler states such as the United States and Australia, or the Iberian colonies in the Americas, which became independent at a relatively early stage. Moreover, colonial capitalism is by definition restricted to the period of formal colonial rule, whereas, as indicated, I want to argue that in a weaker sense white supremacy continues to exist into the postcolonial period today. In the second place, and perhaps more importantly, these terms are, for my purposes, not sufficiently focused on the *racial* dimension of European domination. Both in the standard liberal and the standard Marxist analyses of imperialism there has been an economism that fails to do theoretical justice to race, with race being seen as an irrelevancy to the ontology of the liberal individual or the class membership of workers and capitalists. But the racial nature of the system is precisely what we want to highlight. As Gordon Lewis (1983) has pointed out in his magisterial study of Caribbean ideologies:

The Caribbean society, in sum, was not only a mercantilist-based capitalist society. It was also a racist society. Racial insult was added to economic injury. That explains why a theory of economic exploitation alone – of which there is a substantial literature by Caribbean authors of the Marxist persuasion – is insufficient to explain the totality of Caribbean exploitation . . . It was two dimensional. And the racial exploitation left behind it deep psychic wounds quite different in character and quality from those derived from economic-class exploitation. (6–7)

Still in the spirit of a friendly amendment, it might then be argued that, in that case, 'racism' or 'white racism' is the term appropriate to the conceptual task. My response here is, first of all, that after decades of divergent use and sometimes abuse, the term is now so fuzzy, with such a semantic penumbra of unwelcome associations surrounding it, that unless a formal definition is given, no clear denotation can be readily attached to 'racism' or 'white racism'. Second, one of the crucial ambiguities in its usage is precisely that between racism as a complex of ideas, values and attitudes, and racism as an institution-alized politico-economic structure for which the ideas are an ideological accompaniment. If the term 'white racism' were consistently employed in the latter sense, then we might not need another locution, but this is not at all the case. On the contrary, it is usually the *ideational* sense that is meant. And this has the theoretical disadvantage of making it possible for everybody to be 'racist', in a Hobbesian scenario of equipowerful atomic individuals with bad attitudes, thereby deflecting attention away from the massive power differentials actually obtaining in the real world between non-white individuals with bigoted ideas and institutionalized white power. 'White supremacy' and 'global white supremacy', on the other hand, have the semantic virtues of clearly signalling that one is referring to a *system,* a particular kind of polity, which is structured so as to advantage whites.

A more hostile objection might be that to speak of 'white supremacy' as a political system necessarily implies its complete autonomy and explanatory independence from other variables. But I do not see why this follows. The origins of white racism as an elaborated complex of ideas (as against a spontaneous set of naive prejudices) continue to be debated by scholars, with various rival theories – ethnocentrism on a grand scale, religio-culturalist predispositions, the ideology of expansionist colonial capitalism, the rationalizations of psychosexual aversions, calculated rational-choice power politics – contending for eminence. We do not need to make a commitment as to the truth of any of these theories; rather, we can just be agnostic on the question, bracketing the issue, and leaving it open as to which explanation, or complementary set of explanations, turns out to be most adequate. All that is required is that, whatever the origins of racism and the politico-economic system of white supremacy, they are conceded to have attained at least a partial, relative autonomy, so that they are not immediately reducible to something else.

Correspondingly, it is not being claimed that to speak of white supremacy as a political system implies that this *exhausts* the political universe. The idea is not that white supremacy must now replace previous political categorizations but that it should *supplement* them. In other words, it is possible to have overlapping, interlocking, intersecting, systems of domination. The argument is – in the same way that feminist theorists have convincingly shown that, no matter what their other differences, existing polities have *also* been patriarchies – that the globally dominant political regimes in the West for the past few hundred years have *also* been white-supremacist states. Utilizing the concept of white supremacy focuses our attention on the dimension of racial oppression in these systems; it is not being claimed that this is the *only* dimension. In some contexts, the focus on race will be illuminating, while in other contexts it will not be. So the idea is to correct the characteristic methodological omissions of the past and present, not to prescribe an exclusivist theoretical attention just to this one aspect of the polity.

Nor does use of the term imply that white supremacy is either synchronically uniform or diachronically static. There will be different forms of white supremacy in different parts of the world – native expropriation and enclosure on reservations here, slavery and colonial rule there, formal segregation and antimiscegenation laws in one place, mixing and intermarriage in another. The privileging of whites is compatible with a wide variety of political and institutional structures: it is this privileging that is the key element. Similarly, the depiction of non-whites within the system can vary tremendously – from exterminable savage to colonial ward to second-class citizen – without this threatening the crucial premise of non-white inferiority.

Moreover, white supremacy evolves over time, in part precisely because of the other systems to which it is articulated, in part because of the political struggles against it of non-whites themselves. So in a detailed treatment, one would need to develop a periodization of different forms, with one obvious line of temporal demarcation being that between the epoch of *formal* white supremacy (paradigmatically represented by the legality of European colonialism and African slavery) and the present epoch of de facto white supremacy (the aftermath of slavery and decolonization, with formal juridical equality guaranteed for whites and non-whites). The basic point, then, is that it would be a mistake to identify one *particular* form of white supremacy (for example, slavery, juridical segregation) with white supremacy as a family of types and then argue from the nonexistence of *this* form that white supremacy no longer exists. The changing nature of the system implies that different racial organizations of labour, dominant cultural representations and evolving legal standings are to be expected.

This would also pre-empt the objection that if global white supremacy ever existed, it is now clearly long past, since – especially with the recent demise of apartheid in South Africa – we live in a world where yellows, browns and blacks rule their own countries, and non-whites in First World 'white' nations are no longer formally subjugated. The answers would be: first, even if global white supremacy were completely a thing of the past, it would still be a political system of historical interest. Second, even if there were complete good faith on the part of whites about the desirability of abolishing this system, the comparative historic recency of its *formal* demise (slavery in the Americas ended only a century to a century and a half ago, while global decolonization and desegregation in the United States are essentially postwar phenomena) would mean that it would continue to affect the New World for a long time to come simply through institutional momentum and unconscious attitudinal lag. Third, of course, it is clearly politically naive to argue from the mere fact of the abolition of de jure racial subordination to the reality of genuine de facto equalization, and to conclusions about the genuine commitment of all or most whites to relinquish their historic racial privileges. An objective look at the world today shows that independent Third World nations are part of a global economy dominated by white capital and white international lending institutions; that the planet as a whole is dominated by the cultural products of the white West; that within many First World nations there has been a resurgence of racism, including biologically determinist ideas once thought to have been definitively discredited with the collapse of Nazi Germany; and that, in general, the dark-skinned races of the world, particularly blacks and native peoples, continue to be at or near the bottom of the socioeconomic ladder in both metropolitan and Third World polities.

So a case can easily be made that white supremacy continues to exist in a different form, no longer backed by law, but now maintained through inherited patterns of discrimination, exclusionary racial bonding, differential white power deriving from consolidated economic privilege, and so on.[3] Thus Kimberle Crenshaw (1988) emphasizes (with specific reference to the United States, though I would claim the point is more generally valid) the importance of distinguishing between "the mere rejection of white supremacy as a normative vision" and "a societal commitment to the eradication of the substantive conditions of Black subordination": "[A] society once expressly organized around white supremacist principles does not cease to be a white supremacist society simply by formally rejecting those principles. The society remains white supremacist in its maintenance of the actual distribution of goods and resources, status, and prestige" (1336). Indeed, in the United States, the disappointment of the hopes raised for genuine black inclusion in the polity by the formal victories over 'Jim Crow' segregation in the 1950s and 1960s has led some black Americans to begin to speak pessimistically of "the permanence of racism" (Bell 1992).

A different kind of objection might be not to the principle of the notion of race as a political system but to the details, that is, to the 'white' in 'global white supremacy'. The racial rules in the United States basically dichotomize the polity according to the 'one drop' principle by which any black descent makes you black. But elsewhere, particularly in our own region of the Caribbean and Central and South America, there is a more complicated ladder, with many rungs rather than just two. Moreover, in the postcolonial period, there is at least a partial transition in which 'browns' come to rule rather than just whites. I think the response here would have to be as follows:

1. The colour and shade hierarchies in these countries (for example, the former slave states of the West) have themselves been established by global white supremacy, in that ascent up the ladder strongly correlates with a greater degree of white ancestry and a greater degree of assimilation to

European culture, so that these systems are essentially derivative, and would still need to be related to it.

2. Though in many of these countries 'browns' govern, economic power often continues to be controlled by a white corporate elite, whose presence and interests constrain the dimensions of the political space in which browns can operate, thus delimiting the real possibilities for independent action and the democratizing of racial access to socioeconomic opportunities.

3. In addition, as mentioned, the larger world – the global economy, the international financial institutions – is dominated by First World powers that (except for Japan) are themselves white, and thus linked by various political, economic and cultural ties to local whites, thus differentially privileging them.

Another objection might be to the imagined theoretical presuppositions of such a notion. The invocation of 'race' as explanatory in politics has historically been most strongly associated with discourses (nineteenth and twentieth century imperialism; Nazism) explicitly predicated on biologically determinist assumptions (Social Darwinism; *Rassenwissenschaft*). These bodies of thought were, of course, officially (though never completely or thoroughly) discredited with the collapse of the Third Reich and postwar decolonization. The widespread employment of a racialized discourse in oppositional popular black and Third World theory may then be assimilated by hostile critics to racist theorizing of this kind, even if the charge is sometimes softened by the prefatory 'reverse racism' or 'antiracist racism'.

But this pre-emptive rejection of race as a respectable theoretical category is illegitimate, because the dichotomization between a mainstream methodology (liberal or radical) that is largely insensitive to race and a racial determinism with ludicrous pseudoscientific assumptions (whites as evil 'ice people' driven to dominate the planet) does not exhaust the actual alternatives. A growing body of literature is beginning to recognize both the *reality* (causal significance, theoretical centrality) and the *politicality* (socially constructed nature) of race. It is not the case, in other words, that a focus on race, white supremacy, and corresponding 'white' psychology necessarily commits one to racist assumptions *about* whites, though admittedly lay thought will not always make these distinctions. So although I said earlier that I wanted to bracket and suspend the question of theoretical explanations for racism, I am at least theoretically committed to the extent of seeing race in *constructivist* rather than biologistic terms.

For 'whiteness' is not natural; rather, infants of a certain genealogy or phenotype growing up in a racist society have to *learn* to be white. Correspondingly, there have always been principled and morally praiseworthy whites – those sometimes termed 'white renegades' – who have thrown off their socialization and challenged white supremacy, whether as imperialism, slavery, segregation or apartheid, in the name of a colour-blind humanity. So these could be described as whites who have rejected 'Whiteness'. The important point is, then, that – as 'race men' have always appreciated – a racial perspective on society can provide insights to be found neither in a white liberalism nor a white Marxism, and, when suitably modified and reconstructed, such a perspective need not imply biological generalizations about whites or commit the obvious moral error of holding people responsible for something (genealogy or phenotype) they cannot help.

A specifically Left objection, correspondingly, might be that to see 'race' as theoretically central really implies a return to a pre-Marxist conception of the social order and ignores class.

To begin with, of course, in the largely postcommunist world at the start of the twenty-first century, the explanatory credentials of Marxism are hardly unchallengeable. But in any case, as noted above, the conception of race presupposed is a constructivist one, which *does* leave open the possibility that a convincing historical materialist account of the creation of global white supremacy can be developed. Making race central does not mean making race *foundational*; it just means taking seriously the idea of an at least partially autonomous racial political system. (For those with Left sympathies, the traditional explanatory route will be through the European conquest, the imposition of regimes of superexploitation on indigenous and imported populations, and the differential *motivation* and cultural/ideational *power* of local and metropolitan ruling classes to ensure that 'race' crystallizes as an overriding social identity stabilizing the resultant system [Roediger 1991; Allen 1994].)

Nor does the notion of white supremacy imply that there are no class differences within the white and non-white populations, or that *all* whites are materially better off than all non-whites. The implication is rather that whites are differentially privileged *as a group*, which is compatible with the existence of poor whites and rich non-whites. It also leaves it open for the Marxist case to be made that, in the long term, white supremacy is of greater political and economic benefit to the white elite than the white working class, and that though by the baseline of existing white-supremacist capitalism, white workers are better off than non-whites, they are poorer than they would be in a *non*racial order. Since white supremacy is not being put forward as denoting a comprehensive political system, it does not, as earlier emphasized, preclude there being *other* systems of domination (class, gender and so on).

Finally, it might be objected that the concept – 'global white supremacy' – is pitched at a level of abstraction too high to be useful. But one has to differentiate appropriate realms of investigation. Capitalism as a concept has obviously been found useful by many generations of thinkers, both lay and academic, as a general way of categorizing a certain kind of politico-economic system with a core of characteristic traits, despite the fact that there are evidently vast differences between the capitalism of a century ago and the capitalism of today, or the capitalist systems of Japan, the United States and Jamaica. For detailed case studies, one must, of course, descend empirically to the investigative level of the political scientist, the economist, the sociologist. But for the purposes outlined above – that of supplementing the conceptual apparatus of the political philosopher – this distance from empirical detail does not seem to me to be problematic. At this level, what one is concerned with is the general logic of the abstract system, the overarching commonalities of racial subordination between, say, colonial Kenya and independent Australia, slave Brazil and the postbellum United States, that warrant the subsumption of these radically different polities under a general category. 'White supremacy' captures these usually ignored racial realities, and it is on this basis that I would argue that it should take its rightful place in the official vocabulary of political theory along with other political abstractions such as absolutism, democracy, capitalism, fascism, patriarchy.

In conclusion, having considered all these objections, it should be noted that the great virtue of this account is that race is no longer residual, a concern to be awkwardly shoehorned into the structure of a theory preoccupied with other realities, but central. And by virtue of the social-systemic rather than ideational focus, it directs our theoretical attention to the important thing, which is how racial membership privileges or disadvantages one *independently* of the particular ideas one happens to have. (In that qualified sense, race is 'objective'. Even white renegades need to face the fact that, no matter what their racial politics, they will be privileged by their social classification.) The attitudinal and atomic-individualist focus of at least some varieties of liberalism reduces the issue to bigotry which needs to be purged through moral exhortation; the class-reductivist focus of at least some varieties of Marxism reduces the issue to the imposition of a variant of ruling-class ideology which needs to be purged through recognition of class identity. In neither case is there an adequate recognition of the fact that the system under scrutiny is *also* a racial one with its own dynamism and autonomy, its own peculiar social ontology.

Moreover, whereas Marxism's claims about the intrinsically exploitative character of capitalism, and the viability and attractiveness of socialism as a solution, have always been – and are now more than ever – highly controversial, all good liberals should oppose racism. So if, as many would now argue, the events of the last decade have conclusively demonstrated that capitalism is the only feasible option for humanity, then what one wants is a capitalism that lives up to its advertising. Liberals as well as radicals should therefore enthusiastically *endorse,* rather than raising objections to, the analysis and exposure of global white supremacy as a political system, since this is clearly in contravention to the ideal of a colour-neutral, racially accessible market society. The Marxist anticapitalist project is currently of limited appeal, but in theory, at least, one would like to think that *all* people of good will would support the critique and ultimate elimination of white supremacy, including the whites privileged by it.

The Politics of Personhood

Let us suppose, then, that this is accepted as a useful concept that needs to be taken account of by orthodox political philosophy. How would mainstream theory then have to be transformed to take race – that is, global white supremacy – seriously in its conventional discourses? What would it mean for the standard terminology, scenarios, frames of reference, characteristic terms and favourite preoccupations of Western political philosophy? What new phenomena would come into theoretical view? What old phenomena would have to be transformed?

Now obviously there are many ways to approach these questions, but the issue I am going to focus on, which I believe to be the key to many of the others, is that of *personhood.* As stated most eloquently in the writings of Kant, persons are rational self-directing entities whose rights must be respected and who must be treated as ends-in-themselves rather than merely instrumentally (Kant 1964). Kant here is the philosophical spokesman for the Enlightenment moral and political egalitarianism that ushers in the modern epoch. Thus in the bourgeois revolutions, American and French, that resonate around the world, it is classically stated that "We hold these truths to be self-evident, that all men are created equal." So by contrast, with ancient and medieval hierarchies, the starting point is the freedom and equality of all men (*sic*). (Feminist theorists, of course, have long since demonstrated that the 'men' in these theories are indeed male rather than gender-neutral 'persons'. See, for example, Okin 1979 and Clark and Lange 1979.)

The social contract tradition that dominates political theory over the period (1650–1800: Hobbes, Locke, Rousseau, Kant) begins from a social ontology of the equality of (those counted as) persons, and though contractarianism then disappears for the next century and a half (to be surprisingly revived by John Rawls' *A Theory of Justice* [1971]), this equality is henceforth installed as the normative ground floor of the edifice of Western political philosophy. All humans within the scope of the theory are persons, and the preoccupations of First World theory then centre on different theories of justice, competing constitutional models, rival economic arrangements and the like, for this population.

What difference does taking race seriously intrude into this picture? Basically, it directs our attention to what is happening *beneath* the 'normative ground floor', in (so to speak) the moral/political basement. My argument is essentially that for most of Enlightenment First World political theory, what seems like a *neutral* starting point, which begs no questions, is actually *already* normatively loaded, in that the population of 'persons' has been overtly or covertly defined so as to really be coextensive with the white (male) population. They are the respectable occupants of the building. So in the period of de jure global white supremacy (European colonial rule, African slavery), the scope of European normative theories will usually extend just to Europeans at home and abroad. That is, there will be theories about the rights, liberties and privileges of 'all men', which are really intended to apply only to 'all white men', non-whites being in the moral basement which is covered by a *different* set of rules.

The present period of de facto global white supremacy is characterized by a more complicated normative arrangement, in which there is an *abstract/formal* extension of previously colour-coded principles to the non-white population, but genuine equality is pre-empted by, for example, lack of enforcement mechanisms, failure to allocate the necessary resources for implementation of the law, evasion of juridical proscriptions by legal manoeuvrings,[4] and the continuing consequences of those ethno-class concentrations of economic power that in a capitalist economy violate no law in the first place. Thus while such an extension is a real normative advance, by no means to be downplayed, it will not constitute a genuine challenge to white supremacy unless and until the means to correct for the effects of past racial subordination are included in the rewriting. And this will require, *inter alia,* a frontal recognition of the white-supremacist nature of the polity in its various manifestations.

To take Rawls as an example: even if (as he does) Rawls (1971) declares race to be morally irrelevant to personhood, knowledge of which is accordingly stripped from us by the veil of ignorance, this will not be sufficient in the real life, *non*ideal polity of the United States to redress past inequities. Failure to pay theoretical attention to this history will then just reproduce past domination. In other words, one does not confront white supremacy by ignoring it, since this will just incorporate it, through silence, into the conceptual apparatus. One is then beginning from a starting point that is *not* neutral but biased in ways about which the theory is silent, thereby guaranteeing that these systemic inequities will not be addressed and that the measures objectively necessary to achieve genuine equality will not become theoretically visible. (Compare Okin on the illusory, merely 'terminological' gender neutrality of most contemporary political theory, such as that of Rawls, and the need to develop concepts sensitized to the specific situation of women in the *non*ideal family, for example to reflect the ways in which women are made "vulnerable by marriage" [Okin 1989: esp. chaps. 1, 7].)

A more realistic starting point, which takes white supremacy into account, would therefore not be the abstract egalitarian Kantian ontology (Figure 18.1a), but what I have called elsewhere the dark ontology of *Herrenvolk* Kantianism (Mills 1994b). (The term is inspired by Pierre van den Berghe's description of the white settler states such as the United States, Australia and South Africa as "*Herrenvolk* democracies", polities that are democratic for the master race, the *Herrenvolk,* but not the subordinate race[s] [van den Berghe 1967].) Here the political population is explicitly characterized as it actually is, that is, as a two-tiered, morally partitioned population divided between white 'persons' and non-white 'subpersons' (Figure 18.1b).[5]

From this cognitively advantaged perspective – the view from the basement – First World political theory can then be seen for what it is, that is, primarily the limited theorizing of the privileged 'person' subset of the population about itself. For those in this tier, personhood is not in contention in any way; personhood is taken for *granted,* so that in the internal dialogue between members of this population, the real-life second tier can generally drop out of the picture, and it will seem to them as if the situation is as represented in Figure 18.1a. Abstract raceless colourless persons – *who are concrete, raced,*

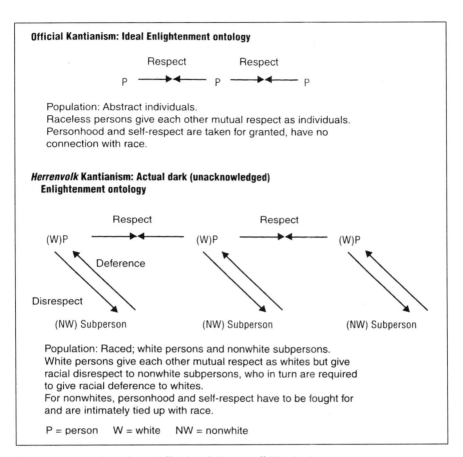

Figures 18.1a and 18.1b   Official and *Herrenvolk* Kantianism

white persons – will then, in their egalitarian moral/political theories, such as those of Kant, relate to one another with reciprocal *respect* as moral equals. Because of the representation of this system in their own minds – because the basement second tier is usually presupposed as invisible – they will think of this respect and this personhood as disconnected from anything else but rationality; race, colour, history, culture will generally play no role in the overt theory, not because they play no role overall – they are in fact *crucial* to the architecture of the two tiers – but because their commonality to the white population means they can be eliminated as a common factor.

We can now appreciate, then, why this conceptual terrain is so apparently inhospitable to the concerns of Third World theory. For if race is not even acknowledged to make a difference, how can these two discourses be located in the same universe? The way to bring them together, accordingly, is to point out the *illusory* character of abstract Kantianism and to recognize the actual *Herrenvolk* moral theory appropriate for a white-supremacist polity, one in which the difference race makes is precisely to demarcate persons from subpersons. Individuals are in fact raced, coloured, bearers of a certain history and culture, and this is what indicates their location in the racial polity. And if, paradigmatically, in the Kantian normative framework, persons are not to be treated merely instrumentally, as means to others' ends, then subpersons (Native Americans, blacks) can be regarded as precisely those for whom such treatment *is* morally appropriate.

It should be noted that this has always been recognized by black and Third World theory: antislavery, antisegregationist, anticolonial. Thus in the introduction to his classic *Black Skin, White Masks* (1967), Frantz Fanon says bluntly: "At the risk of arousing the resentment of my colored brothers, I will say that the black is not a man" (8). And this is because, as he points out elsewhere, the colonial world is "a Manichean world", "a world cut in two", "divided into compartments . . . inhabited by two different species", and "it is evident that what parcels out the world is to begin with the fact of belonging to or not belonging to a given race, a given species", on the one hand the "governing race", on the other inferior creatures to be described in "zoological terms" (Fanon 1961: 38–42).

Similarly, from the other side, a white Alabaman speaker addressing a northern audience in 1860 describes with admirable clarity the actual founding principles of the United States: "Your fathers and my fathers built this government on two ideas; the first is that the white race is the citizen and the master race, and the white man is the equal of every other white man. The second idea is that the Negro is the inferior race" (Fredrickson 1981: 155). And this, of course, far from being an idiosyncratic perception, is accurately reflected in the 1857 *Dred Scott* v. *Sanford* US Supreme Court decision that blacks were "considered as a subordinate and inferior class of beings, who had been subjected by the dominant race . . . so far inferior, that they had no rights which the white man was bound to respect".

So I am not making any claims to theoretical *discovery* here; what I am arguing for is the formal recognition of these realities within the framework of an orthodox theory that generally ignores them. Race has been a problematic 'deviation' for both liberal individualist and Marxist class-centred mappings of this system, because they have both failed to take seriously the objective partitioning in the social ontology produced by global white supremacy.

Once this expanded moral topography has been acknowledged, and not evaded or defined out of existence, it immediately becomes obvious that the transactions in moral and political space are far more complicated, involving many other dimensions, than those sketched in the standard First World cartography. Focusing exclusively on the lateral person-to-person relations of the ideal Kantian population, mainstream theory misses the dense vertical network of the person-to-*sub*person relations, and also elides the ways in which even the horizontal relations are structured by their positioning with respect to the latter. So there will be political struggles that are, if not invisible, at least not readily detectable by the lenses of orthodox theory's conceptual apparatus. Or if they are seen, the tendency will be to assimilate them to something else, missing their true significance; it will not be appreciated that they constitute struggles (affirmations/repudiations) around the *Herrenvolk* ethic, because the existence of this ethic is not formally acknowledged in mainstream philosophy to begin with.

Here, then, are some theses on the politics of personhood within the framework of white supremacy, in a *Herrenvolk* ethics:

1. *Personhood and subpersonhood are reciprocally defined, and manifested on several different planes.*

   In ideal Kantianism (predicated on a population of white individuals), the person can be abstract, raceless, colourless. In *Herrenvolk* Kantianism, on the other hand, the criteria for being a person will necessarily have to be developed in contrast to the criteria for being a subperson. So there will be a dynamic interrelation between the two. As Richard Drinnon (1980) observes about the early colonial settlements in the United States, "Indian-hating identified the dark others that white settlers were not and must not under any circumstances become" (xvii–xviii). Moreover, where abstract Kantianism is focused solely on rationality, *Herrenvolk* Kantianism will have a richer set of metrics of assessment – cognitive, moral, cultural, somatic – numerous axes along which one can measure up to, or fall short of, full personhood. The result, in part, will be that (white) persons will look to (non-white) subpersons as an inverted mirror, a reflection of what they should not be, and (non-white) subpersons who accept the *Herrenvolk* framework will in turn have (white) persons as their (unreachable) ideal, a norm by definition never to be achieved, but one that can at least be aspired to as far as possible.

2. *Subpersonhood has to be enforced, and racial deference from subpersons maintained.*

Because of the self-sustaining symmetry of ideal Kantianism, the system is inherently a stable one, since it rests on reciprocal relations between persons of acknowledged equal worth, involving a respect voluntarily given. *Herrenvolk* Kantianism, on the other hand, requires that a subset of the human population learn to regard themselves as subpersons, and as such *not* really human, *not* of equal worth. Thus the system will be potentially an *un*stable one, requiring subjugation and ideological conditioning to ensure its ongoing reproduction. Subpersons are not born, but *made,* and the making is not a once-and-for-all event, such as slave breaking, or even an extended process of indoctrination, such as colonial education, but an ongoing political operation involving routine daily transactions of various kinds.

Moreover, people's sense of self-worth will obviously be influenced by the peculiarities of this system. In the ideal Kantian community, self-respect is fortified by reciprocal symmetrical relations of respect from others who are our moral equals. In this *non*ideal racially hierarchical 'community', on the other hand, the self-respect of those designated as full persons will be linked with moral relations on *two* levels, white peers and non-white inferiors. Not merely must one's fellow-persons respect one but one must also be paid what could be termed *racial deference* from the subperson population. Failure to receive this deference then becomes a threat to one's sense of self-worth, since self-worth has been defined hierarchically in relation to the class of inferior beings. So it will then be crucial to the reproduction of the system that the moral economy of deference is maintained, with a watchfulness for signs of insubordination in the subperson population. By posture, body language, manner, speech and gaze, subpersons need to be constantly demonstrating that they recognize and accept their subordinate position.

3. *The resistance to subpersonhood requires a struggle at all levels, including the carnal battlefield of the body.*

Correspondingly, the *resistance* to this status will be an ongoing subterranean tension within the racial polity. The persons of mainstream philosophy, being ghostly disincorporate individuals, can take their personhood for granted. But this, as argued, is because they are really *white* persons conceptualized without reference to the non-white subperson population. For subpersons, on the other hand, personhood has to be fought for (against the opposition of the white population, who will have a vested material, psychic and ontological interest in continuing non-white subpersonhood). Sometimes this struggle will be overt; at other times circumstances will make it necessary for resistance to be clandestine, coded. But in all these white supremacist states, it will be a constant presence, a standing threat to the dark ontology of racial hierarchy.

Because of the multidimensionality of the stigmatization of non-whites, this resistance will have to be of a corollary breadth: moral, epistemic, somatic. Morally, one has to learn the basic self-respect that can be casually assumed by white Kantian persons, but whose attainment for subpersons will require the repudiation of the official metaphysic. Epistemologically, a cognitive resistance to *Herrenvolk* theory will be necessary: the rejection of white mystification, the sometimes painful and halting development of faith in one's own ability to know the world, and the articulation of different categories, the recovery of vanished or denied histories, the embarking upon projects of racial 'vindication'. Somatically, since the physical body has itself become the vehicle of metaphysical status, since physiology has been taken to recapitulate ontology, resistance may also involve a physical transformation of the flesh, or of one's attitude towards it. The deviant standing of the flesh of the non-white body means that the body itself is experienced as a burden, as the lived weight of subordination. So one gets what could be called a 'carnal alienation', more ontically central to one's being than any Marxist notion, since what is involved is not the estrangement of the worker from his product but the estrangement of the person from his own physical self. The subperson will then not be at home in his or her own body, since this is the carnal sign of his or her subpersonhood, so that one will be haunted by corporeal spirits, the ghost of the white body. Resistance to subpersonhood will thus require an exorcism of this ghost, and a corresponding acceptance and celebration of one's own flesh.

Revisionist Ontologies

My claim is, then, that this model provides us with a generally useful trope for expanding and transforming traditional political philosophy, extending our conception of what is to count as political. If global white supremacy is conceptualized as a political system, then a wide variety of phenomena can now be illuminatingly seen as attempts respectively to enforce and to resist this system. In particular, once we recognize that 'personhood' itself has been overtly or tacitly racially normed, we can appreciate that a central focus of the struggles of the peoples of the 'New' World, particularly Native Americans and Africans, has always been the defiant assertion of their personhood, the repudiation and reinvention of the selves imposed by white supremacy (the white man's Negro, the white man's Indian) (Jordan 1977; Berkhofer, Jr 1978). One will then be able to see as political that "the mere act of rebellion required, on the part of the slave-person, the capacity to purge himself of the white bias, and its accompanying slavish deference to everything that the white system stood for; to perceive himself, in his self-image, as equal, or even superior, to the white master-person" (Lewis 1983: 225).

'Revisionist ontologies' can then be taken in one or both of two ways: the necessary formal recognition in political theory of the actual dark ontologies constructed by the *Herrenvolk,* the metaphysical infrastructure of global white supremacy, and/or the revisionist challenges *to* these ontologies by the subordinated population contemptuously categorized as subpersons. As Rex Nettleford (1976) has pointed out about the Rastafari,

At the heart of his religious system is the notion of his own divinity and the first-person image of self. As if for emphasis the terms 'I-n-I' and 'I-man' are used as a constant reminder of the final transformation of a nonperson (as the old slave society and the new Babylon would have it) into a *person,* as is defined by 'Jah Rastafari' and asserted by the Rastaman himself. (xiv–xv; emphasis in original)

(And think, in this context, of the significance of the Jamaican creole term *smaddification.*)

Conceptualizing 'personhood' as itself a battlefield, a terrain of political contestation, thereby enables us to locate and understand as 'political' an array of phenomena not readily apprehensible as such either through liberal or Marxist prisms. Whatever their other differences, these theories are both predicated on taking personhood for *granted.* But in fact, from the time of the first European incursion into the Americas, the personhood of Native Americans was in doubt, with the controversy over whether they were really human culminating in the great 1550–51 debate at Valladolid (Hanke 1959), while throughout the period of African slavery, of course, abolitionists and antiabolitionists continued to ask the question of whether blacks were really equal to whites. So the historical record is clear enough; I am not revealing anything that people do not know. The burden of my claim is that the *philosophical* and *political* significance of these well-known facts has not been sufficiently appreciated. What I am arguing for is an explicit reconceptualization of political philosophy that would enable us to situate these struggles appropriately, that is, as defences and subversions of a political system of global white supremacy that is insufficiently, if at all, discussed within the body of theory within which most of us have been trained and within which we continue to operate intellectually.

I want to conclude by indicating, necessarily somewhat schematically, some possible directions of research for political theorists.

1. *Herrenvolk* History: The black oppositional tradition in the Americas has always pointed out the significance of what has been called the 'bleaching' or 'whitewashing' of history. It would be worthwhile to take this as a theoretical object for political philosophy. Thousands of articles have been written in the Marxist tradition on so-called bourgeois ideology and its influence on diverse fields of study. But what Third World political theorists need to start doing is self-consciously theorizing about what could be called white settler ideology, *Herrenvolk* ideology, and its influence both on historiography (Young 1990) and on fictional representations of the European conquest ('discovery', 'colonization', 'founding of a new world', 'the civilizing mission' and so on).

It would be an interesting exercise, for example, to investigate and chart a history of 'holocaust denial', not the familiar neo-Nazi denial of the facts about the World War II mass murder of the Jews but white scholarship's depiction of the fate of native peoples, from the response to the original claims of Las Casas onwards through characterizations of the 'Indian Wars' of the eighteenth and nineteenth centuries. David Stannard's *American Holocaust* (1992) is an important revisionist work, timed for the Columbian quincentenary, that draws on demographic research that has dramatically increased estimates of the pre-conquest population of the Americas, so that – with figures ranging possibly as high as one hundred million victims – this would be "far and away, the most massive act of genocide in the history of the world" (x). The historic downplaying, and even moral justification, of this foundational feat of mass murder would repay study for what it reveals about *Herrenvolk* theory.

Similarly, the distortions about Africa's past need to be contextualized not as contingently racist descriptions by individual bigots, but as an organic part of the project of denying African personhood. Correspondingly, we need to research and valorize the long 'vindicationist' tradition in the pan-Africanist movement, locating it as a crucial part of the intellectual political struggle against the system of global white supremacy (Campbell 1987).

2. **Language and Culture:** The colonized have often argued that the languages of the mother countries are not neutral but to a significant extent the carriers of imperial culture. For this reason, the Kenyan writer Ngugi wa Thiong'o no longer writes in English, choosing instead to write in his native Gikuyu (Thiong'o 1986). In the Caribbean, where creoles of various kinds have developed, part of the resistance to white racism has simply been the affirmation of the worth of these languages, from the work of J.J. Thomas (1869) onwards. But it might also be illuminating to examine them for evidence of conceptual opposition to dominant semantics, alternative categorizations of reality that to a certain extent challenge existing frameworks – an "antilanguage" appropriate for an "antisociety" (Alleyne 1988: chap. 6). And if not here, in the creole languages that developed more or less spontaneously, then certainly in the self-consciously created 'dread talk' of the Rastafari (Pollard 1994).

3. **'Raced'/Third World Epistemology:** Mainstream liberal political theory has seldom been epistemologically self-conscious, taking for granted the universal perceptiveness of the abstract Enlightenment cognizer. The challenge of Marxism was seen in part as the attempt to develop a radical theory from the putatively epistemically privileged position (with respect to possibilities for differential experience, alternative conceptualization) of the proletariat. Contemporary feminism has adopted and adapted this notion in the form of so-called feminist standpoint theory, perhaps the most influential version of 'feminist epistemology'.

   A plausible case can surely be made, then, that a racially informed/'black'/'Third World' epistemology can be developed as part of this political project, an epistemology that would self-consciously take the standpoint of those racially subordinated by the system of white supremacy as a source of conceptual inspiration and experiential guidance. This would recognize that there is such a thing as a 'black' experience and perspective on reality while simultaneously, through its social-structural rather than biologistic conceptualization, repudiating the mystifications of contemporary 'melanin theory' (Mills 1988).

4. **The Body:** In the racial polity, by contrast with the colourless polity of abstract Western theory, the body necessarily itself becomes politicized, giving rise to a 'body politics'. White supremacy subordinates the body as

the indicator of diminished personhood, a subordination manifested both in the derogation of the non-white body (Russell, Wilson and Hall 1992) and, especially during the regimen of slavery, the impositions of certain postures and body languages.

What form has resistance to these negative valorizations and these carnal impositions taken? Within the region, Rastafari is perhaps the most striking case of the deliberate transformation of the black body, and its revisionist reinscription into an alternative narrative of captive warriors in Babylon. The very fact that the flashing locks of the strutting dread are now a media cliché is a remarkable testimony to the transformation of the rules of the somatic space of the *Herrenvolk* polity. Within this expanded vision of the subject matter appropriately to be investigated by political philosophy, an evolving phenomenology of the black body would no longer seem out of place, being clearly tied in with the contested carnalities of politicized personhood. In addition, popular dance could be scrutinized for signs of reinventions of the postures of the body, micropolitics of assertion, stiffenings of the spine, against the imposed deferentiality required of subpersons.[6]

5. **Folk Religions:** This new framework would also imply the explicit political recognition of folk religion – vodun, santeria, obeah, Rastafari, candomble – as a primary locus of resistance to the ideology and practice of the regime of white supremacy. (Indeed, this recognition is, ironically, more clearly manifested in the suppressive policies of colonial governments towards these religions than in academic intellectual theorizing itself.) The crucial role black religion historically played in slave uprisings is, of course, well known; but even well into the postemancipation period these religions have continued to be important as oppositional sites. The church, or the informal meeting place, has functioned as an epistemological fortress, a place where the community could freely meet away from the white gaze and collectively synthesize insights to forge a countervailing ideology. It has served as a source of spiritual strength reinforcing conceptions of self-worth within an alternative narrative, a different cosmology, in defiance of the official status of subpersonhood (Murphy 1994). And in some cases, as discussed in the previous section, it has arguably contributed through the rituals of song, dance and spirit possession to the generation of oppositional physicalities, the rebuilding of an alternative self differently related to its material body.

6. Intersection with Gender: Finally, all of these would need to be examined in connection with the intersecting system of gender domination, which necessarily shapes both the structures of oppression and the patterns of resistance (Mohanty, Russo and Torres 1991). The valorization of precolonial tradition against European erasures, for example, may foster an uncritical embrace of a past remembered less fondly by women assigned to traditional roles, so that a double rethinking may be necessary. The male assertion of personhood in a sexist society becomes the assertion of *manhood* against *emasculation*, a 'manhood' that is itself likely to be at least partially conceptually conflated with a certain positioning over subordinated women. Sexuality and sexual relations will necessarily be racialized in a white-supremacist order involving the privileging of certain somatotypes in a hierarchy of desirability and prestige (Fanon 1967; Hernton 1988). Thus non-white women will in general be engaged in a politics of both transgender unity and intergender division, fighting on shifting fronts that are both racial and sexual (Collins 1991; Reddock 1993).

Conclusion

The idea, then, would be for black philosophers in political theory – or rather, all philosophers interested in the elimination of racism and in bringing mainstream philosophy down from its otherworldly empyrean musings – to take global white supremacy as a political system, and begin to map its contours. An interdisciplinary approach will obviously be called for, in which one moves back and forth across the boundaries of formal philosophy, drawing on recent work in cultural studies, 'critical race theory' and socioeconomic research, to keep the abstractions in touch with empirical reality. (The problem is not abstraction itself but an idealizing abstraction that abstracts away from crucial determinants. No serious theorizing is possible without abstraction.)

There is nothing at all new in the observation that for the past several hundred years, race and racism have been central to the histories of the Caribbean region in particular and the West in general. But the profound implications of this fact for the categories and explanatory schemas of mainstream Western political philosophy have not properly been worked out. In effect, Anglo-American theory needs to catch up with what has always been perceived by the racially subordinated in the West: that the local intra-European ontology was never the general one, and that the revision in both theory and practice of the actual *Herrenvolk* ontology has always been as worthily 'philosophical' an enterprise as any of the preoccupations of orthodox textbook white theory.

Notes

Support for writing this chapter was provided by the Institute for the Humanities, University of Illinois at Chicago. An earlier version of this chapter was presented at the nineteenth annual conference of the Caribbean Studies Association in Merida, Yucatán, Mexico (May 1994).

1. The October 1993 figures from the American Philosophical Association Committee on the Status of Blacks in Philosophy show that black philosophers constitute less than 1 percent of the North American total.
2. A special triple issue of *The Philosophical Forum* (Pittman 1992–93) looks at some contemporary issues in developing African American philosophy. For my own reflections on the matter, see Mills 1994a.
3. For data for the United States, see, for example, Hacker 1992. For a discussion of the Jamaican situation, see Stone 1988.
4. See, for example, Massey and Denton 1993 for an account of the mechanisms by which de facto US segregation continues to be maintained a quarter of a century after the 1968 passage of the Fair Housing Act.
5. In a more detailed treatment one would, of course, have to look at internal differentiations within the non-white population itself. My statement here is obviously just meant to be programmatic, drawing what I take to be the central line of conceptual demarcation.
6. For example, Sebastian Clarke (1980) (drawing on Fanon) argues that in Jamaican rock steady, "the dancer could remain on his spot of earth, shake his shoulders, make pounding motions with his arms and hands (at an invisible enemy, an anonymous force), without recourse to or consciousness of a partner. The internal tension was demonstratively and explosively released" (81).

References

Allen, Theodore W. 1994. *The Invention of the White Race,* vol. 1. London: Verso.

Alleyne, Mervyn. 1988. *Roots of Jamaican Culture.* London: Pluto Press.

Bell, Derrick. 1992. *Faces at the Bottom of the Well: The Permanence of Racism.* New York: Basic Books.

Berkhofer, Jr, Robert. 1978. *The White Man's Indian: Images of the American Indian from Columbus to the Present.* New York: Knopf.

Campbell, Horace. 1987. *Rasta and Resistance: From Marcus Garvey to Walter Rodney.* Trenton, NJ: Africa World Press.

Clark, Lorenne, and Lynda Lange, eds. 1979. *The Sexism of Social and Political Theory: Women and Reproduction from Plato to Nietzsche.* Toronto: University of Toronto Press.

Clarke, Sebastian. 1980. *Jah Music: the Evolution of the Popular Jamaican Song.* London: Heinemann.

Collins, Patricia Hill. 1991. *Black Feminist Thought: Knowledge, Consciousness, and the Politics of Empowerment.* New York: Routledge.

Crenshaw, Kimberle Williams. 1988. "Race, reform, and retrenchment: Transformation and legitimation in antidiscrimination law". *Harvard Law Review* 101.

Drinnon, Richard. 1980. *Facing West: The Metaphysics of Indian-Hating and Empire-Building.* New York: Meridian.

Fanon, Frantz. 1967 [1952]. *Black Skin, White Masks,* translated by Charles Lam Markam. Reprint, New York: Grove Press.

Fanon, Frantz. 1968 [1961]. *The Wretched of the Earth,* translated by Constance Farrington. Reprint, New York: Grove Press.

Fredrickson, George M. 1981. *White Supremacy: A Comparative Study in American and South African History.* New York: Oxford University Press.

Greene, J. Edward, ed. 1993. *Race, Class and Gender in the Future of the Caribbean.* Kingston, Jamaica: Institute of Social and Economic Research.

Hacker, Andrew. 1992. *Two Nations: Black and White, Separate, Hostile, Unequal.* New York: Charles Scribner's Sons.

Hanke, Lewis. 1959. *Aristotle and the American Indians: A Study in Race Prejudice in the Modern World.* Bloomington: Indiana University Press.

Hernton, Calvin. 1988 [1966]. *Sex and Racism in America.* Reprint, New York: Grove Press.

Jaggar, Alison. 1983. *Feminist Politics and Human Nature.* Totowa, NJ: Roman and Allanheld.

Jordan, Winthrop D. 1977 [1968]. *White Over Black: American Attitudes Toward the Negro, 1550–1812.* Reprint, New York: Norton.

Kant, Immanuel. 1964 [1948]. *Groundwork of the Metaphysic of Morals,* translated by H.J. Paton. Reprint, New York: Harper and Row.

Kiernan, V.G. 1981 [1969]. *The Lords of Human Kind: Black Man, Yellow Man, and White Man in an Age of Empire.* Reprint, New York: Columbia University Press.

Kymlicka, Will. 1990. *Contemporary Political Philosophy: An Introduction.* Oxford: Clarendon Press.

La Guerre, John Gaffar. 1982. *The Social and Political Thought of the Colonial Intelligentsia.* Kingston, Jamaica: Institute of Social and Economic Research.

Lewis, Gordon. 1983. *Main Currents in Caribbean Thought.* Kingston, Jamaica: Heinemann Caribbean.

Lewis, Rupert, and Patrick Bryan, eds. 1988. *Garvey: His Work and Impact.* Kingston, Jamaica: Institute of Social and Economic Research.

Massey, Douglas S., and Nancy A. Denton. 1993. *American Apartheid: Segregation and the Making of the Underclass.* Cambridge, Mass.: Harvard University Press.

Mills, Charles W. 1988. "Alternative epistemologies". *Social Theory and Practice* 14, no. 3 (Fall).

Mills, Charles W. 1994a. "Non-Cartesian *sums*: Philosophy and the African-American experience". *Teaching Philosophy* 17, no. 3 (October).

Mills, Charles W. 1994b. "Dark ontologies". Paper presented at the Joint Symposium and Public Lecture Series, Race and the City. Toronto, Canada, 2–3 May.

Mohanty, Chandra, Ann Russo, and Lourdes Torres, eds. 1991. *Third World Women and the Politics of Feminism*. Bloomington: Indiana University Press.

Murphy, Joseph M. 1994. *Working the Spirit: Ceremonies of the African Diaspora*. Boston: Beacon Press.

Nettleford, Rex. 1976. Introduction. *Dread: The Rastafarians of Jamaica*, by Joseph Owens. Kingston, Jamaica: Sangster's.

Okin, Susan Moller. 1979. *Women in Western Political Thought*. Princeton: Princeton University Press.

Okin, Susan Moller. 1989. *Justice, Gender, and the Family*. New York: Basic Books.

Owens, Joseph. 1976. *Dread: The Rastafarians of Jamaica*. Kingston, Jamaica: Sangster's.

Pittman, John, ed. 1992–93. "African-American perspectives and philosophical traditions". *Philosophical Forum* 24, nos. 1–3 (Fall–Spring).

Pollard, Velma. 1994. *Dread Talk: The Language of Rastafari*. Kingston, Jamaica: Canoe Press.

Rawls, John. 1971. *A Theory of Justice*. Cambridge, Mass.: Harvard University Press.

Reddock, Rhoda. 1993. "Primacy of gender in race and class". In *Race, Class and Gender in the Future of the Caribbean*, edited by J.E. Greene. Kingston, Jamaica: Institute of Social and Economic Research.

Roediger, David. 1991. *The Wages of Whiteness: Race and the Making of the American Working Class*. London: Verso.

Romano, Carlin. 1993. "The unbearable whiteness of being/critique of pure whiteness". *Lingua Franca* 3, no. 5 (July–August).

Russell, Kathy, Midge Wilson, and Ronald Hall. 1992. *The Color Complex: The Politics of Skin Color Among African Americans*. New York: Harcourt Brace Jovanovich.

Said, Edward W. 1993. *Culture and Imperialism*. New York: Knopf.

Stannard, David E. 1992. *American Holocaust: The Conquest of the New World*. New York: Oxford University Press.

Stone, Carl. 1988. "Race and economic power in Jamaica". In *Garvey: His Work and Impact*, edited by R. Lewis and P. Bryan. Kingston, Jamaica: Institute of Social and Economic Research.

Thiong'o, Ngugi wa. 1986. *Decolonising the Mind: The Politics of Language in African Literature*. London: James Currey.

Thomas, John Jacob. 1869. *The Theory and Practice of Creole Grammar*.

van den Berghe, Pierre L. 1967. *Race and Racism: A Comparative Perspective*. New York: Wiley.

Young, Robert. 1990. *White Mythologies: Writing History and the West*. London: Routledge.

19

On Reconstructing a Political Economy of the Caribbean

CLIVE THOMAS

Introduction

While in the 1960s and 1970s Caribbean scholarship had made significant contributions to the radical critiques of received doctrines in development economics, that period is perhaps best remembered as the golden age in the construction of 'alternative' models of political economy of the region. This constructionist period produced a number of innovative models and, indeed, schools of thought on political economy: plantation, New World, dependency, Marxist, neo-Marxist, structuralist, plural society, petroleum economy, open economy and Arthur Lewis, to name a few. By the late 1980s, however, a noticeable shift in emphasis had occurred. Radical social analysis was centred more and more on critiques, that is, the deconstruction of the neoliberal paradigm, and less on constructing alternatives. In retrospect, this might have been anticipated, for by the late 1980s neoliberalism had emerged as the predominant framework within which economic ideas evolved and public policies framed within the region.

The deconstructionist critique since the late 1980s remains important nevertheless, since it serves as a reminder of the fact that, despite its pretensions otherwise, neoliberalism is in essence a deeply ideological and political project.

As Bienefeld (1995) observed in his review of International Monetary Fund–World Bank commissioned reviews of their own policies: "empirical evidence plays only a minor role in the justification of the neoliberal policy prescriptions, which are largely derived by deduction from certain assumptions of human behaviour" (9). He then goes on to point out that the very theories that were developed from these unrealistic but axiomatic behavioural assumptions, and from which neoliberal prescriptions are derived, indicate that unless all of their assumptions hold, a 'second best' situation of market imperfection obtains. And, where market imperfections are widespread, the removal of some of these (that is, a 'second best' solution) may or may not improve welfare and efficiency. In other words, from a purely theoretical standpoint the net effect of neoliberal policies is unknown and undemonstrable. This therefore underscores the critical importance that empirical evidence should play in the justification of these policies.

Not surprisingly, as they have developed, critiques of neoliberalism in the region have been considerably influenced by postmodernist ideas – a situation that is common to scholarship in many other parts of the world. One notable consequence of this has been that, while several of the 'alternative' models of political economy had embraced a 'class' approach (while recognizing that the traditional classes of capitalism were underdeveloped in the region and that existing class structures were therefore very complex and fluid, and generally in a state of very early formation, so that nonclass factors such as race, culture and religion played exceptional roles), the influence of postmodernist literature has led to a retreat from this approach. Developed in the industrialized world, postmodernism speaks to contemporary postindustrial consumer-driven societies in which, it is argued, class is an antiquated concept. Bipolar notions of class are portrayed as being incongruent with the living experiences of people in postindustrial societies on the eve of the twenty-first century. For example, it is claimed that in the field of work, 'workers' are increasingly becoming 'part-managers', and they consequently find themselves in a position where they are able to exert unprecedented control over the work process, thereby making their relations to the means of production very different from that of the previous era of industrial capitalism.

In so far as these theories replace class conflicts with what is presented as the more complex and 'sublimated' conceptions of cultural antagonisms, they have found echoes in the contemporary literature of Caribbean societies, even though these societies cannot be realistically portrayed as postindustrial, by any stretch of the imagination. One further noteworthy observation is that postmodernist as well as Marxist/neo-Marxist Caribbean political economies have not only been strongly influenced by the major philosophical and theoretical debates of Western society but in turn they have undoubtedly influenced these wider debates.

At the start of the twenty-first century, however, there is a pressing need once more to embark on sustained scholarship focusing more on reconstructing and devising alternative models of political economy for the region and less on deconstruction. The urgency of this stems in large measure from the radically changed circumstances of today, compared to those of the 1960s and 1970s. These changes are evident in every major dimension of the social life of the region, even though it is perhaps most tellingly revealed at the international level where it is frequently captured in the universal acknowledgement of the fundamental transformations being generated in the region through the catch-all process of 'globalization'.

The theme of this volume is therefore timely: "New Caribbean Thought". This chapter addresses this problematic through an examination of the requirements for the reconstruction of earlier work on the political economy of the region. The basic approach is a discourse with my earlier work, centred in the first instance on identifying its central omissions, limitations and weaknesses at this point in time and, based on this, to proceed to highlight the priorities and directions in which further analysis might be fruitfully pursued.

Historical Periodization

There is no more crucial test of the appropriateness of a model of political economy for any society than its capacity to offer a meaningful periodization of the development of that society, such that the past helps 'explain' the present, whilst *simultaneously* providing guidelines for three dimensions of human activity, namely:

- personal engagement
- collective/group action directed at change
- development policies and programmes, and institutions designed to secure the required change

From the time of Adam Smith, the work of all the great political economists have captured these properties. How then, we may ask, does this test apply to extant work on the political economy of the Caribbean? My own work has suggested four definite periods in the 'modern' history of the region, each with its own distinctive methods and systems of economic organization and production as well as social arrangements. While the first three of these have been substantially explored in earlier work, the fourth has only very recently received attention.

It is commonly acknowledged that the 'modern' history of the Caribbean begins with the effective decimation of the pre-Columbian peoples and their societies in most territories. The first period of this modern history covers the destruction of the indigenous communal societies and the subsequent imposition of a system of forced labour (slavery). This was a long period, which had two distinct phases. It started with an 'early' phase of European conquest, plunder and colonial settlement, which lasted from the late fifteenth century to the early seventeenth century, and which witnessed the effective subjugation of the indigenous communities. This phase therefore paved the way for 'tribute' to be plundered from the region, a tribute that contributed substantially to the financing of commercial capitalist expansion in Europe, thereby establishing an indissoluble link between developments in the region and the expansion of commercial capitalism in Europe.

The subsequent phase I have described as a colonial slave mode of production, which lasted from the mid seventeenth century to the early nineteenth century (Thomas 1988). Its distinctive characterization is that, on the one hand, slave labour predominated as the legal and customary status of the overwhelming majority of the direct producers, while, on the other, colonial rule was the mediating structure through which evolving capitalism in Europe impacted on the region. It was the particular combination of these two features that gave the system of production its distinctive form. In general, the first feature indicates that although the region had been producing commodities for sale in a capitalist world market, the direct labour used in this process was not subject to the laws of this market, while the second feature generated several peculiarities in the system of production; for example:

- the distinctive role that 'speculative profit' played in plantation investment and production;
- the distinction that developed between earning profit and its productive use (much of the profit was used for 'consumption' purposes outside the plantation);
- the 'commandist' labour management system;
- product concentration and risk;

- the survival of precapitalist attitudes to production as observed in the emphasis on extensive rather than intensive use of the productive factors.

As a consequence of the above it was observed that

Although organically related to the process of capitalist expansion in Europe, colonial mediation took root within specific conditions of geographical environment and of cultural adaptation to a new world that pitted African slaves and European slave masters in deadly antagonism. (Thomas 1984a: 13)

It should be recalled that it was during this period that European capitalism was transmuted from its initial commercial form to an industrial one. Of significance also to the theoretical debates that subsequently emerged is the consideration that while the most typical form in which economic and social life was organized in the region during this period was the plantation, the colonial slave system was more than the plantation writ large. As the historical information reveals, this system embraced the coexistence of the plantation with both 'petty commodity producers' and a variety of forms of 'natural economy' among the surviving indigenous communities and runaway slave populations.

The second period is the one in which the colonial slave economy disintegrated. It was in this period that early breaks with colonialism and the later spread of independence movements, particularly among the Spanish possessions in the Western Hemisphere, also occurred. This period lasted roughly from the early nineteenth century to the second decade of the twentieth century, and was characterized by several other distinctive features, such as the introduction of indentured labour; the emergence of a peasantry among the ex-slave population that was part labourer part small farmer; the development of labour markets and efforts at their regulation by the state; the transformation of the planter class along more capitalist lines making it less and less like a 'landed' gentry; the emergence and development of other classes and social groups, particularly small traders, a thin layer of middle strata and landless unemployed persons; and fundamental changes in the nature and functions of the local state.

Of note, it was during this period as well that the United States emerged as a major capitalist power, even as industrial growth in Europe was being intensified and a new stage of European colonization and overseas investments was reached. Imperialism, as it has since been customarily described, was peaking, and the traditional 'centre/periphery' relations of post–World War II 'dependency theorists' and 'world systems analysts' were being rapidly consolidated.

The third period is that linked to the traumas of the Great Depression of the 1930s, World War II and its aftermath to the 1980s. In this period independence was obtained for most of the English-speaking countries in the region. The nationalist parties that took control of the local state sought to use it to break with colonialism and in the process introduced several important changes in the political economy of the region, particularly through their efforts to consolidate the role of markets *and* the state in economic development. Regrettably, the impact of these efforts has been frequently understated in critical assessments of this period, made by the scholars of the region. This impact, though, is difficult to overstate, since among the changes introduced were: development/encouragement of markets for goods, services and the productive factors; regional cooperation; development of state productive sectors; labour-force training; macroeconomic management and regulation, including the introduction of monetary and fiscal policies, as well as planning and statistical departments; social welfare programmes; population policies; land settlement programmes; investments in research and development, as well as the pursuit of 'independent' national roles in the world economy. It was in this period too that the consolidation of labour markets and the trade union movement occurred as well as the more or less complete transformation of the landed classes into local capitalists. The deepening and consolidation of the role and influence of capital led to the emergence of important conflicts with labour.

Given its colonial origins, it is not surprising to find that in pursuit of these objectives, states in the region have been heavily influenced by social democratic traditions in Europe. As events have unfolded, it has become clear that the capacities and performances of these developmental states have varied within the region to the extent that, although on the eve of independence the territories exhibited roughly similar political, social and economic indicators, since independence these have diverged sharply and are perhaps most dramatically revealed in the wide variation that exists in the two most widely known summary indicators of economic well-being: per capita gross domestic product and the United Nations Development Programme Human Development Index (Thomas 1996b).[1]

There are three points of special importance to this chapter which need to be highlighted about this period. First, it was the political economy of this period that four of my books sought to address (see Thomas 1974, 1984a, 1984b, 1988). Second, with the present emphases on liberalization, export-led growth and outward orientation within the neoclassical paradigm, it has become fashionable to deem the political economy of the 1970s as autarkic and pushing disengagement (translated as isolation) from the world economy as *the* solution to the underdevelopment of the region. This seems both unfair and incorrect. At best it confuses the distinction that has been made between an autocentred and self-directed process of growth with the systemic denial of external trade, finance, labour and technological links with the rest of the world. At worst, it is a case of deliberate misinformation. Thus in Thomas 1974, the much in vogue regional model of import substitution was strongly criticized, as it was again in Thomas 1988. As we shall see later also, the autocentred processes of development that had been proposed were explicitly designed to create a platform for external engagement. This platform was to be based on processes that were self-reinforcing and beneficial to Caribbean well-being as well as supportive of efforts to reform the international economic system. This political economy clearly did not advance a false polarity between internalization and internationalism.

The fourth period is the present one. It can be defined as beginning in the early 1980s and has two definite attributes. One is revealed in the impact of globalization on the region and the second in the recognition that, despite the ending of the cold war and the emergence of the United States as the sole hegemonic power, there has been a resurgence of an assertive geostrategic stance in relation to the region.

The first attribute recognizes the impact on Caribbean societies of global changes that have been occurring at several fundamental levels: at the economic level, as seen in the rapid extension of, and qualitative changes in, the character of production and flow of goods and services at all levels (national, regional and international), combined with similar fundamental changes in the character of the mobile productive factors: capital, labour (including skills), enterprise (including new forms of enterprise arrangements) and 'competition'. At the cultural level, it has entailed the close integration of the world of ideas and information supported by far-reaching innovations in the means of travel and data transmission. The effective demise of the Soviet Union as a challenger to the United States and the removal of the ideological barriers of the cold war have also aided this process. At the political level, changes are seen in the apparent reduction in the autonomy of the nation state; the reduced capacity of nation states to control affairs within their national boundaries, let alone internationally; the rise of private transnational corporations to fill this vacuum; the growing proliferation of regional blocs and its implied 'diminution' of sovereignty; the break-up of old states and the emergence of new ones; and, finally, the restructuring of the majority of states worldwide along neoliberal lines. At the environmental level, changes have been portrayed as 'threats' to the sustainability of human development on Planet Earth.

The resurgence of an assertive US geostrategic stance towards the region, despite the ending of the cold war, is based on certain perceived weaknesses by the United States. Evidence from several sources indicates that the 'official' view of the United States is that

the countries of the region comprise too many small and micro economies all of which are inherently unstable and unviable, with the consequence that Caribbean governments are lacking the effective capability to secure their national territories and to protect their sovereignty from either political or criminal predators. (Thomas 1998: 69)

These security concerns centre on the geographical location of the region in relation to the vital supply routes of the United States (which has been a long-standing concern, going back at least as far as the Monroe Doctrine), immigration into the United States from the area, narcotics production and trafficking, money laundering and terrorism.

The historical periodization of the 'modern' history of the region presented above reveals that, from the very beginning, the internationalization of capital has always been a feature of its development; the region has always had to adapt to the global evolution of capitalism. What is distinctive in the present period is the rapidity of change and the truly fundamental shifts in the qualitative aspects of the global economy. In the Caribbean the combination of these globalization processes and the newly assertive geostrategic stance of the United States has been particularly lethal. It has not only undermined the sovereignty of the region but it has also led to the virtual collapse of the postcolonial developmental state. This is reflected in the effective disappearance of the substantial state productive sectors that had developed in many countries after independence and the considerable waning of the regional culture of resistance, self-advancement and nationalism.

The Earlier Thomas Model

Assumptions

My original model of the political economy of the Caribbean is most fully developed in *Dependence and Transformation* (1974). This work, however, should not be seen in isolation. It has antecedents and was also followed by later work that attempted to address some of its shortcomings. One of the two most important antecedents is my doctoral thesis, which introduced the concept of a dependent monetary economy but did so largely on the basis of the then received development economics (Thomas 1974). In that work an economy is deemed dependent if it lacked resilience factors (that is, a capacity to be resilient to changes taking place in the rest of the world, which would depend in large measure on the level and rate of increases of domestic real per capita incomes and the levels of employment of existing resources) and if also the generating factors (that is, as measured by the dependence of the economy on the rest of the world to maintain and increase internal levels of employment, output, demand and prices) are externally directed. An economy is described as monetarily dependent if monetary and financial agents (including individuals and government) have a high propensity to invest their savings in foreign assets (to the extent that their peculiar types of specialization do not make this impossible) and also where autonomous elements in the financial system have a distinct preference to finance the requirements of the generating factors as distinct from those of the other more independent and autocentred sectors of the economy.

The second antecedent was *The Dynamics of Economic Integration* (coauthored with Havelock Brewster, 1967). This was a programmatic and policy-oriented analysis of Caribbean integration, based on the potential for the selective integration of production structures, as against the more universalistic market approaches of free trade areas, then in vogue.

The crucial assumptions (implicit and explicit) that governed the workings of the original model were:

- The location of the analysis in a definite historical period. The original model was explicitly confined to the third period, as described above, and, as such, it therefore implied an international context of bipolarism, the militant search for a new international economic order, insurgent Third Worldism, as well as an atmosphere of optimism about the willingness and capacities of people to build a better world. These circumstances clearly influenced the model, but they do not obtain in the present period, thereby severely limiting its current relevance.
- The model also isolated the political and social dimensions of change in its prescriptive features. A 'worker-peasant alliance' was given as the precondition for the exercise of governmental authority thereby permitting the model to abstract itself from political concerns and social arrangements.

Presently this would not be tenable, as it is precisely these concerns that dominate our outlook on Caribbean societies.

- The model presumed as well that there was a rough uniformity in regional indicators of economic and social well-being, permitting, therefore, a situation in which all the territories more or less broadly conformed to the essential relationships displayed in it. In other words, the model had assumed that there was *neither* a significant gap between capacity and performance among these countries nor that in the long-run the socioeconomic performance indicators of countries of the region would vary so markedly. This situation no longer operates, as marked divergences in economic, social and political indicators have characterized developments in the region during the past three decades (Thomas 1996b).
- Needs were also defined in the model at the national level. These were in turn derived from individual needs (or, at the very best, family/household needs) grossed up to provide estimates of national requirements. This methodology therefore abstracted itself from many of our present-day concerns with individual, household/family and community issues.

In subsequent research I have tried to develop the analysis of some of the issues raised by the limitations of these assumptions. The areas I have concentrated on so far are:

- Attempts to elaborate on the meaning and content of political democracy, the state, its collapse and recomposition as well as state–civil society relations; these attempts focus on relaxing the assumption in regard to political and social conditions (Thomas 1984b, 1996a, 1998)
- Considerations of race/ethnicity, which also focus on relaxing this assumption (Thomas 1995)
- Focusing on the present conjuncture (the fourth period) (Thomas 1998)
- Highlighting the growing regional differentiation in social and economic performance indicators (see Thomas 1993 and 1996b)

Key Elements

The key elements of the original model may be briefly summed up as follows: first, it posited that the original destruction of the communal and other precapitalist production relations, which was followed by the development of capitalism both inside the region and at the global level, had, over the first three historical periods identified above, led to two systemic divergences in the economy of the region: (1) that between the pattern of resource use and the pattern of demand for goods and services; and (2) that between the pattern of resource inventorization and resources known, mapped and earmarked for immediate production. In other words, the ultimate consequence of colonialism was to tear loose the productive capacities of the region from their roots in the domestic needs of the pre-Columbian peoples and the initial settlers.

In light of contemporary debates, it should be stressed that the model had recognized that historically, similar processes did occur in all colonial territories. What was argued is that by and large it was not advanced to nearly the same extent in the larger colonial possessions (for example, India) because the national markets (needs) of these countries, constituted important areas for capitalist exploitation. The Caribbean therefore displays a unique feature in the combination of its smallness and colonial exploitation. While in the heyday of tribute gathering, the limitations of its small size may not have been readily apparent; as the shift from tribute gathering to installed production systems in the territories progressed, it became increasingly evident that production for export was the only profitable route to follow if the large-scale transnational investments of the plantation were to be sustained. As a result, I argued

that the measure of structural dependence, underdevelopment, and the economic backwardness of the process of production which is important above all others is on the *one hand, the lack of an organic link, rooted in an indigenous science and technology, between the pattern and growth of domestic resource use and the pattern and growth of domestic demand, and, on the other, the divergence between domestic demand and the needs of the broad mass of the population.* This interpretation has both quantitative and qualitative dimensions. Together they demonstrate that the crucial elements in the functioning of an economic system qua economic system (i.e., the linkages between: labor-resources-technology-production-demand-needs) are of such a character and are organized in such a way that these communities have internalized through their social relations of production and the use of their productive forces, a pattern of consumption that does not represent the needs of the consumers and a pattern of production not oriented to either domestic consumption or domestic needs. (Thomas 1974: 59; emphasis in original)

Second, the 'export' sector that was developed not only dominated these small open economies in terms of income and employment generation but quickly became (and has effectively remained) highly specialized in a very narrow range of goods and services sold in one or two principal markets, signifying that this was the private view of the most profitable use of local opportunities and the best way to reap economies of scale. Exports did not develop, therefore, on an initial platform of production for internal requirements. Concurrent with this, the import sector, or the other 'half' of these open economies, provided the wide array of goods and services required to satisfy domestic demand.

Third, the patterns of importation and consumption were derived from the patterns of distribution of wealth and income, with the latter at base being inherently unequal. Over time, this inequality has been reinforced with the persistence of large disparities in urban and rural development and significant levels of poverty and dispossession among major social and ethnic groups.

Fourth, the pattern of property ownership and hence the social arrangements that developed around it are both products of, and in turn reinforce the dynamic relations of, the economic model. However, the divergences have historically manifested themselves in various institutional forms of resource ownership and use, income creation and demand patterns, as well as forms of saving and accumulation over time and among different countries. Generally, because of the small size of these territories, these institutional forms have tended to assume the character of 'total institutions', which is one reason why features such as the 'plantation', 'Crown Colony rule' and 'authoritarian societies' are such common descriptors of Caribbean society.

Finally, the principal focus has been on growth in per capita gross domestic product as the measure of a country's performance, as distinct from such broader conceptions as sustainable human development.

Prescription

The original Thomas model sought to 'explain' the political economy of the third period and to lay out prescriptive features to guide development policy, with considerable emphasis being placed on the role of government in this. It was argued that a prerequisite for reconstructing the economies of the region was the reversal of the dynamics revealed above and that this reversal required policy changes in two main directions: first, in the reconceptualization of the development problematic to take account of:

- the need to develop a system of ownership, control, production and distribution, oriented towards satisfying the broad needs of the masses (this is possible only if there are far-reaching fundamental changes in political and social structures);

- the need to encourage a system of labour use, both waged (salaried) employment and self-employment that is based on equality of access; the absence of coercion and discrimination on any grounds; and a framework of industrial relations that honours collective representation, promotes effective worker involvement while simultaneously providing adequate health, occupational safety, training and education to the work force;
- the need to facilitate the unfettered development of civic/community organizations;
- the need to pursue the relentless pursuit of the democratization of power;
- the requirement to ensure environmentally sustainable forms of production;
- the fact that due consideration must be given to the progressive role of the state in international affairs and the domestic economy.

Second, it was advanced that policy should be aimed at the construction of what was termed: "*a process of accumulation founded on the priorities required to ensure the eventual reversal of these divergences. In other words, accumulation has to be founded on the logic of a dynamic convergence between social needs and the use of domestic resources*" (Thomas 1988: 364; emphasis in original). Three basic tasks were then identified in pursuit of this:

1. Orienting agricultural production towards supplying the needs of the population in the 'first instance' with export specialization occurring as an extension of this.
2. Developing at the national, or more likely the regional level, a capacity to produce (as distinct from the actual production of) a representative bundle of basic materials with which to lay the basis for industrialization, transformation and export growth.
3. Raising the level of economic and technical competencies of the population to secure (1) and (2) above, as well as to pave the way for the development of those services which benefit from a highly knowledgeable and purposeful workforce.

The basic materials referred to above are the modern day equivalents of the Ricardian corn and Sraffa commodities in the theory of value. In this sense, therefore, these basic materials can best be described as the commodities which enter directly or indirectly into the production of all other commodities. A society that does not produce such commodities, or does not have the capability of doing so, it was argued, will have no other recourse but to use world prices as the measure of the domestic value of all traded goods and services, as well as most domestic ones, with the major exceptions being the two productive factors: labour and land, since these are not sufficiently mobile internationally for world market prices to rule.

The Task Ahead

I do not intend to attempt to write a new chapter in the political economy of the region. As I see it, my task at this stage, based on the revisiting of earlier work, is to outline directions for future work. What is indicated below, therefore, remains preliminary and somewhat tentative.

There are two obvious ways of proceeding with the task at hand. One would be to start where the earlier 'radical' political economy stopped or failed, and the second would be to seek to find 'common ground' between the concerns of both neoliberal and radical political economies of the region. The strategic advantage of the former approach is the sharp break and outright rejection that it offers, with what has been described as the 'disingenuousness' of the neoliberal paradigm. Its major disadvantage, however, is that dialogue across the frontiers of these schools may be jeopardized since, at present, these schools reject the premises of each other's work so completely that they pay scant attention to each other's literature. The strategic advantage of the second approach is that a common ground could perhaps be constructively defined around the area where current research and theorizing among these schools, accompanied by the generation of new empirical data, coincide. Its major disadvantage is that it could be plausibly interpreted as either opportunistic, less than revolutionary, or open to co-optation by neoliberalism – a not infrequent occurrence. I have opted for the second choice.

Moral Economy

The one feature common to all schools of political economy, including neoclassical economics with its strong positivist orientation, is that they have a normative or prescriptive aspect. It is in their normative aspect that the three essential guidelines of a political economy referred to earlier (namely, personnel engagement, collective/group action directed at change, and policies and programmes) are most evident. In effect, these guidelines define, as it were, the moral economy that guides the exercise of power and authority and the development and use of society's resources in the workings of the model.

If we hold the axiomatic assumptions of neoclassical economics as given, there is no weakness in its analytical framework that is so fundamental that it cannot in principle be logically or mathematically resolved. The areas of fundamental weaknesses do not lie in its mathematical/logical reasoning but instead can be found in the relationship of the axiomatic assumptions to the realities of the particular society under study. Further, because neoclassical economics holds the view that these axiomatic assumptions adequately define social behaviour everywhere and for all 'modern' times, it advances the proposition that its version of political economy is a universal science, applicable to all societies founded on rationality. The thesis advanced in this chapter, however, is the exact opposite. It is based on two arguments: first, that it is precisely the lack of correspondence between the axiomatic assumptions of neoclassical economics and social behaviour in Caribbean societies that severely (although not entirely) negates the relevance of much of neoclassical economics; and second, this is not a unique occurrence, as societies or groups of societies have everywhere exhibited significant differences in their characteristic modes of behaviour and functioning.

It should be observed, however, that if one seeks to advance a more appropriate political economy for a particular group of societies, as we do here, this lack of correspondence cannot be resolved by arbitrarily substituting the present axiomatic assumptions of neoclassical economics with another set of equally idealist and unrealistic constructs. In the reconstruction of Caribbean political economy, an advance on neoclassical economics is possible only to the extent that the moral economy of authority and power that it develops is rooted in concrete features and characteristic modes of behaviour of the social economy of the region. Since it is my belief that alternative political economies of the region have already adequately (if not exhaustively) identified the main features and characteristic modes in the functioning of Caribbean societies, the task is not so much to identify these but to make advances on them.

Household Economy and Household Rights

In search of a new common ground, the analysis and study of the household economy offers the most logical point of entry in reconstructing the political economy of the region. There are two reasons for advancing this: (1) as a social construct, the household is both a central and common feature of all societies and therefore has special (though different) significance for all political economies; and (2) empirically, its concrete forms vary, and have become increasingly the focus of comparative analysis and reconsideration in the social sciences. The latter has been pursued from a variety of analytical standpoints that have made use of the numerous household surveys and anthropological studies recently concluded.

In neoclassical economics the household enters into the analysis in three principal ways: (1) as a source of supply of labour to the market; (2) as a 'unit' for consuming goods and services that are produced in the business and government sectors; and (3) as a 'unit' of savings, that is, foregoing present consumption in order to acquire, typically, financial assets, that provide finance for capital expansion. Additionally, there has been what is termed the microeconomic household theory of fertility, developed in the 1970s, that offers explanations of population growth, family size and gender preferences in terms of the maximization of households' utility functions, the opportunity cost of rearing children and levels of household income.

Feminist work within the tradition of women and development has recently received much consideration in the region. This has tended to emphasize important neglected dimensions of the household in the neoclassical approach, for example, its role:

- as a unit of production (in addition to consumption) of goods and services for the market, (while this is seen as particularly important in underdeveloped economies, it is also observed as a new trend in postindustrial societies)
- as the unit in which labour is reproduced for the market
- as a unit where unrecognized and unwaged labour occurs (household work)
- as a unit where marked gender differences in the sexual division of labour are dramatically revealed, while constituting at the same time the primary arena in which the position of women (and, increasingly, that of children) in the labour market is mediated.

These features of the household have been diversely interpreted as being integrated, marginalized or exploited through the rhythm of the capitalist economy. All these approaches, however, stress a view of the household in which it is in one way or another subordinated to the logic of the market as a fundamental aspect of capitalism. There is of course much truth in this, and in this regard we might even say that this work is consistent with neoclassical economics that also subordinates the household to the market.

In actuality, however, the household is more than a unit driven by the dictates of the market. Studies have shown that it is also the core within which the main features of the social structure are reproduced. Many of these features, however, are neither exclusively nor largely driven by the logic of the market, even in the circumstances of the most fully developed market economies. In other words, the household is the place in which the extended reproduction of the social structure takes place, and this process, by its very nature, has to occur through a multitude of nonmarket factors and influences. This aspect of the household I hold to be as central to its existence as any other.

This argument is somewhat akin to the analysis of Friedman (1992 and 1996) and others, who have introduced the notion of the household as a centre for the production of livelihood. This notion clearly postulates that the needs of the household do not carry the same unlimited consumerist orientation that characterizes the capitalist market and its unending search for utility and profit maximization. It is important to note that this formulation does not suggest that the household and its needs are static. To the contrary, it explicitly recognizes that these develop over time, particularly over generations. Despite this, households are presented as more needs driven than market driven, and as a consequence it is argued they are not reducible to the logic of capitalist accumulation (Friedman 1996: 164).

The argument I am presenting here goes one step further. It describes the household as being as well the primary agency through which social obligations and other such nonmarket relations thrive, and as such, it is a primary source for the accumulation of social capital, just as it is also for financial capital in the neoclassical formulations (Thomas 1996c). Thus we find that it is in the household of the Caribbean people that survival mechanisms are elaborated, particularly in circumstances where deprivation and dispossession prevail. It should be emphasized that this proposition is not intended to deny the significant interconnections that usually exist between the household and the market. These clearly are there, and indeed it is through their linkage to the market that household members normally acquire their 'command over resources'. What is being emphasized instead is the complementarity in the relation between these two aspects of the household – market and nonmarket – with both aspects simultaneously located within the broader dynamics of the society. This feature is common to all households and, I would argue, should enter into all political economies.

Following the reconceptualization along the lines, the next point of departure in the reconstruction of the political economy of the region would seem to be work along the lines of bringing together the rich and varied data that have been generated by several household surveys and anthropological studies in the region, in order to substantiate a theory of its household economy. Based on what we already know there are several suggestive lines of inquiry. For example, striking differences can be found in the 'quality' of existence of households in the region. This variation of quality is due to a number of factors, ranging from the racial/ethnic composition of households to diversity in cultural traditions and community support structures, but we do not know with any degree of certainty to what extent these factors contribute to this. An examination of survival strategies of households in the region also indicates that jobs for household members may profitably be studied in the broader context of sustainable livelihoods, but we are yet to pursue the opportunities this approach offers in integrating the developmental, sustainable resource management and poverty eradication aspects of work in Caribbean societies.

A third point of departure would be to find a means to translate the needs of the household (or, alternatively, what is required to raise the general quality of households in the region) into a priority claim of households' rights on the economic production and growth of the region. If such a priority can be analytically established, then a moral economy, different in its appeal from 'the survival of the fittest' of neoliberalism, will emerge. This development is important, as in the absence of an alternative moral economy it would be impossible to introduce other moral dimensions into the debates on growth and production. At the moment, the competitive ethic of neoliberalism dominates and appears to be the only one suited to practical efficiency concerns. It does appear, however, that it may be possible, through the claims of households (both market and nonmarket), to ensure this while also requiring markets to be socially accountable and that social policy embraces efficiency attributes.

Friedman represents this idea in the form of a call for the declaration of "a decalogue of household rights". The proposition, however, can be taken further and presented as part of a wider set of social and political struggles for a 'social compact' or 'people's charter' that ultimately seeks to achieve a redefinition of the relationship between state and citizens in the region and a rejection of the logic of state reconstruction under the rubric of neoliberal public choice theory, as it presently obtains (Thomas 1996b); and a popular basis for securing national sovereignty in the face of present assaults on it, particularly in so far as it succeeds in locating economic activity and the production of livelihoods in a sense of community and the encouragement of new and culturally relevant forms of enterprise. In other words, we should seek to promote a bundling of needs, rights, nation, sovereignty and moral economy as the foundation for purposeful social action in the Caribbean.

Size and Integration

A fourth point of departure I would recommend derives from the consideration that the most crucial constraint facing Caribbean countries is their size. Recently this has been heightened by the impact of globalization, changes in world trade and investment rules, and the formation of megablocs. Since independence, the practice of economic integration as a strategic response to this constraint has emphasized two things: (1) a free trade and customs union approach (CARICOM), and (2) various ad hoc forms of functional cooperation within the CARICOM framework. More recently, there has been an emphasis on widening CARICOM. After Suriname, Haiti was admitted to full membership in 1997. Also, CARICOM spearheaded the formation of the Association of Caribbean States (1995). Unfortunately, the free trade/customs union approach has not succeeded in increasing intraregional trade and capital flows as a proportion of regional trade or production significantly above the levels that obtained in the early 1970s when CARICOM was first established. The result of functional cooperation has also been very disappointing, and was particularly evident in the disarray among Caribbean countries in face of the threats to sovereignty posed by the infamous Shiprider Agreements (Thomas 1998).

In recent times two other official initiatives in favour of integration have surfaced. One is to move in the direction of integrated markets based on a single currency and the convergence of macroeconomic policies. This faces enormous difficulties, however, not least of which stems from the highly divergent performances of the regional economies since independence (Thomas 1996b). The other initiative is aimed at preparing the region for its eventual absorption into a hemispheric trade arrangement, either the North American Free Trade Agreement or the Free Trade Area of the Americas. This initiative does not address the problem of size within the region, but displaces the region to a different level of integration into the world economy without its prior transformation.

Two other initiatives have also recently surfaced from individual researchers. Havelock Brewster (1991) has suggested that the focus of integration should be on the development of cooperation in areas of Caribbean life that have strong historical and cultural roots and do not require large expenditure in the creation of bureaucratic structures to service them. A good example is Caribbean citizenship and a common regional passport that goes hand in hand with the continued issuance of national passports. The regional passport will be entirely voluntary, allowing individuals to choose to acquire it if they so wish, and allowing external countries to determine their validity by their acceptance of these. Thus the practical usefulness of the Caribbean passport will develop with time, without any real loss in their symbolic value in reinforcing a regional cultural identity. Apart from its symbolic value, such a union should also pursue joint initiatives wherever feasible, for example, sea, airspace, sport, weather, disease and pest infestations. Also regional public goods, such as regional security, social infrastructure, high technology, medical facilities and advanced scientific training, would also qualify for joint coopera-tion. The corollary of this is that activities with no clear rationale for being carried out as regional intergovernmental initiatives should be avoided.

This sort of approach, Brewster believes, is the only counter to the increas-ingly peripheral and isolated status of the region. He argues that, presently, links with our cultural roots (Africa and Asia), our former colonial masters (Europe) and our neighbours (North and South America) are tenuous and virtually nonexistent. If somewhat overstated, it nevertheless pinpoints the change that has been occurring in our "strategic, colonial and migrant ties of the recent past".

A second approach was developed in the context of a case study of region-alization in the field of biotechnology and sugar. Here again the emphasis is on voluntary forms of regional cooperation, but this time centred around creating new and innovative forms of enterprise development and areas of regional cooperation (Thomas 1995). By emphasizing innovation, the objec-tive of the case study was to root cooperation in the creative and change-focused dimensions of Caribbean economy.

Social Capital and Engendered Economics

There are several further points of departure that I would recommend – for example, the role of social capital, women and development, the role of the state, and environment and sustainability issues – but given the confines of this chapter these cannot be adequately addressed here. The first two are referred to very briefly. The role of social capital in the development of the

518 / New Caribbean Thought

region has been addressed in Thomas 1996c, and an engendered perspective
of the social economy of the region has engaged the attention of a number of
the region's feminist theorists (see Green 1995).

In a recent work I have defined social capital as: "those voluntary means
and processes developed within civil society which promotes development for
the collective whole" (Thomas 1996c: 11). It promotes development through
reducing the costs of social interaction (self-help); by advancing the pursuit of
the collective aspects of social development (empowerment); through engendering social bonding; and, in creating "genuine alternatives and a moral
foundation for human behaviour which does not lead to self-defeating choices,
or the non-cooperative outcomes and opportunism of game theory – a sort of
'tragedy of the commons' effect" (Thomas 1996c: 11).

Starting from the premise that all economic theories utilize a concept of
capital, and that capital takes on a multiplicity of forms which are transform-
able one into the other, a distinctive feature of capital is that it can only be
accumulated to the extent that present consumption is deferred. This distinctive feature is highlighted, above all others, in neoclassical economics. However, it is also true that, traditionally, forms of capital embody: "a definite set
of property relations, so that their values, relative availabilities and substitut-
ability can be determined in the market" (Thomas 1996c: 1).

Social capital is advanced as different in that while it embodies social
relations and all the other defining attributes of capital, it has several definite
characteristics that distinguish it. These are: in its usage, diminishing returns
do not apply, instead, it usually appreciates and does not depreciate with use;
it is collectively produced within civic society; it produces outcomes that are
often desired for their own sake; such outcomes are not subjected to market
valuation; it is a new conceptualization of capital; and, while it recognizes
'giving and rewards' in its accumulation, these do not embody the utilitarian
calculus of traditional market-based theories.

The focus of Green's concern is to develop a Caribbean social economy in
which women are portrayed in their full embeddedness in all of its essential
relations. Simultaneously "their social personhood (indeed, their socially specific womanhood) [is presented] as being *critically* informed by all of them"
(Green 1995: 99; emphasis in original). The essential relations that she
singles out are threefold; namely, those that "map out the particular topography" of the social formation of the region and its modes of re/production; the
way in which structuralist and culturalist perspectives are integrated in the
region; and finally, the way social contradictions, such as national dependency,

race/colour, ethnicity, class and gender, play themselves out in contemporary Caribbean society.

In conclusion, when considering these lines of departure, it should be recalled that the original political economists such as Smith, Ricardo and Marx were political philosophers who studied the ways people made their livelihoods in societies as an essential component of their understanding of the motive factors in the development of the society. They recognized that, to be meaningful, it was imperative that the study of an economy should be framed in the political, social and cultural conditions of its society. Recent tendencies, encouraged by notions of specialization and neoclassical economics' narrow view of 'economic man', have been to separate historical, political, social and cultural conditions from economic analysis and policy design, leading to much inefficiency and social injustice in the latter. This is, however, but one more reason behind the urgency in reconstructing the political economy of the region.

Notes

This article was first presented to the symposium New Currents in Caribbean Thought: Looking Towards the Twenty-first Century, Kellogg Center, Michigan State University, 4–6 April 1997, revised July 1997.

1. Per capita real gross domestic product ranges from US$10,500 in the Bahamas to US$570 in Guyana and US$250 in Haiti. The United Nations Development Programme's index rankings have Barbados at 28, Guyana at 104 and Haiti at 156, from a total of 175 countries (UNDP 1997).

References

Bienefeld, M. 1995. "Prospects for sustainable human development: Averting the threat of social disintegration". Paper submitted to UNIFEM as preparatory material for the Woman's Summit. Beijing.

Brewster, H. 1991. *The Caribbean Community in a Changing International Environment: Towards the Next Century.* Eighth Adlith Brown Memorial Lecture. St Augustine, Trinidad: Caribbean Centre for Monetary Studies.

Brewster, H., and Thomas, C.Y. 1967. The Dynamics of West Indian Economic Integration. Kingston, Jamaica: Institute of Social and Economic Research.

Friedman, J. 1992. *Empowerment: The Policies of Alternative Development.* Cambridge: Blackwell.

Friedman, J. 1996. "Rethinking poverty: Empowerment and citizen rights". *International Social Sciences Journal,* no. 148 (June).

Green, C. 1995. "Gender, race and class in the social economy of the English-speaking Caribbean". *Social and Economic Studies* 44, nos. 2 and 3 (June–September).

Thomas, C.Y. 1974. *Dependence and Transformation.* New York: Monthly Review Press.

Thomas, C.Y. 1984a. *Plantations, Peasants and State. A Study of the Modes of Sugar Production.* Los Angeles: Center for Afro-American Studies, University of California.

Thomas, C.Y. 1984b. *The Rise of the Authoritarian State in Peripheral Societies.* New York: Monthly Review Press.

Thomas, C.Y. 1988. *The Poor and the Powerless: Economic Policy and Change in the Caribbean.* New York: Monthly Review Press and Latin American Bureau.

Thomas, C.Y. 1993. "An innovation-driven model of regional cooperation: Biotechnology and sugar in the Caribbean". In *South-South Cooperation in a Global Perspective,* edited by L. Mytelka. Paris: Organization for Economic Cooperation and Development.

Thomas, C.Y. 1995. "Revisiting theories of race and class in the Caribbean". *Twenty-first Century Policy Review* 2, no. 4.

Thomas, C.Y. 1996a. "A state of disarray: Public policy in the Caribbean". *Bulletin of Eastern Caribbean Affairs* 31, no. 6.

Thomas, C.Y. 1996b. "The inter-relationship between economic and social development". In *Poverty, Empowerment and Social Development in the Caribbean,* edited by N. Girvan. Kingston, Jamaica: Canoe Press.

Thomas, C.Y. 1996c. "Capital markets, financial markets and social capital: An essay on economic theory and economic ideas". *Social and Economic Studies* 45, nos. 2 and 3.

Thomas, C.Y. 1998. "Globalisation, structural adjustment and security: The collapse of the post-colonial developmental state in the Caribbean". *Twenty-first Century Policy Options.*

UNDP (United Nations Development Programme). 1997. *Human Development Report.* New York: Oxford University Press.

20

The New World Order, Globalization and Caribbean Politics

ALEX DUPUY

It is now commonplace in public discourse for people to use the word globalization and the phrase new world order when talking about the seemingly epochal changes that have taken place since the collapse of the Soviet Union and the end of the cold war in 1989. The meanings of these two terms obviously differ according to the perspective of the person using them. My purpose here is not to analyse their various interpretations but to outline what they mean to me and what I see as their implications for the future of politics in the Caribbean. I contend that the new world order and globalization refer to two very different phenomena in the contemporary era and should not be used synonymously. On the one hand, the new world order refers to the global hegemony of capitalism and the absence of any competing noncapitalist or socialist blocs, and the unchallenged status of the United States as the only global superpower. This new configuration is essentially political and origi-nated with the collapse of the Soviet bloc in 1989. The term globalization, on the other hand, has its origins in the early 1970s and refers to a process of integration of all parts of the world in the international division of labour of the capitalist system and a concomitant shift of power from nation states to transnational corporations and agencies of international capital (Evans 1997: 65; Meiksins Wood 1998: 1–2).

If the term new world order refers to a change in the geopolitical configuration and balance of power in the world, and hence to a new era of dominance by a single superpower, the term globalization can be seen as an unfolding of the internal logic of the capitalist system characterized by dramatic new developments in the international financial system, the concentration of capital on a global scale, the internationalization of production and the intensification of competition among the most advanced capitalist economies (Meiksins Wood 1998: 2). Even though these two terms have different etiologies and are not synonymous, I will argue here that their coexistence since 1990 has had serious implications for the ability of the nation state in the less developed economies of the world, such as those in the Caribbean, to devise effective policies that can both stimulate economic growth and meet the growing demands for collective goods and the protection of those who are negatively affected by the operation of market forces (Evans 1997: 84–85). I will summarize my argument in the form of seven hypotheses.

The first hypothesis is that the world is now truly unipolar, not because only one superpower is hegemonic but because two rival political–economic systems that are competing for influence in different parts of the world no longer exist. The demise of the Soviet Union means that all those countries of the Third World that relied on the Soviet bloc as an alternative source of trade and economic and military aid to experiment with socialist or state-centred models of development have had to realign themselves with the West and reinsert their economies in the international capitalist division of labour. If the world is unipolar with the unchallenged dominance of the capitalist system, however, it is multipolar with competing capitalist economic blocs. Three such regional blocs exist; namely, the European Economic Community, North America and East Asia. Within each of the three blocs, one country vies for dominance over others in their bloc, such as the United States in North and South America, Germany in the European zone, and Japan in East Asia.

If, as Immanuel Wallerstein (1985) argues, by hegemony we mean not omnipotence but the ability of a great power to "impose its rule and its wishes (at the very least by effective veto power) in the economic, political, military, diplomatic, and even cultural arenas" (38), then clearly the United States can no longer be considered hegemonic in the post–cold war era. The United States became hegemonic at the end of World War II and remained so until 1973. Its transnational corporations operated without much challenge during that period. Beginning in 1973 Western European and Japanese transnational corporations began to challenge the hegemony of US transnational corporations, and by the mid 1980s they had gained control over production and distribution networks once dominated by US transnationals; and Japanese investments abroad began to rival US investments in extent and in scope (Arrighi 1991: 148–49). The year 1973, then, could be said to have marked the beginning of the process we identify as globalization.

Nonetheless, if it is not hegemonic in the sense described above, the United States remains the single most powerful and competitive economy in the world, and it enjoys today an absolute military superiority. The United States remains the only superpower capable of projecting its military strength globally, and this fact allows it to remind its major European and Japanese competitors that they must still rely on the United States to ensure stability and the continued flow of vital resources, without which their economies could be imperiled. Globalization, then, implies the dominance but not hegemony of a single superpower and intense competition among a transnational elite that is no longer constrained in its global operation by the East–West rivalry of the cold war and whose capital is now freer to penetrate every corner of the world.

The second hypothesis is that, as Marx argued long ago, the tendency of capitalism is to eliminate all spatial barriers to the production and accumulation of capital and to constantly reconfigure the territorial organization of production and exchange (Harvey 1995: 6–7). Thus, what we call globalization today is none other than the formation of a worldwide context of production, trade, communication, investment and accumulation of capital within and between territorial spaces or nation states within the world system (Harvey 1995: 6–7; Storper 1997: 35).

As Michael Storper has shown, globalization is a complex process of intersecting territorialized and organizational dynamics that involves, in some cases, the repositioning of some territorially specific assets or firms into globalized positions of dominance. In other cases, it involves the devaluation of territory-specific assets or products subsequent to the penetration of local markets by imported substitutes resulting from changes in the taste and consumption patterns of middle classes. Globalization also means territorial integration of production and organization to achieve economies of scale, leading to the deterritorialization, market penetration, and devaluation of localized firms or services. And, in still other cases, it leads to the reinvention of territorialized assets due to product differentiation or changes in production standards resulting from territorial integration (Storper 1997: 35).

Globalization, in short, involves the movement of capital, commodities, information and labour across state boundaries. The reconfiguration of the international division of labour associated with the globalization process means that the production, consumption, investment, financing, and trade of goods and services are now dispersed throughout the developed and underdeveloped parts of the world economy. This fact has forced nation states to specialize in different branches of production or even in different stages of production within a specific industry (Manley 1991: 110).

Rather than bridging the gap between the advanced or core industrial economies and the underdeveloped countries in the world economy, however, the new international division of labour is characterized by a shift from capital-intensive to technology- or knowledge/information-intensive production and services in the advanced economies, and capital- and labour-intensive industries in the lower wage semiperipheral and peripheral countries. If the production process is becoming more decentralized in some industries and services, on the one hand, the management, technology, information, service and financial aspects of the global production process are becoming more and more concentrated in the core countries, on the other hand (Robinson 1996a: 31–32). As Michael Manley (1991), the late prime minister of Jamaica, argued, "the globalisation of the world economy . . . has not brought the Third World countries into the power centres of the international division of labour, but has left them marginalised as before and less able to affect their peripheral status by political action" (110–11).

It is in this context that one must locate and appreciate the vulnerability of the Caribbean economies. Their most important economic assets – minerals, agricultural, manufacturing, tourism – are not territory specific, meaning that they are not found or located primarily in the Caribbean but are available, accessible and exploitable elsewhere, thereby increasing competition between the Caribbean and other regions. The region imports most of its manufactured and consumer goods, its food and its technology. Its key economic sectors, principally the agricultural, mineral, assembly and tourist industries, are dominated by foreign firms and are dependent on external demand or foreign consumers for their products or services. The lifestyle, taste, values and consumption habits of the middle and elite classes of the region are very much influenced by those from North America.

In short, the region remains heavily dependent on external trade and the taxes derived from it for most of its fiscal revenues. And much of the trade between the Caribbean and the developed countries occurs under preferential trade agreements, such as in the case of banana exports from the Eastern Caribbean to the European Union under the Lomé agreements, or Caribbean exports to the United States, first under the Caribbean Basin Initiative of the Reagan administration, and then under the Enterprise for the Americas Initiative of the Bush administration. The region as a whole, however, has not benefited from such export-oriented strategies since it failed to use its foreign exchange to finance the development of a productive sector that would allow it to diversify its products and reduce its dependence on assembly production, agricultural or raw materials exports, and services (Wickham 1998: 17; *Caribbean and Central America Report* 1997: 4–5). All these preferential trade agreements are coming under attack under the new free trade rules established by the World Trade Organization and the North American Free Trade Agreement. As these rules are enforced, the region as a whole, which is already saddled with relatively high rates of unemployment that range from 7 to 21 percent in the English-speaking countries (in 1994) to around 17 percent in the Dominican Republic and 70 percent in Haiti (in 1997) (*Caribbean and Central America Report* 1997: 5, 1998a: 4, 1998b: 7), faces even grimmer prospects as its protected domestic industries prove unable to compete with cheaper imports and the attraction of lower wages offered by other countries. Since the North American Free Trade Agreement came into effect in 1994, for example, more than 150 apparel plants closed throughout the Caribbean at the cost of about 123,000 jobs. Many of these plants relocated to Mexico, whose textile exports increased more than threefold since then.

The consequences of the increasing economic vulnerability of the region are twofold. The first is that the region is becoming increasingly reliant on exporting more of its labour force, especially its skilled and semiskilled workers, to North America. Migration, in fact, serves as a safety valve for high unemployment, and many countries are becoming increasingly reliant on the remittances the migrants send back to their homelands. The second is that the region is becoming a larger magnet for and less able or willing to combat illegal drug trafficking and money laundering through the offshore financial sector. It is estimated that about 40 percent of the narcotics trade into the United States and Europe in 1997 passed through the Eastern Caribbean, Puerto Rico, the US Virgin Islands and Haiti. In Haiti alone, where a mere 5 percent of the cocaine destined for the United States passed through that country in 1996, the amount jumped to 15 percent in 1997, representing an increase of 200 percent in one year! Drug trafficking and money laundering bring with them increasing criminal activities, violence and corruption of public officials, all of which threaten the social fabric and the democratic institutions of those countries like Haiti that have limited resources, weak internal institutions and crushing socioeconomic conditions that make people more willing to take the risks associated with involvement in drug trafficking even when the payoffs are smaller (Betancourt 1998: 4; Rohter 1998: 1, 4).

The third hypothesis is that the demise of the Soviet bloc and the unchallenged dominance of the capitalist system exacerbate the polarity between the core countries of the North and the peripheral countries of the South. Some analysts, such as William Robinson (1996b), refer to the process of capitalist globalization as involving a world war between the "global rich and powerful minority against the global poor, dispossessed and outcast majority" (14). If we confine ourselves to the post–World War II period, two directly opposite trends can be observed in the world economy: a growing equality in incomes and living standards among the advanced or core capitalist countries of Western Europe, North America and Japan on the one hand, and a growing inequality in incomes and living standards between these advanced countries and the underdeveloped countries of Africa, Asia and Latin America on the other. According to the United Nations Development Programme, the share of global gross national product for the richest 20 percent of the world's population increased from 70 percent to 83 percent, and the share of the poorest 20 percent of the world's population decreased from 2.3 percent to 1.4 percent between 1960 and 1989. Looked at differently, whereas in 1960 the top 20 percent of the world's population received thirty times more than the bottom 20 percent, by 1990 they received sixty times more. As the United Nations Development Programme argued, if one takes income distribution between rich and poor people rather than the average per capita incomes between rich and poor countries as a measure, then the global ratio between the richest and poorest people is estimated at over 150 to 1 (UNDP 1992).

In Latin America as a whole during the last two decades, the total number of people in poverty increased from 120 million (or 39 percent of the total population) in 1980 to approximately 183 million at the end of the decade (or 44 percent of the total population), and to 230 million in 1995 (or 48 percent of the total population). Of this total, the United Nations Food and Agricultural Organization estimates that 59 million people suffer from chronic hunger (Robinson 1996b: 22). In the Caribbean region specifically, despite impressive gains made in the standard of living in the English-speaking countries especially, poverty continues to endure and is especially chronic in the larger countries. For example, in 1990, 45 percent of the citizens of the Dominican Republic lived below the poverty level, as did 65 percent of Guyanese, 78 percent of Haitians, 43 percent of Jamaicans and 16 percent of Trinidadians

(World Bank 1993). Trinidad and Tobago, it should be mentioned, possesses the highest per capita income in the Caribbean because it is the only producer of oil and exporter of petroleum products in the region. Even though it is not a member of Organization of the Petroleum Exporting Countries, it still benefited enormously from the rise in oil prices in 1973–74 and again in 1979–80, and as a result does not face the same financial constraints as its Caribbean neighbours (Mandle 1996: 126).

The income disparities between the developed countries of the North and the underdeveloped South also reflect real differences in the consumption levels of these two geographic divisions. The developed capitalist countries, which include about one-fourth of the world's population, consume 60 percent of the world's food, 70 percent of its energy, 75 percent of its metals, and 85 percent of its wood (UNDP 1992). Today, about four hundred transnational corporations own two-thirds of the planet's fixed assets and control 70 percent of world trade, and intrafirm trade among the largest 350 transnational corporations account for about 40 percent of world trade. Thus, despite all the talk of globalization, production, trade, investment, financial and consumption activities continue to occur primarily within and among the advanced industrial economies, and between them and parts of East Asia primarily. For example, excluding Japan, the share of world trade in Asia increased from 9 to 15 percent between 1980 and 1991; that of Africa, Latin America and the Caribbean decreased from 28 to 13 percent; and that of the advanced industrial economies decreased from 72 to 63 percent. In 1994 more than half of all investment flows to developing countries went to East Asia. East Asia, therefore, appears to be the main driving force behind much of the globalization process, but even this success story is now at risk with the severe financial crisis afflicting these economies (McNally 1998: 2).

The fourth hypothesis is that the demise of the Soviet Union and the unchallenged dominance of the core capitalist powers deprive progressive or would-be progressive Third World governments of any effective alternative sources of support. The political defeat and eventual dismantling of the Soviet Union has led to the universal discrediting of socialist or state-centred ideologies and government policies on the one hand and the dominance of the Anglo-American ideology of the free enterprise system and its associated free market policies on the other. Some analysts, such as Francis Fukuyama (1989), celebrate this victory by turning Marx on his head and declaring that the victory of capitalism over communism rather than the other way around has brought about the end of history, that is "the end point of mankind's ideological evolution of Western liberal democracy as the final form of human government" (4). Aware of the absence of alternatives, and with nowhere else to go for support, socialist or left-of-centre governments were left with few alternatives but to rethink their politics and accommodate themselves to the imperatives of the world capitalist system.

In the case of the Caribbean region, we have seen the defeat of every progressive government since 1980, whether by means of implosion within the ruling party followed by foreign intervention (the Bishop government and the US intervention in Grenada in 1983), electoral defeat (the Manley government in Jamaica in 1980), or military coup d'état (the Aristide government in Haiti in 1991). All these countries have now embraced the neoliberal economic policies advocated by the United States. In Haiti, where the first Aristide government had proposed a moderate social-democratic economic programme, the government of René Préval, Aristide's former prime minister, is trying to implement a structural adjustment programme sponsored by the United States and the International Monetary Fund (IMF)–World Bank designed to privatize former key government industries and pursue free market policies. Similarly, in Guyana, where the Cheddi Jagan government in 1992 had hoped to avoid caving in to the dictates of the IMF and the Paris Club creditor nations to privatize its state-owned enterprises and liberalize the economy, the successor government headed by Cheddi Jagan's widow, Janet Jagan, is now proceeding with such plans (Bousquet 1997).

Cuba, which, thanks to the support of the Soviet Union, defied the United States successfully for thirty years, is now in the process of reinserting itself into the capitalist system and transforming its economy into a mixed economy. While the state sector continues to dominate the economy, most of the state enterprises are inefficient, uncompetitive, and operate at a loss. To reverse the downward trend of the economy, since 1990 the government has de-emphasized socialist or statist strategies and extended the sectors of its economy that operate according to market principles (Eckstein 1997: 147). These include joint ventures with foreign companies and foreign investment, especially in the tourist sector; some export-oriented industries that are state owned but financially and managerially autonomous; the private agricultural sector, which in 1994 accounted for 14 percent of total agricultural land; the self-employed sector; and the remittance sector, wherein workers and others who participate in it receive and spend dollars primarily in the so-called dollar stores.

The consequences of the dual economy are drastic and undermine the socialist and egalitarian principles of the government. It creates new social classes, such as a new managerial class, the self-employed entrepreneurs and the workers they employ, and those who possess dollars. Those who earn or receive dollars enjoy real incomes that are ten to thirty times more than those who are paid in pesos. The unequal income distribution linked with the emergence of these new groups also changes people's incentives. It not only leads ordinary Cubans to chase dollars but also encourages professionals and other skilled workers to leave the peso (or socialist) sector for the dollar (or market) sector. This fact depresses the socialist sector even more by encouraging the exit of those who are needed to perform functions and services that are of highest value to society, such as in health care and education, to seek employment in the dollar sector that is more remunerative but of lesser value to society as a whole, such as tourism, or to become self-employed and charge market prices for their services (Ritter 1997: 154–57; León 1997: 44).

Moreover, to face its mounting fiscal crisis, the Cuban government reintroduced the use of money to obtain social services and benefits that had been provided freely to the population. Although the government continues to define access to education and health care as basic rights, it is now charging for electricity, sports events and museums, meals at work centres and schools, some school fees and student uniforms, and has reduced or eliminated some student stipends and forced those in need of financial assistance to rely on student loans (Eckstein 1997: 143). In short, as Susan Eckstein put it, there is no free lunch in Cuba anymore, and while the government remains publicly committed to socialism, the socialist characteristics of the Cuban economy declined as market features grew in importance during the 1990s. As this happened, new inequalities in wealth and income distribution increased at the same time that the free cradle-to-grave welfare state eroded (Eckstein 1997: 149).

In short, the increasing use of money and reliance on the dollar have had important social and political consequences. They have given rise to new social classes and social inequalities as well as to new social categories of hucksters, prostitutes, peddlers, muggers, and a sharp increase in criminal activities such as drug trafficking, pornography, kidnappings and even murders. Even if the percentage of people engaged in these types of activities pales in comparison to other countries in the Caribbean and Latin America, the fact that they are happening at all in Cuba is alarming and threatens the social peace, which, along with the universal provision of health care, food, education and other public goods had been considered the hallmark of the Cuban Revolution (*Caribbean and Central America Report* 1998c: 3).

The fifth hypothesis is that at the same time that the Left finds itself constrained in terms of its ability to pursue more progressive alternatives to capitalism, the United States has been promoting the democratization of the region. This support for democratic government, however, especially in countries such as the Dominican Republic and Haiti that have lived under US-sponsored dictatorships for most of the twentieth century, has been accompanied by a general shift to an unregulated version of capitalism. More significantly, this shift is occurring in a context where the globalization process summarized above has shifted the locus and power of decision making from the state to international financial institutions and economically powerful private local and international actors (Robinson 1996b: 18).

Governments everywhere are compelled to surrender the formulation of development, fiscal, and monetary policy to international regulatory institutions such as the World Bank, the IMF, and the US Agency for International Development, and embrace their free market, structural adjustment and privatization formulas. Through these reforms, the state is being transformed into what the World Bank calls a "market friendly state" (World Bank 1991), or what others call less benignly a leaner, meaner state reduced to performing those essential functions necessary for the unregulated operation and accumulation of private and transnational capital.

This process of dissolution of the power of the state, David Harvey (1995) argues, is to be understood in terms of the "unstable processes of globalization/territorialization" of capitalism. Initially, the capitalist state had as its primary function the regulation of "money, law, politics and [the monopolization of] the means of coercion and violence according to a sovereign territorial (and sometimes extraterritorial) will" (7). This process of state formation, however, took a long time to complete, with most state boundaries being drawn between 1870 and 1925, and with most of the contemporary states becoming independent after 1945. Today, however, with the spatial reorganization of the processes of capitalist production that we term globalization, the regulatory power of the state, especially but not exclusively in the South, is being superseded by supranational organizations.

The sixth hypothesis, then, is that at a time when the democratization of the Caribbean region is increasing, the capacity of the state to formulate social policies to meet the basic needs of its citizens and the greater demand for public goods is being eroded by the processes of globalization and the subordination of the nation states of the Caribbean to the imperatives of transnational corporations and financial institutions. The international financial institutions have not only eroded the capacity of the state to formulate and implement its own economic policies but, equally as important, have defined the limits of democracy and the meaning of 'good' governance. Basically, the former is reduced to the holding of periodic competitive elections subject to international supervision and the latter is defined in terms of strict adherence to the market principles and free trade policies established by the international financial institutions who penalize uncooperative governments by withholding or discontinuing aid (Wickham 1998: 23). It is in this double sense that I argue that the current historical conjuncture is characterized by the tendency to reduce politics to a mere problem of technical efficiency and top-down policy implementation. For if by politics we mean the right and the ability of a people to determine the agenda of their government, then both this right and this ability are being severely undermined by the subordination of the region's economies to the dictates of international regulatory institutions and powerful private actors who are not subject to democratic control and accountability. Thus, the formal trappings of sovereignty and democracy notwithstanding, the restructuring of the state into a 'market-friendly' or neoliberal state means the de facto marginalization of the popular sectors from the political process, the election of weak governments with very limited political agendas negotiated among and between the domestic and international elites, and the transfer of ultimate veto power over the state to those elites. William Robinson (1996a) aptly refers to this exclusionary political system as a "low-intensity democracy . . . aimed not only at mitigating the social and political tensions produced by elite-based and undemocratic status quo, but also at suppressing popular and mass aspirations for more thoroughgoing democratization of social life" (6).

The above point may be illustrated by the recent example of Haiti. In May 1996 the Haitian Parliament was debating the economic programme that President Préval had submitted for ratification. Uncertain about the outcome of this debate, the managing director of the IMF, Michael Camdessus, travelled to Haiti specifically to remind the parliamentarians of their responsibility toward the government's economic programme that had been devised by the international financial institutions. Camdessus made it clear to the members of Parliament that unless they voted to adopt the programme, the $1.2 billion in foreign aid promised to Haiti by the international financial institutions over the next five years would be given to other countries waiting in the wings, and of which there were many at a time of crisis in international aid (*Haiti en Marche* 1996: 1).

A substantial number of parliamentarians had voiced opposition to the structural adjustment programme because they believed it would wreak havoc among the poor and the working classes. But they also knew that over 40 percent of the government's budget depended on the foreign aid monies and that to vote against the structural adjustment programme would be tantamount to committing economic suicide. The parliamentarians knew also that they had nowhere else to turn to for support if they defied the IMF. Thus, the hands of Parliament were tied and there did not seem to be any alternative but to vote for the government's programme.

That the IMF undermined the democratic process by adopting this arrogant posture did not seem to bother its director in the least. In fact, I would argue, whether a government is democratic or not is ultimately immaterial to the international financial institutions. What really matters to them is that the state, particularly in the peripheral or semiperipheral countries, behaves or can be made to behave as a 'market-friendly' state. Since the international financial institutions view countries in the world economy as mere sites of production, investment and trade, and seek to limit as much as possible the capacity of the state to act autonomously, the same formulas developed by the dominant core powers, especially the US Treasury Department which really calls the shots with the IMF (Sanger 1998: 5), can be applied universally regardless of a country's specific characteristics or needs. Thus, democratic Haiti is treated in the same way as dictatorial Indonesia, irrespective of the fact that the former is trying to regulate private interests to maximize the provision of public goods while the latter's crisis stems largely from the decisions of private actors seeking to maximize their self-interest rather than those of the majority. In fact, because the stakes for private interests, both domestic and foreign, are greater in Indonesia than in Haiti, the IMF was willing to pour in tens of billions of dollars to rescue that faltering economy even if this meant shoring up an undemocratic government and tolerating its family-based system of crony capitalism.

This, then, leads me to the seventh and final hypothesis. My argument here is that while the globalization processes described above limit the ability of states to exercise full sovereignty in decision making, it does not follow that the only state possible is the lean and mean version that places private interests over the provision of public goods and the protection of citizens from the vagaries of the market. Such a view of the state corresponds to the "ideological proclivities of both the only remaining superpower and the private firms that dominate the global economy" (Evans 1997: 72). Thus, despite the constraints of globalization, especially on the small countries of the Caribbean, it is possible to conceive of alternatives to the Anglo-American and international financial institutions's vision of the minimalist state.

The alternative vision of the state I would like to propose involves at least two aspects. First, one needs to rethink the nation state as the locus of development and consider seriously the idea of regional integration. The heads of state of CARICOM are already taking some steps in that direction by trying to broaden membership in the regional organization beyond its original thirteen-member English-speaking country composition. Haiti and the Dominican Republic have recently been added as new trading members, and efforts are underway to extend membership to Cuba, a move that has earned the leaders of CARICOM the ire of the United States. The advantage of such integration is that it would create larger economies of scale for economies that share many similar characteristics and strengthen the region by concentrating trade and investments among them and "develop[ing] the human resources to provide the skills required to cope with the fast-changing technological environment" of the globalized economy (Patterson 1997: 19).

However, if regional economic integration is to benefit the majority of citizens rather than mostly the local elites and foreign corporations and investors, the regional governments would have to break with the current vision of the 'market-friendly' state to create a stronger, more interventionist, and social democratic state. Such a state is necessary to devise and implement an industrial strategy that may require subsidies to and protection of regional industries to allow them time to grow and become competitive. The lesson of the more successful East Asian economies that the World Bank hailed until recently as the model to be emulated by the less developed countries is not that they restricted the involvement of the state in economic affairs and adhered to the free market and free trade policies championed by that institution. Leaving aside the special relationship that these countries had with the United States because of the geopolitics of the cold war, their development successes resulted largely from the central role that the state played in economic planing and development policies. Thus, contrary to the neoliberal ideology, the East Asian experience suggests that success in global market competition may best be achieved through more rather than less state involvement in the economy (Evans 1997: 69–70).

Second, the relationship between the state and the economy needs to be reconsidered. The objective here is to conceive of ways to democratize both and to shift the locus of participation to the public sphere and away from an elite-centred view of politics. I have in mind here the increasingly important role that progressive groups and networking nongovernmental organizations, such as the Caribbean Policy Development Centre, have been playing in formulating "an alternative development model that is grounded in the concerns, needs and aspirations of the region's peoples" (Wedderburn 1998: 63). Established in 1991, the Caribbean Policy Development Centre is a network of twenty-one nongovernmental organizations from across the region that includes organizations of women, youths, workers, farmers, ecumenical communities, human rights groups, intellectuals and indigenous groups, and encompasses all the major languages of the area: English, French, Spanish, Dutch and Creole. The Caribbean Policy Development Centre is organized around the principles of consensus building; grass-roots participation in pro-gramme design and implementation; research, public education and advocacy; and building the confidence of Caribbean peoples to influence public policy (Wedderburn 1998: 63). Of equal significance for my purposes is the Carib-bean Policy Development Centre's understanding that

the present economic and societal crisis in the region has its roots in the structuring of these economies during the colonial period to be producers of goods for export and to be importers of consumer goods. This historical pattern of underdevelopment continued into the postcolonial period and contributed to the region's increased vulnerabilities . . . [And,][j]udging from the regulations and provisions of the GATT [General Agreement on Tarriffs and Trade] and WTO [World Trade Organization], the contemporary situation, rather than envisioning the possibilities of a more humane, sustainable and holistic development effort for the region, suggests a period of recolonisation. (Wedderburn 1998: 64)

As promising as the emergence of these grass-roots movements is, however, it can succeed only if it can democratize the state more rather than undermining its role as a strong regulatory institution. In my view, the state remains essential in its ability to regulate the exercise of individual property rights and in providing public goods and encouraging more public participation at the local and national levels by forging new relations between organized groups of citizens and the public sector. In short, the argument here is that democracy and a healthy civil society that facilitates greater civic participation in economic and political life require a state that is capable of responding to collective needs and serving as an intermediary between private citizens and organized groups (Evans 1997: 80–81).

Thus, rather than rejecting out of hand the experiments with more demo-cratic and statist forms of development during the 1970s and 1980s in Jamaica,

Grenada and Nicaragua, as well as the achievements of the Cuban Revolution, these ought to be re-examined critically without losing sight of the new geopolitical and international economic realities and constraints of the post–cold war era. There are encouraging signs that this is happening, as the example of the Caribbean Policy Development Centre mentioned above suggests. In my view, only a move in the direction summarized above could reverse the trend toward the eclipsing of the state and the atomization of social life that are associated with the neoliberal project.

References

Arrighi, Giovanni. 1991. "Marxist century, American century". In *After the Fall: The Failure of Communism and the Future of Socialism,* edited by Robin Blackburn. London: Verso.

Bousquet, Earl. 1997. "Settling down after Jagan: Guyana now under three-prong leadership". *Caribbean Week,* 12–25 April.

Betancourt, Carlos. 1998. "Drugs, Haiti and the Caribbean". *Washington Report on the Hemisphere* 18, no. 16 (5 September).

Caribbean and Central America Report. 1997. "Tough decisions ahead for Caribbean". *Latin American Regional Reports: Caribbean and Central America Report,* 15 July.

Caribbean and Central America Report. 1998a. "Dominicans lead growth league". *Latin American Regional Reports: Caribbean and Central America Report,* 20 January.

Caribbean and Central America Report. 1998b. "Haiti: Lavalas factions locked in dispute". *Latin American Regional Reports: Caribbean and Central America Report,* 20 January.

Caribbean and Central America Report. 1998c. "Cuba: Crime threatens to get out of hand". *Latin American Regional Reports: Caribbean and Central America Report,* 3 November.

Castañeda, Jorge G. 1993. *Utopia Unarmed: The Latin American Left After the Cold War.* New York: Knopf.

Eckstein, Susan. 1997. "The limits of socialism in a capitalist world economy: Cuba since the collapse of the Soviet bloc". In *Toward a New Cuba? Legacies of a Revolution,* edited by M.A. Centeno and M. Font. Boulder: Lynne Rienner.

Evans, Peter B. 1997. "The eclipse of the state? Reflections on stateness in the era of globalization". *World Politics* 50 (October).

Fukuyama, Francis. 1989. "The end of history". *National Interest* (Summer).

Haiti en Marche. 1996. "Visite houleuse du PDG du FMI au Parlement", 29 May–4 June.

Harvey, David. 1995. "Globalization in question". *Rethinking Marxism* 8, no. 4 (Winter).

León, Francisco. 1997. "Socialism and *socialísimo*: Social actors and economic change in 1990s Cuba". In *Toward a New Cuba? Legacies of a Revolution,* edited by M.A. Centeno and M. Font. Boulder: Lynne Rienner.

Mandle, Jay R. *Persistent Underdevelopment: Change and Economic Modernization in the West Indies.* Amsterdam: Gordon and Breach.

Manley, Michael. 1991. *The Poverty of Nations.* London: Pluto Press.

McNally, David. 1998. "Globalization on trial: Crisis and class struggle in East Asia". *Monthly Review* 50, no. 4 (September).

Meiksins Wood, Ellen. 1998. "Capitalist change and generational shifts". *Monthly Review* 50, no. 5 (October).

Nef, Jorge. 1995. "Demilitarization and democratic transition in Latin America". In *Capital, Power, and Inequality in Latin America,* edited by S. Halebsky and R.L. Harris. Boulder: Westview Press.

Patterson, Percival J. 1997. "Caribbean unity is crucial for success". *CaribNews,* 26 August.

Przeworski, Adam. 1991. *Democracy and the Market: Political and Economic Reforms in Eastern Europe and Latin America.* Cambridge: Cambridge University Press.

Ritter, Archibald R.M. 1997. "The Cuban economy in the mid-1990s: Structural/monetary pathology and public policy". In *Toward a New Cuba? Legacies of a Revolution,* edited by M.A. Centeno and M. Font. Boulder: Lynne Rienner.

Robinson, William I. 1996a. *Promoting Polyarchy: Globalization, US Intervention, and Hegemony.* Cambridge: Cambridge University Press.

Robinson, William I. 1996b. "Globalization: Nine theses on our epoch". *Race and Class* 38, no. 2.

Rohter, Larry. 1998. "Haiti paralysis brings a boom in drug trade". *New York Times,* 27 October.

Sanger, David E. 1998. "Dissension erupts at talks on world financial crisis". *New York Times on the Web,* 7 October.

Storper, Michael. 1997. "Territories, flows, and hierarchies in the global economy". In *Spaces of Globalization: Reasserting the Power of the Local,* edited by K.R. Cox. New York: Guildford Press.

UNDP (United Nations Development Programme). 1992. *Human Development Report.* New York: Oxford University Press.

Wallerstein, Immanuel. 1985. *The Politics of the World-Economy: The States, the Movements and the Civilizations.* Cambridge: Cambridge University Press.

Wedderburn, Judith. 1998. "Organisation and social actors in the regional process". In *Critical Issues in Caribbean Development,* no. 6. Kingston, Jamaica: Ian Randle Publishers.

Wickham, Peter. 1998. "Towards recapturing popular sovereignty in the Caribbean through integration". In *Critical Issues in Caribbean Development,* no. 6. Kingston, Jamaica: Ian Randle Publishers.

World Bank. 1991. *World Development Report 1991: The Challenge of Development.* Washington, DC: World Bank.

World Bank. 1993. *Caribbean Region: Current Economic Situation, Regional Issues, and Capital Flows, 1992.* Washington, DC: World Bank.

Contributors

Brian Meeks is senior lecturer and head, Department of Government, University of the West Indies, Mona, Jamaica. He is the author of *Caribbean Revolutions and Revolutionary Theory: An Assessment of Cuba, Nicaragua and Grenada* (1993), *Radical Caribbean: From Black Power to Abu Bakr* (1996) and *Narratives of Resistance: Jamaica, Trinidad, the Caribbean* (2000).

Folke Lindahl is associate professor of political theory, James Madison College, Michigan State University. He is the author of *Tocqueville's Civil Discourse: A Postmodernist Reading* (1994) and of many articles on Caribbean political thought.

Alex Dupuy is professor of sociology, Wesleyan University, Connecticut. He is the author of *Haiti in the New World Order: The Limits of the Democratic Revolution* (1997), *Haiti in the World Economy: Class, Race, and Underdevelopment since 1700* (1989), and of many articles on Haiti and the Caribbean.

Maribel Aponte Garcia is professor of economics at the Graduate School of Business Administration and researcher at the Social Science Research Center, University of Puerto Rico, Río Piedras. She is co-editor, with Carmen Gautier, of *Postintegration Development in the Caribbean* (1995) and co-author, with Carlos A. Alvarez, of *Economic Globalization and Regional Integration: A Problematic Discourse for the Caribbean and Latin America* (forthcoming). She is also the director of the project The Economics of Comparative Production Systems: A Multimedia Project on Cuba and Puerto Rico.

Norman Girvan is secretary general of the Association of Caribbean States. He was previously professor of development studies and director of the Sir Arthur Lewis Institute of Social and Economic Research, University of the West Indies, Mona. He is the author of *Foreign Capital and Economic Underdevelopment in Jamaica* (1971), *Technology Policies for Small Developing Countries*

(1983), editor of *Poverty, Empowerment and Social Development in the Caribbean* (1997) and numerous other books and collections on Caribbean political economy and development.

Obika Gray is professor of political science, University of Wisconsin–Eau Claire. He is the author of *Radicalism and Social Change in Jamaica* (1991) and *Demeaned but Empowered: The Social Power of the Urban Poor in Jamaica* (forthcoming).

Cecilia Green is assistant professor of sociology, University of Pittsburgh. She has published widely on gender, labour and development, the politics of globalization, and Caribbean politics.

Stuart Hall is emeritus professor of sociology, Open University, United Kingdom. He helped shape the Centre for Contemporary Cultural Studies at the University of Birmingham as a research associate and as director from 1969 to 1979. He is widely regarded as both a founder of the discipline of cultural studies and a leading spokesperson for the British Left. Hall has co-edited and co-authored numerous volumes, including *Culture, Media, Language* (1980), *Politics and Ideology* (1986) and numerous articles on Marxism, modernity, popular culture and Caribbean identity.

Paget Henry is associate professor of sociology and Afro-American studies, Brown University. He is the author of *Caliban's Reason: Introducing Afro-Caribbean Philosophy* (2000), *Peripheral Capitalism and Underdevelopment in Antigua*, the co-editor of C.L.R. *James's Caribbean* (1992) and the editor of the *C.L.R. James Journal.*

Percy C. Hintzen is the former chair of the Department of African American Studies and director of peace and conflict studies, University of California, Berkeley. He is the author of *The Costs of Regime Survival* (1989) and *West Indians in the West* (forthcoming).

Winston James is associate professor of history, Columbia University. His publications include *Holding Aloft the Banner of Ethiopia: Caribbean Radicalism in Early Twentieth Century America* (1998), *Claude McKay: The Making of a Black Bolshevik, 1899–1923* (2000), *A Fierce Hatred of Injustice: Claude McKay's Jamaica and His Poetry of Rebellion* (2000), and, with Clive Harris, co-editor of *Inside Babylon: The Caribbean Diaspora in Britain* (1993).

Linden Lewis is associate professor of sociology, Department of Sociology and Anthropology, Bucknell University, Pennsylvania. He has published widely in the areas of Caribbean political economy, labour relations, gender relations and the postcolonial state.

Rupert Lewis is professor of Caribbean political thought, University of the West Indies, Mona, Jamaica. He is the author of *Walter Rodney's Intellectual and Political Thought* (1998), *Marcus Garvey: Anti-Colonial Champion* (1987), and co-editor of *Garvey: Africa, Europe, the Americas* (1986) and *Garvey: His Work and Impact* (1991).

Charles Mills is professor of philosophy, University of Illinois, Chicago. He is the author of *The Racial Contract* (1997) and *Blackness Visible* (1997) and many other articles on race, philosophy and the Caribbean.

Patricia Mohammed is senior lecturer and director, Mona unit of the Centre for Gender and Development Studies, University of the West Indies, Mona, Jamaica. She is editor of *Feminist Review,* no. 59: *Rethinking Caribbean Difference* (1998) and co-editor of *Gender and Caribbean Development* (1988) among many other publications.

Rhoda Reddock is senior lecturer and director, St Augustine unit of the Centre for Gender and Development Studies, University of the West Indies, St Augustine, Trinidad. She is author of *Women, Labour and Politics in Trinidad and Tobago* (1994), *Elma Francois: The NWCSA and the Workers Struggle for Change in the Caribbean in the 1930s* (1988), and editor of *Ethnic Minorities in Caribbean Society* (1996).

Gordon Rohlehr is professor of West Indian literature, University of the West Indies, St Augustine, Trinidad. Among his many publications are *Pathfinder: Black Awakening in the Arrivants of Edward Kamau Brathwaite* (1981), *Calypso and Society in Pre-Independence Trinidad* (1990), *My Strangled City and other Essays* (1992) and *The Shape of that Hurt and other Essays* (1992).

Selwyn Ryan is director of the Sir Arthur Lewis Institute of Social and Economic Studies, University of the West Indies, St Augustine, Trinidad. Among his many publications are *Race and Nationalism in Trinidad and Tobago* (1972), *Pathways to Power: Indians and the Politics of National Unity in Trinidad and Tobago* (1996), *Revolution and Reaction: A Study of Parties and Politics in Trinidad and Tobago 1970–81* (1989), *The Muslimeen Grab for*

Power in Trinidad and Tobago (1991), and *Winner Takes All: The Westminster Experience in the Caribbean* (1999).

David Scott is associate professor of anthropology, Columbia University. He is the author of *Refashioning Futures: Criticism after Postcoloniality* (1999) and *Formations of Ritual: Colonial and Anthropological Discourses on the Sinhala Yaktovil* (1994), and he is the editor of the journal *Small Axe*.

Clive Thomas is the director of the Institute of Development Studies, University of Guyana. He recently served as the George Beckford professor of Caribbean economy, University of the West Indies, Mona, Jamaica. Among Thomas's many books are *Dependence and Transformation: The Economics of the Transition to Socialism* (1974), *The Rise of the Authoritarian State in Peripheral Societies* (1984), *Plantations, Peasants and State* (1984) and *The Poor and the Powerless: Economic Policy and Change in the Caribbean* (1988).

Hilbourne Watson is professor of international relations, Bucknell University, Pennsylvania. He is editor of *The Caribbean in the Global Economy* and has published extensively on the new globalization, global industrial restructuring and Caribbean political thought.